D0203888

Jim Crow

Jim Crow

A Historical Encyclopedia of the American Mosaic

Nikki L. M. Brown and Barry M. Stentiford, Editors

GREENWOOD

AN IMPRINT OF ABC-CLIO, LLC
Santa Barbara, California • Denver, Colorado • Oxford, England

Library of Congress Cataloging-in-Publication Data

Jim Crow : a historical encyclopedia of the American mosaic / edited by Nikki L. M. Brown and Barry M. Stentiford.

pages cm

Includes bibliographical references and index.

ISBN 978-1-61069-663-0 (hard copy : alk. paper) — ISBN 978-1-61069-664-7 (ebook) 1. African Americans—Segregation—History—Encyclopedias. 2. African Americans—Segregation—Southern States—History—Encyclopedias. 3. African Americans—Civil rights—History—Encyclopedias. 4. African Americans—Civil rights—Southern States—History—Encyclopedias. 5. United States—Race relations—History—Encyclopedias. 6. Southern States—Race relations—History—Encyclopedias. I. Brown, Nikki L. M., editor. II. Stentiford, Barry M., editor.

E185.61.J526   2014

305.896'073003—dc23   2014013921

ISBN: 978-1-61069-663-0
EISBN: 978-1-61069-664-7

18 17 16 15   2 3 4 5

This book is also available on the World Wide Web as an eBook.
Visit www.abc-clio.com for details.

Greenwood
An Imprint of ABC-CLIO, LLC

ABC-CLIO, LLC
130 Cremona Drive, P.O. Box 1911
Santa Barbara, California 93116-1911

This book is printed on acid-free paper ∞

Manufactured in the United States of America

Contents

List of Entries, vii

List of Primary Documents, ix

Guide to Related Topics, xi

Preface, xv

Acknowledgments, xix

Introduction, xxi

Jim Crow Chronology, xxix

The Encyclopedia, 1

Primary Documents, 447

Selected Bibliography, 457

Index, 461

About the Editors, 473

List of Entries

Abernathy, Ralph David
Advertising
Affirmative Action
Alabama
Alabama Council on Human Relations
Albany Civil Rights Movement
Arkansas
Armed Forces
Atlanta Compromise, The

Baldwin, James
Bates, Daisy
Baton Rouge Bus Boycott
Berea College v. Kentucky
Bethune, Mary McLeod
Birth of a Nation, The (1915)
Black Cabinet, The
Black Codes
Black Like Me and John Howard
    Griffin
Black Nationalism
Blues
Brown v. Board of Education
Brown v. Board of Education, Legal
    Groundwork for
Buchanan v. Warley (1917)

Chicago Race Riot of 1919
Churches

Cinema
Civil Rights Act of 1875
Civil Rights Act of 1964
Civilian Conservation Corps
Cold War
Colored Farmers' Alliance
Confederate Flag
Congress of Racial Equality (CORE)

Democratic Party
Detroit Race Riot of 1943
Disenfranchisement
Double V Campaign

East St. Louis Riot of 1917
Eugenics
Evers, Medgar
Executive Order 9981

Fair Employment Practices
    Commission (FEPC)
Federal Bureau of Investigation
    (FBI)
Florida

Garvey, Marcus
Georgia
Great Depression
Great Migration

Health Care
Historically Black Colleges and
    Universities
Housing Covenants
Humor and Comedic Traditions

Jim Crow
Johnson, Jack

Kentucky
King, Martin Luther, Jr.
Ku Klux Klan

Labor Unions
Lawson, James Morris, Jr.
Little Rock Nine
Louisiana
Lynching

Malcolm X
March on Washington Movement
Marriage, Interracial
Marshall, Thurgood
Meredith, James
Minstrelsy
Mississippi
Montgomery Bus Boycott

Nadir of the Negro
National Association of Colored
    Women
Negro League Baseball
New Deal
North Carolina

Parks, Rosa
Passing
Plessy v. Ferguson
Poll Taxes
Prisons

Racial Customs and Etiquette
Reconstruction
Red Summer
Republican Party
Robinson, Jackie
Roosevelt, Franklin D.
Rustin, Bayard

Segregation, Residential
Sharecropping
Sit-Ins
South Carolina
Sundown Towns

Texas
Till, Emmett
Truman, Harry S.
Tuskegee Syphilis Experiment

Virginia
Voting Rights Act of 1965

Wallace, George
Washington, Booker T.
Wells-Barnett, Ida B.
White Citizens Council
World War I
World War II

List of Primary Documents

Excerpts from *Plessy v. Ferguson* (1896), 447
Executive Order 9981 (1948), 448
Excerpts from *Brown v. Board of Education* (1954), 450
The Southern Manifesto, *aka* Declaration of Constitutional Principles (1956), 452
Excerpts from Civil Rights Act of 1964, 455

Guide to Related Topics

Culture

Birth of a Nation, The (1915)
Blues
Churches
Cinema
Humor and Comedic Traditions
Minstrelsy
Racial Customs and Etiquette

Education

Berea College v. Kentucky
Brown v. Board of Education

Employment

Atlanta Compromise, The
Colored Farmers' Alliance
Fair Employment Practices
  Commission (FEPC)
Great Depression
Great Migration
Labor Unions
Washington, Booker T.

Health

Tuskegee Syphilis Experiment

Ideas

Confederate Flag
Eugenics
Passing

Institutions and Organizations

Alabama Council on Human
  Relations
Colored Farmers' Alliance
Congress of Racial Equality (CORE)
Historically Black Colleges and
  Universities
National Association of Colored
  Women
Prisons

Legislation

Black Cabinet, The
Buchanan v. Warley (1917)
Civil Rights Act of 1875
Civil Rights Act of 1964
Civilian Conservation Corps
Executive Order 9981
Fair Employment Practices
  Commission (FEPC)
Federal Bureau of Investigation (FBI)
Health Care
Plessy v. Ferguson
Poll Taxes
Reconstruction
Voting Rights Act of 1965

Movements

Brown v. Board of Education, Legal
  Groundwork for

Double V Campaign
Jim Crow
Sit-Ins

Policies
Affirmative Action
Armed Forces
Black Cabinet, The
Black Codes
Buchanan v. Warley (1917)
Civilian Conservation Corps
Disenfranchisement
Fair Employment Practices
   Commission (FEPC)
Federal Bureau of Investigation (FBI)
Housing Covenants
Lynching
Marriage, Interracial
New Deal
Segregation, Residential
Sharecropping
Sundown Towns

Politics
Bethune, Mary McLeod
Black Nationalism
Democratic Party
Marshall, Thurgood
Republican Party
Roosevelt, Franklin D.
Truman, Harry S.
Wallace, George

Popular Culture
Baldwin, James
Black Like Me and John Howard
   Griffin
Johnson, Jack
Negro League Baseball
Robinson, Jackie

Protest and Resistance
Abernathy, Ralph David
Alabama Council on Human
   Relations
Albany Civil Rights Movement
Baldwin, James
Bates, Daisy
Baton Rouge Bus Boycott
Chicago Race Riot of 1919
Congress of Racial Equality (CORE)
Detroit Race Riot of 1943
East St. Louis Riot of 1917
Evers, Medgar
Garvey, Marcus
King, Martin Luther, Jr.
Lawson, James Morris, Jr.
Little Rock Nine
Malcolm X
March on Washington Movement
Meredith, James
Montgomery Bus Boycott
Parks, Rosa
Red Summer
Rustin, Bayard
Till, Emmett
Wells-Barnett, Ida B.

Racism and Stereotypes
Advertising
Ku Klux Klan
Nadir of the Negro
White Citizens Council

States
Alabama
Arkansas
Florida
Georgia
Kentucky
Louisiana

Mississippi
North Carolina
South Carolina
Texas
Virginia

**War, Military, and Law
    Enforcement**
Cold War
World War I
World War II

Preface

Jim Crow: A Historical Encyclopedia of the American Mosaic is geared toward the needs of high school students, with a focus on the most important people, events, and institutions involved in the creation, maintenance, and eventual dismembering of Jim Crow. The entries explore the complex system of segregation by race, affecting African Americans, Native Americans, Latino Americans, and Asian Americans in the United States that was created beginning in the mid-1880s and that remained in existence until the mid-1960s. The encyclopedia describes Jim Crow's effects on politics, people, and culture with a heavy focus on the key people, events, and documents related to Jim Crow. The encyclopedia entries herein examine the era from the following vantage points: concrete and abstract, as in religious beliefs and art; majority and minority, as in educational institutions; legal and illegal, as in suffrage and violence; working class and middle class, as in housing and employment; and traditional and modern, as in forms of political protest.

The Jim Crow encyclopedia ends its catalogue of events and people with the 1965 Voting Rights Act. Though the story of Jim Crow, much less racial inequality, did not end in 1965, a new form of black protest group emerged in the mid-1960s, best explained by the phrase "black power." As civil rights organizations shifted their emphasis to challenging the lingering social and economic consequences of Jim Crow, they also embraced more strident forms of resistance. Yet, the conversation about civil rights in American public life continues to expand, to gain greater nuances, and to redefine itself to the next generation of students and scholars. The Jim Crow encyclopedia serves as a springboard to this and future discussions on the history of racial subordination and the triumph of social justice.

Readers can quickly identify entries of interest through the alphabetical list of entries and the topical list of entries in the front matter, or from the index. A chronology of the Jim Crow era is also in the front matter. Each entry also offers Further Readings, often including web resources. Each entry includes "See also" cross-reference to other entries of interest. A selected bibliography rounds out the coverage.

Students, and the general public, who strive to understand the full impact of Jim Crow are the primary audience of the *Jim Crow*. The contributors have been drawn from a diversity of intellectual environments. They are professors, teachers, journalists, and lawyers, among others. Their fields of study are similarly diverse, but they are experts on Jim Crow and its impact on American life.

The rise and maintenance of Jim Crow followed what, in hindsight, was a simple pattern of using extralegal and often violent means to prevent black men from voting (women were not allowed to vote when Jim Crow was established) during the final days of Reconstruction. The federal government withdrew from the South and abrogated any responsibility to ensure that civil rights were guaranteed. Once established, all-white state legislatures, courts, sheriffs' departments, and juries could perpetuate Jim Crow largely without the need to employ extralegal means. The dismantling of Jim Crow was likewise founded on ensuring blacks could and did vote.

The popular narrative of the African American experience in the United States is often oversimplified to one of "slavery, emancipation, freedom, and slow but steady progress into mainstream American life." The rise of prominent African Americans in the late twentieth and early twenty-first centuries such as General Colin Powell, Condoleezza Rice, Eric Holder, and especially the election of Barack Obama as president in 2008 put a neat cap on the myth of the slow but steady progress. Left out of that comforting framework are the rise of legally mandated segregation, disenfranchisement, abuse, and almost constant humiliation suffered by most blacks during the Jim Crow decades, and the long and dangerous struggle for civil rights that eventually saw the rise of the black voter, the return of federal enforcement of civil rights, and the dismantling of Jim Crow. The editors and contributors hope that this volume serves several purposes. Foremost is the desire for a succinct ready reference for students seeking an understanding of Jim Crow and related issues. Second, the editors hope to shed light on a period of American history often overlooked by much of society. Finally, the editors hope this volume encourages students to find new ways of looking at that troubling era, and to seek a deeper understanding of particular topics through the *further reading* included with each entry.

Students should, through this volume, understand that while problems faced by the black community in the early twenty-first century are related to the issues of the Jim Crow years, and even slavery before it, current and future generations face a different set of issues. Students should also understand that Jim Crow did not just happen, nor did it simply fall apart on its own. Real flesh-and-blood humans, some famous, many not famous or largely unknown, created and maintained Jim Crow, where others resisted and challenged Jim Crow and eventually brought it down.

The generations-long struggle to end legally sanctioned discrimination and humiliation involved the heroic and the banal. The phenomenon was too long ignored by society at large and simply accepted as the natural order of things. The Civil Rights Movement began the long process of peeling back the layers of ignorance and myth that surrounded what the historian C. Vann Woodward called the "strange career of Jim Crow." The editors hope that the current edition of the encyclopedia adds to the understanding of that shameful period in American history.

Acknowledgments

Jim Crow is the result of collective efforts. Writers for the various entries were sought among college professors, school teachers, doctoral candidates, lawyers, and independent scholars. The editors sought experts from the fields of African American history, civil rights, racism, and related areas. Writers became involved in the project for myriad reasons, but most simply wanted to be part of this important work. The editors, Dr. Nikki L. M. Brown and Dr. Barry M. Stentiford, are deeply grateful that such an especially qualified group of scholars chose to be part of this project. We are especially indebted to Simon T. Cuthbert-Kerr, Olethia Davis, Rutledge M. Dennis, and James W. Loewen, recognized experts in their fields, who wrote several of the cornerstone entries, giving the *Jim Crow Encyclopedia* an authority it might otherwise have lacked. We would also like to thank Dr. Steven Reich and Dr. Ronald Stephens, who served as advisors to the project, for their many valuable suggestions regarding entries and groupings, and allowing us to bounce ideas off of them and occasionally vent.

The editors are pleased to recognize the professionals at ABC-CLIO, especially former senior acquisitions editor Wendi Schnaufer, and Marian Perales, race and ethnicity editorial manager, who understood the need for an encyclopedia documenting Jim Crow. ABC-CLIO has consistently been a strong supporter of creating a useful reference work for students who sought a deeper understanding of this complex and important aspect in the development of American society. We also would like to thank our families and co-workers for tolerating us during the time we were deeply involved in this project.

But most of all, the editors acknowledge, respect, and thank the Americans from many generations who kept alive the dream that Jim Crow would be eventually be deconstructed as it had been constructed. At the risk of their freedom, security, and even lives, they ensured that the dream became a reality, to the benefit of all Americans. For without them, this encyclopedia would simply document a tragedy.

Nikki L. M. Brown
Barry M. Stentiford

Introduction

The term "Jim Crow" refers to a set of laws and customs adopted in many states, predominantly in the American South, after the end of Reconstruction in 1877 that placed severe restrictions on the rights and privileges of African Americans. The name "Jim Crow" originated with a stock character in minstrel shows dating from before the Civil War. The Jim Crow character was usually portrayed by a white actor as a happy, simple minded, country slave. The name was later extended to refer to blacks in general, and then to laws restricting the rights of blacks in particular. As a caste system of enormous social and economic magnitude, the institutionalization of Jim Crow was the most significant element in African American life from the end of Reconstruction until the 1960s.

The attempt during Reconstruction to usher 4 million African Americans from slavery to freedom could simply not compete with the systematic marginalization of people of color under Jim Crow that emerged in the subsequent 70 years. Indeed, what slavery was to the generations after the Civil War, Jim Crow was to the generations following the Civil Rights Movement. Racial segregation, as well as responses to it and resistance against it, dominated the African American consciousness and reinforced long-held beliefs in white supremacy. Division, exclusion, and integration—all based on racism—influenced some of the most important cultural and historical works in African American life. The poetry of Paul Laurence Dunbar, the sociological texts of W.E.B. Du Bois, the literature and art of the Harlem Renaissance, the establishment of historically black colleges and universities, and the growth of the black middle class are just a few of ways in which African Americans have sought to navigate around and dismantle Jim Crow. Although the important watershed events such as the 1954 *Brown v. Board of Education* decision, the 1964 *Civil Rights Act,* and the 1965 *Voting Rights Act* eventually made racial segregation and discrimination illegal, the full impact of Jim Crow is still being measured by academics, teachers, and intellectuals.

Evolution of the Racial Caste System

Immediately after the Civil War ended in 1865, most states of the former Confederacy adopted Black Codes, which were former slave laws refitted in the war's wake to restrict the movement and rights of the former slaves, and eventually all African Americans. Despite constitutional amendments and legislation that abolished slavery and guaranteed African American political rights, the Black Codes instituted a system of racial subordination. The Black Codes also laid the groundwork for the era of Jim Crow. Indeed, Black Codes nullified the Thirteenth Amendment to the U.S. Constitution, which had prohibited slavery, by imposing a similar system under a different name. Radical Republicans, who controlled Congress after the Civil War, were incensed at this flagrant attempt by the Southern states to re-impose a socioeconomic caste system, and placed the defeated states of the former Confederacy under Army occupation during Reconstruction from 1866 to 1877.

Validation of Racial Segregation

During Reconstruction, Southern whites increasingly turned to extralegal means to deny the black vote. Embittered whites created several terrorist organizations, the most infamous of which was the original Ku Klux Klan, created in 1866. The Klan and other groups used the threat of deadly force to instill fear in blacks, and to subdue whites who might dare to openly assist African Americans. Reconstruction officially ended in 1877, with the removal of the last Union troops from the Southern states. The 1880s were marked by the growth in racial violence, which reinforced the subordinate economic status of people of color. Once black men had been prevented from voting for a single election cycle using violence, the white Democrats regained control of state governments and used the mechanism of the government to impose Jim Crow.

Coupled with the violence, political shifts in the legislative and judicial branches led to the exclusion of people of color from the Democratic Party by 1890 and the entire political process by 1900. The Democratic Party in the South had become the organization of white small farmers, disgruntled former Confederates, poor whites, and supporters of states' rights, and it controlled the South after Reconstruction. The resumption of white Democratic control of the South and the adoption of laws restricting the rights of African Americans came to be known as *Redemption*—the salvation of the South. As the Democratic Party thrived after Reconstruction, the declining will of the federal government to protect the civil rights of blacks was reflected in *U.S. v. Cruikshank* (1875). That influential Supreme Court ruling eliminated the power of the federal government to interfere in what was seen as state affairs, and the law allowed states to legislate racial segregation without federal intervention. Congress passed the *Posse Comitatus Act* in 1878, specifically to bar the Army from enforcing law, which stripped away the last power of the federal government to protect blacks—especially those who attempted to vote—from white mobs.

Jim Crow became law of the land with one Supreme Court case of enormous significance. *Plessy v. Ferguson* (1896) signified the complete surrender of the federal government to the white South on matters of civil rights for African Americans, though it also affected other minority groups. The ruling allowed the states the right to segregate blacks from whites, indeed to make segregation mandatory in most aspect of life, as long as the accommodations for each race were "separate but equal." Federal acquiescence reflected weariness on the part of Northerners in dealing with social issues of the South, a struggle that was then in its fourth decade. *Plessy v. Ferguson* was not the first attempt to legislate racial segregation and discrimination. (The first state to segregate public transportation was Tennessee in 1881.) But *Plessy v. Ferguson* was a watershed in American racial and ethnic history. By 1910, every former Confederate state had enacted laws restricting African American political rights, social movement, and economic development.

Normalization of "Separate but Equal"

The phrase "separate but equal" would long burn in the ears of African Americans, who knew intimately that while whites would uphold the "separate" part with zeal, the "equal" part was a complete fiction that no one, black or white, even pretended to believe. Rail cars for white passengers were almost always better than the single-class car reserved for blacks, the "Jim Crow car," or "smoke car." Whites who could afford the higher price of a first-class ticket would have even greater comfort, while no amount of money could buy a black passenger out of the Jim Crow car. Similar dual standards existed in schools, where white children had lower student-to-teacher ratios, newer textbooks, and even sometimes a longer school year, than black students. Restaurants would not allow black customers to eat in the dining room, but required them to use the take-out counter only. Jim Crow dominated almost all aspects of black life in the South, from subjecting blacks to substandard health care and education to daily humiliations of being served last in stores and having to make way for whites on public sidewalks.

Jim Crow became a self-perpetuating system for several decades. The system was particularly degrading to the black middle class. Regardless of income level or intellectual achievement, blacks were instilled with the understanding that they challenged their low status at the peril of their lives. Black landownership remained low compared to whites, as did education levels. Thus the relative poverty and low educational levels of blacks were used to justify their continued exclusion from politics.

Racial stereotypes became a common fixture in the popular American media. American theater, film, and later television became vital instruments in the widespread acceptance of racial segregation. Minstrel shows, comics, cartoons, newspaper stories, and later movies reinforced two divergent images of blacks, both of which underscored the need for white supremacy and the need for Jim Crow laws to control blacks. One image was of blacks as simple, happy-go-lucky, and often child like. The other image was the black beast, the wild emotional creature of hellish lusts, always ready to rape the virtuous white woman, or expressed in the black woman as a wanton woman always ready to seduce a healthy but naive young white man. Such people obviously were not fit for the voting booth, let alone to sit at the same table as white people.

The period from the 1890s into the 1910s, the Nadir of the Negro, was the high point of institutionalized racism. Added to that was a myriad of customs, rules, and unwritten laws, called racial etiquette, that reinforced white supremacy. White men would be addressed as "Mister," while black men would be addressed as "boy," "Uncle," or, if in a newspaper or magazine, as "Negro," but never as "Mister." Blacks would be served last, paid less, required to give way in public places, enter white homes through the back door, and above all, black men would interact socially with white women at the risk of their lives. While legal means enforced the most important foundation of Jim Crow—denying blacks the vote—extra legal means were often employed to enforce the other daily humiliations of blacks. Accusations of rape or murder of whites by blacks brought the most violent response, usually in the form of a lynch mob, although torture and lynching were also applied for a host of lesser transgressions.

The Nadir of the Negro coincided with the high point of European imperialism and so-called scientific racism. Although the foreign policy of the United States had long been officially opposed to European nations taking formal colonial control over other areas of the world, by the end of the nineteenth century, all of Africa except for Ethiopia and Liberia was under the domination of Europe, and even the nominally independent Republic of Liberia was not under the control of indigenous Africans. Additionally, most of Asia was under direct European rule, or part of a sphere of influence of Europeans or the Japanese. With few exceptions, white people were in charge over most of the world. After the Spanish-American War in 1898, the United States itself ruled a small overseas empire of nonwhite colonies. This imperialism and scientific racism dovetailed neatly with Jim Crow in the United States, making the idea that whites ruled nonwhites appear part of the natural order of the world.

Opposition and Survival in the Era of Jim Crow

African Americans struggled against Jim Crow through protests, writing, and other acts of defiance. In general, African Americans sought the elimination of segregation and the recognition of their human and civil rights as American citizens. Some African Americans responded to Jim Crow by advocating a complete separation from American society. Such individuals and groups proposed a spectrum of radical solutions to Jim Crow, ranging from the complete economic and social removal of blacks from American society to the establishment of a separate black nation on the American continent to the removal of blacks to their ancestral homelands in Africa. Most African Americans, however, desired recognition of their basic human and civil rights and to participate in American democracy.

By the 1920s, forces subtle but of lasting importance were underway that would seriously weaken the ability of Jim Crow to continue. Labor shortages in the Northern industrial economy lured African Americans to the North in large numbers during the World War I and World War II, creating a profound demographic shift as the number of African Americans living in the rural South declined. The Harlem Renaissance offered literature and art heralding a New Negro, who militantly challenged the structures of white supremacy. While Northern white racism could at times be as virulent and even as violent as Southern racism, Northern states had few Jim Crow laws that denied blacks the most important civil right—the right to vote. African American voters in the North became an increasingly important constituency for Northern politicians. African American veterans of the world wars had often experienced a world beyond the narrow confines of the Jim Crow South or Northern ghettos. They had experienced the obligations of citizenship, while remaining consciously aware that they were systematically denied the rights of citizenship.

Demolition of Structural Racial Inequality

The history of Jim Crow is interwoven with the threads of resistance, agitation against lynching, the realignment of the Great Migration, and the moral authority of nonviolent civil disobedience, to name a few social movements. These all became crucial parts of the narrative of Jim Crow's downfall. In the original ruling of "separate but equal" lay the Achilles's heel of Jim Crow laws. Had the white South been as scrupulous in maintaining "equal" facilities as they were about "separate," dismantling the system would have been more problematic. But six decades of Jim Crow had amply demonstrated that separate was inherently unequal.

A shift in the outlook of the Supreme Court, combined with vigorous legal assaults launched by the National Association for the Advancement of Colored

People (NAACP), mounted crippling attacks on Jim Crow and the subordination of people of color. World War II, and the patriotic service of African Americans, escorted the transformation of the 1950s. The struggle against Nazism during the war, and the ideological struggle against communism after the war, made many white Americans increasingly aware of the divergence between American rhetoric and practices regarding equality. The eventual result was the landmark 1954 *Brown v. Board of Education,* the Supreme Court ruling that initiated the dismantling of Jim Crow. Although *Brown v. Board of Education* would not in and of itself eradicate all vestiges of Jim Crow and segregation from the United States, it did undermine state laws mandating segregation. The implementation of *Brown v. Board of Education* proved emotional, traumatic, and occasionally violent, but the days of Jim Crow were numbered.

The slow dismantling of Jim Crow came in two phases, from 1955 to 1961, and 1963 to 1965. In the first phase, the Montgomery Bus Boycott and its predecessor, the Baton Rouge Bus Boycott, proclaimed a new conviction to nonviolent resistance and civil disobedience. Civil rights workers focused most of their attention on securing a literal and figurative seat at the table. The world in the 1950s and early 1960s was changing. Glossy magazines such as *Life* brought images of small neat black children being screamed at by angry white adults, or police dogs and fire hoses being used on young black adults, into the living rooms of many Americans who had seldom thought about Jim Crow or race problems.

The second phase of the Civil Rights Movement is marked by the 1963 March on Washington, the 1964 Civil Rights Act, and the 1965 Voting Rights Act. By the summer of 1963, the five main civil rights groups—the Urban League, the Southern Christian Leadership Conference, the Student Non violent Coordinating Committee, the Congress of Racial Equality, and the NAACP—had decided to pool their efforts and organized a march on Washington for jobs and freedom. The March on Washington took place on August 28, 1963. More than 250,000 people gathered at the Lincoln Memorial to hear the various speeches. It was the largest political assembly in American history, and where Dr. Martin Luther King, Jr., gave his famous "I Have a Dream" speech, which brought the entire march to an emotional climax.

In July 1964, President Lyndon B. Johnson signed the Civil Rights Act—the most significant civil rights legislation since Reconstruction. Among many implications in it, the Civil Rights Act of 1964 outlawed discrimination in public accommodations, outlawed discrimination in employment based on race, sex, or national origin, and made the continual segregation of schools illegal.

At great risk to their lives, blacks and whites pushed for voter registration of blacks, and blacks, also at great risk to their lives, began to vote. Johnson then signed the Voting Rights Bill of 1965, which abolished all forms of discrimination in voting, including the poll tax, literacy test, understanding clauses, and grandfather clauses, all of which had been used to prevent blacks from voting. With the passage of these two pieces of legislation, Jim Crow, institutionalized discrimination, and racial segregation were officially illegal.

Jim Crow Chronology

1862	Emancipation Proclamation abolishes slavery in areas under rebellion against the Union.
1865	The Thirteenth Amendment to the Constitution is ratified, abolishing slavery nationwide.
1865–1866	States of the former Confederacy adopt laws that place free blacks in a condition similar to slavery.
1866	Congress passes the Reconstruction Acts that suspend civilian government in the South and place the former Confederacy under military occupation.
1868	The Fourteenth Amendment to the Constitution is ratified, granting equal protection under the law to all American citizens. It also confers citizenship to every person born in the United States, including former slaves.
1875	U.S. Supreme Court ruling in *U.S. v. Cruikshank* strips the federal government of the authority to ensure the protection of citizens attempting to vote.
1877	The Compromise of 1877 removes the last federal troops from the former Confederate states. Reconstruction ends, but the Jim Crow period is not underway fully.
1880	Black migration from the South to the West, begun in 1865, ends. The "Exodusters" sought to escape emerging Jim Crow in the former Confederacy.
1881	Tennessee enacts the first law requiring racial segregation on public trains.
	Booker T. Washington founds the Tuskegee Institute, which builds on the example set by the Hampton Institute founded in 1868.

Washington's leadership of the school would inspire his nickname, the "Wizard of Tuskegee."

1882 The Chinese Exclusion Act drastically limits the number of Chinese immigrants to the United States and requires all Chinese residents who leave the United State to reapply for reentry.

1887 Congress passes the Dawes Severalty Act, beginning official efforts to detribalize the Indians and eliminate reservations. The government divides ancestral and tribal lands and sells the portions not used for capital development.

Major League Baseball imposes racial segregation on all its member teams.

1890s Blues, ragtime, and jazz develop in Southern cities, particularly New Orleans, as the most popular musical forms among African Americans.

The "Nadir of the Negro," a historical period named by historian Rayford Logan, begins in 1890 and runs to the mid-1910s. Lynchings, legal disenfranchisement, and the absence of political equality institutionalize white supremacy and African American subordination.

1890 Mississippi imposes a poll tax, understanding clause, and literacy test for all voters. The state's methods spread to the Alabama in 1893, Virginia in 1894, and South Carolina in 1895. By 1910, all former Confederate states have some provision in place for proscribing black voting.

1895 Booker T. Washington addresses a predominantly white audience at the Atlanta Exposition. Washington pledges African American accommodation to racial abuse in return for economic security.

1896 The National Association of Colored Women (NACW) is founded in Washington, D.C. An African American women's middle-class organization, the NACW would soon become the largest black organization in the country until the 1920s.

The Supreme Court decision *Plessy v. Ferguson* upholds racial segregation on public transportation. In the 8–1 ruling, the majority reasons that legislation "is powerless to eradicate racial instincts or to abolish distinctions based upon physical differences." Segregation, or Jim Crow, quickly spreads to education, public accommodations, housing, and employment.

In a spirited election year, which brought up issue of agrarian rights, race, sectional divisions, and the economy, the Populist Party loses its presidential bid. The breakup of the Populist Party leads to a Southern backlash against African American political activism. The Democratic Party triumphs in the South by promising white supremacy at the polls.

1898   *Williams v. Mississippi* legalizes literacy tests for voter registration. The Supreme Court ruling paves the way for Jim Crow in politics, authorizing legal disenfranchisement and the use of poll taxes, character clauses, and understanding clauses in voting registration.

Race riot in Wilmington, North Carolina, erupts after the Democratic Party tries to oust African American elected officials.

1899   *Cumming v. Richmond County* (Georgia) upholds segregation in public schools by allowing for inequitable funding for black and white secondary schools.

1900   Race riot in New Orleans is sparked by a shoot-out between the police and an African American laborer. Twenty thousand people are drawn into the riot that lasted four days.

1903   W.E.B. Du Bois publishes his landmark polemic, *The Souls of Black Folk*. It pronounces that the "problem of the twentieth century is the problem of the color line."

1905   The Niagara Movement forms. An organization of black intellectuals who opposed Booker T. Washington and his Tuskegee Machine, the Niagara movement promoted black political equality and voting rights.

1906   Rumors of black assaults on white women lead to a race riot in Atlanta. The riot claims the lives of 25 blacks and one white. Hundreds are injured.

1909   National Association for the Advancement of Colored People (NAACP) is founded in New York City. Some of the members of the Niagara Movement contribute to the founding of the NAACP. The board of directors of the NAACP includes several white progressives.

1914–1918   World War I engulfs Europe, and involves much of the world through colonial empires and alliances.

1915   The Great Migration begins. Many African Americans move first from rural areas to cities in the South, then to Northern cities. The Great Migration peaks in the early 1940s.

	D. W. Griffith's film *The Birth of a Nation* is released. Based in part on Thomas Dixon's novel, *The Clansmen,* it depicts the terrorist Ku Klux Klan as heroic defenders of white womanhood and civilization.
1917	The United States enters World War I; in October 1917, 1,000 African American officers are commissioned. Black soldiers win the Croix de Guerre, the French medal for bravery on the front.
June 1917	A race riot in East St. Louis, Illinois, erupts over housing and jobs between working-class whites and blacks. Eight whites and about 100 blacks are killed in the riot. Thousands of residents fleeing the city lose their possessions and homes in the aftermath.
August 1917	A race riot in Houston erupts between the African American soldiers stationed at Camp Logan and the white residents and police officers in nearby Houston. Over 100 soldiers are arrested, and 63 of them are court-martialed. Twenty are later executed, seven are set free, and the rest are given life sentences.
1919	Race riots across the nation claim more 200 lives. The biggest riot is in Chicago.
1920s	Marcus Garvey's Universal Negro Improvement Association (UNIA) gains thousands of followers, until the group's dissolution in the late 1920s. The popularity of UNIA stems from the Black Star Line, a shipping company, founded in 1919.
August 1920	The Nineteenth Amendment passes, granting the right to vote for women.
1921	A race riot in Tulsa, Oklahoma, nearly wipes out the entire African American area, including the "Black" Wall Street.
1925–1935	African American literature, art, and criticism form the Harlem Renaissance, an influential cultural movement. The Harlem Renaissance leads to similar cultural movements in Chicago and Kansas City.
1925	A. Philip Randolph forms the Brotherhood of Sleeping Car Porters.
1926	Historian Carter G. Woodson founds Negro History Week, later evolving into Black History Month.
1929	The crash of the stock market reveals serious problems with the economy.

1932	Franklin D. Roosevelt is elected president. His promise of a New Deal and a "Black Cabinet" in 1933 attracts many black voters to the Democratic Party.
1934	The Nation of Islam comes under the leadership of Elijah Muhammad.
1935	Ethiopia, the last African nation under native rule, is attacked by Italy.
	The National Council of Negro Women is formed.
1936	Jesse Owens wins four gold medals at the Summer Olympics in Berlin.
1938	Boxer Joe Louis defeats Max Schmeling in a rematch from a 1937 fight.
1939	On the personal invitation of Eleanor Roosevelt, Marian Anderson sings at the Lincoln Memorial.
1940	Author Richard Wright publishes *Native Son,* a chilling novel about youth, poverty, and Jim Crow. It is called the "new American tragedy."
1941–1945	The United States joins the Allies and wages war against the Axis Powers of Germany, Japan, and Italy in World War II. African American activists call for a Double V campaign, the defeat of enemies abroad and racism in America.
January 1941	The War Department announces plans to create a "Negro pursuit squadron," which was the beginnings of what became the 332nd Fighter Group—Tuskegee Airmen—of the Army Air Forces.
June 1941	A. Philip Randolph threatens a march on Washington to protest Jim Crow in employment in defense industries.
1941	President Roosevelt signs Executive Order 8802, prohibiting racial discrimination in hiring in government of defense industry during World War II.
1942	Internment of Japanese Americans from West Coast states begins, lasting until 1946.
	James Farmer founds the Congress of Racial Equality.
1945	Nat "King" Cole launches the first black radio variety show on NBC.
1947	Jackie Robinson becomes the first black player in Major League Baseball since 1887, playing for the Brooklyn Dodgers.

1948 President Harry S. Truman orders the desegregation of the U.S. military with Executive Order 9981.

Larry Doby integrates the American League in Major League Baseball, playing for the Cleveland Indians.

1949 Essayist James Baldwin critiques Richard Wright's depiction of African American protest to racism in his short essay, "Everybody's Protest Novel."

Jackie Robinson wins the National League's Most Valuable Player Award.

1950s The first segment of the Civil Rights Movement is underway by 1954.

1950 The Supreme Court decides for both the plaintiffs in *Sweatt v. Painter* and *McLaurin v. Oklahoma.* The lawsuits were a huge success for the NAACP Legal Defense Fund.

1952 Ralph Ellison publishes *Invisible Man,* a stinging critique of Jim Crow.

1954 The Supreme Court decides for the plaintiffs in the landmark *Brown v. Board of Education.* The ruling makes illegal segregation and discrimination in the nation's public schools.

Brown II requires the desegregation of American public schools. The decision is met with massive resistance from the states.

1955 Chicago teenager Emmett Till is lynched while visiting relatives in Mississippi.

Rosa Parks is arrested in Montgomery, Alabama, for not giving up her seat to a white passenger. The Montgomery Improvement Association launches a yearlong boycott. It is the first national protest movement for Martin Luther King, Jr.

1956 Billie Holliday, acclaimed jazz singer, publishes her autobiography, *Lady Sings the Blues.*

1957 The Civil Rights Act of 1957 commits the federal government to prosecute abuses of African American civil rights.

Nine black students in Little Rock, Arkansas, attempt to desegregate Central High School. The Little Rock school board closes the school in protest the next year.

1958 Martin Luther King Jr., Ralph Abernathy, and other African American ministers form the Southern Christian Leadership Conference.

1960	John F. Kennedy is elected president with large support from African American voters.
	Four African American students at North Carolina A&T begin a national movement with their sit-in at a segregated lunch counter at Woolworth's.
	The Student Nonviolent Coordinating Committee forms, a follower of Martin Luther King's program of nonviolence.
1961	The Freedom Rides begin. They last for approximately four weeks.
1962	James Meredith enters the University of Mississippi.
1963	Essayist and author James Baldwin publishes *The Fire Next Time*, a critique of the national resistance to the Civil Rights Movement.
	Medgar Evers, president of the Mississippi chapter of the NAACP, is shot and killed in his driveway.
August	The historic March on Washington for Jobs and Freedom converges in August. Martin Luther King Jr. delivers his "I Have a Dream Speech."
November	President John F. Kennedy is assassinated.
1964	Nobel Peace Prize is awarded to Martin Luther King Jr.
	Malcolm X makes his pilgrimage to Mecca. Upon his return, he forms the Organization of Afro-American Unity.
	The Civil Rights Act of 1964 is passed. The landmark legislation outlawed racial segregation in all public transportation, public accommodation, employment, and education. It also prohibited government financial support of any institution or agency practicing Jim Crow.
1965	Malcolm X is assassinated.
	The last legal vestiges of Jim Crow are removed. The Voting Rights Act abolishes all forms of legal disenfranchisement and pledged to prosecute illegal disenfranchisement.

A

Abernathy, Ralph David

Considered one of the "Big Three" leaders of the Civil Rights Movement, Ralph David Abernathy joined Martin Luther King Jr., Fred Shuttlesworth, and a long list of African American clergymen who defeated Jim Crow using the doctrine of nonviolence. Born in Linden, Alabama, in 1926, Abernathy was the 10th of the 12 children born to William and Louivery (Bell) Abernathy. Abernathy's parents named him David, which family members called him throughout his youth; he registered as Ralph David Abernathy when he enlisted in the U.S. Army in 1944.

The Abernathy family was solidly middle class, in comparison to other residents of Marengo County in rural Alabama in the 1930s and 1940s. William Abernathy owned several hundred acres of fertile land, from which the family drew most of its food and resources. The family also enjoyed an elevated status in Linden, Alabama, as William Abernathy was a deacon at Hopewell Baptist Church and a successful farmer. At the insistence of Louivery Abernathy, all of the Abernathy children attended primary and secondary school. World War II erupted while Abernathy was still in high school, but he enlisted in the army in 1944. Abernathy was honorably discharged at the rank of sergeant in the summer of 1945.

In September 1945, Abernathy entered Alabama State College (now Alabama State University) in Montgomery. At Alabama State, Abernathy studied mathematics and the political activism of civil disobedience. As president of the Student Council, Abernathy met with the president of Alabama State to protest the living conditions of veteran-students, who lived in barracks with no heating and poor plumbing. After the meeting, promises for improvements were made and kept. Abernathy later remarked that his meetings with the intimidating president of Alabama State prepared him for debates over civil rights with future presidents John F. Kennedy, Lyndon B. Johnson, and Richard M. Nixon. Abernathy graduated in 1950 with a BS in mathematics.

Baptist clergyman Ralph Abernathy was Martin Luther King Jr.'s closest coworker during the Civil Rights Movement and the leader of the Southern Christian Leadership Conference after King's death. (National Archives)

Abernathy also found a religious calling while he was a student at Alabama State. He gave a number of sermons at First Baptist Church in Montgomery. When he enrolled at Atlanta University to earn a master's degree in sociology in 1950, he attended the historical Ebenezer Baptist Church. There he met two influential figures in Atlanta's church community, Vernon Johns and Martin Luther King Jr. After graduating in 1951, Abernathy returned to Alabama, where he took two positions, one as dean of men at Alabama State College, and another as the primary pastor at First Baptist Church. Three years later, King and his family moved to Montgomery, where he was named chief pastor at Dexter Avenue Baptist Church. Abernathy and King had similar political interests, including a fascination with the writings of Mahatma Gandhi and the peaceful withdrawal of the British from colonial India after World War II. The two pastors became close friends, and their relationship remained steadfast until King's death in 1968.

Abernathy and King's first organized attack on Jim Crow was the Montgomery Bus Boycott of 1955–1956. Set off by the arrest of Rosa Parks, a seamstress and secretary of the National Association for Advancement of Colored People (NAACP) Montgomery chapter, the boycott of Montgomery's segregated city buses quickly galvanized African American support. Jo Ann Gibson Robinson, leader of the Women's Political Council of Montgomery and a professor of English at Alabama State, had expertly organized a complex network of carpools and private transportation for a one-day boycott in December 1955. Abernathy and King joined with Robinson's network to form the Montgomery Improvement Association (MIA). Arranging a system of phone banks, reduced fare taxis, private cars, and escorts, the MIA extended the boycott over 12 months. The MIA also professed nonviolent resistance and civil disobedience. The Montgomery Bus Boycott emerged successful in December 1956, when the city surrendered to the demands of the MIA and the abolished segregation on its public transportation. After the boycott, King became the charismatic scholar and pastor of the Civil Rights Movement, and Abernathy became its chief tactician.

The success of the Montgomery Bus Boycott led to the founding of the Southern Christian Leadership Conference (SCLC) in Atlanta, Georgia. Abernathy joined King, Fred Shuttlesworth, Joseph Lowery, and other prominent clergymen to establish an organization dedicated to the eradication of Jim Crow and to nonviolence. The SCLC's mission differed from that of the NAACP and the NAACP Legal Defense and Education Fund. The SCLC focused on gathering moral and religious objections to Jim Crow, while the NAACP Legal Defense Fund broke down the legal structures of segregation and white supremacy. Together, the two groups worked to dismantle Jim Crow and change American consciousness, which had tolerated the worst abuses in white supremacy.

Yet Abernathy's activism in the state of Alabama drew harassment and violent backlash. In 1957, while he attended a planning session of the SCLC in Atlanta, his home and church were bombed. His pregnant wife, Juanita, and Juandalynn, their child, narrowly escaped injury, but the arsonists were never caught. Moreover, three other churches were bombed the same night, Bell Street Baptist, Hutchison Street Baptist, and Mt. Olive Baptist. The bitter resistance to the Civil Rights Movement in Montgomery forced Abernathy to move his family to Atlanta in 1960. In 1962, Abernathy and three other clergymen were sued for libel by the attorney general of the state of Alabama. The lawsuit claimed that Abernathy, Joseph Lowery, S. S. Seay, Fred Shuttlesworth, and the *New York Times* had slandered the city by supporting an advertisement in the newspaper to raise funds for King's legal defenses. In *Sullivan v. New York Times,* the jury initially found for the plaintiffs, but the Court overturned the ruling on appeal in 1964.

In Atlanta, King, Abernathy, and the SCLC launched their most memorable, nonviolent attacks on Jim Crow. They maintained their conviction that nonviolence, primarily surrendering to inevitable suffering, would transform the hearts and minds of segregationists and white supremacists. Abernathy's faith and his adherence to nonviolence shaped the critical involvement of the SCLC in the Civil Rights Movement of the mid-1960s. They supported the Freedom Rides of 1961 by taking the riders and their families into the West Hunter Street Baptist Church. They organized the marches against segregation in Birmingham and Selma, and were arrested several times. Abernathy saw King and the SCLC through the difficult period following the Albany marches, and the high point of the 1963 March on

Washington. He also rallied for protests in St. Augustine, Charleston, and Chicago in the latter half of the decade.

Eventually, the violence following the leaders of the Civil Rights Movement caught up with the two leaders. In April 1968, the SCLC members traveled to Memphis to support a sanitation workers' strike. Standing on the balcony at the Lorraine Hotel, King was shot and killed by James Earl Ray on April 4. Abernathy was the last person to see King alive. The assassination of King left a profound void on the Civil Rights Movement, particularly on newer, more militant incarnations. After King's death, Abernathy was vaulted into the presidency of the SCLC. His immediate task was to assess the popularity of groups that had turned to Black Power for answers. Once a close political ally, the Student Nonviolent Coordinating Committee (SNCC) had become increasingly dissatisfied with nonviolence and the goals of integration. The Black Panthers and the U.S. movement amassed a large following of young African Americans, and college students across the country rallied for changes in university curricula to reflect African American contributions. The SCLC had a difficult time appealing to the newer recruits to the Civil Rights Movement, and nonviolence appeared to lose its place as the nation struggled with the assassination of Robert F. Kennedy and the escalation of the Vietnam War.

Stepping into King's shoes as president of the SCLC proved exceedingly difficult for Abernathy. Not only did national events necessitate a response from the organization, but Abernathy's style and leadership were often unfavorably compared with that of King. For example, Abernathy carried on King's program for a Poor People's March on Washington, DC, but the 1968 march attracted much less interest and the tent city, Resurrection City, was taken down by the National Guard. Though Abernathy and the doctrine of nonviolence took the moral high ground amid the violence of the late 1960s, the SCLC competed with the increasingly popular Black Power movement and its militant message. The SCLC was also under considerable pressure to raise funds to continue its work, and it needed new, dues-paying members to fund its activism. The difficulty confronting Abernathy was the type of activism a post-King SCLC should undertake to preserve the organization and the movement.

By the mid-1970s, the SCLC split into two distinct halves—a section of older, middle-class protestors espousing nonviolence and marches, and a section of younger students espousing direct action and self-protection from the police, especially gun ownership rights. In 1977, a vote on the future of the organization was put to the members of the SCLC. The older generation of activists won out, and the SCLC continued its program of nonviolence. Yet, the dispute took its toll on Abernathy's presidency, and he resigned later that year. He ran for a congressional seat representing Georgia in 1977, but his bid was unsuccessful. A fellow cofounder of the SCLC, Joseph Lowery, followed Abernathy as president of the SCLC.

Abernathy later returned to his position as pastor of West Hunter Baptist in Atlanta. He served there from 1977 to 1990. His church deepened its commitment to empowering black communities in Atlanta, by establishing the Foundation for Economic Enterprises Development. In 1989, Abernathy published his autobiography, *And the Walls Came Tumbling Down,* a moving description of the highs and lows of the Civil Rights Movement from 1955 to 1968 with King and the SCLC. Abernathy's autobiography also disclosed some embarrassing mistakes in King's personal life, which drew much criticism from other members of the movement. Abernathy died a year later in Atlanta.

Nikki L. M. Brown

See also: King, Martin Luther, Jr.; Montgomery Bus Boycott.

Further Reading

Abernathy, Ralph David. *And the Walls Came Tumbling Down.* New York: Harper & Row, 1989.

Branch, Taylor. *Parting the Waters: America during the King Years, 1954–63.* New York: Simon and Schuster, 1988.

Fairclough, Adam. *To Redeem the Soul of America: The Southern Christian Leadership Conference and Martin Luther King, Jr.* Athens: University of Georgia Press, 1987.

Garrow, David J. *Bearing the Cross: Martin Luther King, Jr., and the Southern Christian Leadership Conference, 1955–1968.* New York: Morrow, 1986.

Advertising

The use of images of African Americans in advertising has a long history in American marketing. However, even before such images were used for promotional purposes in the United States, images of blacks made for popular advertisements in European marketing campaigns. In both cases, early advertisements featuring blacks relied heavily on popular racist stereotypes that changed little over time. In the United States, these changes came largely as the result of changing social attitudes about race, increased involvement of African Americans in the advertising industry, the growing purchasing power of black markets, and activism on the part of concerned African Americans.

African Americans were first used in commercial imagery in the United States during the 1870s. Utilizing recent developments in color lithography technology that made it possible to produce colorized images cheaply, manufacturers featured images of African Americans on trade cards, a very popular form of advertising in the years between 1870 and 1900. Trade cards were used to advertise a wide variety of consumer items and were included with the product at the time of purchase as an incentive for the consumer.

From the earliest manifestations in America, images of blacks in advertisements frequently drew on existing demeaning, racist stereotypes that had once served to justify the enslavement of blacks. While some nineteenth-century advertisements depicted African Americans in a positive or neutral way, they were much more likely to be represented as ugly, subservient, or ignorant, and were often utilized to depict acts of domestic or manual labor. One popular example of this type of image can be found in a long-lived Lever Brothers advertising campaign featuring the Gold Dust Twins. Designed by the Chicago advertising firm N. K. Fairbanks & Co. in 1884 for a line of cleaning products, advertisements using the Gold Dust Twins showed the twins, two young black children named Goldie and Dustie, diligently cleaning household surfaces for white consumers.

Advertisements for soaps and cleaning products in general were especially likely to utilize images of blacks, creating a popular theme in which the efficacy of the product being promoted was demonstrated by its ability to remove or wash away blackness from skin. The most well-known advertisement of this kind is a 1903 advertisement for Pear's soap, an English product also sold in the United States. In this advertisement, Pear's promotes itself as "powerful enough to clean a black child," and features a before-and-after image in which a young white boy helps a young black boy into a tub of soapy water, causing the body of the black child to turn white. While this is one of the most commonly cited images of this sort in the modern era, it is only one example of a great number of advertisements that utilized this motif.

For white consumers who associated black domestic servants with a life of leisure and status, or who were nostalgic for the enslaved domestic help of decades past, advertisers created a multitude of smiling black mammies, butlers, and other servants. Corporate logos like Aunt Jemima, Uncle Ben, and Rastus are among the most well known of these figures, as their use has persisted into the modern day, but they were certainly not the only images of this type. Convenience products, a relatively new category of consumer item, were particularly likely to adopt these images, as they could suggest that the time and effort saved by the product was akin to having personal domestic help.

Most early nineteenth-century advertisements that depicted images of blacks were for products intended for white consumers. Few industries at this time thought of African Americans as a consumer base worth courting. Those products that were marketed directly to black consumers were usually items that only blacks purchased, such as products designed to lighten skin or straighten hair. These products, which were created for the purposes of altering black features to better adhere to white standards of beauty, were often no less racist than advertisements marketed to white consumers. Depicting images that showed black features as ugly or undesirable, especially when compared to idealized images of white features, these images tapped into an American racial discourse that pathologized the black body while holding up the white form as a normative model of health and perfection. At its most extreme, this practice presented the image of the golliwog, a caricature of blackness and minstrelsy imported from England. The golliwog was an often-subhuman figure recognizable by its black-colored skin, large, exaggerated facial features, and wild, bushy hair.

Despite the political and socioeconomic restrictions placed on African Americans by Jim Crow laws in the South and informal systems of racial segregation and discrimination in the North, the decades following emancipation saw a dramatic increase in the population of middle-class African Americans. While increased buying power did little to alter the popularity of demeaning images in advertising, it did catch the attention of businesses and advertisers, and a marketing industry targeting black customers began to develop in earnest.

In 1916, a gas company in Rock Hill, South Carolina, became one of the first companies to create an advertisement designed to target African American consumers of a race-neutral product. These advertisements promoted the company's collaboration with a local church group to create a cooking school for African Americans looking for employment as servants. As a result of this promotional campaign, the gas company sold 12 kitchen stoves to African American customers, a significant number at the time.

Other companies soon developed African American marketing campaigns of their own. Some, like the Fuller Brush Company in 1922, even began hiring African Americans as salespersons and representatives for markets within black communities. Other companies that discovered unexpected markets among African America consumers began altering not only their marketing strategies but their production as well.

Companies' desires to tap into the purchasing power of African Americans intensified further in the 1930s. This was in no small part due to a study commissioned by Montgomery Ward, Anheuser-Busch, and the Lever Brothers, and conducted by the National Negro Business League. This study, one of the first to investigate the national income, spending, and living habits of African Americans, placed the disposable income of African American consumers at approximately $1.65 million. That same decade, Paul K. Edwards, a professor of economics at Fisk University published "The Negro Commodity Market" in the May 1932 issue of the *Harvard Business School Bulletin,* the first academic study to offer a systematic evaluation of African Americans as consumers.

Through the 1930s, despite decades of increasing corporate interest in African Americans as targeted customers and the business practice of employing African Americans as sales representatives to black markets, all major American advertising firms were owned and managed by whites. This began to change in the 1940s, helped along in no small part by the establishment of black-owned magazines such as *Ebony,* which were willing and eager to work with other black-owned businesses.

Vomack Advertising of Inwood, New York, was the first black-founded advertising agency, but others soon followed, including Fusche, Young, and Powell in Detroit and David Sullivan in New York City, both founded in 1943. Meanwhile, in white-owned advertising agencies, some African Americans began making inroads against long-standing racist hiring policies, acquiring jobs not only as entry-level sales representatives but also as advisers and marketing consultants.

Despite these advancements, the power of African Americans in the advertising industry remained very limited. Images of blacks in popular advertisements continued to represent racist, derogatory stereotypes. In fact, many historical analyses suggest that the number of these kinds of images only increased in the years following the Great Depression. Furthermore, those African Americans who were able to establish themselves in the advertising industry were almost exclusively limited to the creation of marketing for other black-owned companies, for advertisements designed to target African American customers, or for promotions intended to run only in African American media outlets. Industries who wanted to market their products outside the African American market rarely employed blacks in their advertising campaigns, which limited the input African American advertising companies had on mainstream advertisements.

The limited opportunities faced by black advertisers also presented financial difficulties that many advertising firms could not overcome. Many black-owned advertising agencies failed as a result of their inability to compete with larger firms that could attract business from both black- and white-owned companies. The David Sullivan Agency, one of the earliest black-owned advertising firms, was forced to close under these conditions in 1949, only six years after it opened.

White-owned advertising firms could affect African Americans in other ways as well. In 1956, NBC began running a television series starring the popular singer Nat "King" Cole. In the years before the program aired, Cole had established himself as an immensely popular African American performer, with 4 number-one hits, 13 top-ten hits, and a history of performances on a number of television variety programs. Most people expected that Cole's television series would become a substantial success, and ratings for the program were favorable. The series presented a problem for advertisers, however. Contemporary studies had enticed marketers with descriptions of African American consumers as being particularly likely to be brand-loyal customers with strong brand consciousness. For many African American consumers, especially those in the black middle class, the freedom of choice in the marketplace was one of the few social or political arenas in which the rights of African Americans were not restricted, and purchasing brands that suggested prestige or status could be a means of laying claim to these qualities, which were denied to them elsewhere.

Given the implications of these studies, advertisers were eager to find opportunities to appeal to black consumers, and a nationwide broadcast featuring a popular and successful black performer would have been an excellent way of reaching that market. Despite this potential appeal, Cole's program was cancelled after his yearly contract expired due to its inability to attract advertisers, as white-owned companies were unwilling to ally with African American products or advertisements in mainstream media. Despite Cole's popularity among black and white Americans alike, advertisers feared that buying time on his program would upset whites or cause them to associate the advertised products with African Americans, thereby devaluing their appeal to white consumers.

The first significant changes regarding images of blacks in American advertising and the role of African Americans in the advertising industry began to happen in the 1960s. As movements for social change began to exert a presence in the national consciousness, blacks who had long objected to these images began to use these organizations to exert change. Initially, most of these changes were found in advertisements marketed to or created by African Americans. In keeping with the larger African American cultural ethos of black pride that was popularized in this decade, for the first time, these advertisements began to reject the use of models or images with fair skin, straightened hair, or Caucasian features in favor of models and positive images of blacks with dark skin, natural hairstyles, and nonwhite facial features.

Organizations like the Congress of Racial Equality (CORE), the National Association for the Advancement of Colored People (NAACP), and People United to Save Humanity (PUSH) arranged meetings with groups like the American Association of Advertising Agencies to convince advertisers to fundamentally alter the way that they represented, marketed to, and provided sponsorship opportunities for African Americans. In addition to holding meetings, these organizations also helped to organize boycotts of products whose advertising and marketing strategies continued to promote racism against African Americans.

While most white advertisers were slow to respond to these efforts in any substantial way, the efforts of civil rights activists to change the way the media represented blacks did result in gradual but meaningful transformations. By 1970, the images of blacks in American advertisements were considerably different from those seen a decade earlier, and a number of significant milestones had been reached. In 1963, the New York Telephone Company released a newspaper advertisement that was so revolutionary that many newspapers that carried it felt moved to include articles about it the next day. The advertisement was the first of its kind to run in a mainstream media publication and featured a professionally dressed black man entering a telephone booth, bearing none of the stereotypically black attributes that had been commonly present in American advertising.

Some images of African Americans in advertising have proved more durable than others. Studies of the black image in advertising have found it particularly useful to focus on two of these images, Aunt Jemima and Uncle Ben, as their early creation, changes over time, and survival on popular modern products has made them useful case studies for the study of the ways in which the African American relationship with advertising has changed over time.

As the most popular and enduring image of the mammy figure in popular American advertising, Aunt Jemima has been the focus of a great many scholarly and popular studies on the image of black women in American advertising. Chris L. Rutt developed the Aunt Jemima trademark in 1889 after seeing a similar character of the same name in a blackface performance. The original Aunt Jemima image featured a smiling, chubby black woman wearing a kerchief over her hair, and was understood to be a slave. In 1890, the R. T. Davis Milling Company hired Nancy Green, an emancipated slave from Montgomery County, Kentucky, to play Aunt Jemima for public promotions. After Green died in 1923, she was replaced by a new Aunt Jemima, a practice that continued into the 1960s. In total, R. T. Davis and Quaker Oats, which purchased the brand in 1926, hired seven different women, sometimes simultaneously, to play the character of Aunt Jemima for radio, television, public appearances, and promotional images.

The image of Aunt Jemima has been a brand logo for over 100 years, and has been redesigned a number of times. Many of these changes have been in response to changes in the identity of the public spokesperson. Aunt Jemima was first redesigned in 1933 to better match the image of Anna Robinson, Quaker Oats' second Aunt Jemima; again in the 1950s for Ethel Ernestine Harper, the fourth Aunt Jemima; and once again in the 1960s, when Aunt Jemima was redrawn as a composite character.

Objections to the sexism and racism inherent to the Aunt Jemima logo began to appear in the black press and the national consciousness as early as the 1920s. African Americans who saw the figure as a demeaning representation of white desires for blacks to smilingly accept servile, socially inferior roles began adopting the phrase "Aunt Jemima" as a feminine version of the derogatory term "Uncle Tom." Despite these objections, which became increasingly intense in the decades following 1950, few major changes were made to the image of Aunt Jemima. While

Aunt Jemima was made to appear younger and more physically attractive during these decades, these changes were largely intended to increase her appeal to white consumers.

In 1989, following boycotts by the NAACP and attacks in popular works by black artists, Quaker Foods responded to the continued objections of social rights activists by replacing Aunt Jemima's kerchief with pearl earrings and a lace collar, an update intended to rid the figure of connotations of slavery. This change was supplemented in 1992 by another change that straightened the tilt of Aunt Jemima's head, which many people had interpreted as a symbol of deference and docility. While these changes have done much to decrease the intensity of objections to the advertising image of Aunt Jemima, the logo is still capable of provoking controversy and unease, as many consumers see the corporate retention of the brand image as a troubling reminder of the logo's history.

The corporate logo of Uncle Ben is another advertising image that has been the subject of much debate and study. The image was created in the 1940s by Gordon L. Halliwell during the planning stages of what would later become Uncle Ben's Converted Rice Company. According to corporate history, the inspiration for the character came from an actual individual, a rice farmer from Houston, Texas, referred to as Uncle Ben, who, before his death, had been locally famous for the high quality of his product. The actual image of Uncle Ben was supplied by Frank Brown, maitre d' at a restaurant that the founders of the company patronized.

Critics of the Uncle Ben image objected to the logo for reasons that were mostly similar to objections to the image of Aunt Jemima. Activists for black social and civil rights argued that the continued use of the addresses "Aunt" and "Uncle" promoted a racist naming tradition in which Southern blacks had been denied the use of courtesy titles reserved for whites, such as "Mr." and "Mrs." Further objections were raised regarding Uncle Ben's association with rice, an agricultural product stereotypically associated with African Americans based on the heavy use of enslaved black labor on the large rice plantations of the South.

In 2007, Mars Inc., the corporate owner of the Uncle Ben's line of products, attempted to address the racial concerns associated with the image by giving the character a promotion, making him the symbolic chairman of the board for the company. As in the case of Aunt Jemima, this change in image has been met with a mixed response from consumers concerned about the representations of blacks in American advertising. While there has been positive responses to the elimination of a black figure as a servant and his reemergence as a successful businessmen, many people see this symbolic promotion as a cosmetic improvement that cannot make up for the image's longer history of racist symbolism, especially given the retention of the title "Uncle," a decidedly unbusinesslike honorific.

Skylar Harris

See also: Jim Crow; Minstrelsy.

Further Reading

Elliot, Stuart. "Uncle Ben, Board Chairman." *New York Times,* March 30, 2007.

Kern-Foxworth, Marilyn. *Aunt Jemima, Uncle Ben, and Rastus: Blacks in Advertising Yesterday, Today, and Tomorrow.* Westport, CT: Greenwood Press, 1994.

Manring, Maurice. *Slave in a Box: The Strange Career of Aunt Jemima.* Charlottesville: University of Virginia Press, 1998.

McElya, Micki. *Clinging to Mammy: The Faithful Slave in 20th Century America.* Cambridge, MA: Harvard University Press, 2007.

Moss, Janice Ward. *The History and Advancement of African Americas in the Advertising Industry, 1895–1999.* Lewiston, NY: Edwin Mellen Press, 2003.

Motley, Carol M., Geraldine R. Henderson, and Stacy Menzel Baker. "Exploring Collective Memories Associated with African America Advertising Memorabilia: The Good, the Bad, and the Ugly." *Journal of Advertising* 32 (2003): 47–57.

Museum of Public Relations. *Moss Kendrix.* 2006. November 26, 2007, http://www.prmuseum.com/kendrix/moss1.html.

Affirmative Action

In March 1961, President John F. Kennedy set the first steps of affirmative action in motion when he began his term with Executive Order 10925, creating the Committee on Equal Employment Opportunity. The edict compelled contractors to cease all discrimination against employees or employment applicants based on "race, creed, color, or national origin" while taking "affirmative action" to "curb unfair employment practices" due to such discrimination. The phrase "affirmative action" was thus conceived and has since been used to refer to all counter-discriminatory practices.

The Civil Rights Act of 1964, an initiative of President Lyndon B. Johnson, took the idea of equal opportunity employment to the national level. Under the act, affirmative action was bolstered when it demanded the aforementioned discriminated groups the full ability to participate in, benefit from, and be free from all discrimination "under any program or activity receiving federal financial assistance." The statute was pivotal in the rights of discriminated groups, but highly contentious across the United States. Within a year, Johnson believed that it was working to level the playing field of employment, since many minorities had long been hobbled by racism and racist practices.

Johnson gave a speech on June 4, 1965, at Howard University regarding civil rights, and in particular, he argued for the necessity for social programs that benefited minority members of the American public. He hoped the Civil Rights Act

President John Kennedy and Vice President Lyndon Johnson pose with executives of 12 corporations after the executives signed agreements to provide equal employment opportunities to all, at the White House in Washington on November 30, 1961. (AP Photo/William Smith)

would provide discriminated groups, particularly African Americans, equal prospects with "every other American to learn and grow, to work and share in society, to develop their abilities—physical, mental and spiritual, and to pursue their individual happiness." He thought that affirmative action was the most effective way to achieve this end, adding that "Negro [African American] poverty is not white poverty." Though "many of its causes and many of its cures are the same," there are glaring differences. Johnson held that these differences are not based on ethnicity, "but the result of a long history of oppression prejudice and brutality," with effects that "[radiate] painful roots into the community, into the family, and the nature of the individual." Those afflicted by white poverty had not been endowed with a "cultural tradition which had been twisted and battered by endless years of hatred and hopelessness" or exclusion "because of race or color—a feeling whose dark intensity is matched by no other prejudice in our society." His powerful words led to the conclusion that African Americans "just cannot do it alone," and would require the help of their government to achieve the equality that they deserve.

In 1965, President Johnson issued another directive, Executive Order 11246, which furthered affirmative action even more. The order appended to the fray pressure to the "action" side of affirmative action within government. Johnson demanded "positive, continuing program in each [government] department and agency" to "promote the full realization of equal employment opportunity" for "all qualified persons" regardless of national, cultural, or racial background. The act was later amended to include sex, and altogether it further established affirmative-action policies.

Arthur Holst

See also: Historically Black Colleges and Universities.

Further Reading

Cahn, Stephen. "Stephen Cahn on the History of Affirmative Action" (1995). http://aad .english.ucsb.edu/docs/Cahn.html (accessed December 23, 2003).
"The History of Affirmative Action Policies," July 7, 2002. In *Motion* magazine. http:// www.inmotionmagazine.com/aahist.html (accessed September 6, 2002).
Johnson, Lyndon B. "To Fulfill These Rights": Commencement Address at Howard University, June 4, 1965. http://score.rims.k12ca.us/activity/lbj/lbjspeech.html (accessed September 6, 2002).
Sykes, Marquita. "The Origins of Affirmative Action." http://www.now.org/nnt/08-95/ affirmhs.html (accessed December 23, 2003).

Alabama

Alabama, a Deep South state in the "Heart of Dixie," was also one of the centers of Jim Crow. In several respects, Alabama followed the lead of other states in establishing Jim Crow legislation, but once Jim Crow was established in the state, eradicating it would be a long, painful, and at times bloody ordeal. During the 1960s, Alabama became the focal point of the Civil Rights Movement, while white resistance and violence brought the state notoriety.

After Reconstruction, Alabama followed the lead of Mississippi in using white Democratic control of the courts, legislature, and governor's mansion, to establish legal means to prevent black suffrage. With blacks rendered negligible as a political force in the state, Jim Crow laws proliferated by the beginning of the twentieth century. During the 1920s, the revived Ku Klux Klan became a powerful force in Alabama, but with poll taxes and other means keeping blacks off juries and out of the polling places, the Klan in Alabama focused more on Populist causes, such as better public schools for white children, and Prohibition. Many poorer whites flocked to the new Klan, seeing it as a way of breaking the monopoly on political power of the large landowners and the factory owners in cities such as Birmingham, the so-called Big Mules. Hugo Black, who would later be appointed to the U.S. Supreme

Court, was elected senator in 1926 with the backing of the Klan. As a senator, he wholly supported the New Deal. Governor Bibb Graves was elected governor in 1926, also with Klan backing, and he instituted some of the most progressive programs for poor whites in the state's history.

However by the late 1920s, the Klan lost much of its popular support in Alabama. Their heavy-handed attempts to enforce a strict moral code harassed many whites. As long as the Klan focused its violent urges on blacks, it was tolerated. But with Alabama's blacks essentially rendered powerless by Jim Crow, the Klan had found new white targets, white people who could vote and serve on juries. After Klansmen stripped to the waist a divorced white woman, tied her to a tree, and whipped her for immorality, the Klan lost much of its grassroots support.

Moderate and liberal whites had never totally disappeared from the state. The 1938 Southern Conference on Human Welfare met in Birmingham, bringing together 1,200 black and white Southerners, including labor leaders, political and business leaders, newspaper editors, and academics. The group supported paying black and white school teachers equally, and endorsed passing a federal antilynching law. First Lady Eleanor Roosevelt attended. However, despite such meetings, the overwhelming majority of white Alabamans supported Jim Crow.

Still, the years after World War II were a time of optimism for opponents of Jim Crow. The growth of Redstone Arsenal at Huntsville, in the northern part of the state, and its concurrent influx of German scientists involved in the federal government's rocket programs, indicated that the state's future was perhaps to be more cosmopolitan and high-tech oriented, than the state traditionally had been. The Montgomery Bus Boycott, begun in December 1955, eventually resulted in an ending of the system of segregation on that city's buses. Governor James Folsom, who served two nonconsecutive terms from 1947 to 1951 and from 1955 to 1959, raised hope among blacks and white liberals that change might come relatively painlessly. A Populist, Folsom often expressed his desire to help "the common man" and unite the people of his state. He sought to abolish the poll taxes that kept many poor whites as well as blacks from voting. He publicly spoke against the formation of a White Citizens Council in Alabama.

However Folsom's moderate stance on Jim Crow proved too soft for many of Alabama's white residents, who, after all, made up most of the voters. When Folsom tried to accommodate the increased federal involvement in civil rights, his political base dissolved. Poorer whites, often fearing any lessening of Jim Crow, switched their support to candidates they thought would oppose federal intrusion and maintain the status quo on racial issues. In the 1962 gubernatorial election, George C. Wallace defeated Folsom. Wallace had previously been a moderate and had even been backed by the National Association for the Advancement of Colored People in his 1958 bid for the governorship. Wallace lost that election to John

Patterson, who had the support of the Ku Klux Klan. Learning from his defeat, Wallace adopted a strict segregationist stance, which propelled him to the governor's mansion and, eventually, into the national spotlight.

The 1960s turned out to be much different from the 1950s. White supremacist elements in the state saw the gains in black civil rights in the 1950s as a call to stiffen their resistance to further gains by blacks. Birmingham, a city located in the center of the state with an economy based on steel mills, was one of the most segregated cities on America. Police Chief "Bull" Connor, who took office in 1957, swore to use all means to enforce segregation. In 1963, he directed his forces to use police dogs and fire hoses on demonstrators. When photographs of Birmingham police attacking blacks were published in *Life* and other national magazines, Connor became the national face of official white resistance to the Civil Rights Movement. When bombs planted by three Ku Klux Klan members killed four girls at the Sixteenth Street Baptist Church on September 15, 1963, Connor publicly speculated that members of the Civil Rights Movement themselves had planted the bomb to stir up sympathy. He later closed all public parks and golf courses in the city, rather than allow their integration, as ordered by the federal courts.

Connor was only one man, but he represented an entrenched system with wide support among Alabama whites. Given the tension in the state, more confrontations were perhaps inevitable. On February 18, 1965, during a civil rights demonstration on the town of Selma, a state policeman shot Jimmie Lee Jackson in a café, where he and his mother and grandfather had sought shelter from the police. He died of his wounds eight days later. The incident cast Selma into the spotlight. When Civil Rights Movement leaders focused on the town of Selma for voter registration a few weeks after Jackson's death, official opposition turned the event into a national spectacle, and furthered Alabama's violent reputation.

The town of Selma was half black, but only about 1 percent of black residents were registered voters. In an attempt to draw attention to this incongruity, Amelia B. Robinson organized a march along U.S. Highway 80 to the state capital in Montgomery. The march itself was led by civil rights leaders John Lewis, Hosea Williams, and Bob Mants. Rosa Parks was one of the marchers. However, the first attempt, on March 7, 1965, ended shortly after it began with local and state police beating marchers as they crossed the Edmund Pettus Bridge in town, an incident that became known as "Bloody Sunday." The event was again duly recorded by the national media. The second march, on March 9, led by Martin Luther King Jr., and involving the Southern Christian Leadership Conference, did not attempt more than a symbolic short march, in order to obey a court order and not alienate federal judges. The third march was successful, and the marchers reached the state capital on March 24 after a five-day hike.

When Wallace ran for governor in 1962 on a platform of support for segregation, he promised his political base to stand personally "in the school house door" to prevent the desegregation of schools. When Wallace won, he and Alabama solidified their status as symbols of resistance to federally ordered integration. On June 11, 1963, he lived up to his campaign rhetoric by standing in front of a doorway at the University of Alabama's Foster Auditorium to prevent the registration of two black students, James Hood and Vivian Malone. After fulfilling his promise, Wallace stood aside when ordered to by the adjutant general of Alabama, who had been federalized by the Kennedy administration. The incident was largely theatrical in that it had been arranged beforehand to allow Wallace to save face. He would again symbolically attempt to prevent integration, in September 1963, when he tried unsuccessfully to prevent four black children from attending white public schools in Huntsville. Wallace would continue to speak against integration, usually couching it in terms of anticommunism, states' rights, and the rhetoric of the Civil War.

In retrospect, federal enforcement of the Civil Rights Acts of 1957, 1960, and 1964, and the Voting Rights Act of 1965 ensured that black Alabamians regained the right to vote, and with blacks forming a large block of voters, the end of Jim Crow was all but inevitable. The violence of the 1960s, when whites used both official and subversive means in an attempt to prevent blacks from exercising their civil rights, left the state with a tarnished image, but did not prevent blacks from regaining their civil rights. The negative image of Alabama would take at least a generation to overcome.

Barry M. Stentiford

See also: Democratic Party; Ku Klux Klan; Wallace, George.

Further Reading

Carter, Dan T. *The Politics of Rage.* New York: Simon and Schuster, 1995.

McMillen, Neil R. *The Citizens' Council: Organized Resistance to the Second Reconstruction, 1954–64.* Urbana: University of Illinois Press. 1971.

Rogers, William Warren. *Alabama: The History of a Deep South State.* Tuscaloosa: University of Alabama Press, 1994.

Alabama Council on Human Relations

The Alabama Council on Human Relations (ACHR) originated as a state affiliate of the Commission on Interracial Cooperation (CIC), a biracial federation organized in 1919 in response to 26 post–World War I race riots that shook the nation.

While its board was composed of blacks and whites and offered a forum for inter-racial dialogue, the CIC was not a radical organization. The leadership, whose primary goal was to prevent violence, maintained that segregation and reform could coexist.

Although the CIC created the Southern Commission on the Study of Lynching in 1930 and placed black advisors in several New Deal agencies, it was increasingly criticized for its efforts to "improve segregation." In February 1944, the CIC merged with the Southern Regional Council (SRC), an early think tank whose founders believed that racial animosity could be alleviated by improving economic conditions for all Southerners. From its Atlanta headquarters, it reorganized the CIC state affiliates and put volunteers to work gathering economic data and monitoring race relations. Detailed reports and research papers were published several times a year. Alabama's CIC affiliate became the Alabama Division of the Southern Regional Council in 1944, and the Alabama Council on Human Relations in 1954.

Like the CIC, the SRC was slow to attack segregation because it hoped to attract white moderate support, and the SRC did not publicly declare its opposition to segregation until 1949. Regarded as the preeminent Southern race relations organization, after the U.S. Supreme Court's 1954 *Education* decision declaring segregated public education unconstitutional, the Ford Foundation's Fund for the Republic granted the SRC $240,000 to support race relations education. These funds were used to hire 13 full-time regional directors to organize and support local biracial committees, which would in turn assist local communities in achieving school desegregation without violence. The SRC's leadership, perhaps naively, maintained that the Deep South would voluntary desegregate if the alternative was submitting to federal intervention.

On February 8, 1955, 26-year-old Methodist minister Robert Hughes, a graduate of both the University of Alabama and Emory University, was appointed executive director of the Alabama Council on Human Relations headquartered in Montgomery. Thomas Thrasher, rector of the city's largest Episcopal church, served on his board, as did white activists Clifford and Virginia Durr, Aubrey Williams, and Martin Luther King Jr. The membership was composed almost exclusively of middle-class black and white businessmen, ministers, teachers, and housewives. Hughes marketed the council's role as "bridge building," and meetings were held on the campus of the black Alabama State University or in the basements of black churches, since integrated public meetings violated the capital city's municipal code. When King established his Montgomery Improvement Association (MIA) later that year, he recruited Hughes.

The Montgomery Bus Boycott began on Monday, December 5, 1955, and initially the city commissioners refused to meet with the protest leaders. Hughes offered his services as a mediator and he and Thrasher brought the MIA, the city commissioners, and representatives from the bus company together on December 8. Their attempts to broker a settlement were not only unsuccessful, but interpreted by the white community as a betrayal of white interests.

Montgomery's chapter of the White Citizens Council (WCC) was organized in October 1955, shortly after the implementation order for the *Brown* decision was delivered and two months prior to the bus boycott. Its purpose was to resist any attempt to desegregate schools, public transportation, or public facilities. The leadership charged that "human relations" was merely a euphemism for integration, and that Hughes and his council members were communists.

On February 10, 1956, state senator Sam Engelhardt Jr., executive secretary of the Alabama Association of Citizens' Councils, hosted a recruitment rally in Montgomery to celebrate the successful defense of segregation at the University of Alabama that month when black graduate student Autherine Lucy was prevented from attending classes, and to encourage continued opposition to the bus boycott. The audience of 12,000 included farmers, mill hands, businessmen, municipal workers, teachers, attorneys, and students.

The following evening, the Alabama Council on Human Relations celebrated its first anniversary on the campus of Alabama State College. The contrast was stark. Of the 300 who attended, fewer than half were black. Unlike the mix of middle class, working class, and poor whites at the WCC rally, most of the HR Council delegates were white, middle class and lived outside Montgomery. In July, when the ACHR's lease for its headquarters on South Court Street expired, the WCC pressured the landlord not to renew. Hughes subsequently relocated to Birmingham, where the ACHR was once again compelled to hold meetings in the basements of black churches. It was the only biracial organization in the city at that time.

In October 1957, the Birmingham city police broke up an ACHR meeting and wrote down the names and addresses of all present. Their employers subsequently received anonymous letters reporting their attendance at a "communist front" meeting, which violated the municipal ordinance against integrated gatherings. The ACHR lost most of its members and half its officers that evening, and it did not meet again for several months. The Methodist Laymen's Association, organized to oppose the Council of Methodist Bishops' support of the *Brown* decision in 1954, also viciously attacked Hughes. The group sent letters to every Methodist congregation in Birmingham accusing him and the ACHR of supporting racial integration of the congregations. Hughes received death threats, and the Ku Klux Klan burned a cross on his front lawn.

It was evident that the ACHR was too small and too weak to effect any meaningful change. Hughes grew frustrated as he presided over meaningless sessions with a few middle-class blacks and whites who politely discussed issues of little consequence, then fled when segregationists called them communists. It angered him too because he knew that several members of the affluent Young Men's Business Club, who had spoken with him privately, supported the SRC's mission, but were reluctant to declare themselves. Hughes was aware that negative publicity about the Magic City made them nervous since it discouraged new business investment. In a last-ditch effort to force these business progressives into the open, Hughes began to copy the national press on his monthly reports to the SRC. These reports documented the violence and fear that prevailed in Birmingham. On December 15, 1958, *Time* magazine carried an article describing Birmingham's ugly racial climate, based almost entirely on information provided by Hughes. In April 1960, Harrison Salisbury of the *New York Times* met secretly with the minister and subsequently produced a scathing exposé charging that in Birmingham, "Every channel of communication, every medium of mutual interest, every reasoned approach, every inch of middle ground has been fragmented by the emotional dynamite of racism." When the Birmingham and Bessemer City commissions sued Salisbury for criminal libel, Hughes was subpoenaed by a Jefferson County grand jury and directed to submit the ACHR's membership and correspondence files. He refused, knowing that they would be published, and was cited for contempt and jailed for four days. While prominent Birmingham attorney Charles Morgan successfully defended him, Hughes had destroyed his career with the Methodist Church. When the North Alabama Conference convened its 1960 annual meeting in Birmingham that year, the angry Methodist Laymen's Association prevailed on the conclave to demand that Hughes resign from the ACHR. When he refused, they voted to defrock him, a decision supported by Bishop Bachman Hodge on September 5, 1960. After Hughes was released from jail, he personally appealed to Hodge, who agreed to rescind the decision on the condition that Hughes accept a missionary assignment to Salisbury, Rhodesia. He and his family left for Africa before the end of 1960 and remained there for four years until the Rhodesian government expelled him for supporting a national liberation movement.

Years of frustration and failure had radicalized Hughes. He believed that he and the council had accomplished little through their local efforts at mediation and bridge building. By engaging the national press, however, he had made Americans outside of Alabama aware of what blacks and white progressives were coping with. The articles captured the nation's attention and gave Americans some sense of the seething resentments that were brewing in Birmingham just one year before the beatings of the Freedom Riders, and two years before the brutalization of the demonstrators, and the bombing of the Sixteenth Street Baptist Church. Although Hughes was not in Birmingham to see it, his actions also spurred the progressive white business community to action. Men like Charles Morgan, David Vann, and Sid Smyer became involved in negotiating the desegregation of downtown

Birmingham in 1963. By that time, it was too late. Two years after Hughes was banished from the Magic City, Birmingham imploded.

Mary Stanton

See also: Alabama; White Citizens Council.

Further Reading

McWhorter, Diane. *Carry Me Home: Birmingham, Alabama, the Climactic Battle of the Civil Rights Revolution.* New York: Simon & Schuster, 2001.

Sosna, Morton. *In Search of the Silent South: Southern Liberals and the Race Issue.* New York: Columbia University Press, 1977.

Stanton, Mary. *Journey toward Justice: Juliette Hampton Morgan and the Montgomery Bus Boycott.* Athens: University of Georgia Press, 2006.

Thornton, J. Mills. *Dividing Lines: Municipal Politics and the Struggle for Civil Rights in Montgomery, Birmingham, and Selma.* Tuscaloosa: University of Alabama Press, 2002.

Albany Civil Rights Movement

A branch of the extensive Southern Civil Rights Movement took place in the city of Albany, Georgia. One of the largest cities in southern Georgia, Albany was the nexus of protest and demonstrations against the segregated practices in place throughout southwest Georgia. Black Albanians grew tired of the prejudiced practices of the city. Segregated bus stations, eateries, and even classified advertisements divided the city by race. The local newspaper, the *Albany Herald,* ran "Negro Only" classifieds for African Americans in search of a job. The Albany Movement was the first attempt to desegregate an entire city. Prior to the organization of the 1960s movement, war veteran C. W. King established Albany's branch of the National Association for the Advancement of Colored People (NAACP). In the 1950s, a group of concerned black citizens formed the Lincoln Heights Groups and demanded change.

In 1961, members of the Student Nonviolent Coordinating Committee (SNCC) descended into Albany. Charles S. Sherrod, Cordell Reagon, and Charles Jones began organizing mass meetings and protests. The Albany Movement organization was established on December 17, 1961, and elected William G. Anderson as its president. To give motivation to those participating in the movement, Martin Luther King Jr. and Ralph Abernathy were invited to participate in the events. King and Abernathy arrived in December 1961. After delivering a speech at Shiloh Baptist Church and crossing the street to address the overflow of the mass meeting in Mount Zion Baptist Church, King marched with Albany protesters. He was jailed

An African American passenger exits the "colored waiting room" at a Trailway Bus Terminal. The Albany Movement was formed to fight segregation in public interstate travel. (Bettmann/ Corbis)

and refused to post bail. Other prominent members of the black Albany community, including attorney C. B. King and his brother Slater King, a successful real estate broker, participated in the outcry for civil rights and contributed their services to those ready to protest. C. B. King provided legal services to imprisoned protesters, including Martin Luther King and Ralph Abernathy. Slater King served as the vice president of the Albany Movement. After being beaten by Sheriff Cull Campbell while trying to check on a jailed protester, C. B. King's bloodied and battered body was photographed and sent across newswires throughout the country, and published in *The New York Times*.

Mass protests and outcries continued in Albany. Major factors in the Albany Movement continuation included college students and youth who participated. Students from the historically black Albany State College (now Albany State

University) demonstrated and protested in Albany's streets. Many students, including Janie Rambeau and Bernice Johnson Reagon, were expelled from Albany State because of their actions. Students transferred to other surrounding schools, including Fort Valley State College (now Fort Valley State University) in Fort Valley, Georgia, and Spelman College in Atlanta, Georgia. The Freedom Singers, a capella group established by Reagon, sang spirituals to keep protestors uplifted. McCree Harris, a teacher at Monroe Comprehensive High School, also participated with the Freedom Singers. Harris encouraged her students to participate in Albany's fight for equality and rights. Many Freedom Singers were jailed because of their protest and sang songs to keep themselves and other imprisoned protesters positive and committed to their cause. Supporters of the Albany Movement who did not publicly demonstrate diligently worked behind the scenes making signs, fixing meals, and giving monetary donations.

In an effort to squelch the growing influence of equality protests and events, Albany sheriff Laurie Pritchett encouraged police officers to not use violent reproach against protesters in public spaces or in front of media. He contacted jails in the surrounding counties of Mitchell, Baker, and Lee counties to cover the overflow of protestors in Albany's jails. Over 1,000 protestors or supporters of Albany's movement were jailed. When Martin Luther King and Abernathy returned in the summer of 1962 for sentencing on their December convictions, they chose to be jailed instead of paying fines. Pritchett organized for King's and Abernathy's fines to be paid so that both were released unwillingly. After continuing unsuccessful efforts through August and being jailed once more, King left Albany feeling defeated. Albanians, however, felt successful. Albany's black community rallied to support Thomas Chatmon, a successful black businessman and director of voter registration for the Albany Movement. Votes for Chatmon resulted in a runoff election. The following spring, all segregation laws were removed from Albany civil codes.

Using Albany as a guide, King continued his fight for civic equality by staging demonstrations in Birmingham, Alabama. Members of SNCC expanded to other areas of southwest Georgia, including Americus and Camilla, calling for the end of legal segregation. C. B. King continued the fight for social equality in legislation and other civic venues. He unsuccessfully ran for the House of Representatives in 1964, the first African American to do so since Reconstruction. He later was supported by black legislators to run for governor in 1969. In 2002, Albany's newly constructed courthouse was named after the late civil rights attorney. A scholarship for minority aspirants in law was also established in his honor. Slater King continued to advocate literacy and integration efforts in southwest Georgia. After his untimely death in 1969, an adult learning center he designed was named in his honor. Bernice Johnson Reagon continued the legacy of the Freedom Singers through the establishing the popular gospel group Sweet Honey in the Rock.

As a whole, the Albany Movement has been memorialized in Albany's Civil Rights Museum, opened in 1998. The building was formerly Mount Zion Church, one of the sites of the numerous mass meetings during the movement. A memorial dedicated to participants in the Albany Movement was also erected in 1998. It is located in Charles S. Sherrod Park, named after the SNCC member who helped organize the movement in 1961.

Regina Barnett

See also: Georgia; Montgomery Bus Boycott.

Further Reading

Lyon, Danny. *Memories of the Southern Civil Rights Movement.* Chapel Hill: Published for the Center for Documentary Studies, Duke University, by the University of North Carolina Press, 1992.

Tuck, Steven G. N. *Beyond Atlanta: The Struggle for Racial Equality in Georgia, 1940–1980.* Athens: University of Georgia Press, 2001.

Arkansas

Arkansas is in the Southern United States and is bordered by Tennessee, Mississippi, Missouri, Oklahoma, Texas, and Louisiana. It became the 25th state to join the Union in 1836. However, its incorporation into the United States was initially short-lived. In 1861 Arkansas became one of only three states west of the Mississippi to attempt to secede from the Union, to join the Confederate States of America, and to fight in the Civil War against federal forces. This action boldly signifies that Arkansans have historically viewed themselves as Southerners, even though the state serves as something of a borderland between different regions of the country. Indeed, many aspects of the history of the state, including slavery, the advent of Jim Crow, and the eventual move to dismantle both of these institutions, place it firmly within the Southern tradition.

Prior to the Civil War, Arkansas was the sixth-largest producer of cotton in the United States. The cultivation of the crop was dependent upon the efforts of slave laborers. In the decades leading up to the Civil War, the slave population swelled from less than 5,000 in 1830 to more than 110,000 in 1860. Plantation owners exercised political power disproportionate to their numbers. Most white Arkansans owned small farms and few, if any, slaves. Most plantation owners resided in the eastern part of the state. However, in the mountainous northwest, very few Arkansans owned slaves, and many resented the influence that slave owners held in state and national politics. In fact, during the Civil War, pockets of strong

Union sentiment were present in the northwest part of the state, and as many as 10,000 men fought for the Union during the conflict.

Nonetheless, as elsewhere in the South, after defeat in the Civil War, white Arkansans tried to extract the easiest terms of surrender possible and to reassert the same power structure established before the Civil War. Maintaining white supremacy was seen by many as the linchpin of an attempt to maintain elements of their prewar identity. Right after the war, Arkansans passed laws designed to define narrowly the meaning of freedom as described in the Thirteenth Amendment, which outlawed slavery.

For a brief time period, known as Reconstruction, these repressive measures were rolled back. The Republican Party, backed by powerful allies in Washington, D.C., and bolstered by the Union Army that continued to occupy the state, came to power in the state. The Republicans passed a number of progressive measures—including founding educational institutions and building railroads and other much-needed infrastructure. Most importantly, the government in Reconstruction Arkansas sought to protect the civil rights of the former slaves, who had been granted citizenship with the Fourteenth Amendment. Furthermore, the Fifteenth Amendment gave black men the right to vote.

This trend toward greater democratization was short-lived. By 1872, Democrats had regained control over the state government and quickly curtailed the rights of the freedpeople. As early as the 1870s, laws appeared mandating separate educational facilities for whites and blacks, setting the stage for legalized segregation in other areas as well. Jim Crow was further codified during the 1890s as laws were passed with the intention of restricting the freedoms granted to the former slaves and to unambiguously restoring white supremacy.

In 1891, a new election law stated that only election officials could mark the ballots of illiterate voters, opening the door for greater voter intimidation and fraud. In 1892, the Arkansas General Assembly passed a measure creating a poll tax, which further disenfranchised numerous black would-be voters along with some poor whites. An 1891 law, similar to those passed elsewhere in the South, called for separate coaches for white and black passengers riding streetcars. A 1903 version of the law somewhat liberalized this policy by mandating white and black sections of the streetcar rather than separate coaches. Nonetheless, black passengers in Little Rock, Pine Bluff, and Hot Springs staged a several-weeks-long boycott of the streetcars in protest against the legislation.

Although the strike provides evidence that African Americans protested the growth of segregation and disenfranchisement during the 1890s in Arkansas, the time was not yet ripe for an effective challenge of these inequalities. Increasingly, black Arkansans found themselves excluded from the political arena. By 1893, there were no blacks serving in the state's General Assembly. The growing trend toward racial separation and the willingness of whites to use coercive measures—including lynching—to enforce segregation caused many in the black community to turn inward.

Middle-class women joined clubs, including the Mothers League, founded in Pine Bluff in 1893, and the Ladies Relief and Missionary Corps, founded in Fort Smith in 1898. These and other clubs combined a social agenda with charitable activities. Black women's clubs throughout the South adopted the motto "lifting as we climb" and attempted to cure a wide range of social problems in the black community—ranging from inadequate health care and hygiene to poor access to education.

Many black men focused their energies on economic advancement, clinging to Booker T. Washington's model of racial uplift in realms outside the political arena. Black entrepreneurs created a thriving business district centered on Ninth Street in Little Rock. One of the most significant structures on the street was headquarters of the Mosaic Templars, a fraternal and mutual aid organization founded by two former Arkansas slaves in 1882. At its height in the 1920s, the organization had over 100,000 members.

Most African Americans did not live in urban areas, however. Most lived in rural Arkansas, where they continued to grow and harvest cotton as they had before emancipation. Most blacks longed to own their own land and, like many Americans, associated land ownership with freedom. However, land was not redistributed at the end of the Civil War, and most blacks lacked the capital to purchase farms of their own. The freedpeople and plantation owners struck up a compromise of sorts, in which African Americans would farm and inhabit small plots of land, which they could cultivate working family units. This gave them the semblance of independence. At the end of the growing season, the black farmers would pay the landowners for the use of the land with either cash or a portion of the crop. Gradually, more and more white Arkansans began to work as sharecroppers too, but in general, blacks were poorer than white farmers and worked on smaller, less productive plots.

This system had the potential to be exploitive. Some plantation owners deliberately fixed their books so that their croppers would end the year in debt, regardless of how the harvest turned out. Others charged high interest rates on the annual loans that croppers would have to acquire in order to survive in a cash-poor economy, assuring their continued economic vulnerability. Some planters also interpreted Arkansas law in such a way as to suggest that indebted sharecroppers could not leave their place of employment while they owed money. This interpretation left some blacks mired in debt peonage, indicating that some white Arkansans were determined to revisit the institution of slavery well into the twentieth century.

There was a documented case of peonage in Arkansas as late as 1936, when Paul Peacher, an Arkansas planter and town marshal of the small Delta town of Earle, arrested eight black Arkansans and accused them of "vagrancy." T. S. Mitchell, mayor of this town with a population of 2,062 and a justice of the peace, ordered the incarcerated men to pay a $25 fine or spend 30 days in jail. The eight men lacked the necessary capital to pay their fines and were ordered to work off both their fines and their 30-day sentences on Peacher's farm.

The case caught the attention of the national media. Responding to this national humiliation, Governor J. Marion Futrell freed the eight men after 20 days, and Peacher was brought to trial. A Crittenden County jury was unwilling to convict Peacher and quickly returned a "not guilty" verdict.

However, Peacher's case did not fare quite as well when it reached a federal grand jury in Little Rock. The jury indicted Peacher for violating an 1866 law designed to enforce the Thirteenth Amendment, which had ended slavery, levied a $3,500 fine, and sentenced him to two years in prison. Despite this stern warning, Peacher's jail term was quickly transformed into probation as long as he paid the fine. Peacher was easily able to do so thanks to many of his fellow white Arkansans, who quickly raised in excess of $5,000 to pay not only his fine, but his legal fees as well. This incident reveals that most white Arkansans were not yet ready to see blacks regain the legal protections they had lost at the end of Reconstruction.

An even more notorious incident had taken place in Elaine in 1919, when a group of black sharecroppers gathered together to form the Progressive Farmers and Household Union in the hopes of collectively bargaining for better terms from the local planters at the end of the cotton season when they sold their crops. Local whites became fearful when they saw blacks beginning to organize. Whites soon began to form posses to put down what they labeled as a black insurrection. In one of the greatest tragedies in Arkansas history, at least 100, and perhaps more, black Arkansans were massacred.

Despite this attempt at forming a labor union, black Arkansans working in the agricultural sector continued to fight for economic justice. Many joined the Southern Tenant Farmers' Union (STFU), a biracial organization founded in Tryonza in 1934. Although STFU members too faced violent reprisals from local landowners, they achieved some modest successes and were able to attract the attention of the national media to the plight of the sharecropper.

Although some black Arkansans remained attached to the land and interested in pursuing a career in agriculture, regardless of the difficulty, many began to migrate to urban areas, and increasingly to the North. They left seeking a better racial climate and industrial jobs, particularly as the nation geared up for World War I and World War II. Those who stayed behind eventually became displaced from the cotton fields as plantation owners began to mechanize and to reduce their need for a large labor force. Simultaneously, as planters began to loosen their grip on the region's sharecroppers, local African Americans began to make greater strides in the area of civil rights.

In 1918, members of the black elite in Little Rock founded a local chapter of the National Association for the Advancement of Colored People (NAACP), which started out small but began to grow in size and in militancy in the coming decades. NAACP members L.C. (Lucius Christopher) and Daisy Lee Bates founded the *Arkansas State Press,* a black newspaper, in 1941. They drew attention to many of the issues facing local blacks, including police brutality and various kinds of discrimination. Increasingly, Daisy Bates became interested in securing black access to equal education, and she entered the national spotlight in 1957, when she became an advisor to the nine young people who valiantly integrated the city's Central High School that year.

Arkansas, despite incidents in its troubled history such as the Elaine Massacre, was known for relatively harmonious race relations in the middle decades of the twentieth century. It certainly was not known for the same kind of sustained racial violence and intimidation associated with, for example, the state of Mississippi. Thus it came as a surprise to many of the state's inhabitants—both white and black—when Little Rock became the site of one of the first dramatic showdowns between the forces of Southern massive resistance and civil rights advocates.

The Little Rock school board came up with a token plan for integration in order to give lip service to the Supreme Court's 1954 *Brown v. Board of Education* decision, which declared that segregated schooling was unconstitutional. The white citizens who endorsed this modest plan were surprised when, in September 1957, Governor Orval Faubus called out the state's National Guard to prevent nine hand-selected students from entering the school. After a showdown with federal authorities, the students were allowed to enroll in the school. Eight out of nine students managed to make it through the tumultuous 1957–1958 school year despite being the victims of protracted campaign of harassment by many of the students and their parents.

Arkansas became the subject of national and international ridicule as pictures of a racist, jeering, spitting white mob were contrasted with the well-dressed, demure black students. The crisis in Little Rock revealed that race remained a contentious issue among Arkansans despite the veneer of civility that had been carefully crafted to hide those fault lines. The incident was a milestone in the history of the Civil Rights Movement. The intervention of the federal government showed that Washington could be used as a powerful, albeit reluctant, adversary against Jim Crow. The ability of the Little Rock Nine to overcome adversity and persevere even in the face of virulent white resistance inspired activists all over the South and helped jump-start the Civil Rights Movement, which was about to transform Arkansas and the rest of the South.

Jennifer Jensen Wallach

See also: Little Rock Nine; Sharecropping.

Further Reading

Conrad, David Eugene. *The Forgotten Farmers: The Story of Sharecroppers in the New Deal.* Westport, CT: Greenwood Press, 1965.

The Encyclopedia of Arkansas History and Culture. http://encyclopediaofarkansas.net (accessed August 1, 2007).

Whayne, Jeannie M., Thomas A. DeBlack, George Sabo III, and Morris S. Arnold. *Arkansas: A Narrative History.* Fayetteville: University of Arkansas, 2002.

Armed Forces

The armed forces of the United States had a mixed record in dealing with African Americans and Jim Crow. While blacks served in parts of the American military prior to Jim Crow, from 1866 until the Korean War, the military upheld segregation. Units and installations were rigidly segregated, usually with few recreational facilities for black soldiers. In general, the military is a conservative institution, and is naturally resistant to change. Southerners have often been overly represented in the officer corps, and the military as a whole tended to accept Jim Crow as a matter of course. American military leaders traditionally have attempted to resist what they saw as attempts by politicians to use the military for domestic social agendas. The professional ethos of the American military officer includes subordination of the military to civilian control and the avoidance of political involvement; however, the military often uses its allies in Congress to avoid policies or missions that the military hopes to avoid. When ordered to desegregate in 1948, each branch took a different approach, with mixed results.

Blacks fought in almost all American wars from settlement to the present. During the colonial wars, free blacks often served in colonial regiments, especially those from areas with few black slaves. While General George Washington originally attempted to keep blacks out of the Continental Army during the War for Independence, political pressure from Northern colonies and dwindling recruitment forced him to allow blacks in, where in general they served in the same units as white soldiers. After the Revolutionary War, blacks were not allowed to serve in the regular army, but some continued to serve in militia organizations in some states, and the crews of naval vessels were largely integrated, although the officers were all white.

Despite often-heroic conduct of black soldiers during war, the achievements of blacks, and even their presence in battle, was largely forgotten by society after the end of war. Use of black soldiers in American wars brought short periods of celebrations for the units that performed heroically, followed by increased repression and later denial of black military contributions when wars ended. Any shortcomings were magnified and applied to all black soldiers. During peacetime, the very idea of black participation was usually purged from public memory. Maintaining the fiction of black absence from American military history was necessary for Jim Crow. The right to vote has long been tied to military service in republics. Only by denying the presence of black men in the wars of the United States could they be denied the vote. To have acknowledged that black men traditionally performed their duty of defending the nation would have brought a concurrent moral obligation to allow them the vote.

In 1866, Congress allowed for the first time blacks to serve in the regular army, in four segregated regiments. These four regiments—two infantry and two cavalry—were later known as the "Buffalo Soldiers," although the black soldiers at the time did not use that term except as an insult. They constituted about 10 percent of the regular army until the turn of the century. The black regiments were stationed on the frontier, and were not used in the South during Reconstruction. The creation of the black units was originally a liberal idea, a reward for the faithful service of blacks in the Union Army during the Civil War. Black soldiers were paid equally to white soldiers—one of the only places in American society where this was true—although very few blacks were allowed into the officer corps.

The high tide of racism in the military ran from the 1890s through World War II. Despite the professional service of the black regular army regiments and the state-raised black volunteer regiments during the Spanish-American War, black soldiers were increasingly subjected to Jim Crow–style restrictions and humiliations. The regular army expanded after the Spanish-American War, but no additional black regiments were formed, meaning that blacks formed a decreasing percentage of the regular army.

Racism within the army created the self-fulfilling prophecy of failure of black soldiers in battle. The most notorious example was the black 92nd Division during World War I. The division suffered from little training, equipment shortages, no artillery, and uneven officer quality. Many of the white officers assigned to black units were racists, in the belief that they "knew how to handle blacks." Thrown into battle on unfamiliar terrain, two battalions from the division failed in combat, while others performed well. The failure of some elements of the 92nd was projected to the entire division, and then to all black soldiers. The failure of the

92nd was cited as "proof" that blacks were naturally cowards and unfit for combat. As a result, most black combat units were redesignated to perform manual labor, especially as stevedores. The "natural coward" stereotype was also used to justify the exclusion of all but a token few from the officer corps. This stigma would last through World War II.

Blacks had supported the United States fully during World War I, partially in hope that such service and loyalty would be rewarded after the war with increased political and social acceptance. Instead, in the years after the war, blacks suffered the worst oppression and violence since Reconstruction. During World War II, black leaders had to use political pressure to ensure that black men served in combat arms—infantry, armor, artillery—as well as the air forces and Marine Corps. Blacks had the irony of having to fight politically in order to be able to fight and perhaps die against the Germans, Italians, and Japanese. But black leaders sought to avoid the results of World War I, using the slogan of the Double V for a while, to emphasis victory over America's enemies abroad and over Jim Crow at home. While blacks served loyally throughout the war, they continued to serve in segregated units, and with relatively few black officers. Pressure was building for desegregating the armed forces, but military leaders were able to hold off any radical changes in the structure of the military until after the war ended in 1945.

The watershed occurred with President Harry S. Truman's Executive Order 9981 in 1948, which desegregated the military. Truman had been especially bothered by a photo of a black victim of a lynch mob, whose U.S. Army uniform and sergeant's stripes were plainly visible on the lifeless body. All the services, with the exception of the Coast Guard, hesitated at implementing the order, but Truman's insistence forced them to accept integration as inevitable and accommodate themselves to it. The air force simply never created separate black units when it became an independence service in 1947. The war in Korea brought actual integration to the army and Marine Corps, and by the late 1950s, the military was satisfied that it had segregated smoothly and created a model the rest of the nation could follow.

In retrospect, much of the integration was superficial. Basically, the military allowed black men into white organizations, where they were expected to follow white rules or suffer the consequences. Still, for many blacks, the military did provide a sort of haven from Jim Crow. Colin Powell, later a four-star general and the nation's first black chairman of the Joint Chiefs of Staff, recalled that as a young officer stationed in Georgia in the early 1960s, he was able to go on base and eat at the officers club, and escape the world of Jim Crow that existed off base.

However, large-scale U.S. involvement in the war in Vietnam during 1965–1973, following immediately on the heels of the Civil Rights Movement, exposed serious racial problems in the armed forces. The military, which believed that it had solved all problems of integration, found itself beset by racial violence. Various programs that allowed better-educated, middle-class whites to avoid military service meant that the average soldier became poorer, less educated, and younger as the Vietnam War dragged on. And increasingly, the average soldier was less white, as the draft took in larger numbers of poor whites, blacks, and Hispanics to make up for the decrease in middle-class draftees. Among black soldiers too, their average age and education dropped during the war, although less so than among whites. Racial tensions began to break down unit cohesion by 1969, when soldiers began forming covert Ku Klux Klan and Black Panther groups in the military. The Air Force, although it was a far whiter branch than the army, saw itself as immune to race problems, but four days of racial turmoil on Travis Air Force Base, May 21–24, 1971, served to alert the Air Force that it still had a long way to go. Ironically, the unpopularity of the Vietnam War among middle-class whites meant greater use of black soldiers in frontline roles than in any previous war. Vietnam broke the tendency to confine blacks to rear-echelon support roles, as had been common in the world wars. With Jim Crow crumbling, and blacks voting in higher numbers, the impetus to keep blacks from direct combat disappeared.

By the end of direct American involvement in the Vietnam War in 1973, Jim Crow was officially dead, although racial divisions continued. Concurrent with the end of the direct involvement of the United States in Vietnam was the creation of the All-Volunteer Force. The government would no longer draft men into the military. With the prestige of the military at an all-time low, recruiting sufficient white men proved impossible, and for the first time ever, the military began to actively recruit black men, and eventually Hispanic men and even women. The military began a myriad of programs to address racial issues within the ranks. For many nonwhites, the armed forces became an attractive career, although the ratio of black enlisted personnel to officers remains much higher than that of whites.

Barry M. Stentiford

See also: Executive Order 9981; World War I; World War II.

Further Reading

Buckley, Gail L. *American Patriots: The Story of Blacks in the Military from the Revolution to Dessert Storm.* New York: Random House, 2002.

Donaldson, Gary A. *The History of African-Americans in the Military.* Malabar, FL: Krieger Publishing Company, 1991.

Edgerton, Robert B. *Hidden Heroism: Black Soldiers in America's Wars.* Boulder, CO: Westview Press, 2001.

MacGregor, Morris J., Jr. *Integration of the Armed Forces 1940–1965.* Washington, DC: Government Printing Office, 1989.

Atlanta Compromise, The

The so-called Atlanta Compromise derives its name from the famous speech by Booker T. Washington at the Cotton States Exposition in Atlanta in September 1895, where the eminent black educator and leader addressed a racially segregated audience and advocated that African Americans focus on economic advancement rather than social and political equality. In other words, according to Washington in the Atlanta Compromise, African Americans would accommodate themselves to segregation and disfranchisement.

Reflecting the worsening situation facing African Americans in the 1890s—the rise of Jim Crow, disfranchisement, lynching, and economic hard times—Washington firmly believed that African Americans should focus on learning trades and skills and thus build up the black community. Washington was heavily influenced by the educational and sociological theories of the day and the education he received at Hampton University in Virginia. Washington bought into the notion that industrial education and self-help would lead to success. At the Tuskegee Institute in Alabama, from 1881 onward, Washington put these ideas into practice with much success. For example, the graduates from Tuskegee played key roles at the local level in scores of black communities across the South and built up successful black businesses and prosperous farms. At Tuskegee, black students learned new farming techniques and skills that stood them in good stead for the future.

Although Washington was well known in the South by 1895, mainly through good press and close relations with leading white politicians as well as the fine reputation of Tuskegee, it was the Atlanta Compromise that brought Washington national acclaim. In his brief speech to hundreds of onlookers, including the governor of Georgia, Washington contended that African Americans should be given a chance to succeed in business and commerce, that African Americans had shown great loyalty to whites over the generations and therefore deserved the opportunity to be successful. He urged those who complained about the slow nature of change to focus on small improvements and the future, even if the pace of transformation was gradual. He believed that justice, peace, and economic opportunity would lead to a new era of prosperity for all in the South—black and white. Washington argued that cooperation between the races did not threaten segregation at all and, in the most famous quote from the speech, he postulated: "In all things that are purely social we can be as separate as the fingers, yet one as the hand in all things essential to mutual progress." In a nutshell, this was the Atlanta Compromise—accommodation with racism and Jim Crow and disfranchisement—for economic success. Washington also believed that economic prosperity would eventually lead the way to civil and political rights. Whites and African Americans in the crowd cheered the speech and rushed to congratulate Washington.

The Atlanta speech and Compromise propelled Washington into the position of the national spokesman and leader of African Americans in the United States—Frederick Douglass had died earlier in the year. All across the nation, scholars, politicians, and industrialists praised Washington and his ideology. It has been noted that Washington gained ascendancy because his ideas reflected the time. For the next 20 years, until his death in 1915, Washington and the Atlanta Compromise dominated race relations in the United States. At the time, most whites in the South and North and most African Americans supported the tenants of the Atlanta Compromise. Millions of dollars from Northern philanthropists poured into the coffers of black colleges and businesses that adhered to industrial education and self-help programs. Washington became known as the Wizard of Tuskegee—indeed, the institution served as the model for the Atlanta Compromise. Washington built close relations with Republicans, particularly Theodore Roosevelt, as well as wealthy industrialists, such as John D. Rockefeller.

In private, Washington did not always follow the Atlanta Compromise of accommodation with racism and the second-class status of African Americans. Indeed, Washington often completely opposed his professed public pronouncements. It is clear that he rejected white racism. He spoke of his opposition to segregation, his outrage against lynching, and the illegality of disfranchisement. He supported black defendants (in private) with monies in cases dealing with discrimination. He lobbied hard for positions in the federal government for qualified black aspirants. However, due to his accommodationist approach, conciliatory attitude, and public deference to whites, these efforts were kept secret from most African Americans and whites.

The Atlanta Compromise made Washington the leading spokesman for African Americans, and his accommodationism made him very popular within the black community. This approach to racial progress at a very difficult time for African Americans did yield success—for example, increased spending on black schools and more black colleges in the South, as well as increased black business activity throughout the South. However, criticisms of the Atlanta Compromise did emerge. The voice of opponents in the 1890s was muted; perhaps the most famous black opponent at this time to the Atlanta Compromise was Bishop Henry McNeal Turner. However, a more determined opposition to accommodationism formed as the new century dawned. It was clear to many black intellectuals and white liberals that the Atlanta Compromise did not lead to increased opportunities for African Americans. Successful black businesses and businessmen were often the target for racial violence—for example, in the Atlanta Riot of 1906—and the lives of the majority of African Americans were one of poverty and lack of opportunity. Self-help did not seem to work for many. Thus from 1900, the voices of opposition grew. William Monroe Trotter, a black leader from Boston, criticized Washington's ideology as delusional. The most famous critic was W.E.B. Du Bois, who advocated full civil rights and integration immediately and that African Americans needed to build up a talented tenth of well-educated men and women to lead the fight for equality. The death of Washington in 1915 and the changing nature of race relations in the United States also heralded the passing of the Atlanta Compromise and the policy of accommodation. The Atlanta Compromise had become discredited. A new approach of integration and full civil and political rights, exemplified by the National Association for the Advancement of Colored People, took the place of the Atlanta Compromise.

For 20 years, the Atlanta Compromise and accommodationism with racism was the leading black ideological and pragmatic position in the age of Jim Crow. Although it is now discredited by most scholars and civil rights activists, it is clear that the Atlanta Compromise both reflected the mood and beliefs of time and also enabled many African Americans to cope, economically, during the nadir of race relations in the United States. Washington's belief that African Americans should build up their own communities and support one another in economic advancement holds true today. Washington never agreed with the white racists who believed in the natural inferiority of blacks. Washington always believed in equality and advancement. He espoused hard work, self-help, and Christian morality. But his belief that this could come while civil and political rights remained on the back burner was misguided at best, and perhaps a product of black powerlessness at the height of Jim Crow.

James M. Beeby

See also: Washington, Booker T.

Further Reading

Harlan, Louis. *Booker T. Washington: The Making of a Black Leader, 1856–1901.* New York: Oxford University Press, 1972.

Harlan, Louis. *Booker T. Washington: The Wizard of Tuskegee, 1901–1915.* New York: Oxford University Press, 1983.

Meier, August. *The Negro Thought in America, 1880–1915: Racial Ideologies in the Age of Booker T. Washington.* Ann Arbor: University of Michigan Press, 1963.

Washington, Booker T. *Up from Slavery.* New York: Doubleday, 1901.

B

Baldwin, James

James Arthur Baldwin, author, activist, and critic, was born to Emma Birdis Jones on August 2, 1924, in Harlem, New York. Though Baldwin never knew his biological father, he was adopted by David Baldwin at three years of age. Baldwin's strained relationship with his stepfather was the core influence for the pseudo-autobiographical *Go Tell It on the Mountain* (1955), a story of the religious and spiritual development of a young black man in Harlem, New York. A religious fanatic, David Baldwin would often force his beliefs on young James. At the age of 14, Baldwin became a preacher but later denounced religion after moving to Greenwich Village in New York City. Focusing on his literary craft, Baldwin began to write stories, essays, and reflections on his life. While developing his writing, Baldwin also began to recognize and acknowledge his homosexuality. In order to escape racial and sexual intolerance, Baldwin moved to Paris, France, where he would spend the majority of his life.

Though he spent most of his time abroad, Baldwin was very active in the desegregation movement in the American South. He would eloquently speak out against the racial injustices blacks faced during the mid-twentieth century. In *Notes of a Native Son* (1955, 6), Baldwin called for the racial injustices in American society to cease. In the "Autobiographical Notes," Baldwin criticized the body of literature available about black society and culture. "From this point of view, the Negro problem is nearly inaccessible. It is not written about so widely; it is written about so bad," Baldwin wrote. Because of the lack of quality literature for and about African Americans, Baldwin used his own experiences as a black man and molded them into a literary art, both fictitious and critical. At the climax of the Civil Rights and Black Power movements, Baldwin released two powerful collections of essays—the best-selling *Nobody Knows My Name* (1961) and *The Fire Next Time* (1963). In these collections, Baldwin analyzed the race relations between blacks and whites and demanded racial justice and

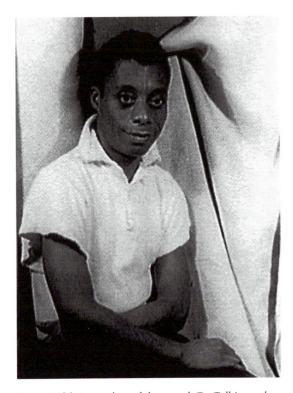

James Baldwin, author of the novel *Go Tell It on the Mountain* (1953). (Library of Congress)

tolerance. The critical and biting essay "Down at the Cross" critiqued the growing severance between Christianity and the Nation of Islam. Baldwin argued the need to eradicate the oppression of blacks through the joining of both religious camps. After returning to Europe and a vicious attack by Eldridge Cleaver in *Soul on Ice,* Baldwin's insight into the black American struggle was questioned.

Baldwin ignored his critics and continued to write. Heavily represented in the nonfiction genre during the 1960s and 1970s, Baldwin also continued writing works of fiction. Several novels were released during this time period, many focusing on and critiquing America's outlook on racial relations. *Another Country* (1962) focused on the role of race in interracial friendships. *If Beale Street Could Talk* (1974) looked at the relationship between black men and women, and the role of family against the socially oppressive system faced in Harlem, New York.

Baldwin returned to the United States in 1983 to accept a teaching position at the University of Massachusetts–Amherst, in the African American Studies Department. After his tenure at Amherst, Baldwin spent his remaining days in France, where he died in 1987 at the age of 62.

Regina Barnett

See also: Jim Crow.

Further Reading

Baldwin, James A. *The Fire Next Time.* New York: Dial Press, 1963.
Baldwin, James A. *Notes of a Native Son.* New York: Dial Press, 1955.

Bates, Daisy

Daisy Lee Gatson Bates is best known for her role in the struggle to desegregate Little Rock's Central High School in 1957. She and her husband, L.C. (Lucius Christopher) Bates, also published the newspaper the *Arkansas State Press,* which served the local Arkansas black community. Both Daisy and L.C. Bates were active members of the National Association for the Advancement of Colored People (NAACP) as well.

Daisy Lee Gatson was born in the sawmill town of Huttig, Arkansas, and was raised by adoptive parents Susie Smith and Orlee Smith, who was an employee at the local mill. The greatest trauma of Gatson's childhood took place when she learned that her birth mother had been raped and killed by three white men. Gatson was incensed that these criminals had not been brought to justice. In her autobiography, *The Long Shadow of Little Rock,* she suggests that this and other childhood experiences propelled her into her future role as a civil rights activist.

When Gatson was 15 years old, she met L.C. Bates, a traveling insurance salesman. After a lengthy courtship, the couple moved to Little Rock in 1941, where they founded the *Arkansas State Press.* The weekly newspaper proved to be a powerful

Civil Rights leader and journalist Daisy Bates with four students in front of her home in Little Rock, Arkansas, September 1957. (Time & Life Pictures/Getty Images)

advocate on behalf of the black community, as it publicized instances of police brutality and other injustices faced by black Arkansans.

Daisy Gatson and L.C. Bates married on March 4, 1942. While working for the newspaper, Daisy Bates also began taking classes at nearby Shorter College and Philander Smith College. She also became increasingly involved in the local chapter of the NAACP and was named president of the Arkansas Conference of Branches in 1952.

In 1954, the U.S. Supreme Court declared that the enforced segregation of schools was unconstitutional in the *Brown v. Board of Education* ruling. Afterward, Bates channeled the majority of her energy toward securing the integration of public schools in her native Arkansas. Most famously, she became a confidant, mentor, and spokesperson for the group of students known as the Little Rock Nine, who integrated the city's working-class Central High School.

Although the local school board designed a very limited plan for integration, ultimately allowing only a handful of handpicked black students to enter the large urban high school, their plan was still met with stiff resistance. Arkansas governor Orval Faubus called out the Arkansas National Guard to prevent the black students from physically entering the school. After a showdown between federal and state authorities, President Dwight D. Eisenhower used federal troops to make sure that the court-mandated integration would take place. However, even after the Little Rock Nine were reluctantly admitted to the school, the drama was not over. Large crowds of angry whites gathered outside the high school to heckle the black students, and a dedicated group of white members of the Central High School student body waged a year-long campaign of harassment in an attempt to force the black students to withdraw.

During this ordeal, Bates met regularly with the students, frequently serving as a liaison between them, the national NAACP, the press, administrators of the high school, and the school board. She ultimately paid a high price for her visibility. Bates was the victim of constant threats, and her home was attacked by angry segregationists on more than one occasion. In addition, the crisis in Little Rock adversely impacted the Bates' newspaper. Many businesses withdrew their advertisements as a form of protest against the Bates' activism. Because of the ensuing economic hardship, the couple was forced to close the *Arkansas State Press* in 1959.

In the aftermath of the events in Little Rock, Bates became well known, one of the few prominent women to be frequently included in the pantheon of civil rights heroes. Capitalizing on her fame, in 1960, she published her well-received autobiography, *The Long Shadow of Little Rock*. In 1963, she spoke at the Lincoln Memorial at the March on Washington. Bates continued her activism when she moved to Mitchellville, Arkansas, becoming an advocate for the poor through the aegis of a federal antipoverty program. In 1984, she realized one of her long-held dreams when she reopened the *Arkansas State Press,* managing the paper for four years before selling it in 1988.

For the rest of her life, she remained a beloved civil rights icon and participated in a wide variety of ceremonies honoring the Little Rock Nine and other pioneers of the movement. Bates died of a heart attack on November 4, 1999, but her legacy was not forgotten. Streets as well as an elementary school have been named after her. Perhaps most dramatically, the state of Arkansas has declared the third Monday of every February a holiday in her honor.

Jennifer Jensen Wallach

See also: Little Rock Nine.

Further Reading

Bates, Daisy. *The Long Shadow of Little Rock.* Fayetteville: University of Arkansas Press, 2007.

Stockley, Grif. *Daisy Bates: Civil Rights Crusader from Arkansas.* Oxford: University of Mississippi Press, 2005.

Baton Rouge Bus Boycott

The Baton Rouge Bus Boycott in 1953 was the first bus boycott in the American South that attempted to end segregation on city buses. The boycott served as an illustration of what could be achieved through peaceful resistance. The methods adopted in Baton Rouge were taken up by the bus boycott that occurred in Montgomery, Alabama, in 1955, which many historians view as the beginning of the Civil Rights Movement in the American South.

African Americans made up the vast majority of bus passengers in Baton Rouge, Louisiana, yet they were consigned to seats on the back of the bus while the first 10 rows of all city buses were reserved for white passengers. Frequently, seats on the front of the bus remained empty while African Americans went toward seats in the rear. A fare increase served as the spark for the protest. Shortly after the city council instituted the increase, which hit African Americans harder as they were the buses' primary passengers, Baptist minister T. J. Jemison spoke against the city council's fare increase and proposed ending segregation on Baton Rouge buses. The city council on March 19, 1953, instituted Ordinance 222 for Baton Rouge buses that allowed blacks to sit in the front seats so long as they did not take any seats in front of white passengers. In addition, African Americans had to enter the bus from the rear rather than the front.

Despite the city council's change of policy, bus drivers failed to observe the new rules. The Reverend Mr. Jemison tested the new policy by refusing to give up his seat when ordered to by a driver. The driver then took the bus to the police station, but given the city council's ordinance, the police failed to take action against Jemison. Given the decision of the city of Baton Rouge's authorities, the bus drivers then chose to go on strike to protest Ordinance 222. The Louisiana attorney general found the Baton Rouge ordinance to be in violation of state segregation law, whereupon the strike ended.

In reaction, Jemison and the African American community of Baton Rouge formed the United Defense League, which on June 19, 1953, called for a boycott of the Baton Rouge public transportation system. The United Defense League grew out of the African American churches. Church buildings also served as nightly meeting places during the bus boycott. At these meetings, money was raised for the boycott and the United Defense League organized a system of rides for those engaged in the boycott, though many chose to walk. The United Defense League politically united the African American community of Baton Rouge. The United Defense League and the city of Baton Rouge quickly reached an agreement, and the boycott ended on June 24, 1953. Despite Jemison and the United Defense League's agreement, many people who had engaged in the boycott were disappointed with the settlement, which preserved segregated seating and reserved the first two rows for white passengers, though the back seat was also reserved for African American passengers. Still, despite the limited achievements of the boycott, the methods adopted in Baton Rouge would be utilized in Montgomery in 1955 and later boycotts.

Michael Beauchamp

See also: Louisiana.

Further Reading

Parent, William. *Inside the Carnival: Unmasking Louisiana Politics.* Baton Rouge: Louisiana State University Press, 1996.

Williams, Juan. *Eyes on the Prize: America's Civil Rights Years, 1954–1965.* New York: Penguin, 1988.

Berea College v. Kentucky

Berea College, located in Berea, Kentucky, was founded to educate former enslaved African Americans and poor Appalachian whites. In 1859, the college obtained its charter from the state. However, no classes were offered at the facility until 1866, after the Civil War ended. Initially the college was started as an independent, non-sectarian Christian institution by John G. Fee, an evangelical, abolitionist minister from Bracken County who had moved to the area when he received several acres of land from Cassius M. Clay, a fellow Kentucky abolitionist. Because the college held close ties with numerous Presbyterian, Congregational, and Baptist churches, between 1855 and 1859, the institution functioned as a nondenominational mission school.

Simultaneously, the founders of Berea introduced a completely integrated curriculum to try to attract men and women, as well as African American and Caucasian students, to its facility. However, before the college could implement its educational plan, the fear of abolitionist-led uprisings, similar to John Brown's assault on the federal armory in Harpers Ferry, Virginia, in 1859, led many local citizens to organize a grassroots group that forced Fee and his supporters to leave the city of Berea. It was not until the early years of Reconstruction, on March 6, 1866, when Berea opened an integrated elementary school, with the enrollment of three African American female students, that Fee returned and the college quickly enacted its integrated educational plan. The following year, the first completely integrated class, taught by Ellen P. T. Wheeler, the wife of a missionary Fee had known during his visits to Camp Nelson, Kentucky, was offered at the institution.

In 1869, Edward Henry Fairchild, a graduate of Oberlin College, became the first president of Berea College. Under his leadership, several buildings were constructed and an enormous endowed funding campaign was started, led by money donated by the American Missionary Association as well as various private donors. During these years, Berea's enrollment also flourished with its highly ambitious educational philosophy that rested on the creation of an entirely integrated and socially equal instructional experience for all races, from kindergarten through college. For example, from 1866 to 1889, at least half of Berea's student body was African American. However, in late 1889, with the departure of President Fairchild, the educational environment of the institution began to change. For instance, with the appointment of William Goodell Frost as Berea's third president, more emphasis was placed on the recruitment and retention of poor white Appalachians, not the enhancement of the institution's integrated educational curriculum and overall plan. Soon, segregated classrooms and dorms began to appear. Also, the percentage of African American students who enrolled and continued their education at Berea College declined greatly.

On October 8, 1906, a grand jury in Madison County, Kentucky, indicted Berea College for violating the state's Day Law. The Day Law, proposed by state representative Carl Day, of Breathitt County, Kentucky, in 1904, made it illegal to educate African American and Caucasian students in the same facility.

Despite its conviction, Berea continued to challenge Kentucky's Day Law in court until the Court ruled in *Berea College v. Kentucky* (1908) that the Commonwealth of Kentucky had the right and authority to alter any educational charter it issued. Moreover, the Court also noted that Berea still had the ability to educate any students who enrolled at its institution, just not at the same time or place.

Eric R. Jackson

See also: Historically Black Colleges and Universities; Kentucky.

Further Reading

Harrison, Lowell H., and James C. Klotter. *A New History of Kentucky.* Lexington: The University Press of Kentucky, 1997.

Heckman, Richard A., and Betty Jean Hall. "Berea College and the Day Law." *Register of the Kentucky Historical Society* 66 (1968): 35–52.

Nelson, Paul David. "Experiment in Interracial Education at Berea College, 1858–1908." *Journal of Negro History* 59 (1974): 13–27.

Peck, Elisabeth S. *Berea's First Century, 1855–1955.* Lexington: The University of Kentucky Press, 1955.

Sears, Richard. *A Utopian Experiment in Kentucky: Integration and Social Equality at Berea, 1866 to 1904.* Westport, CT: Greenwood Press, 1996.

Bethune, Mary McLeod

Mary McLeod Bethune was one of the most prominent educators and civil servants of the twentieth century. "The First Lady of the Struggle," as she was known, worked indefatigably to guarantee the right to education and freedom from discrimination for African Americans. She was the 15th of 19 children born to former slaves in Maysville, South Carolina, on July 10, 1875. Growing up on her parents' farm, where she picked cotton, Bethune did not attend school until she was 11 years old at the Presbyterian mission school in Maysville. Then she attended Scotia Seminary, an African American girls' school in Concord, North Carolina, and subsequently attended the Moody Bible Institute in Chicago.

Upon receiving her degree, Bethune taught at the Presbyterian mission school in Maysville and then the Haines Institute in Augusta, Georgia, in 1896. At the Kindell Institute in Sumpter, South Carolina, she met Albertus Bethune, whom she married. In 1904, she opened a school for African American girls in Daytona Beach, Florida. Starting with five girls and her son, she began the school with virtually nothing: crates were used for desks, charcoal for pencils, and crushed elderberries for ink. To raise money for the school, she and her students held many bake sales. As the school developed, Bethune sought financing help. She was able to get James M. Gamble, of Proctor & Gamble in Cincinnati, Ohio, to become a benefactor. He would contribute to the school until his death.

In 1923, Bethune's Daytona Literacy and Industrial School for Training Negro Girls merged with the all-boys Cookman Institute of Jacksonville, Florida, to form a coeducational high school. In 1924, the school became affiliated with the Methodist Church. In 1931, it became Bethune-Cookman College, a junior college. Bethune-Cookman became a four-year college in 1941. Bethune was pres-

Mary McLeod Bethune fought for social, economic, and educational opportunities for African American women. (Library of Congress)

ident until 1942 and from 1946 to 1947. By 2007, the school achieved university status. As of 2007, the school had an enrollment of more than 3,700 students and an endowment of almost $40 million.

As president of the National Association of Colored Women, Mary McLeod Bethune was also a leader of the National Council of Women. In 1927, at a luncheon she hosted, Bethune met Eleanor Roosevelt and began a lifelong friendship. As a result of this contact, Bethune was named director of Negro Affairs in President Franklin D. Roosevelt's National Youth Administration (NYA) in 1936, a position she held until 1944. This organization, a part of Roosevelt's second New Deal, helped youth obtain employment. Thus she became the highest-ranking African American in the Roosevelt administration. She also was part of Roosevelt's Black Cabinet, an informal group of prominent African Americans that included Ralph Bunche, Eugene K. Jones, Rayford Logan, and Truman K. Gibson Jr. Their goal was to plan strategy and set priorities regarding African Americans for the Roosevelt administration.

Bethune was a champion of civil rights and pressed for antilynching legislation and abolition of the poll tax. During World War II, she also served as a special assistant to the secretary of war and assistant director of the Women's Army Corps. She left government in 1944 when the NYA disbanded. As president of the National Council of Negro Women, a position she held until 1949, she attended the founding conference of the United Nations. Even in her retirement, she spoke out on civil rights issues until her death on May 18, 1955. She was buried on the campus of Bethune-Cookman College.

Sanjeev A. Rao, Jr.

See also: Black Cabinet, The; Roosevelt, Franklin D.

Further Reading

Gelders, Sterne Emma. *Mary McLeod Bethune.* New York: Alfred A. Knopf, 1957.

Holt, Rackham. *Mary McLeod Bethune: A Biography.* Garden City, NY: Doubleday and Co., Inc., 1964.

McCluskey, Audrey Thomas, and Elaine M. Smith, eds. *Mary McLeod Bethune: Building a Better World.* Bloomington: Indiana University Press, 2000.

Birth of a Nation, The (1915)

After a private screening of the D. W. Griffith film *The Birth of a Nation* in early 1915, President Woodrow Wilson reportedly declared, "It is like writing history in lightning. My only regret is that it is all so terribly true." Wilson, a trained historian whose scholarship was cited in the film, identified with the power of the new medium of film and the popular perception of Congressional Reconstruction as a chamber of horrors were accurate. The film propagated white Southern memories of this tragic era outside the South and validated the institution of Jim Crow as a necessary form of racial control.

As early as 1911, Thomas Dixon pursued a screen adaptation of his novel *The Clansman: An Historical Romance of the Ku Klux Klan* (1905). The novel was a best seller when it was published, and Dixon had already adapted it into a successful stage play. He dramatized Southern memories of Reconstruction as a fatal error committed by Radical Republicans who unleashed freed slaves upon their former masters. In particular, Dixon emphasized the dire threat that the so-called hypersexual black brute posed to white women. According to the popular Southern narrative, whites, left with no other option, formed the Ku Klux Klan to restore order and preserve the purity of their race. The tale legitimized measures Southern legislators and lynch mobs took at the turn of the century to separate the races and suppress "lawless" and "uppity" blacks. Dixon proposed that Northern and Southern whites should reforge the nation free of this black menace. He hoped to spread these memories to millions more through the burgeoning film industry.

Dixon's original plan for the film version failed to materialize, but he found enthusiastic partners when he met producer Harry Aitkin and director D. W. Griffith. Griffith had recently broken free of the Biograph Company, where he had established his reputation making one-reel films. However, Griffith displayed a determination to also break free of the small production scale typical of films in the early twentieth century. His films grew longer and more costly. In 1914, he left Biograph and joined Aitkin. Like Dixon, Griffith was a Southerner; born in Kentucky, the son of a Confederate veteran, the director credited his father with passing on tales of the Civil War and Reconstruction that inspired the film. Contrary to this assertion, Dixon provided the film's historical perspective. Griffith developed the technical innovations that brought the past to life for millions of moviegoers.

The Birth of a Nation introduced audiences to the troubled history of the biracial nation created by slavery. Its tale of Reconstruction depicted an era in which a white nation was born. The film began with a brief scene depicting a slave auction that places responsibility for the race problem squarely upon the shoulders of Northern slave traders and the abolitionists who wished to liberate the Africans. The film then shifted attention to the intersecting lives of the Southern Camerons and Northern Stonemans. The Stoneman boys visited the Cameron plantation in Piedmont, South Carolina, an idyllic setting in which whites presided over loyal, content slaves. The young men were friends before the war, yet they enthusiastically marched to war out of a sense of duty to their homelands. The conflict shattered the old Southern order, and

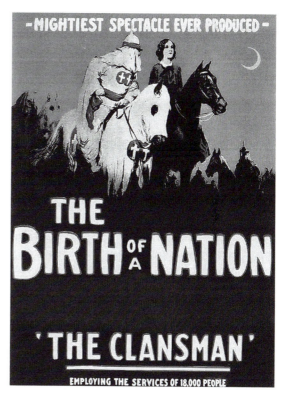

The Birth of a Nation poster highlighting that the film was based on Thomas Dixon Jr.'s novel *The Clansman*. The film and novel created a heroic image of the Ku Klux Klan of Reconstruction and denigrated the freedmen as not fit to vote or serve in office. (Getty Images)

Piedmont's whites suffered from poverty and the constant threat of Union raids. As the war neared its end, Ben Cameron and Phil Stoneman met on the battlefield. Ben proved his honor by assisting a wounded Union soldier and charging enemy lines despite the futility of the action. Wounded in battle, Ben awoke in a military hospital, where he awaited execution for the crime of treason. Phil's sister, Elsie, comforted him, and the pair began a romance that eventually sealed the reunion of North and South. However, Elise's father, Austin Stoneman, obstructed that reunion by crafting a vengeful policy designed to destroy the Southern aristocracy and uplift the freed slave. Stoneman's reign of terror is temporarily checked by President Abraham Lincoln, who expressed his compassion for the South by pardoning Ben and resisting Stoneman's plot. The assassin's bullet doomed the South, conferring control of Reconstruction to Stoneman, who oversaw his work of his mulatto protégé, Silas Lynch, in Piedmont.

Lynch initiated a reign of terror in which ex-Confederates were stripped of property and political rights as their former slaves were elected to the state legislature. During this minstrel session, black legislators, among them actors in blackface, drink, squabble, practice graft, and finally pass a bill permitting interracial marriage. The town of Piedmont suffered under the boot of black federal soldiers. The freedman Gus stalked young Flora Cameron. Unable to escape him, Flora chose to commit suicide rather than succumb to the black beast rapist. Her death inspired the emergence of the Ku Klux Klan, led by her brother, Ben. The Klan initially sought to administer justice for Flora's death; by the end of the film, the Invisible Empire restored white supremacy in Piedmont.

The film's ending emphasized the racial reunion of North and South. Lynch seized power from his mentor and unleashes the black militia upon the unreconstructed Camerons. Phil Stoneman realized that his true loyalty lies with his Southern brethren and comes to the aid of his former adversaries. Austin Stoneman underwent a similar conversion and embraces the Southern cause when he discovered that his mulatto protégé intends to marry Elsie. The film concluded with a double marriage of Phil and Margaret and Ben and Elsie, signifying the reunion of Northern and Southern whites.

The film attracted protest wherever it was screened. The National Association for the Advancement of Colored People (NAACP) organized protests across the country. The organization challenged the violent outbursts against blacks that the film's negative portrayals of the race might inspire. Municipal governments and censorship boards also opposed the film. Griffith protested that those who denied his film a permit violated the First Amendment's protection of the freedom of speech. Dixon capitalized on the White House screening as well as another screening for the Cabinet and the Supreme Court to defeat the film's opponents. In response to those critics who questioned the film's representation of Reconstruction, Dixon offered a reward to anyone who could disprove the film's historical perspective.

Millions saw *The Birth of a Nation*, and the film affected audiences in a variety of ways. NAACP fears proved valid; several white men assaulted black men they encountered after viewing the film. In addition, the film's release provided William J. Simmons the opportunity to fulfill his goal to revive the Ku Klux Klan. In November 1915, Simmons led a group to the top of Stone Mountain, outside Atlanta, where they set fire to a cross, signifying the return of the Klan. The novelist and the director both denounced this Second Klan, although they deserved credit for inspiring its rebirth. The film's ability to teach millions about Reconstruction was its most significant impact. Moviegoers learned that the suppression of the freed slave during Reconstruction required the formation of the Klan. They also understood that in the absence of social controls once provided by slavery, Southern whites required a new system to manage the former slaves. The film educated audiences outside the South that all Americans shared an interest in the purity of the race, and Jim Crow presumably achieved this goal.

The Birth of a Nation continued to attract audiences decades after its release. As civil rights activists demanded the fulfillment of federal promises made during the period Dixon and Griffith damned, the film became a rallying cry for Southern whites who resisted this Second Reconstruction. *The Birth of a Nation* still provided powerful images in defense of Jim Crow.

J. Vincent Lowery

See also: Ku Klux Klan; Reconstruction.

Further Reading

Franklin, John Hope. "*Birth of a Nation:* Propaganda as History." *Massachusetts Review* (Autumn 1979): 417–34.

Lang, Robert, ed. *The Birth of a Nation*: *D. W. Griffith, Director.* New Brunswick, NJ: Rutgers University Press, 1994.

Litwack, Leon F. "The Birth of a Nation." In *Past Imperfect: History According to the Movies,* edited by Mark C. Carnes, 136–41. New York: Henry Holt, 1995.

Slide, Anthony. *American Racist: The Life and Films of Thomas Dixon.* Lexington: University Press of Kentucky, 2004.

Black Cabinet, The

Officially known as the Office of Negro Affairs, the Black Cabinet, or "Black Brain Trust," was a group of African American public policy advocates informally established during the first term of President Franklin D. Roosevelt. Originally created under the direct auspices of Secretary of the Interior Harold L. Ickes, the Black Cabinet came to serve the U.S. government from the early to mid-1930s and sporadically, and often unofficially, during the following decade. Consisting of a number of associates with diverse expertise in fields ranging from law, education, and political science, the Black Cabinet boasted as many as 45 members in 1935 and worked within the departments of the executive branch toward strengthening New Deal agencies to provide federal relief and civil justice for African Americans in the midst of a racially segregated nation.

The Black Cabinet originated largely as a response to the racially polarizing effects of Jim Crow segregation, as well as the lingering outcome of the Great Depression and its ravaging consequences for the African American community. Stemming from the stock market crash of 1929, rural African Americans were devastated as cotton prices dropped dramatically from 18 cents a pound to 6 cents a pound. As more than 2 million African American farmers went into enormous debt, a number of Southern black sharecroppers left the fields for the cities of the North in order to find work. Occupying largely menial jobs such as train porters, maids, sanitation workers, and cooks, African Americans competed directly with whites, leading toward increased economic and racial tensions within the tumultuous and segregated environment of the United States.

Although largely neglecting the plight of African Americans during the first half of his first term, President Roosevelt began to take notice and acted to address the instability that resulted from this cultural convergence. To work within his New Deal programs, Roosevelt sanctioned the Black Cabinet to directly address the issues of African Americans in the age of the Depression. President Roosevelt's motives for endorsing the Black Cabinet were numerous in their design. Inspired by the words and actions of black orators such as Sojourner Truth and the grace and dignity of Marian Anderson, an African American singer who performed for state functions in spite of segregation, First Lady Eleanor Roosevelt became an effective antilynching activist and advocate for ending Jim Crow segregation. The First Lady also served as a primary influence on President Roosevelt, compelling him toward the cause of racial justice as well as addressing the social, economic, and political inequalities of Jim Crow segregation. President Roosevelt's authorization of the Black Cabinet was a controversial yet distinctly political move. The creation of a Black Cabinet conflicted directly with the interests of Southern senators, angering those who were to serve as potential allies for Roosevelt as he doggedly pursued his New Deal plan for Depression relief. However, the formation of the Black Cabinet effectively secured Roosevelt's growing interest in acquiring the African American vote, as the Cabinet came to represent among African Americans a viable and concerted effort to integrate blacks within the working political, economic, and social spheres of mainstream society.

The Black Cabinet worked directly with various government programs for farm subsidies, wider employment opportunities, and better housing and education options for poor and disenfranchised African Americans. The Black Cabinet also worked within the judicial branch to effectively challenge Jim Crow's grip on the legal system. Among its more prominent members were Ralph Bunche and Mary McLeod Bethune, both of whom served successfully as international representatives of the U.S. government. Other members included the National Urban League's Eugene K. Jones, and Robert Weaver, who would become the first U.S. secretary of housing and urban development. The Black Cabinet ended upon President Roosevelt's death in 1945.

Kevin Strait

See also: Bethune, Mary McLeod; Democratic Party.

Further Reading

Gibson Truman, Jr., and Steve Huntley. *Knocking Down Barriers: My Fight for Black America.* Evanston, IL: Northwestern University Press, 2005.
"New Deal Agencies and Black America." http://www.lexisnexis.com/documents/academic/upa_cis/1399_NewDealAgenciesBlackAm.pdf (accessed June 9, 2008).

Black Codes

The Black Codes was the term applied to laws enacted throughout the former Confederate states between 1865 and 1867. The Black Codes set out the specific rights of blacks following the end of the Civil War; in practice, they were used to restrict and control the activities of black people in these states, particularly in relation to their labor. The Black Codes were gradually ended by the actions of the federal government, including through the Freedmen's Bureau, and the establishment of Reconstruction governments. The creation of new state constitutions erased the Black Codes from the statutes. Nonetheless, the motivation that underlay the Black Codes survived and continued to shape the development of black-white relations in the years after Reconstruction. The Black Codes were distinct from the Jim Crow laws that succeeded them after Reconstruction, although both sought to limit the behavior of black people, and there were significant similarities.

In the chaos that followed defeat in the Civil War, the South struggled to make sense of its new reality. Of particularly grave concern to the white South was the position of blacks, particularly those who had recently been emancipated. Across the former Confederate states, whites were concerned that blacks would take revenge for slavery, and rumors of uprisings such as those fermented by free blacks in Haiti were rife. At the same time, many former slaveowners believed that blacks owed them gratitude and loyalty for the perceived benefits extended to them during slavery. Many planters felt betrayed when former slaves left their plantations; the return of former slaves to a plantation was a source of particular satisfaction, an apparent endorsement of the benevolence of Southern slavery. Nonetheless, former slaves were at pains to distinguish between their slave lives and their new freedom; although most were polite and courteous to former masters, they now expected the same in return, a courtesy which many whites were loath to extend. Blacks who continued to live on plantations often preferred to create new houses, rather than to live in former slave quarters, and few were keen to establish close relations with former masters.

While concerns over the potential for black revenge and the loss of the Southern way of life were tangible, at the heart of the South's concerns was that emancipation would lead to the loss of the majority of the region's agricultural labor force. The antebellum Southern economy had relied on slave labor, and without that workforce, Southern agriculture was stymied. After the Civil War, many whites assumed that former slaves would leave the South, as, indeed, many did, draining the region of agricultural labor. More, however, remained in the South, and this raised different anxieties. Antebellum attitudes persisted, and fears that blacks were naturally inclined to idleness and vagrancy increased doubts over their willingness to work without coercion. Many farmers were reluctant to plant a crop when they did not know whether there would be a labor force to harvest it. While many whites complained that blacks were indolent and reluctant to work, it is perhaps more true that blacks recognized the parallels between paid agricultural work and slavery, and were reluctant to enter into agreements whereby they would work on the same plantation as they had during slavery, growing the same crop for the same planter.

Whites failed to acknowledge this fear. Agricultural labor was considered to be the only purpose for which blacks were fit, and most whites assumed that the natural inclination of black people was to idle, unless put to work specifically. The prospect of using white labor on a large scale was never considered seriously; indeed, a more serious prospect was the importing of Chinese labor or other immigrants, such as Germans and Irish. However, such ideas were contrary to Southern orthodoxy, and, in any case, the preference of the white South was for the slave labor force to be reestablished in freedom. The example of the West Indies, where former slaves had taken up small plots of land, causing the decline of the plantation system, was further reason to ensure that blacks were compelled to work on large plantations. However, the need for a guaranteed labor force, even more than the need to reinstate antebellum social and cultural norms, was the key determinant in the creation of the Black Codes.

Despite emancipation and its attendant fears, many Southerners assumed that the patterns of antebellum life would be reestablished quickly. Slavery may have been abolished, but white people continued to believe that blacks were inferior and should be subordinate to white society, and thus expected to retain control over their activities. Moreover, the abolition of slavery and the presence of so many freedmen threatened to undermine both the traditional Southern social structure and the South's main economy. Many arguments that had been used to defend slavery were once again brought to bear. Emancipation was derided as a Northern folly that had misjudged the disposition of blacks and given them unrealistic hopes and ambitions. Southerners argued that Northerners understood nothing of the black character, which was inherently unsuited to freedom without the paternalistic framework of slavery, or some other form of white supervision. Blacks, particularly those who had been emancipated recently, would struggle to survive. Thus, they contended, it fell to the South to once again intervene to provide the necessary direction required by black people.

Presidential Reconstruction made it easy for Southern state legislatures to pass laws that placed blacks into a twilight world between slavery and freedom. The Black Codes set out the rights of blacks, but they also established pernicious labor requirements that severely limited their freedoms. Northerners accused Southern states of attempting to reestablish slavery, but the Black Codes, while impinging on many aspects of freedmen's lives, never went that far. Instead, freedmen in the South found themselves in an awkward position between the full freedom that they expected upon emancipation and the complete subordination of slavery. The Black Codes were a stern response to concerns in the aftermath of the Civil War, but they drew on diverse legal precedents. The slave codes and the laws that had governed the behavior of free blacks during slavery were easy models to reach for. So, too, were the codes that had been implemented in the British West Indies after the abolition of slavery there. Other existing laws, particularly vagrancy statutes, were used in the formulation of the Black Codes.

The first Black Codes were introduced in Mississippi and South Carolina in late 1865, and these two states had the most far-reaching codes. As well as being the first, they were also among the harshest, since the lack of agricultural labor would be hardest felt in these states. The Mississippi Black Codes applied to anyone who was one-eighth or more black. In setting out the rights of blacks in Mississippi, the Black Codes recognized slave marriages, allowed black people to own property (although with limitations on where they could own land), make contracts, sue and be sued, and be witnesses in cases in which a black person was involved. However, the Black Codes also set out that Mississippi blacks could not hold public office, serve on juries, or bear arms. Interracial marriage and cohabitation was forbidden. As in other former Confederate states, blacks were not given the vote. Mississippi also reenacted laws that had formerly applied to slaves, but extended them to all blacks.

The specific details of the Black Codes in each state differed, but across the South as a whole, the purpose and operation of the Codes was the same (in North Carolina, no formal Black Codes were passed). The Black Codes set out particular rights and freedoms that could be expected by blacks, but these were in essence restrictive measures that underlined the fact that the South intended to maintain the distinction between the races, with blacks in a position of impotent subservience. The Black Codes left no doubt that former slaves had become not free men, but free blacks, while the position for blacks who were not freedmen invariably became worse. This was most true in relation to labor, where states sought to ensure an adequate agricultural workforce. In all Southern states, the Black Codes were expressed in such a way that freedmen had little choice but to enter into agricultural labor contracts, and despite protestations to the contrary, there was no doubt that the white South considered blacks to be suitable for nothing other than field work.

Nonagricultural work was not closed to blacks, but was severely restricted, even for those who were not freedmen. In South Carolina, a license was required, along with a certificate signed by a local judge to guarantee the skill and moral character of the bearer. Furthermore, the employment opportunities of blacks in South Carolina were limited by a tax of between $10 and $100 for anyone who wished to engage in an occupation outside agriculture. This tax applied to all blacks and had a damaging effect on the well-established black artisan community in places like Charleston. In Mississippi, blacks who wished to engage in "irregular" work required a certificate. In conjunction with laws that prevented them from renting or leasing land outside towns or cities, and the refusal of the Freedmen's Bureau to provide relief rations to blacks who refused to sign labor contracts, these requirements left agricultural labor as the only option for blacks in several Southern states.

In seeking to protect the interests of planters in Mississippi, anyone who sought to entice a contracted black worker to break his or her contract could be imprisoned or fined $500. Various other aspects of the Black Codes served the same purpose. Blacks who broke labor contracts would forfeit wages already earned, and could be arrested by any white person. While protecting employers, this also severely limited the options available to black workers, who, despite their freedom, were denied economic mobility and were faced with little choice other than agricultural labor. The parallels with slavery were clear, and in most states, these were underlined by codes of behavior expected of black agricultural workers, and the definition of the hours of work from sunup to sundown. In South Carolina, the line between slave labor and free labor was blurred further through references to "masters" and "servants" on employment contracts. The Freedmen's Bureau rarely sought to prevent such obviously biased contracts, not because it favored the planters, as some blacks suggested, but because it viewed them as a temporary measure required to establish blacks in free labor.

The primacy of the South's concerns over labor, as well as its conviction that it could continue to intervene in the lives of blacks, was demonstrated amply by the introduction of apprenticeships. Apprenticeships allowed planters to compel black children to work for them if they were orphaned or were not being supported by their parents. Courts had the power to bind a child to an apprenticeship, for which the consent of the child's parents was not required. Former slave masters had first option on such children, and much about the system perpetuated white beliefs that they had the right to control the lives of blacks. The apprenticeship system was abused widely, and many children were bound into apprenticeships by Southern courts against the wishes of their parents. Since these children were bound under apprenticeships, planters were not required to pay them, further compounding the system's similarities to slavery. The apprenticeship system was a particular source of angst for freedmen, many of whom petitioned the Freedmen's Bureau and other federal officials for the return of children bound to such contracts.

In all states, blacks were required to have legitimate employment; those who did not were considered vagrants and could be fined or jailed. Vagrancy laws worked in conjunction with restrictions on the employment opportunities of blacks to further ensure a ready supply of agricultural labor. In many cases, people arrested under vagrancy laws were forced to work to pay off fines, thus further perpetuating the South's manipulation of free blacks for its own labor needs. In Mississippi, the vagrancy laws were expanded to include any black person who had run away, was found drunk, considered wanton in conduct or speech, had neglected his or her job or family, handled money carelessly, or was considered to be idle or disorderly. Similarly, anyone unable or unwilling to pay a new tax, the purpose of which was to support poor blacks, was considered a vagrant. Blacks were required at the beginning of each year to present written evidence of employment for the forthcoming year, or risk being classed as vagrants. In Alabama, vagrancy laws extended to runaway or stubborn servants and children, workers who worked too slowly, and workers who failed to adhere to the terms of their employment contract.

The introduction of the Black Codes established particular limitations to the employment opportunities available to blacks. As white Southerners sought to tighten their control over the means of production and force blacks into labor contracts, they also restricted activities and freedoms that had existed during slavery and that gave blacks some means of economic independence. In some states, hunting and fishing, as well as the grazing of livestock, were banned by the Black Codes. Some states ended the free ranging of livestock, requiring instead that animals be grazed on fenced land; such laws excluded those who did not own land from keeping animals. Other states banned blacks from owning guns and dogs, or imposed taxes on them. All of these laws were designed to further separate blacks from the ability to provide for themselves, compelling them ever further into agricultural labor contracts.

Other laws that supported the spirit and letter of the Black Codes were introduced across the South. Tax laws were reformed, ostensibly to assist planters amid concerns over the availability of labor, so that even the largest landowners were required to pay only extremely small taxes—as small as one-tenth of 1 percent in Mississippi. At the same time, high poll taxes were applied to freedmen. As with many crimes during this period, failure to pay was punishable by enforced labor. Those who did not pay the tax could be hired out to any planter willing to pay the outstanding tax. This system led to the development of peonage—whereby people (predominantly black) were required to work to pay off a debt. The peonage system was open to abuse by planters, and many blacks found themselves in virtual slavery, forced to work to pay off debts with no way of knowing how much they still owed, or even if they had paid the debt in full. Thus, the Black Codes were part of a system designed to keep blacks powerless and economically dependent.

Despite emancipation, Southern institutions continued to be set against blacks. The Black Codes expressly set out the rights that blacks could expect. In most Southern states, blacks were now able to testify in court, although often they could not sit on juries. This did not change the way in which justice was served, and courts routinely found in favor of white people and against black people. In cases in which whites were accused of crimes against blacks, typically the accused were acquitted. Where whites were found guilty, sentences tended to be lighter than those given to blacks for similar crimes, and in several states, including Mississippi, South Carolina and Louisiana, convicted blacks could be whipped, but convicted whites could not. Just as during slavery, the murder of a black person by a white person was rarely punished: of 500 whites tried for the murder of a black person in Texas between 1865 and 1866, none were convicted.

Although the Black Codes provided a range of laws intended to ensure an adequate agricultural workforce, planters continued to experience labor shortages, particularly through workers being attracted elsewhere by better conditions. In response, some planters tried different means of keeping workers on the land. This included paying laborers a share of the crop instead of a monthly wage, in the hope that workers would remain on the plantation until the crop was harvested, lest they lose what they had already earned. This system was ripe for exploitation, and many laborers complained that they were given a smaller share of the crop than that to which they were entitled. This system would develop into sharecropping, which would be used to keep many blacks landless and poor during the Jim Crow years. Indeed, aspects of many of the Black Codes were identifiable in Jim Crow laws.

The Black Codes were aimed primarily at ensuring that the South maintained an adequate agricultural labor force, but few Southerners were willing to accept that freed blacks should have access to the rights they assumed would be theirs upon emancipation. Many states created Black Codes that went beyond controlling the employment status of free blacks. In Louisiana, the behavior expected of agricultural workers bore strong resemblance to slavery. Bad work, failing to obey reasonable orders, and leaving home without permission were considered acts of disobedience, as were acting impudently or using bad language to or in the presence of the employer or his family. A sliding scale of punishments existed for transgressing these rules.

Restrictions were also imposed outside of work. In the town of Opelousas, Louisiana, freedmen needed the permission of their employer to enter town; any black person found without a pass after 10:00 at night was subject to imprisonment, and no black person was allowed to have a house within the city. In most parts of the South, large gatherings of blacks were forbidden for fear of fomenting sedition or inciting riots. In Mississippi, Black Codes made it a misdemeanor for blacks to engage in a host of activities, including making insulting gestures, preaching the gospel without a license, and selling alcohol. Similar restrictions were imposed by Black Codes throughout the South.

Black Southerners did not allow the Black Codes to go unchallenged. In Mississippi, freedmen petitioned the governor to assure him of their desire to work and to point out that they had no desire to rise up against former masters. The Mississippi petition asked the governor for clarification of the status of blacks in the state, given the apparent contradiction between the abolition of slavery and the terms of the Black Codes. In South Carolina, too, blacks requested recognition of their status as free men and asked for equal treatment. Despite the moderate language of such petitions, they were easily ignored by Southern legislatures in which planters had significant influence, but such petitions were noticed in the North and were a key factor in Northern criticism of the Black Codes.

The Black Codes were short-lived as a legal entity. The large number of laws enacted throughout the South, and their openly prejudiced nature, made them an easy target for the Freedmen's Bureau and the federal government. From their introduction, many Black Codes had been struck down throughout the South, mainly as a result of being too blatantly discriminatory. From their inception, the Black Codes had provoked ire outside the South. Northerners considered them to be a barefaced attempt to re-create slavery and so contrary to the spirit of emancipation that many people, even those who did not necessarily support civil rights for blacks, demanded that the South respect the ideology of free labor. The pleas of Southern blacks for evenhanded treatment and recognition of their status were well publicized in the North, and helped to galvanize support for action.

Even within the South, there had been some concern over the Black Codes, at least over the speed and severity with which they had been applied, if not necessarily their purpose. In 1866, several Southern legislatures had reduced the severity of some Black Codes, largely as a response to the failure of the anticipated outward migration of former slaves, but also in response to concerns that their continued operation would attract unwanted Northern intervention.

The Civil Rights Act of 1866, which defined citizenship and established the civil rights of citizens, and the Fourteenth Amendment, were intended in part to check the effects of the Black Codes. The establishment of full Congressional Reconstruction from 1867 onward saw the formal end of the Black Codes throughout the South, and Reconstruction governments removed the remains of the Black Codes from the statutes. Of particular significance, and as a reminder of the extent to which the Black Codes had been driven by a desire to control black activity in the labor market, the last vestiges of controls over black employment opportunities were removed.

Black children could no longer be apprenticed to an employer without parental consent. Perhaps the most insidious example of the Black Codes, vagrancy laws were rewritten to remove many existing definitions that had been used to ensnare innocent blacks, and it was no longer permissible to put someone to work to pay off a debt. Reconstruction laws also relaxed statutes concerning the enforcement of labor contracts, removing, for example, punishments for enticing a black laborer to break his or her contract.

Nonetheless, the Black Codes continued to have effect in many parts of the South, even when they had been abolished officially; this was particularly true where the Freedmen's Bureau and other federal officials had little presence. While the rescinding of many Black Codes prevented them from being acknowledged and advertised publicly, they often continued to be exercised. Vagrancy laws were particularly persistent, and blacks who refused to enter into a labor contract or who broke such a contract could still expect to be punished as though the Black Codes remained untouched.

While the legal instruments of the Codes had been dismantled, the spirit that had driven them remained. Throughout the South, arguments continued to be put forth that blacks would not work without being compelled to do so, lacked the skills and temperament to work for themselves, and, perhaps most significantly for planters, were required as agricultural labor to sustain the Southern economy. It is undeniable that the Black Codes and their application were driven by more than a desire to maintain the Southern economy. Nonetheless, the demands of Southern agriculture and the influence of planters allowed the Black Codes to continue being applied, legally or otherwise, in the face of black protests and Northern condemnation.

The Black Codes sought to continue to hold blacks in a state of powerlessness and dependence on whites. The need for labor was urgent, but arguments to suggest that blacks would not work unless compelled to do so were largely fallacious and a convenient prop for the white South, which also wanted to perpetuate antebellum socioeconomic patterns. That the Black Codes reached into areas of black life beyond work was a clear indication that the South refused to recognize the freedom of blacks and expected to continue to treat them as they had during slavery. After Reconstruction's end, the Jim Crow laws that were instituted throughout the South bore many similarities to the Black Codes, particularly those that sought to keep blacks as a landless servile class. Although short-lived, the underlying impetus of the Black Codes belonged to a deep-rooted racial ideology that continued to shape the lives of Southern blacks well into the twentieth century.

Simon T. Cuthbert-Kerr

See also: Ku Klux Klan; Racial Customs and Etiquette.

Further Reading

Foner, Eric. *Politics and Ideology in the Age of the Civil War.* New York: Oxford University Press, 1980.

Foner, Eric. *A Short History of Reconstruction.* New York: Harper and Row, 1988.

Franklin, John Hope. *From Slavery to Freedom: A History of American Negroes.* New York: Alfred A. Knopf, 1974.

Litwack, Leon F. *Been in the Storm So Long: The Aftermath of Slavery.* London: Athlone Press, 1979.

Litwack, Leon F. *Trouble in Mind: Black Southerners in the Age of Jim Crow.* New York: Alfred A. Knopf, 1998.

Woodman, Harold. "The Reconstruction of the Cotton Plantation in the New South." In *Essays on the Postbellum Southern Economy,* edited by Thavolia Glymph and John J. Kusma. College Station: Texas A&M University Press, 1985.

Woodward, C. Vann. *The Strange Career of Jim Crow.* New York: Oxford University Press, 1966.

Black Like Me and John Howard Griffin

In late 1959, John Howard Griffin (June 16, 1920–September 9, 1980), a white author, writer, and journalist, traveled through Louisiana, Mississippi, and Alabama disguised as an African American. His account of the journey was serialized in *Sepia* magazine and published in 1961 as *Black Like Me,* the title of which comes from Langston Hughes's poem "Dream Variations." Griffin's stated reason for the

White author John Howard Griffin darkened his skin and spent six months in the American South as an African American, an experience he later wrote about in *Black Like Me*. (Ben Martin/Time Life Pictures/Getty Images)

trip was to investigate suicide among black men in the South, but his real reasons were more complex. In experiencing life as a black man, he believed that he was bridging a gap between white society's perception of the black experience and the reality to which few white people were exposed. Griffin also regarded the journey as a challenge to his own beliefs and to his understanding of his own culture and, indeed, his own self.

Griffin was born into a middle-class Texas family, whom he regarded as "genteel southerners." His family considered themselves above the brutal racism of many white Southerners, but Griffin was nonetheless raised in an air of prejudice in which blacks were considered to be different from whites and therefore inferior. This sense of the otherness of black people would stay with him for many years, and would be both a motivation for and a theme of *Black Like Me*. For much of his life, Griffin wrestled with his own attitude to race and that of white society. At age 15, he traveled to France to take up a place at the Lycee Descartes in Tours. There, he prided himself on the fact that he shared the classroom with black Africans—something that would not happen in Texas— yet he was uncomfortable with their presence in the dining room, which his white peers accepted unquestioningly. Griffin reconciled this by accepting the French attitude to race as a cultural difference. When the Nazis invaded France, Griffin helped to smuggle Jews out of the country and recognized the Nazis' persecution of the Jews as groundless and inherently wrong, although he did not see parallels with the treatment of blacks in the United States.

While serving in the U.S. Army Air Forces during World War II, Griffin was tasked with studying a remote island tribe, to ensure that they would ally themselves with the United States and not the Japanese. Griffin was fascinated by the islanders' society and fully immersed himself in their way of life, although he regarded them as he had black people in Texas, and as a white man considered himself to be superior. He accepted that the islanders had knowledge and skills that he lacked to survive on the island, but concluded that this was merely a cultural superiority, borne from their knowledge of that specific way of life. As nonwhites the islanders were "other," just as blacks were in the United States, and he remained convinced of the inherent superiority of white people.

After the war, Griffin returned to Texas. His eyesight had been damaged in a bombing raid during the war, and in 1946, he lost the use of his eyesight completely. Griffin did not allow his blindness to restrain him: during this period he married, had two children, and published two novels. Arguably the most important event of this period was that Griffin came to realize that he could judge people only by how he interacted with them, not by their skin color. Moreover, as a blind person, Griffin himself became the "other" that he had always considered black people. In 1957, Griffin's eyesight returned, and in 1959, he decided to undertake a trip into the South, disguised as an African American, an idea that had gestated during his sightlessness.

Griffin darkened his skin by using medicine typically used to treat vitiligo and exposing himself to sunlamps for up to 15 hours each day. In facing his own racial attitude, Griffin was anxious about confronting his own image with different colored skin. He was particularly concerned by what his new appearance would mean for his relationship with his family, and wondered whether their racial prejudice—however mild—was so deep that they would be unable to accept his new self. Indeed, Griffin's first glimpse of himself as a black man forced him to confront his own racial prejudices; so stunned was he by his transformation, Griffin struggled to reconcile his appearance with his own sense of self. This loss of self is a recurring theme throughout the book.

Griffin began his journey in Louisiana in November 1959. During his time in disguise, one of Griffin's stiffest challenges was to stop thinking as a white person and to experience life as a black Southerner. He was skeptical that he would pass as an African American, not least because he believed that he did not have typically African American features. Griffin soon realized the diversity of face shapes, eye colors, and bone structures in the African American community, and he was accepted unquestioningly as an African American by everyone he encountered. Griffin disclosed his identity only to Sterling Williams, a black shoe shiner whom Griffin had befriended in New Orleans before he made his transformation. Although Williams accepted that Griffin had to be the white man to whom he had spoken several times in the past few days, he continued to doubt that Griffin was, in fact, white. Nonetheless, Williams became Griffin's mentor in entering into black life.

Griffin's account of his experience reveals his horror at both the nature of the black ghetto and the open racism he encountered from almost every white person he met. He struggled to cope with the character of black life he experienced, even though he recognized that this was a reality forced upon black people by Jim Crow. The poverty and desperate situations in which he found himself regularly led him to despair and doubt about his ability to complete the trip (indeed, on at least two occasions, Griffin took brief breaks from his journey, spending time with P. D. East, a liberal white Mississippian, in his home in Hattiesburg, and an Episcopalian priest in New Orleans). Many of Griffin's bleakest moments were a result of his treatment at the hands of white people, and he encountered regularly the humiliation that attended the daily experiences of black Southerners.

Trying to find work, Griffin was rejected out of hand, often told bluntly that he would not be hired because of his race. His experiences of segregation—often de facto—saw him moved on in public spaces and making use of inadequate separate facilities. On a bus journey into Mississippi, he was prevented from leaving the bus to use the bathroom at a rest stop and came to recognize these humiliations in the faces and behavior of the black people he met. His encounters with white men often revealed their level of sexual depravity and fascination with the sex lives of black people. On one occasion, he was tacitly, but clearly, threatened with murder. In particular, he was stunned by the racism he encountered from white women, having believed strongly in the inherent virtuousness of Southern womanhood.

Griffin's experience left him despairing for white people who subjected blacks to a reality that was founded entirely on prejudices based on skin color. Griffin found that by the end of his trip, he had become reconciled with his appearance and his place in society as a black man. While he had not lost his sense of self as he feared he might, he had been transformed by his experience—he recognized that he had started to look and think differently, hardening himself against the next expected indignity. With black skin, he found that he struggled to talk to his wife, having assimilated the understanding that black men did not address white women. Just as Griffin's entry into black society had been anxious, so was his reentry into white society. However, just as he found that he was immediately accepted as black because of his skin color, so he found that his white skin instantly gave him access to all that had been denied him as a black man.

Although *Black Like Me* received generally positive reviews, and entered the best-sellers list, *Negro Digest*—the only black publication to review the book—was lukewarm, wondering whether a white man could truly understand what it meant to be an African American in the South. The publication of *Black Like Me* led to Griffin and his family being subjected to death threats to the extent that they spent nine months living in Mexico during 1960 and 1961. In the years following its publication, there was strong media interest in the book, and Griffin became a spokesman on race issues for much of the rest of his life. Until his death in 1980, Griffin continued to write and lecture on the question of race in various contexts, including the Christian faith.

Simon T. Cuthbert-Kerr

See also: Passing.

Further Reading

Bonazzi, Robert. *Man in the Mirror: John Howard Griffin and the Story of* Black Like Me. New York: Orbis, 1997.
Griffin, John Howard. *Black Like Me.* San Antonio, TX: Wings Press, 2004.

Black Nationalism

Jim Crow laws explain the various ways in which American society was divided based on skin color and ancestry. Jim Crow laws also show how public facilities were regulated and how resources were distributed unevenly to American citizens. African Americans through black nationalism confronted Jim Crow laws and institutionalized racism and practices that were perpetuated by white power structures. They include unequal access to education and wealth as well as systematic attempts to deny nonwhites of their civil liberties and human rights. Black nationalism can be viewed from three angles: as a form of mobilization in opposition to white supremacy, as a platform for promoting black aesthetics, and as a call to all people of African descent to create a separate homeland and country without whites. This radical philosophy also called for economic independence for all black people.

Black nationalism is the process in which people of African descent—individuals, groups, and institutions—responded or continue to respond to the legacy of slavery, Jim Crow laws, neocolonialism, apartheid, racial prejudices, discrimination, and all forms of white supremacy. Black nationalism also speaks to the idea of promoting black racial pride, black cultural identity, and African heritage. In African American history, black people have mobilized in different eras to defy notions of white power and black servitude as well as notions of white civilization and black "primitiveness." Through these processes, black nationalism was able to change the ways in which whites and blacks interacted socially, politically, and economically.

The tradition of black nationalism and resistance dates back to the time of the transatlantic slave trade, when African slaves resisted attempts to capture them as slaves and how those who were captured unified on slave ships to fight their captors. Other forms of black nationalism emerged when Africans rebelled during their tenure as slaves in plantations in the New World—North America, South America, Central America, and the Caribbean—to register their protest against bigotry. Jim Crow laws, on the other hand, had their origins in racial ideologies that were developed during and after the introduction of chattel slavery in Africa and the institutions of slave plantations in the Americas. Jim Crow laws can also be traced through eugenics projects—the idea that the white race is endowed with positive hereditary qualities while the nonwhite race is bestowed with negative human attributes. Advocates of eugenics believe that a better human stock could develop through breeding or through the process of wiping out the weaker race. Institutional racism is built on the premise of eugenics and has provided justifications for Jim Crow laws or other forms of white supremacists projects. To look at it from another angle, the binary system created by oppression and resistance has defined contacts and relations between whites and blacks since their first contact.

During the period of slavery, African American slaves mobilized strategically based on their shared racial and African ancestral history, and through these efforts, they created a form of racial consciousness that served as a recipe for future black nationalism. Resistance by pioneers of the African American struggles against slavery and different forms of racism created a racial pride that has continued since the time of Nat Turner, the African American slave who initiated slave rebellions to challenge white supremacy and exploitations. Other resistance that was led by abolitionists such as Harriet Tubman and Frederick Douglass are all part of a tradition that developed at the height of white supremacy in America. Others have credited Marcus Garvey, the founder of the United Negro Movement Association (UNIA) in the 1920s, as one of the major architects of black nationalism in the twentieth century because of the ways in which he mobilized millions of black people all over the world to resist Jim Crow laws and all vices of white supremacy.

Also, black nationalism appeared in different shapes after the demise of slavery—especially in the post-Reconstruction era. At the height of Jim Crow laws in the late nineteenth century and early twentieth century, several international events such as the Spanish-American War, World War I and World War II, and decolonization campaigns also energized and radicalized black nationalism, giving it a stronger foothold. These mobilization strategies brought to the fore contradictions between Jim Crow laws and attempts to enforce democratic ideals in other parts of the world. For instance, African American soldiers who fought on the side of Europeans to liberate them from other oppressive regimes or ideology such as Nazism returned home to face racial segregation under Jim Crow laws. The lynching of African American war veterans gave additional meaning and impetus to the lasting effects of Jim Crow laws and the severity of racial hatred in America. Black nationalism in the early 1900s was also prompted by terror that was created by the Ku Klux Klan—a white supremacist group that was based mostly in the Southern belt of the United States. Ku Klux Klan members not only infused racial hatred, but they also employed intimidations and lynching to silence any African American racial mobilization and to stifle black nationalism in America.

World events continued to spur black activism and militancy around the globe. In the 1930s, black organizations such as the Council on African Affairs (CAA) which was founded by African American leftists such as Paul Robeson, W.E.B. Du Bois, Alpheus Hunton, Max Yeargan, and others energized black nationalism during the Italian-Ethiopian crisis (1934–1937).

The CAA also served as a political bridge that linked both black nationalism in America and others on the African continent as well as the African Diaspora—especially the Caribbean and Europe. Domestically, the CAA worked alongside African American–towering institutions such as the National Association for the Advancement of Colored People (NAACP) in the 1930s to challenge Jim Crow laws in labor unions, corporate America, and educational institutions. These institutions became advocates for African Americans who left the agrarian South to industrial regions in the North during the great migration eras and around the period of the Great Depression. On the national front, the success of the CAA paved a way for international black radicalism, such as the Pan African Congress in Manchester, England, in 1945. The African Diaspora conference brought black nationalist leaders such as Du Bois, Kwame Nkrumah, Jomo Kenyattah, and scores of leaders from the Caribbean to forge new alliances to strengthen black nationalism worldwide.

Vigorous crusades that were promoted by the Council on African Affairs, the NAACP, and other campaigns by black nationalists leaders around the globe in the 1930s through the 1950s bore many fruits abroad. These groups challenged Jim Crow laws in the United States and contributed to the demise of colonialism in Africa and Asia. Domestically, the surge of black nationalism at both home and abroad influenced the development of different forms of black activisms.

The germination of civil rights groups and student sit-in movements were all motivated by black consciousness that continued to increase in the mid-1950s. Most civil rights groups, including the Student Nonviolent Coordinating Committee, were adherents of Mahatma Gandhi's nonviolent approach—a strategy that Martin Luther King Jr. and other religious-based black nationalists also subscribed to during this era. Although these groups opposed Jim Crow laws to its core, they spoke against any group that used violent means to end white oppression. Resistance by African American women, including Rosa Parks and other women leaders in the Montgomery Bus Boycott (1955–1956), also shows how Jim Crow laws were resisted in various public spaces.

Black nationalism to some degree also gave birth to black radical groups such as the Black Panther Party, one of the most assertive organization in the history of black nationalism. The expression "Black Power" became synonymous with resistance against white oppression. Black Power also emphasized the creation of a separate black nation in North America as a form of rebellion against Jim Crow laws. The Black Panther Party was formed by Huey B. Newton and Bobby Seale in Oakland, California, in 1966. The Black Panther Party emerged at the height of the Civil Rights Movement, and although they shared a lot in common, they differed enormously on strategies for toppling Jim Crow laws.

Leaders of nonviolence groups and the Black Panther Party did not agree on how to end white oppression; yet, the two groups worked side by side to challenge Jim Crow laws. Although black nationalist traditions were tainted by numerous violent clashes between the police, the National Guard, and the Federal Bureau of Investigation, as well as government propaganda between the 1960s and the 1970s, the Black Panther Party remained popular because the party appealed to the consciousness of most young African Americans who remained marginalized in American society.

The Black Panther Party's emphasis on self-defense attracted many men and women into the party because they were able to express their freedom and manhood through their dress code and the use of arms. Specifically, the Black Panther Party's Ten Point Program exposed flaws in Jim Crow laws. They included lack of employment, unequal housing facilities for whites and blacks, poor health care systems for nonwhites, and police brutality. The Black Panther Party also provided clothes, food, free health services, and numerous resources to minimize the plight of poor people in the country. Adherents to self-defense, such as Malcolm X and Robert F. Williams, influenced black nationalism and radicalism in many ways because they held similar views about strategies for reforms in America. Despite resistance by the federal government, the Black Panther Party forced the federal government to act by making social reforms.

Black nationalism is expressed in other ways. In terms of aesthetics, it generated notions of black pride, black beauty, and black religiosity. Disciples of this form of black nationalism use the "black body" to make political and cultural statements. For example, the use of Afro hair, the celebration of African cultural holidays such as *Kwanzaa,* the use of African names, the wearing of African clothes and ornaments, and the folding of the fist are all expressions of "Black Power." Other forms of black nationalism were visible in the works of literary writers or poets such as Amiri Baraka (formerly known as LeRoi Jones).

Musicians such as James Brown also used music as a forum for advocating black pride and black beauty.

Kwame Essien

See also: Garvey, Marcus; Malcolm X.

Further Reading

Collier-Thomas, Bettye, and V. P. Franklin, eds. *Sisters in the Struggle: African American Women in the Civil Rights—Black Power Movement.* New York: New York University Press, 2001.

Eschen, P. Von. *Race against Empire: Black America and Anticolonialism, 1937–1957.* Ithaca, NY: Cornell University Press, 1997.

Forman, James. *High Tide of Black Resistance and Other Literary Political Writings.* Washington, DC: Open Hand, 1994.

Gaines, K. Kevin. *American Africans in Ghana: Black Expatriates and the Civil Rights Era.* Chapel Hill: University of North Carolina Press, 2006.

Lazerow, Jama, and Yohuru Williams, eds. *In Search of the Black Panther Party: New Perspectives on a Revolutionary Movement.* Durham, NC: Duke University Press, 2006.

Meriwether, H. James. *Proudly We Can Be Africans: Black American and Africa, 1935–1961.* Chapel Hill: University of North Carolina Press, 2002.

Weisbrot, Robert. *Freedom Bound: A History of American Civil Rights Movements.* New York: Norton Press, 1990.

Blues

The blues emerged in the rural segregated South, and particularly in the Mississippi Delta, in the early years of the twentieth century. African American blues pioneers such as Henry Sloan (1870–?), "Blind" Lemon Jefferson (1893–1929), and Charley Patton (1891–1934) developed a raw interpretive style that contrasted sharply with the compositional structures of ensemble playing featured in contemporaneous traveling shows. Performers could collaborate, but the performance featured a singer, self-accompanied on guitar, or in more urban venues, on piano. A few professional traveling musicians like Gertrude "Ma" Rainey (1886–1939) and W.C. Handy (1873–1958) quickly incorporated and adapted the style for ensemble performance, but retained the harmonic structure of the blues and, importantly, the individual voice of the lyric.

Blues developed out of a musical tradition that included the work songs of antebellum slavery, but blues is by no means a continuation of that tradition. Metrically, the

Blind Lemon Jefferson (1897–1930), American country bluesman, singer, and guitarist, 1925. He had a profound influence on later rock guitarists. (Hulton Archive/Getty Images)

work songs follow the rhythms of labor; the subject of the songs is often quite literally the work at hand. Blues, in contrast, utilized a distinctive 12-bar pattern, often with a simple verse pattern in which the first line of lyrics repeats in the second line and a third line concludes. Musically, the blues employed a scale with flatted thirds and sevenths, although in vocal and instrumental performance, there were extraordinary and subtle variations. The subject matter of blues is the individual, alone or in relationships. It is the individual at leisure—loving, fighting, drinking, crying—not at work.

Likewise, blues music draws upon the call-and-response traditions of African American spirituals, but has little use for the spiritual content. Occasionally, God might be called upon, but not to bring salvation—spiritual or worldly—but simply to witness the trials of the individual suffering. Nor is there a parallel in African American spirituals to the boast of Robert Johnson (1911–1938) of a personal encounter with the devil in "Cross Road Blues" or "Me and the Devil Blues."

The early blues musicians of Mississippi and Southern states to the west would have been identified as "songsters," and their repertoire also included popular dance tunes and ballads. Charley Patton was such a versatile and prolific musician that when he recorded for the Paramount label in 1929, several recordings were released pseudonymously so that he would not so dominate the catalog that year. His two-part "Prayer of Death," a more traditional spiritual, was released under the name "Elder J. J. Hadley." Even so, his distinctive vocalizations and complex guitar playing mark the rise of a new style of music. Most blues musicians learned from one another, playing in "jook" joints or informal dances in all-black sections of rural communities. Others took to street corners, working individually or in small groups for tips, learning techniques and songs from one another. In addition to Paramount, the Okey record company recorded a number of early blues artists, and these recordings, released as "race records" and intended for sale primarily in

African American communities, further expanded the market for the new music and attracted other musicians to the style. These early recordings were particularly important in the careers of female artists, who, unless they were employed full time as musicians in traveling shows, were less likely than their male counterparts to reach wide audiences.

More important even than the musical innovation was the radical individualism of the blues. The feelings and experiences of an individual blues composer were in themselves significant and offered a challenge to the racist underpinnings of the Southern social order in the early decades of the twentieth century. The racial hierarchy of the Jim Crow South precludes the individual case. Exceptions were outlaws, and extraordinary measures were available to guarantee their elision. The blues singer, in contrast, expressed feelings that mattered to a person and, by expressing the worst of them, could undermine the stereotype of the African American content with his or her lot. The artist also expressed an autonomy that challenged racial strictures. A man with the "walkin' blues" asserted the right to go anywhere he wanted. A female artist could assert her sexual independence. Even songs about fighting and killing asserted a right to one's own black body that would have been unachievable a half-century earlier.

Recent scholars have criticized blues artists for avoiding important social issues, for creating complaint songs rather than protest songs. W.C. Handy, often described as the "Father of the Blues," for his popular success in composing music based on blues patterns, generally avoided controversy both in his lyrics and in his professional life. But his most famous composition, "St. Louis Blues," opens with the line, "I hate to see that evenin' sun go down." The song is the lament a woman abandoned by her man, but Handy in his autobiography offered another context: "More than once during my travels in the North and South I had passed through towns with signs saying, 'Nigger don't let the sun go down on you here'" (Handy 1941, 86). Handy also reported that he left the South for good after an experience in Memphis. A lynch mob had murdered a young man named Tom Smith, putting out his eyes with hot irons and burning his body. The killers tossed the skull into a crowd of African Americans that had gathered at the square on Beale Street, which subsequently would be named for Handy. "They'd look for me on Beale Street, up and down the river, along the Yellow Dog and the Peavine, but I would not be there," he wrote. "Somebody else would have to play" (Handy 1941, 178).

In a region where African Americans could face lengthy jail time for minor or fictional offenses, blues artists often sang of life behind bars. The narrator of an Alger "Texas" Alexander (1900–1954) song complains that he is falsely accused of murder and forgery even though he can neither read nor write. Another Texan, Sam "Lightnin'" Hopkins (1912–1982), who had firsthand experience in the matter, addresses his jailer in one song, asking vainly for a key to his cell.

Mississippi's infamous state penitentiary, Parchman Farm, housed at least two important bluesmen. Musicologist Alan Lomax (1915–2002) recorded inmates there in 1939, including Booker T. Washington "Bukka" White (1909–1977), composer of "Parchman Farm Blues." In "Country Farm Blues," Edward James "Son" House Jr. (1902–1988) recalled an experience that echoed the cruelties of slavery. Arbitrary and harsh treatment were so common as to hardly merit comment, but House warned listeners that any who were unlucky enough to find themselves at Parchman Farm likely would endure whippings that would scar them long after their release.

Blues artists could not afford to address openly the most egregious injustices that Southern society offered, at least not in a venue that might include a white audience. In the Jim Crow South, a singer who sang about lynching likely would be lynched. With cautious producers, recorded blues were even less likely to venture a critique of the social order. But there are cases of allusion, such as a variation of a traditional blues lyric "Hesitating Blues," recalled by blues artist Sammy Price (1908–1992). Price reported that following a lynching in Robinsonville, Texas, near the town of Waco, people began singing a new version of the song with a verse that threatens a labor boycott in response to the mob's actions. There is even a subtle revision of the "hesitation" of the original song, suggesting a threat to the white establishment. The promise to "get you" in the original no longer has an apparent romantic connotation, but now promises something more revolutionary. The contextual change would be evident only to an audience familiar with the lynching and sympathetic to the possibility of an African American's violent response.

The critique of white-on-black violence was coded, but even with recorded music, a change of color in the lyrics could make the message plain. Erreal "Little Brother" Montgomery (1906–1985) recorded "The First Time I Met You" in 1936. The only characters in the song are the narrator and "Mr. Blues." An inattentive audience might hear Mr. Blues as a personification of the singer's feelings, but in Montgomery's song, the character's actions betray another allusion. The blues, and then Mr. Blues particularly, chase the narrator through the woods. They chase him into his home and harm him. The narrator ends the song begging Mr. Blues not to murder him. A black audience would know that every African American in the South was obliged to address every white adult male as "Mister." This is not just a singer trying to shake off a depressive gloom. It is a black man confronted with the real dangers of a white mob.

Other artists sang about tragic events that affected black communities in particular. Songs that highlighted the suffering of African Americans during the flooding of the Mississippi River in 1927 rarely dealt explicitly with racism, but the unequal treatment of black victims in the floods would have been a part of an audience's response to those songs. Sippie Wallace's (née Beulah Thomas, 1898–1986) "Flood Blues," Bessie Smith's (1894–1937) "Backwater Blues," and Charley Patton's "High Water Everywhere" catalogued the sufferings of folks whose homes were destroyed when the levees failed. Black audiences knew that black men were conscripted at gunpoint for relief work, and that mob violence against African Americans increased following the floods. Patton's "High Water Everywhere," recorded in 1929, pointedly observed that the homes of African Americans were most likely to be in the flood plain. The hill country, safe from the floodwaters, was off limits to African Americans.

Blues musicians accompanied, physically and musically, the Great Migration of African Americans out of the rural South to the cities of the North in the decades including the two world wars. On occasion, the farewell critique of the Jim Crow South was explicit, as in the case of Charles "Cow Cow" Davenport's (1894–1955) 1929 recording, "Jim Crow Blues," about leaving the Jim Crow South for Chicago. Other artists were more cautious. In "L&N Blues," Clara Smith (1894–1935) sang in 1925 about going the other direction, but she makes the point that in returning to the South, she will have to relinquish her Pullman berth for less comfortable accommodations.

In Northern cities, particularly in Chicago, blues artists extended their craft and found a wider audience. Race records were advertised prominently in the *Chicago Defender,* the nation's premier African American newspaper. There was also a greater opportunity for employment for blues artists, both as musicians and as laborers. With urban life came changes in the music, although the radical, subversive individualism that characterized its earliest formulations remained at its core. Exchanging their acoustic guitars for electric, a new generation of blues artists reached a wider audience than their rural predecessors. Muddy Waters (né McKinley Morganfield, 1913–1983), a migrant from Mississippi, became an internationally acclaimed star, although many of his first white fans were young musicians in England rather than in his home country. The urban music scene that finally embraced blues music in the decades following World War II was by no means color-blind, but it was a far cry from the music's roots in Jim Crow Mississippi.

James Ivy

See also: Great Migration; Jim Crow.

Further Reading

Davis, Angela Y. *Blues Legacies and Black Feminism: Gertrude "Ma" Rainey, Bessie Smith, and Billie Holiday.* New York: Random House, 1998.

Evans, David, Edward Komara, and Dick Spottswood. Liner notes to *Screamin' and Hollerin' the Blues: The World of Charley Patton.* 6-CD boxed set. Revenant, 2001.

Floyd, Samuel A. *The Power of Black Music: Interpreting Its History from Africa to the United States.* New York: Oxford University Press, 1995.

Gussow, Adam. *Seems Like Murder Here: Southern Violence and the Blues Tradition.* Chicago: University of Chicago Press, 2002.

Handy, W.C. *Father of the Blues: An Autobiography.* New York: The Macmillan Company, 1941. Reprint, New York: Da Capo Press, 1985.

Oakley, Giles. *The Devil's Music: A History of the Blues.* New York: Da Capo Press, 1997.

Oliver, Paul. *Broadcasting the Blues.* New York: Routledge, 2006.

Oliver, Paul. *The Meaning of the Blues.* New York: Collier, 1960.

Palmer, Robert. *Deep Blues.* New York: Viking Press, 1981.

Brown v. Board of Education

Brown v. Topeka, Kansas Board of Education, 347 U.S. 483, was decided by the U.S. Supreme Court in 1954. Two years earlier, *Brown* along with four other companion cases—*Belton v. Gebhardt (Bulah v. Gebhardt),* Delaware; *Bolling v. Sharpe,* 347 U.S. 497, D.C.; *Briggs v. Elliott,* South Carolina; *Davis v. Prince Edwards County School Board,* Virginia—were filed by the National Association for the Advancement of Colored People (NAACP) attorneys—Thurgood Marshall, Robert Carter, Jack Greenberg, Charles Bledsoe, Charles Scott, John Scott, and James Nabrit)—on behalf of plaintiffs challenging the legality of de jure or state-mandated racial segregation of black and white children in public schools.

By 1949, at least 17 states—Alabama, Arkansas, Connecticut, Florida, Georgia, Kentucky, Louisiana, Massachusetts, Mississippi, Missouri, North Carolina, Oklahoma, Rhode Island,

Lawyers for the National Association for the Advancement of Colored People celebrate outside the Supreme Court after successfully challenging school segregation in *Brown v. Board of Education* (1954). From left to right are George E. Hayes, Thurgood Marshall, and James Nabrit. (Library of Congress)

South Carolina, Tennessee, Texas, and West Virginia—and the District of Columbia had enacted laws requiring the racial segregation of public school children. Four other states—Arizona, Kansas, New Mexico, and Wyoming—provided for a local option in determining whether to segregate public education. Wyoming was the only state that did not exercise this option.

In Delaware (*Belton/Bulah*), a 1935 state law required that "[t]he schools provided shall be of two kinds; those for white children and those for colored children. The schools for white children shall be free for all white children between the ages of six and twenty-one years, inclusive; and the schools for colored children shall be free to all colored children between the ages of six and twenty-one years, inclusive. . . . The State Board of Education shall establish schools for children of people called Moors or Indians." This dual system of public education was contested because of the inferior conditions of the black schools.

In *Bolling,* the Court concluded that:

> the Equal Protection Clause of the Fourteenth Amendment prohibits the states from maintaining racially segregated public schools [Note: *Bolling* was decided on the same day as *Brown*]. The legal problem in the District of Columbia is somewhat different however. The Fifth Amendment, which is applicable in the District of Columbia, does not contain an equal protection clause as does the Fourteenth Amendment which applies only to the states. But the concepts of equal protection and due process, both stemming from our American ideal of fairness, are not mutually exclusive. The "equal protection of the laws" is a more explicit safeguard of prohibited unfairness than "due process of law," and, therefore, we do not imply that the two are always interchangeable phrases. But, as this Court has recognized, discrimination may be so unjustifiable as to violative of due process. . . . In view of our decision that the Constitution prohibits the states from maintaining racially segregated public schools, it would be unthinkable that the same Constitution would impose a lesser duty on the Federal Government. We hold that racial segregation in the public schools of the District of Columbia is a denial of the due process of law guaranteed by the *Fifth* [emphasis added] Amendment to the Constitution. For the reasons set out in *Brown v. Board of Education,* this case will be restored to the docket for reargument on Questions 4 and 5 previously propounded by the Court.

In *Briggs,* Article 11, Section 7 of South Carolina's 1895 constitution required racial segregation of its public schools. According to the language of this article, "[s]eparate schools shall be provided for children of the white and colored races, and no child of either race shall ever be permitted to attend a school provided for children of the other race." Similarly, Section 5377 of the 1942 Code of Laws of South Carolina made it "unlawful for pupils of one race to attend the schools provided by boards of trustees for persons of another race." The emphasis in this case was on inequities—facilities, transportation, and teachers' salaries—that existed between white and black public schools.

Even though *Davis* was one of *Brown's* companion cases, this case differed from the other cases in that the *Davis* challenge was initiated by a 1951 student protest against the disparities that existed between white and black public schools in the state of Virginia. The NAACP later joined the students to challenge various disparities.

The *Brown* plaintiffs brought suit to enjoin "a Kansas statute [Kan. Gen. Stat. 72–1724 (1949)] which permit[ed], but d[id] not require, cities of more than 15,000 population to maintain separate school facilities for Negro and white students." This case was brought on behalf of 20 black children who were denied admissions to public schools reserved for white children.

Brown was not the first legal challenge to racially segregated public education for white and black children. It is instead the most successful and well-known challenge to this form of segregation because of the final decree of the U.S. Supreme Court. The earliest challenge to segregated public schools dates back to 1849 in *Robert v. the City of Boston,* 59 Mass. 198. In fact, the *Brown* Court noted that "the [application of the separate-but-equal] doctrine apparently originated in *Roberts v. City of Boston,* 59 Mass. 198, 206 (1850), upholding school segregation against attack as being violative of a state constitutional guarantee of equality. [As a result], [s]egregation in Boston public schools was [not] eliminated [until] 1855."

Between 1881 and 1950, many lawsuits were filed challenging the constitutionality of racially segregated public schools. These lawsuits were as follows:

1881 *Elijah Tinnon v. The Board of Education of Ottawa, KS* (26 Kan. 1)
1891 *Knox v. The Board of Education of Independence, KS* (45 Kan. 152)
1903 *Reynolds v. The Board of Education of Topeka, KS* (66 Kan. 672)
1906 *Richardson v. The Board of Education of Topeka, KS*
1906 *Cartwright v. The Board of Education of Coffeyville, KS* (73 Kan. 32)
1907 *Rowles v. The Board of Education of Wichita, KS* (76 Kan. 361)
1908 *Williams v. The Board of Education of Parsons* (79 Kan. 202)
1916 *Woodridge v. The Board of Education of Galena, KS* (98 Kan. 397)
1949 *Webb v. School District No. 90, South Park Johnson County* (167 Kan. 395).

Since this decision, there have been two other *Brown* decisions—*Brown* II, 349 U.S. 294 (1955), and *Brown* III, 84 F.R.D. 383 (D. Kan. 1979). In *Brown* II, the

Court ruled that "the cases are remanded to the District Courts to take such proceedings and enter such orders and decrees consistent with this opinion as are necessary and proper to admit to pubic schools on a racially nondiscriminatory basis *with all deliberate speed* [emphasis added] the parties of these cases." *Brown* III was brought by attorneys requesting that the courts revisit *Brown* I and *Brown* II to determine whether Kansas's public schools had been desegregated. The U.S. Supreme Court denied the appellants a *writ of certiorari* and remanded the case for implementation of the Tenth Circuit's ruling on behalf of the *Brown* III plaintiffs. Years later, magnet schools were built in an effort to eliminate the remaining vestiges of segregation in the public schools of Topeka, Kansas.

What distinguished *Brown* from previous attempts to integrate public education was the role played by the NAACP in working with community activists and parents in order to initiate class action lawsuits in specific localities. Beginning in the 1920s and specifically under the leadership of Walter White, the NAACP began developing a strategy to challenge the constitutionality of legally mandated racial segregation. In the 1930s, Charles Hamilton Houston replaced White and later became director of counsel for the NAACP. It was Houston's experience with Jim Crow laws during his military service that served as an impetus in his attack on segregation. Thus, the NAACP viewed *Brown* as the first of many steps toward the goal of integrating every aspect of American society.

Brown reached the Court in 1951 but was not argued until December 9, 1952. Rather than providing a ruling in 1952, the Court scheduled reargument of the case. This reargument was scheduled for December 8, 1953. In preparation for reargument, the justices asked the lawyers to consider five specific questions. Three of these questions focused upon the applicability or lack thereof of the Fourteenth Amendment to the issue of racial segregation, and two questions focused on the procedures and timetable for possible integration of public education. The attorneys were asked to address the following questions:

1. What evidence is there that the Congress which submitted and the State legislatures and conventions which ratified the Fourteenth Amendment contemplated or did not contemplate, understood or did not understand, that it would abolish segregation in public schools?
2. If neither the Congress in submitting nor the States in ratifying the Fourteenth Amendment understood that compliance with it would require the immediate abolition of segregation in public schools, was it nevertheless the understanding of the framers of the Amendment:
    (a) that future Congresses might, in the exercise of their power under section 5 of the Amendment, abolish such segregation, or

(b) that it would be within the judicial power, in light of future conditions, to construe the Amendment as abolishing such segregation of its own force?

3. On the assumption that the answers to questions 2(a) and (b) do not dispose of the issue, is it within the judicial power, in construing the Amendment, to abolish segregation in public schools?

4. Assuming it is decided that segregation in public schools violates the Fourteenth Amendment:

(a) would a decree necessarily follow providing that, within the limits set by normal geographical school districting, Negro children should forthwith be admitted to schools of their choice, or

(b) may this Court, in the exercise of its equity powers, permit an effective gradual adjustment to be brought about from existing segregated systems not based on color distinctions?

5. On the assumption on which questions 4(a) and (b) are based, and assuming further that this Court will exercise its equity powers to the end described in question 4(b),

(a) should this court formulate detailed decrees in these cases;

(b) if so, what specific issues should the decrees reach;

(c) should this Court appoint a special master to hear evidence with a view to recommending specific terms for such decrees;

(d) should this Court remand to the courts of first instance with directions to frame decrees in these cases, and if so what general directions should the decrees of this Court include and what procedures should the courts of first instance follow in arriving at the specific terms of more detailed decrees?"

Prior to the reargument of *Brown*, Chief Justice Fred Vinson died and was replaced by Earl Warren. Warren eventually persuaded fellow justices of the importance of rendering a unanimous decision in the *Brown* case. On May 17, 1954, the Court issued a unanimous decision on behalf of the *Brown* plaintiffs.

When presenting their arguments in *Brown*, the attorneys relied upon the doll experiment of Professor Kenneth B. Clark and Mamie Clark to support their inferiority complex thesis. Professor Clark found that black children were consistently more likely to prefer a white doll to a black one, which they classified as "bad" or "looking bad." The attorneys successfully employed the contention relied upon by Attorney Robert Carter in *Westminster School District of Orange County v. Mendez*, 161 F.2d 774 (9th Circuit 1947), to convince the Court that racially segregated public schools resulted in black children feeling inferior to their white counterparts and experiencing psychological harm. In agreement, the Court stated:

> To separate them from others of similar age and qualifications solely because of their race generates a feeling of inferiority as to their status in the community that may affect their hearts and minds in a way unlikely ever to be undone. The effect of this separation on their educational opportunities was well stated by a finding in the Kansas case by a court which nevertheless felt compelled to rule against the Negro plaintiffs:
>
> > "[s]egregation of white and colored children in public schools has a detrimental effect upon the colored children. The impact is greater when it has the sanction of the law, for the policy of separating the races is usually interpreted as denoting the inferiority of the negro group. A sense of inferiority affects the motivation of a child to learn. Segregation with the sanction of law, therefore, has a tendency to [retard] the educational and mental development of negro children and to deprive them of some of the benefits they would receive in a racial[ly] integrated school system."

In addition to their emphasis upon an inferiority complex thesis, the *Brown* attorneys challenged the "separate-but-equal" doctrine established in *Plessy v. Ferguson,* 163 U.S. 537 (1896). This strategy forced the Court to determine whether black and white public schools were in fact equal under the Fourteenth Amendment and allowed plaintiffs' attorneys the opportunity to address the relevance of the Fourteenth Amendment to the case.

Interestingly, the Court's interpretation of the Fourteenth Amendment in *Brown* differed considerably from its interpretation of this amendment in *Plessy.* Unlike the *Plessy* Court's application of the separate-but-equal doctrine, the *Brown* Court opined that:

> In approaching this problem, we cannot turn the clock back to 1868, when the Amendment was adopted, or even to 1896, when *Plessy v. Ferguson* was written. We must consider public education in the light of its full development and its present place in American life throughout the Nation. Only in this way can it be determined if segregation in public schools deprives these plaintiffs of the equal protection of the laws. Today, education is perhaps the most important function of state and local governments. Compulsory school attendance laws and the great expenditures for

education both demonstrate our recognition of the importance of education to our democratic society. It is required in the performance of our most basic public responsibilities, even service in the armed forces. It is the very foundation of good citizenship. Today it is a principal instrument in awakening the child to cultural values, in preparing him for later professional training, and in helping him to adjust normally to his environment. In these days, it is doubtful that any child may reasonably be expected to succeed in life if he is denied the opportunity of an education. Such an opportunity, where the state has undertaken to provide it, is a right which must be made available to all on equal terms. We come then to the question presented: Does segregation of children in public schools solely on the basis of race, even though the physical facilities and other "tangible" factors may be equal, deprive the children of the minority group of equal educational opportunities? We believe that it does.

Therefore, the *Brown* Court concluded "that in the field of public education the doctrine of 'separate-but-equal' has no place. Separate educational facilities are inherently unequal. Therefore, we hold that the plaintiffs and others similarly situated for whom the actions have been brought are, by reason of the segregation complained of, deprived of the equal protection of the laws guaranteed by the Fourteenth Amendment."

Even though the Court ruled that the "segregation of children in public schools solely on the basis of race . . . deprive the children of the minority group of equal educational opportunities," it failed to order states to immediately desegregate public schools. Instead, the Court once again asked *Brown* attorneys to address questions focusing on the implementation of his desegregation order. Of course, the attorneys argued that the integration of public schools should occur immediately rather than in "gradual adjustments" or increments. Therefore, in 1955, the Court issued a directive in *Brown* II requiring lower federal courts to "enter such orders and decrees consistent with [its] opinion as are necessary and proper to admit to public schools on a racially nondiscriminatory basis *with all deliberate speed* [emphasis added] the parties of these cases (*Brown* I).

White segregationists used the Court's "with all deliberate speed" phrase as a loophole in their efforts to delay the implementation of *Brown*. As a result, in many localities, integration of public schools did not occur until many years after the *Brown* decision. Despite obstacles—the infamous actions of Governor Orval Faubus of Arkansas, enactment of school closing laws, repeal of compulsory attendance and student placement statues, "freedom of choice" student plans, and passage of anti-NAACP laws—encountered in the implementation of the *Brown* ruling, the significance of this decision cannot be exaggerated.

This ruling had a far-reaching impact on civil rights in the United States and led to the eventual dismantling of Jim Crow laws throughout the United States. The Court's declaration in *Brown* that the separate-but-equal doctrine adopted in *Plessy* did not apply to the field of public education resulted in efforts to eliminate all forms of segregation—the initial and ultimate goal of the NAACP. As a result, post-*Brown* attention has focused on segregated housing, public accommodations, public transportation, voting, and employment.

Olethia Davis

See also: *Brown v. Board of Education,* Legal Groundwork for.

Further Reading

Brown v. Board of Education of Topeka, Kansas, 347 U.S. 483 (1954).

Brown v. Board of Education of Topeka, Kansas, 349 U.S. 294 (1955).

Brown v. Board of Education Orientation Handbook (Brown Foundation for Educational Equity, Excellence, and Research, 1996–2003), available at http://brownvboard.org/research/handbook/overview/overview.htm

Ogletree, Charles J., Jr. *All Deliberate Speed: Reflections on the First Half Century of Brown v. Board of Education.* New York: W. W. Norton & Company, 2004.

Patterson, James T. *Brown v. Board of Education: A Civil Rights Milestone and Its Troubled Legacy.* New York: Oxford University Press, 2001.

Plessy v. Ferguson, 163 U.S. 537 (1896).

Brown v. Board of Education, Legal Groundwork for

In a series of Supreme Court decisions that paved the way for black students to pursue graduate degrees at state universities, lawyers working for the National Association for the Advancement of Colored People (NAACP) laid the groundwork for extinguishing the legal basis for Jim Crow segregation in other public arenas. The architect of the NAACP's legal strategy was Charles Hamilton Houston, who has since become known as "The Man Who Killed Jim Crow." Houston, a graduate of Harvard Law School, eventually became dean of the Howard University Law School. Houston trained a significant portion of the nation's black lawyers during the middle of the twentieth century.

Houston considered the U.S. Supreme Court's "separate but equal" doctrine, established in *Plessy v. Ferguson* (1896), to be the legal foundation of Jim Crow. Houston's strategy was to undermine incrementally this doctrine in a series of lawsuits brought by NAACP lawyers beginning in the 1930s, and culminating in 1954 with *Brown v. Board of Education.* Houston aimed to demonstrate that "separate but equal" doctrine led to inequality, and thus violated the Fourteenth Amendment right to equal protection under the law. Houston's primary target was segregation in the American education system.

One of the NAACP's first significant victories was *Pearson v. Murray* (Md. 1936). Donald Gaines Murray, a black graduate of Amherst College, was denied admission to the University of Maryland Law School. Future U.S. Supreme Court Justice Thurgood Marshall served as Murray's attorney. Marshall had also been denied admission to the same school years before, and had instead obtained his law degree from Howard University.

Maryland argued that it could meet the requirements of "separate but equal" doctrine by providing scholarships for black students to fund their graduate education at out-of-state schools. The trial court held that the legislature's appropriation for the scholarship fund was obviously inadequate to support the population of black law students in Maryland. Nor could black students study Maryland law and court procedures at out-of-state law schools. The state appealed the case to Maryland's highest court, which affirmed the lower court's ruling in favor of Murray. The court required the University of Maryland Law School to admit black students. Because the NAACP prevailed in Maryland's Supreme Court, thus ending the litigation, the court's judgment was not binding outside of Maryland.

In 1938, the U.S. Supreme Court decided *Missouri ex rel. Gaines v. Canada.* Lloyd Gaines, a black student represented by the NAACP, complained that Missouri had no grounds to exclude him from the state university's law school, because Missouri provided no alternative state law school for him to attend. He argued that this condition thus violated his Fourteenth Amendment right to equal protection. The Court agreed, and held that states that provide a public legal education to white students must also make a comparable education available to black students. However, this did not end segregation nationwide. The decision permitted states to continue to maintain segregated graduate schools by creating additional law or medical schools for blacks. Thus states could avoid Fourteenth Amendment challenges by fulfilling the requirements established by *Plessy's* "separate but equal" doctrine.

Ada Lois Sipuel, a black student, applied to the School of Law at the University of Oklahoma, and was turned down on the basis of race. Oklahoma had no alternative state-funded law school that admitted blacks. In *Sipuel v. Oklahoma State Regents* (1948), the U.S. Supreme Court held that in such circumstances, states must admit black applicants to white law schools. Thus the Court upheld and extended *Gaines.*

With *Gaines* and *Sipuel,* Houston and the NAACP legal team had successfully established that black students had an equal right to a legal education at state universities. Their next challenge was to overturn the "separate but equal" doctrine that segregated white and black law students into separate schools. They came close to accomplishing this by winning *Sweatt v. Painter* (1950). Herman Sweatt, a black mail carrier, applied to the University of Texas Law School and was denied admission on the grounds that the Texas Constitution prohibited racially integrated public education. There were no other law schools in Texas that admitted black students. Thus Texas was in violation of the rule set in *Gaines* and *Sipuel.*

The Texas trial court attempted an end run. The court set aside the case for six months, to give the state time to create a law school for blacks (which eventually developed into what today is Texas Southern University). Sweatt complained that the makeshift facility—a few rooms staffed by underqualified teachers—was clearly unequal compared with the University of Texas Law School.

The Supreme Court agreed with Sweatt, and overturned the lower court in 1950. The Supreme Court held that if a state establishes separate black schools, they must be "substantially equal" to the comparable white schools. The Court held that the new black law school was clearly inferior on objective criteria. It also held that intangible factors must also be considered, such as the graduates' isolation from the broader population of future lawyers. These intangibles were a component of the new doctrine of substantive equality, along with the objective criteria used to evaluate schools. Thus, in *Sweatt,* the principle of "separate but equal" was seriously undermined. The Court now held states to the "equal" part of the rule, which states had been evading for decades. As a result, segregation was effectively eliminated with regard to higher education at state law schools, because funding two fully equal law schools made segregation too expensive to be practical, and because the intangible aspects of substantive equality were nearly impossible to re-create in a segregated system of graduate education.

The Supreme Court heard another significant case in Oklahoma the same year, in *McLaurin v. Oklahoma State Regents for Higher Education* (1950). A retired black professor, George McLaurin, had successfully sued the University of Oklahoma for admission into the school's PhD program in education, after the university denied his admission on the basis of race. Because Oklahoma had no other state-funded graduate school in education, the Court forced the university to admit McLaurin. The university reluctantly complied, but relegated McLaurin to segregated facilities within the university. He was required to sit at a designated desk in an anteroom next to his classroom, and was not permitted to sit in the classroom itself. He was given another designated desk on the mezzanine in the library, and was not permitted to study on the main floor. In the school cafeteria, he was forced to sit at a designated table and eat at a separate time from the white students.

The U.S. Supreme Court held that such restrictions violated McLaurin's Fourteenth Amendment rights under the equal protection clause, because they prevented McLaurin from interacting with other students in a meaningful fashion, thereby impinging on his education. Thus the Court overturned segregation within the facilities at state universities, and established the principle that students of different races must be treated equally.

These cases were at the core of the NAACP's attack on Jim Crow. While the NAACP attacked segregation in other cases outside the arena of graduate education, the education cases incrementally undermined the "separate but equal" doctrine. Education cases in general were highly symbolic, in that the issue of segregation in public schools tended to inflame emotions among Southern whites more so than any other aspect of Jim Crow, save interracial sex and marriage. The cases outlined in this entry created the groundwork for the *Brown v. Board of Education* decision. By establishing the necessary precedents for *Brown* at the graduate school level, the NAACP lawyers prepared the way for the Supreme Court to drive the final nail into the coffin of the "separate but equal" doctrine in *Brown*.

Thomas Brown

See also: *Brown v. Board of Education.*

Further Reading

Kluger, Richard. *Simple Justice: The History of Brown v. Board of Education and Black America's Struggle for Equality.* New York: Knopf, 2004.

McNeil, Genna Rae. *Groundwork: Charles Hamilton Houston and the Struggle for Civil Rights.* Philadelphia: University of Pennsylvania Press, 1983.

Buchanan v. Warley (1917)

Buchanan v. Warley was a unanimous U.S. Supreme Court decision that prohibited racial segregation in residential areas. By upholding the rights of African Americans and whites to sell residential property to each other, the case marked the first exception to segregation laws permitted under *Plessy v. Ferguson* (1896). Lauded as ensuring the personal and property rights of African Americans, the *Buchanan* decision is considered as the legal precursor to the renowned case prohibiting segregation in public schools, *Brown v. Board of Education* (1954).

In 1914, the city of Louisville, Kentucky, enacted a state law that prohibited African Americans and whites from residing in areas where members of another race were the majority. Charles H. Buchanan, a white real estate agent, sued William Warley in 1916 for breach of contract. Warley, the president of the Louisville chapter of the National Association for the Advancement of Colored People (NAACP) and an African American purchaser, stated that their contact was void because the Louisville ordinance prevented him from buying the home. He refused to pay the full price for the property and withheld $100 from the $250 amount. Since Warley could not use the property as a residence, he further claimed that the ordinance prevented him from benefitting from the property's full value.

After the Kentucky Court of Appeals upheld the Louisville ordinance, Warley appealed the decision and the case moved to the U.S. Supreme Court in 1916. Represented by Moorfield Storey, the first president of the NAACP, Warley finally prevailed. Storey argued that the ordinance denied the legal rights of African Americans, had adverse social consequences for African Americans and whites, and prohibited landowners the right to sell their property to whomever they wanted. In 1917, the Supreme Court unanimously found that the Louisville ordinance violated the Fourteenth Amendment because this law entitles African Americans to have property without state discriminatory practices based on race. The decision, written by Justice William Rufus Day, also stated that race as a motive for the Louisville ordinance was insufficient to make the law constitutional and laws cannot deny rights protected by the Constitution. The Court separated its decision in *Buchanan v. Warley* from its previous ruling of legalizing racial segregation in *Plessy v. Ferguson* and *Berea College v. Kentucky* (1908) by finding these cases equitably apply the separate but equal provision of the Fourteenth Amendment.

While *Buchanan v. Warley* prevented many cities from limiting black migration in residential areas and placing fixed boundaries on black neighborhoods, the case was faulted for drawing too much attention to upholding property rights rather than the equal protection of human rights. The case also promoted buyers and sellers of property to have private restrictive covenants, which effectively created residential segregation by race and did not legally violate the Equal Protection Clause of the Fourteenth Amendment. Even with these criticisms, the *Buchanan* decision garnered awareness to the fundamental rights of African Americans set forth in the Fourteenth Amendment. Most importantly, the case signaled the emergence of the protection of the liberties and rights of African Americans by the U.S. Supreme Court.

Dorsia Smith

See also: Segregation, Residential.

Further Reading

About, Inc. *Buchanan v. Warley* African-American History Web site http://afroamhistory
.about.com/library/blbuchanan_v_warley.htm (accessed June 9, 2008).

Fairclough, Adam. *Better Day Coming: Blacks and Equality, 1890–2000.* New York: Penguin, 2002.

Klarman, Michael J. *From Jim Crow to Civil Rights: The Supreme Court and the Struggle for Racial Equality.* New York: Oxford University Press, 2004.

C

Chicago Race Riot of 1919

The Chicago Race Riot of 1919 was the most destructive race riot of the early twentieth century. The violence began along the shores of Lake Michigan, adjacent to Chicago's South Side, as a black teenager named Eugene Williams and his friends maneuvered a makeshift raft past a "white" beach. Rock-throwing whites attacked them, and Williams drowned. Fighting quickly broke out among whites and African Americans. Between July 27 and July 31, mobs of angry whites and blacks battled with fists, knives, and guns. Order was ultimately restored, but the costs were high: 23 African Americans and 15 whites had been killed, while another 573, including 342 blacks, were injured. Hundreds more lost their homes as a result of arson. As the boundaries of Chicago's black communities rapidly expanded during the era of the Great Migration, white-black tensions over access to public spaces and white anxieties about the growth of the African American population sparked the riot.

The riot unleashed many years of pent-up frustrations among whites and African Americans in Chicago. Throughout the early twentieth century, whites struggled to limit black access to schools, housing, trolleys, parks, and beaches. These tensions escalated during World War I, as more than 330,000 African Americans moved from the Jim Crow South to Northern cities in order to take advantage of expanding wartime job opportunities. With its many factories, Chicago was a key destination. The black population of the city doubled during the 1910s, reaching 109,000. The Chicago Commission on Race Relations, which published a study of the riot in 1922, pointed to whites' unease about the expanding African American presence in the city's factories and public spaces. For example, black employment in 62 Chicago factories increased by more than 1,000 percent between 1915 and 1920, and some whites complained the large meatpacking firms intentionally brought in blacks from the South and were subsequently responsible for the city's racial tensions. On the street cars, which transported black and white

White children cheer outside a burning African American home, Chicago, summer of 1919. (Bettmann/Corbis)

workers into the South Side meatpacking district, white office workers complained about having to share the elevated trains with grimy African American stockyard workers. Other whites complained about rural blacks from the South—the newest element of the city's growing population—who were supposedly guilty of talking too loudly, wearing grubby clothing, and taking up too much space in the seating areas of the trains. During the era of the Great Migration, urban life was crowded, contested, and racially charged.

Tensions among whites and blacks reached a crescendo during the summer of 1919. On July 27, as African Americans and whites spent a hot summer day on adjoining beaches in the vicinity of 29th Street on the South Side, Eugene Williams and his companions drifted on their raft near the "white" beach. On shore, whites loudly voiced their anger at Williams and his friends, and they began throwing stones in the boys' direction. One of the rocks, said to have been thrown by a man named George Stauber, struck Williams in the forehead and knocked him into Lake Michigan. Nearby, African American men and women who witnessed the attack tried to move into the water to help him. However, the mob of whites impeded their efforts and the boy drowned. The African Americans then tried to convince a white policeman, Dan Callahan, to arrest the man who had thrown the rock, but he refused. Tensions worsened quickly: the black men and women who witnessed the attack began berating and assaulting Stauber. Whites rushed to his aid, and the rioting was underway. The violence rapidly expanded throughout the entire South Side.

The beatings, stabbings, fire bombings, and gunshots tore through the Chicago streets for five days. The experiences of individual riot victims point to the unpredictable nature of the violence. To illustrate: a roving gang of white teenagers battered Frederick Smith, a 33-year-old African American and wounded World War I veteran of the Canadian army. Since he was a decorated soldier of the recent war, Smith believed the mobs of whites would not bother him. He was mistaken. Luckily, army officers at a nearby recruiting station rescued Smith from the gang. On the first night, as violence accelerated, white gangs attacked street cars as they carried African Americans home from work, dragged them into the streets, and beat them mercilessly. A white policeman named John O'Brien exchanged gunfire with a group of armed black men, resulting in the death of one African American. O'Brien himself was wounded, along with two others. But even those who remained behind closed doors were not safe. As the shooting of guns crackled in the streets near Charles Cromier's home, a stray bullet crashed through the front window and struck the man in the head. Guy Hubblestone, a daring Irish taxi driver, warned a journalist who wanted to tour the riot scene that several cabs had come out of the embattled neighborhoods with bullet holes in the roofs. Despite the obvious danger, Hubblestone audaciously agreed to take the reporter into the South Side. After four days of rioting, the chaos eventually began to subside when Governor Frank O. Lowden ordered the Illinois militia into the city of Chicago. Periodic clashes still occurred in the coming days, however.

The Chicago Race Riot of 1919 did not occur in a vacuum. There were numerous confrontations between whites and African Americans in the United States during the first two decades of the twentieth century. Between 1900 and 1921, major riots erupted in Southern cities and towns such as Atlanta (1906), Brownsville, Texas (1906), East St. Louis, Illinois (1917), Charleston, South Carolina (1919), Longview, Texas (1919), and Tulsa, Oklahoma (1921). Riots struck Northern cities and smaller communities as well: New York City (1900), Springfield, Ohio (1904), Greensburg, Indiana (1906), and Springfield, Illinois (1908). The violence of the summer of 1919, however, was so widespread that the National Association for the Advancement of Colored People's (NAACP) secretary and *New Negro* author James Weldon Johnson described those stressful months as the "Red Summer." Even Washington, D.C., experienced racial violence in 1919. For four days in July, members of the U.S. military—Marines, soldiers, and sailors—roamed the streets of the city and viciously assaulted African Americans on sight. Blacks fought to defend themselves. Between June and

December 1919, there were an estimated 25 race riots in the United States, and these clashes led to 120 deaths.

In response to the alarming destruction of Red Summer, some civic leaders suggested that Chicago's racial tensions could be resolved only by adopting a Southern approach to race relations. Chicago authorities quickly proposed a system of formal segregation for the city. Newspaper editorials endorsed the idea. In the city council chambers, Alderman Terence F. Moran introduced a resolution that called for the racial segregation of public accommodations. However, the resolution did not pass. Despite the terror produced by the riot, tension and mistrust would continue to overshadow race relations in twentieth-century Chicago and the United States as a whole. As an October 7 editorial in the *Chicago Daily Tribune* noted, "Both north and south have had enough violence. Both may have more."

Gregory Wood

See also: World War I.

Further Reading

Chicago Commission on Race Relations. *The Negro in Chicago: A Study of Race Relations and a Race Riot* (1922). Excerpts reprinted in Ronald H. Bayor, *The Columbia Documentary History of Race and Ethnicity in America,* 543–69. New York: Columbia University Press, 2004.

Grossman, James R. *Land of Hope: Chicago, Black Southerners, and the Great Migration.* Chicago: University of Chicago Press, 1989.

Tuttle, William M., Jr. *Race Riot: Chicago in the Red Summer of 1919.* New York: Atheneum, 1970.

Churches

The history of black churches and legalized discrimination predates both the mid-nineteenth-century minstrel show, from which the term "Jim Crow" was derived, and the U.S. Supreme Court's legalization of "separate but equal" in *Plessy v. Ferguson* (1896). It is tied to the complex relationship between racial oppression and black resistance to it, as well as in the quest among blacks for self-determination and valuation.

Black churches of the eighteenth and nineteenth centuries mounted their first collective act of resistance by embracing their own interpretation of the Bible, one distinct from that of white slaveholders. Slaveholders contended that the system of slavery reflected divine order. They based their supposition on "the Hamitic curse," according to which Africans were the descendants of Ham, the son whom Noah had cursed for mocking rather than covering Noah as he lay naked in a drunken stupor. Noah vowed that Ham would serve his brothers, Shem and Japeth, for failing to conceal his shame. The Hamitic curse laid the foreground for white slaveholders to stress biblical passages in the Old and New Testaments that seemed to sanction slavery and separatism, or verses that implied a hierarchy privileging whiteness and condemning blackness. Blacks, by contrast, embraced passages and narratives that emphasized liberation and egalitarianism, particularly the Exodus in the Old Testament, and New Testament themes of redemption and inclusion. Despite the theological differences expressed over time in the proliferation of black churches and denominations, black Christians reflected a collective commitment to autonomy and valuation by establishing religious organizations that addressed their spiritual, social, and political needs, and afforded them unprecedented opportunities to develop leadership skills, musical gifts, and myriad talents.

African American resistance to racism and appreciation for autonomy is readily expressed in the establishment of the African Methodist Episcopal Church (AME). In the aftermath of the American Revolution, Richard Allen precipitated the first wave of independent black religious expression among mainline worshippers by establishing the Bethel African Methodist Episcopal Church in 1793 in Philadelphia. Allen and a fellow worshipper were told that a room in which they prayed was off-limits to blacks. Allen responded to discriminatory treatment by establishing a church where African Americans could worship freely. Although Allen's vision unfolded in a barn, by 1816 it had engendered the first independent black denomination in the country, one that by the dawn of the twentieth century claimed congregations throughout the United States, Africa, and the Caribbean. The separation Allen initiated was based on social as opposed to theological differences and was a harbinger of the commitment to social justice and uplift remained important tenets of the Black Church from the birth of the AME onward.

Subsequent willing separations of blacks from predominantly white churches and denominations occurred after the Civil War, when thousands of African American Southerners, especially Baptists and Methodists, initiated a grand exodus from white congregations. From the late nineteenth century onward, blacks continued to form denominations independent of white hierarchy and control. The six largest independent black denominations include the African Methodist Episcopal Zion (AMEZ) Church, Christian Methodist Episcopal (CME) Church, National Baptist Convention, USA, Inc. (NBA), National Baptist Convention of America, Unincorporated (NBCA), Progressive National Baptist Convention (PNBC), and the Church of God in Christ (COGIC). The establishment of all but the COGIC and PNBC predated the legal birth of Jim Crow.

In the immediate aftermath of slavery, black churches focused on education, which they believed offered the surest defense against poverty and exploitation. They worked to establish educational institutions to serve newly emancipated African Americans. By 1952, independent black denominations had established numerous church-affiliated historically black colleges and universities, including Wilberforce (AME), Paul Quinn (AME), Tyler College (AME), and others. These institutions were springboards for a variety of social, civic, and self-help organizations. They were also cauldrons of social and political activity, where members were encouraged to engage in the political process. For example, members of the AME church in Florida played a key role in the election of black political officials during Reconstruction.

Black Methodist, Baptist, and Pentecostal women were indispensable parties to projects initiated by their respective denominations. They helped raise funds for educational institutions, mission projects, orphanages, convalescent homes, and other social outreach efforts at home and abroad despite their persistent encounter with various degrees and expressions of gender discrimination within the polities they served. The long-term impact of their involvement and the complexity of the projects they initiated usually depended on the general economic and educational standing of the church or organization to which they belonged. Generally, the richer and more educated the church, the more sophisticated the outreach.

When African American members of the various denominations traveled to state and national conventions, they had to make prior arrangements to live in the homes of blacks residing in the area of a given convention. Within the COGIC, for example, members attending conventions would agree to attend the services in shifts. Some attended the night services and slept during the day; others attended the daytime meetings and slept during the night. Regardless of the position held within the denominations served, blacks were expected to respect the rules of Jim Crow. Just as members endured the day-to-day indignities of Jim Crow, independent black denominations were barred from joining predominantly white religious organizations.

This unyielding backdrop of racism and bigotry helped precipitate the Great Migration, a period during which individuals, families, and sometimes even entire churches decided to leave the South. Black pastors, sometimes following their members, headed to the Midwest and West, where all hoped to find greater social, political, and economic opportunity. Black Southerners in migration helped create the progressive social era that emerged with the election of President Franklin D. Roosevelt, whose administration set the stage for future civil rights reform. Black churches in Chicago were challenged to establish a variety of programs to assist new arrivals. Churches and denominations that offered adequate responses to the needs of migrants experienced phenomenal growth during the Great Migration.

Those that failed to adapt to the changing needs of Chicago's black migrant community experienced notable decline.

The gospel music tradition was one of the most dynamic examples of cultural creativity and resistance to emerge during the Jim Crow era. Black church musicians and songsters, particularly of Pentecostal and Baptist traditions, began to shy away from the accepted repertoire of sacred music approved by leaders of mainline churches, who at the turn of the century generally sought to facilitate black assimilation into American culture. This new generation of church musicians opted to compose songs that reflected the cultural and spiritual experiences of African American Christians. Using fast-paced rhythms and expressive lyrics, they treated a variety of themes in their songs, including struggle and triumph, suffering and healing, and, perhaps most importantly, power, especially the transcendent nature of divine power.

Black churches of the Jim Crow era experienced perhaps some of their greatest triumphs and trials during the Civil Rights Movement, when ministers, churches, laymen, and organizations responded to the call for civil rights. Baptist ministers and others founded the Southern Christian Leadership Conference in response to the Montgomery Bus Boycott, with Martin Luther King Jr. serving as the first president of the organization. Although black Baptist ministers were at the forefront of the movement, members and individual churches affiliated with the COGIC, the largest predominantly black Pentecostal organization, made important contributions to the pre-civil rights and civil rights efforts as well.

Mamie Till Mobley, the mother of Emmett Till and a member of Robert's Temple COGIC in Chicago, fueled the movement when she permitted *Jet* magazine to publish a photograph of her son's mutilated remains. Mason Temple COGIC in Memphis, Tennessee, the headquarter church of the COGIC, organized musicals and political rallies in support of the Sanitation Workers Strike. Suggesting the role Martin Luther King thought the COGIC organization might play in the continued struggle for justice, it was at Mason Temple COGIC that King roused the audience with his famous "mountaintop" address, the last speech he gave before his assassination.

In essence, black churches of the Jim Crow era provided refuge against the social, political, and economic storms confronting blacks throughout the period of legalized discrimination. Churches fostered important opportunities for blacks to exercise leadership and organizational skills as they established churches, schools, and organizations to address the needs of the communities they served. They also provided critical space for aspiring soloists, groups, and musicians to nurture and hone their creative musical gifts despite the opposition.

Karen Kossie-Chernyshev

See also: Congress of Racial Equality (CORE); King, Martin Luther, Jr.

Further Reading

Best, Wallace. *Passionately Human, No Less Divine.* Princeton, NJ: Princeton University Press, 2005.

Butler, Anthea D. *Women in the Church of God in Christ: Making a Sanctified World.* Chapel Hill: University of North Carolina Press, 2007.

"Churches v. Jim Crow." *Time,* December 13, 1948. Printed at Time Incorporated, 2008, http://www.time.com/time/magazine/article/0,9171,799481,00.html (accessed June 12, 2008).

Cornelius, Janet Duitsman. *Slaves Missions and the Black Church in the Antebellum South.* Columbia: University of South Carolina Press, 1999.

Gomez, Michael A. *Reversing Sail: A History of the African Diaspora: New Approaches to African History.* New York: Cambridge University Press, 2005.

Kossie-Chernyshev, Karen. "Constructing Good Success: The Church of God in Christ and Social Uplift in East Texas." *East Texas Historical Journal* 1 (2006): 49–55.

Kossie-Chernyshev, Karen. "A Grand Old Church Rose in the East: The Church of God in Christ in East Texas." *East Texas Historical Journal* 41, no. 2 (2003): 26–36.

Rivers, Larry Eugene, and Canter Brown. *Laborers in the Vineyard of the Lord: The Beginnings of the AME Church in Florida, 1865–1895.* Gainesville: University Press of Florida, 2001.

Robeck, Cecil M., Jr. *The Azusa Street Mission and Revival: The Birth of the Pentecostal Movement.* Nashville, TN: Thomas Nelson Reference and Electronic, 2006.

Sernett, William. *Bound for the Promised Land: African American Religion and the Great Migration.* Durham, NC: Duke University Press, 1997.

Cinema

Films depicting the era of Jim Crow or produced during its time tended to reinforce white supremacy until a more nuanced portrait began to emerge following the victories of the modern Civil Rights Movement.

For all of its pioneering impact in graphic realism and establishing cinema as a competitive choice for entertainment, *The Birth of a Nation* (1915) attested to a virulent racism and its hold upon the former Confederacy. This silent epic chronicled the evolution of two families (one Northern and one Southern) from their cordiality in the antebellum years through the maelstrom of the Civil War and the onset of Reconstruction. Relying upon an exaggerated portrayal of corruption and ineptitude among Reconstruction officials as well as depredations against white women by blacks, the film treated the formation of the Ku Klux Klan as a reasonable response. White supporters of reform in the South appeared merely as craven opportunists willing to make any alliance that secured power. The film's only suggestion of

Vivien Leigh and Hattie McDaniel in a scene from *Gone with the Wind* (1939). The popular film, and novel on which it was based, reinforced the idea that enslaved people were basically happy and devoted to their owners. (MGM/Photofest)

evenhandedness was found in the brutality of white Southerners punishing blacks. President Woodrow Wilson, a proponent of segregation, enjoyed the production during a private screening at the White House. Despite temporary successes by the National Association for the Advancement of Colored People (NAACP) in banning the film in some metropolitan areas, director D. W. Griffith helped cement a façade of the genteel Old South united in a quixotic pursuit of the "Lost Cause."

Following *The Birth of a Nation,* the cinematography of the South remained mired in the plantation myth as the sole motif around which to shape a production. The plantation was often depicted as a bucolic refuge from the clamor, filth, and degradation of urban life. This agrarian world appeared run by noble landowners and worked by docile slaves. Such fabled portrayals paralleled the lack of serious scholarship on the region's turbulent political, social, and economic conditions.

The early cinematic forays into Southern life were shallow in their portrayal of blacks and romantic to the point of being maudlin. A partial explanation lies with the impact of the Great Depression, fostering a desire for escapism and nostalgia. *Hearts in Dixie* (1929) was Hollywood's first all-black feature film with its sketches of African American life. But the fawning Stepin Fetchit rendered the plotline surreal and reflected a society still preoccupied with a hierarchy of race. The film culminated in a grandson being shipped North for schooling so as not to end up like his lazy, ignorant father. *So Red the Rose* (1934) bombed at the box office due to its blatant pro-Confederate bias, as exemplified by slaves exhorting Southern troops to battle. Thanks in part to this debacle, studios began rejecting Civil War projects, such as the eventual hit *Gone with the Wind* (1939). The romanticization of the small-town South was evident in *Steamboat 'Round the Bend* (1935) starring Will Rogers, with Stepin Fetchit adding comic relief. *The Littlest Rebel* (1935), designed primarily to showcase child star Shirley Temple, promoted the imagery of blacks as the idiotic, slavish Sambos. Such productions left no room for a textured examination of Southern culture, as the Civil War seemed little more than the product of harmless miscommunication.

Stepin Fetchit built one of the most contradictory, controversial, and successful careers in entertainment history. A master of physical comedy, he managed to become a millionaire during the Great Depression of the 1930s, playing the unmotivated, dim-witted "coon" that has rankled African Americans ever since. Yet, the black community has gradually recognized him as an innovator, paving the way for other actors of color.

Born Lincoln Perry, he briefly wrote for a newspaper before developing a two-man vaudeville act for white audiences featuring a character known as "The Laziest Man in the World." As he ventured into solo performances, his soon-to-be infamous stage name stuck. Despite the widespread belief that this moniker formed a contraction for "step and fetch it" in the spirit of the subservient "Tom" persona (from *Uncle Tom's Cabin* by Harriet Beecher Stowe), Perry linked the name to a racehorse. Scholars have differentiated the Stepin Fetchit character from a "Tom" by noting its more rebellious characteristics as a "coon," that is, a black who feigns slothfulness and ignorance to resist white repression and disrupt economic activities. Integral to the "coon" persona was speaking in apparent gibberish that blacks appreciated as insults aimed at the pretensions of white society. Many whites accepted Stepin Fetchit as a mainstream characterization of African Americans. Yet, he found a way to turn the situation to his advantage. In a case of life imitating art, Perry grew adept at adopting the "coon" persona when auditioning for roles while imitating the Stepin Fetchit character during rehearsals. If he found particular lines offensive, he would omit or mumble them so as to discourage their survival in the script. He succeeded in frustrating paternalistic whites by confirming their low expectations. As segregationists consolidated their post-Reconstruction gains, entertainment offered one of the few avenues for blacks to wage this subtle form of rebellion. Even in *Steamboat 'Round the Bend*, Stepin Fetchit maintained a screen presence on a par with Rogers. Wasting his fortune by the late 1940s, Perry no longer could land roles in "white" cinema. Boxer Muhammad Ali took up his cause in the 1960s and added him to his entourage. Perry joined the Nation of Islam that promoted the black nationalism of the era. Because of the visceral reactions of many black viewers to Stepin Fetchit's seemingly degrading roles, his appearances have often been excised from films, even if doing so created plot confusion. But in *Amazing Grace* (1974), Perry made his final showing with a scene and soundtrack that acknowledged the contributions made by his often-overlooked generation of African Americans.

Based upon Margaret Mitchell's sweeping novel of the Civil War, *Gone with the Wind* emerged as an international hit and the most popular film of the South ever produced. Scarlett O'Hara (played by the British actress Vivien Leigh) had to decide between the dashing, scandalous Rhett Butler (Clark Gable) and the faithful, aristocratic Ashley Wilkes against the backdrop of a war that would consume her Georgia plantation. Ultimately abandoned by Butler and unfulfilled by Wilkes, Scarlett grew to accept that the antebellum South could be no more. Integral to the plot was a celebration of the land that numerous Americans still down on their luck could appreciate.

The mobilization of resources necessary for a global war on fascism created opportunities for black empowerment and weakened white supremacy in the South. Proud of their military service and contributions to defense production, African Americans were poised to assume leadership roles in a burgeoning Civil Rights Movement. President Harry S. Truman, in a modest attempt to reorient the Democratic Party with its powerful Southern wing, desegregated the Armed Forces in 1948 and banned discrimination in federal employment.

Hollywood responded slowly but steadily to a changing national mood on race. Although the most obvious caricatures disappeared from post–World War II films, a dearth of positive black roles was evident. In the 1950s and 1960s, most black characters were limited to productions in which race figured prominently in the plot. Films that featured primarily black actors were designed solely for black audiences. Only gradually were "color-blind" parts, such as black policemen and professionals, created for movies without a racial focus. Over time three categories emerged for films with African American stars or costars: mainstream productions, serious films with the potential for "crossover" appeal, and projects aimed at resonating solely with black popular culture.

Despite a trend toward progress, *Song of the South* (1946) enraged the black community, as the normally astute Disney Company employed James Baskett as Uncle Remus to amuse and enlighten a young white boy. In the eyes of many African Americans, the "Tom" stereotype had been resurrected. The film, based on Joel Chandler Harris's folk tales, was designed to recapture an earthiness and dignity amid the impoverished.

Stimulated in part by revulsion over the Holocaust, the postwar period saw the rise of "social problem" films that confronted questions of race among other contested issues. *Intruder in the Dust* (1949), adapted from William Faulkner's novel, showed an African American veteran (Lucas Beauchamp) returning home to Mississippi only to be accused of murdering a white man. An unlikely alliance composed of a white teenager, his African American friend, the white boy's lawyer uncle, and an elderly white spinster proved Beauchamp's innocence and spared him a lynching.

For much of the 1950s, the ideological fixation with anticommunism engendered by the Korean War and McCarthyism militated against racially based films and the awarding of key roles to African Americans. But films on the South contributed to a growing trend toward probing the darker side of human nature to include portrayals of a violent lust for power, explicit sex, and moral decay.

In the wake of the civil rights triumphs of the 1960s, a series of films on the South proved more honest in their portrayal of white excesses, even if sometimes promoting stereotypes of their own. The earliest of these productions reflected the genre of "blaxploitation" that cast slaves as inveterate plotters in the spirit of the Nat Turner rebellion and whites as sexual predators with no redeeming qualities or conflicted emotions. This era marked the appearance of the strapping "buck" as the dominant characterization of black men by whites. This persona served as an embodiment of lingering anxiety over racial and sexual aggression. Michael Caine starred in *Hurry Sundown* (1967) as a soulless Southerner so hell-bent on purchasing his cousin's farms that he provoked a mob of whites into destroying a dam that flooded nearby farms, including one that belonged to his wife's feeble, African American nurse. The film was notable for its employment of a largely black cast.

A predominantly black production with a more sophisticated treatment of Southern life was *Black Like Me* (1964), starring James Whitmore as a Texas journalist who went undercover with darkened skin to get the scoop on life for blacks. Despite unconvincing special effects, the film displayed the virtually unrelenting hostility of Southern whites as Whitmore found himself incredibly moved by the smallest degree of kindness. Although the production dodged many of the thornier questions of race relations in America, *Guess Who's Coming to Dinner* (1967) highlighted the ascension to mainstream status of Sidney Poitier. He played a world-renowned surgeon residing in Switzerland whose betrothal to a middle-class, white woman threw both families into an uproar. With the couple planning to live overseas, all of the pressing racial issues of the time were completely irrelevant to the story, for which Poitier took a good deal of criticism from the black community for accepting only saintly roles.

Yet that same year, Poitier contributed to the Best Picture Oscar for *In the Heat of the Night*. He played a Philadelphia homicide detective wrongfully arrested for murder by a prototypical sheriff (Rod Steiger) while visiting Mississippi. Much to the consternation of both men, they were ordered to collaborate in identifying the killer. The two solved the crime while gradually learning to understand and respect each other.

As a concurrent trend, other productions presented the harmless stereotype of the Southern "good 'ol boy" content with fast cars, moonshine, and outwitting hapless police officers. In *Thunder Road* (1958) Robert Mitchum's character, Lucas Doolin, rejoined the family's bootlegging business after service in the Korean War.

Based on a novel by Harper Lee, *To Kill a Mockingbird* (1963) reflected the maturation of the white South beyond its segregationist past. Gregory Peck played a lawyer (Atticus Finch) almost singlehandedly defying racism in a small Southern town by defending an African American accused of raping a white girl. Although he lost the case and his client was killed in an "escape" attempt, Finch won the respect of local blacks. Peck won an Academy Award in this portrayal of a rural community in the Great Depression making its painfully slow transition to racial equality.

By the early 1970s, Hollywood retreated from civil rights projects as the movement splintered and a white backlash grew evident in electoral politics. With the exceptions of *The Man* (1972) and *The Klansman* (1974), television would lead the way with progressive advocacy until the 1980s.

Mississippi Burning (1988) provided a powerful account of the circumstances surrounding the disappearance of three civil rights volunteers (one black, two white) participating in the Mississippi Summer Project in 1964, whose bodies were eventually found in Neshoba County. But the film's focus on two FBI agents, played by high-profile actors Gene Hackman and Willem Dafoe, relegated the contributions of black activists to obscurity.

Ghosts of Mississippi (1997) traced the long-overdue justice provided to the family of slain NAACP leader Medgar Evers, through the conviction of his white supremacist killer. But the film avoided any serious treatment of the racial conflicts of the early 1960s by focusing on the retrial decades later.

Jeffrey D. Bass

See also: *Birth of a Nation, The* (1915).

Further Reading

Bogle, Donald. *Toms, Coons, Mulattoes, Mammies, and Bucks: An Interpretative History of Blacks in American Films.* New York: Viking Press, 1973.

Campbell, Edward, Jr. *The Celluloid South: Hollywood and the Southern Myth.* Knoxville: University of Tennessee Press, 1981.

Heider, Karl. *Images of the South: Constructing a Regional Culture on Film and Video.* Athens: University of Georgia Press, 1993.

Kirby, Jack. *Media-Made Dixie: The South in the American Imagination.* Athens: University of Georgia Press, 1986.

Smith, Stephen. *Myth, Media, and the Southern Mind.* Fayetteville: University of Arkansas Press, 1985.

Civil Rights Act of 1875

The Civil Rights Act of 1875 could have been a step forward in attempting to ensure that all U.S. citizens would be able to use public accommodations without discrimination. This legislation was controversial for its granting of a fuller place in American society for African Americans.

The first part of the act stated:

> That all persons within the jurisdiction of the United States shall be entitled to the full and equal enjoyment of the accommodations, advantages, facilities, and privileges of inns, public conveyances on land or water, theaters, and other places of public amusement; subject only to the conditions and limitations established by law, and applicable alike to citizens of every race and color, regardless of any previous condition of servitude.

However ambitious and noble the aims of the law may have been, there was minimal enforcement of the act after its passage. This was especially true after the withdrawal of federal troops from the South and the collapse of Reconstruction. Moreover, the lack of enforcement of the law was indicative of the deep historical chasm over race and rights that had come to a head in the Civil War and that did not disappear in the post–Civil War period.

This division in American politics was represented in the debates and negotiations of earlier versions of the Civil Rights Act of 1875. Senator Charles Sumner of Massachusetts, a leader of the Radical Republicans, had originally proposed a bill to protect the rights of African Americans in public settings of all kinds, including schools and churches, in 1870. That bill faced considerable opposition from less radical Republicans who feared the loss of political power in Congress. The bill also found substantive opposition from Southern senators and representatives who disagreed with the bill's wide-sweeping integrationist policy. As such, the bill was not taken up by the House of Representatives at that time even in a watered-down form.

Sumner reintroduced the bill in 1873, which was voted for by the Senate after Sumner's death in 1874. The House of Representatives took it up and passed it in a form that dropped the sections that would have made segregation in education illegal. The actions by Congress were that of a lame-duck legislature that had lost control over the House of Representatives in part because of Republican support for the bill and other Reconstruction efforts. Yet, the legislative victory of the Civil Rights Act of 1875 was a hollow one without effective enforcement in the regions of the country most plagued with racial prejudice and institutionalized injustice.

There was occasional and inconsistent enforcement of the law, but even when citations and penalties were issued, they were often challenged in court. Five such cases arose in which African Americans did not receive the same treatment as other persons by private entities, including theaters, hotels, and other facilities. Those businesses appealed the enforcement of the law on the constitutional ground that Congress could not pass a law that would control their private business decisions. Although Congress had passed the Civil Rights Act of 1875 to enforce the Fourteenth Amendment's equal protection clause and specifically to prevent the kind of discrimination that was apparent in these cases, the U.S. Supreme Court sided with business owners and held that Congress's power did not reach into the world of discrimination in private business.

The lone dissenter was Justice John Marshall Harlan, who found the case to be an end run around the congressional intent of the law and the Fourteenth Amendment. Furthermore, he saw the case as a matter of a poorly written law, in that the legal basis cited by the majority implied that states had no interaction or regulatory interest in business, when in fact they did have such an interest through the issuing of permits and licenses for business establishments. Therefore, claiming that the Fourteenth Amendment only had bearing on state action and had no bearing on private business action was fallacious. At the time of the decision, there was little public outrage, but in succeeding generations, the words of Justice Harlan resonated as a marker of another missed opportunity for the advancement of social and political equality in the United States.

Aaron Cooley

See also: Jim Crow; Reconstruction.

Further Reading

Franklin, John Hope. "The Enforcement of the Civil Rights Act of 1875." *Prologue: The Journal of the National Archives* 6, no. 4 (1974): 225–35.

Klarman, Michael. *From Jim Crow to Civil Rights: The Supreme Court and the Struggle for Racial Equality.* New York: Oxford University Press, 2004.

Civil Rights Act of 1964

Not since Reconstruction had there been such a muscular and sweeping federal law designed to protect African Americans. It is similar to the Civil Rights Act of

1875 in that the major portion of the act is designed to provide and guarantee equal access for blacks to public accommodations and transportation; it also gives the federal courts the authority to hear cases brought under the act.

During World War II, African Americans had embraced the concept of the Double V campaign: victory against fascism aboard and against racism at home. Post–World War II, the Civil Rights Movement had accelerated, buoyed by favorable rulings from the U.S. Supreme Court and high-impact civil rights battles in Montgomery, Alabama, and Little Rock, Arkansas. By the 1960 presidential election, the fight for black civil rights was in the forefront of the nation's conscience for the first time in nearly 100 years.

Vice President Richard M. Nixon was the Republican nominee; his opponent was the Democratic junior senator from Massachusetts, John F. Kennedy. Both men understood the importance of the Civil Rights Movement. Moreover, Nixon had worked to help pass the Civil Rights Act of 1960 and had met with Martin Luther King Jr. to discuss civil rights; he even had the support of the beloved Jackie Robinson. Kennedy was viewed by black Americans with suspicion because he was Catholic, and although he was the chairman of the subcommittee on Africa, his civil rights record was perceived as thin to nonexistent.

President Lyndon B. Johnson signs the Civil Rights Act of 1964, legislation intended to eliminate racial discrimination in places of public accommodation and employment. (Lyndon B. Johnson Library)

Both men had opportunities to establish their civil rights credentials during the campaign. On February 1, 1960, four black students from North Carolina A&T College conducted a sit-in at a segregated Woolworth's lunch counter. The sit-in movement spread throughout the South. On October 19, King was arrested along with a group of students while conducting a sit-in at an Atlanta department store. The charges connected with the sit-in were dropped, but on October 25, King was transferred to the notorious Reidsville State Prison. A pregnant Coretta Scott King contacted Harris Wofford, the civil rights coordinator for the Kennedy campaign, and Woffford spoke to Robert F. Kennedy, who was managing the presidential campaign of his brother. Robert Kennedy convinced his brother to call Coretta King, and he contacted the Georgia governor and the judge assigned to Martin Luther King's case. King was released, and Kennedy was seen as a hero in the black community. Richard Nixon had refused to comment on the situation.

Kennedy soon found that it would be difficult to stay away from the civil rights issue. The socialist Michael Harrington led demonstrations for civil rights outside the arena where the convention was held. The Democrats inserted a mild civil rights statement in the Democratic platform, and Kennedy found himself answering questions about civil rights for the duration of the campaign.

The administration, which had no plan for civil rights legislation in spite of Kennedy's ringing campaign rhetoric, repeatedly found itself scrambling to control a movement they did not understand. Less than six months after being elected, an integrated group of civil rights activists dubbed the Freedom Riders decided to test the Supreme Court decision in *Boynton v. Virginia* (1960), which had outlawed segregated facilities in interstate travel. When they arrived in Anniston, Alabama, they were beaten by a white mob and their bus was firebombed. The Kennedy administration was forced to act, and Robert Kennedy, now the U.S. attorney general, convinced the Interstate Commerce Commission to write regulations prohibiting Jim Crowism in interstate bus terminals. In November 1961, the regulations went into effect.

In January 1961, James Meredith applied to the University of Mississippi, which had never admitted a black student. Supported by the National Association for the Advancement of Colored People (NAACP), Meredith sued; on September 25, 1962, the U.S. Supreme Court ordered Meredith to be admitted. Two weeks later, Governor Ross Barnett blocked Meredith's admission. A riot broke out on September 30; Kennedy was forced to send federal troops, and two people were killed. Meredith began class the next day.

The summer of 1963 proved pivotal in the Civil Rights Movement. On June 11, Alabama governor George C. Wallace appointed himself the registrar and stood in the doorway of the University of Alabama to block the admission of two black students, Vivian Malone and James Hood. Kennedy federalized the National Guard, and the students were admitted. That same day, the Kennedy administration sent a civil rights bill to Congress, and the president spoke on national television that evening. He defined civil rights as a moral issue and urged Americans to ensure that the promise of America was available to all its citizens. The next evening, Mississippi field secretary Medgar Evers pulled into his driveway after meeting with the NAACP. He was assassinated as he stepped out of his car, carrying a stack of shirts emblazoned with the logo "Jim Crow Must Go." Evers had worked in Mississippi for years and had attempted to enter the University of Mississippi in the 1950s. In the weeks preceding his death, he was heavily involved in boycotts of local businesses; his home was bombed and he had received numerous death threats.

Birmingham, Alabama, one of the most segregated cities in the South, was the target of massive demonstrations against Jim Crow business practices in the spring of 1963. After being arrested, King wrote his famous "Letter from Birmingham Jail," in which he decried white moderates who encouraged blacks to wait for their rights to be handed to them. In response to the arrest of King, and with the leadership of the Southern Christian Leadership Conference, schoolchildren joined the demonstrations, which were quickly renamed the Children's Crusade. Hundreds of children as young as six skipped school to participate; they were met by police commissioner "Bull" Connor with fire hoses, police dogs, and mass arrests. The Kennedy Justice Department intervened, and on May 10, the city of Atlanta capitulated. It agreed to establish a biracial citizens committee, desegregate downtown businesses, and release the protesters on bond.

The conscience of the nation was again shocked and sickened by an incident that resulted in the murders of four young girls. On August 28, the Sixteenth Street Baptist Church was firebombed by the Ku Klux Klan, claiming the lives of Addie Mae Collins, Denise McNair, Carol Robertson, and Cynthia Wesley. The church had long been a gathering place for civil rights workers. The apogee of that violent year in civil rights history was the March on Washington, held on August 28. President Kennedy had been fearful that the march, which drew an interracial crowd estimated at 250,000 people, would descend into chaos in that violent summer and that it would endanger passage of his civil rights bill, which he sent to conference and which faced tough opposition. Instead, it was an entirely peaceful demonstration and undoubtedly showed Congress that the American people supported the dismantling of Jim Crow.

As summer turned into autumn, opposition to the bill increased and it appeared that it might not pass. On November 22, Kennedy was assassinated in Dallas, Texas, and African Americans had little confidence in the new president, Lyndon B. Johnson, a Southerner. Yet in his first message to Congress, Johnson urged it to pass the civil rights legislation as a memorial to the slain president. Johnson, helped by liberal Republican congressmen, labored mightily and the bill, which had for months been stalled in the rules committee of the House of Representatives, was reported out on February 10, 1964, and sent to the Senate. It was next destined for the Judiciary Committee chaired by ardent segregationist James O. Eastland. A clever parliamentary maneuver by Mike Mansfield, the Senate Majority Leader, bypassed the Judiciary Committee and sent the bill to the full Senate on March 30, in spite of a 14-hour filibuster by Robert C. Byrd, the Democratic senator from West Virginia. On July 2, President Johnson signed the landmark bill into law.

The Civil Rights Act of 1964 dealt the death knell to Jim Crow in the United States. Title I prohibited unequal application of voter requirements, although it did not bar literacy tests. Title II, the heart and soul of the bill, ended discrimination in public accommodations engaged in interstate commerce; Title III barred that practice on account of race, religion, or ethnicity by state and city governments. Title IV encouraged the desegregation of public schools and gave the U.S. attorney general the authority to file suits to force desegregation. The focus of Title V of the bill was procedural changes with the operation of the Commission on Civil Rights, including requiring hearing notices be published in the *Federal Register* and gave those testifying before committee the right to be accompanied and advised by counsel. Title VI outlawed discrimination by private companies that receive federal funding and provided for the loss of that funding if violations occurred. Finally, Title VII prohibited covered employers from discrimination based on race, sex, color, national origin, or religion.

Passage of the law did not immediately end Jim Crow practices. Congress passed the law under the authority of the commerce clause in the U.S. Constitution instead of the equal protection clause of the Fourteenth Amendment so that the law would have the broadest possible reach. The first challenge of the law quickly appeared in the case of *Heart of Atlanta Motel v. United States* (1964), giving the Supreme Court an opportunity to uphold the constitutionality of the Act. Heart of Atlanta Motel refused to admit black patrons, and based its refusal on what it read as a Fifth Amendment right to do business as it saw fit without government interference or just compensation. Furthermore, counsel for the motel it argued that the act had violated the Thirteenth Amendment right to be free from involuntary servitude by forcing it to rent rooms to African Americans. The Supreme Court ruled that because interstate travelers used the motel, it was part of the fabric of interstate commerce, which Article I, Section 8, of the Constitution gave Congress broad authority to regulate; that the Fifth Amendment did not prohibit a reasonable regulation of commerce, and that since no property was taken from the motel, its owners' rights to just compensation and due process had not been violated. It also reasoned that the Thirteenth Amendment was meant to apply to slavery and the conditions it created. Thus, the Civil Rights Act of 1964 was held to be constitutional.

It took more than a decade for Jim Crow to be dismantled, and on occasion, incidents of it continue to surface. But the importance and scope of the Civil Rights Bill of 1964 is such that it is on the list of the National Archives 100 milestone documents in American history.

Marilyn K. Howard

See also: Civil Rights Act of 1875; Voting Rights Act of 1965.

Further Reading

Branch, Taylor. *Pillar of Fire: America in the King Years 1963–1965.* New York: Simon and Schuster, 1999.

Kotz, Nick. *Judgment Days: Lyndon Baines Johnson, Martin Luther King Jr., and the Laws That Changed America.* Boston: Houghton Mifflin Company, 2005.

Whalen, Charles, and Barbara Whalen. *The Longest Debate: A Legislative History of the 1964 Civil Rights Act.* Washington, DC: Seven Locks Press, 1985.

Civilian Conservation Corps

In an attempt to ease the devastating levels of joblessness during the Great Depression, President Franklin D. Roosevelt proposed a series of legislative acts to Congress. One of these acts, *the Emergency Conservation Work Act,* passed by Congress in 1933, formed the Civilian Conservation Corps (CCC). The Department of Labor recruited young people to the CCC to be employed on public works projects, primarily in rural areas. These work projects varied across the country but mainly focused on erosion control, forestry, flood control, recreation, wildlife, transportation, and structural improvement. Initially only single, physically fit unemployed males between the ages of 18 and 25 whose fathers were on relief were accepted into the CCC. These young men could enlist for a six-month period and reenlist for up to two years. They would work 40 hours each week at $30 per week, with most of that wage sent home to family or held in escrow for the enlistee until leaving the CCC. In addition to providing jobs, an underlying reason for the CCC was to give young men in urban areas something to occupy them to keep them out of trouble, such as turning to crime or radicalism in response to the Depression. Courses were also offered, ranging from basic literacy and vocational skills to college-level courses. Later in 1934, young women were recruited in small numbers, and by 1935, the age range was expanded to between 17 and 28. A series of residential camps were created in each state, as well as the territories of Alaska, Hawaii, Puerto Rico, and the Virgin Islands, to house the CCC members. These camps, which eventually numbered 4,500, were under the control of the War Department and run in a quasimilitary manner. During its existence, approximately 3 million men and 8,500 women served in the CCC.

The act that established the CCC forbade discrimination based upon race. All enrollees received the same pay and benefits. Black membership was set proportional to their population at 10 percent, and they could not serve in camps outside their home state. Approximately 250,000 African Americans and 80,000 Native Americans served during the life of the program. The CCC camps were integrated until July 1935, when the War Department reversed the policy, claiming complaints from locals around the camps. In addition to these complaints, there was violence within some integrated camps between various ethnic and racial groups. Also, many administrators of the army and CCC held racist views. Neither of these realities was used as a public reason for segregation. There were at least 150 all-black camps, and although most Native Americans enrollees did not live in camps (instead living and working around their home reservations), there was at least one separate camp for Native Americans, Camp Marquette in Michigan; there they lived on the camp and worked in the area near the camp.

Vocational training for members of the Civilian Conservation Corps (CCC), circa 1931. The CCC was an agency of the New Deal, a massive set of programs launched by President Franklin D. Roosevelt to counter the effects of the Great Depression through the infusion of massive federal funds into the economy. CCC camps in most, but not all, states were segregated. (Franklin D. Roosevelt Library)

Civil rights activists, such as NAACP leader Thomas Griffith, complained about the Jim Crow policy, yet CCC director Robert Fechner replied that segregation was not discrimination. Quite a few others in FDR's administration, like Harold Ickes, vehemently disagreed. Jim Crow also impacted minorities in that many states ignored highly qualified applicants in preference of white applicants. African Americans were also overlooked for supervisory positions within the CCC. In September 1935, President Roosevelt ordered Fechner to appoint a few more African Americans at CCC camps on National Park Service properties. Fechner ignored the order and leaked Roosevelt's mandate to some prominent white Southern Congressmen. In the culminating uproar, Roosevelt revoked the demand. A more welcoming approach to minorities did not exist until 1941, when recruitment was more encouraged because of dropping enrollment among whites, due to their taking jobs in the developing wartime industry. With the rapid mobilization toward war, by 1942, the CCC program ended.

Julieanna Frost

See also: Armed Forces; New Deal.

Further Reading

Cole, Olen. *The African American Experience in the Civilian Conservation Corps.* Gainesville: University of Florida Press, 1999.

Hill, Edwin. *In the Shadow of the Mountain: The Spirit of the CCC.* Pullman: Washington State University Press, 1990.

Cold War

One feature of American standing in the Cold War was the argument that democratic capitalism represented a better world order than Soviet-style communism. Racism and Jim Crow undercut that claim. American leaders found it difficult to attack Soviet injustices and demand equality and the rule of law worldwide when African Americans endured systematic segregation throughout much of the nation. Facing Soviet propaganda that declaimed such hypocrisy, and fearful it would alter the status of the Cold War enabling the Soviets to lure African, Asian, and Middle Eastern states into their orbit, American politicians made halting efforts against Jim Crow and racial inequality. The Cold War thus acted as one factor influencing politicians to support domestic racial reform. At the same time, the Cold War limited the framework of those reforms. The focus for politicians was as much diplomatic as domestic, so symbolism that undercut Soviet rhetoric often was favored over substantive reforms that actually attacked segregation. Over the course of two decades, the Cold War thus both constrained and encouraged the fight against Jim Crow.

The impact of domestic racial issues on the global scene arose during World War II, when the Germans and Japanese made note of racial conflict in America. The segregation of the U.S. Army, violence at Southern encampments between African American soldiers and local whites, and the internment of Japanese Americans all served as fodder for the Axis. The Japanese and Germans used these issues as propaganda designed to destroy the morale of African American soldiers. Those propaganda efforts had little impact on the battlefield, but when the soldiers returned from overseas, many began to demand the democracy at home for which they had fought abroad. Most Southern states determined to prevent such a domestic revolution, and reinforced the already entrenched system of Jim Crow.

The Soviet Union, the nation's new enemy, readily picked up on the domestic racism and growing desire of African Americans to oppose it, and used both as propaganda against the United States. The administration of President Harry S. Truman quickly realized the danger of such propaganda. In 1946, Secretary of State Dean Acheson issued a study of the damage domestic racism had on American diplomacy. In 1947, Truman's Presidential Committee on Civil Rights issued a report entitled *To Secure These Rights,* in which it argued that the nation needed to address civil rights issues not simply because discrimination was morally wrong, but because of the damage done to foreign relations.

Truman agreed with these assessments and, in public speeches, continually stressed the need for civil rights reform as a part of the nation's Cold War struggle. While he occasionally invoked morality, Truman consistently placed civil rights within the international arena. That placement proved especially prophetic when dignitaries from developing countries visiting the United States encountered American-style racism. In 1947, Mahatma Gandhi's physician was barred from a restaurant. In November of that year Haiti's Secretary of Agriculture Francois Georges traveled to Georgia for a conference. Although he had a reservation, the hotel refused to allow him to room or to dine with his fellow conference attendees. Georges returned to Haiti rather than endure the indignity. The foreign press railed against such outrages, and the nation's moral standing sank.

African American leaders viewed such treatment, and the mingling of civil rights with diplomacy, as an opportunity. In 1947, W.E.B. Du Bois authored a document entitled *An Appeal to the World,* which the National Association for the Advancement of Colored People (NAACP) issued to the United Nations (UN). In it, Du Bois argued that Mississippi, not the Soviet Union, threatened the United States, and that Theodore Bilbo (former governor and U.S. senator from Mississippi) and John Rankin (U.S. congressman from Mississippi) were greater dangers than Stalin. When additional African Americans spoke out, the State Department revoked their passports and worked with host countries to cancel international appearances. Thus, Paul Robeson, Richard Wright, James Baldwin, and Josephine Baker faced harassment and interruptions in their careers as a result of their efforts to protest a Jim Crow America.

Fearful that this domestic unrest and the furor over the treatment of diplomats would aid the Soviets, the Truman administration issued a rebuttal to Du Bois's essay and sent African American leader and executive secretary of the Council on African Affairs Max Yergen on an international goodwill tour. Truman also appointed the first African American ambassador when he stationed Edward Dudley in Liberia. When such efforts failed to improve the nation's image abroad, Truman made more substantive attempts to help African Americans. In 1948, he desegregated the military, and in the years leading up to the *Brown v. Board of Education* Supreme Court decision, his Justice Department filed numerous amicus curie briefs that pointed out the negative impact segregation had on the nation's ability to wage the Cold War.

Despite these achievements, in 1949, the American ambassador to the Soviet Union noted that the Soviet press continued to pound away on the topics of segregation, racial violence, and the lack of social equality. The continuation of this racial injustice, the Soviets explained, proved that the U.S. Constitution did not guarantee liberty, but rather enabled capitalists to exploit racial divisions for their own economic gain. Faced with such enduring criticism, in 1950, Massachusetts senator Henry Cabot Lodge Jr. dubbed racism America's diplomatic Achilles heel.

In 1951, the U.S. Information Agency (USIA) created a pamphlet for American ambassadors designed to help them depict American race relations in a positive manner. Entitled *The Negro in American Life,* this work portrayed the nation's racial history as one of redemption. The pamphlet did not hide the legacy of racial strife, but rather depicted it openly as a means of showing how far the nation had advanced. It also made clear that only the openness of American society allowed for such a frank depiction of the nation's past. The pamphlet thus created an overly optimistic picture of race relations that served to offset the overly negative image created by Soviet propaganda.

The outbreak of the Korean War made the claim of racial improvement difficult to sustain. During the war, the Soviets continued to denounce the United States for its segregation, and rhetorically asked how the nation could force black soldiers to fight for the freedom of foreigners when they had no freedom at home. Domestic events helped prove this point, as in July 1951, when 3,000 people rioted to prevent the integration of a Cicero, Illinois, neighborhood. By this point, ordinary Americans realized the damage such events had on diplomacy, and one citizen wrote to the *New York Times* to suggest that every rioter deserved an Order of Lenin for the harm they caused the nation.

The Truman administration responded to these wartime developments with a new propaganda campaign that moved a step beyond the USIA report. The Voice of America (VOA), American diplomats, and federal writings admitted that the task of racial reconciliation was not complete and that segregation remained, but tried to depict the racial issue as a sectional problem, not an American one. Racism, in other words, was not a deeply held American ideal, but rather a Southern flaw that could be corrected. As a part of this new campaign, Nobel Peace Prize winner Ralph Bunche and Edith Sampson, a member of the American delegation to the UN, travelled abroad extensively to sell the concept and shore up the nation's image.

The Truman administration thus sought to undercut Soviet propaganda with a few well-placed reforms and a mass of counterpropaganda. President Dwight D. Eisenhower had a similar path in mind when he succeeded Truman in 1953. Eisenhower had little interest in civil rights and actually testified against desegregating the military. At the same time, he understood the damage racism inflicted on America's international image and recognized the need for at least symbolic improvements. Thus, between 1953 and 1955, the president desegregated the public areas and schools in Washington, D.C. Although a step forward, Eisenhower took it for the image desegregation provided rather than for larger moral or ethical principles.

The same was true when the U.S. Supreme Court issued the *Brown v. Board of Education* decision in May 1954. The Eisenhower administration quickly used it to counter Soviet propaganda. The VOA announced the decision in 34 languages worldwide, implied that it had ended segregation forever, and suggested that race relations thereafter would be perfect. The *Brown* decision did not end racial strife in America, however, and the Soviets continued to pummel the nation with propaganda that focused on the white backlash known as "massive resistance."

While American diplomats pointed to the *Brown* decision and the peaceful settlement of the 1955 Montgomery Bus Boycott as evidence that the political system was working to end Jim Crow, the refusal of Southern states to desegregate and the continuing racial discord remained problematic. The Emmett Till case, in particular, created a powerfully negative international reaction and served as evidence of the nation's dilemma. NAACP chairman Channing Tobias understood as much when he claimed the Till jury deserved a Soviet medal for its role in undercutting the nation's standing. A year later, in 1956, the failure of Autherine Lucy to integrate the University of Alabama provided additional fodder for Communist propaganda as yet more evidence of "massive resistance."

The most problematic development during the Eisenhower administration emerged in 1957 with the Little Rock Nine crisis. The Soviets quickly broadcast news of the violence surrounding the effort of the nine African American children to integrate Central High School. The Soviet newspaper *Pravda* carried a headline declaring "Troops Advance against Children!" while *Izvestia* described the event as a "tragedy" that displayed the "façade" of American democracy. The Soviets also mockingly included Little Rock in the itinerary of cities over which *Sputnik* orbited. The mass coverage led the American magazine *Confidential* to suggest mockingly that Arkansas governor Orval Faubus was a Communist agent, since his actions had provided the Soviets with such a useful Cold War tool.

This international outrage was one of the reasons Eisenhower, who was loath to intervene, finally did so. In his September 24, 1957, speech on the crisis, he made specific note of the damage events in Little Rock had on the nation's standing and the use being made of them by the Communists. Once Eisenhower sent in federal troops, he ordered diplomats to explain the crisis as an aberration that was being attended to by the full power of the federal government. They were to present Little Rock within the context of continued gains for African Americans and as a part of the ongoing struggle for racial equality, a struggle supported by the Eisenhower administration. The Soviets were unconvinced, however, and Radio Moscow presciently noted that the president and American diplomats seemed more interested in the international impact of Little Rock than with the underlying causes of the crisis.

Beyond these domestic issues, Eisenhower faced an additional diplomatic reality that forced him to confront American racism. Soviet Premier Nikita Khrushchev sought to extend Communist influence into the nonaligned world and, by the late 1950s, was using Jim Crow to woo African, Asian, and Middle Eastern nations to the Communist fold. In 1957, Illinois senator Paul Douglas responded to this Soviet effort by explaining that not only was every riot, bombing, and racial clash immoral and antithetical to the nation's founding, but each crisis assisted Khrushchev in his effort to broaden the Soviet sphere of influence. Douglas was not alone, and the fear that the nonaligned world might accept Communist guidance because of American racism permeated the nation.

In spite of that fear, Eisenhower did little to affect civil rights and left a festering domestic and diplomatic situation for President John F. Kennedy. The new president considered the need to win the Cold War as his primary mission, but he also understood that the Soviets would continue to use racial unrest in their effort to win support in the colored community of the world. Kennedy thus determined to control and moderate the Civil Rights Movement so it did not interfere with his diplomacy. Proof of this came when he backed down from a campaign pledge to desegregate the National Guard. Faced with a crisis in Berlin in 1961, Kennedy refused to order integration, and explained that he could not risk a "social revolution" in the military while he was on the brink of nuclear war with the Soviet Union.

The violence surrounding the Freedom Rides of 1961 further threatened his control. Kennedy was upset with the Rides because he was on the verge of a summit meeting with Soviet leader Khrushchev in Vienna. Kennedy feared that his already weakened position, due to the Bay of Pigs fiasco, would be weakened further by the violence in Anniston and Birmingham, Alabama. When the Rides continued into Mississippi, the Kennedy administration convinced Senator James Eastland to find a peaceful solution by warning of the dangers of sending a weak, young president to the Vienna summit. Mississippi officials acquiesced to Kennedy's wishes and arrested the Riders without violence, thus allowing Kennedy to meet Khrushchev without this millstone around his neck. The damage had already been done, however, as Soviet papers played up the Freedom Rides as further proof that racial violence was a way of life in America.

In 1962, Kennedy faced another threat with the effort of James Meredith to integrate the University of Mississippi. In his address to the nation in the midst of the crisis, Kennedy appealed to the citizens of Mississippi for calm by noting that the eyes of the world were on them. When his appeal failed and he was forced to send in federal marshals, Kennedy, like Eisenhower before him, wanted to display to the world that the federal government would go to great lengths to enforce the law of the land. Kennedy thus hoped to control the story so that the enforcement of federal authority would overwhelm the images of racial violence. After the fact, administration officials believed they had achieved this goal, and claimed that during the ensuing Cuban Missile Crisis, several African nations had refused to allow Soviet planes to refuel on their territory due to Kennedy's handling of events in Mississippi.

Events closer to Washington caused Kennedy further concerns, however, and laid the foundation for a potentially more damaging international spectacle. With the explosion of independence movements in Africa in the early 1960s, large numbers of African diplomats appeared in Washington, D.C., as ambassadors, and in New York City as representatives to the United Nations.

Many of those diplomats experienced great difficulty finding acceptable accommodations in the D.C. area, and the White House soon learned that only 8 of 200 apartments available for rent in the capital were open to blacks. As Kennedy feared, the Soviets exploited the issue by offering to rent apartments for African ambassadors who might otherwise have been refused. At the same time, many African diplomats faced the humiliation of being denied service at hotels and restaurants on Route 40 between Washington and New York City. The problem came to a head in June 1961 when Ambassador Adam Malik Sow of Chad was denied service and then physically abused at a Howard Johnson's along Route 40. Fearing the Soviet Union again would exploit this treatment to win the support of African nations, Kennedy searched for a solution. He first angrily asked why African ambassadors simply did not fly from Washington to New York to avoid the problem. More usefully, he created a Special Protocol Service Section of the State Department. Led by Pedro Sanjuan, the Section's goal was to convince restaurant and hotel owners along the route to desegregate. Sanjaun visited every restaurant on Route 40, but after nine months, fewer than half of the 70 restaurants had complied. Only in January 1963 did Maryland pass a law forcing desegregation of public accommodations, thus alleviating the problem.

Violence in Alabama, however, soon subsumed this accomplishment. In response to the Southern Christian Leadership Conference's effort to demonstrate in Birmingham, Sheriff "Bull" Connor called out attack dogs and water hoses and arrested thousands of peaceful demonstrators. The images offered the Soviets yet another propaganda tool. According to USIA studies, Soviet radio spent one-fifth of its news coverage in late April and early May 1963 on the violence in Alabama. Not only did Birmingham offer the Soviets an opportunity, it also potentially threatened America's standing in Africa. In May 1963, leaders of the various African states met in Addis Ababa, Ethiopia, to create a series of resolutions setting a framework for the continent's standing in the world. On the second day of the conference Ugandan prime minister Milton Obote issued an open letter to President Kennedy protesting the treatment of blacks in Alabama. He tied the treatment of African Americans to imperialism and colonialism, and portrayed the American civil rights struggle as part of the larger worldwide battle for the rights of people of color. Many in the Kennedy administration feared this letter would lead African nations to break relations with the United States and potentially turn to the Soviets. No such break occurred, but the fear once again reinforced the connection between civil rights and the Cold War.

Realizing that his government simply had been reactive to events that threatened the nation's standing, in the summer of 1963, Kennedy became proactive and began work on a civil rights bill. In trying to sell the bill to Congress, the administration noted that the Soviets continued to use racial issues in the global struggle and that passage of the bill would provide a diplomatic benefit. As Congress debated the bill, the March on Washington occurred. Kennedy knew this march posed dangers, but also offered a propaganda opportunity. If the march was peaceful, it would offer further proof of the strength of the American system, which allowed people the free expression of their opinions. When the march did go off peacefully, Kennedy encouraged diplomats to compare the United States, where the government allowed protest, with the Soviets, who brutally crushed all dissent. The problem was that the civil rights bill remained tied up in Congress, and only days after the march, a bomb explosion at a Birmingham church killed four black girls. Although Kennedy met with Martin Luther King Jr. and issued a statement denouncing the attack, the violence and the failure to achieve civil rights legislation again demonstrated that the struggle against Jim Crow was not over.

For Kennedy, the struggle was more about the Cold War than about moral integrity, yet his administration oversaw a number of civil rights victories. After the Kennedy assassination, Lyndon B. Johnson carried on and expanded his predecessor's policies. He also carried on the practice of viewing civil rights through the prism of diplomacy. That view helped Johnson exploit the landmark Civil Rights Act of 1964. Soviet papers covered the congressional debate over the act, and noted the Southern intransigence with glee. Once the act passed, however, the Johnson administration used it against the Soviets as evidence of the nation's racial progress.

Tragically, events soon threatened to subsume that progress once again. The June 1964 murders of Freedom Summer activists Andrew Goodman, James Chaney, and Michael Schwerner in Neshoba County, Mississippi, drew massive international coverage. More trouble erupted in July, when racial violence exploded in New York City. For a decade, American efforts to counter Soviet propaganda had explained racism as a regional problem. The riot, which began after a white police officer shot a black teenager in Harlem, proved the fallacy of that claim. To make things worse, civil rights activists sent a letter to the UN asking it to bring the issue of violence before the Security Council and suggesting the use of UN peacekeeping forces in Mississippi. At the same time, Malcolm X appealed to the international community to pressure the United States toward racial reform. The USIA tried to depict the violence and the African American protest to it within the context of continued racial progress, but the world was skeptical.

The spasm of racial confrontation continued in March 1965 in Selma, Alabama. Surprisingly, the violence at the Edmund Pettis Bridge received only minimal worldwide coverage. USIA studies contended that the reasons were the passage of the Civil Rights Act of 1964 and Johnson's open and uncompromising promise to bring civil rights to the nation. According to a USIA report, earlier foreign editorials had condemned the United States for allowing racial violence to occur. By 1965, however, the international community condemned the violence, but not the United States. As a result, instead of seeing Selma as a symptom of national pathology, the world purview was that it was the final spasm of white racism. In other words, racial strife no longer threatened the nation's standing. Instead, the international community acknowledged the American position that the federal government supported equality, that racism was an aberration not part of mainstream society, and that democracy was the system best suited to facilitate racial reconciliation. Even the Soviets accepted this changed paradigm.

The passage of the Voting Rights Act in 1965 offered the United States another opportunity to enhance this new worldview, but only five days after Johnson signed the bill into law, more racial violence erupted with the Watts riots and the onset of the "long, hot summers." Despite the urban chaos, the new paradigm held. The connection between domestic racial issues and international affairs thus had diminished considerably, despite the obvious fact that serious racial problems remained. In 1966, the USIA explained that this diminished reaction did not mean the world had changed its view on how the nation treated African Americans. Most people worldwide continued to hold a negative impression of the nation's racial issues. What had changed was that this impression no longer affected the overall image of the United States. Racism had become a blot, rather than the defining national characteristic.

Proof that the nexus between the Cold War and Jim Crow had collapsed for good was more evident by 1968. The assassination of Martin Luther King and the ensuing violence received wide international coverage, with the Soviet press contending that the nation was on the verge of civil war. The focus of the foreign press, including the Soviets, however, was on the issue of violence in America, not race. The same was true with international coverage of the Vietnam War. Unlike the coverage of the Korean War, by 1968 the foreign focus on the war in Vietnam was the nation's militarism rather than the disproportionally high number of African American soldiers who saw combat or the fact that the United States was once again fighting a people of color.

This changed international perspective, combined with détente and the thawing of the Cold War under Nixon, gave the federal government less incentive to push for racial reform. At the same time, the major legal issues had been addressed, and the goal became implementation. Struggles over how to implement racial equality found little international interest, and by the end of the 1960s, the world abided by American claims of racial improvement.

Although the impact of the Cold War on the struggle against Jim Crow waned by the late 1960s, during the previous 20 years the two issues were linked intimately. The need to address foreign criticism served as one powerful factor in pushing the federal government to support civil rights reform. Once that criticism waned, however, federal support for change diminished as well. The Cold War thus helped instigate the campaign to end American segregation, but it also helped constrain the depth and breadth of that campaign according to diplomatic needs.

Gregory S. Taylor

See also: New Deal; World War II.

Further Reading

Borstelmann, Thomas. *The Cold War and the Color Line: American Race Relations in the Global Arena.* Cambridge, MA: Harvard University Press, 2001.

Bryant, Nick. *The Bystander: John F. Kennedy and the Struggle for Black Equality.* New York: Basic Books, 2006.

Dudziak, Mary. *Cold War Civil Rights: Race and the Image of American Democracy.* Princeton, NJ: Princeton University Press, 2000.

Mann, Robert. *The Walls of Jericho: Lyndon Johnson, Hubert Humphrey, Richard Russell, and the Struggle for Civil Rights.* New York: Harcourt Brace, 1996.

Nichols, David. *A Matter of Justice: Eisenhower and the Beginning of the Civil Rights Revolution.* New York: Simon and Schuster, 2007.

Colored Farmers' Alliance

The Colored Farmers' Alliance (CFA) was one of the largest black organizations in American history, with a membership of about 1 million—though this number is in dispute and difficult to verify. Indeed, one leading scholar argues that the number was probably close to 250,000. However, it does appear that the membership peaked from about 800,000 to 1,200,000 members. Evidence on the CFA is fragmentary at best, but it is clear that it had a large and active membership and a strong cadre of leaders who organized the black community in an attempt to improve the lot of African American farmers at the end of the nineteenth century, during a period of economic stagnation in the rural South. The CFA preached self-help and cooperation. The CFA existed from the late 1880s into the 1890s. The CFA was an independent organization connected to the Southern Farmers' Alliance—with a separate leadership and dues-paying members. Reflecting the times and the racism of whites, the two organizations did not formally unite with each other; rather, they would meet in separate conventions. However, the organizations would cooperate on economic matters—to help farmers, black and white. In addition, at the national level there was a great deal of communication and planning between the various groups.

The CFA formed in Texas in 1886, and its rank-and-file members were African Americans in the South who farmed their own land or more commonly were sharecroppers and tenants. The foundation of the CFA came at a farm in Lovelady in Houston County, Texas. The CFA quickly spread outward across the South and, more often than not, it followed the rapid expansion of the Southern Alliance across Dixie. The CFA focused its recruiting and organizing activities in rural areas, such as the black belt, but exchanges also existed in Southern cities such as New Orleans, Mobile, Charleston, and Norfolk. The Alliance emphasized both economic and political education for farmers at a time when farmers faced deteriorating conditions, such as rising freight costs, rising interest rates, the crop lien, declining prices for cash crops, such as cotton, and debt peonage. These problems affected all small farmers, but African Americans faced even greater problems—fewer African

Americans owned land, and those who did often had the poorest land. The overwhelming majority of black farmers either rented poor-quality farms at high prices or worked as sharecroppers. If this was not bad enough, to compound these problems, African Americans had to deal with racial injustices, discrimination in the prices of goods and availability of credit, and white hostility to success. Advocating "producerism"—that is, that the producer deserves the fruit of his or her work—the Alliance quickly found an attentive audience and a massive following for its mission to improve the lives of the common farmer. The Alliance was the last (and largest) in a long line of farming organizations in the second half of the nineteenth century, including the Grange and the Agricultural Wheel.

Traveling lecturers in the CFA educated black farmers on the need for economic cooperation to alleviate the worst effects of the farm crisis. For example, buying in bulk to offset high freight rates, using fertilizers and practicing modern farming techniques, and building exchanges where farmers could buy products at reduced costs were all remedies advocated by the CFA. Indeed, in exchanges black and white farmers often cooperated with one another. The exchanges often failed, due to lack of money and poor planning, but the cooperative element installed a movement culture based on producerism that ultimately radicalized many farmers into independent political action. By early 1888, the CFA was so large that it needed to procure a federal charter and after a convention at Lovelady, the Colored Farmers' National Alliance and Cooperative Union was born.

Not surprising, perhaps, the CFA also quickly entered the political realm. Although it began as a nonpartisan organization, the CFA voted and campaigned for politicians who were sensitive to the needs of farmers and who promised to effect change. At this time, the Bourbon Democrats largely ignored the pleas of small farmers and paid even less attention to the plight of black farmers. Still, the CFA educated and organized African Americans to use their votes effectively and strategically.

The success of the CFA in the Southern states reflected the nature of local politics and conditions on the ground as well as the activism of local leaders. For example, North Carolina witnessed a strong CFA due in part to the foundational work of the Knights of Labor and the indefatigable leadership of Walter Patillo. Patillo was a black Baptist minister from Granville County and he quickly rose to position of lecturer and secretary of the North Carolina CFA with close associations with leading white Alliance leaders, such as state president Elias Carr. Patillo worked very hard to educate black farmers and organize them in local cooperatives and also in politics. It is highly probable that other such leaders and close relationships existed in other states in the South.

Reflecting the racism of the times, the national leader of the CFA was Richard M. Humphrey, a notable white Texas Allanceman and farmer. He was originally from South Carolina, but by the mid-1880s, he was a leading member of the Alliance in Texas—he was present at the founding of the CFA in Lovelady in 1886. Humphrey was a Confederate veteran and Baptist preacher who built a career as an ally with black congregations in East Texas. Humphrey had a long history of political activism, running as a congressional Union Labor candidate in Texas. Although Humphrey was the titular head of the CFA, it appears that much of the local leadership held the power to effect change and increase membership. As the CFA grew, it absorbed other black farming groups including, in 1890, the Consolidated Alliance led by Andrew J. Carothers, another white leader from Texas.

Many white members of the Southern Farmers' Alliance held negative views of African Americans—most white Southerners at this time were racist and believed in the inferiority of blacks. In addition, many did not believe in black leadership and feared a return to black power and the days of Reconstruction. As a result, in several states, such as Alabama, Virginia, and North Carolina, the state leadership of the CFA was white. But in other states, such as Georgia, Louisiana, and Mississippi, the CFA leadership was black. For example, Frank Davis, the black leader of the CFA in Alabama, was well respected and held some power. Most of the local leaders within all the Southern states were African American, and they worked to organize black farmers as best they could.

In each state, the CFA organized suballiances at the local level. Although evidence at the local level is sparse, it does appear that the CFA followed the same organizational structure of the white Alliance—it was a secret fraternal organization that welcomed women, met regularly, discussed issues facing farmers, and welcomed traveling Alliance lecturers. The suballiances across the South organized local cooperatives and exchanges and attempted to improve the lot of the local farmers. However, perhaps in part to avoid white violence or reprisals, most of the local CFA activities were covert. Many cooperatives failed in economic terms, but they provided leadership opportunities in the black community and fostered a movement culture that aided in the politicization of the black belt in the 1890s.

As the CFA rapidly expanded in size and scope by the end of the 1880s, it faced increased hostility from entrenched Democrats who were both unsympathetic to the plight of farmers and opposed to African Americans. Economic and political unions between organized labor and farmers were ridiculed by Democrats. In some locations, Democrats attacked and even killed CFA leaders. The Mississippi Delta witnessed one such terrible incident. In addition, Republicans opposed the formation of the Alliance because they worried that the CFA would weaken the GOP in elections—this was a justified fear. Thus it appears that in Alabama, North Carolina, South Carolina, Texas, and Virginia, black Republican leaders stymied the CFA at every turn.

In late 1891, as conditions for black farmers worsened, particularly in the cotton economy, the CFA debated supporting a cotton pickers strike. The CFA's national leader, R. M. Humphrey believed a strike across the South was the only way to improve pay and conditions for black farmers, and so he worked with other CFA members to organize the Texas CFA to strike. These developments were kept from the white Southern Farmers' Alliance. However, the strike was poorly planned and executed and occurred only in a few isolated places in Texas, South Carolina, and Arkansas. The CFA did not have the funds to mount a strike and the merchants were too powerful. Violence also followed; for example, in Texas, 15 strikers were killed. The planned strike outraged the Southern white leadership of the Alliance, and they refused to back any attempts at striking. In Georgia, for example, the Alliance opposed the strike. The strike was a complete failure. The strike debacle exacerbated internal problems within the CFA, and by the end of 1891, the organization was in terminal decline.

As the Alliance moved toward political insurgency in 1892—culminating in the formation of the People's Party—the CFA and its members faced a choice: either support the Populists or remain within the Republican Party. The CFA's leader, Humphrey, supported the People's Party and urged African American members to join the nascent party. From the evidence, it seems that in many locations, African Americans voted or campaigned for the Populists in 1892; for example, John B. Rayner became a black Populist leader in Texas, while in North Carolina, Walter Patillo supported the Populists. However, a larger number of African Americans stayed with the party of Lincoln. Even if many black members of the CFA supported the Populists' economic and political platform, they could not abandon the Republican Party.

Following the formation of the People's Party, the Alliance witnessed a period of rapid decline, due in part to the internal divisions within the Alliance, the fallout over outright political action, and the worsening economic situation facing farmers across the South. The CFA mirrored this decline. Indeed by 1892, the CFA was an empty shell, with little or no power. Black farmers now faced worsening economic conditions as rates of tenancy and sharecropping increased and foreclosures and debt peonage abounded. As the 1890s continued, African Americans faced political disfranchisement and Jim Crow. The CFA was no more. By the end of the 1890s, the numbers of African Americans owning farms decreased, and many began to move to cities in the South, move out West to look for work, and later many began the Great Migration northwards as industrialization and urbanization took a hold of the United States. The heyday of black farming was over.

For a brief time, African Americans worked together in the CFA and achieved some notable victories, but these successes proved short-lived. The CFA was the largest black organization in the history of the United States, and from the evidence, it is clear that it helped to organize black farmers to cooperate with one another and to alleviate some of the problems facing agrarians.

James M. Beeby

See also: Sharecropping.

Further Reading

Gaither, Gerald. *Blacks and the Populist Revolt: Ballots and Bigotry in the New South.* Tuscaloosa: University of Alabama Press, 1977.

Goodwyn, Lawrence. *Democratic Promise: The Populist Movement in America.* New York: Oxford University Press, 1976.

Holmes, William F. "The Demise of the Colored Farmers' Alliance." *Journal of Southern History* 41 (1975): 187–200.

McMath, Robert. *Populist Vanguard: A History of the Southern Farmers' Alliance.* Chapel Hill: University of North Carolina Press, 1975.

Confederate Flag

The banner widely recognized as the flag of the Confederacy is one of the most controversial symbols in America. The flag consists of a blue Saint Andrews Cross, or diagonal cross, on a slightly wider white Saint Andrews Cross, against a red background. On the blue cross are 13 white stars. The use of the flag by the Ku Klux Klan and other white supremacist groups makes it offensive. However, this flag never served as the flag of the Confederate States of America, and the military used several versions of the battle flag. In the early twentieth century, Confederate heritage societies standardized the flag and popularized its use as a symbol of regional pride, states' rights, and white supremacy. In the middle of the century, the battle flag became a symbol of massive resistance to the Civil Rights Movement. Many white Southerners believed that they faced the same struggle the Confederate generation endured. Although the Civil Rights Movement succeeded, some states continued to display the flag, inspiring heated debates about the history and symbols of the South. Critics of the flag's display on public grounds argued that it symbolized the legacy of slavery, segregation, and disfranchisement. In essence, "Whites Only" signs disappeared, but the Confederate flag remained.

After the Civil War, the Confederate battle flag represented an important symbol of Southern identity. In 1865, Father Abram J. Ryan penned "The Conquered Banner," a poem that advised Southerners to accept the defeat of the Confederacy through the metaphor of the furled Confederate flag. Although other Southerners refused to furl the flag and accept the costs of defeat, federal military command-ers banned its display during Reconstruction. After the Compromise of 1877 re-stored home rule in the South, the flag became an increasingly pervasive symbol of regional identity. Confederate heritage societies honored the dead and marked the Southern landscape with monuments to the Lost Cause. The United Confeder-ate Veterans and the United Daughters of the Confederacy erected monuments to promote regional pride and transmit lessons on racial and social hierarchy to the children of the South. The Confederate battle flag was an important part of this campaign; Southern boys and girls learned that the flag symbolized the Confeder-ate defense of states' rights and white supremacy.

After World War II, the children who were raised to revere the Confederacy displayed the flag as a symbol of their resistance to the Civil Rights Movement. In 1948, the States' Rights Democratic Party, often referred to as the Dixiecrats, utilized the flag as a symbol of the party's commitment to states' authority over matters of race. In parts of the South, the Dixiecrats inspired supporters to purchase battle flags in record numbers. The Dixiecrats failed to prevent the reelection of Democrat Harry S. Truman, but their campaign popularized the use of the Con-federate battle flag as a symbol of massive resistance. White Southerners formed White Citizens Councils across the region and employed the flag as a symbol of their constitutional, economic, moral, and racial arguments in defense of segrega-tion. Students at the University of Mississippi waved the flag in protest against the enrollment of African American James Meredith in 1962. The flag was a prominent symbol of the Confederate spirit at the University of Mississippi, but it assumed greater importance as the National Guard and federal officials protected Meredith in his attempt to enter the university. The Ku Klux Klan employed the flag at its rallies, establishing an association between the flag and racial terrorism. A variety of Southerners waved the Confederate battle flag, but they all unfurled the flag as a symbol of their defense of the racial status quo.

Southern state leaders also employed the flag as a symbol of their resistance to federal action on behalf of African Americans' civil rights. Mississippi established the precedent in 1894 when the legislature incorporated the battle flag into the state banner. The decision followed the introduction of Jim Crow legislation that eventually swept the South. Sixty years later, the U.S. Supreme Court overturned Jim Crow schools in its ruling in *Brown v. Board of Education* (1954). The Geor-gia state legislature adopted its plan to resist the ruling and blended the battle and state flags in the same session. The South Carolina legislature raised the flag over the state capitol building in 1962, claiming that the flag was raised to commemo-rate the Civil War centennial. The centennial provided an opportunity to interpret the Civil War as a precedent for their struggle to preserve states' rights over mat-ters of race. On the day Alabama governor George Wallace met Attorney General

Robert F. Kennedy at the University of Alabama to discuss integration, the flag was raised over the dome of the capitol building. In this context, the flag symbolized Wallace's determination to preserve state sovereignty against the threat of federal intervention.

Despite the failure of massive resistance, the Confederate flag continued to be a pervasive symbol throughout the South. African Americans who gained a political voice as a result of the Civil Rights Movement challenged the symbol at the turn of the twenty-first century. Georgia, Mississippi, and South Carolina endured controversies over the states' use of the battle flag. Defenders argued that the flag represented a distinct Southern heritage, while critics suggested that it symbolized the desire to oppress African Americans in slavery and freedom. The controversy surrounding the battle flag was part of a larger public debate about expressions of Confederate heritage in public spaces. As one of the most visible symbols of white resistance in the South, the Confederate battle flag's removal was an important part of the modernization of the Southern landscape. Those who defended the flag as symbol of Southern tradition often struggled to respond to the assertion that it represented white supremacy.

J. Vincent Lowery

See also: Jim Crow; Reconstruction.

Further Reading

Coski, John M. *The Confederate Flag: America's Most Embattled Emblem.* Cambridge, MA: Belknap Press of Harvard University Press, 2005.

Cox, Karen L. *Dixie's Daughters: The United Daughters of the Confederacy and the Preservation of Confederate Culture.* Gainesville: University Press of Florida, 2003.

Goldfield, David. *Still Fighting the Civil War: The American South and Southern History.* Baton Rouge: Louisiana State University Press, 2002.

Congress of Racial Equality (CORE)

During the spring of 1942, the Congress of Racial Equality (CORE), initially called the Committee of Racial Equality, was founded by a group of blacks and whites on the campus of the University of Chicago. James L. Farmer Jr., Bernice Fisher, Joe Guinn, George House, Homer Jack, Bayard Rustin, and James R. Robinson are credited with the establishment of CORE. The initial leaders of CORE were George Houser, a white student, and James Farmer, the Race Relations Secretary for the Fellowship of Reconciliation (FOR).

James Farmer, national director of the Congress of Racial Equality (CORE), leads a demonstration at the 1964 New York World's Fair. (Library of Congress)

Many of CORE members were also members of FOR, its parent organization founded in 1914. Like CORE, FOR was a pacifist organization concerned with promoting justice with nonviolent civil resistance based upon the philosophical teachings of Mahatma Gandhi. Consequently, CORE members embraced such nonviolent disobedience techniques as sit-ins, picketing, jail-ins, and freedom rides to fight Jim Crow laws.

The earlier membership of CORE consisted mainly of white college students from the Midwest. To date, "[m]embership in CORE is open to anyone who believes that 'all people are created equal' and is willing to work towards the ultimate goal of true equality throughout the world." Therefore, CORE's mission remains "to bring about equality for all people regardless of race, creed, sex, age, disability, sexual orientation, religion or ethnic background." In pursuing its aim, CORE seeks to identify and expose acts of discrimination in the public and private sectors of society.

CORE's mission statement continues, "CORE is the third oldest and one of the 'Big Four' civil rights groups in the United States. From the protests against 'Jim

Crow' laws of the 40s through the 'Sit-ins' of the 50s, the 'Freedom Rides' of the 60s, the cries of 'Self-Determination' in the 70s, 'Equal Opportunity' in the 80s, community development in the 90s, to the current demand for equal access to information, CORE has championed true equality. As the 'shock troops' and pioneers of the civil rights movement, CORE has paved the way for the nation to follow" (CORE official web site).

CORE began organizing sit-ins in 1942 to protest segregated public accommodations. Its first sit-in occurred at a coffee shop in Chicago. These sit-ins were the first such nonviolent resistance activities in the United States. Based upon the success of this technique, CORE is credited with desegregation of public accommodations in cities in many Northern and border states. It was this success that resulted in CORE turning its attention to the segregated South.

In 1947, George Houser and Bayard Rustin organized a two-week Greyhound and Trailways bus journey, referred to as the Journey of Reconciliation, to the South in order to test the U.S. Supreme Court's *Morgan v. Commonwealth of Virginia,* 328 U.S. 373 (1946), ruling that forbade racial segregation of bus passengers engaged in interstate travel. In 1944, 10 years before the arrest of Rosa Parks and the Montgomery Bus Boycott, Irene Morgan, a resident of Baltimore, Maryland, was arrested and incarcerated in Virginia for resisting arrest and refusing to give up her seat on a Greyhound bus to a white person.

CORE sent a team of eight white and eight black men on the Journey of Reconciliation through the states of North Carolina, Kentucky, Tennessee, and Virginia. Members of the team were Louis Adams, Dennis Banks, Joseph Felmet, George Houser, Homer Jack, Andrew Johnson, Conrad Lynn, Wallace Nelson, James Peck, Worth Randle, Igal Roodenko, Bayard Rustin, Eugene Stanley, William Worthy, and Nathan Wright. The members were arrested several times for violating state-imposed Jim Crow bus statutes. Despite the members' arrest, the Journey of Reconciliation marked the beginning of an arduous national campaign against racial segregation.

After the *Brown v. Board of Education* ruling, CORE began focusing on segregated public accommodations in the Deep South by engaging in similar nonviolent disobedience tactics as those used in Northern cities. CORE also launched several voter registration drives for black Southerners. CORE member Bayard Rustin served as an advisor to Martin Luther King Jr. during the Montgomery Bus Boycott.

In response to Southern resistance, CORE organized student sit-ins in 1960 and provided assistance to college students throughout the country in their attempts to challenge racial segregation. These sit-ins successfully ended racial segregation of restaurants and lunch counters in some Southern cities. CORE also targeted other segregated public facilities such as parks, beaches, transportation, swimming pools, theaters, libraries, churches, and museums.

On May 4, 1961, CORE and the Student Nonviolent Coordinating Committee (SNCC) organized Freedom Rides throughout the Deep South. These Freedom Rides were similar to the Journey of Reconciliation. The Freedom Rides tested the *Boynton v. Virginia*, 364 U.S. 454 (1960), ruling that extended the *Morgan* decision to bus terminals used in interstate bus service. The original participants were six whites and seven blacks who rode buses from Washington, D.C., to New Orleans, Louisiana. Over a thousand people participated in these rides. Despite violent attacks and incarcerations, CORE maintained its overall mission and continued to grow as an organization. Additionally, the Freedom Rides were viewed as having some measure of success because the Interstate Commerce Commission passed new regulations to desegregate bus terminals.

In 1963, CORE played an instrumental role in the March on Washington and in President John F. Kennedy's Voter Education Project. One year later, CORE, in collaboration with SNCC and the National Association for the Advancement of Colored People (NAACP), organized the Freedom Summer campaign in Mississippi. The purpose of this campaign was to increase black voter registration and to promote civic literacy in Mississippi. CORE, SNCC, and the NAACP formed the Mississippi Freedom Party and established 30 Freedom Schools in order to teach civic education.

The participants of Freedom Summer experienced a rash of violence. In fact, three members of CORE—James Chaney, Andrew Goodman, and Michael Schwerner—were killed. Ironically, their deaths resulted in Freedom Summer receiving national publicity. Hence, one year later, President Lyndon B. Johnson requested passage of his Voting Rights Act. Despite opposition, in 1965, the Voting Rights Act was successfully passed.

By the mid-1960s, as CORE began opening chapters in the North and West, it experienced both an ideological and membership shift. During this time period, CORE membership became increasingly black and its ideology shifted more toward "Black Power." The ideological change was welcomed by the new national director Floyd McKissick, even though it alienated some of CORE's previous allies.

In 1968, Roy Innis became the national director of CORE. Innis restructured the organization and improved its financing health. He also promoted what was considered a less radical approach than McKissick and involved the organization in black economic development and community self-determination efforts—Black Nationalism.

Olethia Davis

See also: Montgomery Bus Boycott.

Further Reading

Arsenault, Raymond. "'You Don't Have to Ride Jim Crow': CORE and the 1947 Journey of Reconciliation." In *Before Brown: Civil Rights and White Backlash in the Modern South,* ed. Glenn Feldman, 21–67. Tuscaloosa: University of Alabama Press, 2004.

Bell, Inge P. *CORE and the Strategy of Non-Violence,* New York: Random House, 1968.

CORE Official Web site. http://www.core-online.org.

Meier, August, and Elliott Rudwick. *CORE: A Study of the Civil Rights Movement 1942–1968.* New York: Oxford University Press, 1973.

D

Democratic Party

A bastion of support for maintaining the repressive conditions of the Jim Crow South, the Democratic Party turned almost completely around from Reconstruction to the mid-1960s into a vehicle for the empowerment of Southern blacks and the use of federal power for social advocacy.

The end of Reconstruction in 1877 signified the dominance of the Democratic Party in the South despite its defeat in the recent Civil War. With Congress deadlocked over resolving the disputed presidential election of 1876, a tacit agreement stipulated that, in exchange for the triumph of Republican Rutherford B. Hayes, the new president would evacuate the remaining federal troops from the former Confederacy and offer no obstacles to the assumption of political power by Southern Democrats. The latter group vowed (despite its already obvious propensity for violence) to respect the civil rights embodied in the Thirteenth, Fourteenth, and Fifteenth Amendments to the Constitution, but gradually subverted their intent. The South was fast deteriorating into a one-party political system, with most Northerners inclined to emphasize other issues than the divisive question of race relations.

The rise of the Southern Alliance in the 1880s threatened the regional hegemony of the Democratic Party. This agrarian-dominated movement appealed to small farmers frustrated by vast market forces beyond their control and institutions unresponsive to their needs. At a time when laissez-faire economic principles seemed to apply only to those without lobbying influence in Washington, the Alliance promoted government intervention with such measures as adjusting the money supply and providing warehouses to store crops until prices climbed to more favorable levels. Some Democrats paid lip service to the movement while hoping that they could retain its support without delivering on its demands. Southern farmers agonized over whether to compete independently in politics. The resulting People's Party (1891) anticipated a fusion of blue-collar and agricultural workers to attack entrenched power in government and make the political process viable for the entire American public. In reality, support for the People's Party proved strongest in the South and West among farmers, with little progress among eastern industrial workers. Eager for any opportunity to wield power, Southern Republicans banded together with Populists in North Carolina to control the general assembly. Leery of a political realignment, Democrats across the South responded to this challenge with a combination of co-optation and the tried-and-true practices of fraud and violence.

As the 1896 presidential campaign commenced, reformers in the Democratic Party secured the nomination of William Jennings Bryan on a platform highlighting the monetarization of silver as a boon for cash-starved farmers and enough class-based rhetoric to encourage the downtrodden. This maneuver left the Populists torn over whether to nominate Bryan themselves in the hope of participating in a reform-focused coalition, continue to merge with Republicans, or maintain their distinctive identity and sense of mission. Although Bryan supported the subtreasury plan of supplying government warehouses and low-interest loans for farmers, he chose a fiscally conservative running mate to unify his party. The Populist convention, fractured over a strategic vision, nominated Bryan while tapping a radical Georgian, Tom Watson, as the vice presidential candidate. This paradoxical choice left Bryan scarcely able to present a coherent and consistent message to voters. Although many Southern Populists had set aside old anxieties and prejudices to rally both black and white farmers, Democrats capitalized on lingering fears to undermine this crusade in political utopianism. Following Bryan's defeat at the hands of the Republicans, many Populist leaders reverted to habit with denunciations of Jews, Catholics, and blacks. The path stood clear for Southern Democrats to imitate the Mississippi Plan (1890), whereby poll taxes, literacy tests, and residency requirements could disenfranchise the black population without violating a narrow interpretation of the Fifteenth Amendment. With these barriers in place, Southern Democrats celebrated their progressive credentials thanks to a new primary system that included the secret ballot, direct election of U.S. senators, the standardization of voting procedures, and a crackdown on corruption. Of course, this expression of democracy could function only with the virtual exclusion of African Americans. With blacks evicted from the political process by the early twentieth century, the Republican Party ceased to be an effective regional force and existed primarily to provide federal patronage in the event that one of its own occupied the White House.

As Southern Democrats solidified their gains, poor whites perceived their salvation in the heyday of the one-eyed, irascible demagogue, "Pitchfork" Ben Tillman. Although a race-baiter of the most outrageous variety, he emerged as a champion of the white underclass. His nickname stemmed from a promise to impale

President Grover Cleveland (a fellow Democrat) for a lethargic response to an economic downturn plaguing the Southern economy. He honed his political survival skills through manipulating the racially motivated violence of the 1870s and the Southern Alliance of the ensuing decade. Tillman organized a political machine that catapulted him into the governor's mansion in South Carolina from 1890 to 1894 and ultimately to the U.S. Senate. He served as inspiration for notable politicians of the New South, such as James Vardaman of Mississippi and Jeff Davis of Arkansas. In a moment illustrative of the passing of a torch between generations, one of Strom Thurmond's proudest childhood memories was of meeting Tillman.

The ascendancy of Franklin D. Roosevelt in 1932 owed itself in no small part to Southern Democrats, who turned out in droves for him and backed much of his legislation in Congress. As Southern blacks migrated northward in search of industrial jobs during World War II, their traditional allegiance to the Republican Party weakened considerably. In a step away from the states' rights heritage of the party, Southern Democrats cautiously began to appreciate the federal government as a positive force for economic development. A future Democratic president, Lyndon B. Johnson, ran the National Youth Administration in Texas as a showpiece for the possibilities of FDR's New Deal. Mindful of Southern seniority in Congress and the unusual instability of the times, the president avoided the sort of social policy that might have eroded the foundation of the Jim Crow South.

Despite his respect for white Southern prerogatives, FDR's greatest challenge from within his own party originated from the meteoric Louisianan, Huey Long. While governor from 1924 to 1928, he overhauled his state's economic infrastructure and uplifted its poor like no politician of the Depression era. In the process, he ran roughshod over the Louisiana constitution and oversaw a political machine potent enough to allow him to continue running the state even after he occupied his U.S. Senate seat in 1932. Originally a New Dealer, Long grew to argue that the president's measures constituted a halfhearted effort to produce anything beyond superficial reform. His Share Our Wealth Plan included fantastic promises of government stipends for struggling Americans and likely encouraged FDR to introduce a social security plan in 1935. Angling for a presidential bid the following year, Long distanced himself from the White House in the hope that he could divide the Democratic vote nationally while making a sufficiently prominent name for himself to triumph in the next campaign. He seemed the one politician who could surpass Roosevelt at his own game of connecting with the masses. Gunned down in 1935 by the relative of a political rival, Long lost an opportunity to test the national mood for its willingness to embrace radicalism.

Upon FDR's death in 1945, President Harry S. Truman was personally moved to address black grievances. But with a Congress dominated by conservatives after the 1946 midterm elections, he was loath to take dramatic action. Confining himself to matters well within the purview of the executive branch, Truman established a Committee on Civil Rights and issued executive orders desegregating the military and mandating fair employment practices in the federal government. The Democratic convention of 1948 witnessed a deterioration of sectional relations. Senator Hubert Humphrey of Minnesota spearheaded an effort to include a vigorous civil rights plank in the party platform. Congressman Sam Rayburn of Texas failed to engineer a mass walkout by Southern delegates, but 13 percent of them departed the proceedings. Shortly thereafter, roughly 6,000 Southern Democrats convened in Birmingham to form the States' Rights Party (dubbed the "Dixiecrats") with South Carolina governor Strom Thurmond atop its ticket. Thurmond ran a vitriolic campaign linking racial integration with communism as anxiety over the emerging Cold War gripped the U.S. public. Despite South Carolina, Alabama, Louisiana, and Mississippi going for Thurmond, Truman won an improbable victory that emboldened Northern Democrats to elevate the importance of the civil rights issue. As a measure of Southern disaffection, Republican Dwight D. Eisenhower took five and six states, respectively, in his successful presidential campaigns of the 1950s. Yet his effort to desegregate a Little Rock high school in 1957 cemented the distrust of segregationists for the Republicans. Estranged from both parties at the national level, Southern Democrats retained their stranglehold on local organizations and political offices.

The 1960 presidential campaign heightened Southern Democratic suspicions surrounding their party. In a highly symbolic move, John F. Kennedy worked through his brother, Robert F. Kennedy, to save Martin Luther King Jr. from incarceration and the prospect of a sentence at a Georgia labor camp. The leader of the Southern Caucus, Senator Richard Russell of Georgia, pointedly avoided endorsing Kennedy or even remaining in the country during the final weeks of the campaign. Nevertheless, buoyed by the presence of Texan Lyndon B. Johnson, on the ticket, Kennedy carried a majority of white Southern voters. His advantage was much stronger in the electoral college than with the popular vote. Although Kennedy skirted civil rights questions for most of his tragically short presidency, he reacted forcefully when confronted in the spring of 1963 with scenes of beleaguered civil rights demonstrators in Birmingham, Alabama, facing attack dogs and high-pressure water hoses. In what turned out to be the final months of his life, the president put Southern segregationists on notice and introduced meaningful civil rights legislation that Lyndon Johnson would expand on and shepherd through Congress after Kennedy's death.

Johnson represented a bundle of contradictions as he approached race relations in America. He was deeply committed to eliminating the mutually reinforcing scourges of poverty and racism even while he bandied about epithets in his phone conversations with Southern leaders. With an eye toward the stature of his mentor's New Deal, Johnson showcased a Great Society that would include racial equality. Capitalizing on sympathy for a fallen president, he successfully urged Americans to make the Civil Rights Act of 1964 a tribute to Kennedy's legacy. As Johnson prepared to run for a term of his own, Governor George Wallace of Alabama hit the trail with a broader message of states' rights than Thurmond had employed before him. For Wallace, civil rights advocacy formed just one of a wide variety of abuses of federal power that he believed would resonate with voters beyond the South. In 1963, he had prompted the federalization of the Alabama National Guard with his threat to bar entrance to the University of Alabama at Tuscaloosa should two recently admitted black students attempt to enroll. But Wallace dropped out of the race when it became clear that the Republicans would nominate ultraconservative Senator Barry Goldwater of Arizona. With such a polarizing opponent, Johnson could select Hubert Humphrey as his running mate and still position himself as relatively centrist.

The Democratic convention was marred by a dispute over the credentials of rival Mississippi delegations. The Mississippi Freedom Democratic Party (MFDP) argued that it was the only Democratic organization from its state that actually supported the national party, since white Democrats clearly preferred Goldwater. Making both an exhaustive legal case and a poignant emotional appeal, the MFDP seemed assured of bringing its status to a floor vote in Atlantic City. But Johnson thwarted the effort by compelling Humphrey to broker a "compromise" whereby the MFDP would provide only two delegates to the convention. MFDP activists, such as the outspoken Fannie Lou Hamer, rejected the token gesture in a move symbolic of the growing militancy of blacks in the Civil Rights Movement and their distrust of white liberals. Although progressive in his personal views on race, Goldwater vehemently opposed the Civil Rights Act of 1964 as an infringement upon states' rights. During this campaign, Thurmond switched his party affiliation to Republican and barnstormed the South on Goldwater's behalf. Although Johnson won in a landslide, he sparked a tectonic shift in the Southern political landscape. His opponent took five Deep South states as many segregationist Democrats transferred their allegiance. As Johnson subsequently backed the Voting Rights Act of 1965 with his exhortation that "we shall overcome" (quoting a popular civil rights song), the Republicans secured the white Southern vote. But the milestones achieved by the Civil Rights Movement and its political allies began to return Southern blacks to the polls as the South rediscovered legitimate, two-party competition.

Although the Democratic Party would experience severe divisions over race, gender, and the Vietnam War in the coming years, it no longer could be so intimately associated with excesses dating back to Reconstruction. While some segregationists, such as Richard Russell and Ernest "Fritz" Hollings, remained in the party, it could console itself with a degree of credit for translating the sacrifices of civil rights advocates into concrete legislation.

Jeffrey D. Bass

See also: Ku Klux Klan; Roosevelt, Franklin D.

Further Reading

Bartley, Numan, and Hugh Graham. *Southern Politics and the Second Reconstruction.* Baltimore: Johns Hopkins University Press, 1975.

Kousser, J. Morgan. *The Shaping of Southern Politics: Suffrage Restriction and the Establishment of the One-Party South, 1880–1910.* New Haven, CT: Yale University Press, 1974.

Lamis, Alexander. *The Two-Party South.* New York: Oxford University Press, 1984.

Rae, Nicol. *Southern Democrats.* New York: Oxford University Press, 1994.

Detroit Race Riot of 1943

There were 243 instances of racial violence in 47 American cities in 1943, including Los Angeles and New York City, but the two-day race riot in Detroit was the largest and most devastating. The riot began at a city park located on a small island in the Detroit River, and dangerously spilled over into the city itself. As a result of the rioting, 34 people died, 25 blacks and 9 whites, and 675 were wounded. Property damage reached $2 million; more than 1,890 had been arrested. Wartime competition among whites and African Americans for access to defense industry jobs, as well as increasingly scarce housing, limited public recreational spaces, and crowded public transportation, precipitated the racial tensions that produced the riot.

African Americans and poor whites from Southern states, as well as rural whites from the Midwestern countryside, all came to Detroit to find work during the war, and the bulging population of the city deepened tensions among the races. Racial hostilities reached the breaking point on the afternoon of June 20, 1943. On Detroit's Belle Isle, a popular public park, nearly 100,000 whites and African Americans sought refuge from the summer heat by enjoying the day on the island's many beaches and shaded picnic areas. However, following a tense period of racial conflicts in the city over housing and public recreation in 1942 and 1943, angry groups of black teenagers ventured throughout Belle Isle and harassed numerous whites. As skirmishes unfolded throughout the afternoon and into the evening, the

Passengers climb from the rear of a streetcar stopped by a mob during the Detroit Race Riot, June 22, 1943. (Library of Congress)

violence congealed into open race war. The fighting rapidly escalated on the Jefferson Avenue bridge, which linked the park and the city, and the riot spread into Detroit itself. Rioting continued on Belle Isle and in Detroit until roughly 2:00 A.M., June 21, when an understaffed Detroit police department was finally able to scatter the mobs.

While the riot appeared to be over, it was actually just beginning. False rumors—spread by whites and African Americans—precipitated the second phase of the violence. In Paradise Valley, an ironically named black enclave near Woodward Avenue, a young African American man named Leo Tipton stormed onto the stage of the Forest Club, a popular night spot. He announced to the large crowd that a black woman and her baby had been thrown from the Jefferson Avenue bridge by white mobs and drowned. The rumor was false, but its effect was devastating. The crowd at the Forest Club poured into the streets of Paradise Valley. Angry African Americans attacked white-owned stores on Hastings Street, the main thoroughfare in the neighborhood. The mob also assaulted whites in their cars as they tried to drive past, dragging passengers into the streets and violently beating them. Nine whites died. The violence and the casualties continued to increase as members of the Detroit police fired randomly into the crowds of black men and women. Seventeen African Americans were killed.

Simultaneously, another untrue rumor circulated among whites in the vicinity of Woodward Avenue that a group of black men had attacked and raped a white woman on Belle Isle. All along Woodward, large white mobs estimated to be in the thousands assailed blacks on sight, tearing their way through theaters, stores, and the crowded street to search for victims. As the white mobs circulated, police officers remained in the background and did nothing. As night fell on June 21, the white mobs gathered in Cadillac Square in downtown Detroit, preparing for a rampage in Paradise Valley.

Local authorities responded hesitantly. The Detroit mayor, Edward J. Jeffries Jr., initially hoped local and state police, along with the state guard, would be enough to quell the violence, but the worsening crisis ultimately forced him to ask the federal government for troops. Late in the evening on June 21, two military police battalions marched from the outskirts of Detroit to the riot scene with their rifles and bayonets at the ready. As troops moved through Paradise Valley and down Woodward, the mobs finally began to dissolve. Slowly, quiet came to the city. The many casualties and the extent of the property damage made Detroit neighborhoods look more like the battlefields of Europe or the Pacific—rather than the celebrated "Arsenal of Democracy." Paradise Valley and Woodward Avenue were in ruins.

Accusations and conspiracy theories proliferated in the days after the riot, as authorities, residents, and outside observers struggled to identify those responsible. Their various allegations reflected the long-standing resentments of various social groups and wartime fears of subversion. African Americans pointed to the sinister and enduring influence of the Ku Klux Klan, the Black Legion, and other white racists, while many whites in Detroit blamed the National Association for the Advancement of Colored People and "Communists" for inciting black violence. Southern white observers complained that First Lady Eleanor Roosevelt and the Committee of Fair Employment Practice (FEPC) were responsible for the riot, arguing that their reckless calls for social equality among blacks and whites created the turmoil. Still others claimed that a fascist "fifth column" caused the violence in an attempt to embarrass the United States and hinder wartime production.

There were much deeper sources of racial violence in Detroit, however. Whites had long opposed black migration to the city, using violence and discrimination in an effort to marginalize the African American population. In 1925, for example, white mobs attacked a black physician, Ossian Sweet, and his family as they attempted to move into a new house in a "white" neighborhood. During World War II, whites worried extensively about competing with blacks for jobs and homes in an increasingly crowded city. In 1942, as the African American population of Detroit began expanding dramatically, black families confronted white picketing and violence when they tried to take up residence in a new government housing project, the Sojourner Truth Homes, which was situated in another predominantly white section of the city. During June 1943, only a couple of weeks before the race riot, African Americans confronted a massive "hate strike" at Packard Motors, where thousands of white men walked off the job in opposition to only a small number of black promotions. As African Americans battled for victory both in the war against fascism and for racial justice at home, many whites worried about the erosion of white privilege. President Franklin D. Roosevelt's Executive Order 8802, the creation of the FEPC, and the allocation of the Sojourner Truth Homes to African American families distressed many whites in Detroit. In southeastern Michigan, white apprehension about the changing status of African Americans could be heard in frequent complaints about the shadowy "bump club": whites believed that many black men were members of a secret group of especially assertive African Americans, whose purpose was to "bump" and harass whites on crowded buses and streetcars. Throughout the period between World War I and World War II, white demands for the residential and occupational separation of African Americans and whites, white anxieties about an expanding black population, and African American determination to struggle against harassment were the explosive foundations of racial strife in Detroit.

Despite the terrible bloodshed and costly damage to property, the Detroit Race Riot of 1943 was not the end of racial tensions in the city. Persistent racial discrimination and inequalities in employment, housing, and public space continued to define daily life in metropolitan Detroit; and deadly rioting would once again occur in 1967.

Gregory Wood

See also: Fair Employment Practices Commission (FEPC); World War II.

Further Reading

Capeci, Dominic J., Jr., and Martha Wilkerson. *Layered Violence: The Detroit Rioters of 1943*. Jackson: University Press of Mississippi, 1991.

Clive, Alan. *State of War: Michigan in World War II*. Ann Arbor: University of Michigan Press, 1979.

Shogan, Robert, and Tom Craig. *The Detroit Race Riot: A Study in Violence*. Philadelphia: Chilton Books, 1964.

Sugrue, Thomas. *The Origins of the Urban Crisis: Race and Inequality in Postwar Detroit*. Princeton, NJ: Princeton University Press, 1995.

Disenfranchisement

Depriving African Americans the right to vote, or disenfranchisement, was a significant feature of Jim Crow politics for almost a century. It began in the late nineteenth century as a means to curtail the political advantages African Americans had gained during Reconstruction. After the Civil War, three constitutional amendments were ratified to ease the transition from slavery to freedom: the Thirteenth Amendment abolished slavery, the Fourteenth Amendment granted former slaves the right to citizenship, and the Fifteenth Amendment granted black men the right to vote. These three Reconstruction amendments were contested by the former Confederate states because African Americans were no longer under whites' control. This period of relative freedom and equality lasted for about a decade, until Southern states repealed all the Reconstruction Acts created by Radical Republicans, the party once headed by Abraham Lincoln. By the mid-1870s, the Democratic Party had regained much of their former congressional power with the support of a new administration. White Southerners sought redemption for the loss of the Civil War, and their most pressing concern was, as one historian puts it, a "struggle for mastery" once again over African Americans.

In a move to return to the white supremacy status quo, disenfranchisement was a political process that took only a few decades to accomplish. The history of black suffrage began when the Fifteenth Amendment was ratified in 1870. Only a small percentage of free blacks, primarily in the North, had voting privileges prior to then. During Reconstruction, African Americans took full advantage of their voting rights by supporting Republican officials, particularly electing other blacks to office. High-ranking black Republicans during this period included state legislators, governors, and U.S. senators. Congressmen Robert Smalls from South Carolina and John Lynch from Mississippi as well as Louisiana governor P. B. S. Pinchback were among the many black politicians elected by black voters during the 1870s and early 1880s. Such victories were short-lived, as white Southerners began manipulating the elections in various ways. Black voters were often verbally harassed or physically assaulted to prevent them from casting their ballots or even reaching the polls. Violent threats and terror campaigns for voter intimidation usually occurred without legal intervention.

Some African Americans would refuse to be intimidated despite such warnings. If they did succeed at casting their votes, however, white election officials often destroyed these ballots. Black voters were usually unaware that their votes were not counted under such conditions. "Ballot box stuffing" was yet another deceptive tactic used to disenfranchise African Americans. This practice of "counting out" the intended votes of African Americans for an opposing candidate or using phony ballots against the candidate supported by a black majority were ways of "stealing" the vote. This second phase in the history of black suffrage was an age of "Redemption," when white Southerners schemed to regain political control of once Republican-dominated governments.

White Democrats were determined to find other ways of effectively disenfranchising blacks that would prevent them from even registering to vote. They drew a fine distinction between having "the *ability* to vote at *elections*" and "the *right* to vote" at all. The latter option was a more permanent solution to the "race problem" attributed in part to black suffrage. All the political, social, and economic advancements African Americans had made in just a few years since slavery antagonized white supremacist ideas about natural social order. The rallying cry of "Negro domination" signaled the fears of white Southerners in regard to the power wielded by the black vote in support of the Republican Party. African Americans were never in control as white Southerners imagined, because segregation laws upheld white hegemony. Blacks were deemed social inferiors with little or no civil rights to protect. Yet, the idea of blacks ruling whites inspired a revolution. The specter of "Negro domination" could only be replaced by another political obsession, "white supremacy." Complete disenfranchisement resolved the ideological conflict of race by restoring white supremacy.

By the 1890s, Southern states began to deprive African Americans of their voting rights by creating stringent voting restrictions. Property qualifications were required in Alabama, Louisiana, Virginia, North Carolina, Mississippi, Georgia, and South Carolina; the registered voter had to own as much as $300 or more in real estate or personal assets. Poll taxes were imposed in Tennessee, Arkansas, Florida, Texas, and several other states with property qualifications. A third common voting restriction was an education qualification. Literacy tests were administered to prove if a potential voter was capable of understanding his rights. Often these tests included reading and interpreting passages from the U.S. Constitution. Sometimes the election officials would read an article or constitutional amendment and ask the applicant to explain the passages. Such practices were common in Mississippi, South Carolina, Louisiana, Alabama, North Carolina, and Virginia. The voting restrictions were effective not just in eliminating black voters, but some whites could also be disenfranchised too. Therefore, "saving clauses" were often included in voting restriction proposals as loopholes for whites who would be otherwise disqualified by property, poll tax, and educational qualifications. The "grandfather clause" was intended as a nonracial requirement that nevertheless limited black suffrage; it stipulated that any son or descendent of a (Confederate) soldier or any one who had the right to vote prior to 1867 would then inherit his ancestral voting rights. This law of inheritance did not always prevent African Americans from voting, considering the documented participation of black soldiers in both the Union and Confederate armies during the Civil War. Nevertheless, the grandfather clause did eliminate a majority of black voters who were themselves descended from former slaves. Some African Americans just faltered under considerable pressures of disenfranchisement. They would not vote at all or would sell their votes altogether. These two forms are not technically forms of disenfranchisement, since the individual was not prevented from voting but instead chose not to do so. However, the employment qualification and character assessments were two notorious forms of voting restrictions found in Alabama. The black voter would have to prove that he had suitable employment and then that he was of "good character." Both qualifications were judged by a white election official and therefore subject to his discretion.

African Americans responded to the motives and means of disenfranchisement with their actions and words. In record numbers, they continued to vote despite the fraudulent election schemes. Less-educated blacks would sometimes be accompanied to the polls by others to ensure a fair chance at voting. Most African Americans believed that voting was a basic right of U.S. citizenship and were determined to maintain their civil rights at all costs, even to their personal safety. Writer Charles Chesnutt participated in the public debates about the second-class citizenship status being forced on African Americans. In his article, "The Disenfranchisement of the Negro" (1903), Chesnutt challenged the constitutionality of the various voting restrictions imposed in Southern states. He therefore criticized the federal government for being influenced by white Southerners: "Not only is the Negro taxed without representation in the [South], but he pays, through the tariff and internal revenue, a tax to a National government whose supreme judicial tribunal declares that it cannot, through the executive arm, enforce its own decrees, and, therefore, refuses to pass upon a question, squarely before it, involving a basic right of citizenship" (92). Chesnutt believed that the federal government could have taken action by using congressional regulations, under the Fourteenth Amendment, to prevent Southerners from "a district where voters [had] been disfranchised" from ever holding office. Thus, white Southerners' political power would be just as limited as disenfranchised African Americans. The black press also responded to voter manipulation by castigating the perpetrators. The *Richmond Planet* and *Southwestern Christian Advocate* (a Methodist paper in New Orleans), for example, featured editorials about black disenfranchisement that was occurring throughout the South. Between 1902 and 1905, the *Baltimore Afro-American Ledger* led a series of campaigns against the move to segregate public transportation, as an additional consequence of disenfranchisement. It circulated few successful petitions and organized boycotts that would allow blacks to retain at least an illusion of political power.

"Restoration," or the third phase in the history of black suffrage, was completed by the early twentieth century. The black vote was eliminated by amendments to state constitutions. Southern states held conventions to revise their suffrage requirements that could circumvent federal election laws. The Democrats secured their political power through voting manipulation and intimidation. They had also manipulated public opinion against black suffrage as a challenge to white supremacy. Only when organizations such as the National Association for the Advancement of Colored People (NAACP) began to take action did white supremacists lose some footing. By the 1930s and 1940s, organized by the NAACP, black voter registration drives once again appeared as the modern Civil Rights Movement began to take shape. Medgar Evers and other activists challenged the election of racist demagogues in Mississippi and Georgia. It was the black vote that secured the presidential election of Harry S. Truman in 1948. As evidenced in Truman's administration, civil rights legislation was reintroduced to the national public. African Americans staged massive protests against racial discrimination and segregation throughout the 1950s and 1960s. Militant opposition to racial oppression and support of voting rights was signaled by Malcolm X's speech "The Ballot or the Bullet" (1964) to a gathering in Cleveland. Black disenfranchisement, one of the last vestiges of Jim Crow, would finally be overturned by the Voting Rights Act of 1965 when federal authorities would regulate voter registration and blacks could free access to the ballot.

Sherita L. Johnson

See also: Black Codes; Nadir of the Negro.

Further Reading

Chesnutt, Charles. "The Disenfranchisement of the Negro" [1903]. In *The Negro Problem,* edited by Bernard R. Boxill, 77–124. Amherst, NY: Humanity Books, 2003.

Gilman, Glenda Elizabeth. *Gender and Jim Crow: Women and the Politics of White Supremacy in North Carolina, 1896–1920.* Chapel Hill: University of North Carolina Press, 1996.

Perman, Michael. *Struggle for Mastery: Disenfranchisement in the South, 1888–1908.* Chapel Hill. University of North Carolina Press, 2001.

Wormser, Richard. *The Rise and Fall of Jim Crow.* New York: St. Martin's Griffin, 2003.

Double V Campaign

As the United States entered World War II, much of black America was divided in its enthusiasm to sacrifice for a nation that treated African Americans as second-class citizens. It was only a generation earlier, during World War I, that W.E.B. Du Bois had urged African Americans to "close ranks" and support the war effort to, in President Woodrow Wilson's words, "make the world safe for democracy." While Du Bois initially believed that African American service in the war would prove to white America both their patriotism and their worthiness of equal citizenship, he, along with the rest of black America, was bitterly disappointed with the nation's response. Instead of earning acceptance and gratitude for the contributions of the 380,000 black men who served in the war, and the hundreds of thousands of African Americans who worked in war industries and bought war bonds back home, black America was instead met with unprecedented racial violence in the summer of 1919, an invigorated Ku Klux Klan, and a general unwillingness to pursue any change in the racial status quo.

Two decades later, black leaders were determined to be more aggressive in pushing the U.S. government to improve civil rights if it wanted black support for the war effort. In 1940, President Franklin D. Roosevelt appointed William Hastie as his "Aide on Negro Affairs" and promoted Benjamin O. Davis to brigadier general following pressure from both the National Association for the Advancement of Colored People (NAACP) and the Urban League. The next year, Roosevelt issued Executive Order 8802, outlawing discrimination in government and defense employment following A. Phillip Randolph's threatened "March on Washington." Randolph and other black leaders also lobbied the president, unsuccessfully, for the end of segregation in the armed forces, but were successful in opening up opportunities in the service previously off-limits to African Americans, most notably the flight training program at Tuskegee, Alabama. The Marine Corps also accepted its first black recruits in 1942, and the army increased the number of African Americans admitted to officer training programs. Nonetheless, many black leaders, remembering the failure of the nation to reward black America for its service in World War I, were hesitant to urge African Americans to follow the flag in a war against fascist racism in Europe and Asia while fighting in a Jim Crow army and being denied many of the basic tenants of American democracy at home.

The black press, long the nation's watchdog for racial violence and an outspoken critic of the country's discriminatory policies, found itself in a delicate position with the entry of the United States into World War II following the bombing of Pearl Harbor. If it came out in support of the war effort, it risked not heeding the lessons of World War I by failing to pressure the United States to improve life for black Americans at a time when the nation needed them most; however, if it criticized the government at a time of war, it risked being labeled as unpatriotic and unsupportive of the tens of thousands of African American men and women who had already answered the call to service.

This dilemma was solved in January 1942 by James G. Thompson, a cafeteria worker at the Cessna Aircraft Corporation in Wichita, Kansas. In a letter to the editor of the *Pittsburgh Courier,* the nation's most widely circulated black newspaper, he wrote:

> Being an American of dark complexion . . . these questions flash through my mind: "Should I sacrifice my life to live half American?" . . . "Would it be demanding too much to demand full citizenship rights in exchange

for the sacrificing of my life?" "Is the kind of America I know worth defending?"

I suggest that while we keep defense and victory in the forefront that we don't lose sight of our fight for true democracy at home.

The V for victory sign is being displayed prominently in all so-called democratic countries which are fighting for victory over aggression, slavery and tyranny. If this V sign means that to those now engaged in this great conflict, then let we colored Americans adopt the double VV for a double victory. The first V for victory over our enemies from without, the second V for victory over our enemies from within. For surely those who perpetrate these ugly prejudices here are seeking to destroy our democratic form of government just as surely as the Axis forces.

In response to Thompson's letter, the *Courier* instituted the "Double V" campaign, demanding a war to end fascism abroad and Jim Crow at home. Beginning with its February 7, 1942, edition (the first following Thompson's letter), the newspaper exposed the contradictions inherent in the country asking its black men and women to fight against Nazi racism abroad while being subjected to American racism at home, and demanded that African Americans serving their country abroad receive full citizenship rights when they returned. To promote this message, the paper adopted a design for its masthead. Under the word "Democracy," an eagle sat between two large letter Vs, one on top of the other, on a banner that said "Double Victory," while beneath the banner read "At Home—Abroad."

Over the coming weeks, the paper actively promoted the "Double V" campaign. *Courier* columnists wrote pieces prodding the black public to agitate for equality, while numerous letters and telegrams from readers voicing their support for the campaign were published. The *Courier* also began a weekly photo layout of people from around the nation smiling and making the "Double V" sign with their fingers. Soon, the photos began to include famous African Americans who were supportive of the "Double V" campaign, such as Adam Clayton Powell and Marian Anderson, and even included some prominent whites, including Humphrey Bogart and Thomas Dewey, who flashed the "Double V" sign. "Double V" lapel pins were found on men's coats, women sported "Double V" hairdos, "Double V" posters were printed, and the *Courier* even began running a weekly "Double V Girl of the Week." Other African American newspapers picked up on the "Double V" campaign as well, giving it greater exposure and making it a nationwide effort.

The *Courier,* like almost every other black newspaper in the nation, made it clear that it fully supported the war effort and encouraged all African Americans to do the same. Indeed, emphasizing patriotism was central to the "Double V" campaign, as the black press wanted to both promote the loyalty of black Americans to the United States while exposing the contradictions of asking people to fight for the preservation of freedom abroad when it was denied to them at home. The black press also regularly celebrated the achievements of African Americans in the service, which were almost universally overlooked by the mainstream white media.

Despite its unflappable support for the war effort, the "Double V" campaign disturbed members of the federal government, who believed it might undermine support for the war among African Americans. The U.S. military banned the *Pittsburgh Courier* and other black newspapers from base libraries, and even confiscated the papers from some newsboys. Most notably, Federal Bureau of Investigation director J. Edgar Hoover sought to indict black publishers for treason because of their support of the "Double V" campaign; his efforts were foiled, however, by the attorney general's office, which refused to pursue the indictments.

The *Courier* officially abandoned its "Double V" campaign in 1943, as photos and telegrams supporting the campaign began to dwindle, but the paper, along with most of the black press, continued to pursue the ideals of victory against fascism abroad and victory against racism at home throughout the war years. Despite its relatively short run, the impact of the "Double V" campaign in raising black consciousness to the contradictions of being asked to sacrifice for a nation in the name of freedom and democracy while being denied those benefits themselves was incalculable, and helped contribute to the resolve of African Americans to agitate for change in the postwar era.

Thomas J. Ward, Jr.

See also: Roosevelt, Franklin D.; World War II.

Further Reading

Buni, Andrew. *Robert L. Vann of the Pittsburgh Courier: Politics and Black Journalism.* Pittsburgh, PA: University of Pittsburgh Press, 1974.

Eagles, Charles W. "Two Double V's: Jonathan Daniels, FDR, and Race Relations during World War II." *North Carolina Historical Review* 59, no. 3 (1982): 252–70.

Washburn, Patrick S. "The Pittsburgh Courier's Double V Campaign in 1942." *American Journalism* 3, no. 2 (1986): 73–86.

Washburn, Patrick S. *A Question of Sedition: The Federal Government's Investigation of the Black Press during World War II.* New York: Oxford University Press, 1986.

E

East St. Louis Riot of 1917

The brutal violence of the East St. Louis, Illinois, Riot of 1917 was the result of rising tensions between white and black residents. White citizens resented black workers who took jobs as strikebreakers and squeezed the already-tight housing supply, while African Americans were dissatisfied with their unequal access to housing, health care, and jobs, as well as exorbitant rents. Tensions erupted into indiscriminate violence on July 2, 1917, in which at least 39 blacks and 9 whites died and many more were injured or had to flee the city.

Large numbers of African Americans from the South moved north as part of the Great Migration in the early twentieth century. With many men leaving their jobs to serve in the military during World War I, Northern cities offered an abundance of jobs, especially in the industrial sector. Blacks hoped to escape Southern segregation and find new economic opportunities outside of exploitative sharecropping arrangements. By 1917, the African American population of East St. Louis, a city of approximately 70,000 people, had exceeded 10,000. Upon arrival in East St. Louis, however, African Americans found continuing segregation at work. White residents resented black workers, who were willing to take jobs that were vacated by striking whites and often worked for lower wages. Additionally, the city's housing shortage placed black and white residents in close quarters, and whites believed that the vast majority of African Americans owned guns and would use them against their white neighbors.

Throughout the spring of 1917, groups of white people attacked African Americans for various reasons. White citizens feared a race war, rumored to begin on July 4, and vowed to fight. A preliminary attack, spurred by stories of a black man shooting a white man, occurred on May 28 following a public union meeting. White rioters beat several black people and demanded that African Americans not be allowed to carry weapons. When black citizens appealed to Mayor Fred Mollman for assistance, he resisted taking action because he feared losing white supporters.

On July 2, 1917, six blocks of Walnut Street, primarily an African American neighborhood, were burned to the ground during the east St. Louis Riot. (Bettmann/Corbis)

Violence quickly became a daily occurrence. When a carload of whites repeatedly fired at black homes on July 1, black residents eventually fired back and unwittingly shot two police officers in an unmarked police car. Whites interpreted this accident as evidence of black warfare. Following a meeting at the Labor Temple on the morning of July 2, white laborers and other residents armed themselves for violence. The group began shooting black people on the street, pulled victims off streetcars, and beat pedestrians. While white men perpetrated much of the violence, women and children often joined the abuse of injured African Americans.

The mobs spread throughout the city and conducted several lynchings and attempted lynchings. Rioters frequently attacked anyone who tried to interfere or assist victims, including ambulance drivers and sympathetic bystanders. Fire destroyed more than 200 homes, and crowds waited to beat escaping black residents. The National Guard was not available due to its being in federal service for World War I, and the state had raised several new regiments for state emergencies, but home guardsmen from the one regiment mobilized in response to the riot did not deal effectively with the rioters and at times even joined the violence. While white rioters inflicted injuries on African Americans, other white people took black people into their homes to hide until the violence had passed. The True Light Baptist Church rang its bell as a warning for African Americans. As many as

7,000 black people fled the city, and many did not return. While the official death count was 39 blacks and 9 whites, the *Chicago Defender* claimed that between 100 and 200 blacks died.

Following the riot, the state took only small steps to deal with the riot politically and legally. Twelve black people were convicted of murdering the two police officers. Nine whites served time in the penitentiary for homicide, while the courts found 41 whites guilty of misdemeanors, 27 white people paid fines, and 14 served short terms in the county jail. East St. Louis business leaders called for federal intervention to prevent future violence, but President Woodrow Wilson chose not to get involved. In November 1917, a congressional committee held hearings but did not hand down any indictments. The committee condemned the social situation and political corruption in East St. Louis. The 1917 riot had a lasting impact on the city, as fear of future violence hindered population growth, business prospects, educational integration, and other social relations.

Shannon Smith Bennett

See also: World War I.

Further Reading

Asher, Robert. "Documents of the Race Riot at East St. Louis." *Journal of the Illinois State Historical Society* 65 (1972): 327–36.

Rudwick, Elliot M. *Race Riot at East St. Louis, July 2, 1917.* Carbondale: Southern Illinois University Press, 1964.

Sherfy, Michael. "Race Riot at East St. Louis—1917." East St. Louis Action Research Project's Social History Project Web site http://www.eslarp.uiuc.edu/ibex/archive/nunes/esl%20history/race_riot.htm (accessed July 2007).

Eugenics

Eugenics is a philosophy that advocates improving the human race through selective breeding and related strategies. During the Jim Crow era, eugenicists successfully advocated sterilizing individuals thought to be unfit to reproduce. Eugenicists also opposed immigration into the United States by "inferior" races.

Scientific Racism

During the pre–Civil War era, American scientists developed a body of research that has since been labeled "scientific racism." This was an attempt to classify racial categories and to discern the essential differences between the various categories.

These scholars linked race with a host of other characteristics that they thought were inherited, including many cultural and psychological characteristics as well as physiological characteristics. Scientific racism ranked the various races into a hierarchy. People of northern European descent were ranked as superior on all dimensions. People of African descent were ranked at the bottom of the hierarchy. Thus, a pseudoscientific discourse emerged to justify preexisting racial ideologies.

Social Darwinism and the First Eugenicists

The social philosophical world that spawned scientific racism also included "social Darwinism," which extended Darwin's theory of evolution into the social realm. Darwin had theorized that competition between organisms is the basis of biological evolution. Social Darwinism is a conflict theory of society, which seeks to explain social change. It perceives social outcomes as the consequence of competition between individual humans, or between groups of humans.

Social Darwinism formed a basis for the development of eugenics in the 1860s by Darwin's cousin, Francis Galton. From Darwin's observations on the heritability of physical traits, Galton theorized that mental ability was similarly inheritable. Galton viewed humanitarian institutions serving the poor and disabled as enabling the less fit members of society to reproduce more readily. Galton observed that this could lead to a gradual degradation of humanity. While Galton himself did not approve of governmental interference in human reproduction, Galton's followers, the developers of eugenics, argued that human breeding should be engineered to encourage reproduction by the more fit members of society and to discourage reproduction by the less fit members.

Eugenics as Scientific Justification for Anti-Immigration Laws

The concerns about Americans mixing with "inferior stock" were not limited to intermarriages between whites and non-European minorities. Eugenicists also distinguished between Anglo-Saxon and Nordic Europeans on one hand, and eastern and southern Europeans on the other hand. Eugenicists believed the eastern and southern Europeans were racially distinct and inferior from the northerners. In 1924, after hearing testimony from leading eugenicists, Congress passed an act that increased restrictions on immigration from eastern and southern Europe. Congress also banned most immigration from Japan and China based on racial concerns.

Eugenics as Scientific Justification for Antimiscegenation Laws

Eugenics derived from scientific racism and provided a pseudoscientific justification for Jim Crow and related legislation. Eugenicists fretted about the harmful effects that mixed marriages, known as "race mixing" or "miscegenation," would cause to population health. They were especially concerned about the future of the white race if it became diluted with "inferior stock." Eugenicists offered such arguments to justify antimiscegenation laws that forbade marriages between whites and nonwhites.

Many scholars have argued that during the Jim Crow era, American society was organized in a caste system. A person's caste status depended on the racial category into which he or she was born. All caste societies have mechanisms for maintaining the boundaries between castes. These boundaries are reinforced by sanctions that prohibit intermarriage between castes, and that prohibit members of different castes from interacting as equals. The ideology of eugenics became part of the foundation of the Jim Crow caste system during Jim Crow's later period, by providing a pseudoscientific basis for the notorious antimiscegenation laws, which prohibited marriages between people of different races, in order to maintain white racial purity. This obsession with the purity of bloodlines derived from eugenics.

The most notorious example of antimiscegenation law was Virginia's Racial Integrity Act of 1924. This law required the Virginia Bureau of Vital Statistics to record a racial description of every newborn baby. It also outlawed marriages between "white persons" and "non-white" partners. The state legislature enacted this statute on the same day it passed the Sterilization Act, which permitted the state to sterilize institutionalized individuals deemed to be incompetent—an explicitly eugenicist policy. The same activists and legislators were behind the movement to pass both laws. Virginia's notorious Sterilization Act was upheld by the U.S. Supreme Court in *Buck v. Bell* (1927). These two laws were derived from the eugenicist Harry Laughlin's model language for such statues (1922). Laughlin testified on behalf of Virginia in *Buck v. Bell,* and also supported the Racial Integrity Act. Thus, while the main thrust of the eugenicists was to sterilize those defined as unfit, antimiscegenation was also a subsidiary goal of the movement. The U.S. Supreme Court overturned the antimiscegenation component of Virginia's Racial Integrity Act in 1967 in *Loving v. Virginia.* In 1975, Virginia's General Assembly repealed the entire Racial Integrity Act. In 1979, it repealed the Sterilization Act.

Among the American eugenicists most obsessed with race were Arthur Estabrook and his coauthor Ivan McDougle. Estabrook traveled to Virginia to assist the state with research in support of its Sterilization Act, which was contested in *Buck v. Bell.* While in Virginia, Estabrook and McDougle also conducted extensive research on a mixed-race population near Lynchburg. In 1926, Estabrook and McDougle published their study of these people in *Mongrel Virginians: The Win Tribe.* "Win" was an anagram for white-Indian-negro, referring to the hypothesized racial mixture in this population. Estabrook and McDougle detailed all of the negative traits they had observed among these people, attributing their failings to their "mongrel" heritage. For Estabrook and McDougle, this was a case study that legitimated the eugenicists' warnings about race-mixing. Meanwhile, Estabrook and McDougle discounted the intense poverty and racial oppression that their subjects suffered under Jim Crow.

Thomas Brown

See also: Jim Crow.

Further Reading

Buck v. Bell. 274 U.S. 200 (1927).

Estabrook, Arthur H., and Ivan E. McDougle. *Mongrel Virginians: The Win Tribe.* Washington, DC: Carnegie Institution of Washington, 1926.

Laughlin, Harry. *Eugenical Sterilization in the United States.* Chicago: Psychopathic Laboratory of the Municipal Court of Chicago, 1922.

Loving v. Virginia. 388 U.S. 1 (1967).

Osborn, Frederick. "Development of a Eugenic Philosophy." *American Sociological Review* 2, no. 3 (June 1937): 389–97.

Virginia Legislature. *Racial Integrity Act.* SB219 (March 20, 1924).

Evers, Medgar

Medgar Wiley Evers was the first National Association for the Advancement of Colored People (NAACP) field secretary in Mississippi. During the 1950s and early 1960s, Evers was one of the key activists in Mississippi, and was involved in many high-profile challenges to racial subjugation.

Born in Decatur, Mississippi, on July 2, 1925, Evers's early life was shaped by Jim Crow, and these experiences informed his later outlook and activities. The Evers family had a long history of standing up to racial oppression. Evers was named for his maternal great-grandfather, a half-Indian slave who had a reputation for being uncooperative with masters, while his maternal grandfather, the son of a white man, had reputedly shot two white men. Evers's father James instilled both racial and personal pride into Medgar and his older brother, Charles, who himself would become a civil rights activist in Mississippi. James Evers was a public worker and so less susceptible to the seasonal fluctuations of agricultural employment; he owned his own land and built the family home himself, and was therefore not at risk of eviction, as were so many black Mississippians who were tenants of whites. Throughout his childhood, Medgar witnessed his father's refusal to accede to many

Jim Crow customs: he refused to step off sidewalks to allow whites to pass and, on one particular occasion, defended himself with a broken bottle against a white storekeeper who had tried to overcharge him. Several white men witnessed this incident, but no repercussions were directed at the Evers family.

Despite his father's defiance, Medgar was nonetheless exposed to the realities of Jim Crow in Mississippi. Friendships with several white children were abruptly severed as Medgar grew older, and while the Evers brothers had to walk to school, white children travelled by bus. In 1934, Medgar and his brother sneaked into a political rally given by Governor Theodore Bilbo, who singled them out and warned the crowd that unless Jim Crow remained in place, such children

Medgar Evers, Mississippi field secretary for the National Association for the Advancement of Colored People, was shot outside his home after returning from an integration rally on June 12, 1963. (AP Photo)

would grow into adults who demanded the vote. From an early age, Evers developed an attitude to the racial norms of Mississippi that would shape the rest of his life. As children, he and Charles would fantasize about moving to South America, where they would buy land and refuse access to whites, while Medgar's response to the lack of respect shown to local blacks by white traveling salesmen was to let the air out of their car tires.

At the same time as indulging in such childish revenge fantasies, Evers developed an anger at black Mississippians' impotence in the face of Jim Crow. When a local black man was lynched and his clothes left as a reminder to the rest of the community, Evers struggled to understand how such atrocities could occur with no attempt by the black community to intervene or have the perpetrators brought to justice. Evers grew frustrated with black people who accepted the tenets of Jim Crow without challenge, in a way that his father never had. This frustration would stay with him as an adult.

In 1944, Medgar dropped out of the 11th grade to enlist in the army. He was posted to the 325th Port Company, where he served in England and France. As was true for many black Southerners who served in the armed forces, this was Evers's first visit out of his home state, and the contrast with Mississippi was stark. Although his unit was commanded by white officers, Evers found that the entrenched racial attitudes of Mississippi were absent, and his potential was recognized by at least one white lieutenant, who encouraged him to attend college when he returned home. The difference in racial attitudes was particularly noticeable when off duty, and in France, Evers befriended a white family and even dated their daughter. When he returned to Mississippi, however, Evers knew that he could not risk even writing to her, for fear that local whites would find out.

Spurred by their experiences in Europe, Medgar and a group of other black veterans, including his brother Charles, registered to vote, becoming the only blacks on the voters' roll in Decatur. As polling day approached, the Evers family home received both white and black visitors who urged Medgar and Charles not to vote for fear of reprisals. The Evers brothers took these warnings so seriously that on the night before the election, they armed themselves and waited for an expected attack, a familiar Mississippi tactic to dissuade blacks from voting. No attack came, but when the Evers attempted to vote, they were turned away from the polling station by a group of armed white men.

In 1946, Evers enrolled at Alcorn Agricultural and Mechanical College, the oldest state college for blacks in Mississippi. He featured strongly in campus life and participated in a wide range of extracurricular activities. He was a member of the debating team, the campus YMCA, the college choir, and the track and football teams, as well as president of the junior class, editor of the 1951 yearbook, and editor of the college newspaper for two years. In his senior year, he achieved honor-roll grades. Evers's achievements saw him listed in the nationally published *Who's Who among Students in American Colleges and Universities*. At Alcorn, Evers met his future wife Myrlie Beasley, whom he married on Christmas Eve 1951.

While at college, Evers's racial attitude continued to harden, and he became increasingly antagonistic toward white people. Nonetheless, despite having spent time in Chicago in 1951, and in spite of his wife's desire to move away from Mississippi, Evers came to see what the state could be like without Jim Crow and became determined to stay and challenge racial subjugation. Evers's commitment to this ideal grew stronger when he and Myrlie moved to the all-black town of Mound Bayou, where he took a job with the Magnolia Life Insurance Company, operated by T. R. M. Howard, a wealthy black doctor and activist who had helped found the Regional Council of Negro Leadership. Evers's job exposed him for the first time to the entrenched poverty of black communities in the Mississippi Delta, and he soon joined the local NAACP branch, joining a statewide network of activists.

Embers of Evers's earlier radicalism still glowed and, inspired by Jomo Kenyatta's Mau Mau rebels in Kenya, he and his brother toyed with the idea of an armed black uprising in Mississippi. Evers ultimately dismissed this notion and instead became more deeply involved with the NAACP. In 1954, he volunteered as a test case to integrate the University of Mississippi and applied to its law school. The NAACP's Thurgood Marshall represented his case. After nine months, Evers's application was rejected on a technicality. This had brought him to the attention of the NAACP's national office, and in December 1954, he took up a post as the NAACP's first field secretary in Mississippi. His wife, Myrlie, acted as his secretary: in the office, Medgar insisted they refer to each other as "Mr." and "Mrs."

Evers's appointment coincided with the rise of massive white resistance to the *Brown v. Board of Education* (1954) ruling, and over the next few years, intimidation and violence disrupted the network of black activism that had developed in Mississippi. Undaunted, Evers travelled tirelessly throughout Mississippi, organizing NAACP chapters, collecting affidavits from blacks who had been intimidated by the White Citizens Council, urging people to sign petitions supporting school integration, and encouraging witnesses of crimes like the murder of George Lee in Belzoni to testify. Evers was involved in many high-profile incidents in Mississippi. During the trial of the alleged killers of Emmett Till, Evers scoured the delta looking for witnesses, and ferried reporters around so that they could see for themselves the reality of Jim Crow Mississippi.

By the early 1960s, Evers had become one of the most well-known civil rights activists in Mississippi, to both blacks and whites. This made him vulnerable to segregationists: his Mississippi State Sovereignty Commission file grew increasingly thick, and he was beaten while attending the trial of nine students who had tried to integrate a public library. However, his profile also gave him influence, and the Justice Department investigated the beating, signaling an increased federal interest in Mississippi. Evers's profile meant that he was involved in a wide range of civil rights episodes in the state, including James Meredith's attempt to integrate the University of Mississippi and a sustained boycott of downtown Jackson in 1962 and 1963. The boycott made him an even more visible target, and after his house was firebombed, he became increasingly concerned about his family's security. Despite initial wariness, Evers also tried to create links with other civil rights organizations like the Southern Christian Leadership Conference and Student Nonviolent Coordinating Committee during this period, often without the knowledge or approval of the NAACP's national office.

On June 11, 1963, the same evening that President John F. Kennedy gave a televised address in which he announced his attention to bring forward civil rights legislation, Evers was shot dead outside his home by Byron De La Beckwith, a White Citizens' Council member well known for his hatred of black people. He was shot while carrying T-shirts bearing the slogan "Jim Crow Must Go." Over 5,000 people attended Evers's funeral, and he was buried in Arlington National Cemetery. His brother Charles replaced him as NAACP field secretary. Beckwith was tried, although this twice resulted in hung juries and he was freed. In 1990, he was rearrested, and in February 1994, was found guilty of murdering Evers and sentenced to life imprisonment.

Simon T. Cuthbert-Kerr

See also: Mississippi.

Further Reading

Dittmer, John. *Local People: The Struggle for Civil Rights in Mississippi.* Urbana: University of Illinois Press, 1995.

Payne, Charles M. *I've Got the Light of Freedom: The Organizing Tradition and the Mississippi Freedom Struggle.* Berkeley: University of California Press, 1995.

Vollers, Maryanne. *Ghosts of Mississippi: The Murder of Medgar Evers, the Trials of Byron De La Beckwith, and the Haunting of the New South.* Boston: Little, Brown and Company, 1995.

Executive Order 9981

Beginning with the founding of the nation, the role of African Americans serving in their county's military has been hotly debated. At the opening of the American War for Independence, as some Northern colonies began enlisting free blacks into the ranks of their regiments, George Washington declared that no blacks, free or slave, would be permitted to serve in the Continental Army. However, when the Loyalist Virginia governor Lord Dunmore began enticing slaves with the promise of freedom if they left their masters and joined his "Ethiopian Regiment," at a time when the rebels were having difficulty recruiting men, Washington, though a slave owner, reconsidered his earlier prohibition on black troops, and, on January 17, 1776, the Continental Congress approved the enlistment of black troops into Washington's army. Over 5,000 black men fought for the American cause during the War for Independence, and they fought shoulder to shoulder with white soldiers; there was no segregation in the Continental Army.

Black sailors and soldiers also fought for the United States against the British in the War of 1812. Some, like the New Orleans Free Black Militia who served with distinction under General Andrew Jackson, fought in all-black units, but the policy of segregating troops by race was not official. Indeed, the U.S. Navy, whose force was one-sixth African American during the War of 1812, found it almost impossible to segregate sailors on board ship. The aftermath of the War of 1812 saw a dramatic change in the U.S. government's policy regarding blacks in the military. In 1820, reacting in part to the fear of slave rebellion, the U.S. government announced that "No Negro or mulatto will be received as a recruit of the Army." As a result of the ban on black recruits, the 1846–1848 Mexican-American War was the only major U.S. conflict in which no black soldiers participated, although some African Americans served in the navy during the war.

The policy of not accepting African Americans into the armed forces was still in place when the Civil War erupted in 1861. As George Washington had initially done in 1775, in 1861, Abraham Lincoln declared that the war would be a "white man's fight," and that no blacks, free or slave, would be accepted into the Union forces. Pressure from black leaders, most notably Frederick Douglass, combined with mounting losses, convinced Lincoln to accept black troops in 1862. Almost 180,000 African Americans served in the Union armed forces during the Civil War, in segregated units, as it was during the Civil War that the policy of creating separate units for black troops was made official policy. It was the creation of a Jim Crow army that would last until the 1950s.

Following the Civil War, black troops were organized into four units: the 9th and 10th Cavalry, and the 24th and 25th Infantry Regiments. Although often relegated to labor battalions, black troops fought with distinction in the West, in Cuba, in the Philippines, and in the world wars in their segregated units. During World War II—a war fought against Nazi racism—the black press, led by the *Pittsburgh Courier* launched the Double V campaign: victory against racism and fascism abroad, and victory against segregation and discrimination at home. The National Association for the Advancement of Colored People (NAACP) also continued its campaign, begun during World War I, demanding the end to segregation in the armed forces, while black leaders repeatedly pointed out the inconsistencies of black troops fighting for freedom and democracy in a Jim Crow army.

Military leadership resisted desegregation, asserting that the army was not designed to be a social laboratory, and that the military would integrate when the rest of American society did. In 1946, the army reviewed its policy toward black soldiers in what became known as the Gillem Board. This committee acknowledged that the army had failed to make the best use of its black manpower during World War II, and recommended that African Americans should comprise 10 percent of the postwar army (the policy actually included creating new all-black units, thereby increasing segregation), that blacks be given equal opportunity for advancement, and that the use of some base facilities (like recreation centers) be integrated. The board did not, however, challenge the army's traditional policy of segregating troops.

Black leaders such as the NAACP's Roy Wilkins were outraged by the recommendation of the Gillem Board, as it did not take any meaningful steps to end segregation in the army. Led by A. Phillip Randolph, the labor leader whose 1941 March on Washington Movement had pressured President Franklin D. Roosevelt into signing Executive Order 8802, which created the Fair Employment Practices Commission, black leaders began demanding the end of the Jim Crow army. In November 1947, Randolph helped found the Committee against Jim Crow in Military Service and Training to push for the desegregation of the military. Black leaders were encouraged when President Harry S. Truman issued his civil rights message to Congress in February 1948, which, among other things, called for the secretary of defense to end discrimination in the military as soon as possible. But both military leaders and Southern congressmen balked at the message, and it seemed that no progress on desegregation would come without pressure from black America.

Truman's call in March 1948 for the first peacetime draft in U.S. history provided Randolph with the opportunity he was looking for. Stating that "Prison is better than Army Jim Crow," Randolph pledged to lead black youths in a boycott of any universal military training program if the army was not fully desegregated. He kept the issue in the headlines by leading peaceful protests in major cities throughout the summer of 1948, urging young black men to refuse to register for the draft. While this tactic was not endorsed by all black leaders, some of whom thought that Randolph's threat would make black America look unpatriotic and therefore perhaps even harm the drive for civil rights, the president took Randolph seriously, especially as 1948 was an election year. On July 26, Truman issued Executive Order 9981, which stated that "there shall be equality of treatment and opportunity for all persons in the armed services without regard to race, color, religion or national origin," and that "This policy shall be put into effect as rapidly as possible."

While some black leaders, including Randolph, criticized the executive order as weak in not openly ordering the immediate desegregation of the military, it did signal a drastic change by the U.S. government toward supporting integration instead of segregation. Resistance from both Congress and the military persisted, however. Both generals Eisenhower and Omar Bradley publicly criticized the president's order, going as far to say that it compromised national defense. Southern politicians also led the charge against desegregation, culminating in the Dixiecrat revolt at the 1948 Democratic National Convention. Most insidious were military officers who quietly and simply ignored the order, allowing the racial status quo to continue.

After initial resistance, both the navy and air force implemented desegregation rather quickly and easily in 1949. The army, much larger and more deeply entrenched in its traditions than the other two branches, proved to be much more intransigent. By 1950, army leaders still had made no plans for desegregating the units; instead, they had made only token changes regarding increased training and promotional opportunities for blacks. It took war in Korea to finally bring about the integration of the army. When the United States entered the Korean conflict in June 1950, the army was still rigidly segregated. Indeed, some of the first U.S. troops to reach the Korean Peninsula in the summer of 1950 were the all-black units of the 24th Infantry. While some army commanders attempted to maintain the segregated army, the demands of the war made continuing segregation both impractical and inefficient. Moreover, a number of officers came to believe that the all-black units were inferior to those of whites, and should therefore be eliminated and the white units integrated. While black soldiers condemned this assessment, during the Korean War, the all-black units were phased out as black troops were absorbed by the white units. By the end of the war in 1953, the integration of the U.S. military had finally come about, but the historic all-black units were a casualty of the process.

Thomas J. Ward, Jr.

See also: Armed Forces; Truman, Harry S.

Further Reading

Buckley, Gail. *American Patriots: The Story of Blacks in the Military from the Revolution to Desert Storm.* New York: Random House, 2001.

Dalfiume, Richard M. *Desegregation of the U.S. Armed Forces: Fighting on Two Fronts, 1939.* Columbia: University of Missouri Press, 1969.

Edgerton, Robert B. *Hidden Heroism: Black Soldiers in America's Wars.* Boulder, CO: Westview Press, 2001.

F

Fair Employment Practices Commission (FEPC)

The Fair Employment Practices Commission (FEPC) was a World War II–era federal agency created by President Franklin D. Roosevelt to counter a threat of a March on Washington by African Americans opposed to discrimination in the military and in defense industries. It was subsequently replaced by a Committee on Fair Employment Practice (CFEP), which had broader powers than the FEPC.

The FEPC was established by Executive Order 8802, which prohibited discrimination in the defense industry and established the agency to monitor hiring practices. The agency's mandate was to bar discrimination in employment based on race, creed, color, national origin, ancestry, and against aliens by any company holding a government contract or subcontract.

The origins of the agency can be traced to a September 1940 meeting between A. Philip Randolph, the president of the Brotherhood of Sleeping Car Porters, and Roosevelt. Randolph urged the president to promote equal employment opportunities and to desegregate the armed services. When the meeting did not produce a positive response from Roosevelt, Randolph decided that he would bring the case directly to the American people by staging a march on Washington, D.C.

Randolph spent months gathering support for his plan and preparing for the march. Concerned about the political impact of the march, Roosevelt met with Randolph two weeks before the scheduled date of the march to urge him to call it off. Randolph's response to the president was that the march would be called off only if Roosevelt issued an executive order. On June 25, 1941, Roosevelt issued Executive Order 8802, which made discrimination based on race, creed, color, or national origin illegal in the defense industry. In response, Randolph agreed to suspend the march.

The role of the FEPC was "to receive and investigate complaints of discrimination . . . take appropriate steps to redress grievances which it finds to be valid," and to make recommendations to other federal agencies for the purpose of carrying out Executive Order 8802. While this was the first presidential action ever taken to prohibit employment discrimination by government contractors, the agency lacked enforcement authority. The FEPC was established in the Office of Production Management (OPM) and was to consist of a chair and four members appointed by the president. The FEPC was the first government agency in which blacks were all line officers. Prior to this time, blacks were only racial advisors with no line authority.

In January 1942, when OPM was abolished, the FEPC was transferred to the War Production Board (WPB) by Executive Order 9040, and in July, the agency was transferred to the War Manpower Commission (WMC) by a presidential letter to Paul V. McNutt, the chair of the WMC.

The agency was strengthened by Executive Order 9346, issued on May 27, 1943. This new order established a CFEP, replacing the FEPC, and placed it under the Office of Emergency Management (OEM). The order broadened the jurisdiction of this agency to include federal government establishments, employers holding government contracts with antidiscrimination clauses, other employers who were engaged in production-related activities or the utilization of war materials, and labor organizations whose activities affected those employers. Executive Order 9346 also required all government contracts to include a nondiscrimination clause. The committee consisted of a chairman and not more than six other members appointed by the president.

The agency decentralized its operations, establishing 13 regional offices between July and November 1943. A 14th regional office was opened in Los Angeles, California, in February 1945. One of the major problems encountered by both the FEPC and the CFEP were widespread work stoppages by white workers who refused to work beside blacks. The agency also found that employers resisted training African American workers or hiring African American women. While being effective in the North, the agency did not attempt to challenge the practice of segregation in the South.

The CFEP's *Final Report* noted that:

The Committee's wartime experience shows that in the majority of cases discriminatory practices by employers and unions can be reduced or eliminated by simple negotiations when the work of the negotiator is backed up by firm and explicit National policy.

FEPC's unsolved cases show that the Executive authority is not enough to insure compliance in the face of stubborn opposition. Only legislative authority will insure compliance in the small number of cases in which employers or unions or both refuse after negotiation to abide by the National policy of nondiscrimination.

After Roosevelt's death, Congress, in July 1945, abolished the agency through the National War Agencies Appropriations Act of 1946 (59 Stat. 473) by not providing funding for its continued operation. While President Harry S. Truman and some members of Congress sought to reestablish the agency, Republicans and Southern Democrats blocked their efforts in Congress. While five states (New York, New Jersey, Massachusetts, Connecticut, and Washington) created agencies to combat employment discrimination, the federal government would not have another agency dealing with employment discrimination until the establishment of the Equal Employment Opportunity Commission (EEOC) in 1964.

Jeffrey Kraus

See also: March on Washington Movement; World War II.

Further Reading

Daniel, Cletus E. *Chicano Workers and the Politics of Fairness: The FEPC in the Southwest, 1941–1945.* Austin: University of Texas Press, 1991.

Garfinkel, Herbert. *When Negroes March: The March on Washington Movement in the Organizational Politics for FEPC.* Glencoe, IL: The Free Press, 1959.

Kersten, Michael K. *Race, Jobs, and the War: The FEPC in the Midwest, 1941–1946.* Urbana: University of Illinois Press, 2000.

Reed, Merl E. *Seedtime for the Modern Civil Rights Movement: The President's Committee on Fair Employment Practice, 1941–1946.* Baton Rouge: Louisiana State University Press, 1991.

Ruchames, Louis. *Race, Jobs and Politics: The Story of the FEPC.* New York: Columbia University Press, 1953.

Federal Bureau of Investigation (FBI)

In recent years, the release of government records under the Freedom of Information Act (1966) has enabled scholars to study the role of the Federal Bureau of Investigation (FBI) in American society. Declassified FBI files on black leaders and organizations help to put into focus questions of racism, segregation, disenfranchisement, and the role of the federal government in containing social movements. The Bureau, which was founded in 1908 as part of the Justice Department (and was simply known as the Bureau of Investigation until 1935), helped to uphold and perpetuate the system of racial segregation and inequality by undermining racial justice movements, monitoring both black and white critics of Jim Crow. The FBI aligned with city police to protect the color line and refused to prosecute white vigilante attacks against African Americans. In thousands of battles between freedom workers and Southern segregationists during the rise of the modern Civil Rights Movement, the FBI embraced the concept of states' rights and dismissed white violence as a local problem. For the FBI, racism was respectable and tacitly accepted, and it hired very few black agents to work its investigations.

As the nation's top law enforcement agency, the FBI's failure to protect black crime victims set a precedent that local police often followed. For example, the FBI refused to stop the extralegal practice of lynching before the 1960s. Even the liberal Democratic president Franklin D. Roosevelt refused to support antilynching efforts during the 1930s New Deal, in part because of opposition by FBI director J. Edgar Hoover. On the question of police brutality, the FBI refused to investigate Southern lawmen.

Hoover, who oversaw the government's surveillance of radical activities during the Progressive era and then served as FBI director from 1924 to 1972, continued to believe throughout his career that blacks were inferior and harbored a profound animus toward racial justice. He long equated civil rights activism with disloyalty to the nation and narrowly viewed most black resistance as Communist-inspired. He

The burned automobile of Andrew Goodman, James Earl Chaney, and Michael Schwerner, civil rights activists, discovered near Philadelphia, Mississippi on June 24, 1964. (AP Photo)

wanted African Americans to remain second-class citizens and subjected many of their leaders and organizations to extralegal "dirty tricks," including false prosecutions as well as the full array of surveillance techniques: the use of undercover informers, bugs, taps, mail openings, and burglaries. FBI informants in white groups (e.g., the Ku Klux Klan) were permitted to engage in acts of racist violence.

The FBI's monitoring of critics of Jim Crow included many of the leading black figures of the time. FBI surveillance files on A. Philip Randolph, Marcus Garvey, W.E.B. Du Bois, James Weldon Johnson, Jack Johnson, Paul Robeson, Thurgood Marshall, Adam Clayton Powell Jr., Bayard Rustin, Hosea Hudson, Malcolm X, James Baldwin, Mary McLeod Bethune, Fannie Lou Hamer, Ella Baker, Jesse Jackson, Elijah Muhammad, and Martin Luther King Jr. have been released to the public. While the government viewed these leaders as a threat, they on the other hand believed that the FBI stood against them by protecting white Southern rule.

During the First Red Scare (1917–1920), the Bureau created the category of "subversive" to include "Negro Activities" and "the negro agitation movement." When black leaders urged "self-defense," such as fighting back against white rioters, the government labeled it "negro subversion," a radicalism it sought to monitor and suppress. Investigations focused on Randolph and the *Messenger;* Garvey and the United; the African Blood Brotherhood; and black Communists. The Bureau also investigated institutions critical of Jim Crow, especially the black-owned press. The FBI monitored the *Chicago Defender, Negro World,* the *Crusader,* and *Crisis* magazine. Agents interviewed editors, conducted secret surveillance of some journalists, filed regular reports on the content of articles, and added subscriber lists to their intelligence files. By the early 1920s, Hoover remained convinced that the press incited "the negro elements of the country to riot and to the committing of outrages of all sorts."

During the interwar years, the FBI investigated such groups as the National Association for the Advancement of Colored People (NAACP), the National Negro Congress, and the American Negro Labor Conference (ANLC). The ANLC met in October 1925 with the specific goal of ending Jim Crow unions in the American Federation of Labor (AFL) since the exclusion of blacks, with only a few exceptions, posed a major obstacle to black economic advancement. The FBI file runs 87 pages, focusing on the six-day event with complete coverage, including founding documents and lists of delegates and leaders. The FBI field office described the enquiry as part of its surveillance of "Radical Negro Communist Activity." Black Communists in America were perceived as doubly dangerous, as outsiders who demanded justice along both race and class lines. At the height of its popularity during the 1930s and 1940s, scholars estimate that the U.S. Communist Party enrolled about 4,000 African American members.

In 1935, the National Negro Congress was formed with A. Philip Randolph as president. The Communist connections of some of its leaders and its effort to unite black labor organizations prompted FBI surveillance from the 1930s to the 1950s. The FBI's NAACP file covers the years from 1923 to 1957, with intelligence information on each branch of the organization and with attention to the political beliefs and affiliations of members and leaders. The surveillance included wiretaps on office phones, as well as the use of dozens undercover informers and confidential sources. The FBI monitored the Congress of Racial Equality (CORE), which had an interracial membership, for its early work for desegregation. When James Farmer, a CORE founder, organized in Chicago what is probably the first series of civil rights sit-ins in 1943, the FBI opened an investigation looking for the Red Menace, unwilling to view black protest as a legitimate response to oppression. By linking the issue of Communist subversion to civil rights, Hoover hoped to discredit both.

During World War II, surveillance under the Negro Question included weekly reports on "Negro trends" and individuals and groups involved in civil rights activities. The Bureau intensively studied the role of "foreign-inspired agitation" under a program named RACON (Racial Conditions). The Bureau's RACON file totals about 77,000 pages, with reports from around the nation discussing black loyalty and charges of sympathy for the Axis powers. The FBI concluded that "a number of Negroes and Negro groups" have "acted or exhibited sentiments in a manner inimical to the Nation's war effort." Overall, 18 black Americans would be convicted of wartime sedition. The black press continued to pose a threat, according to the government. At a time when the black press enjoyed very high circulation, FBI investigations expanded to include the *Pittsburgh Courier, Baltimore Afro-American, Amsterdam News, People's Voice, Black Dispatch, Atlanta Daily World,* and *Michigan Chronicle.* Hoover claimed that black publications were too favorable toward the Japanese and to American Communists and other radicals.

White critics of Jim Crow, whose position against racial segregation often was part of a broader critique of American society, also faced "political policing." For example, First Lady Eleanor Roosevelt came to the attention of the Bureau chiefly because of her work for racial justice. On the Left, groups as diverse as the Industrial Workers of the World (IWW) and the Communist Party denounced Jim Crow and were targeted for being outspoken. The Bureau spied on Orson Welles, Frank Sinatra, and other white supporters of antilynching legislation as well as the liberal politicians Hubert H. Humphrey Jr. and Henry Wallace. The Bureau monitored the Fellowship of Reconciliation, a pacifist Quaker organization that advocated nonviolent direct action against racism.

During the 1950s and 1960s, the FBI kept a close watch on the Civil Rights Movement. The U.S. Supreme Court's landmark 1954 desegregation case,

Brown v. Board of Education, had little impact on Hoover's views of race relations. After the Montgomery of 1955, FBI officials once again expressed heightened concern about Communist influence in the movement, opening new investigations. During the 1961 Freedom Rides to integrate Southern transportation, the Bureau contributed to the violence by informing segregationist police of the riders' movements, and the FBI was held liable in two civil lawsuits for failing to protect the riders from violent attacks. The volume of political intelligence generated by FBI agents continued to grow. In 1963, Bureau leaders wrote more than 8,000 internal memos on racial matters for distribution to the Justice Department, military intelligence, and other government agencies. The FBI routinely conducted background name-checks on protestors looking for criminal records and radical associations.

At the same time that the FBI fought integration, they tried to preserve disenfranchisement. The Bureau opposed the voting rights campaigns of the early 1960s, sharing the view of white Southerners that granting suffrage would transform a way of life. Once again, the FBI stood on the sidelines when segregationists attacked activists from CORE and the Student Nonviolent Organizing Committee (SNCC), who were trying to register voters. The Bureau forwarded political intelligence on civil rights workers to local police departments, including plans for demonstrations, which helped the police to crack down on protestors.

Young civil rights workers especially came to distrust the federal government, upset at the collaboration with segregationists. The lack of a murder conviction in the June 12, 1963, slaying of Medgar Evers, the NAACP field representative in Mississippi, outraged the civil rights community. Moreover, when the FBI investigated the September 15, 1963, bombing of Birmingham's Sixteenth Street Baptist Church (the 21st bombing attack against blacks in the city during the prior eight years), it took 12 years to get an indictment against a Ku Klux Klan member. The FBI tried to cover up the role of FBI informers inside the Klan who helped plan the bombing. In Albany, Georgia, in 1963, the FBI helped prosecute nine civil rights activists who organized a citywide campaign of civil disobedience. Many activists wondered, as SNCC chairman John Lewis asked, "Which side is the federal government on?" Despite numerous black appeals for protection, federal law enforcement left Southern lawmen on their own to dispense Jim Crow justice.

For nearly a decade, the FBI orchestrated a campaign to smear and harass Martin Luther King Jr. King's FBI file totals more than 17,000 pages, and a separate FBI file on the Southern Christian Leadership Conference (SCLC), which King led, runs more than 13,000 pages. As King's popularity grew, so did the FBI interest to contain him and, hopefully, replace him with a more "moderate" black leader. After the March on Washington in August 1963, at which King gave his "I Have a Dream" speech, the FBI classified him "as the most dangerous Negro leader of the future in this nation from the standpoint of communism, the Negro and national security." The Bureau intensified its surveillance and warned in secret memos of the coming "social revolution." In October 1963, Attorney General Robert Kennedy approved the FBI's request to place listening devices on King's home phone and at SCLC headquarters. Without Kennedy's approval, the FBI also wiretapped King's hotel rooms while he was traveling. King and the SCLC realized they were being bugged, which further strengthened their resolve to change the society.

Hoover tried to discredit King by secretly leaking material from his FBI file to journalists and politicians. Hoover distributed throughout the government a monograph calling King an "unprincipled man" who "is knowingly, willingly, and regularly taking guidance from Communists." Hoover became obsessed with King's sexual life, looking for information to damage his reputation. Hoover's racist views toward King included the description, "King is a 'tom cat' with obsessive, degenerate sexual urges." The FBI sent tape recordings to Coretta Scott King to try to break up their marriage. The Bureau also spread rumors through the use of anonymous telephone calls and letters. Before King received the Nobel Peace Prize in 1964, Hoover publicly called him "the most notorious liar," and a counterintelligence operation urged him to commit suicide.

The FBI's role in what was termed "Mississippi Burning" remains a topic of debate. When CORE activists, aided by Northern white college students, registered black Mississippi voters during the summer of 1964, the Klan went on a rampage. The Klan's murder of Michael Schwerner, James Chaney, and Andrew Goodman brought national attention, and President Lyndon B. Johnson ordered the FBI to investigate. In this case, the FBI helped achieve select convictions, but the FBI's political policing toward civil rights "troublemakers" and "agitators" continued to expand, culminating in the establishment of the Black Nationalism section of COINTELPRO (Counter Intelligence Program) in 1967.

Critics suggest that by grouping surveillance under such categories as "racial matters," "racial conditions," or "black nationalist hate groups," the FBI designated African Americans as special objects of suspicion. Free-speech rights to criticize Jim Crow should not prompt government surveillance and counteractions. When the FBI established its first "White Hate" counterintelligence program in 1964, focusing on the Klan at the urging of the Johnson White House, the FBI's effort remained secret and did not result in increasing black legal protection.

The FBI considered itself a relatively autonomous entity in the government, without subject to outside oversight. Both Republican and Democratic presidents feared to challenge Hoover, who ran the agency as the "boss." Hoover grew up in segregated Washington, D.C., and never outgrew white supremacist attitudes. For nearly five decades, he directed the FBI to suppress racial justice movements, intent on preserving Jim Crow.

Ivan Greenberg

See also: Black Nationalism.

Further Reading

Garrow, David. *The FBI and Martin Luther King, Jr.: From "Solo" to Memphis.* New York: W. W. Norton, 1981.

Hill, Robert A., ed. *The FBI's RACON: Racial Conditions in the United States during World War II.* Boston: Northeastern University Press, 1995.

Kornweibel, Theodore, Jr. *"Seeing Red": Federal Campaigns against Black Militancy, 1917–1925.* Bloomington: Indiana University Press, 1998.

O'Reilly, Kenneth. *"Racial Matters": The FBI's Secret File on Black America, 1960–1972.* New York: The Free Press, 1989.

Theoharis, Athan G. *The FBI and American Democracy: A Brief Critical History.* Lawrence: University Press of Kansas, 2004.

Washburn, Patrick S. *A Question of Sedition: The Federal Government's Investigation of the Black Press during World War II.* New York: Oxford University Press, 1986.

Florida

Jim Crow in Florida followed trends in most other Southern states, yet unique demographic and historical shifts gave unusual aspects to Florida's form of segregation. At the time of the Civil War, Florida was in many ways a frontier state rather than a long-settled state. Most of the white slaveowning class were settled along a narrow band stretching from Jacksonville west along the state's borders with Georgia and Alabama, while much of the peninsula was thinly populated. Relatively large numbers of tribalized Native Americans occupied the Everglades. Although segregationists in Florida proved especially virulent in their support of Jim Crow, as the southern half of the peninsula became more populated with Northerners and Cubans, Jim Crow became increasingly difficult to support politically.

Florida was one of the last states still occupied by federal troops when Reconstruction ended in 1877. Florida had been one of the contested states, along with Louisiana and South Carolina, in the presidential election of 1876 that led to the Compromise of 1877, which removed federal troops from Florida. It also ended the brief period when blacks in Florida had anything resembling civil rights until the 1960s. Florida then became a pioneer in establishing Jim Crow, with laws requiring the segregation of blacks and whites on railroad cars in the late 1880s, before Louisiana's own law that led to the *Plessy v. Ferguson* U.S. Supreme Court decision that made "separate but equal" constitutional. Florida followed neighboring states Georgia and Alabama in using poll taxes as the primary method to disqualify most African Americans from voting without inviting challenges based on the Fifteenth Amendment.

In the first decades of the twentieth century, Jim Crow became firmly entrenched in Florida, to the point that not only were the schools segregated, but state law went so far as to require that schoolbooks used by black students and those used by white students be stored in separate facilities when not issued to students. White populations in Myakka City and other towns drove blacks out during the Great Retreat, when blacks were driven out of towns and areas around the country. In much of the South, such incidents were relatively rare, as blacks represented a sizable portion of the workforce. Its occurrence in Florida demonstrates the different path the state took on some racial issues.

Blacks did not simply acquiesce to these attacks on their rights and dignity. In 1904, Mary McLeod Bethune opened a school for black girls in Daytona Beach. Although McLeod and her handful of students originally had to raise their own funds for the school, it eventually found a backer in James Gamble of Procter & Gamble, who contributed to the school for the remainder of his life. But Daytona was then almost a frontier town, south of the main population belt of Florida, the "Old South" band across northern Florida, and such radical ideas stood a better chance of avoiding direct physical oppression.

On New Year's Day 1919, African Americans in Jacksonville began a statewide voter registration drive. Blacks hoped to increase black voters and perhaps revive the Republican Party in the state. By November 1920, in the wake of the passage of the Woman Suffrage Amendment, around 7,000 black women, plus 1,000 black men, had been registered in Jacksonville. Several thousand other blacks were registered across the state, although Jacksonville remained the center of the movement. In response, white supremacists and ardent Democrats used a variety of means to keep blacks away from the voting booths, from Ku Klux Klan violence to harassment by election officials. Often violence was not required, as officials simply threw away registrations of blacks, thereby preventing blacks from voting by denying that they had registered. A more open tactic was to simply declare that blacks were not allowed into "white" voting booths, although no booths were provided for blacks. The level of violence, and more importantly, charges from congressional Republicans that blacks were systematically prevented from voting in the 1920 presidential election based on their party affiliation, led to congressional hearings on the matter. However, Congress ignored much of the racial basis for the discrimination, and little progress came from the hearings. Republicans in Congress were simply not powerful or committed enough to challenge white Democratic control of the South.

The violence against blacks in Florida would reach truly horrific levels in the 1920s, with the most blatant example of what would by the late twentieth century be called "ethnic cleansing" occurring in the first week of 1923, in Rosewood, when an allegation of a robbery and rape of a white woman by a black man led first to the torture and lynching of a suspect. The murder did not quench but only fed the bloodlust of the mob, and eventually the town's black residents were either killed or driven out over several days of violence.

The 1920s were also a time when demographic forces began to challenge the domination of the state by the large landowning white Democrats from the state's northern tier. On the east coast from Daytona to Miami, the state experienced a land boom that brought in many new residents, mostly from the Northeast and especially from the New York City area. Tourism began its long challenge to agriculture as the state's dominant industry. While the boom eventually went bust, it did leave a permanent population of Northerners, particularly Jews, from the liberal wing of the Democratic Party. They might not challenge the Democratic Party's control of the state, but they would increasingly, especially after World War II, challenge who controlled the party in the state. In 1937, on the grounds that the poll tax disenfranchised more white citizens than black, Florida abandoned it as a method of keeping blacks from the polls. The fight between liberal and conservative Democrats for the control of the party in Florida would last until the 1980s, but while it remained under the control of the conservatives, the state would officially continue to back Jim Crow. Florida's Democratic leadership opposed President Harry S. Truman's tentative approach toward protecting civil rights for blacks, but eventually opted against leaving the party to form a new one.

Beginning in 1959, Florida began a profound demographic shift. After Fidel Castro, the leader of the Cuban Revolution and the new president of Cuba, announced that he was a Marxist, the United States began accepting thousands of Cuban exiles, most of whom settled in southern Florida. Technically, these people were not immigrants, but refugees from Communism, and their presence was of propaganda value for the American government. Although many were already middle class, the U.S. government gave them generous aid in settling into American society, and in a few years, most of them became citizens and voters. The overwhelmingly majority of them became Republicans, and Florida became one of the first states of the South to have a true two-party system since Reconstruction.

The collapse of Jim Crow in the 1950s and 1960s was not without violence and struggle in Florida. But the disjointed nature of the state, with its northern belt that more closely resembled the Deep South, its more cosmopolitan southeast coast, and its heavily Hispanic south, prevented the state from officially attempting to keep Jim Crow alive after 1965. Instead, most opposition to integration came from towns and private groups. Demographic shifts more than attitude shifts doomed Jim Crow in Florida.

Barry M. Stentiford

See also: Cold War.

Further Reading

Gannon, Michael. *The New History of Florida.* Gainesville: University Press of Florida, 1996.

Oesterreicher, Michel. *Pioneer Family: Life on Florida's Twentieth Century Frontier.* Tuscaloosa: University of Alabama Press, 2003.

Ortiz, Paul. *Emancipation Betrayed: The Hidden History of Black Organizing and White Violence in Florida from Reconstruction to the Bloody Election of 1920.* Berkeley: University of California Press, 2005.

G

Garvey, Marcus

Although Marcus Garvey made many contributions to the Black Nationalist Movement in America, his most noted legacy is his unrelenting support for the Back to Africa Movement. Marcus Mosiah Garvey Jr. was born on August 7, 1887, in St. Ann's Bay, Jamaica, to the mason/stonebreaker Marcus Mosiah Garvey Sr. and domestic worker Sarah Jane Richards. His family was of modest means, and Garvey always sought to improve the quality of life for the poor and working-class individuals who were often forgotten by mainstream society. His quest for change began at the age of 16, when he left the Methodist school where he was receiving his education to search for employment. After a series of odd jobs, he became a printer for P. A. Austin Benjamin in Kingston, Jamaica. It was here, during a printers' union strike, that his leadership skills and abilities were first displayed. As the vice president and the Kingston Union and strike leader, he refused to accept financial offers to desert his fellow strikers. Although many of strikers eventually returned to their jobs, Garvey refused to back down on his beliefs. His rebellious protest left him blacklisted by private printers. He later took a job with a government printing office, and in 1907, he produced one of his first periodicals, *Garvey's Watchman.* While the series lasted for only three publications, it showed Garvey's commitment to addressing the economic exploitation of the poor masses and his desire to improve the plight of black workers.

After the collapse of *Garvey's Watchman,* Garvey joined a political group called the National Club and released a second publication, *The Struggling Mass.* Several political activists and scholars, including Robert Love and J. Coleman Beecher, noted Garvey's commitment to improving the plight of the underprivileged and addressing racial discrimination. They encouraged him to continue pursuing his dreams. In 1910, Garvey left Jamaica and traveled to Central America with the hopes of gaining more experience and financial support for his works.

Marcus Garvey, from Jamaica, launched the first mass movement of African Americans based on racial pride, self-help, and separatism. (Library of Congress)

Garvey's travel led him through many Latin American countries, including Costa Rica, Panama, Nicaragua, Honduras, Bocas-del-Toro, Ecuador, Chile, and Peru. In each of the countries, he was shocked and outraged at the treatment of poor black Jamaican migrants who had left their poverty-stricken island in search of employment. In 1911, he returned home to Jamaica and began to protest the harsh treatment of blacks, demanding that the British rulers commit themselves to protecting overseas Jamaican workers. When the British leadership refused to adhere to his request, he traveled to England to protest. His protest fell on deaf ears, as the British rulers refused to take any of the actions that were promoted by Garvey.

Although his protest was unsuccessful, Garvey did expand his knowledge base by taking classes at Birbeck College and meeting with black nationalists from around the world. While these encounters and connections further inspired and motivated Garvey to fight for change, none were more inspirational than Garvey's reading of Booker T. Washington's *Up from Slavery*. Washington's work caused Garvey to ask, "Where is the Black man's government? Where is his king and kingdom?" On July 15, 1914, after two years in England, he returned to Jamaica to establish a base to oppose the extreme racism that dominated the world.

Five days after Garvey returned to Jamaica, he established the Universal Negro Improvement Association (UNIA) and African Community Leagues (ACL). Garvey's mission for the organizations was to bring together African people and establish an independent and sovereign nation. After the organization was established, Garvey made plans to travel to the United States to meet Booker T. Washington and raise much-needed funds for his work. When Garvey arrived in the country in 1916, he was informed that Washington was deceased. Though disappointed, Garvey decided to continue with his journey and meet with other black leaders and view black institutions in an effort to gain more insight on how to improve the infrastructure of his organization in Jamaica. Although his visit led him to the Tuskegee Institute, in an effort to gain insight on how to open a similar school in Jamaica, and other areas in the United States, he was smitten with the environment in Harlem, New York.

After World War I, Harlem was filled with African Americans who had traveled to the North in search of inspiration and hopes of social change. Garvey began to cater to those needs by working as a soapbox speaker on street corners of Harlem. His valiant arguments for black pride, economic stability, and international programs drew in large audiences. Many of these audiences comprised a large segment of the African American poor and working class who thought that organizations such as the National Association for the Advancement of Colored People (NAACP) and the Urban League catered the rich and did not adequately represent their views. They clung to Garvey's messages of hope and daring activism of social change and political restructuring.

Garvey's popularity and support from the community led to the establishment of the first American branch of the UNIA in Harlem. Approximately two years after the Harlem branch was established, 38 other branches of the organization were formed in different states.

Garvey's UNIA-disbursed locations throughout the United States provided the opportunity for him to reach a broader African American audience, build a stronger economic base, expand the mission of the organization, and establish other entities connected to the mission of the group. The UNIA bought and rented property in an effort to build grocery stores, restaurants, laundries, garment factories, dress shops, a greeting card company, and a publishing house.

Three of the more widely noted entities established through Garvey's efforts include Liberty Halls, the Black Cross, and the Black Star Line. Liberty Halls were developed in every city in which the UNIA was located. The entity functioned as a center for political meetings and social functions in the African American community. The Black Cross was a group of African American nurses designed to meet the medical needs of the community. The Black Star Line, a steamship line and one of the more controversial organizations, led to the demise of Garvey's movement in 1925 when he was convicted of mail fraud associated with the ship line. He was sentenced to five years in prison. Two years later, President Calvin Coolidge pardoned Garvey, and he was deported back to Jamaica. Many scholars speculate that the mail fraud conviction was a ploy that was used to silence Garvey's extreme political views and weaken the movement.

Garvey's political views promoted black nationalism. He argued that people of African descent should return back to Africa to establish an economic base and develop an ethnic identity. Without a clear understanding of their identity and economic base, the African race of people was doomed to failure. Only in their own separate nations could blacks realize themselves and develop the tools and characteristics needed to gain worldwide respect from other racial groups. Garvey's desire to promote his Back to Africa Movement often alienated many African American leaders. W.E.B. Du Bois and A. Phillip Randolph strongly opposed his message and tactics, which included meeting leaders of the Ku Klux Klan to discuss their support for the Back to Africa Movement.

Garvey believed that once African Americans returned to Africa, they should develop a mixed economic system and a leadership structure in which the ruling minority promoted the interest of the people. These ruling minorities and their families were to be well provided for so that they would not be tempted by corruption. He noted that the leader also should possess the authority to select all top officials. These top officials were to be held to high standards and would be punished with death by stoning if they disrespected the people's trust and engaged in corrupt leadership practices.

Garvey's movement began to lose strength after his imprisonment for mail fraud and 1925 deportation to Jamaica. He died of a stroke on June 10, 1940. On November 15, 1964, Jamaica named him the country's first national hero and placed a shrine for him in the country's National Heroes Park.

Barbara A. Patrick

See also: Black Nationalism; Malcolm X.

Further Reading

Cronon, Edmund. *The Story of Marcus Garvey and Universal Association.* Madison: University of Wisconsin Press, 1955.

McCartney, John. *Black Power Ideologies: An Essay in African American Political Thought.* Philadephia: Temple University Press, 1992.

Winnick, Jill. "Marcus Garvey: 'A Defiant Symbol of Black Nationalism.'" http://debate.uvm.edu/dreadlibrary/winnick.html (accessed August 2007).

Georgia

After the failure of Reconstruction and the removal of federal troops from the South, Jim Crow gripped Georgia in the 1880s. Separate and unequal, African American schools were characterized by decrepit facilities and poorly paid teachers. African American voters, denied the ballot, were subjected to demeaning tests of intellect and literacy if they attempted to vote or aspired to elected office.

Vigilantes and lynch mobs terrorized black Georgians who threatened elite white Southerners with public displays of wealth, activism, or education.

Particularly in the 1890s, and escalating through the 1920s, the state frequently led the nation in lynching each year. Hundreds of African Americans fell prey to ritualized violence, most commonly at the hands of all-white mobs that claimed that the accused had either murdered a white person or raped a white woman. One of the most infamous of these spectacles was the lynching of Sam Hose on April 23, 1899. Alleged to have murdered his white boss, the Palmetto, Georgia, farmer was tortured and set afire in front of more than 2,000 people. Spectators toted home Hose's burned body parts, and an Atlanta shop exhibited his charred knuckles.

In addition to this climate of social control, economic peonage, and racial violence, one that may have seemed only slightly improved from slavery, black and white Georgians during Jim Crow grappled with poverty. After Reconstruction and through the mid-twentieth century, the state's economy of cotton, peanuts, and other crops was primarily agricultural, and nearly half of Georgia's farm laborers did not own their own land but worked plots they rented as sharecroppers or tenant farmers. They bought equipment, seed, animals, and household necessities on credit, and the bulk profits from what they grew and harvested went toward repaying their debt, which mounted annually. In his book *The Souls of Black Folk* (1903), the African American educator W.E.B. Du Bois documented how black sharecroppers in the cotton country around Albany, Georgia, struggled with high rents, overworked land, and cheating employers, while descendants of white plantation owners fought repossession and diminishing crop prices.

It would be inaccurate, however, to conclude that Jim Crow meant complete ruination for African Americans in the state. As the nineteenth century waned, they logged successes, particularly in education and religion. For example, in 1883, Lucy Craft Laney opened a school for black youth in Augusta, the Haines Normal and Industrial Institute, that lasted 50 years.

Haines's curriculum offered college preparatory courses in languages, math, and science, as well as vocational training. One of its pupils, John Hope, became the first president of Atlanta University. Another Augustan, William J. White, founded a school to train black ministers; the school moved to Atlanta and became known as Morehouse College.

The line between the classroom and the congregation had been porous since slavery, and some of Georgia's most educated African Americans coupled a spiritual calling with political agitation. Bishop Henry McNeal Turner, who pastured St. Phillips's AME Church in Savannah during the 1870s and 1880s, served in the state house of representatives during Reconstruction, the brief period when black men in Georgia could exercise the vote without poll taxes, literacy tests, or other impediments. Turner later contributed essays on voting and other civil rights issues to Republican newspapers such as Savannah's *Colored Tribune*. Emmanuel King Love, who led the flock at Savannah's First African Baptist Church from 1885 to 1900, sermonized on lynching and segregation, and he endured a beating in 1889 while attempting to integrate the whites-only section of a Jim Crow railway car.

In 1897, Du Bois began teaching economics and history at Atlanta University. There he inaugurated the "Atlanta Conferences" for the discussion and publication of scientific research about African Americans. Ever balancing a conviction that racism meant to grind down the race with a curiosity about how the race managed nevertheless to excel in so many endeavors, in 1900, he commissioned black Atlantan Thomas J. Askew to photograph members of the city's African American middle class, their homes, and their businesses. Du Bois featured these photographs at the 1900 Paris Exhibit, along with books, art, and other examples of the intellectual enlightenment, material prosperity, and cultural creativity that asserted themselves in spite of Jim Crow's repression. During a time when African Americans were routinely stereotyped as shuffling, dialect-intoning, kerchief-headed "darkies" in stereoscopic views, sheet music, and other visual and literary material encountered by white Georgians, Du Bois's Paris exhibit challenged negative perceptions of black people in the state that he had described in *Souls* as both the spiritual and spatial center of the African American nation and symbolic Ground Zero for the tensions between the races nationally.

However, it was an address in the 1890s, later dubbed "The," that would establish the most influential blueprint for race relations in Jim Crow Georgia—the Atlanta Compromise. The speaker, Booker T. Washington, was president of Tuskegee University in Alabama, a school to train black students in teaching and vocational skills. His speech, delivered at the Cotton States and International Exposition, before a mixed-race crowd on September 18, 1895, in what is now Atlanta's Piedmont Park, proposed a plan for his fellow African Americans to achieve gradual political parity and more immediate economic security within the social restrictions and climate of distrust created by Jim Crow. To blacks, with the imperative "Cast down your bucket where you are" (Washington 1901, 99), Washington urged a focus on making their labor indispensable in agriculture, domestic service, and skilled trades. By patiently proving their merit as relentless workers and respectable citizens, he argued, they would gradually persuade whites to extend to them political and civic equality. To whites, Washington requested the understanding that African Americans wanted to intermingle socially with them only insofar as this furthered the nation's economic advancement. He also held whites accountable for taking a more active role in mending the racial tensions that were slavery's legacy. Black colleges and universities in Georgia and the Deep South benefited from the resounding welcome Washington's proposal met from white philanthropists, who demonstrated their support by dipping into their pockets to endow and build institutions for industrial training.

The curtain fell on the first half of the Jim Crow era in Georgia to the same note of racial intimidation and illegal rampages that had opened it. Two days in 1906, from September 22 through 24, marked the Atlanta Race Riot, when white mobs committed the most heinous violence against black Georgians since the Sam Hose lynching. False newspaper accounts about white women in the city who had been raped by black men triggered the violence. Angry all-white mobs assembled in the downtown section of Atlanta, which had refashioned itself after the Civil War into Georgia's center of commerce and business, and they exploded in rage and revenge. They trashed black-owned business and homes and set them aflame. They dragged protesting African American passengers from trolley cars and beat them. And they fanned into African American residential neighborhoods and exchanged gunfire in shootouts with the homeowners there. By the time the rioting waned on the third day, scores of black Atlantans had been severely beaten or killed.

Like the lynching of individuals, the multiple assaults and murders of the Atlanta Race Riot underscored that a root cause of racial violence was the African American middle and working classes that threatened to compete with whites for jobs and businesses, and the interracial mingling that came with urban growth and undermined notions of white racial superiority. Nor were African Americans alone in their vulnerability to this vigilante justice. On August 6, 1915, a Jewish man from Marietta named Leo Frank was hanged by a lynch mob for allegedly raping and murdering a factory girl and sharecroppers' daughter named Mary Phagan. Phagan had failed to return home from work one day, and her battered body had been discovered in the cellar of the building where she was employed. A brief police investigation had yielded Frank as the prime suspect, and, based on thin and inconclusive evidence, an all-white jury swiftly found him guilty of murder.

After studying court documents and concluding that justice had been miscarried and an innocent man convicted, Georgia's governor at the time, John Slaton, commuted Frank's sentence from execution to life imprisonment. Yet the court of public opinion already had tried Frank and determined that he was a monster, so lynchers, calling themselves the Knights of Mary Phagan, collected the prisoner from his cell in Milledgeville, carted him back to Marietta, and carried out the sentence that their own governor had reasoned was unjust. On Thanksgiving Day 1915, during a ceremony on Stone Mountain, the Knights of Mary Phagan reestablished themselves as the Ku Klux Klan, the hate group that had been outlawed during Reconstruction.

Like African Americans, recent European immigrants and Jews like Frank represented a challenge to the job security and business ownership of working-class white Southerners. As Jean Toomer would articulate in his *Cane* (1925), a multigenre meditation on racial politics and the meaning of Southern identity, when rural white Georgians lost their farms and their sense of community because of industrialization and urbanization, blacks, Jews, and others with marked differences in skin color and culture became easy and convenient targets for their despair and frustration. Jim Crow policies ensured their oppression. By the end of 1915, when D. W. Griffith's epic film *The Birth of a Nation,* with its drumbeat images of brutish black men attacking fragile white virgins, premiered to sold-out theaters in Atlanta, the specter of the white-hooded posse riding to raise the lynch rope was a customary threat to black Georgians. Emancipation's promise of civic equality lay tattered by the wayside.

The second half of the Jim Crow era in Georgia coincides with the state's ascendancy as an economic, political, and cultural force. These decades are characterized by escalating pressures from members of marginalized races and classes to attain social justice and eliminate poverty, culminating in the Civil Rights Movement of the 1940s, 1950s, and 1960s. Georgians who made significant contributions to race relations at an earlier stage of Jim Crow, during the 1920s and 1930s, include Walter White and Lillian Smith.

From Atlanta, White, who was so fair in complexion that he could pass for white, used his skin color to investigate racial violence in the 1920s as a member of the National Association for the Advancement of Colored People (NAACP). Masquerading as a white man, he infiltrated hate groups and observed race riots throughout the South, gathering information about lynching for the NAACP's campaign to institute national legislation outlawing racial violence and to influence the federal courts to end Jim Crow. He published two books about lynching and its horrors, the novel *Fire in the Flint* (1924) and the nonfiction study *Rope and Faggot* (1929), and in 1929 he earned an appointment as the NAACP's executive secretary, which he held for over 25 years. One example of the lynching crimes that White and other NAACP members documented and pressed President Harry S. Truman to investigate took place near the Moore's Ford Bridge in Walton County, Georgia. On July 25, 1946, four African American sharecroppers—Roger and Dorothy Malcolm and George and Mae Murray Dorsey—were kidnapped and taken to this landmark where they were tortured and shot to death. Although Truman responded to the NAACP by ordering the Federal Bureau of Investigation to solve the lynching, no one was ever formally charged and brought to justice.

Lillian Smith, who grew up in Clayton, Georgia, also earned a reputation as a civil rights activist through both her community work and her writing. She dedicated her adult life to eradicating prejudice and dismantling Jim Crow, which she did beginning in the 1930s primarily through magazine writing, debates, and conversations with civic leaders and civil rights organizations, and membership in interracial groups, such as the Southern Regional Council, that were committed to progressive social change. She urged influential white Southerners who disapproved of Jim Crow, such as Ralph McGill, the *Atlanta Constitution* editor, to risk a clear and unambiguous stand against segregation. In 1949, her book *Killers of the Dream* galvanized American readers with its meditation on the crippling physical and psychological impact of Jim Crow policies. Smith's account of the bitterness and ignorance that the system had engendered contrasted widely with the nostalgic depictions of the Old South that another Georgia writer, Margaret Mitchell, had imagined to much popular acclaim in her *Gone with the Wind* (1939) a decade earlier.

Instituted in 1942, the interracial, Christian community of Koinonia Farm aspired to realize the integrated society that activist-writers like Smith and White envisioned even while Jim Crow maintained its grasp on Georgia life. The rural southwest Georgia farm, founded by two Baptist ministers, Clarence Jordan and Martin England, was a commune where residents divided chores, ate together, and worked side by side as equals in spite of racial differences. Jordan's antiracist sentiments made Koinonia a target of fire bombings, hate mail, and attempts by local officials to shut it down.

The Albany Civil Rights Movement is one of the most exciting and intensified chapters in Georgia's civil rights history. Taking place primarily over an 11-month period between October 1961 and August 1962, residents of this city in southwest Georgia decided that the time had come to end Jim Crow not gradually, but by simultaneously desegregating as many public facilities as they could: libraries, restaurants, bus terminal waiting rooms, grocery stores, schools, and churches. The leaders of the Albany Movement included William Anderson, a black physician; Charles Sherrod and Cordele Reagon, Student Nonviolent Coordinating Committee (SNCC) field secretaries; and C.B. King, one of a handful of black lawyers in the state and from an affluent business-owning family in Albany's black community.

Inspired by the success of the 1955 Montgomery Bus Boycott and Martin Luther King Jr.'s book about the effort, *Stride toward Freedom* (1958), the organizers of the Albany Movement focused on using nonviolent direct social action as a strategy for exposing the moral deficiencies of Jim Crow and embarrassing segregationists into dismantling the apartheid society. With varying degrees of effectiveness, the Albany Movement attempted to unite civil rights, religious, and civic organizations in the community so as to encourage blacks in the city and neighboring counties to register to vote, and those who joined it employed the power of the dollar to pressure local businesses to welcome the patronage of black consumers. Members of the Albany Movement also perfected the tactic of holding mass meetings in local churches to shore up activists' courage, disseminate information about goals and strategies, and raise bail money and other funds for marchers. The Freedom Singers, four African American students (the SNCC organizer Cordell Reagon; Bernice Johnson, who married Reagon; Rutha Mae Harris; and Charles Neblett) who led the congregation in spirituals and freedom songs at these mass rallies, were invited to tour the nation using their music to rouse the complacent or timid into action.

At the request of the Albany Movement's leaders, King and Ralph Abernathy of the Atlanta-based Southern Christian Leadership Conference (SCLC), which King headed, joined the picketers. The Albany Movement organizers counted on the arrests of these high-profile activists to bring further pressure to bear on city officials to desegregate, but they were undermined by the courtly and respectful manner in which the city's white police chief, Laurie Pritchett, treated both locals and outsiders who had come to demonstrate for social change. What the Albany Movement did convey to organizers of future desegregation campaigns was the important leadership role of local residents and community members, who understood deeply how Jim Crow affected them where they lived. And Albany further ingrained King, Abernathy, SNCC, and the SCLC, all centered in Atlanta, as symbols of the national movement for peace, justice, and racial tolerance.

In the fall of 1961, another civil rights milestone occurred with the integration of the University of Georgia, the state's flagship public institution and, as a segregated school, a symbol to many African Americans of Jim Crow's narrow-minded prejudices and blunted opportunities. The applications of qualified African Americans were routinely denied, and the state instituted a policy to pay the tuition at out-of-state schools for black youth who qualified for entrance, rather than admit them for study in their native state. Hand-picked for their character, impeccable manners, and outstanding academic achievements, Charlayne Hunter-Gault and Hamilton Holmes became the first African American undergraduates admitted to the school, assisted by a legal team led by the Atlanta-based civil rights lawyer Donald L. Hollowell. An African American graduate student, Mary Frances Early, also enrolled.

Barbara McCaskill

See also: Blues; Great Migration; Sit-Ins.

Further Reading

"Atlanta in the Civil Rights Movement." Atlanta Regional Council for Higher Education Web site. http://www.atlantahighered.org/civilrights/index.asp (accessed August 2007).

Brundage, W. Fitzhugh. *Lynching in the New South: Georgia and Virginia, 1880–1930.* Urbana: University of Illinois Press, 1993.

Du Bois, W.E.B. *The Souls of Black Folk.* Chicago: A. C. McClurg and Company, 1903.

Inscoe, John C., ed. *Georgia in Black and White: Explorations in the Race Relations of a Southern State, 1865–1950.* Athens: University of Georgia Press, 1994.

Lewis, David Levering, and Deborah Willis, eds. *A Small Nation of People W.E.B. Du Bois and African American Portraits of Progress.* New York: Amistad Press, 2005.

McCaskill, Barbara, and Caroline Gebhard, eds. *Post-Bellum, Pre-Harlem: African American Literature and Culture, 1877–1919.* New York: New York University Press, 2006.

Unsung Foot Soldiers: The Foot Soldier Project for Civil Rights Studies at the University of Georgia. http://www.footsoldier.uga.edu (accessed August 2007).

Washington, Booker T. *Up from Slavery.* New York: Doubleday, 1901.

Wexler, Laura. *Fire in a Canebrake: The Last Mass Lynching in America.* New York: Scribner, 2003.

Great Depression

The Great Depression was a severe economic downturn impacting the United States and other industrialized countries. Lasting from 1929 through the early 1940s, the period was characterized by bank failures, massive unemployment, and a dramatic decrease in the production and sale of manufactured goods. In the United States, the economic collapse led to a dramatic transformation in the role that the federal government plays in regulating the economy. President Franklin D. Roosevelt's New Deal programs sought to alleviate suffering through unprecedented government intervention. Roosevelt's economic policies proved to be a turning point in the agricultural South, as federal funds led to the mechanization of agriculture and to the eventual displacement of many of the region's agricultural workers.

The Great Depression startled many, coming as it did on the heels of the 1920s, a time of reputed national prosperity characterized by an ebullient national mood and unprecedented consumer spending. Although many people did see an upswing in their standard of living during this decade, many of these changes were only surface-deep. Wealth remained unequally distributed, and many Americans, particularly in the South, continued to live in poverty. In order to maintain the lifestyle promoted by the advertisements of the era, many bought luxury items on credit and were ultimately unable to support their lifestyle. Some investors also borrowed money to buy stocks on margin, initially paying as little as 10 percent of the face value in the hopes of paying off these debts as the stock's value increased. Speculation of this kind led to inflated stock prices, whose values could not be maintained, and on October 29, 1929, the bubble burst. The stock market fell in value by $14 billion in a single day. Industrial production quickly fell by half, and the unemployment rate reached a devastating 25 percent by 1932.

The events on Wall Street and the pain felt by the nation's industrial sector initially meant very little to the inhabitants of the largely rural Southern United States. In 1929, Southerners were already suffering from the decline in agricultural prices that followed the end of World War I as international production outpaced the demand for agricultural goods. Natural disasters in the form of an infestation of boll weevils, which plagued the cotton-producing South, and the devastating

Mississippi River flood of 1927 brought severe damage to the Southern economy well before the onslaught of the nationwide depression.

The federal government dramatically increased its role in regulating the economy and in providing for the needs of its citizens during this era. After his election in 1932, Roosevelt set out to provide needy Americans with the "New Deal" he had promised in his campaign. These government programs were designed to regulate businesses and agriculture, shore up the nation's banking system, provide relief to the needy, and reduce unemployment. In theory, many of these programs prohibited discrimination on the basis of race, but in reality, such discrimination continued to occur.

Throughout the country, African Americans were disproportionately impacted by the Great Depression. They were typically the last hired and the first fired. During the height of the Depression, half of black workers were unemployed. Like other workers, African Americans became increasingly radicalized in response to dire economic need and joined labor unions, such as the biracial Southern Tenant Farmers' Union, which was founded in Arkansas in 1934, in an attempt to protect their economic interests.

Blacks also suffered disproportionately as they were less likely than needy whites to receive aid—in the form either of payments or of food subsidies. Particularly in the South, blacks who did receive relief typically received less money and food than whites. This was due to the prevailing belief that African Americans were prone to laziness and would not work if given too much assistance. To compound matters, prominent Southern whites generally controlled relief funds and supplies, even those donated by the Red Cross, and were able to use their control over these resources to influence black behavior.

One of the federal programs that most dramatically impacted the South was the Agricultural Adjustment Act. Passed in 1933, this bill was designed to increase agricultural prices by limiting production by means of government subsidies to farmers. Southern plantation owners enthusiastically participated in the program, but for the most part, they refused to share New Deal monies with the sharecroppers and tenant farmers who worked on their land. Furthermore, as large landowners began to decrease production, they began to evict unneeded farm workers from the land. The displacement of the agricultural workforce accelerated in the following decades as landowners used federal funds to mechanize agricultural production, further reducing their dependence on individual laborers.

Both black and white farm laborers began to migrate to cities in search of other kinds of work, and many African Americans in particular set their sights on the North. Blacks had begun migrating northward in large numbers to take advantage of opportunities in manufacturing as the stream of European immigrants dried up during World War I. Although many waited out the lean years of the Great Depression in the South, African Americans began migrating again in great numbers as the country mobilized in preparation for World War II. In the process, African Americans went from residing primarily in rural areas of the South to becoming a predominately urban population that resided in increasing numbers in the North.

As the 1930s progressed, the South continued to lag behind other parts of the nation on the road to economic recovery. The South failed to measure up in terms of per capita income. The region's inhabitants also suffered from a lack of access to adequate health care and a lackluster commitment to providing quality public education for all Southerners. In 1938, Roosevelt soberly labeled the region "the nation's No. 1 economic problem."

Recovery did come to the nation after the United States entered World War II and the effort to prepare for war jump-started the economy. The South began increasingly to industrialize, and machinery such as tractors and mechanical cotton pickers continued to displace laborers as the dramatic transformation in the Southern economy that began in earnest during the lean years of the Great Depression continued.

Jennifer Jensen Wallach

See also: Civilian Conservation Corps; New Deal; World War II.

Further Reading

McElvaine, Robert S. *The Great Depression: America, 1929–1941.* New York: Crown, 1984.

Shlaes, Amity. *The Forgotten Man: A New History of the Great Depression.* New York: HarperCollins Publishers, 2007.

Great Migration

The epic "great" migrations of African Americans to Northern areas and the West from the South during the first half of the twentieth century ultimately impacted America's economic, social, political, and even religious landscape as those blacks sought the proverbial "Promised Land" to escape the searing and relentless Jim Crow racism of Southern states. African Americans themselves were greatly impacted demographically and socially, for better or worse, depending on their destinations and the racial climate that was often hostile once they arrived.

From 1916 to 1970, some 6.5 million African Americans came from the South and headed north and west. During one phase of the first migration between 1910 and 1940, about 1.5 million black Americans fled the South for Northern territory. The second mass movement, occurring between 1940 and 1950, involved another 1.5 million people.

As blacks began to move in proximity to whites in Northern urban areas, causing virulent and widespread white resentment that led to Jim Crow–like responses, including violence and segregation, the black urban population still exploded between 1930 and 1950. Cities such as Pittsburgh and others in the Ohio Valley experienced black population increases ranging from 25 percent to 64 percent. Similar increases were reported in New York City, Philadelphia, Chicago, and Washington, D.C.

The changes caused by such mass movements of African Americans from the South—often ignited by substantial Southern lynching, riots that led to the destruction of entire black communities, and the determination of whites to hamper or eliminate black economic advancement and suffrage—were at times cataclysmic for both the Southern areas they left and the Northern sanctuaries that blacks sought. The impact nationally was extraordinary.

There had always been migrations of blacks in America, at first to escape Southern slavery during colonial years. The first enslaved Africans brought to American shores by the Spanish during the 1500s often escaped from what is today Georgia and South Carolina and traveled southward to the Florida swamps where they allied with the Seminole Indians. Black migrations also occurred just before and after the American Civil War that erupted in 1861 and ended in 1865. During the antebellum period, the movement consisted of forced movement of slaves, fleeing runaway slaves, and free persons looking for better opportunities in the North.

Even earlier, during the American Revolution of the late 1770s, blacks who were offered their freedom by the British became "loyal" to the English crown, with many moving to Canadian territory or New England states. Some settled in Pennsylvania and New York. There were, however, additional pressures to move to the North. By the 1830s, free blacks in such states as Virginia were required to leave within one year of being emancipated. In other Southern states, including North Carolina, liberated blacks were prohibited from entering. And in South Carolina and Maryland, there were reports of free blacks being sent back into slavery if they were found guilty of minor infractions. Often, such states would enact restrictive laws as slave rebellions increased or the black population grew, especially in South Carolina. Blacks were required to adhere to strict curfews, limit group communication, and carry passes while traveling. Such laws, or "Slave Codes," were enforced by marauding white groups, who often evolved into law enforcement authorities or even the militia. By 1850, the notorious Fugitive Slave Act was made law and allowed authorities—and many white citizens—to arrest suspected escaped slaves. In Charleston, South Carolina, if free blacks wanted to work, they had to wear a badge. Growing numbers of blacks began to rebel and to leave Southern plantations. Some scholars contend even that the mass exodus of African Americans during the years leading up to the Civil War was a primary cause of that great conflict.

Even after the Civil War, despite some racial equality progress during the Reconstruction period that ended in 1877 following the departure of federal troops from the South, Southern blacks faced very difficult times. They were relegated primarily to sharecropping or tenant-farming jobs that essentially kept them indebted to unscrupulous white landowners who overcharged them for rent, food, clothing, and other necessities.

When limited black progress was made, the white backlash was often devastating. Numerous black preachers and politicians were murdered by white mobs during Reconstruction, while the African American masses also faced unspeakable violence and atrocities by such groups as the Ku Klux Klan. Thousands of African Americans were lynched as anger from whites became increasingly exhibitionist to establish a climate of utter terror.

For instance, at the dawn of the first Great Migration on October 21, 1916, Anthony Crawford, the richest black man living in the vicinity of Abbeville, South Carolina, where the Confederacy was conceived several decades earlier, was brutally lynched. Crawford's wealth could not save him from a white mob after he was accused that day of insulting a white merchant. He was hanged from a pine tree, and several hundred bullets were fired into his then-lifeless body. There were no subsequent arrests or convictions. Many blacks from the Abbeville-Greenwood area took off for North Philadelphia, Pennsylvania, following the footsteps of other African Americans who had already departed.

Yet, as blacks fled north during Reconstruction and into the twentieth century, often their job prospects were curtailed by discriminatory labor practices demanded by immigrants from Europe competing with African Americans for skilled-labor jobs, a pattern that would continue as the first Great Migration of African Americans northward escalated in 1917 as America entered World War I. That trickle began to stream in the summer of 1916, when the Pennsylvania Railroad sponsored the northern journeys of 16,000 Southern African Americans to perform unskilled labor in the North. Some blacks also found work in Chicago via the Illinois Central Railroad, while others landed employment in the steel mills of Pennsylvania, all important components of the war effort and economy. Many black women followed husbands or partners—who generally ranged from ages 18 to 35—and found work as domestics. Yet, most of the jobs that the men and women found were menial and low-paying, but not as depriving and limiting as the substandard agricultural jobs they had left in the South.

As the number of black migrants grew, white Southerners became so nervous that they even resorted to snatching black travelers from railway stations and trains to keep them in the debilitating South. However, Northern newspapers and letters from home, sometimes with money enclosed, encouraged these travelers to push on. Such letters were often read in Southern churches, linking that first Great

Migration to a religious mission. Meanwhile, black community and church leaders were appointed to communicate with various Northern industries, as well as such newspapers and periodicals as the *Urban League Bulletin, Amsterdam News,* and *Chicago Defender.*

As many of the 400,000 African American soldiers returned from World War I to demand black rights in their Southern hometowns, they were met with certain and often violent racism. The soldiers were particularly angry because many had risked their lives for America overseas, but returned to the boiling kettle of racism and Jim Crow in the United States. Reports of black soldiers being imprisoned or lynched skyrocketed. Memberships in such black civil rights' groups as the National Association for the Advancement of Colored People (NAACP), founded in 1909, and the National Urban League—an organization established in 1910 to fight for black rights in primarily urban areas—began to grow exponentially.

The growth of the black population in major Northern cities during the decade between 1910 and 1920 was staggering. Out of necessity, and due to isolation from whites, black communities in those cities became self-sufficient socially and regarding many needed services.

Due to the restrictions placed upon them in terms of housing, work, and various services, blacks established their own institutions and communities. These included churches, hospitals, nursing schools, and colleges. In addition, the black cultural middle class, including doctors, attorneys, teachers, and religious authorities, focused on providing services to the black working class.

Although middle-class blacks and workers seemed to be a cohesive and unified group, there were certainly divisions. Class separation and even racism among African Americans emerged with respect to religion, ideology, politics, lifestyle, and employment. For instance, some black churches in cities such as Philadelphia reportedly admitted members according to skin tone and professions. Lighter-skinned congregants with middle-class jobs were sometimes accused of excluding darker-skinned blacks who held menial jobs. And sometimes, these dynamics worked in reverse. Meanwhile, such exclusion practices and class separation was monitored in other black organizations, including college fraternities and sororities.

Perhaps the most visible fissure regarding class involved the differences between the black intellectuals W.E.B. Du Bois and Booker T. Washington during the late 1800s and early 1900s. Du Bois believed that blacks must uncompromisingly demand equal rights, promoting college education and intellectual pursuits for those blacks deemed "talented." Meanwhile, Washington believed more in accommodation and that blacks should at first be content to deal with segregation, work hard, and accept agricultural and trade jobs while gradually building trust in white America. Both men had many followers, indicating a line of demarcation within the growing black populace.

Simultaneously, white racism proliferated in the South and North. Yet, many African Americans as early as 1833 set their eyes on the West to avoid the South's racism. Mexican Texas became popular after the third annual Convention for the Improvement of the Free People of Color touted it as a destination. Blacks worked as miners, railway workers, and even cowboys in the West.

Furthermore, the abolition of slavery created great opportunity for blacks who opted to move West. African Americans flocked to Texas, where the black population grew rapidly during the last several decades of the nineteenth century. Blacks also took advantage of the 1862 Homestead Act that allowed Americans— supposedly irrespective of gender or race—to acquire 160 acres from the federal government after paying a small filing fee. Blacks also zeroed in on Oklahoma and its homesteading opportunities. Black ownership of farmland increased dramatically to 1.5 million acres, worth about $11 million.

However, when Oklahoma gained statehood in 1907, such progress was hampered when Jim Crow practices in hiring, education, and voting were instated. Still, by the early 1900s, some blacks had moved further west to the Dakotas and

Exodusters in Nicodemus, Kansas, circa 1880. Such pioneers were the beginnings of a much more massive movement of African Americans out of the rural South during World War I and beyond. (Library of Congress)

Nebraska, especially in the Omaha area. By the 1920s, those black families began to move to urban centers. Many blacks found work in such booming towns as Las Vegas, Nevada, and Denver, Colorado, despite the comparatively low population of African Americans in such places when sized up with Northern urban centers. However, the largest concentration of blacks out west eventually settled in Los Angeles, many in what is today the South Central area. Meanwhile, the great African American woman entrepreneur, Madam C. J. Walker, who was a native of Louisiana and moved to Denver before journeying to Indianapolis, settled in New York City in 1916. By then, many black Southern immigrants began to move into Harlem when she amassed a fortune from her black beauty-aid products that allowed her to construct a mansion on the Hudson River.

Although most African Americans could not even dream of Walker's riches, they began to journey north in prodigious numbers. Although at first Southern blacks could face difficulties getting jobs upon their arrival, large manufacturing businesses began to use them as strikebreakers who were willing to work for cheaper wages than whites. This created terrific racial difficulties in such urban centers as New York City, Philadelphia, and Chicago, as black men moved from agricultural, domestic, and service jobs to the manufacturing sector. Although wages for black men could sometimes be quite adequate—with black Pullman porters taking home as much as $35 per work week—many black men earned wages so low that their wives were forced to work too.

Yet, somehow, despite the pressures, many black families began to thrive with black churches and other groups providing substantial support. In Harlem, the influx of Southern blacks during the 1920s brought about what became known as the Harlem Renaissance, despite blacks' earlier major contributions to the development of jazz, the blues, and soul music. The struggles of these people gave the likes of writer Langston Hughes, as well as poets, artists, and musicians, plenty to write about and increased the prominence of such black intellects as Alain Locke who would become known as "the father of the Harlem Renaissance." He published and wrote about many of the developments concerning African Americans during this period that included editing a special edition of the magazine *Survey,* an in-depth study of Harlem.

Yet, the 1920s also reflected the diversity of black thinking, politics and social movements, as reflected in the Back to Africa Movement of Marcus Garvey, a Jamaican-born black activist who believed that blacks should create their own society in Africa. Many Southern immigrants, after realizing the deep racism in the North, began to follow Garvey, despite his ultimate fall due to pressure from the federal government. In fact, many blacks from the Caribbean made America their home during the first and second Great Migrations, often assuming leadership roles because they found black subservience in America so unacceptable—sometimes because they had come from societies ruled totally by their black brethren.

Meanwhile, blacks followed diverse religious leaders—ranging from the evangelistic "Daddy Grace," or Charles Emmanuel Grace and Father Divine or George Baker to the Black Muslim leader, Elijah Muhammad, originally named Robert Poole and born in Sandersville, Georgia. However, as Muhammad undoubtedly witnessed, although the Great Depression of 1929 and the early 1930s certainly severely hurt blacks nationwide, including Southern African American migrants, the new black communities of the North—bolstered by self-sufficient professionals, community cohesiveness, and the mighty church—managed to survive the storm. President Franklin D. Roosevelt's New Deal programs, although they helped many blacks, also hurt many of them.

Like many of his fellow black Southern migrants, Muhammad found work at one of Detroit's auto plants and, by 1931, met "Master Wallace Fard," who began to develop the black-separatist tenets of the Black Muslim movement. Almost two decades later, the movement would attract the likes of Malcolm X, whose father had migrated from the South to Michigan in 1929 before being killed by suspected white supremacists for his black nationalist views as a Baptist preacher. Malcolm's father, Earl Little, had followed the teachings of Marcus Garvey. In fact, Malcolm X's 1940s conversion to the Black Muslim movement, as well as migration to New York City and rise to power under the leadership of Elijah Muhammad during the 1950s after his imprisonment, coincided with the second Great Migration of Southern blacks to Northern cities.

Black churches of the African Methodist Episcopal and Baptist faiths rose and prolifically expanded, becoming vibrant pillars of the community, shepherding to millions of the blacks in the North and South. Those churches would become the backbone of the spawning Civil Rights Movement, soon to be led by the likes of such supremely educated preachers as the Southern-based pastors Vernon Johns and Martin Luther King Jr., as well as Adam Clayton Powell of New York City and Leon H. Sullivan of Philadelphia. Most of those leaders had Southern roots and many had been educated in Northern schools.

The second Great Migration from 1940 to 1970 started as America entered World War II with the influx of blacks to Northern and Western cities quite notable. For instance, the black population in California continued to rise, primarily nourished by African Americans coming from Louisiana, Texas, Arkansas and Oklahoma. Jim Crow racism directed at black World War II soldiers returning from overseas and to Southern locales in the United States helped to reignite the mass migration of blacks from the South. There was major unrest in several Southern states, including Texas, that resulted in the killing and even executions by the U.S. government of black soldiers accused of crimes that ranged from not obeying Jim Crow laws to murdering marauding whites. Furthermore, the dwindling number of agricultural jobs brought on by mechanization—most notably machines that processed cotton—as well as the cotton-producing competition from such countries as India and Brazil made it necessary for Southern blacks to look elsewhere for work. Simultaneously, the mass industrial mobilization needed to produce war goods during World War II drew many blacks away from the still-inflamed racism of Jim Crow in the South, where lynching was still practiced, although not as much as in the past. The federal government's spending in California grew, attracting many black migrants, as factories producing airplanes, such as Boeing, increased black employment. Black migrants also found work at Pacific Coast shipyards.

As World War II raged and later, when President Harry S. Truman began to integrate the U.S. armed forces, the barriers of segregation started to break down a bit in the broader society despite persistent elements of Jim Crow, including the segregation of some public facilities even in the North. Blacks soon began slowly moving toward Truman's Democratic Party, despite the antiblack and Jim Crow segregationist pronouncements of such Dixiecrats as Strom Thurmond of South Carolina and George Wallace of Alabama. Indeed, many African Americans still voted Republican in the South—when they were permitted to vote and not stopped by so-called poll taxes and bogus literacy tests—because white Democrats had consistently backed such racist policies. Furthermore, the party of the "Great Emancipator," Abraham Lincoln, and many antislavery abolitionists, was Republican. That party had sponsored many newly elected black politicians of the Reconstruction period during the 1870s.

But, as the Civil Rights Movement sped forward during the 1950s, led by the likes of Martin Luther King Jr., black Southern migrants who had settled in Northern cities changed their voting registration to Democratic. African Americans, many with Southern roots, fervently supported the Democratic ranks after the assassination of King in 1968 and the Democratic president Lyndon B. Johnson signed into law crucial civil rights acts. They were also pleased with Johnson—although during his early political career in Texas, he campaigned as a conservative with racist overtones—appointing as an associate justice a black NAACP legal warrior, Thurgood Marshall, to the U.S. Supreme Court. Marshall had tremendous stature in the black community because he had won the landmark 1954 case that outlawed legal segregation in America, *Brown v. Board of Education.* Much of Marshall's career was spent fighting the segregationist laws that many black Southern migrants had endured.

Meanwhile, as the black population in Northern cities exploded, the first African American mayors of major metropolitan areas in Chicago, Philadelphia, New York City, Detroit, Newark, and other cities were elected due to the growing and substantial black pluralities expanding from the 1960s onward.

Donald Scott

See also: World War I; World War II.

Further Reading

Dodson, Howard, and Sylviane A. Dioue. *In Motion: The African-American Migration Experience.* Washington, DC: National Geographic, 2004.

Gates, Henry L., and Evelyn Brooks Higginbotham, eds. *African American Lives.* New York: Oxford University Press, 2004.

Katz, Michael B., and Thomas J. Sugrue. *W.E.B. Du Bois, Race, and the City.* Philadelphia: University of Pennsylvania Press, 1998.

Sernett, Milton C. *Bound for the Promised Land: African American Religion and the Great Migration.* Durham, NC: Duke University Press, 1997.

Taylor, Henry L., and Walter Hill. *Historical Roots of the Urban Crisis: African Americans in the Industrial City, 1900–1950.* New York: Garland Publishing, 2000.

H

Health Care

One of the most devastating effects of discrimination during the Jim Crow era was the effect on the health care of African Americans. The combination of poverty and racism put black Americans, especially in the segregated South, in a precarious position regarding their health. Blacks were far more likely than whites to die of ailments such as tuberculosis (TB) and heart disease in the Jim Crow South, because of both poor living conditions and the lack of available medical care. The malnutrition of poor blacks had a tremendous effect on their susceptibility to diseases like TB, and the lack of concern for black health from state governments kept those infected from receiving treatment. For example, while the black death rate for TB was three to four times that of whites in South Carolina in the early twentieth century, it took five years before the state TB sanitarium even admitted blacks, and it was not until the 1950s that blacks were admitted to the hospital on a par with whites.

In addition to exclusion from proper care, during the Jim Crow era, many African Americans, especially from poverty-stricken rural areas of the South, rarely sought professional medical care, even if it was available. Doctors were people one saw only when they were "really sick," many believed, and hospitals were places where people went to die. Others refused to patronize physicians because of the cost involved. "I was really sick enough for a doctor, but I didn't call one," recalled one black Southerner. "They say they won't come less you have money." Poor people knew they could not afford proper medical care, and therefore did not seek it, resorting instead to patent medicines, folk healers, or unlicensed practitioners when they were ill. Because of both the lack of access and the unwillingness to seek professional medical care, "unknown causes" was a leading explanation for black deaths in many parts of the South well into the twentieth century, as so few African Americans in the South died in a physician's care.

The use of homemade remedies and "conjure doctors" to supplement health care needs was a legacy of slavery that was still common in many black communities, especially in rural areas, during the Jim Crow era. Many rural blacks went through a type of "lay referral system" in attaining health care, first taking home remedies or patent medicines, then seeking the aid of friends and relatives before moving on to traditional healers, and only turning to the services of a professional physician when a condition persisted.

Midwives were also central to the health care system of African Americans in the Jim Crow era. Well into the twentieth century, the majority of black children born in many Southern states were delivered by midwives. Accessibility, cost, and tradition were the main reasons for the persistence of midwifery in the South. There were very few hospitals open to black patients in the rural South, and even if there was a hospital bed available, few Southern blacks could—or would—pay for a hospital stay for something as "routine" as childbirth. Midwives typically charged less than half of what physicians did to attend to a birth, and were usually more willing to accept payment in kind. The midwife, not the physician, was also the traditional birth attendant in Southern black culture. Many black women expressed a dislike for male physicians delivering their babies, preferring instead to have women attend to births. While a mother was in confinement, midwives also often performed numerous household duties, such as cooking and cleaning, that a physician would not be expected to do. In addition to delivering infants, midwives were often called in to administer all types of health care—usually, but not exclusively, to women. One woman interviewed by sociologist Charles S. Johnson in the 1930s stated:

> When I gets sick, [my husband] don't take me to no doctor. He'll buy medicine and bring it to me . . . Last time I was sick I had stomach trouble and he kept getting me medicine and I got worse, so he got me a midwife and she said my womb had fallen. She fixed it up and I got all right.

While traditional healers continued to care for many Southern blacks during the Jim Crow era, the desire by most Americans to be treated by professionally trained physicians increased dramatically during the early twentieth century. African Americans in the Jim Crow South sought care from white and black physicians alike, although most white physicians treated only those blacks who could pay their fees, while subjugating them to segregated service. "All of the white doctors and white dentists have separate waiting rooms for colored people," recalled T. M. Bibbs of Cleveland, Mississippi. "Most of the time they work out all of the white people and then they get to the colored." Physician Ranzy Weston remembered that similar practices were used by white physicians in Georgia. A white doctor, he recalled, "would see all of his white patients first and then he would see his black patients afterwards. In the meantime some patients did sit up and die; black patients." While not all white practitioners treated their black patients poorly, Weston believed "white doctors would not give the same type of service to the black patients as they did to the white patients."

While no public medical school in the South admitted African Americans before the 1950s, in the late nineteenth century, a number of institutions were founded to train black doctors in the South. However, as a result of medical reforms, in the first three decades of the twentieth century, medical schools for African Americans in New Orleans, Louisiana, Raleigh, North Carolina, Chattanooga, Tennessee, Louisville, Kentucky, and Memphis, Tennessee, all closed their doors, leaving Howard University in Washington, D.C., and Meharry Medical College in Nashville, Tennessee, as the only institutions south of the Mason-Dixon line where African Americans could receive a medical education. While some medical schools outside of the South, most notably Harvard University and the University of Michigan, did accept a limited number of African Americans, up until 1969, Howard and Meharry together annually produced more than 50 percent of the nation's black medical graduates.

Black physicians often tried to exploit the lack of dignity and respect that white doctors showed African Americans as a means to lure those patients into their own offices. South Carolina's black medical leaders publicly criticized the state's African American population as late as the 1950s for "seeking aid from sources where segregated waiting rooms are not much more than broom closets with a few chairs." However, African Americans did have a host of legitimate reasons for choosing white physicians, despite the humiliations of segregated waiting rooms and Jim Crow care. Because of either discrimination or expense, black doctors often could not provide patients with the same services as their white counterparts, as white doctors usually had better-equipped offices with more modern facilities and medicines than did black doctors. Some drug companies even refused to sell medicine to black physicians. Outside of Washington and Nashville, there were almost no black specialists in the South before the end of World War II, so African Americans who wanted and could afford specialized treatment had to go to white physicians.

Economic pressure also played a role in the decision of Southern blacks to choose white doctors. Many African Americans went to the doctor their employer told them to go, and, more often than not, white employers steered their employees to white physicians—especially if the employer was paying the bill. "Most of the people are in domestic service and their white bosses and mistresses influence them to use their doctors," bemoaned a black New Orleans physician in the 1930s. The economic pressure of the Jim Crow South that was used to keep blacks out of the voting booths and "in their place" therefore also aided white professionals in competition for the black dollar. White physicians, recalled Mississippi's B.L. Bell in 1939, had an advantage in soliciting black patients because white doctors "can work through the people that the Negroes work for."

Access to hospital care was another factor in African Americans' decision to patronize white doctors. Because black physicians were rarely allowed to treat their patients in Southern hospitals, African Americans often needed to have a white physician in order to receive hospital treatment, even though that treatment would most always be in a segregated, basement ward. "The rural Negro physician is simply unable to practice modern medicine," wrote Milton Roemer in 1949, because "when his patient needs hospitalization he is nearly always compelled to release the case to a white practitioner." Montague Cobb, the dean of black medical history and long-time editor of the *Journal of the National Medical Association,* concluded in 1947 that because of the lack of facilities and professional opportunities, "the Negro doctor [in the South] tends to retrogress." Black patients understood this, and therefore, according to Cobb, "the majority of Negro patients will seek medical attention from white physicians, whom they believe better, no matter how badly they are treated or even exploited."

As a result of discrimination, violence, lack of opportunities, and the migration of Southern blacks from the region, by 1930, 40 percent of the nation's 3,805 black physicians resided outside of the South, where 80 percent of the nation's almost 12 million African Americans still lived, and the vast majority of those who remained in the South were located in urban areas. In rural states, the situation was most acute. Mississippi saw its number of black physicians decline from 71 in 1930 to 55 in 1940, and the bulk of those physicians were located in the cities; 56 of the state's 82 counties had no black physicians at all. Even Southern cities saw a decline in their number of black physicians as the century progressed. For example, New Orleans, once a hub of the black medical community, saw the number of black physicians practicing in the city decline from 50 in the 1930s to only 16 by the mid-1950s.

Even if attended to by a white physician, African Americans were barred from many hospitals in the Jim Crow South, and most that admitted black patients usually did so only in segregated basement wards. In 1910, 30 percent of all hospitals in the South refused black patients entirely; in some states the exclusion rate was much higher. Some hospitals, moreover, regarded black patients, especially indigent ones, as training subjects for white interns and residents, contributing to black distrust of white-run health care facilities.

Excluded from most of the larger, better-equipped hospitals of the South, a number of African American physicians founded their own small, private hospitals and clinics to serve their communities and keep their patients from abandoning them for white doctors. These hospitals were often little more than clinics set up in physicians' offices or homes, sometimes having only 5 or 10 beds. Unlike public or nonprofit hospitals, these institutions were often designed to generate income for the proprietor. Most of these small hospitals did not meet the minimum standards set by the American Hospital Association in the early twentieth century in regards to size, equipment, resources, or even cleanliness. Yet, in this time and place, these small clinics met a valuable need for both doctors and patients, especially in the more rural areas of the South. In some areas, in fact, they were the only hospital facilities for persons of any race for dozens of miles in any direction.

By the 1930s, more than 200 small, independent black-run hospitals had opened in the United States. Serving an impoverished clientele with little or no outside financial help, physicians constantly struggled to keep their small hospitals open. Many private black hospitals of the Jim Crow South did not prove to be the moneymaking ventures that their proprietors had initially hoped, but instead consumed not only the bulk of the fees collected but often the physician's savings as well. Others, like the Burruss Sanitarium in Augusta, Georgia, prospered and grew during the early twentieth century. G. S. Burruss's private hospital eventually had 27 rooms, modern equipment, and a staff of a dozen black physicians, making Burruss a wealthy man. Despite the fact that, unlike the Burruss Sanitarium, many of the proprietary hospitals opened by black physicians were ill-equipped, poorly staffed facilities that survived only a few years, they represent an assault on the unjust exclusion of black physicians from white-run public and private hospitals, and serve as a striking example of the self-help mentality of many black physicians who made the tough choice to practice in the Jim Crow South.

In addition to small hospitals built and owned by physicians, African American organizations in some Southern communities built their own hospital facilities. Many of these hospitals were owned and run by fraternal organizations, churches, or independent boards. Two of the most successful black fraternal hospitals were located in the Mississippi Delta towns of Yazoo City and Mound Bayou. The first fraternal hospital opened for Mississippi's black population was the Afro-American Sons and Daughter's Hospital in Yazoo City. Fraternal hospitals provided both inexpensive medical care for the working classes and private care—without the indignities of Jim Crow—for the black middle classes. Because of the success of society hospitals, a number of fraternal organizations built their own hospitals in the South during the first half of the twentieth century. In addition to those in Mississippi, there were black fraternal hospitals in Arkansas, South Carolina, and Florida. Arkansas alone had four such hospitals by the end of the 1920s, including the 100-bed facility of the Woodmen of the Union in Hot Springs. Other black-run hospitals were administered by black colleges and medical schools, some of which survived even after the medical school folded.

At Booker T. Washington's Tuskegee Institute, a hospital was established in 1892 to care for the school's faculty and students and to train black nurses. The hospital expanded after the appointment of John A. Kenney as director in 1902 and began serving the surrounding African American community as well. During the early twentieth century, the hospital was renamed the John A. Andrew Memorial Hospital, in honor of the Civil War governor of Massachusetts, and became a center for the postgraduate training of black physicians in the Deep South.

Like Tuskegee, a number of the South's black hospitals also served as training centers for black nurses. These facilities filled a need for both young women looking for a career in nursing, and for physicians who desperately needed black nurses to aid them, as the caste system of the South strictly prohibited white nurses from working with—and taking orders from—black doctors. In Charleston, South Carolina, Alonzo B. McClennan proposed the establishment of a nurse training school in 1896 to Charleston's black medical community, which at that time consisted of six physicians and one dentist. With a great deal of community support, McClennan opened the Cannon Street Hospital and Training School for Negroes in 1897. The hospital and nurse training facility survived until 1949, when it closed because the 26-bed facility did not meet the state's new minimum patient load requirements for a nursing program.

With the aid of philanthropic organizations such as the Julius Rosenwald Fund and the Duke Endowment, a number of all-black hospitals, or all-black wings to existing hospitals, were built in the South between the 1920s and 1960s. In Kansas City, Missouri, City Hospital #2 (City Hospital #1 was for whites) was opened exclusively for black patients in 1930, while across the state in St. Louis, Homer G. Phillips Hospital was opened for blacks in 1937. In Winston-Salem, North Carolina, the Kate Bitting Reynolds Memorial Hospital was opened in 1938 for the city's African Americans with both public and private funding. The construction of black hospitals, or the renovation of older hospitals for black patients, was seen by many whites and blacks as an answer to the hospitalization needs of the South's black community, the demands of black physicians for hospital access, and white insistence of racial separation. Many black leaders, however, deemed such facilities as "Deluxe Jim Crow," which only served to make discrimination more palatable to the general public.

Hospital care, even at all-black hospitals, was often an expense black Southerners could not afford in the Jim Crow South, however. Many physicians, white and black, therefore gave of their time and expertise to bring health care and education to African American communities at little or no cost. Some of the public health work done for the African American community was sponsored by private industry, black medical hospitals and schools, or philanthropic organizations, where physicians donated their time and services; still other doctors spent significant sums out of their own pockets in order to fill the glaring public health need of Southern black communities. Public health projects conducted by black physicians serve as a shining example of the self-help movement within African American communities during the segregation era, and is evidence of the desire of many physicians to reach across class lines to aid their less fortunate neighbors.

Booker T. Washington was one of the first African American leaders to understand fully the need for improved public health if Southern blacks were going to be able to lift themselves up and gain equal opportunity in American society. In conjunction with Howard University, the National Medical Association (the African American counterpart to the American Medical Association), the National Insurance Association, and the National Business League, Washington started National Negro Health Week at Tuskegee Institute in 1915 to raise consciousness to proper health care. Negro Health Week was patterned on a program begun in 1913 by the Negro Organization Society of Virginia called "Clean-Up Day," which encouraged black communities to improve the sanitary conditions of their homes and schools. Clean-Up Day was such a success that the following year, Hampton Institute president Robert Russa Moton sponsored a "Clean-Up Week." By the 1930s, counties throughout the United States celebrated Negro Health Week every April, with lectures and demonstrations pertaining to health and sanitation concerns at home and school, and rallies designed to persuade local white health authorities to give more attention to their black citizenry. On the national level, special commissions were appointed in conjunction with Negro Health Week to study a number of diseases as they related to blacks, including a tuberculosis commission, a hookworm commission, and a pellagra commission. Support for the program was bolstered in 1921 with the sponsorship of the U.S. Public Health Service. Twenty years after its inception, Negro Health Week programs were conducted in over 2,000 communities, reaching over a million black families.

Churches were another vital element in the health care delivery system in black communities of the Jim Crow South, as African American churches were much more than simply religious centers; they were often the center of black society as well. "The church has been the one place that black people had control of," recalled the Reverend William Holmes Borders of Georgia. "Black people never controlled the school. . . . The school belongs to the white folks. So they dictated its use, and you got turned down." Black churches, however, were "always open." Because the churches were always open to black physicians and nurses, whereas other public buildings—schools, hospitals, auditoriums, gymnasiums—were not, churches were a natural place to hold health clinics. They were not only large enough facilities to handle the need, but also symbols of black autonomy and self-reliance—owned and operated by the black community, free of white control. Black churches were also centers of communication, especially in the rural areas of the Deep South. In a time before television, among poor and sometimes illiterate populations without access to radios or newspapers, the minister was not only the mouthpiece of the Lord, but also the town crier. Ministers announced coming events, like health clinics, and encouraged their congregations to attend. Preachers often participated in health education as well, instructing their flock to get immunized, eat properly, and maintain a clean home. A church also had another great advantage as a community health center—everyone knew where it was located.

Church clinics were founded in many areas of the Jim Crow South. In 1907, physicians from Washington, D.C.'s Medico-Chirurgical Society opened a free dispensary clinic at the 19th Street Baptist Church. Twelve physicians, along with two dentists and two pharmacists, donated their time to the clinic. The White Rock Baptist Church of Durham, North Carolina, opened a health clinic at its community center in conjunction with the city health department in 1939. The next year a similar program was begun in Jackson, Mississippi, when the Galloway Memorial Church opened a community center in a cottage on its property. A small room was added to the center, and a retired physician donated his office equipment for a health clinic, which was conducted every Wednesday morning for the local community. The state board of health provided a public health nurse, and local black doctors donated their services. Children received free examinations and vaccines at the church clinic, and one day a month was dedicated to prenatal care for expectant mothers.

In addition to free treatment, many African Americans during the Jim Crow era paid for their health care through a variety of methods known as contract medicine. Contract medicine represented any one of a number of agreements that physicians entered into to treat groups of people for a fixed price. Sometimes these were prepaid arrangements; at other times, flat rates were assessed to members of the group for certain medical treatments and procedures. Insurance companies, fraternal and benevolent societies, private clubs, factory and shop organizations, and even some plantations made health care provisions for their members and workers, and physicians competed for the often lucrative contracts to serve these clients. Black physicians in particular saw contract medicine as a means both to build a reputation and to secure a steady income. While contract medicine was openly denounced by most American physicians and medical associations, physicians of all races participated in different forms of contract service in the nineteenth and twentieth centuries.

The most common form of contract medicine entered into by African Americans in the Jim Crow South was through fraternal and benevolent societies. Many of these societies were sponsored by local churches, while others were fraternal, neighborhood, or even drinking clubs. New Orleans, for example, had African American benevolent societies as far back as the eighteenth century, but in the immediate post-Reconstruction era, they became an integral part of life in black New Orleans. While these clubs provided benefits only for those who were able to pay their dues, it was estimated that as much as 80 percent of the city's population belonged to such groups in the late nineteenth century. Outside of churches, more black New Orleanians belonged to benevolent societies in the early twentieth century than to any other type of voluntary association.

Many of the medical services benevolent societies provided to black communities in the South were eventually replaced by industrial insurance agencies. These companies provided benefits similar to those of fraternal organizations, affording limited protection against sickness, accident, and death, usually for a weekly premium. As African Americans were typically unable to afford ordinary life insurance policies, and white companies were unwilling to insure them at the same rates as whites, the insurance industry created an opportunity for black entrepreneurs. One of the forerunners in the industrial insurance industry was the Sun Mutual and Benevolent Association, organized in the 1880s by J. T. Newman and Constantine Perez in Louisiana. It provided the services of a physician, supplied pharmaceuticals, and offered a burial contract to members. Joseph Hardin ran the Metropolitan Relief Association in New Orleans. Along with Hardin, the Metropolitan employed three other physicians who treated patients for a weekly assessment of 15 cents. The company also had contracts with six drug stores that provided its members with pharmaceuticals.

While prevalent in urban areas, contract medicine was by no means limited to the cities. Plantations were the most common areas that physicians formed contracts for service in the rural South. Carter Woodson found that "occasionally a Negro physician may be engaged by a rich man to visit his tenants on his plantation from time to time." Daisy Balsley recalled that her father, Robert Fullilove, "did a large plantation practice" in the area around Yazoo City during the early twentieth century. "Those who could bring their patients in from the farms did so," she remembered, but he had to go out to the plantations to treat those who were unable to make it to town.

Throughout the Jim Crow era, black leaders fought for both an end to segregated medical facilities and to improve health care for African Americans. The National Association for the Advancement of Colored People and the National Medical Association led the charge for change, agitating governmental bodies and the American Medical Association to desegregate, and by bringing lawsuits to enforce desegregation. In 1963, the federal bench handed down the landmark case in the fight for hospital integration in *Simkins v. Moses H. Cone Memorial Hospital*. It took the enforcement of the *Simkins* case, along with the Civil Rights Act of 1964, to finally bring integration to the South's hospitals. Between 1964 and 1970, most Southern hospitals accepted the integration of both black patients and staff without the application of federal sanctions. Along with the Civil Rights Act of 1964, another major incentive for Southern hospitals to integrate was the advent of Medicare in 1965. This federal program, part of President Lyndon B. Johnson's Great Society, provided financial support to hospitals for the medical care of elderly patients, costs that had previously often gone uncompensated. In order to qualify for Medicare funding, however, hospitals were required to abide by Title VI of the Civil Rights Act, which forbade the federal government from allocating funds to any institution that discriminated on the basis of race, creed, or national origin. Providing the carrot to the Civil Rights Act's stick, Medicare funding helped sway the last segregated hospitals into compliance with the law by the end of the decade.

Thomas J. Ward, Jr.

See also: Jim Crow; Tuskegee Syphilis Experiment.

Further Reading

Beardsley, Edward. *A History of Neglect: Health Care for Blacks and Mill Workers in the Twentieth-Century South.* Knoxville: University of Tennessee Press, 1987.

Morais, Herbert M. *The History of the Negro in Medicine.* New York: Publishers Co., 1967.

Smith, David Barton. *Health Care Divided: Race and Healing a Nation.* Ann Arbor: University of Michigan Press, 1999.

Ward. Thomas J., Jr. *Black Physicians in the Jim Crow South.* Fayetteville: University of Arkansas Press, 2003.

Historically Black Colleges and Universities

The term "historically black colleges and universities," or "HBCUs," became a descriptor for what had previously been termed "Negro" or "black" colleges. Colleges thus designated were institutions that existed prior to 1964, and were established specifically to educate African American students. Prior to the 1954 *Brown v. Board of Education* ruling, most states with a substantial black population and Jim Crow laws maintained at least one "Negro college" or other institution for educating black residents beyond the high school level. The existence of such schools fulfilled, at least in theory, the "separate but equal" doctrine. The first Negro colleges were established for generally benevolent reasons in the decades after the end of slavery, but many became bulwarks of Jim Crow, both through their existence as "separate" institutions and through their curricula, which tended to prepare black graduates for the occupations deemed suitable for blacks by white-dominated society. At the same time, Negro colleges became centers of black middle-class respectability and intellectual identity in the South. Students at black colleges often established lifetime networks of mutual support.

Most of the first black colleges were founded without a specific categorization of higher education, and many continued to maintain secondary educational programs as well as collegiate programs throughout their existence. Modern HBCUs offer a wide assortment of programs, from junior colleges to full universities with medical and business schools. The federal government recognizes 110 HBCUs. Other modern colleges with a predominantly black student body exist, but they either were founded after 1964 or were formally white colleges that have experienced a demographic shift in their student body.

Most black colleges existed in the South, where Jim Crow laws prevented black students from attending college with whites at either public or private schools. However, a few black colleges existed outside of the South, such as Wilberforce University in Ohio and Lincoln University in Pennsylvania. In general, private black colleges were usually founded or largely supported by Northern-based church groups during Reconstruction, whereas public black colleges were usually founded after the establishment of Jim Crow, specifically to thwart legal challenges to all-white public colleges. Some colleges were established from genuine

Students in the library of Fisk University in Nashville, Tennessee, circa 1900. (Library of Congress)

grassroots efforts, such as what became Grambling State University, where black farmers in northern Louisiana created a college for their children. However, Grambling, like some other private black colleges, was eventually absorbed into the state system.

While the establishment of black colleges by states fulfilled the "separate" clause of the "separate but equal" doctrine, black public colleges were funded far below the level of white public colleges and so failed to maintain the "equal" clause of the doctrine. Black colleges were additionally handicapped by the poor primary and secondary education provided for black students at most segregated public schools. But as the ratio for seats for black students at black colleges was far lower than that for white students at white colleges, many black colleges were able to be somewhat selective in their admissions and to maintain a high quality of graduates.

Most black colleges followed Booker T. Washington's model, and focused on subjects that were immediately practical for blacks, such as agriculture and home economics, rather than liberal arts or the sciences. Educating primary and secondary teachers soon became a major role for many of the schools. With the declining acceptance of Washington's ideas in the 1950s, as well as the rapidly declining percentage of African Americans involved in agriculture, black colleges began shifting toward liberal arts, social work, and business. Black public colleges usually had mostly black administrations and faculty, but many private colleges had white faculties and administrations. Increasingly, private colleges came under pressure from students and alumni to employ greater percentages of blacks in faculty and administrative roles. Howard University in Washington, D.C., generally considered to be the most prestigious of the black colleges, received its first black president in the 1920s, but other colleges would take much longer.

The *Brown* decision forced public and private colleges to end racial segregation. Negro colleges were increasingly called historically black colleges and universities. The new term reflected the post-*Brown* reality, as the formerly black colleges accepted students from any ethnic group, while not forgetting their origins as schools for blacks. While the efforts to desegregate previously all-white colleges such as the University of Alabama and the University of Mississippi received wide publicity, the integration of formerly black colleges passed with little notice. More significant were the efforts of black colleges to be integrated into state university systems. The case of *Geier v. Tennessee* dragged on from its initial filing in 1968 until its conclusion in 2001, when a federal district court ordered the state to dismantle its de facto two-race system. The desegregation of mainstream universities had the ironic effect of weakening many HBCUs. Top black academic achievers and student athletes were increasingly recruited by formerly all-white colleges. Some HBCUs have been successful in recruiting significant numbers of non–African American students, while others find competing for students more problematic, as a century of financial neglect and the legacy of Jim Crow left a stigma of inferiority for HBCUs. However, most have built on their legacy and have adapted to the competition from mainstream universities, carving out new niches in higher education.

Barry M. Stentiford

See also: Jim Crow; Reconstruction.

Further Reading

Anderson, James. *The Education of Blacks in the South, 1860–1931.* Chapel Hill: University of North Carolina Press, 1988.

Betsey, Charles L. *Historically Black Colleges and Universities.* Edison, NJ: Transaction Publishers, 2008.

Gasman, Marybeth. *Envisioning Colleges: A History of the United Negro College Fund.* Baltimore: Johns Hopkins University Press, 2007.

Willie, Charles V., Richard J. Reddick, and Ronald Brown. *The Black College Mystique.* Lanham, MD: Rowman and Littlefield, 2005.

Housing Covenants

Housing covenants, also known as restrictive covenants, are legal documents designed to ensure that blacks do not move into white neighborhoods. Rather than deed restrictions, which are enforced by individuals, housing covenants must be agreed upon by some majority of neighborhood residents (usually about 75%) after which most others are pressured to comply. These covenants forbid the property owners, as well as their heirs, from selling their property to blacks as well as other racial and ethnic minorities. Because of these covenants, if they sold to a minority person, neighbors had the right to go to court to ensure that property and homes did not change hands and become the property of minorities. Therefore, courts in these cases, for generations, were complicit in ensuring and maintaining residential segregation of suburban and urban neighborhoods.

After World War II, a number of historical events and practices of the government, realtors, and private citizens resulted in the suburbanization of former white ethnic city-dwellers, particularly white ethnics, and the ghettoization of urban blacks. First, heavy industry and low-skill but high-paying jobs moved to the South and West, while high-paying service-sector jobs located in the suburbs. Second, the government offered housing loans to veterans, while the growth of interstate highways ushered in a new age of suburbs surrounding central cities. Third, as whites left the cities, they sought to ensure that blacks did not follow. Blacks were unable to gain access to low-income loans to buy new homes or improve existing homes through redlining by realtors, resulting in increasing isolation in rapidly deteriorating urban centers. Housing covenants, in conjunction with loan restrictions and urban renewal projects, increasingly locked blacks into public housing as their former homes, which had been in redlined areas, were bulldozed. By locking blacks into urban centers, they were also locked into poor-quality social services, education, housing, and job opportunities, thereby perpetuating social and economic inequality and replicating their place in the Jim Crow racism of America.

To ensure residential segregation between blacks and whites in urban and newly suburban areas, many realtors and residents used housing covenants forbidding the owners to sell the home or its land to blacks (as well as Jews, Asians, and other racial groups). These covenants appeared throughout the country in cities as disparate as Seattle, Los Angeles, and Chicago as well as nearly all Southern states. While most were directed at blacks, other cities used housing covenants to ensure that Jews, Asians, or Hispanics did not purchase property in white neighborhoods. For example, in Los Angeles, covenants were used almost exclusively to bar Mexicans from entering white neighborhoods.

Housing covenants were developed primarily by members of "neighborhood improvement associations." Many of these organizations existed to "improve" the neighborhoods by ensuring that blacks and other minorities did not buy homes within them. These covenants were then institutionalized by realtor organizations that encouraged and often required residents to sign to ensure high profits for themselves because of increased house values due to residentially segregated neighborhoods. Conversely, an increase in blacks would lower the values of the homes. Local real estate boards collaborated nationally on the development of model covenants to provide to white homeowners throughout the country as well as conducted citywide drives to ensure all "desirable" neighborhoods were ensured against black encroachment and the maintenance of high property values. Finally, the Federal Housing Administration (FHA) advised, encouraged, and then required residents to use covenants if they wanted to gain access to home loans and mortgages.

These covenants, though not written into law, often appeared in conjunction with state laws prohibiting residential proximity between blacks and whites and, therefore, were similar to the Black Codes enacted during and after Reconstruction that restricted blacks' rights and liberties. These restrictive covenants coincided with a wide variety of laws, statues, and municipal codes prohibiting blacks from building or buying homes in white neighborhoods or in the same building that were found in Delaware, Illinois, Louisiana, Kentucky, New York, Virginia, and Washington. Chicago was a leader in using restrictive covenants to ensure that blacks remained on the South Side of the city in what was, and continues to be known as, the "Black Belt." These legally binding affirmations of black and white difference served to entrench racial attitudes outside of the South, where black and white residential segregation was deeply ingrained in culture and custom, as well as ensure that blacks did not gain access to higher-quality schools, jobs, and public services often found in and around white neighborhoods. They also allowed for the perpetuation of Jim Crow laws and attitudes in otherwise "liberal" places. Therefore, these covenants reveal whites' real fear of black encroachment on their neighborhoods, in the schools, and in their daily lives.

Blacks recognized the insidious nature of these covenants in limiting their access to educational, social, economic, and political opportunity and challenged their constitutionality in a number of cases. The first of these was *Shelley v. Kraemer* initially brought by a black family who purchased a home in St. Louis, Missouri. White neighbors seeking to halt their move into their new home argued that the Shelley's purchase of the home was illegal due to the restrictive covenant barring blacks from purchasing the home. The court argued that the covenants were state-sponsored discrimination, but there were no penalties for those who engaged in this practice, and the ruling was effective only when suits were brought to court and the courts enforced the law. As such, they did not forbid their existence, only with using the courts to ensure their enforcement. The rights and racial attitudes of property owners ensured that this practice persisted well into the twenty-first century, as many deeds continue to have these clauses written into them.

The 1948 *Hurd v. Hodge* case reaffirmed *Shelley v. Kraemer,* finding it illegal to fail to sell to blacks in Washington, D.C. Congress officially outlawed the practice in the 1968 Fair Housing Act, which also addressed redlining and other discriminatory practices by realtors. The U.S. Supreme Court reaffirmed these previous rulings in the 1968 *Jones v. Alfred H. Mayer* case based in St. Louis, emphasizing the 1866 and 1968 Civil Rights Acts that barred racial discrimination in all housing, both public and private. In doing so, the Court declared restrictive covenants "a relic of slavery" that perpetuated the badge of slavery suffered by all blacks.

Although ruled unenforceable in the *Shelley v. Kraemer* decision, and reaffirmed numerous times since then by both rulings and Constitutional amendments, housing covenants continue to exist. Restrictive covenants, though repeatedly ruled to be illegal, continue to preclude blacks' access to suburbs. In 2007, the House of Representatives sponsored a resolution condemning the use of restrictive covenants and urging states to follow California's lead in complying with existing legislature and rulings (including the Fair Housing Act of 1968; *Shelly v. Kraemer;* and *Hurd v. Hodge*) addressing the issue in proactively removing these clauses from housing documents and urging the Department of Housing and Urban Development to educate the public about these issues and collect date on any continued use of covenants.

One of America's most well-known and its first preplanned neighborhood, Levittown on Long Island, New York, offered working-class Americans the opportunity to own homes, but employed housing covenants to ensure that the development would remain white. Built almost entirely during the five years between 1946 and 1951, Levittown comprised nearly 18,000 almost identical homes, which began as an initial 2,000 in Hempstead, spilled into neighboring Wantagh, Hicksville, and Westbury. Many credit Levittown with the beginning of suburban sprawl and the movement away from cities as it fulfilled the American dreams of many families in the 1950s by providing them with affordable homes, plenty of space for children to play, access to good schools, and all the latest appliances.

But Levittown had a dark side for minorities longing to live there. The Levitts, particularly William, enforced racial segregation by restricting the purchase of homes to only whites using restrictive covenants forbidding "any person other than members of the Caucasian race" from living in Levittown homes. After restrictive covenants were outlawed in 1948 and the FHA announced that they would not back mortgages linked to such covenants, Levitt continued to practice discrimination in renting and selling Levittown homes. Levittown was not integrated until the late 1970s.

Melissa F. Weiner

See also: Segregation, Residential.

Further Reading

Lipsitz, George. *The Possessive Investment in Whiteness: How White People Profit from Identity Politics*. Philadelphia: Temple University Press, 1998.

Massey, Douglas S., and Nancy A. Denton. *American Apartheid: Segregation and the Making of the Underclass*. Cambridge, MA: Harvard University Press, 1993.

Vose, Clement E. *Caucasians Only: Supreme Court, the NAACP, and the Restrictive Covenant Cases*. Berkeley: University of California Press, 1973.

Humor and Comedic Traditions

As a characteristic element of black culture, humor has played an important role in the lives and experiences of African Americans since slaves first encountered the New World. Historically, African American comic performances have appeared in slave shanties and on plantation fields, on the minstrel stage and in vaudeville, on the radio and television, in films and literature, in nightclubs, barbershops, and salons, in kitchens and living room parlors, and on the street corner. In short, comedy has always permeated every inch of African American culture, from the spectacular to the quotidian. Humor has historically served the purposes of emotional and spiritual survival and of gaining recognition of black humanity at the same time that it was a source of the stereotypes of black people that would impede this process. Indeed, the blurred line between black humor and black people as a source of humor generates a complex relationship of African Americans to comedy.

African American comic sensibilities originate with traditions of humor carried with slaves from Africa. Clever, ironic speech, signifying, tall tales or "lies," and animal stories featuring the trickster in various guises, for example, maintained a prominent role in the rich oral cultures of the Western and Central African countries from where the majority of black slaves were taken. While the humor of African comic traditions was reserved primarily for joyous occasions, the humor of black slaves took on a tragicomic tone that reflected the misfortune of chattel slavery. Thus, African American comedy in its earliest form developed in direct response to conditions on the plantation.

The comedy of slaves manifested as both a form of redress and a form of resistance. In 1851, Samuel A. Cartwright wrote in *Diseases and Peculiarities of the Negro Race* of a particular ailment which he called "dysaethesia aethiopica," referring to the tendency of some slaves toward "rascality." Cartwight was observing, albeit through the distorted lens of white racist culture, the comic act of "playin' the fool" or "puttin on ole massa." In other words, slaves employed a misleading naïveté and subversively engaged in Sambo-like behavior, completed work at an agonizingly slow place, stole from the plantation, and were generally duplicitous in order to sabotage the enterprise of forced servitude. Cartwright was not able to understand how this behavior, which he took to be a pathological condition, actually exhibited politically tinged irony, subterfuge, distortion, and contradiction. The comic mask of the slave would continue to resurface in black culture as mode of resistance and as a strategy for negotiating the limits of popular representation.

A staple of the black comic tradition, folktales featuring the trickster slave and powerful but ignorant master recorded in oral literature the comic resistance of those that would be considered nonhuman objects. "John and Ole Massa" tales overtly criticized the culprits of the peculiar institution and thus were performed in slave quarters for the purposes of entertainment and redress. However, these same tales appeared in disguise as adaptations of traditional African animal tales. Brer Rabbit and Brer Fox stood in for the trickster and the slave master, respectively, the camouflage of which enabled these tales to eventually become well known among white Southerners who had constant contact with black slaves and their culture. One such white Southerner, Joel Chandler Harris, famously attempted to transcribe this impressive body of folklore in his collections of "Uncle Remus stories." Harris's collections, which feature the happy-go-lucky slave Uncle Remus, bring up the problem of when African American humor comes up against what Ralph Ellison called "comedies of the grotesque," or those white performances of black culture that served to ridicule black people through crude, racist impersonations and stereotypes. The parallel legacy of black comic traditions that feature blacks as humorous individuals finds its origins on the plantation as well.

The laughter of slaves was originally taken as a threat by whites who, perhaps rightly at times, assumed they were the source of amusement. Additionally, whites publicly expressed undue anxiety at the sound of black laughter, which they found to be unusually raucous and mysterious, so much so that on plantations one might find a "laughing barrel" into which slaves were required to channel their amusement. On the other hand, the sight of the happy-go-lucky grinning and laughing slave became the source of endless amusement for the planter class. Slaves who evinced such a disposition were often prized highly as commodities. The black clown became the target of impersonation within blackface minstrelsy, America's first form of popular entertainment.

Minstrelsy, a burlesque of impersonated black performance and caricature performed originally by white actors in blackface makeup, began appearing as early as the 1820s. The humor of the minstrel stage consisted primarily of one-liners, riddles, quips, gibes, malapropisms, parodic and nonsensical stump-speeches, as well as slapstick comedy and antic humor, and centered on the popular myth of the happy slave and a romanticization of the plantation. The minstrel show generally had an established format featuring the interlocutor, a straight man, and the comic "endmen," Mr. Bones and Mr. Tambo, so named for the instruments they played. The form consisted of a "walkaround" and opening song, followed by the "circle" or comic exchange between the interlocutor and endmen, the olio, and finally a plantation skit or farce of well-known play; Harriet Beecher Stowe's abolitionist novel *Uncle Tom's Cabin,* for example, was frequently parodied.

With the popularity of the stage performances of Edwin Forrest and British actor Charles James Matthews (known, strangely enough, as the father of American humor), two of the first known blackface entertainers, "Negro impersonation" began to gain prevalence. Around 1828, Thomas Dartmouth (T. D.) Rice invented a caricature that would leave a lasting mark not only on the minstrel imaginary but also on the entire conception of U.S. race relations for over a century to come. Rice relates the story of having seen a disabled, black stable groom singing to himself and dancing a peculiar dance. Impressed by the spectacle, Rice alleges to have copied the song and dance, and even to have bought the clothes off of the stable groom's back, bringing song, dance, and character to the stage. Performing the song and impersonation between acts of *The Rifle,* "Jim Crow" Rice became one of America's best-known comedians. Likewise, the popular representation of "Jim Crow" soon came to stand in for all black people.

The conspicuous link between popular entertainment and legal apartheid reflects the impact of precarious representations of blackness on the conditions of unfreedom for blacks in the United States. Remarkably, many of the official institutions of apartheid culture find their influence in the minstrel tradition. For example, the Confederate rallying song "Dixie" was written by one of the Virginia Minstrels, Dan Emmett. As well, "Carry Me Back to Old Virginny" by James Bland became Virginia's state song in 1940.

Between the 1840s and 1850s, minstrelsy sprang up from coast to coast with professional troupes such as the African Melodists, the Congo Minstrels, the Buckley Serenaders, the Ethiopian Mountain Singers, and Bryant's Minstrels generating extreme popularity for this form of entertainment. Minstrelsy in its original form began to disappear as early as the 1880s, with the closing down of the Al D. Field Minstrels in 1928 possibly signifying the official end, a few troupes continued to tour into the first couple of decades of the twentieth century. As well, the minstrel show appeared in vaudeville, on the radio, in film, and eventually on television after World War II. While minstrelsy is properly remembered for its lasting impact on the misrepresentation of black people, the form is simultaneously responsible for the emergence and popularity of black entertainers and the comic tradition they would instantiate. While the early minstrel stage was racially restricted to white actors, the early white minstrels report being highly influenced by the black performers Signor Cornmeali (or "Old Corn Meal") and John "Picayune" Butler of New Orleans. Occasionally, black performers found their way into white troupes—for example, when William Henry "Juba" Lane, known as the father of tap dancing, performed with minstrel troupes in the 1840s. Thomas Dilward, or "Japanese Tommy," a dwarf, also performed with white minstrels in from the 1850s to the 1860s.

Black minstrel troupes, which were less successful than their white counterparts, began to appear around 1855. These troupes catered to both black and white audiences, and in either case to the lower levels of society. The small number of black bourgeoisie strongly protested these performances, while the white gentry expressed distaste in the minstrel show's lack of refinement. One of the best-known black troupes, Brooker and Clayton's Georgia Minstrels, which eventually became Sam Hague's Slave troupe of Georgia Minstrels, featured the talented Charles "Barrey" Hicks, Bob Height, and Billy Kersands at different points in time. The Georgia Minstrels were very popular in the 1870s and, over the course of the next few decades, were eventually joined by several other black troupes. F. S. Wolcott's Rabbit Foot Minstrels would continue to tour through the middle of the nineteenth century, and featured famous black blues singers such as Bessie Smith, Gertrude

"Ma" Rainey, Big Joe Williams, Ida Cox, and Rufus Thomas, as well as the comic duo Butterbeans and Susie.

Billy Kersands of the George Minstrels, who had started his own black minstrel troupe in 1885, represents one of the first black comic stars. He was well known for his comic singing, dancing, acrobatics, and drumming, but most of all for his comic facial contortions and unusually large mouth. He was known to put objects, such as billiard balls, in his mouth while dancing, for a thunderous reaction. Other well-known black minstrels include Tom Fletcher, Sam Lucas, Tom McIntosh, A. D. Sawyer, Charles Hicks, the self-proclaimed inventor of the cakewalk Billy McClain, and the prolific songwriter and cerebral comedian James Bland. Starting with these actors, the dilemma of black comedians could be characterized by the fine line between satirizing white stereotypes and contributing to those very stereotypes. What remains true of minstrelsy in the black comic tradition is that it became the arena for black performers to create and test out comic tropes and antics that would remain into the present day.

Into the first part of the twentieth century, servile examples of black comedy continued to fuel performances on the mainstream stage, in vaudeville, in print, on the radio, and in the new medium of silent film. Comic shorts such as *Laughing Ben, A Nigger in a Woodpile,* and *Who Said Chicken?* that played in nickelodeon theaters around the turn of the century would establish film as a prominent medium for such examples. While popular black comedians and film stars employed the stereotypes and comic devices of minstrelsy, including the use of blackface, they often did so with hints of subversion. Such has been said of the celebrated comedian and film actor Stepin Fetchit (born Lincoln Theodore Monroe Andrew Perry) and his comic offshoot Mantan Moreland, as well as Hattie McDaniel, Willie Best, and others. In addition, the comic duos of Bert Williams (America's first black comic superstar) and George Walker and of Flournoy Miller and Aubrey Lyles perpetuated these "comedies of the grotesque" in the musical theater, even as they were able to experiment and expand their comic repertoire.

At the same time, however, black comedy directed primarily toward black audiences began to reflect pent-up resentment and a more irreverent critique of white racist society. Bombastic performances of mythic "Bad Nigger" ballads and toasts like "Shine and the Titanic," "The Signifying Monkey," "Dolemite," "Stackolee," and those featuring actual African American cultural heroes like the racially controversial boxing champion Jack Johnson began surfacing at black, predominantly male venues. Moreover, the "John and Ole Massa" stories reappeared in the oral literature of this period and replaced animal representations and childish portrayals of the trickster. For obvious reasons, these more overtly critical folktakes did not get printed by the mainstream white press in the way that the Brer Rabbit tales did. However, Zora Neale Hurston, Arthur Huff Faucet, and other black ethnologists began accumulating in print such folklore in the context of people's everyday lives.

Some of the best achievements in black comedy during the early decades of the twentieth century occurred through the literature of the New Negro Movement, starting with the breakthroughs of Paul Lawrence Dunbar's dialect poetry and Charles W. Chesnutt's recasting of Harris' Uncle Remus tales in *The Conjure Woman.* Rudolph Fisher, George Schuyler, and Wallace Thurman presented the culture with satirical novels that leveled the absurdity, on both sides of the equation, of American race relations. The prolific writer Langston Hughes eventually gained recognition as a notable humorist with the publication of his novel *Not without Laughter* in 1930 followed later on by the creation of his wartime serialization of "Simple" stories in the *Chicago Defender*. Zora Neale Hurston's literary renderings of the folklore she amassed as an anthropologist, such as those recalled in her celebrated collection *Mules and Men* (1935), brilliantly and hilariously capture the comic sensibilities of traditional African American humor—sensibilities that would continue to shape the acts of black comedians to this day.

African American comedy took a notable turn in the 1950s when the mounting frustration over racial injustice finally came to a head with the mass organization of civil rights struggle in the South and across the nation. Tolerance for popular representations of black people as coons and buffoons finally met its limit. Protests against these portrayals became more regular and more successful due in part to the backdrop of televised atrocities streaming out of the Jim Crow South into the living rooms of white Northerners. Protests against the *Amos 'n' Andy* television program organized by the National Association for the Advancement of Colored People, for example, generated enough pressure to force the show's cancellation after just two seasons in 1953. Continuing pressure would eventually prompt the CBS Corporation to cease all reruns in 1966.

In literature, Ralph Ellison's *Invisible Man* paved the way for a new kind of satirical novel that employed African American comic sensibilities to deeply explore the absurdity of American racism and critique the problems of black protest without restraint or fear of censorship. Over the course of the tumultuous decades of the Civil Rights and Black Power movements, comedic novels of this sort would be produced by Chester Himes, Ishmael Reed, Charles Wright, Cecil Brown, and others. Similarly during this era, black stand-up comedians with politically charged humor began to dominate the popular scene. Slappy White, the "father of the integrated joke," Moms Mabley, "the funniest woman in the world," Redd Foxx, with his raunchy nightclub acts, and others unleashed their unrestrained wit on stages along the "chitlin' circuit." In the 1960s, Dick Gregory reached comic superstar status with his cerebral and overtly political humor. Gregory, as well as the collective contributions of comedians of the Civil Rights era, had a great influence on the comic genius Richard Pryor. Pryor, who channeled the entire African American comic tradition in his sharply political stand-up act, set the tone for the comic greats of the last part of the century, including Whoopi Goldberg, Bill Cosby, Eddie Murphy, Chris Rock, and Dave Chappelle.

Danielle C. Heard

See also: Cinema; Jim Crow.

Further Reading

Beatty, Paul. *Hokum: An Anthology of African-American Humor.* New York: Bloomsbury, 2006.

Boskin, Joseph. *Sambo: The Rise & Demise of an American Jester.* New York: Oxford University Press, 1986.

Dance, Daryl Cumber. *Honey, Hush! An Anthology of African American Women's Humor.* New York: W. W. Norton, 1998.

Levine, Lawrence W. *Black Culture and Black Consciousness: Afro-American Folk Thought from Slavery to Freedom.* New York: Oxford University Press, 2007.

Schechter, William. *The History of Negro Humor in America.* New York: Fleet Press Corp., 1970.

Watkins, Mel, ed. *African American Humor: The Best Black Comedy from Slavery.* Chicago: Lawrence Hill Books, 2002.

Watkins, Mel. *On the Real Side: A History of African American Comedy.* Chicago: Lawrence Hill Books, 1999.

J

Jim Crow

The term "Jim Crow" refers to the system of racial segregation and oppression that existed primarily in the South from 1877 to the mid-1960s. Segregation existed in some parts of the North, yet by the turn of the century it had become a distinctly Southern phenomenon. In *Plessy v. Ferguson* (1896) the U.S. Supreme Court declared that "separate but equal" was constitutional and this provided the legal backbone for segregation until it was overturned by *Brown v. Board of Education* (1954). In reality, "separate but equal" was never really equal. Racial segregation violated the intent of the Fourteenth Amendment, but the federal government continued to sanction the state laws and practices of Jim Crow until the passage of the Civil Rights Act of 1964. The Jim Crow era marked the ascendancy of white supremacy and not only consisted of the social separation of the races, but more broadly included lynching and mob violence, the manipulation of the justice system, inequality in education, economic subjugation, and the elimination of black suffrage.

The term Jim Crow is derived from the name of a character in a minstrel song performed by Thomas Dartmouth Rice in the 1830s. Blackface minstrelsy was a form of popular entertainment in which white actors blackened their face with cork and imitated what they considered to be authentic African American dialect, dance, and song. These theatrical performances frequently ridiculed African Americans and exaggerated alleged black characteristics. Rice named his act "Jump Jim Crow" and claimed to have based it on a dance he saw performed by an aged crippled slave in Louisville, Kentucky, owned by a Mr. Crow. Wearing ragged clothing representative of a field hand, Rice sang and danced to lyrics that included the stanza "Weel about and turn about / And do jis so, / Eb'ry time I weel about / And jump Jim Crow." The routine was immensely popular during the antebellum period, and the figure of Jim Crow became a recognizable and enduring icon in American popular culture. In the 1840s, abolitionists used the phrase Jim Crow to describe segregated

African American men march in the 1940s with a casket symbolizing the imminent dismantling and "death" of Jim Crow laws. (Library of Congress)

railroad cars. By the end of the nineteenth century, the term came to signify the social separation of the races.

Two forms of Jim Crow existed in the South: *de jure* and *de facto*. De jure segregation referred to the separation of the races as mandated specifically by law and de facto segregation occurred by custom or tradition. In the 1880s, laws such as the segregation of street cars appeared sporadically across the South. Between 1890 and 1915, Southern states enacted an array of statutes that led to a more rigid and universal framework for the social separation of the races. This explosion of de jure segregation reflected Southern whites' growing unease about a younger, more assertive generation of African Americans who demanded respect and recognition of their rights. In addition, the intent of widespread codification was to solidify custom and to eliminate uncertainty about the social status of blacks and whites. Signs labeled "For White" and "For Colored" dominated the Southern landscape, and Jim Crow regulated social contact in such places as restaurants, hotels, movie theaters, parks, schools, libraries, hospitals, and waiting rooms. In many cases, separation often meant total exclusion. State legislatures also enacted antimiscegenation laws prohibiting interracial marriage and passed laws or rewrote the state constitutions to make voter registration difficult, if not impossible.

Although Southern states passed an elaborate network of laws, de facto practices of segregation endured. Patterns of de facto segregation varied depending on the location, the traditions of a community, or even the whim of a white person. In most places, whites and blacks were expected to abide by an unspoken racial etiquette. For example, blacks could not enter a white home through the front door, address a white person by his or her first name, or refuse to give way to a white person on a sidewalk. Courtrooms often swore in black witnesses with separate bibles, and in many stores, blacks could not be served until white customers were finished. Whites did make exceptions for black domestic workers, but only because a black servant tending to white children in a space marked as white still clearly retained a position of inferiority. For many African Americans, Jim Crow caused incredible apprehension about the repercussions of crossing the color line. Any action taken by a black man or woman that whites perceived to be impudent or disrespectful could lead to swift and violent retaliation.

After World War II, the edifice of Jim Crow began to break down. Black soldiers questioned the logic of having to fight for democracy abroad while returning home to face continued racial inequality. Protest on the grassroots level as well that initiated by institutions and celebrated leaders spread in the 1950s and early 1960s. The growing Civil Rights Movement ultimately pressured the federal government to take action. In 1964, the U.S. Congress answered President Lyndon B. Johnson's call to support racial equality and end Jim Crow. Congress enacted the Civil Rights Act of 1964, which forbade discrimination in public places; provided funding for assistance to further desegregate schools; created the Equal Employment Opportunity Commission; and gave the attorney general more authority to prosecute civil rights violations involving voting, the use of public facilities, government, and education. It was the most extensive piece of federal legislation in support of civil rights ever ratified by Congress. While racial discrimination and oppression did not entirely disappear following the passage of the Civil Rights Act, it truly marked the end of the widespread legal and social system of Jim Crow.

Natalie J. Ring

See also: Reconstruction.

Further Reading

Ayers, Edward. *The Promise of the New South: Life after Reconstruction.* New York: Oxford University Press, 1992.

Chafe, William Henry, Raymond Gavins, and Robert Korstad, eds. *Remembering Jim Crow: African Americans Tell about Life in the Segregated South.* New York: New Press, 2003.

Educational Broadcasting Corporation. *The Rise and Fall of Jim Crow.* Public Broadcasting Service TV series, 2002. http://www.pbs.org/wnet/jimcrow/ (accessed May 23, 2008).

Lhamon, W. T. Jr. *Jump Jim Crow: Lost Plays, Lyrics, and Street Prose of the First Atlantic Popular Culture.* Cambridge, MA: Harvard University Press, 2003.

Litwack, Leon F. *Trouble in Mind: Black Southerners in the Age of Jim Crow.* New York: Alfred A. Knopf, 1998.

Johnson, Jack

Jack Johnson was the first African American heavyweight boxing champion. As champion from 1908 to 1915, Johnson held the most important athletic title in all of American sports. Before him, white heavyweight champions refused to fight African American contenders. Battering whites in the ring, Johnson shattered the myth that white men were physically superior to African Americans. Outside the ring, he rebelled against white authority by defying the law and flaunting his relationships with white women. Johnson embodied a physical challenge to Jim Crow.

A poster from *The San Francisco Chronicle* advertises the July 4, 1910, heavy-weight championship match between James J. Jeffries (left) and Jack Johnson. (Library of Congress)

Arthur John "Jack" Johnson was born a year after the collapse of Reconstruction, in 1878, in Galveston, Texas. Johnson's father, Henry, labored as a school janitor, while his mother, Tina, worked as a laundress to support their six children. For five or six years, Johnson attended elementary school. His boxing education began when he started fighting in battle royals. In these humiliating contests, white men formed a circle around black youths, who were sometimes blindfolded, and forced them to fight each other until only one was left standing. The victor won a handful of pennies. By his late teens, Johnson traveled throughout the country boxing against minor professionals.

In 1901, Johnson fought Joe Choynski, an experienced fighter, in Galveston. After Choynski knocked out Johnson, both were locked behind bars for nearly a month for violating Texas laws that prohibited prizefighting. Freed from jail, Johnson continued to fight, defeating the best contenders Galveston had to offer. Later that year, he left for California to fight new opponents. At that time, Johnson had no chance at the heavyweight title. In 1892, champion John L. Sullivan drew the color line, refusing to enter the ring with African American challengers. Although African Americans fought white champions in other divisions, heavyweight title bouts remained segregated. For many Americans, the heavyweight champion represented the "king of men," and as long as a white man wore the crown, whites continued to believe in their own inherent racial superiority.

As a premier African American heavyweight, Johnson earned a shot at the Negro heavyweight championship against Denver Ed Martin in 1903. After defeating Martin, he defended his title against the best African American fighters, including Sam McVey, Sam Langford, and Joe Jeannette. Holding the Negro championship brought Johnson little fame and fortune. For the next three years, he fought the best black and white boxers in the country, but white champions ignored him.

By 1905, boxing seemed to decline in popularity. Five years earlier, reform-minded politicians banned the sport by law, claiming that prizefighting promoted corruption, gambling, and immoral behavior. With little interest in boxing, purses shrank, and the heavyweight champion Jim Jeffries retired undefeated. At the same time, Johnson fought against less-talented white fighters, often carrying his opponents round after round in order to dish out more punishment. He also hired a white manager who had the kind of connections that would help Johnson break the color barrier. Significantly, Johnson began traveling openly with white women, most of whom were prostitutes.

Johnson journeyed to Australia in 1907 to build up his international reputation. Later that year, he earned a match in Philadelphia against an aging former champion, Bob Fitzsimmons. Johnson dropped Fitzsimmons in two rounds and celebrated with a white prostitute named Hattie McClay, who became his travel companion over the next four years. The next year, Johnson chased heavyweight champion Tommy Burns to Australia hoping to arrange a title fight. Burns rejected his overtures, but Johnson persisted. The champ eventually gave in, after Johnson agreed to let the white fighter keep $30,000 of the $35,000 purse.

From the opening seconds of the first round, it was clear Johnson would win. Toned and powerful, Johnson toyed with Burns. He laughed as Burns wailed away at his midsection, dispelling the myth that African American men lacked intestinal fortitude. Burns fought back with racial epithets. Johnson hammered him until the 14th round. For the first time in history an African American held the heavyweight championship.

Almost immediately, promoters searched for the "Great White Hope," a boxer who could restore the crown to the white side of the color line. As the search began, Johnson returned to America in 1909, more determined to live by his own rules. He bought flashy suits, fancy hats, and fast cars. The American public began to hear stories about his nightlife carousing with white women. In Chicago, he met a young prostitute named Belle Schreiber, who became one of his closest mistresses. Johnson lived recklessly, racing cars, ignoring speed limits, and racking up unpaid tickets. Jack Johnson insisted on being free.

After Johnson easily discarded every white challenger he faced, America finally found its White Hope, pressuring Jim Jeffries out of retirement. Now 35 years old and extremely overweight, Jeffries was far from prepared to save the white race. Nonetheless, the astronomical $101,000 purse and the fight's movie revenue provided plenty of motivation for him to lose more than 70 pounds before the match.

Originally scheduled for San Francisco, promoters moved the battle for racial supremacy to Reno, Nevada. The media depicted Johnson in Sambo cartoons, stereotypically portraying him as childlike and cowardly. More than 20,000 people traveled to Reno to witness the "fight of the century." Drunken gamblers placed bets right up until the opening bell. When the two men finally raised their gloves on July 10, 1910, it was clear that Johnson was the stronger boxer. He unleashed a series of counterpunches and uppercuts on Jeffries. By the 15th round, Jeffries's face had swollen as he struggled to stand upright. Finally, Johnson drilled him until he fell to the canvas. Jeffries's corner threw in the towel. The Great White Hope had fallen.

After Johnson's victory, white mobs attacked celebrating African Americans in numerous cities. To prevent further riots, authorities banned the showing of the fight film, while others called for an end to boxing all together. The new champion struck fear in whites who viewed Johnson as a dangerous role model for African Americans. Johnson hoped his fame would translate into a successful vaudeville career, but theater promoters feared boycotts or riots would follow the champion on stage. Johnson added to his controversial reputation by marrying Etta Terry Duryea, a previously wed white woman. He angered his new wife by continuing his relationship with Belle Schreiber. Duryea could not share her husband, or stand his physical abuse, and eventually committed suicide.

Nearly two months after his wife's death, Johnson married another young white woman, Lucille Cameron. Cameron's mother charged Johnson with abduction and white slavery, a federal violation of the Mann Act, which forbade the transportation of women in interstate travel for immoral purposes. The case fell apart when Cameron admitted to practicing prostitution before she met Johnson. Although the federal government knew he was not guilty, they pursued conviction, persuading Schreiber to testify against him. In May 1913, Johnson was convicted of trumped-up Mann Act charges. The judge sentenced him to 366 days in prison and a $1,000 fine. Defiantly, Johnson fled to Montreal, Canada, and then set sail for France. Over the next year and a half, he staged shows, boxing exhibitions, and wrestling matches throughout Europe, but struggled to earn money with the onset of World War I.

After defending his title three times in Paris, Johnson arranged a fight with another White Hope in Cuba. On April 5, 1915, Johnson squared off against the six-foot-six "Pottawatomie Giant," Jess Willard. In the 26th round, Willard took advantage of the aging champion and landed a long right punch that knocked Johnson down. Many reporters believed that the fight was fixed. Johnson later maintained that he threw the match for a large sum of money and a lenient return to the United States. Historians doubt Johnson's claim. Nonetheless, Willard reinstated the color line, and not until 1937 did another African American, Joe Louis, win the heavyweight championship.

Jack Johnson's boxing career basically ended after the Willard fight. Over the next five years, he fought unspectacular boxers and took up bullfighting in Spain and Mexico. After seven years in exile, he turned himself in to U.S. marshals in July 1920 at the California border. Thereafter he served one year in prison at Leavenworth, Kansas. For the rest of his life he worked a variety of jobs, as a boxing promoter, museum lecturer, preacher, and nightclub owner. During World War II, he fought an exhibition at the age of 67 to raise money for the war effort. Johnson was no longer the fighter he once was, but he could still race cars. On June 10, 1946, his life ended when he crashed his speeding automobile in North Carolina.

John Matthew Smith

See also: Jim Crow.

Further Reading

Roberts, Randy. *Papa Jack: Jack Johnson and the Era of White Hopes.* New York: Free Press, 1983.

Ward, Geoffrey C. *Unforgivable Blackness: The Rise and Fall of Jack Johnson.* New York: A. A. Knopf, 2004.

K

Kentucky

The Commonwealth of Kentucky was admitted in the Union on June 1, 1792, becoming the nation's first state west of the Appalachian Mountains. Isaac Shelby was elected the state's first governor, and Frankfort was chosen the capital. During the first half of the nineteenth century, Kentucky was primarily a state of small farms rather than large plantations. In 1833, the state's General Assembly passed a law that made the importation of slaves into the state illegal. In 1850, however, the legislature repealed this restriction, and Kentucky, while slave trading had began to redevelop during the mid-1840s, was converted into a huge slave market for the Lower South. At the same time, the overall population of African American Kentuckians began to increase. For example, in 1800, of the 220,955 people who resided in the Bluegrass State, 41,084 were black Americans who lived mostly in the state's major urban centers. Thirty years later, in 1830, the number of African Americans throughout the state had increased to 24.7 percent of the overall population (170,130 of the 687,917 inhabitants of Kentucky were black Americans).

Antislavery and abolitionist sentiment began in the state as early as the late eighteenth century. In various churches and other civic organizations, people such as John G. Fee, James G. Birney, Delia Webster, Calvin Fairbank, and Cassius M. Clay worked vigorously throughout Kentucky to eliminate the system of human bondage. This group was joined by a cadre of African Americans, like Eliza Harris, Henry Bibb, Lewis Hayden, John Rankin, John Parker, and Margaret Garner, who set out to prove that slavery could not stand in a state as well as a nation that rested on the principles stated in the Declaration of Independence. Soon Kentucky, like other border states, was torn by conflict over the issue of slavery. With the onset of the Civil War, with 30,000 Kentuckians fighting for the Confederacy, and about 64,000 serving in the Union ranks, including some 23,000 African Americans, the institution of slavery came to an end.

In 1865, as a result of the passage of the Thirteenth Amendment, black Americans in the Bluegrass State gained citizenship. However, many white Kentuckians, retaining their racist views about African Americans, sought to prove that they still were in charge. More specifically, with the help of various white supremacist groups like the Ku Klux Klan, the enormous gains African Americans made in Kentucky during Reconstruction, as well as nationwide, came to an unceremonious end. Very quickly, the state began to enact a series of Jim Crow laws such as the 1892 Separate Coach Law, which required separate coaches for blacks and whites on interstate railroads. Although a group of African American Kentuckians tried to challenge the constitutionality of this law in court, in 1900, the U.S. Supreme Court ruled that the law was valid.

During the early 1900s, state politicians continued to enact Jim Crow laws to curtail the educational accessibility and limit the mobility of African American Kentuckians. For example, in 1904, the state passed the Day Law, which required the segregation of all public and private schools. Ten years later, in 1914, the Louisville Board of Alderman passed an ordinance designed to promote residential segregation. This law declared that if the majority of a specific community was one race, then only members of that race could purchase a home in the area. Despite the overturning of this law by the U.S. Supreme Court in *Buchanan v. Warley* (1917), residential segregation unremitting characterized most of the Bluegrass State until the late 1960s. However, the stern walls of legal segregation had started to crumble during the late 1940s.

In 1949, a federal court ordered the University of Kentucky to admit African Americans to its engineering, graduate, law, and pharmacy schools. A bill was defeated in the Kentucky General Assembly to rescind the Day Law in 1954; however, the landmark *Brown v. Board of Education* on May 17, 1954, made this challenge moot. Most educational facilities throughout the state quickly complied with this ruling, thus avoiding the harsh battles that erupted throughout the Deep South. Although unwritten discrimination practices continued in Kentucky during most of the 1950s and early 1960s, most of the overt forms of residential segregation gradually disappeared mostly as a result of the pressure garnered by civil rights–led boycotts and marches throughout the state. For example, in March 1968, Kentucky became the first state to enact a statewide anti-housing discrimination law.

Eric R. Jackson

See also: Jim Crow.

Further Reading

Harrison, Lowell H., and James C. Klotter. *A New History of Kentucky.* Lexington: University Press of Kentucky, 1997.

Klotter, James C. *Our Kentucky: A Study of the Bluegrass State.* Lexington: University Press of Kentucky, 1992.

King, Martin Luther, Jr.

Martin Luther King Jr. was a theologian, social activist, lecturer, and author. Born into a middle-class family in Atlanta, Georgia, King, during the decades of the 1950s and 1960s, first represented the social, moral, and political aspirations and struggles of black Americans during the age of segregation and would become the leader of the Civil Rights Movement generally organized in black churches and supported largely by middle- and working-class blacks throughout the South. Later, as white resistance in the South organized to oppose desegregation on all levels and violence against blacks and Northern whites who traveled to the South to support desegregation, the movement took on national as well as international importance.

King was a precocious youngster, both mentally and physically, and grew up in a Christian home. His father, Martin Luther King Sr. was the pastor of Ebenezer Baptist Church, the largest black church in Atlanta, and his mother,

The Reverend Dr. Martin Luther King Jr. at a press conference in Birmingham, Alabama, on May 16, 1963. King led the African American struggle to achieve full rights of U.S. citizenship and eloquently voiced the hopes and grievances of African Americans and the poor before he was assassinated in 1968. (Library of Congress)

Alberta Williams King, was the organist. At home, the young King was doted on, was loved and told that he was special, and enjoyed middle-class comforts. Though his parents, especially his father, railed against racism and segregation, they made it a point to remind him that it was very important to transcend hate, even from those who publicly humiliated you. King joined the church when he was five, received his first experience of racism when he was six when his white friend, with whom he had played since King was three, suddenly informed him that he could no longer play with him. At eight, he was slapped by a white female on whose feet he accidentally stepped. Before enrolling in Morehouse College at the age 15, King would witness and experience many examples of racial and social injustice that prevailed in Atlanta. He was mostly undaunted by such examples, and all visible and overt examples of racism he experienced in the world outside of the home were largely negated by the expressions of love and devotion directed toward him by his parents and others who recognized his talents: he won an oratory contest when he was 14 on the theme "The Negro and the Constitution."

Enrollment at the all-male Morehouse College (1944–1948) for a BA in sociology and Crozer (1948–1951) for his BD threw King into an intellectual and academic world that, he claimed, shattered his fundamentalist upbringing. For in these worlds, he rediscovered Thoreau and discovered Hobbes, Marx, Locke, Mill, Nietzsche, and the writings of Christian theologians, W.E.B. Du Bois, and the Satyagraha theory of Mahatma Gandhi. This exposure prompted King to reflect on two features of religion he would seek to attain: the infusion of more intellect, not just emotion, in black sermons, and his view that religion should be used to challenge and change the existing society, not simply adapt to its ongoing values and norms. He later attended Boston University (1951–1955), where he received a doctorate in theology. There, he met Coretta Scott, who was studying to become a concert singer. They were married in Marion, Alabama, in June 1953.

In April 1954 King accepted an offer to become the pastor at Dexter Baptist Church in Montgomery, Alabama, while completing his dissertation at Boston University. He was installed as pastor in October of that same year. King, however, was indecisive with respect to his future career. He was torn between a career in education and a career as a pulpit minister, just as he was once torn between living in the North or living in the South. He chose living in the South because he pledged himself to work to resolve racial and human rights problems in the area. On December 1, 1955, Rosa Parks was arrested for refusing to give up her bus seat to a white man, though no other seats were available in the bus. After her arrest, the ministers assembled and elected King president of the Montgomery Improvement Association (MIA). After a judge deemed Parks guilty and fined her $100, the MIA agreed to launch a bus boycott. The news of the boycott spread like wildfire throughout the South; the boycott was successful, and it was the beginning of

King's problems with justice in the South. Between the beginning of the boycott and November 1956, when the U.S. Supreme Court struck down the segregation law as unconstitutional, King was arrested for speeding—30 miles per hour in an area with a 25 miles per hour speed limit—and received more than 40 death threats, and, on January 30, 1956, his home was bombed. During this time, King was solidifying two approaches that would be a part of his strategy in resolving social issues: a Christian approach that emphasized Christian love and forgiveness, and Gandhi's method of winning through nonviolence. He visited Gandhi's India in February 1959, where he got a close look at the world of the untouchables, those at the bottom of the Indian caste system. King's leadership was recognized by many in the Civil Rights Movement, for he was elected president of the Southern Christian Leadership Conference.

As demonstrations against racial segregation in the South began to spread, King was called upon to lead these demonstrations and to help organize the protests. The demonstration against segregation in Birmingham, Alabama, would be the next test case after Montgomery. It was here after his arrest in April 1963 for protesting racial segregation in the city that King wrote his famous "Letter from a Birmingham Jail."

This letter, written on the margins of old newspapers, scraps of paper, and legal pads, was first of all a castigation of the Christian ministers who criticized King for leading the protest in the city. It was also the beginning of King's assertion that there were just laws (God's Laws) and unjust laws (human laws), and citizens had an obligation to disobey unjust laws. In August 1963, King made his famous "I Have a Dream Speech" to the more than 300,000 people assembled on the Mall in Washington, D.C. King reminded the nation that it was time to put an end to segregation, that Americans had to be conscious of the importance of the Declaration of Independence and the Constitution in the making of the nation, and that blacks have come too far to give up or permit the freedoms they had won to disappear. The speech was an often stern message to both whites and blacks: for whites, to judge Americans not by their color but by their character; for blacks, the advice was to stay strong and remain disciplined in their protests.

In 1964, King was honored as *Time* magazine's Man of the Year, published the book, *Why We Can't Wait,* and, in December of that year, received the Nobel Peace Prize in Oslo, Norway. Then overt racial strife began to break out in the North, the Vietnam War was heating up, and critics of the war began to overtly question the government's war policy. Young blacks, more impatience than their elders, began to utter the cry of Black Power as a new approach to power and diversity in American life. Younger members of the movement had long expressed their discontent with older leaders, withdrew from their association with older members of the movement, and formed the Student Nonviolent Coordinating Committee in April 1960.

King began to compare the war in Vietnam as an example of the attempt by the large Western nations to colonize Third World nations of color. First, he raised the issue of spending billions for war while the poor were not being sufficiently cared for at home. King's public antiwar declarations strained the racial alliance he had formerly created to address issues of poverty and discrimination, for there were whites who favored the war as a necessary war against Communist aggression, while supporting all efforts to abolish segregation in the United States. King also raised the issue of "guns vs. butter" and whether it was possible for the nation to spend billions abroad and not neglect its problems at home. King opposed the war on moral and economic grounds. Like Malcolm X before his death, King wanted to move from civil rights to a more universal human rights movement and struggle, and he saw nothing wrong in linking the American Civil Rights Movement to international political and war matters.

King understood the importance of the idea of Black Power for black youth given the historical legacy of slavery and segregation. He believed the slogan "Black Is Beautiful" to be positive and asserted the right of any group to be proud of itself. He was simply afraid of "excessive" racial or ethnic pride, one that might short-circuit attempts to forge social and political alliances with others. He was particularly concerned that young blacks were raising the cry of race precisely at the moment the rest of the world was focusing on the changing world economy and the impact of automation on all aspects of life. Above all, King hoped to forge alliances between all segments of American society—poor whites, Hispanics, Asians, and Native Americans. That he was unable to forge such alliances would be one of his greatest disappointments.

The year 1967 was one of massive urban devastation as riots occurred in a number of large American cities, and King's last book, *Where Do We Go from Here? Chaos or Community,* seemed to mirror some of his disappointments due to notable progress in racial and human relations and the lack of great progress in alleviating abject poverty in the nation. Despite these shortcomings, King continued to believe that the nation would right the wrongs perpetuated against blacks and other minorities. He was a moral leader who believed white Americans could and would step up to the plate and do the right thing, and he also believed that blacks would not give up their quest for greater freedoms in the nation. He also believed that black Americans would link their struggles at home to the struggles of others abroad, and thereby strengthen the politics of one type of power confronting another power, but with love, patience, and forgiveness in the forefront.

When King agreed to travel to Memphis, Tennessee, to join others in support of the striking sanitation workers, he was warned to be careful, and he, himself, had a degree of uneasiness, though he did go. His speech in the Memphis Masonic Temple, "I've Been to the Mountain Top" was revealing in that he vowed to fight on and to look death in the face and remain unafraid and unbowed. On April 4, 1968, he was shot and killed on the balcony of the Lorraine Motel in Memphis by James Earl Ray.

Rutledge M. Dennis

See also: Abernathy, Ralph David; Montgomery Bus Boycott.

Further Reading

Branch, Taylor. *Parting the Waters: America in the King Years, 1954–1963.* New York: Simon and Schuster, 1988.

King, Coretta Scott. *My Life with Martin Luther King, Jr.* New York: Holt, Rinehart and Winston, 1969.

King, Martin Luther, Jr. *Letter from Birmingham City Jail.* Philadelphia: American Friends Service Committee, 1963.

King, Martin Luther, Jr. *Where Do We Go from Here: Chaos or Community?* New York: Harper and Row, 1967.

Lincoln, C. Eric, ed. *Martin Luther King, Jr.: A Profile.* New York: Hill and Wang, 1984.

Walton, Hanes. *The Political Philosophy of Martin Luther King, Jr.* Westport, CT: Greenwood Press, 1971.

Ku Klux Klan

The Ku Klux Klan (KKK) is the name of various terrorist organizations originally created in late 1865 to restore white Democratic rule to the recently defeated states of the former Confederacy. In order to realize their goal, the KKK used violence and the threat of violence to prevent blacks from exercising their civil rights, and to cower or drive out whites who assisted blacks or in any way supported Republican rule in the South. The original Ku Klux Klan can be interpreted as a continuation of the Civil War by insurgency. The original Klan and other white supremacist terrorist groups such as the White League were able to drive blacks away from the voting booth in large enough numbers to allow the legal disenfranchisement of blacks. The original Klan largely disappeared by the mid-1870s. It revived in 1915, and reached new heights of influence in the 1920s, when the Klan became politically strong in several states, particularly in the Midwest. The new Klan focused on Jews, Catholics, and immigrants as much as blacks. After declining into obscurity in the 1930s, new, more violent organizations calling themselves the KKK began to thrive in the 1950s, ostensive defending traditional American values against communism, but in practice attempting to use violence to prevent integration and black voting.

The original Ku Klux Klan was created by six former Confederate soldiers on Christmas Eve in 1865, in Pulaski, Tennessee. According to later accounts, several former Confederates dressed in white sheets pretending to be the ghosts of Confederate dead and rode around in the night to frighten the local black population. After seeing the effect of their actions, the night riding continued. The men, all college educated, chose the name *Ku Klux Klan,* based on the Greek word *kyklos,* meaning circle, and the word *Clan,* which reflected the commonly held idea that white Southern culture was transplanted Scottish Highlander culture. Originally, the Klan focused on terrorizing blacks who attempted to change their social, economic, and political subordination. However, the Klan also targeted white Republicans who assisted blacks.

The Klan relied on grassroots organization and newspapers stories of Klan activities to spread its message across the occupied South. From 1866 until 1869, many groups with little or no formal coordination between them referred to themselves as the Ku Klux Klan. Their tactics were similar, including face coverings, the use of horses, and the tendency to attack during the night. While the original group dressed in white, other groups began using a wide variety of costumes to conceal their identity. Soon almost all areas of the South under federal control had at least one group claiming to be part of the KKK, although some groups were more bent on theft, revenge killing, or general mayhem than restoring white Democratic rule to the South.

Despite attempts to create a hierarchy, the movement remained decentralized and not subject to any central direction. Most KKK groups agreed broadly on ending Republican rule over the South. To accomplish that goal, the Klan used extra-legal means such as murder, arson, whipping, and intimidation to keep blacks from voting, and assuring that blacks remained socially inferior to whites. Most victims were black and white Republicans. Arkansas congressman James M. Hinds and three members of the South Carolina legislature were only the most prominent Republicans killed by the Klan. Enraged by this lawlessness and flagrant attacks on its political base, Republicans in Congress passed the Civil Rights Act of 1871, also known as the Ku Klux Klan Act, which empowered civil and military authorities to use federal power to destroy the Ku Klux Klan. President Ulysses S. Grant backed the Radical Republicans and used the act to bring the Klan to bay. However, other forces also worked against the Klan. Middle- and upper-class Southern whites increasingly feared the lack of control over the Klan by the "better" elements in society. Additionally, Reconstruction was drawing to an end, and some areas had been returned to civil control. Once Klan activity helped white Democrats to assume control of all elected offices, extra-legal methods to keep Republicans from voting were no longer needed. Indeed, some Democrats began to argue that the continued violence and even existence of the Klan only served to keep federal troops in the

South longer. By 1873, the original Ku Klux Klan was largely defunct. However, it had largely fulfilled its purpose. With the declining federal presence in the South, white Democrats increasingly gained control of state and local governments. Thus state laws, state courts, and sheriff's departments could increasingly be used to oppress blacks lawfully.

The rebirth of the Ku Klux Klan came as part of a general romanticization of the Civil War era. The novels *Leopard's Spots* (1903) and *The Clansman* (1905) by Thomas Dixon presented a heroic interpretation of the Klan as chivalrous gentlemen who fought blacks, carpetbaggers, and scalawags to return civilization to the South during Reconstruction. The novels introduced the concept of the burning cross as a symbol of the Klan, something that was never used by the original Klan. The burning cross borrowed on Scottish highlander traditions of using burning crosses on hilltops as a way to call together the Highland clans in the event of invasion or other crisis, although the Scots used a diagonal St. Andrews cross. Dixon probably got the idea of the Scottish Highlander clans burning crosses from Sir Walter Scott's 1810 poem the *Lady of the Lake,* which had been popular among white Southerners. The images of the Ku Klux Klan in the novels became even more entrenched in popular culture as a result of D. W. Griffith, who used the novels as the basic of one of the first truly modern motion pictures, *The Birth of a Nation* in 1915.

The Klan was reborn in 1915 in a wave of nostalgia, nativism, and anti-Semitism. The immediate cause for the revised Ku Klux Klan was the trial and conviction in Georgia of a Northern Jewish factory owner named Leo Frank for the rape and murder of a young factory worker named Mary Phagan. Although little evidence connected him to the crime, he was a Northerner, wealthy, and Jewish. After his appeals in the trial failed, the governor commuted his death sentence to life in jail. However, the threat of mob violence had surrounded the case from the beginning, and after the commutation, a group of vigilantes calling itself the Knights of Mary Phagan took Frank from the prison farm where he was being held and lynched him.

Many Southerners, especially in Georgia, saw the death of Phagan at the hands of a Northern Jew as synonymous with the suffering of white womanhood under Reconstruction as depicted in the film *The Birth of a Nation.* Although blacks in the South remained relatively powerless through Jim Crow, some white Southerners believed a revived Klan was needed against a new host of perceived enemies, such as Catholics, Jews, immigrants, and the decline of sexual morality. The new Klan was inaugurated in 1915 at a meeting led by William J. Simmons on top of Stone Mountain, Georgia. Along with the Knights of Mary Phagan, some men attending claimed to have been members of the original KKK. The new group, calling itself the Knights of the Ku Klux Klan, was more organized than the original

Klan, but still had little central control and no one executive leader. New terms and offices were invented, and Klan attire became more regular. While the members of the original Klan wore a variety of costumes, often in colors other than white, members of the new Klan tended to wear the familiar white robe with pointed top.

While Southern Klansmen could act more openly, the Klan found its most fertile recruiting grounds in the Midwest, areas in which the black population was increasing due to the Great Migration, but without formal Jim Crow laws to oppress blacks. In the South, the Klan orchestrated lynches, or members participated as individuals, but much of the Klan's attacks were in the form of arson, beatings, or whippings. Most Klan activity was more psychological, using the burning cross or simply announcing its presence to instill fear. With blacks in the South excluded from government and the judicial process, Klansmen could act with a sense of impunity. Klan groups seldom participated in overtly violent acts together, and unlike the former KKK, almost never wore Klan regalia during acts of racial violence. Instead, through rhetoric and public spectacle of the rally and mass meeting that featured a burning cross, Klan leaders spread their message of using violence against blacks, Jews, Catholics, or whoever angered the local group. Then Klansmen, working in small groups, would carry out specific acts of violence. In the case of an allegation of rape or murder of a white by a black, Klan members often acted in concert with non-Klan members in lynching suspects. Outside of the South, secrecy was more important, as courts were often less sympathetic. In the Midwest and West, the Klan was often more overtly antiblack, although Catholics, Jews, and other enemies were also targets of Klan activity.

The new Klan grew as a for-profit fraternal organization, pitching itself as the friend of the common man. Klan support for Prohibition made it many friends among rural Protestants, but its real strength came from urban areas, where many old-stock whites saw themselves awash in new peoples, new ideas, and new morality. Many people who did not join the Klan at least tolerated it and even admired it for the Klan's purported support for sexual morality, Protestant Christianity, and opposition to corruption and Communism. The new Klan had dominated some state governments during the 1920s, specifically in Oklahoma, Oregon, and Indiana. In the South, Klan support for honest government and assistance for poor whites against big city corruption also brought it much popular support.

In 1928, the Klan made a showing of its power by a large march down Pennsylvania Avenue in Washington, D.C., but in retrospect, the Klan had already peaked and its influence was on the wane. Klansmen's sense of their own power caused several serious missteps. Their attempt to take control of the Democratic Party in 1924 alerted many who had been ambivalent in the past to the political threat of the Klan. The Klan's use of overt violence against whites believed to be acting immorally in the South lost it much of its political support. Several sexual and financial scandals, including one particularly salacious rape and murder by Grand Dragon David Stephenson of Indiana, destroyed the Klan's claim to represent integrity and morality. The Klan declined in strength and influence throughout the 1930s. By the end of the 1930s, the Ku Klux Klan was again a spent force. Scandals, a recovering economy, and the example of Nazi Germany all helped bring a decline in numbers so that the Klan was negligible as a social or political force.

The Klan did not remain fallow for long. Following the *Brown v. Board of Education* ruling in 1954, new Ku Klux Klan groups formed, taking advantage of white fears of integration. While the Klan in the 1920s drew heavily from the lower middle class, the new Klan was more working class, and its growth reflected the anxiety many poorer whites felt at their relative loss of status and privilege as Jim Crow was dismantled. While not as numerous or as politically powerful as the Klan in the 1920s, the Klan in the 1950s and 1960s used murder, bombs, and arson to spread fear through the Civil Rights Movement. The Klan in the 1950s was not unified in any meaningful sense. Several distinct organizations claimed to be the "true" Ku Klux Klan, with the largest, the Invisible Empire, Knights of the Ku Klux Klan, controlling only a minority of Klansmen. While the Klan in the 1950s and 1960s continued to list the old enemies of Catholics, Jews, and immorality, in practice it was more focused on opposing integration as its main goal. In much of the South during the Jim Crow era, courts and police did an effective job of enforcing segregation. But with the crumbling of Jim Crow, the Klan assumed that mission. The Klan advertised itself as a patriotic organization, dedicated to protecting America against Communism. The Klan used broadsheets, billboards, posters, and speeches to equate integration with Communism, thus taping into Cold War fears about the Soviet Union and Communism to gain a measure of respectability. In reality, the existence of the KKK and similar groups and racial violence as a whole were powerful propaganda issues for the Soviets, who often used the term "Negro lynchers" to refer to non-Communist white Americans. The Soviets publicized throughout the world, especially in the newly independent nations in Africa, lynchings, bombings, and other incidents of American race violence.

The Civil Rights Movement struck directly at white supremacy, and the Klan reacted with increased savagery. One of the most horrific acts of the new Klan came on the early morning of Sunday, September 15, 1963, when a bomb set by Bobby Frank Cherry, Thomas Blanton, and Robert Chambliss, all members of United Klans of America, exploded at the Sixteenth Street Baptist Church in Birmingham, Alabama, killing four girls and wounding another 22. Although some whites in Birmingham, including police chief "Bull" Connor, blamed the bombing on blacks themselves, or on the U.S. Supreme Court for its *Brown* decision, many moderate whites throughout the nation were horrified by the attack. Political pressure built for the federal government to become more involved in protecting blacks and prosecuting terrorists at the federal level. Beginning with Attorney General Robert F. Kennedy, and increasing after the passing of the Civil Rights Act of 1964, the federal government increasingly took an active role in persecuting people who attempted to use violence or the threat of violence against blacks and whites who attempted to ensure that blacks were able to vote. Although deprived of the de facto immunity offered by all-white juries in state courts the Klan had long enjoyed, Klan members continued to use violence in an attempt to maintain white supremacy in the South. In January 1966, a group of white men, led by Samuel Bowers, an Imperial Wizard of the Ku Klux Klan, firebombed civil rights leader Vernon Dahmer's home, killing him.

Although the violence of Klan groups and individual Klansmen in the 1960s and into the 1970s could often be bloody and shocking, their power, as limited as it had been, was again on the wane. With the ending of Jim Crow, blacks in the South formed a formidable voting bloc, which would hold Southern governments accountable for prosecuting Klansmen involved in violent acts. Black voters meant the end of sympathetic all-white juries for Klansmen accused of crimes. The legacy of Klan violence during the Civil Rights Era left the Klan with a poor reputation among middle-class and even most working-class whites. Klan groups that continued to exist increasingly drew from the most marginalized whites in the South, and had little political power.

Barry M. Stentiford

See also: Jim Crow; Lynching.

Further Reading

Carr, Cynthia. *Our Town: A Heartland Lynching, a Haunted Town, and the Hidden History of White America.* New York: Three Rivers Press, 2007.

Chalmers, David. *Backfire: How the Ku Klux Klan Helped the Civil Rights Movement.* Lanham, MD: Rowman & Littlefield, 2005.

Jackson, Kenneth T. *The Ku Klux Klan in the City, 1915–1930.* Chicago: Elephant Paperbacks, 1992.

L

Labor Unions

Labor unions in the United States are affiliated organizations that function as the legal representatives for a multiplicity of workers in various industries. The history of labor unions during the era of Jim Crow is the history of struggle to overcome racism and discrimination within labor unions and the labor movement. It is also a history spotted with episodes of biracial activism. Because racial exclusionary policies are a very effective way to control the labor supply and, consequently, exercise bargaining power over the wages of workers, labor unions, particularly during the era of Jim Crow, have a long history of racial discrimination on their hands. Racial discrimination is fundamental to understanding labor unions during the era of Jim Crow, and, vice versa. Discrimination within unions during the Jim Crow era is unique given the fact that a majority of union leaders' rhetoric and theories were are always quick to include, or at least not explicitly exclude, African Americans by arguing that working-class consciousness would ultimately trump racism. However, in practice and organization techniques, they often fell short and were quick to embrace exclusionary policies that stemmed from Jim Crow policies.

Slavery and Free Labor

The budding relationship between black workers and organized labor movements began to take form during the periods of the Civil War and post–Civil War Reconstruction. The Civil War not only freed three and a half million people of African descent from a life of bondage and oppression by dismantling the institution of slavery but also transformed millions into free laborers, and resurrected union activity that had been static since the depression of 1837. However, it has been noted that was not until the post–Civil War era that the United States completed abolition and had defined civil rights. The politically established principles of free labor had to confront the first nationwide labor organization by the late 1860s.

African American Bricklayers union, Jacksonville, Florida, circa 1900. (Library of Congress)

Unions, arguably, were from the start not concerned with the plight and struggle of Africans Americans. That labor unions and early working-class peoples' opposition to slavery rarely rested on the claim that slavery was a moral injustice imposed upon bond(wo)men is testament to their peculiar strand of racism. Indeed, working-class people of the Midwest and the West became aware and raised concern over the pro-slavery 1854 Kansas-Nebraska Act—an act that would soon allow the expansion of slavery to proceed and expand into the open Midwestern and Western territories—and the Dred Scott decision—a court decision that declared that people of African descent, slaves and nonslaves alike, could never become citizens and declared that Congress had no authority to prohibit slavery in federal territories—not as an expression of the immorality of slavery or commiseration for those enslaved, but rather, expressed outrage over the fact that the expansion slavery might affect their working-class status. To be sure, working-class opposition to slavery was not so much against slavery per se, but against the expansion of slavery that would ultimately jeopardize their status as workers.

Knights of Labor

While the National Labor Union (NLU) and the National Colored Labor Union (NCLU) fought unsuccessfully to preserve their respective unions during the devastating depression of 1873, the Noble Order of the Knights of Labor (KOL) successfully avoided the union-crushing depression and survived to see the early beginnings of Jim Crow. Uriah Stephens, a Philadelphia tailor and antislavery Republican, formed the KOL in 1869. Blacks were loyal to the Republican Party due to its abolitionist past. Originally, the KOL was formed as a secret union that embraced both trade and industrial unions. Moreover, the KOL's rhetoric of racial inclusiveness, Christian evangelicalism, and abolitionist heritage, backed by an unwavering appreciation for class unity, ultimately made the organization acceptable to black workers.

Although the Knights of Labor at their birth practiced exclusionary policies vis-à-vis the black worker, they did lift their ban on black workers during the early shaping of Jim Crow in 1883. The fact that the Knights of Labor boasted an agenda of racial inclusiveness may have led to the dramatic increase in their union membership. By putting worker dissatisfaction, low wages, and class unity across racial lines at the front of their agenda, the Knights of Labor's membership increased dramatically throughout the 1880s. By the mid-1880s, the KOL had won several important strikes and saw its membership increase to approximately 750,000 official union members, of which 60,000 to 90,000 were black. The KOL's commitment to interracial activism trickled down to the workers and created cooperation across the color line. Due to the efforts of the KOL, throughout the Jim Crow South, episodes of interracial working-class unity were at work. Indeed, in the mid-1880s, the heyday of the KOL, the KOL and other unions saw a dramatic increase in the amount of interracial class unity experienced. KOL District Assembly 194 sought negotiations with the nearby black Louisiana Sugar Planters Association in an effort to increase wages and better methods of pay, while white and black miners of Alabama, under the auspices of the KOL, stood unified in strike against wage cuts for mine operators. In the end, prison laborers and Italian immigrants broke the miner's strike.

Although the KOL's rhetoric preached about racial inclusiveness, and while at times they even practiced racial inclusiveness, they too practiced a major policy that defined the Jim Crow South: separatism. While union leaders stood at the pulpit recommending black-white worker unity, they constantly and consistently advocated separate but unified black and white local organizations. Moreover, the KOL were ardent supporters of the anti-Chinese movement and refused to admit Chinese workers. In 1885, in Spring Rock, Wyoming, the KOL led a riot that resulted in the deaths of 28 Chinese railroad workers. They also did not support European immigrants.

In retrospect, the KOL's racial inclusiveness may have been as much responsible for the union's increase in membership in the mid-1880s as much it was responsible for its decrease in the late 1880s. By 1890, 100,000 members remained in the KOL; few of whom were black. The violence of the KOL's strikes caused a decrease in support from blacks, who were once attracted to their peaceful revolutionary style. Despite the KOL's efforts, the period put blacks and the labor movement at further distance.

American Federation of Labor

That the more racially restrictive American Federation of Labor (AFL) replaced the KOL and took control of the labor movement during the nadir of race relations—a racially complex time period starting in 1890 and enduring throughout the Jim Crow era until 1930, when blacks were forced back into noncitizenship and race relations, indeed, got worse—is evident in their workings as an organization. AFL delegates took their cue from the KOL's broad social vision of racial inclusiveness by focusing their efforts on securing higher wages, shorter working days, and improved working conditions for the unions and union members they represented across racial lines. Throughout the early 1890s, the KOL and AFL engaged in bitter disputes around the country as to what the goals of labor movement should be. The AFL rejected the KOL's favoritism of workers' cooperatives, and criticized their simply defined economic agendas. By the 1890s, the AFL became the dominant national labor organization.

While open to socialist and Marxist thought concerning the economic structure and the direction of the labor movement, AFL leaders, like the KOL leaders before them, remained perplexed about the race issue within the labor movement during the racial hostile period of Jim Crow. The AFL was an umbrella organization with which separate trade unions were affiliated. The AFL's constitution was quiet on race issues and implicitly included African Americans. AFL founder Samuel A. Gompers initially opposed the inclusion of racially exclusive organizations under the AFL's umbrella. However, due to the fact that the AFL focused on skilled labor, many African Americans, who were barred from such jobs and relegated to perform "unskilled" labor due to racial discrimination, received very little attention from the AFL.

Like the KOL leaders before them, AFL leaders were quick to spout rhetoric in favor of racial egalitarian ideals. Gompers, who led the AFL from 1886 until his death in 1924, affirmed his commitment to racial egalitarianism at the 1891 annual convention. Although the AFL's commitment to racial egalitarianism remains suspect, there were episodes of biracial activism. In 1892, white and black longshoremen of New Orleans rallied behind the AFL banner and supported each other's strikes at substantial risk to themselves. Gompers would constantly herald the event as a landmark case of biracial union activism. More scattered episodes of interracial union activism carried on throughout the World War I era and into the 1920s. During the war, in Little Rock, Arkansas, the white-controlled labor council supported black women who worked in the city's steam laundries that served a nearby army base. Meanwhile, the black longshoremen labored on the docks of Philadelphia and became attracted to and strongly affiliated with the radical, Marxist, and, above all, racial egalitarian Industrial Workers of the World (IWW), African Americans and their white counterparts struggled, with varied success, to form unions that rose above the color line in places such as Chicago, rural Louisiana, and Memphis. For example, AFL carpenter unions in rural 1919 Bogalusa, Louisiana, struggled together in an effort to preserve their biracial union. In the South Side of Chicago's packinghouses and stockyards, World War I–era interracial unity reached its peak. Fifty thousand men and women, both black and white, rallied behind the AFL's Amalgamated Meat Cutters (AMC), a very powerful AFL organization of skilled workers that did not ban blacks, side by side with the AFL's Chicago Federation of Labor (CFL) between 1916 and 1922 in a long-drawn-out struggle for equal rights and better working conditions in Chicago's meat packinghouses.

The president of the CFL, John Fitzpatrick, and a Railway Carmen Union organizer, William Z. Foster, both radical syndicalists who dedicated their efforts to turn the AFL on to socialism, led the Chicago labor activists and workers' struggle to effectively organize industrial unions and stockyards across the color line. Together they formed the Stockyard Labor Council (SLC) in an effort to unite all packinghouse workers regardless of color and gender. As a result of other, less-skilled unions segregating and banning blacks, the SLC and AFL became locals that blacks could join. The successful organization of meat industry workers was vital to the success of the labor movement as a whole. It presented the opportunity for the AFL to enlarge its influence by expanding from craft unions into one of the country's largest mass production industries. AMC affiliates, one of the AFL organizations that did not ban black workers, were ardent supporters of organizing across racial lines and continually, with mixed success, advocated the importance of nondiscrimination in the labor movement. The AMC, in an effort to show its commitment to black workers, created a black local. In fact, all the AMC locals representing workers in the South Side of Chicago included African Americans. The SLC shared the AMC's commitment to African American workers. The SLC pressed for dramatic changes, such as its call on the federal government to nationalize the meatpacking industry, the implementation of the eight-hour workday, and increased pay for unskilled workers, a category into which most African American workers fell. As the end of the Great War approached its demise, the SLC started pressing for a 100 percent union agreement with the packers, with blacks being the primary hurdle. Ninety percent of white workers and a meager 25 percent of African American workers were members. However, black gains in union membership and wages came at the cost of increased racial hostility between blacks and native-born and immigrant whites, which culminated in the vicious Chicago Race Riot of 1919.

The Chicago race riots might, indeed, be reflective of the collective conscious-ness of the American public at large during the racially daunting years of Jim Crow. Although a causal claim between the SLC's effort to organize black work-ers in Chicago cannot be verified, there is, no doubt, information that makes such a causal connection attractive. On the packinghouse floors, where native-born and immigrant whites toiled side by side with their African American coworkers and fellow union supporters, whites expressed their hostility and contempt for African Americans. European immigrant laborers who were "working toward whiteness" by reminding their native-born white coworkers that African Americans were, in-deed, the "other" and the real problem met African Americans with intense racial tension. In the summer of 1919, racial tension erupted onto the streets and an all-out riot ensued. The riot was sparked when a black boy was drowned for crossing into a white neighborhood on Lake Michigan beach. The event triggered racial violence that would last for weeks. Most of the mayhem was attributed to gangs of Irish immigrants. In the end, 23 blacks and 15 whites lay dead. The July race riots, arguably, ended the hope of the SLC to successfully organize black workers. Rac-ist policies, although not explicitly written in the constitution, was a tradition for the AFL and its affiliated organizations from the beginning.

As Jim Crow policy tightened its grip on everyday life in the South, and newly arrived immigrants began competing with native-born whites and blacks for jobs, exclusionary policies vis-à-vis immigrants and African Americans increased. Im-migrants were not welcome into the AFL or any affiliated organizations from the start. Gompers, a Jewish immigrant from Great Britain and once a supporter of racial egalitarianism, stated that the AFL's policy was to protect whites from the "evils" of the Chinese invasion. Chinese immigrants who toiled on the railroads were banned from unionization outright. While white workers led vicious, bloody massacres and anti-Chinese riots, writers and editors of union and labor newspa-pers were busy constructing the Chinese and other immigrant groups as "savage" and "uncivilized." As early as 1897, AFL leaders urged the adoption of a draconian literacy test in an effort to curtail immigrant labor. They argued that the plethora of early European immigrants who emigrated had not proved themselves assimi-lable or fit for union organization ultimately posed a threat to the American worker whose wages they undercut.

The AFL's putative commitment to racial egalitarianism was a sham. They, like much of American society, had elements of both de jure and de facto segre-gation along with a history of violence against African American and Chinese laborers. The railroad unions proved to be the least accepting of African Ameri-cans and Asian immigrants. Blacks were often barred from unions or were forced to form separate unions. In fact, the early radical W.E.B. Du Bois, in a publica-tion on union activity, revealed that of the 1 million AFL members, 40,000 were black. Moreover, 43 unions practiced Jim Crow policy to the point that they had no African Americans at all. The National Association of Machinists, an umbrella organization affiliated with the AFL, is a case in point to the AFL's ultimate commitment to party building, not to racial egalitarianism. The National Association of Machinists was founded in 1889 in Atlanta as an organization dedicated to organizing skilled railroad laborers. For five years, the AFL denied the admittance of the National Association of Machinist into the organization to do its constitution declaring white-only membership. However, in an effort to build union membership, AFL officials backed down from their commitment to racial egalitarianisms and biracial activism and admitted the National Association of Machinists in 1895. In the 1890s, firemen stood with the Brotherhood of Railway Trainmen in an effort to organize against the admittance of African Americans into their unions on a national scale. In 1899, the trainmen's union voted for the exclusion of African Americans from railroads worldwide.

Violent means were often used to ensure that railroad unions remained as segregated and off-limits to African Americans as possible. Violent outbreaks against African American railroad workers often sprung from strikes advocating white-only hiring policies. In an effort to maintain the color line, white workers in 1911 organized a strike against New Orleans, Cincinnati, and Texas Pacific railroads for employing African Americans. In the end, 10 African Americans were murdered. As a result, the strikers and the railroad companies decided that African Americans would not be employed north of Oakdale and Chattanooga, Tennessee. More still is that the railroad companies concurred that the overall percentage of African American firemen would not rise on a national level. The AFL continued to ignore, or at least place secondary to increasing union numbers, African Americans and their complaints of racial discrimination into the 1920s. When union officials refused to make the Railroad Brotherhood of Railway Carmen strike the words "white only" from its constitution, and when they refused to grant international charter to the black Railway Coach Cleaners, blacks took the jobs of whites during the 1922 shopmen's strike. The results were tragic. Over 1,500 cases of attempted murder, kidnapping, dynamiting, and vandalism occurred in an effort to curtail blacks from acting as strikebreakers. African Americans' willingness to act as strikebreakers increased the AFL's hostility toward them. The AFL often blamed its lack of attention to African American workers on the African Americans themselves. As the Depression began to take a grip on the economy, and as racial tensions increased due to the lack of job opportunity, increased competition, and Jim Crow laws, African Americans made up only 50,000 of the nation's 2.25 million union members. However, as the Congress of Industrial Organization (CIO), arguably the most egalitarian significant union to emerge since the KOL, emerged as the primary labor organization in 1935, African Americans saw increased racial tolerance, and labor unions saw a dramatic increase in the number of African American affiliates.

The Congress of Industrial Organization

While Jim Crow laws began to cripple the South, the CIO presented a viable opportunity to organize African Americans within a largely racist labor movement. CIO leaders took a divide-and-conquer, radical, Marxist approach to the racial question vis-à-vis the labor movement by contending that racial division was created by bourgeois employers who wished to disrupt working-class solidarity so as to keep wages low and create "super profits." Thus, the CIO's primary goal was to organize industrial sectors of the labor force, which, they realized, necessitated the inclusion of African American workers who by the 1930s made up a significant portion of the industrial labor. In the South, where labor union representation was comparatively weak to that of the North, unions desperately needed the support of African American workers if they wished to succeed in mining, steel, and a multiplicity of agriculture sectors of which African Americans dominated. As such, the CIO sought to reach out to African American workers and civil rights groups to create interracial, working-class solidarity. And reach out they did. The CIO, in a remarkable effort to preserve and create racial harmony, formed the Committee to Abolish Racial Discrimination, and encouraged blacks to reject and speak out against the AFL and other independent unions.

The CIO took its cue from the United Mine Workers Association (UMWA), which had been promoting and practicing racial egalitarianism under the presidential leadership of John L. Lewis since the late nineteenth century. By the turn of the twentieth century, African Americans made up one-quarter of UMWA's membership and enrolled at a much higher rate than their white comrades. The UMWA consisted of more than 20,000 black miners, approximately half of the AFL's black membership. In the depths of the Great Depression in 1934, the UMWA boasted 90 new locals and 20,000 men, of whom 60 percent were African Americans. Even in the hostile time and space of Jim Crow Alabama in the 1890s, the UMWA struggled to create interracial unity in the union locals of Alabama and other Southern states. Furthermore, Irish immigrants along with British immigrants made up a significant portion of union leadership. To be sure, the UMWA did, indeed, have its share of racial turmoil, but it was their effort to forge class unity across racial lines that caused the CIO to adopt the UMWA's organizing techniques. For example, UMWA organizers in Alabama made it clear that their commitment to African American workers did not embrace the idea of social equality, simply better wages and working conditions. At one point in 1920, white mine workers bombed the houses of a dozen black strikebreakers. Despite a few episodes of interracial hostility, the UMWA proved its commitment to black workers.

Indeed, the CIO's efforts and commitment to African American workers did not go unnoticed. Unlike the AFL, which practiced Jim Crow policy if not in rhetoric or theory then in practice, the CIO transcended racial lines in its organizing process and made its way into Piedmont region—southern Virginia to northern Alabama—and had organized 200,000 cotton textile workers. From the early stages of the Great Depression to the end stages of World War II, African American union membership increased radically from 60,000 to an impressive 1 million. African Americans became the CIO's main supporters. Other unions such as the KOL and AFL tried to organize across racial lines but ultimately fell pray to Jim Crow practices. The CIO represented the first massive effort to organize workers across racial and ethnic lines for a common movement. This was indeed the case in Chicago's meatpacking industry, in which African Americans made up 20 to 30 percent of the labor force. Thanks to the efforts of CIO and others, mostly Communist activists, the Packing House Workers Organization Committee brought together several unions to reach out to blacks by promising designated seats for blacks on the executive board, and by mandating a quota equivalent to the local population.

As World War II emerged, the labor movement more broadly, and labor unions in particular, would again have serious consequences for African American workers. Blacks were direly needed in the industrial sector to produce goods for the war effort; however, their employers were very hesitant to hire them due to long-standing Jim Crow practices within the industrial sector. By the end of 1944, it is estimated that at least 1.25 million African American workers, a quarter of which were women, were performing industrial work, a 150 percent increase from 1940. During World War II, both the AFL and the CIO grew dramatically. The AFL expanded its union affiliates from 4.2 million to just shy of 7 million. The CIO grew to 4 million members from 2 million members from 1940 to 1945. In all, union membership doubled from 1940 to 1945 to 15 million.

However, Jim Crow policies that pervaded the labor movement and unions would tighten their grip during the war effort, and blacks were forced to overcome racism and discrimination on a multiplicity of levels. Their struggle in the railroad unions and craft brotherhoods is a case in point. Railroad unions have a history of Jim Crow policy under the tutelage of the AFL, and they continued this tradition during the course of the war. While railroad employment increased to meet the demands of the war effort, so too did discrimination against black workers in labor unions. Black workers faced severe forms of discrimination, including contracts that limited the number and locations where blacks could work. The Brotherhood of Locomotive Firemen, for example, pushed to rapidly accelerate the removal of black workers. This culminated in the Brotherhood successfully winning Southeastern

Carriers agreement, which limited the employment of "unpromotable" firemen to 50 percent and ended the increased hiring of blacks. While the Brotherhood of Locomotive Firemen practiced a strict form of Jim Crow by virtue of job elimination, the International Boilermakers Brotherhood (IBB) did admit blacks, albeit in a Jim Crow fashion that separated black and white union members into separate locals. Black workers paid dues to the union but were denied membership. Additionally, the hierarchal structure of the union did not allow all black unions to exercise autonomy and set up "parent" all-white unions to dictate their organization techniques and behavior. In short, the IBB openly practiced Jim Crow policies.

AFL-CIO at the End of Jim Crow

The postwar effort to organize across racial lines in the Jim Crow South proved fruitless. The Taft-Hartley Act—an amendment passed in 1947 to amend the National Labor Relations Act of 1935—provided little protection for black union members who were already in unions. The act permitted Jim Crow segregation in union locals and weakened the efforts of the AFL and the CIO to organize across racial lines. The act was effective. Black and white union members in the South remained largely segregated despite the fact that the AFL had 60 percent of its 7 million African American members located in the South. Soon after Jim Crow began to loosen grips on the policy and consciousness of the United States with the *Brown v. Board of Education* case in 1954, the AFL and CIO merged in 1955.

Both the AFL and the CIO strongly and openly endorsed the black Civil Rights Movement that emerged in the South in response to Jim Crow. The AFL-CIO led charges in favor of Civil Rights Acts throughout the late twentieth century, and played a significant role in bringing civil rights to the fore of national consciousness. Indeed, the Civil Rights Act of 1964—an act that outlawed public school, public workplace segregation, and guaranteed fair employment practices—and the Voting Rights Act of 1965 were all endorsed by the AFL-CIO, who now began to understand the Civil Rights and labor movements as organically linked phenomena, and acknowledged that biracial activism is the life's blood of the labor movement.

Jack A. Taylor III

See also: Fair Employment Practices Commission (FEPC); Great Depression; New Deal.

Further Reading

Bernstein, David. *Only One Place of Redress: African Americans, Labor Regulations, and the Courts from Reconstruction to the New Deal.* Durham, NC: Duke University Press, 2001.

Honey, Michael. *Southern Labor and Black Civil Rights: Organizing Memphis Workers.* Urbana: University of Illinois Press, 1993.

Moreno, Paul. *Black Americans and Organized Labor: A New History.* Baton Rouge: Louisiana State University Press, 2006.

Nelson, Bruce. *Divided We Stand: American Workers and the Struggle for Black Equality.* Princeton, NJ: Princeton University Press, 2001.

Obadele-Starks, Ernest. *Black Unionism in the Industrial South.* College Station: Texas A&M University Press, 2000.

Roediger, David. *Working toward Whiteness: How America's Immigrants Became White: The Strange Journey from Ellis Island to the Suburbs.* New York: Basic Books, 2005.

Zieger, Robert H. *For Jobs and Freedom: Race and Labor in America since 1865.* Lexington: University Press of Kentucky, 2007.

Lawson, James Morris, Jr.

James Morris Lawson Jr. was a minister, teacher, and activist who performed an influential role during the Civil Rights Movement. As an officer in the Student Nonviolent Coordinating Committee (SNCC), Lawson changed the tactics by which Americans fought for integration and racial equality. As a leading proponent and theorist of the resistance tactics of Indian leader Mahatma Gandhi, Lawson trained hundreds of young people to use nonviolence as a tool of mass protest. A close confidant of Martin Luther King Jr. and other important leaders, Lawson led the lunch counter sit-ins in Nashville, Tennessee, participated in the 1961 Freedom Rides, and advised the Memphis sanitation workers strike in 1968.

Born on September 22, 1928, in Uniontown, Pennsylvania, Lawson was the oldest son of a preacher who was heavily involved with the National Association for the Advancement of Colored People (NAACP). Lawson grew up in Massillon, Ohio, and attended schools with mostly white students. Just out of high school, Lawson got his first license to preach in 1947 and traveled a good deal for Methodist training and prayer meetings, soon coming to see race and poverty as the major divisive elements in American society. As a freshman at Baldwin-Wallace College in Berea, Ohio, Lawson joined the pacifist Fellowship of Reconciliation (FOR) in 1947. Lawson began to learn more about Ghandian resistance, or using nonviolent means to struggle against oppression, from the FOR's executive director A.J. Muste. Increasingly committed to pacifism, Lawson refused to comply with the military draft at the start of the Korean War and spent 13 months in federal prison beginning in 1950.

Following his parole, Lawson graduated from Baldwin-Wallace and became a professor at Hislop College in Nagpur, India, in April 1953. In India, Lawson studied Ghandian tactics and considered their usefulness for combating segregation, while reading eagerly of the Montgomery Bus Boycott (1955–1956) in Indian newspapers. Lawson returned to the United States to begin graduate work in theology at Oberlin College and met Martin Luther King Jr. in February 1957. The two men connected instantly over discussions of nonviolent mass action, and King urged Lawson to move to the South. At Lawson's request, the FOR made him a field secretary in Nashville, Tennessee, where he also joined the Southern Christian Leadership Conference (SCLC). Upon his arrival in Nashville in January 1958, Lawson became the second African American student ever to enroll at Vanderbilt University's divinity school. Soon after Lawson's arrival, he met Dorothy Wood, whom he would marry in 1959.

If moderate by Tennessee standards, Nashville remained largely segregated in 1958, which included restaurants, the bus station, lunch counters, restrooms, hotels, cabs, neighborhoods, and schools. Lawson began holding workshops in nonviolent philosophy in November 1959 in the basement of Kelly Miller Smith's First Baptist Church. Sponsored by FOR, Lawson's workshops stressed the importance of complete pacifism in order to provoke a moral crisis in their opponents. Lawson trained students in actual protest tactics as well as the philosophy of peace. Students also began to test policies in different stores in late 1959 to choose targets for a sit-in protest. Among Lawson's mentees were Diane Nash, James Bevel, Bernard Lafayette, Marion Barry, and John Lewis, all of whom went on work for civil rights through the 1960s with the SCLC, SNCC, and other organizations. The Nashville movement relied primarily on young people because they would be less vulnerable to pressure or stricture from white employers once they began protests against segregation.

When students in Greensboro, North Carolina, staged a sit-in on February 1, 1960, the Nashville students sprung into action. One hundred twenty-four students, all trained and prepared by Lawson, staged an initial sit-in at downtown Nashville lunch counters on February 13, 1960. On February 27, Nashville police allowed mobs of angry whites to physically assault the activists and then arrested 81 demonstrators. However, the sit-ins had been organized such that replacements stood ready to fill empty seats at lunch counters. Lawson's strategy of "jail, no bail" meant that protestors remained in overcrowded jails for some time, financially costing the city of Nashville and forcing the local government to become involved in the conflict. Segregationists on Vanderbilt's Board of Trustees, including *Nashville Banner* publisher James Stahlman, demonized Lawson in the press and in private meetings. Vanderbilt chancellor Harvey Branscombe subsequently expelled Lawson on March 3,

1960, and Nashville police arrested Lawson the next day for his involvement in the demonstrations.

Lawson and the Nashville leaders soon called for an Easter boycott of downtown stores that depended on African American business but refused access to restrooms and lunch counters, which heightened the pressure on Nashville mayor Ben West to intervene. On April 19, 1960, reactionaries bombed the home of Z. Alexander Looby, the attorney representing the arrested students. The Loobys were unharmed, but the furious Nashville students and ministers initiated a silent march toward the courthouse downtown. Confronted by Diane Nash on the courthouse steps, West publicly acquiesced that downtown lunch counters should be integrated, effectively ending the symbolic reign of Jim Crow in city restaurants. By May 10, 1960, six downtown stores had integrated, and more gradually followed. Over the next two years, the Nashville Movement built by Lawson integrated movie theatres and restaurants in Nashville as well.

A few days before the Looby bombing, on April 15 and 16, Lawson delivered the keynote address at a conference organized by SCLC member Ella Baker in Raleigh, North Carolina. Baker had called the meeting to build upon the work of students activists in Nashville and throughout the South. On the podium, Lawson criticized the NAACP for being too conservative and timid in its methods, and pointed to direct action as the only way to defeat Jim Crow. The Shaw University conference marked the birth of SNCC, and also began a period wherein Lawson advised ever greater numbers of activists. In 1960, the SCLC made Lawson its director of nonviolent education. At the same time, Lawson finished his master of divinity degree at Boston University (1960) and accepted an appointment to tiny Green Chapel Methodist Church in Shelbyville, Tennessee, just south of Nashville.

When the U.S. Supreme Court banned segregation in interstate travel facilities in *Boynton v. Virginia* (1960), the Congress of Racial Equality (CORE) organized "Freedom Rides" to test the integration of transportation facilities throughout the Deep South. Leaving Washington, D.C., on May 4, 1961, the Freedom Rides nearly dissolved in Anniston, Alabama, when the bus was firebombed. Activists from SNCC and CORE chapters reinforced the original riders in Birmingham and Montgomery after additional attacks. Lawson joined the riders in Montgomery, where he was made spokesperson for the initial bus sent to Jackson, Mississippi. Authorities in Jackson arrested Lawson and many others, and sent them to notoriously brutal Parchman State Penitentiary. Waves of Freedom Riders followed to attempt to integrate the Jackson bus station and nonviolently resist arrest. After repeated violence and national attention, Attorney General Robert F. Kennedy ordered the desegregation of bus terminals in November 1961.

In 1962, Lawson assumed the pastorship of Centenary Methodist church in Memphis, where segregation was more ingrained than Nashville. In June 1966,

King asked Lawson to organize a replacement march after James Meredith was shot by a sniper on his solo walk against fear from Memphis to Jackson. During the march, Lawson became dismayed by increasing factionalism between SNCC and the SCLC and wary of the separatist strain adopted by SNCC under Stokely Carmichael's leadership. Lawson thought that greater militancy belied a turn away from nonviolence, a shift that Lawson could not support. Lawson also served as a counselor for King in Chicago, where he saw increasing weariness among nonviolent activists struggling to fight the more complicated forms of Jim Crow that existed outside of the South.

Lawson also helped to fight racial injustice in Memphis as an advisor for the Memphis Sanitation Workers strike in 1968. Long underpaid, denied access to higher-paying jobs, and without benefits, African American sanitation workers' frustration boiled over on February 1, 1968, when two workers were killed due to a short circuit in a garbage truck's crushing mechanism. Under Lawson's guidance the workers commenced a strike on February 12, making their slogan "I AM A MAN" as visible as possible. Lawson reached for national exposure by inviting King to Memphis, suggesting the sanitation strike fit perfectly with King's burgeoning Poor Peoples Campaign against poverty. After a March 28 demonstration fell apart due to a number of disruptive elements, King agreed to return to lead another march. Fatefully, King was assassinated the day before he was to lead the second march. City officials and the sanitation workers settled the strike one week later.

Lawson moved with his wife and three sons to Los Angeles in 1974, and became pastor of Holman Methodist Church. Lawson continued to work for peace education and racial justice throughout the latter decades of the twentieth century, and retired from the ministry in 1999. In the fall of 2006, Lawson returned to Vanderbilt University as a visiting professor.

Brian Piper

See also: King, Martin Luther, Jr.

Further Reading

Ackerman, Peter, and Jack DuVall. *A Force More Powerful: A Century of Nonviolent Conflict.* New York: St. Martin's Press, 2000.

Halberstam, David. *The Children.* New York: Random House, 1996.

Inskeep, Steve, and James Lawson. "James Lawson: An Advocate of Peaceful Change." Radio interview, National Public Radio Web site. http://www.npr.org/templates/story/story.php?storyId=6676164&sc=emaf (accessed July 2007).

Lovett, Bobby L. *The Civil Rights Movement in Tennessee: A Narrative History.* Knoxville: University of Tennessee Press, 2005.

Little Rock Nine

The term "Little Rock Nine" refers to the group of nine students who in September 1957 became the first African Americans to attend Central High School in Little Rock, Arkansas. The nine students were Melba Pattillo, Minnijean Brown, Elizabeth Eckford, Ernest Green, Gloria Ray, Carlotta Walls, Thelma Mothershed, Terrence Roberts, and Jefferson Thomas. The Nine, who had been carefully selected for their role, submitted themselves to humiliation and physical danger in order to help desegregate the public schools of Little Rock.

On May 24, 1955, the Little Rock School Board unanimously approved a plan drafted by Virgil Blossum, the superintendant of schools, for the gradual integration of the city's schools, in compliance with the U.S. Supreme Court, which had ruled in the 1954 decision *Brown v. Board of Education* that segregated schools were unconstitutional, and that all schools were to be desegregated. The initial

Elizabeth Eckford surrounded by journalists after she was prevented from entering Little Rock's Central High School by the Arkansas National Guard. She was one of nine black students chosen to integrate Little Rock's Central High School in 1957. (Bettmann/Corbis)

phase, when nine black students would begin attending classes at the previously all-white Central High School, would begin in September 1957. Local civil rights leaders and the Little Rock School Board understood that the first black students to attend the school would be under intense scrutiny, with any deficiency in academics or conduct used as an excuse to label the entire movement to integrate the schools a failure. The nine students were carefully selected by the local chapter of the National Association for the Advancement of Colored People (NAACP) for their high grades, solid attendance records, and lack of discipline problems in their previous school records. Daisy Lee Bates, a journalist and publisher who was active in the Civil Rights Movement in Little Rock, provided continual advice and support to the Nine. The students were instructed to dress neatly, not to overreact to provocation, and in general to give segregationists no excuse to use them as an argument against integration.

White residents of the city formed "citizen's councils," which pledged themselves to uphold segregation, with force if necessary. Governor Orval Faubus, a former liberal who had come to support segregation, promised white voters that he would keep Central High an all-white school. By inclination, President Dwight D. Eisenhower disliked heavy-handed government approaches, and preferred to remain aloof from the Civil Rights Movement. However, he saw a crisis building in Little Rock, as segregationists rallied and planned during the 1956–1957 school year. Hoping to avoid a showdown between state and federal authorities, Eisenhower met with Governor Faubus to discuss the approaching integration. While Faubus remained noncommittal, Eisenhower apparently believed that although Faubus might speak against integration, he would ensure that federal laws were obeyed.

The initial attempts of the Nine to attend classes at the school on September 4, 1957, brought out large crowds of white adults, mostly parents of students attending the school, bent on maintaining segregation. The crowds had assembled around the school in the early morning to keep the black students out of the school. Governor Faubus mobilized part of the Arkansas National Guard with the mission to physically block the nine black students from entering the school. Faubus explained his actions as stemming from his concern for maintaining law and order, but the white mobs were the people violating the law, not the black students. Photographs of the day's events were published nationally, with the image of a row of white armed Guardsmen and the mobs of angry adult white adults blocking the small group of neatly dressed black students, all of whom were in their mid-teens, making a powerful impression throughout the nation. Eisenhower was furious at the actions of Faubus, seeing his stance as a direct challenge to federal authority. Eisenhower had the U.S. Department of Justice request an injunction against the use of the National

Guard in U.S. District Court for the Eastern District of Arkansas. The injunction was granted, and Faubus was ordered to withdraw the National Guard or face contempt of court.

Faubus, having shown his commitment to his political base while holding himself and his city up to national ridicule, complied and withdrew the Guard on September 20, and city police took over the mission of ensuring the safety of the Nine. However, the situation at Central High School was still tense, as a large crowd of whites, estimated in the hundreds, kept a vigil at the school in an attempt to ensure that the Nine did not enter the school. On September 23, the police were able to sneak the Nine into the school to begin attending classes. However, when the surrounding mob learned that the Nine were in the school, order began to break down. The police, seriously outnumbered, feared for the safety of the Nine, and escorted them away from the school.

Supporters of integration, as well as people who supported the rule of law and not the rule of mobs, realized that a stronger show of authority would be needed, or else the mobs around Central High School would continue to keep the Nine away from school. Woodrow Mann, the Democratic mayor of Little Rock, formally requested that Eisenhower use federal soldiers to maintain order and ensure that the Nine were able to attend classes. On September 24, Eisenhower sent in the U.S. Army's 1,200-man 327th Battle Group of the 101st Airborne Division to Little Rock to take control of the campus. At the same time, he federally mobilized the entire Arkansas National Guard, about 10,000 Guardsmen, mainly to prevent Governor Faubus from attempting to use the Guard to oppose the federal soldiers. With this overwhelming show of disciplined soldiers, the threat from the mobs abated, although the shouting continued. The Nine were able to enter the school and begin attending classes on September 25.

The federal soldiers were deployed for the immediate crisis, but Eisenhower and the army wanted them to return to Fort Campbell, Kentucky, as soon as the situation allowed it. Originally, most of the National Guardsmen were ordered to remain at their armories. However, the army began organizing some of the federalized National Guardsmen into what became Task Force 153 on Camp Robinson, in North Little Rock, with the long-term mission of ensuring order at the school, while demobilizing most of the remainder of the Arkansas National Guard. By the end of November, the 101st soldiers were all withdrawn, and Task Force 153 assumed full control of the campus.

Although the Nine attended classes under tight security, they were still subjected to a host of threats, harassments, and even assaults, from white students throughout the year. Despite the hostile environment, the Nine remained at the school through the fall semester. Minnijean Brown was the only one of the Nine not to complete the school year. In December, a group of white male students began hassling her in the cafeteria. In the confrontation, she dropped her tray, in the process splashing some of her chili on one of the white students. For this, she was expelled from the school. Melba Pattillo suffered injury when acid was thrown in her face by a white student, but continued to attend Central and finished the school year.

However, the opponents of integration were not finished. With the support of the governor and the state legislature, the school board closed all public high schools in Little Rock after the end of the 1957–1958 school year. The public high schools remained closed only for one year, though. Under pressure from the Little Rock Chamber of Commerce, as well as the enormous negative publicity the city and state received nationally over the crisis, the school board reopened the high schools, as integrated schools, in the fall of 1958.

Of the eight black students who completed the first year, Earnest Green was the only senior and, at the end of the 1957–1958 school year, became the first African American to graduate from Central High School. Elizabeth Eckford moved to St. Louis in 1958 and completed her college preparation there. Jefferson Thomas returned when Central reopened, and graduated from Central High in 1960. Terrence Roberts moved to Los Angeles after the end of the first year, and graduated from Los Angeles High School in 1959. Carlotta Walls, the youngest of the nine, also returned to Central High School when it reopened in 1959 and graduated in 1960. Thelma Mothershed completed most of her coursework by correspondence during the year the public schools were closed. She received her diploma from Central High by mail. Melba Pattillio moved to California after the first year and completed her high school program there. In 1999, each of the Little Rock Nine was honored with Congressional Gold Medals presented by President Bill Clinton, in recognition of their courage and their important role in knocking down segregation.

Barry M. Stentiford

See also: Arkansas; *Brown v. Board of Education;* White Citizens Council.

Further Reading

Fitzgerald, Stephanie. *Little Rock Nine: Struggle for Integration.* Mankato, MN: Compass Point Books, 2006.

Freyer, Tony. *The Little Rock Crisis: A Constitutional Interpretation.* Westport, CT: Greenwood Press, 1984.

Jacoway, Elizabeth, and C. Fred Williams, eds. *Understanding the Little Rock Crisis: An Exercise in Remembrance and Reconciliation.* Fayetteville: University of Arkansas Press, 1999.

Louisiana

Louisiana holds an important place in the history of Jim Crow. It is where the landmark case *Plessy v. Ferguson* originated. The *Plessy* case established the doctrine of "separate but equal," which legalized Jim Crow in America. According to the U.S. Supreme Court, it was constitutionally permissible to maintain a regime of racial segregation if the services a state provided were equal. This ruling justified several Jim Crow laws, while opposition to it began the modern Civil Rights Movement.

The city in Louisiana responsible for the *Plessy* case was New Orleans. New Orleans had a unique history that made it one of the most interesting places in Louisiana and the entire South. Its unique demography began to take shape as early as 1720 with the first mass importation of African slaves. By the end of the eighteenth century, New Orleans was home to several ethnic groups and had the largest free black community in the Deep South. Most of the free black population in New Orleans considered themselves Creoles of Color. They were Catholic, educated, born in New Orleans, and could trace some family ties to white Creoles of the city. Their wealth, social standing, education, and unique history set them apart not only from slaves but also from free persons of color elsewhere. Most were descendants of unions between Native Americans, French, Spanish, and Africans. Before the Civil War, they owned property and dominated skilled crafts like bricklaying, cigar making, carpentry, and shoemaking. The Creoles of Color provided the leadership for the black community in Louisiana after the Civil War. They were instrumental in bringing about the *Plessy* case.

At the end of the Civil War in 1865, the federal government had to come up with a plan to govern former Confederate states, reunite the nation, and recover from the destruction of the war. The 1865 passage of the Thirteenth Amendment to the U.S. Constitution ensured that blacks would no longer be held in bondage by abolishing the institution of slavery in America. Newly freed slaves dreamed of a new South that would allow them their basic rights as freedmen, while white Southerners looked for ways to retain as much control over former slaves as possible. After the passage of the Thirteenth Amendment, former slave states, including Louisiana, implemented the infamous Black Codes. The Black Codes consisted of a series of laws aimed at restricting the rights of freedmen by making them second-class citizens. The Black Codes enraged Northerners, who pushed for radical changes in the South. In 1866, Congress began a new phase of reconstruction, called Radical Reconstruction. Under Radical Reconstruction, all Black Codes were repealed, and the South was put under military rule. To ensure that nothing like this could ever happen again, Congress granted all freedmen citizenship rights by drafting what became the Fourteenth Amendment to the Constitution and pressuring the states to pass it. In 1870, Republicans continued their Radical Reconstruction by pushing the Fifteenth Amendment through the states, which gave blacks the right to vote. From 1870 to 1875, Southern blacks voted in record numbers for Republicans. In 1875 this changed with the adoption of the Mississippi Plan, which was made by the Democratic Party to overthrow Republican rule in the South. The plan relied on organized violence, intimidation, and fraud.

Louisiana was one of the first Southern states to adopt the Mississippi Plan. Redeeming Louisiana government was very important to the Democratic Party. In 1872, Louisiana had for the first time ever a black governor, courtesy of the Republican Party. P.B.S. Pinchback became governor of Louisiana after the impeachment of Henry Clay Warmoth. Pinchback served as governor of Louisiana for 35 days, from December 9, 1872, to January 13, 1873. With the help of the Mississippi Plan and the Compromise of 1877, which ended Reconstruction in the South, the Democratic Party had taken over in Louisiana and proceeded to reverse the constitution of 1868 and all of the work of the Creoles, including integrated schools, integrated public accommodations, and voting rights. Reconstruction was over, and the nation was united once again. The national Republican Party was tired of the problems in the South and had abandoned blacks, leaving them powerless to white redeemers.

Between 1877 and 1900, racist politicians in the South gained control of Southern governments and began infringing on the rights of black citizens. Southern redeemers believed in the ultimate supremacy of the white man, especially in matters concerning social and political equality. It was accepted as a fact to many white people that blacks were inferior to whites, and incapable of any real social or political equality; however, Southern whites more so than Northern whites were committed to making racial policies reflect that belief. Although, their beliefs rested upon prejudice, emotion, and ignorance, they acted upon the assumption that they were correct, and made sure that their premises justified their policies of social segregation, economic discrimination, and political subordination. In 1890, the state of Louisiana took things a step forward by passing the Separate Car Act, which stated that railroad companies provide separate but equal train cars for blacks and whites. This act provided for the basis of several Jim Crow laws.

In 1891, two Creole of Color leaders, Rudolph L. Desdunes and Louis A. Martinet, began a grassroots attempt to form a committee of black citizens to fight against the Separate Car Act. Desdunes and Martinet believed that there could be no accommodating the rights of a U.S. citizen. They saw the Separate Car Act as the first of many acts that would hinder those rights. Through their efforts, the Citizens Committee was formed. The goal of the committee was to end the infringing practice of racial segregation in the South. In 1892, the committee chose Homer Plessy a light-complexioned Creole of Color who worked as a shoemaker in New

Orleans, to test the validly of the Separate Car Act. The committee instructed Plessy to board a designated white train car of the East Louisiana Railroad. Officials of the East Louisiana Railroad told Plessy that he could not ride on the white train car because he was not white. They asked him to take a seat on the black train car. Plessy refused to do so. He was arrested and jailed.

Once Plessy was arrested the Citizens Committee began to work on his defense. At his trial, *Homer A. Plessy v. State of Louisiana,* lawyers argued that the railroad company denied Plessy his constitutional rights under the Thirteenth and Fourteenth Amendments. The judge presiding over the case, John Ferguson, ruled that Louisiana did not infringe on Plessy's rights. According to Judge Ferguson, the state of Louisiana had the right to regulate railroad companies that operated in their state. Judge John H. Ferguson found Plessy guilty of violating the Separate Car Act and fined him $300.

Many members of the Citizens Committee were not pleased with the verdict of Judge Ferguson. They decided to take the case to the Supreme Court of Louisiana, where the ruling was upheld. In 1896, the committee tried one last time to have the ruling overturned by bringing the case all the way to the U.S. Supreme Court. The U.S. Supreme Court ruled the same way as Judge Ferguson and the Louisiana Supreme Court. According to the U.S. Supreme Court, it was constitutionally permissible to maintain a regime of racial segregation if the services a state provided were equal. The *Plessy* case became the landmark case that established the doctrine of "separate but equal," which legalized Jim Crow in America.

"Separate but equal" was the law. Even though the doctrine specified that all facilities and accommodations were to be equal, generally the facilities for blacks were inherently unequal. The National Association for the Advancement of Colored People (NAACP), founded in 1909, tried from its beginning to destroy the constitutional doctrine that the *Plessy* case established. They gradually began to develop a plan for coordinating litigation to fight against Jim Crow laws. Unequal education systems provided the NAACP with the first cases it needed to challenge the *Plessy* decision. The fight to overturn the *Plessy* decision began the modern Civil Rights Movement.

Sharlene Sinegal DeCuir

See also: Black Codes; *Plessy v. Ferguson.*

Further Reading

Fairclough, Adam. *Race & Democracy: The Civil Rights Struggle in Louisiana, 1915–1972.* Athens: University of Georgia Press, 1995.

Foner, Eric. *A Short History of Reconstruction 1863–1877.* New York: Harper & Row, 1984.

Hirsch, Arnold R., and Joseph Logsdon, eds. *Creole New Orleans: Race and Americanization.* Baton Rouge: Louisiana State University Press, 1992.

Medley, Keith Weldon. *We as Freemen:* Plessy v. Ferguson. Gretna, LA: Pelican Publishing Company, 2003.

Lynching

Scope

Mark Twain (1835–1910), the prolific writer and observer of American life and culture, once sarcastically noted that America had become the "United States of Lyncherdom" and other social commentators observed that "America's national crime was lynching." Lynchings were extralegal murders carried out by a mob or a group of vigilantes. It functioned to summarily and severely execute individuals accused of heinous crimes. Depending upon the period and region, individuals were lynched for both trivial and serious allegations, such as whistling or sexual assault.

Historians have been extremely skeptical of any attempt to define, reconstruct, or accurately measure the scope of lynching given the geographical, racial, and ethnic variations. For example, black Southerners were lynched for almost 100 offenses; however, on the whole, Southern lynch mobs primarily lynched blacks suspected of murder or rape. While lynching served to punish particular criminals and crimes, it also functioned as a kind of mass communication in which the objective was to produce and enforce social conformity with respect to racial hierarchy, social status, and gender norms. Lynching constituted state- and community-sanctioned violence for which federal, state, and local governments and courts rarely prosecuted the individuals involved, and even those prosecutions seldom resulted in fines or prison sentences. Lynch mobs and vigilante groups murdered with impunity because lynching occurred within a culture of violence that embraced popular conceptions of repressive violence.

Lynching in the United States has a long and tragic history. Lynch mobs expeditiously executed alleged criminals and perceived social deviants from the colonial period (1619–1781) through the Civil Rights era (1955–1975). While present throughout all periods of American history, lynching occurred sporadically prior to the American Civil War (1860–1865). In post–Civil War America, lynching increased dramatically, so that by the end of the nineteenth century, it had engulfed virtually every region in the nation. Between 1882 and 1930, approximately 4,760 men, women, and children fell pray to lynch mobs. No individual or group was entirely safe from lynching. White Americans, Mexicans, Chinese, Italians, and other racial-ethnic groups were all victims of lynching.

Members of the National Association for the Advancement of Colored People call for a federal antilynching law at the National Crime Conference in Washington, D.C., on December 11, 1934. (Library of Congress)

Lynching was indeed a national crime, but it was also a Southern hysteria that targeted African Americans, who represented approximately 70 percent of all lynching victims. Lynching was so pervasive and commonplace in the South that 10 Deep South and Border South states lynched more individuals than all other states and regions combined. During the peak of Southern lynching (1882–1930), approximately 2,800 Southerners perished as a result of lynch mobs, accounting for nearly 60 percent of all lynching victims in the United States. Moreover, Southern lynching stretched far beyond punishing particular individuals for heinous crimes and became a systematic and constitutive component within Jim Crow segregation—an expansive system of racial subordination and oppression.

Between 1882 and 1930, African Americans constituted 94 percent of lynching victims. Lynching came to symbolize black oppression within the system of American race relations. Regardless of region, lynch mobs desired to swiftly and brutally punish individuals who violated seemingly sacred community norms and provided a mechanism by which communities could collectively participate in apprehending and punishing criminals. In this way, lynching was as much a form of community-building as it was extralegal violence.

Geography

While lynching occurred in every region and period in American history, it was concentrated within particular subregions and social groups. Generally speaking, in the South, lynching functioned as an instrument for racial control and terror; however, depending upon the Southern subregion in which lynching occurred, African Americans perished "at the hands of persons unknown" at varying rates and for differing reasons. Southern lynching was concentrated and occurred most frequently within Black Belt counties, a contiguous cross-section of several Deep South states (Louisiana, Mississippi, Alabama, and Georgia) with dense black populations, cotton monocultures, and plantation economies. The Southern agricultural elite employed lynching to exploit and manipulate black sharecroppers and tenant farmers, whereas lynching beyond Black Belt counties were generally targeted at African Americans who ostensibly violated the labyrinth of racial taboos of Jim Crow etiquette. For instance, lynching in Louisiana and Georgia was most prevalent in their respective cotton-producing regions. Louisiana's cotton-producing regions accounted for 60 percent of lynching incidents in the state between the years 1878 and 1946. Between the years 1880 and 1930, 458 lynchings occurred in Georgia, of which 84 percent were concentrated in Georgia's Cotton Belt region. White planters did not always resort to mob violence to punish unruly black workers, particularly when racial demographics did not work in their favor. Within Louisiana's black-dominated Mississippi River Delta parishes, white elites employed state-sanctioned executions because they believed African Americans' numerical superiority made the outcome of lynching unpredictable. State-sanctioned executions took the form of legal trials in which African Americans were unable to offer testimony and were at the mercy of all-white jury pools that often were unconcerned with the rules of a fair trial. Extralegal executions could lead to widespread quitting, work stoppages, or even retaliatory violence. White planters believed sham trials with legal executions or imprisonment were the most effective means to control black labor. In plantation regions, where large numbers of blacks and whites labored as sharecroppers and tenant farmers, plantation elites less frequently employed lynching as a means to intimidate and control black laborers for fear of retaliation by blacks and the perceived threat of poor whites and blacks uniting against the wealthy plantation owners.

Lynching in the Northeast and Mid-Atlantic states was virtually nonexistent and accounted for less than 10 percent of total U.S. lynching incidents. The relative small number of lynchings in the Northeast can be mostly attributed to a civic culture that respected the rule of law. Although lynching was relatively scarce in the Northeast and Mid-Atlantic regions, lynchings could eerily resemble those in the South. For instance, in 1911, Zachariah Walker, a black steel worker, was burned alive in Coatesville, Pennsylvania, for murdering a white man. It is estimated that 5,000 men and women witnessed the spectacle and, in the lynching's aftermath, several onlookers mutilated Walker's body, including taking his fingers and bones as souvenirs. Between 1882 and 1930, only 41 individuals were lynched in the Northeast and Mid-Atlantic states. The vast majority of persons lynched, though, were African Americans such as Walker, who accounted for roughly 87 percent of lynching victims in both the regions. Of the 41 lynching victims, 30 lynchings occurred within Maryland, and the state with the next highest total (Pennsylvania) had only six total lynchings.

In contrast to the Northeast, Midwestern and Western lynching activity was much more prevalent and more evenly distributed throughout the region. For instance, between the years 1882 and 1930, 588 lynchings occurred within the Midwest, for which Oklahoma (160 lynchings), Missouri (116), Nebraska (60), Indiana (52), and Kansas (52) had the highest number of lynching incidents. In addition, Western lynch mobs killed 415 individuals, and at least 7 out of 10 Western states had in excess of 30 mob murders during the height of the lynching epidemic. Unlike Southern lynch mobs, Midwestern and Western lynch mobs primarily lynched whites, who constituted roughly 67 percent of lynchings in the Midwest and 93 percent in the Western United States. Lynching was never entirely utilized for the purpose of controlling a particular ethnic or racial group, but rather to punish individual acts of social deviance such as horse theft, counterfeiting, murder, and rape. In addition, Midwestern and Western lynching was more concentrated in rural areas. For instance, lynching occurred more frequently in rural southern Iowa than the urban centers of northern Iowa because of the lack of influence of capitalist culture and the relative weakness of legal institutions.

Typology of Lynch Mobs

Lynchings were cultural performances that legitimated the values of mob participants and translated its cultural significance through social rituals or patterned practices designed to broadcast their message. However, the form and content of lynching varied significantly and impacted its overall meaning. The key differences between lynch mobs were their organization, planning, longevity, and the extent to which they engaged in ceremonialism or lynching rituals. Private mobs, terrorist mobs, posses, and mass mobs represent the four persistent patterns of mob behavior.

Private and terrorist mobs were composed of 50 or fewer individuals and were most prevalent in Western and Midwestern lynching. Private mobs murdered

75 percent of lynching victims in California, 63 percent of lynching victims in Iowa, 61 percent of lynching victims in Washington State, and 44 percent of lynch victims in Wyoming. In the South, private mobs claimed the lives of less than half of all lynching victims. For instance, in Georgia, private mobs accounted for 30 percent of lynchings and 46 percent of lynchings in Virginia. In addition, private mobs were organized several days or even weeks after an alleged crime occurred. They usually became disillusioned with the legal system and the broader community's failure to lynch an alleged criminal, and consequently they used their anger and disappointment as impetus for their organization. Private mobs were usually comprised of friends and family members of the victim, and their participation was motivated by their desire to exact revenge due to their sense of collective loss. Since private mobs generally did not seek community support, the lynching was carefully premeditated, secretive, and less preoccupied with ritualism associated with other lynchings. Despite private mobs' penchant for premeditation and secrecy, their vengeance killings were usually discovered; however, very few private mobs were ever prosecuted or received jail sentences. Similar to private mobs, terrorist mobs operated clandestinely and rarely gained community support for lynching. Extensive or broad-based community support guaranteed personal anonymity for mob participants and immunity from criminal prosecution.

When private and terrorist mobs believed community support was negligible, they wore masks in order to conceal their identities. Unlike private mobs, terrorist mobs did not disband after an accomplished lynching. Rather, their modus operandi was to use lynching as a means of achieving a broader social agenda. The Ku Klux Klan, arguably the most famous and long-lived terrorist organization, is one example of a terrorist mob that used lynching and other forms of repressive violence. While these groups and organizations boasted hundreds or even thousands of members, the impact upon lynching was fairly minimal. In the South, terrorist mobs were responsible for 59 of 460 lynchings in Georgia and only 3 of 86 lynchings in Virginia between the years 1880 and 1930.

Posses and mass mobs usually received the broadest community support. Unlike private mobs and terrorist mobs, posses had quasi-legal status and operated with near-immunity. In most communities, posses were respected and viewed as heroes because they were central to apprehending and punishing dangerous criminals. Often, they had the support of local elected officials, including the sheriff and mayor as well as community leaders. Mass mobs occurred most frequently during the 1880s and 1890s and consisted of hundreds or even thousands of participants and spectators. White men dominated leadership positions within mass mobs, while women and children often occupied supporting roles, such as cheering and gathering rope used in the lynching. Despite their sheer size, mass mobs often displayed sophisticated organization, planning, and ritualism. During the zenith of mass mob activity in the American South, it was routine for mob leaders to adver-tise an impending lynching so as to guarantee a "festival of violence." Furthermore, mob leaders orchestrated these large gatherings with the intention of demonstrat-ing the lynching's cultural significance as well as the community's collective sup-port. Mass mobs encompassed 34 percent of lynchings in Georgia and 40 percent of lynchings in Virginia. Southern mass mobs were usually reserved for African Americans who were accused of rape or murder of white men, women, and chil-dren. These lynchings placed a premium upon performing racial domination, hu-miliation, and eliciting excruciating pain. Typical ritual aspects of Southern mass mobs included taking the lynching victim to the scene of the crime, forcing them to confess or pray for forgiveness, mutilating their body parts, and burning the lynch-ing victim's corpse. Individuals who evaded or resisted capture were often pursed by mobs. Posses killed approximately 42 lynching victims in Louisiana, 51 lynch-ing victims in Georgia, and 31 persons in Virginia. Importantly, the families of ac-cused individuals were also subjected to threats and violence as mobs pursed the accused.

Lynching and Identity

If lynchings were indeed cultural performances that legitimated the values of mob participants, sexuality, race, class, and gender identity were cornerstones of those cultural performances. Lynch mobs were organized and carried out by men who believed lynching was an honorable masculine duty that demonstrated their mas-tery over inferior men and by extension the home, the workplace, and community institutions. Lynching as a ritual of masculine domination and authority was at its root a critique of the legal system and its inability to effectively dramatize or per-form collective notions of crime, punishment, and justice. In the Midwest, West, and South, proponents of lynching espoused a "rough justice" ethos that embraced and valorized extralegal vigilantism and violence. Rough justice advocates favored lynching because the legal system seemed remote, abstract, and ineffective in pun-ishing criminal behavior. They tended to emanate from rural working-class com-munities in the West, Midwest, and South, and in many cases, working-class social ties facilitated lynchings.

While Midwestern, Western, and Southern lynch mobs were informed by a working-class "rough justice" ethos, racial, gender, and sexual cultural scripts more heavily influenced Southern lynch mobs. Southern lynchings were often gendered performances that criss-crossed racial lines. With respect to black Southerners, the ritual of lynching served as a dramatization of unequal racial and gender power relationships. Through lynching, white lynch mobs asserted and enforced white masculine dominance. It confirmed for white men their right to emasculate black men by demonstrating their impotence as public citizens. Black women were also targets as white men employed sexual violence against black women as a means to demonstrate black men's inability to protect black women and their combined racial and masculine authority over black men as patriarchs. Lynching's ability to efficiently communicate racial and gender subordination constituted "lynching's double message."

Racial and gender mythologies structured rationalizations for lynching black men and sexual violence against black women. In the Southern racist imagination, black women were viewed as naturally sexually promiscuous, and therefore sexual relationships between white men and black women were always consensual. Moreover, lynching apologists persistently trumpeted black men as lustful and sex-crazed rapists who only desired to rape virginal white women. The black male rapist syndrome represented an "emotional logic of lynching," which meant that only swift and sure violence, unhampered by legalities, could protect white women from sexual assault. Some lynching proponents so vehemently believed black men were innate rapists that they suggested black genocide! Even though Southern whites tirelessly clung to the rape myth as the basis for lynching, contemporary scholarship has overwhelmingly demonstrated that murder rather than rape was the most frequent accusation for lynching black men and women.

Karlos K. Hill

See also: Jim Crow; Till, Emmett

Further Reading

Brundage, W. F. *Lynching in the New South: Georgia and Virginia, 1880–1930.* Urbana: University of Illinois Press, 1993.

Dray, Philip. *At the Hands of Persons Unknown: The Lynching of Black America.* New York: Random House, 2002.

Hall, Jacqueline D. "The Mind That Burns in Each Body": Women, Rape, and Racial Violence. *Southern Exposure* 12 (1984): 61–71.

Hall, Jacqueline D. *Revolt against Chivalry: Jesse Daniel Ames and the Women's Campaign against Lynching.* New York: Columbia University Press, 1979.

Pfeifer, Michael J. *Rough Justice: Lynching and American Society, 1874–1947.* Urbana: University of Illinois Press, 2004.

Tolnay, Stewart E., and Beck, E. M. *A Festival of Violence: An Analysis of Southern Lynchings, 1882–1930.* Urbana: University of Illinois Press, 1995.

Malcolm X

Malcolm X, or El-Hajj Malik El-Shabazz, was a charismatic religious leader, a relentless activist for black liberation, a brutally honest public speaker, a social scientist, an international revolutionary, and an unequivocal cultural icon during the mid-twentieth century of the United States. He ascended to prominence through his public speaking appointment with the Nation of Islam (NOI, or "The Nation"), the heterodox religious black nationalist/separatist North American organization, during the mid-1950s and early 1960s. He traveled the nation, and the globe, speaking on behalf of the NOI, and its spiritual leader, Elijah Muhammad (d. 1973), while critiquing the remnants of white supremacy, questioning "civil rights," and advocating black self-defense. Along with speaking to ethnically mixed audiences in public forums, Malcolm participated in countless interviews and debates, which appeared on numerous popular television programs and in print media, such as newspapers and magazines, at the time. His oratory abilities forced people to listen to him, though his eloquence and terse way of speaking did not translate into prolific writing. Indeed, Malcolm was not known as an author, but he was deeply involved in the publication of the once-popular NOI newspaper, *Muhammad Speaks.*

He was born Malcolm Little on May 19, 1925, in Omaha, Nebraska, to a Baptist minister, the Reverend Earl Little, and his wife, Louise Little, who were members of the "Universal Negro Improvement Association and African Communities League" (UNIA). The organization was founded in the early twentieth century by the provocateur of rights for all people of African descent in the United States, Marcus Garvey. The seventh child of 10, Malcolm spend his early life growing up in foster homes, and with family members, after the murder of his father at the hands of the local Ku Klux Klan. Subsequently, Louise was institutionalized years later on the diagnosis of insanity.

Once older, he worked menial jobs amid traveling between Lansing, Michigan, Boston, Massachusetts, and New York City during the early 1940s, but was

Malcolm X (1925–1965) in 1964. (Library of Congress)

eventually lured by the desire for bigger profits through criminal means in the street life of the big city. Influenced by lack of opportunity sanctioned by a Northern version of Jim Crow, and the survivalist mentality born from a environment of criminality, Malcolm experimented with peddling dope, larceny, running numbers (gambling), and *pimpin'* (procuring prostitution). Consequently, he was arrested in 1946 and served a brief period of imprisonment as a young adult. While serving an eight-year prison term for larceny and burglary, Malcolm was introduced by his brother Reginald to the teachings of Elijah Muhammad.

The NOI, or the "Black Muslims" as the press called them, was an organization founded in Chicago during the Great Depression of the 1930s by Elijah Poole. He was taught "Islam" and the "legacy" of blacks by a mysterious man, Wallace D. Fard, who appeared in the Chicago slums. Fard was a silk peddler who claimed to be a messenger of God from the East, and would "convert" would-be followers to Islam for a nominal fee. However, when law enforcement officers began to question neighborhood inhabitants for information on Fard, he fled. Poole, who was a staunch believer in Fard's rhetoric, recognized an opportunity, and developed a palatable theology for the growing numbers of uneducated former Christian-turned-Muslim followers. Now as Elijah Muhammad, he began to spread the message to blacks that Fard was God incarnate, and that he was to be considered God's (Fard) prophet. Thus, the then "Lost-Found Nation of Islam in the American Wilderness" was founded, which was essentially an amalgamation of three other preceding movements: Marcus Garvey's Pan-Africanism, Noble Drew Ali's Moorish Science Temple, and, to a lesser extent, the Ahmadiyyah Movement. The confluence of these three movements was important, because they served as "pillars" for the NOI's religious-based Black Nationalism. For example, the Moorish Science Temple was more religious than political in its ideologies, while Garvey's program through UNIA was strictly political. A considerable number of followers from both organizations were among those who joined the NOI at its inception during the 1930s. Both organizations, and their leaders in particular, prioritized agendas for "escape" from the "implications of being black in a white-dominated society."

Noble Drew Ali founded the Moorish Science Temple of America, which was a sect of Islam influenced by Buddhism, Christianity, and the Freemasons. The Moors, as they were often called, maintained the reactionary ideology that whites were naturally demonic, and expressed that the only way for minority salvation was through conversion to Islam. Drew Ali decided to change the mental condition of blacks by introducing a new nomenclature of Arabic names and new cultural symbols such as "Nationality and Identification" cards for his followers—that is, Black Moors—while Garvey believed in secession in, or complete emigration from, predominately white America.

The Ahmadiyyah Movement came to the United States during the late nineteenth century from the Punjabi region of British-ruled India, and was led by spiritual leader and Indian Muslim Mirza Ghulam Ahmad. As a studious young man, Ahmad was convinced he was a prophet and a messiah sent to earth to receive and disseminate, what he believed to be, revelations from God. This claim drew tremendous criticism from orthodox Punjabi Muslims, who believed that the descention of revelation was completed when the final verses of the Holy Qur'an came down from heaven to the Arab prophet, Muhammad ibn Abdullah, during the later years of his life in seventh-century Arabia. Thus, Ghulam Ahmad and his followers, who would later spread their teachings to America's shores, were violently persecuted for their heretical beliefs.

The introduction to the NOI was pivotal in young Malcolm's life considering the context of the United States at the time. Affronted with a system that infringed on their inclusion in cultural and political participation within America, historically blacks had found solace in the Christian church. The black church was a refuge from the misery of white racism, a cornerstone of any black community, and a crucial, relatively safe haven for public discussion. And as Malcolm would often point out through his later speeches, what was surprising to him was that Christianity was a religion given to blacks by their enslavers, and yet they clung to it tightly.

The dilemma was that in the church, some black Americans discovered an equivalent difficulty to challenge oppression in American Christianity, because it remained dominated by a similar white supremacy to that of the secular society. Thus, in a race-conscious society in which blacks were disproportionately imprisoned, openly discriminated against by Jim Crow laws in the Southern, as well as Northern states, unprotected by a biased legal system, collectively held the least amount of property, and terrorized by the Ku Klux Klan with the constant threat of death, American Christianity's appeal as the path to liberation was contested.

Growing weary of the treatment they received from their Christian brethren, some black Christians debated whether Christianity was a source of liberation or oppression for their peoples. Few black Americans decided to challenge the white supremacy in Christianity from within, while others "took a leap of faith," and left Christianity completely. As other black Americans before him sought an alternative path to cultural and political equity, the teachings offered by the NOI ignited something in Malcolm, and served as a catalyst for his program of self-education on subjects, such as world and U.S. histories, literature, and philosophy.

Once released from prison on early parole in 1953, Malcolm began to attend NOI temples and, shortly after, was given responsibility as a minister under the guidance, and personal attention, of Elijah Muhammad. After spending time in NOI temples in New York City, Philadelphia, and Chicago, Malcolm later ascended to the position of national representative for the NOI from the late 1950s until 1963, which allowed him to further the organization's black separatist rhetoric. Through the heterodox interpretation of the religion of Islam, blacks sought out an alternative cultural and religious experience not to become honorary Arabs or whites, but truer, more authentic black men and women. The author of the seminal book, *Black Muslims in America,* C. Eric Lincoln, had the opportunity to conduct first-hand research on the Nation during the height of its popularity, and conducted personal interviews with Elijah Muhammad and Malcolm. Lincoln wrote that the NOI espoused ideas such as self-reliance, economic empowerment, and high morality, and was an exemplar of black social protest for social change. Malcolm, with the teachings of Elijah Muhammad, and the NOI as his base, exemplified these characteristics.

Furthermore, the NOI promoted ideas such as: "getting equality now instead of salvation in heaven later"; prohibition of consuming harmful food products, for example, pork, alcohol, cigarettes, and other narcotics; refrain from gambling; chastity, responsibility, and honesty, which were all the ills that plagued the black community. Additionally, the NOI offered a discourse of black superiority to challenge white supremacy, and they firmly believed that Islam was the natural religion of black people.

Along with the rather docile empowerment concepts, there were two theories that distinguished Malcolm and the NOI. One of the most disturbing theories asserted by Malcolm was the race-tinged generalization of white Americans based on the world history that all white peoples were "devils," as taught to Elijah Muhammad by his teacher, W.D. Fard. The second was their call for a separate area in North America for blacks, because they rejected the idea of integration as a ploy to re-subjugate blacks. This was a departure from the ideas of Garvey's Back to Africa Movement, and was an obvious break from orthodox Islam's historical tradition of leaving a home to establish a society that would abide by justice, or egalitarian principles not available. Due to the persecution they experienced in their home city of Makkah (Mecca), Allah (God) commanded His believers through the Prophet of Islam, Muhammad, to establish a truly Muslim community in Madinah in 622 CE.

In a move to emulate tradition, the NOI prioritized connecting Black Muslims in the West to the broader Muslim world community. Their slant was that they emphasized "brownness" of the larger community, who had been, in most cases, oppressed like blacks on the North American continent. In a constructed prophesy, Elijah Muhammad "foretold" of America's destruction for its treatment of the darker humankind. Likewise, he tried to make the case for black non-Muslims to see their condition in America as a microcosmic representation of what was happening globally wherever the "white man" went. Earlier, Muhammad even admonished his followers to not fight against Japanese military forces in World War II, because they were victims of white racism also.

Continuing this rationale, the analysis of the political infrastructure of the United States' government by the NOI, and Malcolm in particular, was a lucid interrogation of U.S. history, U.S. domestic policies, and the claim of democracy in the United States for its citizens. Malcolm, in his eloquent manner of oration, took the government to task, delivering now infamous speeches, such as "The Message to the Grassroots," "A Declaration of Independence," "The Ballot or the Bullet," and "The Black Revolution." Through his words, whether speaking to audiences in Detroit, Harlem, Cleveland, or London, Malcolm also questioned the intellectual coherence of blacks who desired to be in the political establishment, and spoke suspiciously of the loyalty of white liberals.

In terms of political philosophy, he considered Democrats to be identical to Republicans in that they supported the white supremacist infrastructure. It made no difference whether the discussion was on the Northern or the Southern states, because where the North provided more economic opportunities, there was unemployment and disparate housing. Alternatively, in the South, blacks faced those conditions in addition to threats of being terrorized by the Ku Klux Klan, or even lynched, or murdered, for no serious reasons. Being a critic of the altruistic tactics of protesting nonviolently, Malcolm advocated the constitutional right to bear arms for all blacks in the United States as a means to protect their bodies, families, and communities where the government had failed to do so.

For these reasons, Malcolm argued that Democrats, or as he called them, "Dixiecrats," were most often "Southern" in political orientation, and not really friends of blacks. In numerous speeches, he directly referenced the absence of voting rights for Southern blacks as an abomination to democracy, being that the Civil Rights

Act had been signed in 1957. Malcolm continuously emphasized being aware of the words by white liberals (Dixiecrats) in Washington, D.C., and the actions of the Republicans and their constituents in the Southern states, because white liberals kept blacks disenfranchised with no hope of casting votes in the best interest of themselves. As the March on Washington took place in 1963 where Martin Luther King Jr. gave the famous "I Have a Dream" speech, Malcolm only witnessed a ploy to appease the frustrated blacks around the country with no real gains.

In early 1964, he left the NOI after being silenced for making unauthorized comments about the assassination of President John F. Kennedy, and over confirmed reports that the person who saved his life, his father-like figure, Elijah Muhammad, had fathered several children with young secretaries within the Nation. He formed a new organization, Muslim Mosque Inc., in Harlem, New York City, to support the smaller Muslim community outside of the NOI. In the spring of 1964, through the financial generosity of his sister Ella, he traveled to Makkah, Saudi Arabia, to perform the *hajj* (the required pilgrimage of all orthodox Muslims). Also on this extended trip, he was able to make contacts in foreign countries such as Egypt, Morocco, Algeria, Nigeria, Ghana, and Lebanon.

While on hajj, Malcolm was struck by the sense of "brotherhood" he experienced, as he witnessed no racial divisions among men and women, but saw only a unity of being for the worship of Allah (God). By observing, and sharing quarters with white European Muslims, Malcolm, now identifying himself as Malik El-Shabazz, concluded that the race problems of the United States could be, potentially, solved by Christian, white America's conversion to Islam. Additionally, the experience of hajj solidified his decision to increase the call for Black Nationalism in black communities in the United States, and to replace efforts for civil rights with a more internationalized consciousness toward human rights for blacks.

Through the contacts he made on his extended trip abroad, Malcolm felt certain that with a Pan-Africanist perspective, his people in the United States could receive more support from partners within the United Nations if the focus was on obtaining human rights instead of civil rights. Upon his return to the United States, he formed a new secular group, Organization of Afro-American Unity (OAAU), to complement Muslim Mosque Inc., and address social, political, and economical issues facing the broader, disenfranchised, non-Muslim black community in the United States.

Malcolm would never see his plan materialize, as an unexplained chain of events began to happen in his life. He was attacked by assailants, was to be evicted from his family home by the NOI, and his house was under constant surveillance by the FBI. In early February 1965, Malcolm's family home was firebombed with Molotov cocktails thrown by assailants in the early morning hours as he, his wife, Betty Shabazz, and their four daughters slept. This was an obvious attempt on his

life by assassins, though who was responsible for sending them was left to speculation. However, while he was giving a speech before an audience of supporters in the
Audubon Ballroom in Harlem, New York City, assassins infiltrated the crowd, and
fatally shot Malcolm several times. El-Hajj Malik El-Shabazz, posthumously called
the "Black Prince" and "our manhood" by film actor, playwright, poet, activist, and
friend, Ossie Davis at his funeral, died from those wounds on February 25, 1965.

Mika'il A. Petin

See also: Black Nationalism; Garvey, Marcus.

Further Reading

Breitman, George. *Malcolm X Speaks.* New York: Grove Weidenfeld, 1990.
Chapman, Mark. *Christianity on Trial: African-American Religious Thought before and after Black Power.* New York: Orbis Books, 1996.
Haley, Alex, and Malcolm X. *The Autobiography of Malcolm X: As Told to Alex Haley.* New York: Ballantine Books, 1964.
Jackson, Sherman. *Islam and the Black American: Looking toward the Third Resurrection.* New York: Oxford University Press, 2005.
Lincoln, C. Eric. *Black Muslims in America.* Boston: Beacon Press, 1961.
Strum, Philippa, and Taratolo, Danielle, eds. *Muslims in the United States.* Washington, DC: Woodrow Wilson International Center for Scholars, 2003.
Turner, Richard Brent. *Islam in the African American Experience.* Bloomington: Indiana University Press 1997.

March on Washington Movement

The origins of the March on Washington movement can be traced to a September 27, 1940, meeting between A. Philip Randolph, the president of the Brotherhood of Sleeping Car Porters; Walter White, head of the National Association
for the Advancement of Colored People (NAACP); T. Arnold Hill of the Urban
League; and President Franklin D. Roosevelt. Randolph urged Roosevelt to promote equal employment opportunities and to desegregate the armed services. When
the meeting did not produce a positive response from Roosevelt, Randolph decided
that he would bring the case directly to the American people by staging a march
on Washington, D.C.

African Americans had benefited less than other groups from New Deal programs during the Great Depression, and continuing racial discrimination was
excluding them from the job opportunities in the defense industries that were expanding as the world plunged into the World War II. At a September 1940 union

convention held at Madison Square Garden, Randolph discussed the problem of discrimination in the defense industry. Government training programs excluded blacks; defense contractors announced that they would not hire blacks or would hire them only for menial positions, and that despite the shortage of construction workers, contractors would not hire experienced blacks. During this time, the armed forces were segregated: in an army of half a million men, there were only 4,700 blacks. There were no blacks in the Marine Corps or the Army Air Corps, and even the Red Cross blood supply was segregated. In the audience the evening of Randolph's speech was First Lady Eleanor Roosevelt, who was going to speak to the convention the following evening. She learned from Randolph that the president's staff had refused to set up a meeting between Roosevelt and Randolph. Through her efforts, the September 27 meeting took place.

At the meeting, Randolph pointed out the discrimination in the defense industry; the refusal of skilled labor unions to admit blacks, and the discrimination in the armed forces. Roosevelt responded that progress was being made, although his secretary of the navy, Frank Knox (who also attended the meeting), asserted that it would be impossible to desegregate the navy. Roosevelt told the black leaders that he would consult his cabinet and military leadership and respond to their concerns. The response they received was not from the president but was instead a statement by Roosevelt's press secretary, Stephen Early, who announced that the military would not be desegregated, and implied that the black leaders Roosevelt had met with agreed with decision. Randolph and the others publicly announced that this was not the case, and the requested another meeting with the president, which was not forthcoming.

This led to a change in tactics. Randolph had sought change through letter writings and meetings with government officials. He now believed direct action was essential, and started making public statements to this effect. Randolph, along with Bayard Rustin, the youth director of the Fellowship of Reconciliation, and A. J. Muste, the executive director of the Fellowship of Reconciliation, proposed a march on Washington to protest discrimination in government and the defense industry as well as segregation in the armed services. They established a March on Washington Committee (MOWC) to organize the march. Their slogan was: "We loyal Negro Americans demand the right to work and fight for our country." By late 1940, Randolph had established a National March on Washington Committee with chapters in 18 cities.

Randolph made his formal proposal in January 1941, and spent months gathering support for his plan and preparing for the march, which was scheduled for July 1, 1941. His union, the NAACP, the Urban League, and the black press played major roles in generating interest in the march. In "The Call to March," which appeared in the May 1941 issue of the *Black Worker,* he wrote that "[o]nly power can effect the enforcement and adoption of a given policy. Power is the active principle of only the organized masses, the masses united for a definite purpose."

Roosevelt, who had continued to refuse to meet with Randolph, became concerned about the political impact of the march, which had originally promised to bring more than 10,000 marchers to the nation's capital and had grown to where more than 100,000 marchers were expected. Randolph had indicated that all the marchers would be black, and Roosevelt feared that there might be violence, and that such a march would then become a precedent for other groups. Also, given the Roosevelt administration's opposition to the fascist regimes in Europe, a march by blacks against discrimination would be embarrassing to the country, which presented itself as a model of democracy. Roosevelt was further concerned about the reaction of Southern Democrats to such a march.

At the president's request, Eleanor Roosevelt wrote to Randolph asking him to call off the march. Randolph refused. Randolph then met with the first lady, who concluded that the only way to stop the march would be for the president to meet with Randolph. President Roosevelt met with Randolph and White on June 18, 1941, to urge him to call off the march. Roosevelt told them that the armed forces would remain segregated, but that he would consider an investigation of discrimination if the march was called off. Randolph's response to the president was that the march would be called off only if Roosevelt issued an executive order. Roosevelt agreed, and Randolph worked with Roosevelt's staff to draft the order.

On June 25, 1941, Roosevelt issued Executive Order 8802, which made discrimination based on race, creed, color, or national origin illegal in the defense industry, and established the Fair Employment Practices Committee (FEPC) to investigate charges of racial discrimination. This was the first executive order concerning the rights of African Americans since President Abraham Lincoln issued the Emancipation Proclamation during the Civil War. In response, Randolph announced in a radio address from Madison Square Garden on June 28, 1941, that he had agreed to suspend the march. In his speech, Randolph said that he had not cancelled the march but had only suspended it. By leaving open the possibility of a march, Randolph asserted that this was the movement's "ace in the hole" to ensure that the government would not backtrack on its commitment.

The decision to suspend the march led Rustin, who believed that Randolph had "sold out" by not holding out for desegregation of the armed forces, to break (temporarily) with Randolph. In 1942, Rustin would help found the Congress of Racial Equality (CORE).

While suspending the march, the effort continued. By December 1941, the MOWC had become a dues-paying organization in order "to help create faith by Negroes in Negroes." In 1942, the MOWC mounted rallies in New York, Chicago, and St. Louis. The goal of the organization was to mobilize African Americans into an effective pressure group. Nearly 2 million African Americans worked in the defense industries by the end of 1944. However, the FEPC did not effectively tackle discriminatory practices in the South, and following Roosevelt's death, the FEPC was abolished as Congress refused to fund the agency. It ceased operation in 1946. Randolph and Rustin would initiate the effort that would culminate in the March on Washington of 1963.

Jeffrey Kraus

See also: Roosevelt, Franklin D.; World War II.

Further Reading

Garfinkel, Herbert. *When Negroes March: The March on Washington Movement in the Organizational Politics for FEPC.* Glencoe, IL: Free Press, 1959.
Goodwin, Doris Kearns. *No Ordinary Time.* New York: Simon and Schuster, 1994.
Pfeffer, Paula F. *A. Philip Randolph, Pioneer of the Civil Rights Movement.* Baton Rouge: Louisiana State University Press, 1990.

Marriage, Interracial

Laws in many states made illegal the marriage between adults of different "races." Specifically, these laws were intended to prevent marriages between whites and nonwhites. State laws banning interracial marriages aimed to keep the "races" separate and identifiable, and sought to buttress white privilege, especially of sexual access to white females. Differences among the states in their laws regarding marriages between whites and nonwhites made being married under the laws of some states a criminal act in others.

Laws preventing marriages between whites and nonwhites predated Jim Crow, dating back to the colonial period, appearing in colonial statutes in the late seventeenth century. Jim Crow simply gave support to such laws, particularly but not exclusively in the South. By 1950, about 30 states still carried such laws, although they were increasingly ignored outside the South. While almost all states of the South had such laws, many Northern and Western states also carried them. No uniform definition of what constituted a nonwhite person existed, and standards varied from state to state. Usually such laws specifically banned marriage between a white person and a person of the opposite sex with at least one black great-grandparent, although occasionally the "one-drop rule" was used. While most such laws were specifically aimed at black-white couples, marriages between whites and other nonwhites such as Asians, Native Americans, and South Asians were also affected by such laws. However, marriages between whites and Hispanics/Latinos were usually not banned under the law, as most state laws regarding racial classification considered Hispanics as white. However, if a Hispanic person looked black, officials usually refused to issue a license.

State laws varied considerably. On one extreme was Virginia, with a 1922 law that made being married itself a crime for black and white couples, regardless of where the marriage occurred. Other states simply refused to issue marriage licenses to couples of different races but did nothing officially against couples who were married in other states. However, local customs and hostility often prevented mixed-race couples from residing in most areas of the South. Western states, especially California, Arizona, and Oregon, focused on preventing unions between whites and Asians and Malays as much as between whites and blacks. Enforcement of anti-interracial marriage laws tended to be less stringent when neither partner was white.

In American territories, such laws either did not exist or were seldom enforced. However, in those situations, the overwhelming majority of white Americans were male, making such unions perhaps inevitable. However, prejudices against such unions usually resulted in the ostracizing of interracial couples from the polite society, which meant white couples. In the Panama Canal Zone, men who married local women were referred to as "squaw men," and became social outcasts. American soldiers who were stationed in the Philippines or Hawai'i and married local women often continued to reenlist in the army to stay out of the continental United States, where they would be unable to take their wives.

Such laws and customs reflected white society's fears of miscegenation, and were specifically aimed at preventing sexual relationships between white women and black men. In a society that depended in part on easily definable categories of "race," children of such unions presented problems that law against interracial marriage attempted to prevent. Children of such illicit unions were often raised by the mother if she were the nonwhite partner, or aborted or given to a black family to raise if the mother were white. However, popular culture abounded with the concept of the "tragic mulatto," indicating that such people were doomed to live miserable lives and thus their creation should be avoided. Of course, that such misery was caused by racism seems to have not occurred to many people. The rise of so-called scientific racism buttressed the belief that the offspring of unions between people of different "races" was genetically inferior, and should be avoided. Such pseudoscientific nonsense found its way into court rulings and legislative debates for decades.

Despite officially being banned in many areas, sexual relationships between white men and nonwhite women were tolerated if kept discreet, and such couples did not seek legal sanction. Many of the states with anti-interracial marriage laws also had laws that defined any sexual contact between black men and white women as rape regardless of the circumstances. Such laws made any indication of sexual activity between black men and white women dangerous for black men. White women caught in a compromising position could always claim rape, which often resulted in the lynching of the black man involved, or any black man, as a warning to all, especially in the South. Even when state laws did not specifically define interracial sexual relations as rape, an allegation of rape against a black man commonly resulted in a lynch mob.

The end of anti-interracial marriage laws began with the marriage of Richard Loving, who was white, and Mildred Jeter, who was black, in 1958. Unable to wed in their native Virginia, the couple wed in Washington, D.C. Upon their return to Virginia as a married couple, they were arrested and faced up to five years in prison for their crime. Under a plea, the couple agreed to leave the state and not return for 25 years. The couple moved to Washington, D.C, and, in 1963, began court action

Richard and Mildred (Jeter) Loving. Legally married in the District of Columbia in 1958, they were arrested when they moved to Virginia. Their case eventually led the U.S. Supreme Court to rule in 1967 that state laws banning "interracial" marriages were unconstitutional. (AP Photo)

against the Commonwealth of Virginia. The lawsuit eventually led to the U.S. Supreme Court, which ruled in 1967 in *Loving v. Virginia* that state laws banning interracial marriages were unconstitutional. At the time, some 16 states still had such laws, as many states had been repealing them in the two decades before the Supreme Court ruling. By the end of the 1950s, an estimated 51,000 mixed black and white marriages existed in the United States, compared to almost half a million by the end of the century.

Such laws could not prevent interracial marriages among committed couples, who traveled to states without such restrictions to marry. But these laws did force interracial couples to choose their state of residence carefully, and made travel in states with such laws problematic and even deadly. Such laws made interracial couples, even in states that permitted such unions, not quite respectable. Official disapproval of such marriages limited their acceptance, and the numbers of interracial marriages began to swell only after such laws were nullified by the Supreme Court.

Barry M. Stentiford

See also: Jim Crow; Racial Customs and Etiquette.

Further Reading

Gay, Kathlyn. *The Rainbow Effect: Interracial Families.* Danbury, CT: Grolier Publishing, 1987.

McNamara, Robert P., Maria Tempenis, and Beth Walton. *Crossing the Line: Interracial Couples in the South.* Westport, CT: Greenwood Press, 1999.

Moran, Rachel F. *Interracial Intimacy: The Regulation of Race and Romance.* Chicago: University of Chicago Press, 2001.

Robinson, Charles Frank, II. *Dangerous Liaisons: Sex and Love in the Segregated South.* Fayetteville: University of Arkansas Press, 2003.

Marshall, Thurgood

The lead attorney for the National Association for the Advancement of Colored People (NAACP) in the 1954 *Brown v. Board of Education* case and the first African American to sit on the U.S. Supreme Court, Thurgood Marshall was born in Baltimore, Maryland, on July 2, 1908. Named for his great-grandfather, Thoroughgood, who had escaped slavery, Marshall grew up comfortably in middle-class, but segregated, black Baltimore (Marshall shortened the name himself to Thurgood as a child because he found his name too long to write out). His father, William, was a Pullman porter and a waiter at a white club, while his mother, Norma, was a schoolteacher.

In 1925, Marshall followed his older brother, Aubrey, to Lincoln University in Pennsylvania, one of the nation's most prestigious black universities. At Lincoln, Marshall was not an exceptionally serious student and was suspended from school for his involvement in hazing freshmen. When he returned to school, his racial consciousness was stoked by a fellow Lincoln student, the poet Langston Hughes, who was leading the charge to have Lincoln's all-white faculty integrated. Marshall, like most Lincoln students, initially opposed integrating the faculty, but he eventually became a supporter of the idea, and took over the campaign when Hughes graduated. As a senior, Marshall pushed a student referendum to force the administration to integrate the faculty, and the school's first black faculty member was hired the following year.

Marshall married Philadelphia native Vivian "Buster" Bury, a University of Pennsylvania student, in 1929. He graduated from Lincoln the following year but was relegated to working as a waiter at Maryland's all-white Gibson Island Club, with his father, as the onset of the Great Depression had left jobs scarce. Marshall, who had been an excellent debater in college, then decided that he wanted to go to law school. He and Buster lived with his parents in Baltimore, so he applied to the all-white University of Maryland Law School, but was rejected because of his race, bringing him face to face with the Jim Crowism that he had mostly avoided growing up in black Baltimore and at Lincoln University. Angered at the rejection, his only other option seemed to be to apply to the historically black Howard University Law School in Washington, D.C. Howard's reputation at this time was poor, as the law school was not accredited by the American Bar Association or the Association of American Law Schools.

Marshall was admitted to Howard Law in the fall of 1930, at a fortuitous time in the school's history. Harvard-educated Charles Hamilton Houston, who had joined Howard's faculty in 1924, had recently been promoted to dean of the Law school, and, along with Howard University's first African American president, Mordecai Johnson, was determined to increase Howard's academic standards and become a fully accredited law school. Despite some opposition to his rigorous policies, Houston succeeded in toughening admission requirements to the school, and by 1931, it was accredited by both the American Bar Association and the Association of American Law Schools. Most importantly, Houston was committed to using Howard Law School to develop a cadre of black lawyers to fight racial injustice. It was into this vigorous academic environment that Marshall entered in 1930.

At Howard, Marshall quickly became a disciple of Houston and fellow Howard faculty member William Hastie. Along with fellow student and future NAACP attorney Oliver Hill, Marshall developed as Houston's protégée, accompanying him to court and sitting in on strategy sessions for NAACP cases. Through Houston's tutelage, Marshall became aware of the power that lawyers could wield in bringing about change, and he wanted to be a part of it. Following his graduation from Howard in 1933, first in his class, Marshall traveled South with Houston to examine the state of black elementary schools throughout the region. The trip was part of Houston's research in developing a legal strategy for the NAACP to challenge segregated education; it was the basis of what would eventually culminate in the *Brown* decision.

Marshall was offered a scholarship to pursue an advanced degree at Harvard Law School in 1933, but instead decided it was time for him to begin his own practice and earn some money for his family, so he opened his own firm in Baltimore. However, the clientele available for a black attorney in Depression-era Baltimore was slim, and Marshall had a very difficult time making ends meet. The clients he did have often had a tough time paying his fees, but he developed a reputation of not turning anyone in need away. His reputation also brought him to the notice of the Baltimore branch of the NAACP, which retained him as its counsel, and in December 1933, Marshall began preparing his first civil rights case, what became *Murray v. Maryland.*

As Marshall knew all too well, the University of Maryland's law school refused to admit black students on account of their race. Marshall and the local NAACP wanted to challenge the legality of this segregationist policy, but they were hampered by the Supreme Court's 1896 *Plessy v. Ferguson* "separate but equal" decision, which ruled that segregation was constitutional. This decision was the great hurdle for black lawyers like Marshall and Houston to overcome, as once the Supreme Court has ruled on a decision, it rarely overturned itself, a practice known as *starre decisis* ("Let the decision stand").

Houston, however, had been working on a different approach to challenge school discrimination, and when Marshall informed him that he planned to sue for the right of Donald Murray to attend the University of Maryland Law School, Houston sought to put his strategy to the test and join his former pupil on the case. He and Marshall would not challenge the *Plessy* decision; they would embrace it. Houston and Marshall argued not that Maryland had to admit Murray to its law school because segregation was unconstitutional (overturning *Plessy*), but instead that Murray had to be admitted under the "separate but equal" statute, because there was no public law school open to African Americans in the state of Maryland. Houston's strategy was relatively simple: in the *Murray* case, he did not have to prove the inequality between black and white law schools (the way he would have to with black and white elementary schools, for instance), because there was no black law school in the state; it was a question of exclusion, not equality, and therefore not allowed by *Plessy.*

Houston and Marshall prevailed in the *Murray* case when the Maryland Court of Appeals upheld the lower court's decision to admit Murray to the law school and the state decided not to appeal the case to the U.S. Supreme Court. It was Marshall's first civil rights victory, and it began a strategy that he and Houston would pursue in attacking school segregation for another 15 years, in cases such as *Missouri ex rel. Gaines v. Canada* (1938), *Sipuel v. Board of Regents of the University of Oklahoma* (1948), and *Sweatt v. Painter* (1950). In all of these cases, Marshall and/or Houston focused on graduate educational facilities and did not challenge the legality of separate but equal, but instead on the lack of education programs provided for black citizens. With each victory, the NAACP lawyers chipped away at the legitimacy of school segregation and laid the groundwork for the eventual assault on *Plessy.*

While Marshall is most famous for his work on school desegregation during this era, he was involved in a host of other cases for the NAACP as well. In 1936, he closed his unprofitable one-man firm in Baltimore and became a full-time employee of the NAACP, focusing on cases in Maryland and Virginia. Many of the cases he pursued successfully were pay-equalization cases for African American public school teachers and employees. In 1938, he took over as head of the NAACP's legal division, replacing Houston, who was in ailing health. Two years later the NAACP Legal Defense Fund Inc. was founded as an organization separate from the NAACP to focus on civil rights litigation, and headed by Marshall from its inception until 1961, when he became a federal court of appeals judge.

With Marshall at the head of the NAACP's legal wing, the organization flourished. In addition to continued work on school integration and pay equalization, he instituted successful litigation that eliminated the white primary (*Smith v. Allwright,* 1944) and restrictive housing covenants (*Shelley v. Kraemer,* 1948). Marshall even traveled to Japan and Korea in 1951 to investigate discrimination by the U.S. Army against black soldiers, who were being court-martialed at much higher rates that whites, mostly on vague charges of "cowardice" and "incompetence." Between August and October 1950, 32 black servicemen in Korea were convicted under the 75th Article of War—"misbehavior in front of the enemy"—in comparison to only two white soldiers; blacks also got harsher penalties for being convicted for the same crimes as whites. Marshall's investigation revealed a pattern of discrimination in the court-martial process, going back to World War I. Marshall blamed the army high command, specifically General Douglas MacArthur, for continued discrimination against African American soldiers, as the army leadership continued to resist integration two years after President Harry S. Truman's Executive Order 9981 mandated the end of segregation in the armed forces.

In 1950, Marshall also believed that the time had finally come for a frontal attack on *Plessy,* and the NAACP announced that it was looking for plaintiffs who would be willing to challenge school segregation. For almost 15 years, the NAACP had pursued the legal strategy developed by Houston of using *Plessy* to gain equal educational facilities for African Americans (with the hope that the cost of making schools truly equal would force school integration). Now, Marshall decided that the Supreme Court was ready to hear a challenge to the constitutionality of school segregation itself. His team compiled five cases—from Kansas, Virginia, South Carolina, the District of Columbia, and Delaware—which became known as *Brown v. Board of Education.*

The cases came before the Supreme Court in 1952. Marshall's strategy in arguing *Brown* was controversial, in that he based much of his argument on evidence provided by psychologists Kenneth and Mamie Clark and their famous doll experiment. The Clarks' study of three- to seven-year-old children revealed that white superiority was so ingrained in society that young black children preferred white dolls (which they identified as "pretty" or "nice") instead of black dolls (which they described as "ugly" or bad"). While derided as sociological garbage by opposing counsel, Marshall's use of the "doll test" proved to be powerful evidence that school segregation caused a sense of inferiority in black children that was a violation of their Fourteenth Amendment right of equal protection of the laws. The justices agreed with Marshall's arguments, and in 1954, the Supreme Court overturned *Plessy,* ruling that "separate is inherently unequal in the area of education."

While the *Brown* decision was a dramatic victory for Marshall and the NAACP, the culmination of almost two decades of legal attacks on segregation in education, it did not bring about the immediate desegregation of the nation's schools. At the conclusion of *Brown,* the Court asked lawyers from both the NAACP and the states to return the next year to present their plans for a timetable on how *Brown* should be implemented. In his brief for the high court, Marshall recommended that integration plans go into effect in 1955, with complete school integration by the fall of 1956. Lawyers for the states asked instead that the Court set no timetable for integration, but to leave the decision on how and when to integrate to local school boards. In what became known as *Brown* II, Chief Justice Earl Warren sided with the gradualist approach of the states in 1955 by refusing to set a timetable for integration, ruling instead that integration should proceed "with all deliberate speed." This infamous order set the stage for massive resistance against school integration, as many school districts throughout the South simply refused to integrate until finally forced to by the federal government following the passage of the Civil Rights Act of 1964.

The same year as his professional setback with *Brown* II, Marshall suffered a personal loss when Buster, his wife of 25 years, died of cancer. His personal fame, however, in 1955, was at an all-time high. Known even before *Brown* in the African American community as "Mr. Civil Rights," he became well known throughout the nation as a result of the *Brown* decision, even appearing on the cover of

Time magazine. As black protests regarding Emmitt Till's murder in Mississippi and the Montgomery Bus Boycott in Alabama developed, Marshall also emerged as a lighting rod in the Civil Rights Movement. He believed that the best way for African Americans to enact change was through the courts, not the streets; he was not always totally supportive of the protest movement, and was highly critical of black separatist organizations.

Despite some of his reservations over public protests, Marshall and the NAACP did provide legal assistance to the protesters. Marshall was directly involved in the Montgomery Bus Boycott case, working with local NAACP attorney Fred Gray as the case was eventually settled in their favor by the U.S. Supreme Court in 1956. He also continued to work for school integration, including representing Autherine Lucy in her fight to integrate the University of Alabama. Marshall, who remarried in 1955 to Cecilia ("Cissy") Suyat, an NAACP secretary, enjoyed a personal joy when his first child, Thurgood Jr., was born in 1956. The couple later had a second son, John.

In 1961, Marshall left the NAACP after a quarter-century of service when President John F. Kennedy appointed him as a federal appeals judge. As counsel for the NAACP, Marshall had argued 32 cases before the U.S. Supreme Court, winning 29 of them. Four years after his appointment as a federal judge, President Lyndon B. Johnson appointed Marshall as U.S. solicitor general. As the nation's top litigator, Marshall won numerous other decisions before the Supreme Court on behalf of the United States. After less than two years in that post, Marshall was appointed by Johnson to the U.S. Supreme Court in 1967, becoming the first African American to serve on the nation's highest court.

During Marshall's 24-year term on the Supreme Court, he consistently supported civil rights, voting with the court's liberal majority in the 1970s on landmark cases regarding affirmative action, abortion, defendant rights, and school desegregation. As the court took a conservative turn in the 1980s, Marshall increasingly found himself arguing with the minority, and many of his written opinions became angry and bitter, especially in regard to cases in which he believed that the Court was trying to turn back the clock on civil rights. Frustrated by the conservative nature of the Court and in failing health, Marshall retired in 1991. The decision to appoint Clarence Thomas, a conservative African American with little experience as a litigator or a judge, hurt Marshall, but he accepted it with dignity, meeting with the new justice for more than two hours when Thomas joined the Court. Thurgood Marshall died the following year, at age 84.

Thomas J. Ward Jr.

See also: *Brown v. Board of Education*; *Brown v. Board of Education*, Legal Groundwork for.

Further Reading

Davis, Michael D., and Hunter R. Clark. *Thurgood Marshall: Warrior at the Bar, Rebel on the Bench*. New York: Carol Publishing Group, 1992.
Tushnet, Mark V. *Making Civil Rights Law: Thurgood Marshall and the Supreme Court, 1936–1961*. New York: Oxford University Press, 1996.
Williams, Juan. *Thurgood Marshall: American Revolutionary*. New York: Times Books, 1998.

Meredith, James

James Howard Meredith was a reluctant civil rights pioneer known for his integration of the University of Mississippi, but he always eschewed such honorific labels as well as the public spotlight.

Meredith was born on June 25, 1933, in Kosciusko, Mississippi. After graduating from high school, Meredith enlisted in the U.S. Air Force, in which he served from 1951 to 1960. During his service, he spent time overseas. Additionally, Meredith began to take college courses offered through military outreach programs. Upon his honorable discharge from the air force, he returned to Mississippi and attended historically black Jackson State College, completing two years of study. On January 31, 1961, Meredith applied to the University of Mississippi. From the outset, university officials stalled the admission process by using, what Meredith would describe in his letter to the U.S. Justice Department in which he appealed for assistance, as "delaying tactics."

Anticipating the struggle he faced in his attempt to be admitted to the University of Mississippi, Meredith also wrote to Thurgood Marshall, seeking representation from the National Association for the Advancement of Colored People (NAACP) Legal Defense and Education Fund. Near the end of May 1961, the NAACP proceeded with litigation to have Meredith admitted, and the case eventually ended up in the U.S. Supreme Court. On September 10, 1961, the Supreme Court decided that Meredith should be allowed to attend the university.

What followed was a showdown between the state of Mississippi and the federal government over states' rights and opportunities for equal education. Segregationist governor Ross Barnett took active steps to prevent Meredith from registering for classes by physically blocking Meredith's entrance into the appropriate university office. Tensions grew in the area and boiled over with riots that encompassed the entire campus. In response to Barnett's defiance of the Supreme Court, President John F. Kennedy ordered the mobilization of federal marshals and federal troops to Mississippi to enforce the order admitting Meredith. This step only further riled the segregationists in the area, and there were several violent clashes between the protesters of Meredith's admittance and the federal authorities. The conflicts were bloody, with two deaths and scores of serious injuries. Finally, the violence abated after pleas from all sides, and Meredith attended his first class on October 1, 1962. He went on to graduate from the University of Mississippi, pursue further studies in Nigeria, and receive an LLB from Columbia University.

Meredith took a leadership role in the March against Fear in 1966. He was shot by Aubrey James Norvell while participating in the march from Memphis, Tennessee, to Jackson, Mississippi. He recovered from the wound and was able to complete the journey. Meredith then retreated from the limelight and became a businessperson who seemed to want to put his contributions behind him. After this period, he relocated to Washington and worked on the staff of Senator Jesse Helms on matters of domestic policy. He made several unsuccessful runs for Congress as a Republican and wrote a number of books and articles.

As the 40th anniversary of Meredith's entry into the University of Mississippi approached, his attendance at the ceremony remained in doubt. In the end, Meredith reluctantly attended the ceremony, but he again expressed his desire to be viewed only as a humble U.S. citizen who sought the protections and opportunities offered by the government and not as a civil rights hero. Nonetheless, many still view Meredith as a significant contributor to the Civil Rights Movement and, at the same time, respect his wishes to be thought of as just another American standing up for himself and others through action.

Aaron Cooley

See also: Mississippi; Segregation, Residential.

Further Reading

Klarman, Michael. *From Jim Crow to Civil Rights: The Supreme Court and the Struggle for Racial Equality.* New York: Oxford University Press, 2004.
Meredith, James. *Three Years in Mississippi.* Bloomington: Indiana University Press, 1966.

Minstrelsy

Minstrel shows were the first form of musical theater that was uniquely American, based on American history and featuring uniquely American social relations. Minstrelsy began in the 1820s and went on to become America's most popular form of entertainment for nearly a hundred years (although blackface depictions date back to the 1750s, before the American Revolution). The very phrase "Jim Crow" came into existence by Thomas D. Rice's depiction of a black man who "Jumped

Jim Crow" and later became *the* image of African Americans in the United States. For these shows, whites used burned cork to darken their skin and lipstick to enlarge their mouths to depict a stereotype of Africans and African Americans in a wide variety of American settings.

General Description

Minstrel shows used stereotypes for white profit by simultaneously constructing black and white identities in the national imagination. Minstrel shows represented the most provocative and, perhaps, revealing form of entertainment in the late nineteenth and early twentieth centuries. Their enticing use of black bodies and representations created, enforced, and disseminated ideas about whiteness and white privilege, and, conversely, black inherent inferiority and subservience. By both portraying blacks a certain way, generally in line with

Poster for Al. G. Field Minstrels, featuring Emmett Miller, the clarinet voiced comedian, circa 1900. Minstrel shows, featuring white performers in blackface make up, were popular throughout the nation and presented white audiences with a broad stereotype of black culture. (Library of Congress)

racial stereotypes of the time, and articulating statements that voiced political, social, and economic concerns, minstrel shows became both a principal site of struggle in and over the perceived culture of blacks.

The image of blacks that appeared in minstrel shows, Jim Crow, was based on a caricature of a black homeless man, dressed in ragged clothes, singing and dancing on stage. Though a gross misrepresentation of blacks, these depictions were perceived as reality and taken as truth when depicted by working-class whites in blackface. During minstrel shows, white audiences witnessed blacks in a wide variety of settings, ranging from slave ships to plantations to the urban North. Nearly all included (mis)representations of "authentic" black dancing styles. To attract large audiences, minstrel shows featured popular American music, most notably "Dixie," a nostalgic song dreaming of the "good old days" of white aristocracy rooted in blacks' plantation life. Contributing to these shows were many famous American songwriters, including Stephen Foster, who wrote lyrics to accompany blackfaced actors' performances.

The content and subjects of minstrelsy changed with each historical epoch in America. The largest shifts appeared after slavery and emancipation and then again during the early part of the twentieth century, which coincided with both the Great Migration of blacks northward and out of the South and mass migration of Southern and Eastern Europeans into America. This inexpensive entertainment for the masses provided many urban dwellers who spent their evenings watching minstrel shows with sufficient information about blacks to develop racial (and racist) attitudes about many of the men and women with whom they often lived in close proximity and/or competed with for jobs. However, traveling minstrel shows, which were extremely popular, brought these forms and ideas to countless Americans in the Midwest who never had any contact with blacks, thereby allowing them to participate in both American cultures and ideologies.

After the Civil War, minstrel shows featured nostalgically longing depictions of the "good old days" of slavery, when slaves were happy and content on the plantations. The new content of minstrel show also resulted in the introduction of new characters into the shows. Prominent characters included Zip Coon, Sambo, the Mammy, and the brute. Characters were depicted as whites' conceptions of good blacks (Sambo and Mammy), the "brute nigger" who delighted in carrying knives and starting fights, and the dandy, who attempted to imitate upper-class white styles of dress and speech. The inhumanity and cartoon-like nature of these characters distanced real blacks from being perceived as equal to whites. Finally, black children, often referred to as "pickaninnies," were ignorant youths often prone to thievery and other forms of deviance with little potential aptitude for the new public education system in America that few wanted to extend to blacks.

Particularly fearful to whites was the black brute intent on raping white women. These depictions of these rapacious black men fueled a century of lynchings that took countless lives of innocent black men and women oftentimes only on the whispered rumor of a rape, or even a sideways glance, deemed inappropriate, at white women. Deeply embossed in American culture, the nation's first feature-length film, *The Birth of a Nation* (based on Thomas Dixon's book, *The Clansman*), featured the black brute, a white man in blackface depicted as chasing after a white woman who would rather jump from a cliff to her death than lose her chastity and virginity to a black man.

Throughout their long history, minstrel acts reflected an admiration and longing for values and characteristics of blackness in line with racial ideologies of the time period. Childish, emotional, and musical and rhythmic characteristics of blacks conveyed to white audiences that blacks were intellectually inferior to whites and lacked the intelligence and other mental resources to succeed in any profession beyond servile positions. In this way, caricatures of blacks in minstrel shows also embodied the past for which whites longed, thus voicing a conscious wish for black social and economic inequality implicit in slavery.

Ideological Functions

Minstrelsy is a useful example of how race was learned and perpetuated through popular culture, entertainment, and media forms. Minstrel shows, like lynchings, focused on a black otherness that unified whites and led to the creation of a unique American identity. These images of blacks supported, dispelled, and reinforced ideologies of white superiority ranging, depending on the time period, from environmental causes for degradation, inherent inferiority, romantic racialism, paternalism, social Darwinism, and progressivism. These images then provided whites, many of whom in the North likely knew few blacks, with the knowledge necessary to shape their own identity to the contrary of this perceived black inferiority.

As black culture developed, whites appropriated parts and pieces of it to use for their own economic advantage and political purposes, thereby shaping their own culture in turn. When blackness was vague and uncertain, whites took what they saw and assumed that it was authentic, combined these visions with previous stereotypes, prejudices, and images about savages in Africa, and created a blackness they could use to their advantage. In this way, blackness became integral to both the American identity and culture, even though most whites rarely maintain any kind of sustained relationship with their black counterparts.

As the first true and realized white entertainment in the nation, and in the world, minstrel shows emphasized the white identity of its audience and actors, and their difference from those whom they were imitating. In line with the racial ideologies of the time, particularly Romantic racialism, minstrel shows usually portrayed blacks as emotional characters who, although they had qualities whites often lacked, had a number of others that made success in America impossible—they were shiftless and lazy, brutish and sex-crazed, dirty and incompetent. In other words, they were everything whites were not, and thus something against which whites could use to measure themselves. Minstrel shows thereby educated Northern whites and new immigrants who may have rarely encountered blacks in their daily lives, as to these characteristics, thereby disseminating a highly damaging and long-lasting racial ideology of white supremacy.

Unskilled immigrants from Europe, particularly Ireland, during the second half of the nineteenth century were flooding America's shores and competing with blacks for the lowest-paying jobs in the North. Mocking blacks through minstrel shows in the late nineteenth and early twentieth centuries ensured that blacks would be considered neither citizens nor workers on the same plane as whites. Instead, minstrelsy further identified the presumed differences between blacks and whites, even among those working in similar positions in the North. The license with which blackface provided whites allowed them to make statements about their own social circumstances that reflected the longing, fears, hopes, and prejudices enmeshed with being among the white working class in the nineteenth century. Minstrel shows inhibited cross-racial coalitions by ideologically suppressing black workers and obscuring any similarities between the two groups.

Lasting Legacies of Minstrel Shows

In addition to existing on the historical stage, minstrel figures continue to exist in many popular forms. For example, the vast majority of television programs and movies lack depictions of blacks in middle-class and professional roles and instead often appear as sidekicks, clowns, or criminals. Advertising, historically, drew on America's longing for the ideal and "simple" days of the plantation era. For generations, stereotyped caricatures of blacks have appeared on a wide variety of popular brands (e.g., the Gold Dust Twins and Nigger Brand oysters, tobacco, and toothpaste) and household products (ashtrays, piggybanks, kitchen accessories, etc.). A trip to a modern supermarket will find the legacies of these products and images in Aunt Jemima and Mrs. Butterworth's (classic examples of the Mammy figure) and Uncle Ben (an Uncle Tom figure) remain on store shelves.

Minstrel figures had also appeared in popular cartoons, particularly Bugs Bunny cartoons by Warner Brothers and a variety of cartoons by Walt Disney (including *Brer Rabbit and the Tar Baby*), through the 1980s. These cartoons often featured happy, smiling, banjo-playing, watermelon-eating, big-lipped, barefoot, blacks in the South in a plantation setting or in Africa, as comic savages, roasting the hero in a pot, alluding to cannibalism. Therefore, while these images appeared from stage shows prior to World War II, their lasting legacy continues to influence new generations of youth, including the current one.

Melissa F. Weiner

See also: Jim Crow.

Further Reading

Dates, Janette L., and William Barlow. *Split Image: African Americans in the Mass Media.* 2nd ed. Washington, DC: Howard University Press, 1993.

Fredrickson, George M. *The Black Image in the White Mind: The Debate on Afro-American Character and Destiny, 1817–1914.* New York: Harper & Row, 1971.

Hale, Grace Elizabeth. *Making Whiteness: The Culture of Segregation in the South, 1890–1940.* New York: Vintage, 1999.

Lott, Evan. *Love and Theft: Blackface Minstrelsy and the American Working Class.* New York: Oxford University Press, 1993.

Roediger, David R. *The Wages of Whiteness: Race and the Making of the American Working Class.* Rev. ed. New York: Verso Books, 1999.

Mississippi

Jim Crow practices were arguably more deeply entrenched in Mississippi than in any other state. The roots of this lie partly in the large number of slaves in the state before 1865. In 1860, there were over 436,000 slaves in Mississippi, who accounted for more than 55 percent of the population, second only to South Carolina. Following emancipation, many freedmen remained in Mississippi and gained the franchise under the 1868 Reconstruction state constitution, the first constitution of Mississippi not to limit voting to whites. Black Mississippians registered to vote in large numbers: in 1868, 96.7 percent of those eligible to register had done so, compared with 80.9 percent of eligible whites. Several blacks held high political office during this period: among others, Hiram Rhodes Revels and Blanche Kelso Bruce were both U.S. senators, while A. K. Davis served as lieutenant governor. Most black office holders held minor local positions.

Despite the large number of registered black voters, black Mississippians made little mark on the state's politics during Reconstruction. This was largely because of white efforts to prevent blacks from taking advantage of the franchise. In 1875, the First Mississippi Plan gerrymandered black majorities into irrelevance, a move that was supported by intimidation and violence to discourage blacks from voting. The results were obvious and immediate: in 1880, 66 percent of registered blacks did not vote in the presidential election. By 1890, when the Second Mississippi Plan redrew the state constitution, black disfranchisement was almost complete. This was achieved by a range of measures that, although they did not expressly mention race, were clearly designed to exclude blacks from the vote. This was particularly true of the understanding clause, which required an individual to read any section of the state constitution, or to be able to understand it, or give a reasonable interpretation of the section, when read to him. While this clause allowed illiterate whites to register, the function of the 1890 constitution was primarily to deny the franchise to black Mississippians. Although some blacks still managed to register, by 1896 only 8.2 percent of eligible blacks were registered.

The large-scale exclusion of blacks from the vote was matched by increasing restrictions on their freedom and rights in other aspects of Mississippi life. Before Reconstruction, Mississippi had introduced a series of repressive Black Codes, and many of these were carried on when home rule returned. In 1888, the first Jim Crow law was passed, segregating railroad coaches. In practice, however, Jim Crow had been in place in Mississippi for many years. Even before it came into law in 1888, most railroad coaches were already segregated, as were many other public facilities, including steamboats, hotels, and restaurants. Biracial education was virtually nonexistent; interracial marriage was forbidden, and in their leisure time, the races were separate. Increasingly, blacks and whites lived in different parts of towns by law, while in some towns curfews defined when blacks could be on the street.

Indeed, while Mississippi did pass other Jim Crow laws, fewer were required than in other states, because the custom of racial separation was so entrenched. There are examples of apparent integration throughout Mississippi in this period (e.g., a soda fountain in Indianola remained integrated until the 1930s), but the subordinate position of blacks was never in doubt and was rarely challenged. Even where blacks and whites shared personal space—such as in working situations—long-established Jim Crow customs made it clear that whites were always superior. The custom of white supremacy was as effective a tool as legal segregation.

Black employment opportunities were severely limited by Jim Crow. In urban areas, blacks worked in a variety of occupations, which tended to be limited to low-paid domestic and manual jobs. In such occupations, blacks could be paid less than whites and worked harder and longer; black labor was less likely to be organized and could more easily be fired. While there were black professionals, they were few in number and tended to exist solely for the black community. The respect afforded white doctors and lawyers was rarely directed toward black professionals: indeed, they were often regarded with suspicion as race agitators.

For many black Mississippians, however, agricultural work was all that could be expected. Few blacks could afford to buy land, and when they were able to do so, such land tended to be on poorer soil: in the Delta region, black landowners were scarce, although they were more numerous in the southwest part of the state. Most black agricultural workers were tenant farmers and sharecroppers. In the first half of the twentieth century particularly, this system bore more than a passing resemblance to slavery in a number of ways. Black tenants relied on white landowners for employment and shelter, were subject to the whims of their landlord, and were vulnerable to punishment for transgressing racial codes. Sharecroppers were routinely swindled by landlords who paid them less than their share; while blacks were often aware of this, they had little recourse. Tenants who sought to leave or to break employment contracts were often forcibly returned to the land, sometimes being punished to serve as peons. Through sharecropping, the Delta planter elite was guaranteed a cheap, pliable, and easily-replaceable workforce.

Sharecropping also did much to perpetuate Jim Crow as a means of social control. The planter class was powerful financially and politically, and many prominent Mississippi politicians relied on the support of working-class whites. Blaming blacks for Mississippi's ills and ensuring that the potential power of a united black and white labor force never came to pass helped Delta planters to protect their position. Race-baiting became a regular tactic on the stump, and politicians like Theodore G. Bilbo and James K. Vardaman were renowned for engendering race hatred among their supporters.

Clear lines of racial etiquette existed in Mississippi, and these were well known to blacks, who were careful to adhere to expected standards of behavior. The punishment for transgressing racial codes was also well known: between the 1870s and 1930s, lynchings were more common in Mississippi than in any other state. The brutality of lynching was matched often by its seeming randomness. While white mobs regularly lynched alleged black criminals before they could be tried legally, countless individuals were lynched based on rumor, suspicion, or mistaken identity. Moreover, as many as lynchings were used to punish blacks who had crossed racial lines, they also served to send a message to the black community; thus, few lynch mobs were concerned if their victim was innocent. It was not uncommon for a crime to be punished by the indeterminate lynching of several black people. Lynching was often a method through which whites reasserted their dominance over blacks and lynching tended to be more frequent during times of economic difficulty.

The second-class nature of black life in Mississippi extended to education. Throughout the Jim Crow period, schools were segregated. State spending on black schools was a fraction of that on white schools. Based on assumptions that black education was an unnecessary and expensive luxury, the proposition that only black taxes should be spent on black schools was popular in the early years of the twentieth century, although never enacted. Black education was also considered a threat to the state's social structure, and many whites feared that educated blacks would challenge Jim Crow; in particular, planters were concerned that black education would reduce the agricultural labor force.

While some black Mississippians believed that education was pointless in a state that denied black people access to jobs where it might be required, many blacks were convinced that education was a cornerstone of black uplift, and money for black schools and teachers' salaries often came from black community efforts and privately owned buildings like churches and stores often served as schools. Few schools, whether private or public, had the resources to provide a high school education, and eighth grade was as far as many black children were able to attend, although many did not reach that mark. Private institutions, whether elementary, high school, or further-education colleges, were often supported by Northern bene-factors, but many still struggled to survive.

While black teachers were noted for their diligence and enthusiasm, they were faced with seemingly unending challenges. Attaining the appropriate training was difficult for potential black teachers. For much of the first half of the twentieth cen-tury the only teacher training available at a public college of higher education was at Alcorn Agricultural and Mechanical College; otherwise, private institutions like Tougaloo College, or unaccredited summer schools, were the only means of obtain-ing training. Black teachers' salaries were routinely significantly smaller than those of white teachers, and resources were scarce. Such difficulties were compounded by the tendency of many black children to attend school for only part of the year, particularly in rural areas where they assisted in the fields, or to attend only until they were old enough to become full field hands.

Black higher education was rare, but private institutions like Tougaloo and Alcorn represented efforts to provide the education that white Mississippi sought to deny. These institutions counted many prominent black Mississippians among their alumni. Eventually, in the 1940s, Mississippi created two state black teacher training institutions, Jackson State College for Negro Teachers and Mississippi State Vocational College. For many blacks, however, particularly in rural areas, Jim Crow ensured that higher education was not a viable option by denying a quality elementary education and regarding blacks as little more than cheap labor.

World War II marked a watershed in race relations in Mississippi. Blacks were offered opportunities that allowed them to escape the restrictions of Jim Crow. Many black men left Mississippi, many for the first time, to serve in the military; financially, this meant that their families no longer needed to work on the land. Others were able to leave agriculture through better-paid factory employment sup-porting the war effort. By breaking their economic dependence on whites, blacks were less curtailed by Mississippi's social structure. In the Delta, planters attempted to counter this by offering higher wages, but few blacks were tempted, and World War II was a time of relative freedoms for many black Mississippians.

These freedoms gave rise to a new determination to challenge racial subju-gation. This was complemented by the return of black veterans, many of whom were all too aware of the irony of fighting for freedoms in Europe that they themselves did not have in Mississippi. During the late 1940s and early 1950s, a statewide network of black activists, organizers, and leaders grew up, often through membership in the National Association for the Advancement of Colored People (NAACP), but also through homegrown organizations such as the Regional Council of Negro Leadership, founded by T. R. M. Howard. Many of these leaders were business owners, giving them the independence and financial security to participate in such activity. These efforts helped to raise the number of registered black voters. Atrocities like the murder of 14-year-old Emmett Till were accompanied by open condemnation from the black community. The number of black people who came forward as witnesses in such cases was unprecedented, and represented the first large-scale challenge to the orthodoxy of Jim Crow since Reconstruction.

Mississippi whites reacted to this in a number of ways. Massive white resistance was a reaction not only to increased black defiance but also to the U.S. Supreme Court's ruling in *Brown v. Board of Education* (1954). The two main instruments by which whites reasserted their dominance were the Mississippi State Sovereignty Commission and the White Citizens Councils. While the Sovereignty Commission operated mainly as a means to monitor activity that was considered to endanger the sovereignty of Mississippi, these councils were primarily responsible for disrupting the network of black activism that had developed. Eschewing the brutality of lynching, the White Citizens Councils used other means to assert its power. Black leaders were particularly targeted, often economically: loans were recalled and credit lines stopped, while business owners found that their customers were taking their business elsewhere. Intimidation and (less often, although not rarely) violence saw NAACP membership dwindle and the number of registered black voters fall sharply. During this period, many prominent black leaders, including Howard, left the state.

By the early 1960s, Mississippi was known as the most brutal enforcer of Jim Crow values in the South. Black life was governed almost entirely by Jim Crow, and whites felt secure in their domination of the state. Signs of black defiance were quickly suppressed, usually without any fear of punishment. In every sphere of public life blacks were cowed by white supremacy. The extent of Mississippi's defiance is illustrated by James Meredith's attempt to integrate the University of Mississippi. Meredith had initially tried to enroll in 1961, only to be physically prevented from doing so by Governor Ross Barnett. When Meredith arrived to enroll in September 1962, after a federal court had ordered his admission, Barnett once again prevented him from entering. Meredith's admission was achieved only with the assistance of federal marshals and the Mississippi National Guard, which had been federalized by President John F. Kennedy to quell a riot in which two people were killed. During his time at the University of Mississippi, a constant troop presence was maintained on campus.

However, the very depth of black subjugation in Mississippi made it a focus for the burgeoning Civil Rights Movement; while Jim Crow was challenged throughout the South, Mississippi received particular attention. Much of this was led by young activists, especially those belonging to the Student Nonviolent Coordinating Committee (SNCC) and the Congress of Racial Equality (CORE), the two organizations that would be most active in Mississippi.

Many activists gained their first experience of Mississippi during the Freedom Rides of May 1961. The Kennedy administration struck an agreement that would allow Governor Barnett to jail the freedom riders, but required that he guarantee their safety. The activists confounded Kennedy by refusing bail and remaining in jail until July. Such intransigence and single-mindedness would mark the attitude of civil rights activists in Mississippi. Another key development in the Mississippi movement was the establishment by SNCC of a voter registration project in McComb. The project was run by Bob Moses of SNCC, who had been directed to McComb by Amzie Moore. The McComb project, particularly the tactics used by Moses, along with the experience of the Freedom Rides, would crucially inform the Mississippi movement.

SNCC soon became the leading civil rights organization in Mississippi. Working at the grassroots level, SNCC activists assisted communities to organize to challenge for equal access to the vote. SNCC's strategy was to encourage the development of local leadership and an activist infrastructure that could sustain a prolonged, community-led challenge to Jim Crow. The role of SNCC was to facilitate, rather than lead, such activity. This approach reached its apogee with the Mississippi Summer Project (often known as Freedom Summer).

During the summer of 1964, thousands of civil rights activists, many of them white Northern college students, entered Mississippi to participate in Freedom Summer, the main focus of which was to increase the number of registered black voters. This was done under the banner of the Council of Federated Organizations (COFO), which included several national civil rights organizations, as well as Mississippi groups. The Mississippi Freedom Democratic Party was formed to challenge the seating of the regular Mississippi delegation at the Democratic National Conference (a challenge that ultimately failed). Freedom Summer addressed many of the problems that had been caused by successive generations of blacks being subjugated by Jim Crow: In addition voter registration, citizenship education classes, community centers, and a range of other projects were created to help black Mississippians access and make full use of the vote.

Freedom Summer provoked strong support from black communities, but also a fierce backlash from whites. Civil rights workers were particularly vulnerable during their time in Mississippi, as were local blacks who participated. Evictions, intimidation, beatings, and bombings were all widespread, and membership of the

Ku Klux Klan increased. Perhaps the most notorious incident of Freedom Summer was the murder of three civil rights workers, Andrew Goodman, Michael Schwerner, and James Chaney; they disappeared in June, but their bodies were not found until August. The national interest in this case brought an unprecedented federal presence into Mississippi and signaled that Mississippi would no longer be able to exercise Jim Crow justice with impunity.

The precise effect of Freedom Summer is hard to gauge: in some communities, it had long-lasting effects and helped the emergence of local leaders (e.g., Fannie Lou Hamer in Sunflower County); elsewhere, it had almost no impact. The poverty that had blighted black Mississippi for so long continued, and for much of the remainder of the 1960s, poverty relief and access to welfare were key campaigns for black communities. Gradually, however, the effects of civil rights legislation, as well as the cumulative impact of the civil rights movement, both in Mississippi itself and more widely, began to erode Jim Crow in its last stronghold. In 1969, *Alexander v. Holmes County* effectively desegregated public schools, and social customs that had separated blacks and whites weakened. Many public facilities that had traditionally been separated became gradually integrated, although often without any single sweeping blow. Nonetheless, in *Ayers v. Fordice* (1992), the Supreme Court held that Mississippi had not yet eradicated fully Jim Crow from higher education.

Crucially, by the end of 1968, 60 percent of eligible blacks were registered to vote, perhaps the most important achievement of the Civil Rights Movement in Mississippi. In the face of such large numbers of registered blacks, and in line with political shifts elsewhere, notably the election of racial moderates in several states, Jim Crow could no longer dominate Mississippi life. As blacks gained the vote, they were able to use it to leverage concessions from white politicians. Even more significantly, increasing numbers of blacks began to run for office. Across Mississippi, black office holders were elected to a variety of posts, including to the Mississippi state legislature, and, in 1986, for the first time since Reconstruction, a black Mississippian, Mike Espy, was elected to Congress.

Simon T. Cuthbert-Kerr

See also: Alabama; Ku Klux Klan.

Further Reading

Dittmer, John. *Local People: The Struggle for Civil Rights in Mississippi.* Urbana: University of Illinois Press, 1995.

Kirwan, Albert D. *Revolt of the Rednecks: Mississippi Politics, 1876–1925.* New York: Harper Torchbooks, 1965.

McMillen, Neil R. *Dark Journey: Black Mississippians in the Age of Jim Crow.* Urbana: University of Illinois Press, 1990.

Moody, Ann. *Coming of Age in Mississippi.* New York: Dell Press, 1968.

Parker, Frank R. *Black Votes Count: Political Empowerment in Mississippi after 1965.* Chapel Hill: University of North Carolina Press, 1990.

Payne, Charles. *I've Got the Light of Freedom: The Organizing Tradition and the Mississippi Freedom Struggle.* Berkeley: University of California Press, 1995.

Montgomery Bus Boycott

Starting in December 1955, the African American community of Montgomery, Alabama, boycotted the city bus system for over a year. Demanding equal and fair treatment, blacks refused to ride until their requests were met. Organized by the Women's Political Council (WPC) and Montgomery's National Association for the Advancement of Colored People (NAACP) branch, this boycott is often referred to as the beginning of the modern Civil Rights Movement.

In the 1950s in Montgomery, the city bus system was segregated. African Americans were not hired as drivers, rode in the back of the bus, and were expected to surrender their seat at a white passenger's request. Black passengers entered the front of the bus to pay the fee, exited the bus, and reentered at the back entrance. At times, bus drivers would leave black passengers standing at the sidewalk after paying the bus fee. Although 75 percent of passengers were African American, they were constant victims of public degradation and humiliation.

For several years, the WPC, led by Jo Ann Robinson, and Montgomery's NAACP branch, formerly led by E. D. Nixon, had discussed the inequalities of the city bus system and possible resolutions. In 1954, Robinson sent a letter to Montgomery mayor W. A. Gayle requesting the buses' Jim Crow practices be put to an end and warned of a potential boycott if the demands were not met. Gayle paid no attention to Robinson's warning.

Even though the WPC had been organizing a possible boycott, the challenge of rallying the entire black community remained. A successful boycott required full participation. Due to fear of losing jobs, harassment, and racial violence, few African Americans publicly acknowledged their discontent of second-class citizenship. These organizations waited for the right person who would stand up against the ways of the south. That day came on Thursday, December 1, 1955, when Rosa Parks stepped on one of the city buses. It had been a long day of work, the bus was almost completely full, and Parks sat in the first row of the black section. At the next stop several white passengers entered the bus. A white male wanted Parks's seat. Parks refused. The bus driver ordered her to move or he would call the authorities.

While National Guardsmen remain on the alert in the background, Freedom Riders board a bus in Montgomery, Alabama, to continue their trip to Mississippi, 1961. The Riders were challenging segregation laws regarding interstate travel. (Library of Congress)

Parks did not move. Parks was arrested, and the inspirational story Nixon and Robinson had waited for arrived. The soft-spoken, respectable Parks served as the perfect symbol to mobilize African Americans for the bus boycott.

Days following the arrest, over 200 volunteers passed out 30,000 flyers calling for a one-day boycott of the Montgomery bus system on Monday, December 5, 1955. The one-day boycott was successful and that evening the black community gathered in Holt Street Baptist Church to decide if the boycott should continue. Thousands attended the meeting. The church overflowed to the outside stairs and sidewalks.

The Montgomery Improvement Association (MIA) was developed to coordinate, support, and organize the demonstration. Martin Luther King Jr., the new preacher in town, was elected MIA's president and chosen to give a speech at the first mass meeting at Holt Street Baptist Church. With less than an hour to prepare, King delivered a speech that inspired the crowd to vote unanimously to continue the boycott. This speech also marked the beginning of King's role as a leader in the Civil Rights Movement.

Through the efforts and sacrifices of the black community, the Montgomery bus boycott lasted 381 days. Boycotters walked to work, established a large car pool system, and ran extensive fund-raisers to finance the car pool system. Even on the coldest of days, some walked as far as 12 miles a day. Only a month after the boycott began, James H. Bagley, the superintendent of the Montgomery City Bus Lines, expressed frustration with the lack of patronage. The bus system was losing close to $400 daily, as expenses greatly outweighed income. Forced to reduce expenses, Bagley cut schedules, fired drivers, and increased the cost of bus fares. However, the movement needed federal legislation to change Jim Crow practices.

On February 1, 1956, NAACP lawyers Fred Gray and Charles Langford filed a lawsuit in the U.S. Circuit Court against Alabama and Montgomery's unconstitutional segregation laws. Gray and Langford filed this suit on behalf of five African American women: Aurelia S. Browder, Susie McDonald, Jeanetta Reese, Claudette Colvin, and Mary Louise Smith. Throughout the year, boycott leaders and participants faced much racial violence. Both King's and Nixon's houses were bombed, crosses were burnt on front lawns, and several blacks were arrested for participating in "illegal" boycotts. Through Alabama's state courts, white Montgomery officials successfully made carpooling illegal. Interestingly enough, this state legislation passed the same day the federal court found Alabama's segregation laws unconstitutional.

On December 21, 1956, African Americans boarded the Montgomery city buses and sat where they pleased. This achievement sparked the modern Civil Rights Movement and heightened racial tensions across the South as more and more blacks demanded freedom.

Emily Hess

See also: Alabama; King, Martin Luther, Jr.

Further Reading

Burns, Stewart, ed. *Daybreak of Freedom: Montgomery Bus Boycott.* Chapel Hill: University of North Carolina Press, 1997.

Robinson, Jo Ann, with David Garrow. *The Montgomery Bus Boycott and the Women Who Started It: The Memoir of Jo Ann Gibson Robinson.* Knoxville: University of Tennessee Press, 1987.

Williams, Donnie, and Wayne Greenhow. *The Thunder of Angels: The Montgomery Bus Boycott and the People Who Broke the Back of Jim Crow.* Chicago: Lawrence Hill Books, 2006.

N

Nadir of the Negro

The Nadir of the Negro is the era from 1890 to the 1930s. In these years, African Americans lost many of the rights they had won during Reconstruction. In the South, whites forced blacks back into noncitizenship, no longer allowed to vote or serve on juries, and cut funding for black schools by as much as two-thirds. In the North, organizations ranging from restaurants to organized baseball to the dormitories of Harvard University that had previously admitted African Americans now rejected them.

Historian Rayford Logan, who earned his doctorate from Harvard in 1936 and chaired Howard University's history department in the 1940s and 1950s, established the term in his 1954 book, The *Negro in American Life and Thought: The Nadir.* The same year, C. Vann Woodward gave a series of lectures, reprinted later as *The Strange Career of Jim Crow,* telling how African Americans lost citizenship and social rights in the South not right after Reconstruction, but after 1890. Since then, the idea that race relations grew worse around 1890 has become well accepted in American history.

Three events in 1890 signaled the new era. Mississippi passed a new constitution, stripping voting rights from African Americans, and although the new law clearly violated the Fourteenth and Fifteenth Amendments, the federal government did nothing. The U.S. Senate failed to pass the Federal Elections Bill, which would have helped African Americans (and white Republicans) to vote freely across the South. Worse, after the defeat, when tagged as usual by Democrats as "niggerlovers," Republicans this time denied the charge and largely abandoned the cause of civil rights. Since the Democrats already labeled themselves "the white man's party," African Americans now found themselves with no political allies. Finally, the Massacre at Wounded Knee, South Dakota, ended the last vestige of Native sovereignty, sending American Indians into their nadir period as well.

What caused the Nadir? The antislavery idealism spawned by the Civil War faded as memories of the war dimmed. By 1890, only one American in three was old enough to have been alive when it ended. Fewer still were old enough to have any memory of the war. Among older Americans, millions had immigrated to the United States long after the war's end and had played no role in it.

Three developments having nothing directly to do with black rights further eroded the position of African Americans. The first was the Indian wars. Although the federal government had guaranteed their land to the Plains Indians "forever," after whites discovered gold in Colorado, Dakota Territory, and elsewhere, they took it anyway. If it was all right to take Indians' land because they were not white, was not it all right to deny rights to African Americans, who were not white either?

Second, immigrants from Europe persisted in voting Democratic, partly because they saw that it was in their interest to differentiate themselves from blacks, still at the bottom of the social hierarchy. Also, Republicans were moving toward Prohibition, hardly a preferred position among Italian, Greek, and Russian newcomers among others. Frustrated politically by the new arrivals from southern and eastern Europe, Senator Henry Cabot Lodge helped found the Immigration Restriction League to keep out "inferior" racial strains. This further sapped Republican commitment to the idea "that all men are created equal."

Third, the ideology of imperialism washed over the United States from Europe. Imperialism both depended upon and in turn reinforced the ideology of white supremacy. The growing clamor to annex Hawai'i included the claim that Americans could govern those brown people better than they could govern themselves. After winning the Spanish-American War, the administration of President William McKinley used the same rationale to defend making war upon our allies, the Filipinos. William Howard Taft, who was made U.S. commissioner over the Philippines in 1900, called the Filipinos "our little brown brothers" and said they would need "fifty or one hundred years" of close supervision "to develop anything resembling Anglo-Saxon political principles and skills." Democrats drew the obvious parallel, "What about our little black brothers in the South?" and Republicans could make no cogent reply.

Seeing that the United States did nothing to stop Mississippi's usurpation of black rights, whites in other Southern states and states as distant as Oklahoma followed suit by 1907. In 1894, Democrats in Congress repealed the remaining federal election statutes, leaving the Fifteenth Amendment lifeless, with no extant laws to enforce it. In 1896, in *Plessy v. Ferguson,* the U.S. Supreme Court declared de jure racial segregation legal. Schools were segregated statewide in Delaware, Maryland, West Virginia, Kentucky, Missouri, Arkansas, Oklahoma, Texas, and Arizona, as well as much of Ohio, Indiana, Illinois, Kansas, New Mexico, and California. The South already had segregated schools, of course.

The new Mississippi constitution required prospective voters to "be able to read any section of the constitution of this State . . . or he shall be able to understand the same when read to him, or give a reasonable interpretation thereof." Other states incorporated similar measures in their new laws. In practice, black would-be voters were required to be able to read a section and interpret it. Local folklore has it that a professor at Tuskegee Institute with a doctorate in political science could not interpret the constitution to the satisfaction of the Macon County, Alabama, registrar, who was a high school dropout. Certainly even jurisdictions like Macon County—84 percent black, and home to two important black institutions, Tuskegee Institute and a large VA hospital—had white voting majorities until the Civil Rights Movement.

Not only did these clauses remove African Americans from voting, and hence from juries, they also linked literacy and education as the mechanism. In their wake, every Southern state cut back on black schooling. Their new constitutions commanded racially segregated schools de jure, so it was easy to set up shorter sessions for black schools, require lower qualifications of black teachers, and pay them a fraction of white salaries.

In 1898, Democrats rioted in Wilmington, North Carolina, driving out all Republican officeholders and killing at least 12 African Americans. Astonishingly, the McKinley administration allowed this coup d'etat to stand. Congress became resegregated in 1901 when Congressman George H. White of North Carolina could not win reelection owing to the disfranchisement of black voters. No African American served in Congress again until 1929, and none from the South until 1973. The so-called Progressive Movement was for whites only. In many Northern cities, its "reforms" removed the last local black leaders from city councils in favor of commissioners elected citywide.

Coinciding with the Nadir and helping to justify it was the ideology of social Darwinism—the notion that the fittest rise to the top in society. It provided a potent rationale not only for white supremacy but also for America's increasing class hierarchy. Its "scientific" handmaidens, eugenics and psychometrics, flourished. Madison Grant, author of the 1916 eugenics tract *The Passing of the Great Race,* helped write the 1924 law that drastically cut immigration to the United States from Asia and southern and eastern Europe. Carl Brigham, concerned that "American intelligence is declining . . . as the racial admixture becomes more and more extensive," developed the Scholastic Aptitude Test in 1926 to select the brightest students for elite colleges. Popular culture also justified the Nadir. In this era, minstrel shows came to dominate our popular culture. They had begun before the Civil War but flourished after 1890 minstrel shows both caused and reflected the increased racism of the period. As author, politician, and activist James Weldon Johnson put it, minstrel shows "fixed the tradition of the Negro as only an irresponsible, happy-go-lucky, wide-grinning, loud-laughing, shuffling, banjo-playing, singing, dancing sort of being." In small towns across the North, where few blacks existed to correct this impression, these stereotypes provided the bulk of white "knowledge" about what African Americans were like. The first epic motion picture, *The Birth of a Nation,* glorified the Ku Klux Klan as the savior of white Southern civilization from the menace of black upstarts during Reconstruction. In 1936, near the end of the Nadir, the Margaret Mitchell novel *Gone with the Wind* sold a million hardbound books in its first month. The book and the resulting film, the highest-grossing movie of all time, further convinced whites that noncitizenship was appropriate for African Americans.

During the Nadir, lynchings rose to their height, and not just in the South, although the main "national" database has never included Northern lynchings. Segregation swept through public accommodations, North as well as South. In 1908, touring the North for an article, "The Color Line in the North," Ray Stannard Baker noted the deterioration even in Boston, the old citadel of abolitionism: "A few years ago no hotel or restaurant in Boston refused Negro guests. [N]ow several hotels, restaurants, and especially confectionery stores, will not serve Negroes, even the best of them." Writing of the day-to-day interactions of whites and blacks in the Midwest, Frank Quillen observed in 1913 that race prejudice "is increasing steadily, especially during the last twenty years." In the 1920s, Harvard barred an African American student from the very dormitory where his father had lived decades earlier when attending the university. Whites ousted African Americans from occupations ranging from major league baseball player and Kentucky Derby jockey to postal carrier, mason, firefighter, and carpenter. Even jobs like department store salesclerk and factory worker were closed to African Americans, and not just in Dixie.

Across the North and throughout the Appalachian South and the Ozarks, whites forced African Americans to make a Great Retreat from hundreds of communities. These then became all-white sundown towns for decades. Communities that had voted Democratic in the 1860s were especially likely to bar African Americans decades later, during the Nadir. Even some previously interracial Republican towns, like Hermann, Missouri, where African Americans had celebrated Emancipation Day in the 1870s, went sundown after 1890.

African Americans thrashed about, trying to cope with their increasingly desperate situation. Early in the Nadir, some left the Deep South for new homes in Kansas and Oklahoma (the Exodus), but Oklahoma entered the Union in 1907 with a constitution modeled after Mississippi's, while Kansas lost its abolitionist edge and developed many sundown towns. Booker T. Washington suggested blacks relinquish claims to social equality, concentrating on hard work and education, but this proved difficult because hostile Southern whites often targeted successful black farmers and businessmen.

W.E.B. Du Bois disputed with Washington, but his refusal to condone loss of black rights proved no more workable. Forming black towns like Boley, Oklahoma, and Mound Bayou, Mississippi, gave no relief, because these communities were ultimately under the white thumbs of county and state governments. The Back to Africa movements organized by Chief Sam and Marcus Garvey also provided no solution.

In this context, the Great Migration provided African Americans with environments in which they could vote freely, and hence could bargain for at least some municipal services and other basic rights. However, cities North and South became much more residentially segregated during the Nadir, and many suburbs formed on an all-white basis. Still, African Americans were able to establish small majority-black settlements on Long Island, New York, west of Detroit, south of Chicago, and on the outskirts of other Northern cities.

During the Woodrow Wilson administration, the Nadir intensified. Wilson segregated the navy, which had not been segregated before. He also replaced blacks who held appointed offices with whites. Responding to his leadership, whites rioted against black communities in Chicago, East St. Louis, Omaha, Washington, and other cities in what James Weldon Johnson called the Red Summer of 1919. The release of *The Birth of a Nation* led to a rebirth of the Ku Klux Klan, this time as a national organization that displayed astonishing if short-lived clout in Georgia, Indiana, Oklahoma, Oregon, and other states during the 1920s. The Klan prompted the expulsion of African Americans from additional Northern towns and counties. The Great Depression of the next decade spurred whites to drive African Americans from additional jobs like elevator operator and railroad fireman.

Anti-Semitism increased as well in the Nadir. Early in the Civil War, people of various religions—including Jews—had founded the Union League Club to combat the pro-secession sentiment that dominated New York City. When white segregationists removed the widow of an African American soldier from a streetcar, the Union League Club came to her defense. Joseph Seligman, a Jew, leading banker, and friend of Ulysses S. Grant, had been a founder of the club. His son Jesse became a member in 1868. Then, during the 1890s, members refused to admit Jews, as well as Italians, Catholics, and others of "incorrect background." In 1893, after 25 years of membership, 14 of them as a vice president, Jesse Seligman had to resign. Members blackballed his own son Theodore because he was a Jew. During World War I, the U.S. Army for the first time considered Jews "a special problem whose loyalty to the U.S. was open to question." Along with other government agencies (and the KKK), the Military Intelligence Department mounted a campaign against Jewish immigrants that helped convince Congress to pass a restrictive immigration bill in 1924.

The Nadir manifested itself in many ways, including treatment of African Americans in Iowa newspapers. During the 1870s, they covered the activities and individual happenings within the African American population. By the 1890s, however, most stories about blacks appeared on the crime page. Even the appointment of an Iowan as ambassador to Liberia, one of the highest posts available to African Americans during the Nadir, drew no notice in the Iowa press.

African American intellectuals despaired of the Nadir. In 1900, African American poet Paul Laurence Dunbar wrote "Robert Gould Shaw," a bitter ode to the white colonel who led the black 54th Massachusetts Volunteer Regiment in its charge at Fort Wagner during the Civil War. The poem ended by suggesting that Shaw's "cold endurance of the final pain" had been pointless. Only with the rise of the CIO unions and some important symbolic gestures by First Lady Eleanor Roosevelt did the Nadir begin to crack. The Great Migration itself helped end it. Coupled with the Great Retreat, it concentrated African Americans into a few large cities. This enabled blacks to win seats in Northern state legislatures and the U.S. House of Representatives, which in turn prompted white political leaders to moderate their racist rhetoric so as not to alienate urban black voters and political leaders. A second crack in the wall of white supremacy came from the crumbling of imperialism. In a Cold War context, America could not afford to offend the nonwhite leaders of newly independent nations in Asia and Africa. Most important of all was the role played by World War II. Germany gave white supremacy a bad name. It is always in victors' interests to demonize the vanquished, but Nazism made this task easy. Americans saw in the German death camps the logical result of eugenics and segregation, and it appalled them. As they sought to differentiate themselves from Hitler's discredited racial policies, the overt racism of the Nadir now made them uneasy. Swedish social scientist Gunnar Myrdal called this conflict our "American dilemma" and predicted in 1944, "Equality is slowly winning."

Although the Nadir reached its lowest point before 1940, it has left the United States with two progeny: sundown towns and warped history. Near the end of the period, in 1935, W.E.B. Du Bois lamented the distorted account of Reconstruction to which it gave rise: "We have got to the place where we cannot use our experiences during and after the Civil War for the uplift and enlightenment of mankind."

James W. Loewen

See also: Atlanta Compromise, The; Jim Crow; Lynching.

Further Reading

Baker, Ray Stannard. "The Color Line in the North." *American Magazine* 65 (1908). Reprinted in Otto Olsen, ed., *The Negro Question: From Slavery to Caste, 1863–1910.* New York: Pitman, 1971.

Bassett, John Spencer. *A Short History of the United States.* New York: Macmillan, 1923.

Bergmann, Leola. "The Negro in Iowa." *Iowa Journal of History and Politics* (1969 [1948]): 44–45.

DeVries, James. *Race and Kinship in a Midwestern Town.* Urbana: University of Illinois Press, 1984.

Du Bois, W.E.B. *Black Reconstruction.* Cleveland, OH: World Meridian, 1964 (1935), 722.

Frederickson, George. *The Black Image in the White Mind: The Debate on Afro-American Character and Destiny, 1817–1914.* New York: Harper and Row, 1971.

Johnson, James Weldon. *Black Manhattan.* New York: Knopf, 1930.

Loewen, James W. *Lies across America.* New York: New Press, 1999.

Loewen, James W. *Sundown Towns.* New York: New Press, 2005.

Loewen, James W. "Teaching Race Relations through Feature Films." *Teaching Sociology* 19 (January 1991): 82.

Logan, Rayford. *The Negro in American Life and Thought: The Nadir.* New York: Dial, 1954.

Myrdal, Gunnar. *An American Dilemma.* New York: Harper & Row, 1944.

Quillen, Frank. *The Color Line in Ohio.* Ann Arbor, MI: Wahr, 1913.

Upchurch, Thomas Adams. *Legislating Racism: The Billion Dollar Congress and the Birth of Jim Crow.* Lexington: University Press of Kentucky, 2004.

National Association of Colored Women

In 1896, the National Association of Colored Women (NACW), one of the first all-black political organizations, was created at one of the lowest points—the "nadir"—of African American history in response to the birth of Jim Crow. It was incorporated as the national affiliate for hundreds of clubs dedicated to the social reform activities of its members. The "race women" who participated in this national club movement were committed to "uplifting the race" or improving socioeconomic conditions for African Americans. By the late nineteenth century, critiques of the nation's "Negro Problem" weighed heavily on the status of African American women, especially as the burden bearers of the race. They were often considered both the source and the solution to the many problems African Americans encountered after slavery. Black disfranchisement, lynch law/mob rule, "peonage slavery," and discriminatory laws and social customs nullified the civil rights and privileges African Americans had gained during Reconstruction. Consequently, the 1890s was a decade plagued by racial prejudice and violence that severely affected African Americans. The 1896 landmark *Plessy v. Ferguson* U.S. Supreme Court case, in particular, stipulated the "separate but equal" laws of segregation that would lay firmly the foundation for white supremacy until the Civil Rights Movement of the 1950s and 1960s. In light of the decree for de jure segregation, African

American women galvanized efforts and collected resources more than ever to overcome obstacles to black survival and racial progress.

Although they stood in the shadow of icons like Frederick Douglass, Booker T. Washington, and W.E.B. Du Bois, black club women nevertheless were actively involved in the gender and racial politics of the period. They worked with white women and black men in the suffrage movement and for racial equality. As a double minority, however, black women of the NACW also concentrated on gender and racial matters apart from those of the national club movement among white women. Black women like Fannie Barrier Williams had encountered racism while participating in predominately white feminist organizations. Sexism was most apparent among black men who evaluated the roles and responsibilities of black women within the limits of patriarchy. The NACW then made it possible and necessary for black women to voice collectively their concerns and secure their autonomy. Within the pages of the *Woman's Era* (and later the *National Association Notes*), the leading publications by and about black women, the NACW campaigned for gender and racial equality.

Another major impetus for NACW activism involved frequent public attacks on African American women in character and body. An infamous letter written in 1895 by a white journalist, for example, ridiculed all black women as prostitutes and thieves. The reputation and image of black women was tarnished by various reports of immorality linked to disease and poverty among the black masses. As during slavery, black women were also vulnerable to sexual violence and harassment with little or no legal protection by the end of the nineteenth century. These are a few justifications for the NACW's call to action to protect black womanhood in particular but to salvage racial pride in general. To address these issues, the first National Conference of Colored Women was held in Boston in July 1895. Led by Josephine St. Pierre Ruffin and other black feminists, the conference had a special agenda to address the needs of black women as wives, mothers, and daughters committed to the race being moral exemplars and civic activists. Their plans mandated a domestic model of racial uplift, making black women responsible for the health care, spiritual welfare, and moral elevation of their families and communities.

A renewed commitment to service and more defined leadership led to the official creation of the NACW following the national conference. Clubs formerly within the National League of Colored Women of Washington, D.C., and the National Federation of Afro-American Women were united as a solid governing body and Mary Church Terrell was elected as the first NACW president in 1896. Other members included Margaret Murray Washington (Booker T. Washington's third wife), Anna Julia Cooper, Frances Harper, Victoria Earle Matthews, and Ida B. Wells-Barnett. Most of the club women were members of the black middle class. They were well-educated professionals distinguished as "New Negroes" who would become race leaders. Their uplift ideology advocated self-reliance *and* defined self-worth in light of Jim Crowism. Like all African Americans, the black elite also experienced discrimination and racial prejudice. When traveling on lecture tours, for instance, Terrell and Wells-Barnett could not always find suitable public accommodations when many hotels, restaurants, and trains catered primarily to white patrons. Inferior rest rooms, seating, and lodging were reserved for blacks only. When faced with such obstacles, club leaders would find black hosts to stay with in the tour cities, hold meetings in black facilities, and, sometimes, travel in Jim Crow cars despite the inconvenience. It has been asserted that some club leaders with fair complexions would, however, pass for white to traverse racial barriers. More formal resolutions were issued by the NACW against segregation, lynchings, and disfranchisement.

Inspired by their motto, "Lifting as We Climb," African American women in the NACW created a legacy of activism and service. They were on a mission to help the massive populations of the black underclass. The NACW members organized to provide adequate day care for children of working black mothers (or in some areas kindergartens), domestic workshops for better household management, shelters for black elderly and/or orphans, and even formed neighborhood patrols to rid the areas most vulnerable to criminal and/or immoral activities. Education was foremost among the objectives of NACW, too. Reading rooms and literary forums were often supported by the NACW and its affiliate clubs. The diverse service work these club women accomplished inspired generations of African Americans as the NACW remained visible within the ranks of black leadership into the twentieth century.

Sherita L. Johnson

See also: Nadir of the Negro.

Further Reading

Giddings, Paula. *When and Where I Enter: The Impact of Black Women on Race and Sex in America*. New York: William Morrow, 1984.

Shaw, Stephanie J. "Black Club Women and the Creation of the National Association of Colored Women." *Journal of Women's History* 3, no. 2 (Fall 1991): 1–25.

White, Deborah Gray. *"Too Heavy a Load": Black Women in Defense of Themselves, 1894–1994*. New York: W. W. Norton, 1999.

Negro League Baseball

Segregation in baseball began in 1858 when the National Association of Baseball Players (NABBP) included in its constitution a clause excluding "persons of color" from playing. After a period of segregation from 1867 to 1871, the rules changed. In 1871, there were no formal rules against blacks in baseball in the newly organized National Association of Professional Baseball Players (NAPBBP). African Americans, including Bud Fowler, Charlie Grant, George Stovey, and Moses Fleetwood Walker, played on professional integrated teams for a short time. In the 1880s, a "gentleman's agreement" shifted acceptance again, creating a color line in baseball. Owners forced the black players off teams and did not sign new ones.

After the reemergence of segregation in the last two decades of the nineteenth century, African American responded by creating their own teams and leagues. With no professional leagues from the late 1880s to 1920, blacks played on semipro teams. Attempts at organizing leagues proved unsuccessful. In 1886, the League of Colored Baseball included teams in Baltimore, Boston, Cincinnati, Louisville, New York, Philadelphia, Pittsburgh, and Washington, D.C. The league lasted for a week, with 13 games played. Other leagues included black teams in their schedule. In 1889, the Penn League included the Cuban Giants and New York Gothams, but lasted for only one season. In 1898, the Acme Colored Giants played for a few months in the Iron and Oil League in Celeron, New York.

After 1898, no other teams of players of color participated in white leagues, and attempts at organizing separate independent leagues began. In 1890, black business owners tried to organize a league with teams in Chicago, Cincinnati, Cleveland, Indianapolis, Kansas City, and Louisville. Finances lacking, the teams never played any games. The International League of Independent Professional

The Pittsburgh Crawfords, 1935 Negro National League Champions. The team included five future Hall of Famers, from left: Oscar Charleston, 1st; Judy Johnson, 5th; Cool Papa Bell, 12th; Josh Gibson, 15th; and Satchel Paige, 17th. Others are not identified. (AP Photo)

Baseball Clubs included teams of Cuban X Giants, Cuban Stars, Havana Stars, and Quaker Giants. In 1907, the league added two white teams, but financial difficulties, again, prevented implementation. Three years later, Chicago lawyer Beauregard Moseley led an effort to create the Negro National Baseball League. At an organizational meeting in December 1910, interested owners elected Moseley president and Felix Payne as secretary/treasurer. This attempt was the most successful in organizing, coming the closest to being a league, but it did not become a reality. Also in 1910, the United States League of Professional Ball Clubs was organized, with teams in Baltimore, Brooklyn, Jersey City, New York, Newark, Philadelphia, and Trenton. Owners would include both black and white players. Financial reasons and the fact that this was an outlaw league hindered its development. In 1901, baseball teams had organized to create the National Association of Professional Baseball Leagues (NAPBL). Members of this organizational structure became "organized baseball," those that were not belonging "outlaw." As different teams and leagues attempted to establish themselves, they also had to contend with a formalized structure that discouraged nonmembers. All of the attempts to establish leagues before 1920 and white teams playing against black teams helped establish a foundation for future successes. In the nineteenth century, approximately 70 blacks played on integrated professional teams, with several hundred playing on other kinds of teams.

During the first two decades of the twentieth century, numerous independent black teams, including the long-lasting Baltimore Black Sox (1916–1934), Chicago American Giants (1911–1958), Hilldale Daisies (1910–1930s), Indianapolis ABCs (1902–1940), Homestead Grays (1911–1950), and Leland Giants (1905–1915), successfully kept African Americans playing baseball.

On February 13, 1920, leaders from eight cities met in Kansas City, Missouri, to establish the Negro National League (NNL). Andrew "Rube" Foster organized the business and sports writers. A former player and manager with the Leland Giants and Chicago American Giants, Foster essentially managed all the details of the new league to ensure its success. Born in 1879 in Calvert, Texas, Rube Foster pitched for semipro and independent teams. In 1908, Foster established his own team because he felt the owner of the team he played on did not respect the players. Foster's Chicago American Giants became part of the new Negro League. The National Association of Colored Professional Baseball came into being, with the team owners signing a constitution that placed Foster as president. Teams included the Chicago Giants, Detroit Stars, Indianapolis ABCs, Kansas City Monarchs, and St. Louis Giants. Owners paid an entrance fee and agreed to league rules. Most of the teams did not own, but rented stadiums from white teams. In addition to the regular league teams, other teams could play as associate teams, but the game would not count in league statistics.

In May 1920, the Negro Southern League played after two months of planning, but was not as organized as the NNL. Teams included the Atlanta Black Crackers, Birmingham Giants, Chattanooga Black Lookouts, Jacksonville Red Caps, Montgomery Grey Sox, Nashville Elite Giants, and New Orleans Black Pelicans. In 1921, the league dissolved due to conflicts among the teams. Other black leagues were the Continental League (based in Boston), the Negro Western League (based in Kansas, Virginia, and Kentucky), and the Tandy League (based in St. Louis). As the NNL continued to develop, teams came into and out of the league. Rube Foster's Chicago American Giants was the only team to compete in all 12 seasons.

In 1923, Ed Bolden of the Hilldale Daisies organized the Eastern Colored League (ECL). To ease the distance in traveling to games and to exert control himself, Bolden's league included the Bacharach Giants, Baltimore Black Sox, Brooklyn Royal Giants, the Eastern Cuban Stars, Hilldale Daisies, and the New York Lincoln Giants. Teams played in the ECL from 1923 to 1928. In 1929, they reorganized as the Negro American League and played for one season.

In the Negro Leagues, contracts with players proved to be an ongoing struggle. Players would move to another team if the owner produced a better offer. Owners of Negro League teams were both white and black. Many team owners held businesses in the community. A handful of them participated in illegal activities. The community loved their local teams, and the team had a central role in the African American community. The community leaders would participate in the games. Games on Sunday would begin after church had ended, and fans would come to the ballpark dressed in their Sunday best.

Baseball teams in the Negro Leagues did not travel by train, but by bus. Play on teams in fluctuating leagues allowed players to play for many teams during the year. With the regular season from April to October, players could continue playing on traveling teams, winter ball teams, or barnstorming against white teams in warmer climates, including the West Coast and Latin America. On average, players began their careers when they were 20 and played professionally for about five years. Some players were older or younger, and some played for two or more decades. Segregation made the extensive travel more difficult. Teams might not find hotels that would accept them or restaurants that would feed them. Members of the black community would regularly house the players in their own homes when a team came to town.

Until 1971, the National Baseball Hall of Fame did not consider Negro League players eligible for election. The initial plan was to place them in a separate wing, but, recognizing that it was the segregation of their time and not their ability as ball players, their achievements are now recognized in the same way as players from organized baseball. Some of the players in the Negro League now in the Baseball

Hall of Fame include Satchel Paige, Josh Gibson, Cool Papa Bell, Oscar Charleston, Ray Dandridge, Leon Day, Monte Irvin, Judy Johnson, Buck Leonard, Alex Pompez, Bullet Rogan, and Willie Wells. Each of these players became a member of the Baseball Hall of Fame based on their career in the Negro Leagues.

The decline of the Negro League came with the integration of major and minor league baseball. After Jackie Robinson signed a contract with the Brooklyn Dodgers in October 1945, played for the minor league Montreal Royals in 1946, and played for the major league Dodgers in 1947, the death knell for Negro Leagues baseball sounded. Fans, players, and owners would choose integration over continued segregation. As more and more players went into major or minor league baseball, fewer top quality players played into the Negro Leagues. One by one, the teams dissolved, and the end of the Negro Leagues was marked in 1960.

Amy Essington

See also: Jim Crow.

Further Reading

Heaphy, Leslie A. *The Negro Leagues, 1869–1960.* Jefferson, NC: McFarland, 2003.

Holway, John. *The Complete Book of Baseball's Negro Leagues: The Other Half of Baseball History.* Fern Park, FL: Hastings House Publishers, 2001.

Lanctot, Neil. *Negro League Baseball: The Rise and Ruin of a Black Institution.* Philadelphia: University of Pennsylvania, 2004.

Peterson, Robert. *Only the Ball Was White.* New York: Gramercy, 1999.

New Deal

The New Deal was put into place by President Franklin D. Roosevelt during the Great Depression from 1933 to 1938. New Deal programs created a radical shift in the role of the federal government vis-à-vis the nation's economic sphere in an effort to reform the U.S. economy torn by the Depression. New Deal policies were guided by the "Three Rs": direct relief, economic recovery, and financial reform. However, New Deal initiatives extended well into the 1940s and 1950s, largely to support retuning World War II veterans. During the New Deal, under the auspices of Roosevelt and largely controlled by the Jim Crow mentality of the South for whom most of the aid was geared toward given the rampant rural poverty of both blacks and whites, the federal government transformed into an activist government that sought to advance human well-being and provide economic security to its citizens. The federal government tightened its grip on the nation's economic sector via New Deal programs. Of all the New Deal programs initiated during the course of this activist government's reign, three social initiatives particularly reveal the New Deal government's commitment to alleviating social ills, albeit in a fashion that was largely racist and indeed Jim Crowed (i.e., exclusionary or separate): welfare, work, and war. Aid to Dependent Children (ADC) was the largest social welfare initiative. In regard to the New Deal's influence on labor laws, three laws are worth examining: the National Industrial Recovery Act, the National Labor Relation Act, and the Fair Labor Standards Act of 1938. In regard to war, the Selective Service Readjustment Act was the largest New Deal initiative, and its effects on the country were enormous. However, all of the New Deal initiatives, whether in the North or the South, were implemented in a race-based fashion that at best favored white Americans over African Americans, and at worst was a segregated system that could not escape the all-pervading influence of Jim Crow segregation and exclusion that divided the nation.

Welfare

Aid to Dependent Children passed as one of 11 titles in the 1935 Social Security Act passed in Congress. The federal programs passed under the act, which was designed to provide 30 million Americans with a safety net by virtue of federal government support, in August during Roosevelt's term were Jim Crowed from the beginning. ADC was designed to offer grants to families in which one of the parents, usually the father, was absent. Aid often went to mothers who were divorced, never married, or abandoned, or whose husbands could not work. ADC, and other programs included within the Social Security Act, was funded by both the federal and state governments. However, the programs were governed at that state level, which ultimately made the programs decentralized from the federal government and subject to Jim Crow exclusion and segregation.

Black mothers were largely excluded from receiving such federal and state aid, often in the Jim Crow South where black population was the highest. The racial exclusionary policies of the landmark Social Security Act were employed in terms of labor performed. The act prohibited qualification for aid to those who toiled in the agricultural or domestic service sectors, jobs that were dominated by blacks and Mexicans. Black mothers often had to fight against locally state-controlled bureaucracies that were partially funded by the federal government. In the United States as a whole, 14 percent of children in the program were black. That the relief would be administered at the state level was detrimental to African Americans in the Jim Crow South. Thirty-seven percent of the children in Louisiana were African American, but only 26 percent were ADC recipients. Throughout the South, blacks were largely excluded.

Work

During the New Deal era, the National Industrial Recovery Act, the National Labor Relations Act, and the Fair Labor Standard Act were passed to increase working conditions. These three very significant acts gave workers, among other things, the right to bargain collectively with unions, a maximum work week, better working conditions, and a minimum wage. These three acts were generally employed in a discriminatory fashion and ultimately harmed African American workers, both male and female.

The National Industrial Recovery Act (NRA) passed during the famous first 100 days of Roosevelt's administration on June 16, 1933. One of the components of the bill was that it guaranteed workers the right to organize and bargain collectively with unions and other representatives without fear of employer coercion. Furthermore, it put forth "codes of fair competition" that guaranteed a minimum wage and a maximum 40-hour work week. Although the act presented itself and had the potential to help African Americans, it ultimately had devastating consequences on African American workers.

The wage provisions guaranteed by the NRA discriminated and harmed African Americans in a multiplicity of ways. After Southern legislators voiced concern over the consequences that increased wages would have on agricultural profits and easily affordable domestic workers, both industries that African Americans dominated, they agreed not to establish "fair labor codes" for agricultural and domestic labor. Wages in the agricultural and domestic fields remained stable, while wages in other sectors of labor, largely dominated by white workers, increased. The NRA determined the minimum wage in relation to the category of work performed. Consequently, when the NRA minimum wage codes happened to apply to occupations that African Americans dominated, the occupations received a lower classification than similar unskilled "white" occupations, and thus were granted a lower minimum wage. In short, the NRA promoted and practiced separate wage differentials for white and African American workers. In the end, the minimum wage provisions dramatically harmed African American workers; it is estimated to have cost half a million African Americans their jobs.

The National Industrial Relations Act (NIRA) also attempted to raise wages through collective bargaining. When it came to collective bargaining with unions, blacks faced the same problems they met with wage provisions. The passage of NIRA, under Section 7a, gave racist unions, those that excluded and segregated African Americans in their locals and federations, exclusive bargaining power on behalf of workers in various industries. Before the passage of the NRA, American unions represented a small but significant, 2.25 million members, of whom 50,000 were black. Two months after the passage of the NRA, union membership increased to a little less than 4 million. Ultimately, the exclusive right to bargain on behalf of workers granted to racist labor unions displaced many African American workers. When African Americans did complain about union discrimination to the National Labor Relations Board, the federal government failed to intrude on their behalf. In response, government officials attempted to pacify African American outrage by pointing out that the act had led to minimum wage laws, the elimination of child labor, and a maximum 40-hour work week, of which some, but by no means a vast majority, African Americans enjoyed.

On May 27, 1935 the Supreme Court declared that the NRA was unconstitutional in *A.L.A. Schechter Poultry Corp. v. United States*. The National Labor Relation Act (NLRA), also known as the Wagner Act of 1935, replaced Section 7a of the NRA. The NLRA guaranteed wage workers the right to organize and bargain collectively with unions, and made illegal "unfair labor practices" used by employers to avoid unionization. Moreover, the act prohibited employer discrimination on the basis of union activity and obliged employers to bargain with these organizations. Additionally, like the NRA's Section 7a, the Wagner Act, through the National Labor Relations Board, made unions the only way to bargain collectively with employers. Union membership rose to 8 million by 1941, and by 1948, union membership surged to 14.2 million.

The Wagner Act, however, did not protect black workers. It was implemented in an exclusionary fashion, as it did not contain a clause that protected African American workers, as a result of racist labor unions, particularly the American Federation of Labor (AFL), that successfully lobbied to keep the clause from protecting African American workers. The Wagner Act also banned company unions, unions that were more racially egalitarian than affiliated unions, and made the hire of strikebreaking workers, usually African American, more difficult. The NLRA, in essence, gave unions governmental validation to exclude black workers from labor agreements.

The minimum wage provisions mandated by the NRA, which were later found unconstitutional by the Supreme Court, were later smuggled in under the Fair Labor Standards Act of 1938 (FLSA). The FLSA guaranteed a minimum wage of 25 cents an hour for the first year of its passage, 30 cents for the second, and 40 cents an hour inside a six-year time period, overtime protections, maximum working hours at 44 hours a week in the first years of its passage, 42 in the second, and 40 hours henceforth, to many wage laborers. The act was designed to advance the cause of white workers. Again, like the New Deal labor laws passed before it, it was implemented in a Jim Crow fashion. Domestic and agricultural workers, an overwhelming majority of whom were African American or Mexican Americans, were not covered under the act. Furthermore, FLSA cost many Africans Americans their jobs. The disemployment of workers was mostly felt by African American laborers in the South who often performed labor at a rate less than the minimum wage mandated by the government. Two weeks after the passage of the FLSA, it is estimated by the Labor Department that 30,000 to 50,000 workers, predominantly black in the South, had lost their jobs as a result of the minimum wage provisions. For example, the percentage of African Americans in the tobacco industry declined from about 68 percent in 1930 to about 55 percent in 1940.

War

Of all the bills passed during the progressive days of the New Deal, the Selective Service Readjustment Act, also known as the G.I. Bill, was implemented in the most discriminatory fashion, and it, more than any other bill, did more to increase the economic gap between African Americans and their white counterparts. The G.I. Bill, passed in 1944, marks the largest social benefit bill ever passed by the federal government in a single initiative. The bill was designed to (re)integrate 16 million returning veterans; it reached 8 of every 10 men born in the 1920s. In a 28-year span from 1944 to 1971, federal spending totaled over $90 billion, and by 1948, a massive 15 percent of the federal budget was geared toward funding the bill. The bill was designed to help returning veterans start a business, buy a home, or attend college. The bill is, no doubt, responsible for the making of the middle class.

The middle class it created was largely white. The G.I. Bill, like the New Deal bills it followed, was written under the patronage of Jim Crow and was prone to practice exclusionary policies that either rejected blacks outright or underfunded them dramatically in comparison to their white counterparts. Upon returning from World War II, many black veterans, no doubt, reaped the fruits of the G.I. Bill and attended colleges, started business, and experienced some upward mobility. However, the entrenched racism in the Jim Crow South and throughout America put many obstacles in front of blacks who sought to secure the benefits of the G.I. Bill. The bill was drafted by the openly racist, anti black, anti-Catholic, and anti-Jewish John Rankin of Mississippi, and had to pass by Southern members of Congress who insisted that the G.I. Bill be decentralized from the federal government. The G.I. Bill left the administrative responsibilities up to the states. Leaving administrative tasks in the hands of policymakers in Jim Crow South, who feared that blacks would use their new status to dismantle segregation, proved to have negative consequences on African Americans. Locals administering the program at the Mississippi Unemployment Compensation Committee strongly encouraged blacks not to apply for social benefits. Two years after the G.I. Bill's implementation, the committee had received only 2,600 applications from African Americans, whereas it received 16,000 from white applicants. When black applicants were rewarded funding, they often had to overcome the discrimination of the institutions they wished to attend. Elite universities in the North were reluctant to admit blacks.

The University of Pennsylvania, the most racially egalitarian university in 1946, boasted only 40 blacks out of an institutional enrollment of 9,000. Black enrollment in the North and the West never exceeded 5,000 African Americans in the 1940s. As a result, 95 percent of black veterans were forced to attend segregated, all-black colleges. However, because of Jim Crow policies that forced blacks to segregated, all-black institutions, and the failure of Southern states to fund black institutions, black colleges failed to keep up with the demand. Twenty thousand eligible blacks could not find an academic institution to attend in 1947, and as many as 50,000 might have sought admission if there would not have been such widespread Jim Crow policies.

Jack A. Taylor III

See also: Great Depression; Roosevelt, Franklin D.; World War II.

Further Reading

Bernstein, David E. *Only One Place of Redress: African Americans, Labor Regulations, and the Courts from Reconstruction to the New Deal*. Durham, NC: Duke University Press, 2001.

Brown, Nikki. *Private Politics and Public Voices: African American Women's Activism from World War I to the New Deal*. Bloomington: Indiana University Press, 2007.

"The Depression, The New Deal, and World War II." African American Odyssey, Library of Congress. http://memory.loc.gov/ammem/aaohtml/exhibit/aopart8.html (accessed May 28, 2008).

Katznelson, Ira. *When Affirmative Action Was White: An Untold History of Racial Inequality in Twentieth-Century America*. New York: W. W. Norton, 2005.

Moreno, Paul. *Black Americans and Organized Labor: A New History*. Baton Rouge: Louisiana State University Press, 2006.

Roediger, David. *Working toward Whiteness: How America's Immigrants Became White: The Strange Journey from Ellis Island to the Suburbs*. New York: Basic Books, 2005.

Sullivan, Patricia. *Days of Hope: Race and Democracy in the New Deal Era*. Chapel Hill: University of North Carolina Press, 1996.

Zieger, Robert H. *For Jobs and Freedom: Race and Labor in America since 1865*. Lexington: University Press of Kentucky, 2007.

North Carolina

North Carolina had a relatively small slave population before the Civil War, with most slaves confined to the coastal plain. Unlike neighboring Virginia and South Carolina, much of North Carolina was covered with hills and mountains, and thus poor plantation country. The state was lukewarm about secession. During the Jim Crow era, North Carolina followed the practices common in much of the South. Despite the entrenchment of Jim Crow in the state, whites took some pride in what they believed were good race relations, and often contrasted the apparently peaceful nature of race relations in North Carolina with those of other states. The Civil Rights Movement, however, drew attention to daily discriminations and humiliations blacks faced, and forced the state to begin to come to terms with its legacy.

The Republican Party remained a force in North Carolina longer after the end of Reconstruction than it had in most Southern states. In 1898, Democrats rioted in Wilmington, killing a dozen black Republicans and forcing out all Republican officeholders. With this use of overt force and violence, the Democrats were able to destroy the two-party system in North Carolina, and institute Jim Crow without political opposition. With blacks stripped of political power, some towns, such as Spruce Pine, used violence to drive out its entire black population. North Carolina adopted the poll tax specifically to deny African Americans the right to vote without invoking challenges based on the Fifteenth Amendment. However, in 1920, as part of the Progressive reform movement, the state repealed the poll tax, largely because it disenfranchised more whites than blacks.

North Carolina's segregated educational system followed those of most of the South, in that the state rigidly enforced "separation," but paid no heed to "equal." During the 1914–1915 school year, the state spent about $4 million for educating whites, and only about $600,000 on black students. Even given the larger white population of the state, the figure represented a significant lower rate per student for black students. In counties with more black students than white students, more funds went for white schools than black schools. White teachers throughout the state in 1910 earned on average three times more than black teachers.

The presence of the Lumbee Indians in North Carolina led to a three-tier educational system, unlike the two-tier system in most of the Jim Crow South. Native Americans opposed state efforts to classify them as "colored," and did not want their children assigned to the black schools. Part of this came from the stigma of black schools as inferior, but also from cultural and political goal of Indians nationwide that were at odds with those of African Americans. Unlike blacks, Indians often resisted attempts to assimilate them, and preferred instead that their children attend schools with other Indians. School districts with tribalized Indian populations created separate schools for blacks, whites, and Indians.

While North Carolina had a medical school for blacks from the Reconstruction era, reforms of medical schools in the early twentieth century closed the school, leaving North Carolina without a source to train black doctors. This was part of a regional trend, until only Howard in Washington and Meharry in Nashville remained as a source of black doctors for much of the South. The result was that black patients either had to see white doctors, or more likely, simply relied on unlicensed folk practitioners, or did without medical care.

Despite the self-image of most white North Carolinians that their state stood separate from most of the South in its race relations, the stirring of the Civil Rights Movement, and the reaction of state officials to challenges to the status quo, exposed the underlying oppression of blacks in the state. In 1946, the U.S. Supreme Court ruled in *Morgan v. Virginia* that state laws requiring segregation on buses involved in interstate commerce were unconstitutional. In 1947, a "Journey of Reconciliation" tested whether states were honoring the decision. An interracial group of passengers attempted to travel by bus through the South. In North Carolina, police arrested many of the riders for violating state laws. When the riders refused to pay the fines, they were placed on the state's prison chain gangs.

The town of Greensboro, in the 1950s, saw itself as a paradigm of peaceful race relations, despite the very real presence of Jim Crow segregation. The years since the start of World War II had actually seen an increase in segregation in the city. On February 1, 1960, four students from North Carolina Agricultural and Technical College, a black state college in Greensboro, walked into the lunch counter at the local Woolworth's department store and sat down for service. The four young men were Ezell A. Blair Jr., David Richmond, Joseph McNeil, and Franklin McCain. Under Jim Crow restrictions in force at the time, only white patrons could use the seats, black patrons had to either get their food to go, or eat it while standing. At the time, the Woolworth's lunch counter was one of the nation's largest restaurant chains, and often was responsible for a large percentage of each store's profits. As a national chain, it was more vulnerable to the negative publicity the incident brought. The use of the sit-in had been used by the Congress of Racial Equality in Chicago in 1942, in St. Louis in 1949, and in Baltimore in 1952, but the Greensboro sit-in caught the attention of the national media. The four students were well dressed and well groomed, polite, and patient. They waited all day, and were not served. The next day they returned, along with about 27 supporters. Within a few days, the number had grown to over a thousand. The movement spread throughout the South, and drew attention to unfairness of many of the daily forms of discrimination most blacks faced. By July, the four were able to sit at the Woolworth's lunch counter and be served.

After the *Brown v. Board of Education* decision in 1954, which ruled segregated schools unconstitutional, states of the South began to desegregate, albeit slowly. In North Carolina, the process more closely followed that of Virginia and the Deep South in opposition and the use of delaying tactics. The eventual integration of public schools, although far from uniformly instituted, resulted in the demotion and displacement of many black teachers. While some of the demotions resulted from the generally lower credentials of many black teachers—itself

Joseph McNeil, Franklin McCain, Billy Smith, and Clarence Henderson, on February 2, 1960, sitting at the Woolworth's lunch counter. (Library of Congress)

a legacy of Jim Crow—the dismissal and demotion of many black principals came more from deep-seated white opposition to having a school where white children attended being run by a black person. Additionally, the idea of white teachers having a black principal also caused fear and opposition from whites. Erasing the effects of Jim Crow would take more than court orders—it would take a change in attitudes and, more often, a change of generations.

In much of the South, patterns of residential segregation worked against integration of public schools. If students attended their local neighborhood public school, and the entire neighborhood was all white or all black as a result of generations of residential segregation, then school integration was a meaningless concept. Proponents of integration proposed using school buses to ensure some black students attended previously all-white schools, and that some white students attended previously all-black schools. Busing was widely unpopular with white parents but also with some black parents, because it meant long bus rides for their children, and taking them away from their neighborhood school. North Carolina passed a law that prohibited school districts form using busing as a means to integrate schools.

The large school district of Charlotte-Mecklenburg reflected the demographic reality of most of the South, where blacks lived in separate neighborhoods from whites. A series of legal challenges beginning in 1965 led eventually to the

U.S. Supreme Court ruling of *Swann v. Charlotte-Mecklenburg Board of Education* (402 U.S. 1) in 1971 that busing was a constitutional and appropriate means of integrating public schools. Busing remained a controversial tactic, but the legality of its use had been settled. As in many other aspects of the long struggle to end Jim Crow, North Carolina provided an unwilling battleground, but its own image of itself as a Southern state spared most of the racial strife of most of the South, made residents uncomfortable with overtly racist politics, and helped bring about the eventual end of Jim Crow.

Barry M. Stentiford

See also: Sit-Ins; South Carolina.

Further Reading

Crow, Jeffrey, Paul D. Escott, and Flora J. Hatley. *A History of African Americans in North Carolina.* Raleigh: North Carolina Division of Archives and History, 1992.

Gilmore, Glenda Elizabeth. *Gender and Jim Crow: Women and the Politics of White Supremacy in North Carolina, 1896–1920.* Chapel Hill: University of North Carolina Press, 1996.

Powell, William S. *North Carolina: A History.* Chapel Hill: University of North Carolina Press, 1988.

Ready, Milton. *The Tar Heel State: A History of North Carolina.* Columbia: University of South Carolina Press, 2005.

P

Parks, Rosa

Known as the "mother of the civil rights movement," Rosa Louise McCauley Parks is one of the most famous historical figures in American history. By refusing to surrender her seat to a white passenger on a segregated bus, Parks violated one of the many Jim Crow laws. Her actions and arrest served as the impetus for the Montgomery Bus Boycott.

On February 4, 1913, Rosa was born in Tuskegee, Alabama, to James and Leona McCauley. Reared and educated in rural Pine Level, Alabama, Rosa was known as a soft-spoken, intelligent student. She continued her education at Montgomery Industrial School for girls and Alabama State Teacher's College High School. However, due to several illnesses in the family, Rosa postponed graduation to help out at home. In 1932, she married local barber Raymond Parks and received her high school diploma two years later. In Montgomery, the couple worked together in the National Association for the Advancement of Colored People (NAACP). Parks served as the branch secretary and youth leader of the NAACP and worked as a seamstress in a downtown department store.

On December 1, 1955, the 43-year-old Parks boarded the city bus after work. Since all of the seats in the back were taken, Parks sat in the first row of the black section. At the next stop a white male passenger asked for Parks's seat. She refused to move. The bus driver ordered Parks to move and threatened to call the cops. Again, she refused to move and was arrested. Parks never thought she would make history that day; her only desire was "to know once and for all what rights I had as a human being."

Parks became the symbol of hundreds of thousands of African Americans who had suffered as second-class citizens. Her actions served as the spark for the Montgomery Bus Boycott. The NAACP and Women's Political Council (WPC) had organized long before this incident but had waited for such an event to rally their cause around. Only days after Parks's arrest, the boycott of the Montgomery bus system began.

Shortly after her arrest, Parks lost her job in the department store, and two years later, Parks and her husband moved to Detroit, Michigan. For more than 20 years, Parks worked as an assistant to Michigan's U.S. congressman John Conyers. In 1987, Parks cofounded the Rosa & Raymond Parks Institute for Self Development, which focuses its efforts on encouraging and leading children to reach their fullest potential.

As an activist, lecturer, and writer, Parks continued to inspire thousands of Americans. In addition to the 43 honorary doctorate degrees, Parks received the NAACP Springarn Medal, UAW's Social Justice Award, the Martin Luther King Jr., Non-Violent Peace Prize, the Medal of Freedom, and the Congressional Gold Medal, to name a few. The strong, soft-spoken woman whose courage changed the nation died at the age of 92.

Emily Hess

See also: Alabama; King, Martin Luther, Jr.

Further Reading

Brinkley, Douglas. *Rosa Parks*. New York: Viking, 2000.

Crawford, Vicki L., Jacqueline Anne Rouse, and Barbara Woods, eds. *Women in the Civil Rights Movement: Trailblazers and Torchbearers, 1941–1965*. Brooklyn, NY: Carlson Publishing, 1990.

Hine, Darlene Clark, Elsa Barkley Brown, and Rosalyn Terborg-Penn, eds. *Black Women in American: An Historical Encyclopedia*. Brooklyn, NY: Carlson Publishing, 1992.

Parks, Rosa, with Gregory Reed. *Rosa Parks: The Faith, the Hope, and the Heart of a Woman Who Changed a Nation*. Grand Rapids, MI: Zondervan, 1994.

Passing

The common perception of passing is of a light-complexioned African American assuming the identity of a white person. Under the conditions of Jim Crow, passing was an opportunity to gain social, political, and economic benefits afforded by white supremacist ideology. This phenomenon occurred regularly during slavery when mulatto slaves wanted to escape or prevent capture once free. In 1848, for instance, William and Ellen Craft devised an elaborate passing scheme when they ran away from a Georgia plantation. Ellen was light enough to pass as a white man; she wore the disguise of a sickly gentleman, accompanied by "his" male slave (her husband William) traveling to the North. They figured that it would be more believable for Ellen to appear as a white man rather than face the impropriety of a Southern white woman accompanied by a black man. The Crafts arrived in Philadelphia undetected, and their story was later documented in *Running a Thousand Miles for Freedom* (1860). In places like New Orleans with large populations of free mulattos, many of them could or did easily assimilate into white society throughout the nineteenth century. Such accounts of racial passing were less frequent during the Reconstruction era (1863–1877), when more liberal circumstances provided less motivation for passing throughout the South. African Americans, for the first time in American history, enjoyed greater political freedom than ever before. However, Reconstruction ended when Southern states that were readmitted to the Union sought revenge for losing the Civil War and the radical Republican policies that destroyed and made amends for slavery. Segregation was codified and enforced as a systematic form of racial oppression, hence the birth of Jim Crow. Many African Americans who passed for white then did so to avoid the hardships of racial discrimination, prejudice, and often violence. Essentially, they could live as free people in a democratic society. Their choices for education, housing, shopping, employment, transportation, and even entertainment would not be limited by their black racial identity. On the contrary, the chance to acquire equal rights and social privileges then reserved for whites only seemed worth the risk.

Passing required life-altering changes based on the kind and length of the experience. Some individuals might have passed involuntarily if their mixed-race heritage was unknown; they could have been born under such pretenses if their family

Ellen Craft, as depicted in a nineteenth-century illustration of her "disguised as a young planter" during her escape from slavery in 1848. Even after the end of slavery, some light-skinned African Americans continued to pass to take advantage of the greater opportunities for whites. (Eon Images)

kept the secret of passing (which they often did). This is the sort of racial tragedy dramatized in fiction, though it occurred often in real life. Others severed ties completely from their black family to live a solitary white life. This separation of family or loss of communal relationships could have been devastating consequences for passing. The disconnection from familiar environments and people could symbolize "passing" as the death of a former life. While investigating race relations in the Deep South during the 1930s, sociologists explained this kind of passing as social death and rebirth. When the truth was revealed or while passing, an individual could likely have experienced psychological conflicts about identifying with either race. Those who fully assimilated, however, may not have suffered emotional distress. Some even married "pure" whites to further dilute their bloodline. The fear of producing "black" offspring could then prevent the passer from having any children at all. So having a white complexion alone did not guarantee the passer success.

The discovery of an individual's true identity was a foremost concern when the "one-drop rule" was used to define blackness. Having a traceable black ancestry (or any "black blood") was enough to classify a mixed-race person "black" despite the dominant white racial traits inherited. Descriptions of biracial individuals as "near-white" or "white Negroes" suggest racial impurities or an invisible blackness that many whites feared. Black-to-white passers were therefore complicit in their attempts to assimilate under white surveillance, especially in the Jim Crow South. Racial ambiguity threatened segregation and sensitized white Southerners to maintain the status quo. They proclaimed an ability to detect any passers with visible or invisible signs of blackness. If the average African American developed a double consciousness as theorized by W.E.B. Du Bois in *The Souls of Black Folk* (1903), passers were even more sensitive to racism. The "peculiar sensation" of "always looking at one's self through the eyes of others" was fundamental to their concealment. Du Bois challenged segregationists' reliance on ocular proof of black inferiority with his American Negro Exhibit at the 1900 Paris Exposition. Many of the photographs on display featured African Americans of questionable racial origins: pale complexions, light eyes, thin noses, and various hair textures. These images of exceptional blacks proved that they could "pass" as model citizens and undermine white peoples' perception of blackness.

Despite close racial scrutiny, the "great age of passing" occurred at the height of Jim Crow during the late nineteenth and early twentieth centuries. Thousands crossed the color line to defy legal segregation, social restrictions, and geographical boundaries. Since the majority of African Americans lived in the South, those wanting to pass would migrate to the North, where they could become "new people" without the burden of race. Or, they could take advantage of the opportunity to live a double life. Alex Manly, a mulatto journalist from North Carolina, fled the South during a race riot in 1898. When he relocated to Philadelphia, he divided his time working as a white man during the day and returned home to his black family in the evening. He eventually decided to live as a black man permanently, though he could not find suitable employment to support his family as such. When passing proved to be a costly venture, other alternatives became attractive options for circumventing the race problem. Some African Americans passed for European immigrants, who would often receive better treatment upon arrival to this country than black people in America. French, Italian, Spanish, and other foreign ethnicities were ideal covers used to explain the variations of colored complexions among African Americans resulting from generations of miscegenation. To appear more convincing, passers adopting a foreign ethnicity would even speak in a native tongue when approached by suspicious whites. Mary Church Terrell, a leading civil rights activist and black feminist, would often pass for white inadvertently or on purpose as she traveled through the South on lecture tours during the late nineteenth and early twentieth centuries. Terrell spoke several languages and easily passed for a European native as well as a cultured, white Southern belle when necessary to avoid traveling in filthy Jim Crow railway cars.

Whether passing on a temporary or permanent basis, an individual who passed for white during the Jim Crow era risked their personal safety. There were (or could have been) violent repercussions after discovery. "Separate but equal" policies of segregation tried to determine the limits of interracial mixing in public spaces. Yet, the culture of segregation depended on the "myth" of absolute racial differences, and passing violated the metaphorical and legal limits of segregation. Cases of mistaken identity did occur when African Americans with Caucasian features did not appear "black." Such individuals were often treated with dignity and respect by whites who were unaware of the racial stigma that defined the passer's blackness. Charles Chesnutt was a popular light-skinned African American novelist who experienced life on the color line in this way. He withheld his racial identity with the release of early works to avoid racial censure and received critical reviews on the basis of his artistry alone and not his ancestry. When done as a conscious or deliberate act, however, others lived as a spy crossing racial boundaries. These African Americans sat or ate in the "white-only" sections of trains, theaters, and restaurants without detection. Walter White, for example, was an investigative reporter for the National Association for the Advancement of Colored People (NAACP) during the 1920s. With light skin, blue eyes, and wavy blond hair, the natural disguise White wore to investigate lynchings throughout the South protected him. His subversive act of passing could have easily made him a victim of the same crimes that he witnessed and reported on in *The Crisis*. Years earlier as a young boy, White and his father survived the 1906 Atlanta race riots also by passing as white men until they reached the safety of their home.

African American writers have often fictionalized passing narratives to depict Jim Crow race relations. In her 1892 novel *Iola Leroy,* Frances Harper's mulatto protagonist passes as a white woman until her black heritage is revealed after the death of her parents. The novel unfolds as Iola learns to survive as a "black" woman facing racial discrimination and prejudice. She decides not to pass as a white woman because of her familial relations and racial obligations. Both she and her brother devote their lives to "uplifting the race" as they identify with all African Americans in the struggle for civil equality. Their commitment to become race leaders instead of "race traitors" is a decision made by real mulattos like Walter White with his NAACP activism. Charles Chesnutt's novels often depict mixed-race or "tragic mulatto" characters that experience biological and social conflicts due to their "warring blood" or inherited racial traits. Those that do not succumb to a tragic end (death, desertion, exile, etc.) cross the color line and disappear into white society. As art imitates life, Chesnutt's stories explore the options for passing presented to light-skinned African Americans who seek the benefits of the privileged class. In *The Autobiography of an Ex-Colored Man* (1912), James Weldon Johnson examines the racial paradox in America through an anonymous protagonist who passes for both white and black: "I know that I am playing with fire, and I feel the thrill which accompanies that most fascinating pastime; and, back of it all, I think I find a sort of savage and diabolical desire to gather up all the little tragedies of my life, and turn them into a practical joke on society." Using social realism to captivate his readers, Johnson's novel was a successful literary hoax initially since many people believed the autobiography was a truthful account of passing. The republication of the novel with Johnson's authorship finally acknowledged appeared in 1927.

Like Johnson, Nella Larsen, Jessie Redmon Fauset, and George Schuyler were other African American novelists who continued to develop the theme of passing during the Harlem Renaissance. Works by Larsen and Fauset are populated by characters with mixed-race ancestries and thus the burden of race. Larsen presents the psychological trauma of mulatto women in her 1929 novel about complex racial, class, and gender identities. Aptly titled *Passing,* the work explores the motivations and consequences of Irene Redfield and Clare Kendry passing as socialites on both sides of the color line. Schuyler's *Black No More* (1931) provides a satirical solution to America's race problem by interrogating the power of whiteness. The plot dramatizes racism when black people are transformed into white people via a commercially successful whitening process invented by a black scientist.

White writers like William Faulkner also experimented with the passing theme. He created mulatto characters in works like *Absalom, Absalom* (1936) and *Intruder in the Dust* (1948) that challenged white Southerners' abilities to sense race under segregation. His Mississippi settings were ideal to dramatize many white

Southerners' racial paranoia. Not only were light-skinned blacks the target of bigots, but liberal whites sympathetic to blacks' civil rights were also labeled "white niggers" like those in Faulkner's fiction.

Reverse passing of "mulattos" with white skin and black behavior made for controversial headlines in twentieth-century divorce cases. The scandalous Rhinelander trial of 1924, as detailed in *Love on Trial: An American Scandal in Black and White* (2002), captured the nation's obsession with racial purity and segregation culture. The marriage of a white New York socialite, Leonard Rhinelander, to a working-class domestic, Alice Jones, was annulled when the husband accused his wife of not being completely white. Jones did have mysterious racial origins, though her family did not try to pass for white. Ultimately, her class status proved more of a moral transgression than the scandalous interracial affair staged for the public. Other examples of white-to-black passers' moral failures were not uncommon in multiracial families. "Pure" white siblings would identify as "black" to keep their family relations with black half-siblings intact. Illegitimate whites would also identify as "black" to avoid the stigma of being born a bastard.

Recently, genealogical research has proven how generations of "white" Americans are actually descendants of light-skinned African Americans who passed for various reasons. Attempts to untangle ancestral roots have resulted in revised historical accounts of slavery, fractured memoirs, and emotional family reunions. Edward Ball, a white descendant of prominent South Carolina slaveowners, documents his tedious research into family records in two books, *Slaves in the Family* (1998) and *The Sweet Hell Inside: The Rise of an Elite Black Family in the Segregated South* (2002). In *Life on the Color Line: The True Story of a White Boy Who Discovered He Was Black* (1996), Gregory Howard Williams recalls his coming-of-age during segregation. Shirley Taylor Haizlip likewise reconstructs the difficult past relations of her multiracial family in *The Sweeter the Juice: A Family Memoir in Black and White* (1995); it chronicles the lives of two sisters who were separated for nearly 70 years as each lived in different worlds. The publication of these works and numerous others signals a sort of revival of passing narratives since the demise of Jim Crow.

While the authors present intriguing exposés of passing, firsthand accounts of passing rarely exist because of the fear of discovery. Anonymous testimonies were published only when necessary as political propaganda. Many "post-passing" narratives are only now being studied as evidence of the pressures to adapt to racist society; these stories and similar reports about the "past" trend of passing were published in popular black periodicals like *Ebony* and *Jet* during the 1950s. A notable example is John Howard Griffin's *Black Like Me* (1960), his autobiography of becoming a "black" man within the last decade of Jim Crow. Like Walter White, Griffin's mission as a white "spy" was to investigate black life in the Deep South and report his findings to promote racial understanding. His white-to-black passing appealed to American racism by dissecting America's own "white" consciousness. Griffin's timely publication appeared on the cusp of a new era in the history of passing. After all, black-to-white passing at least had become "passé" as the Civil Rights and Black Power movements redefined blackness in positive ways. The racial pride anthem "black is beautiful," for instance, proclaimed a new generation of African Americans' acceptance of darker skin complexion and validated black culture in general.

Sherita L. Johnson

See also: Jim Crow; Racial Customs and Etiquette.

Further Reading

"The Adventures of a Near-White." *Independent* 75 (1913): 373–76.

Bay, Mia. *The White Image in the Black Mind: African American Ideas about White People, 1830–1925.* New York: Oxford University Press, 2000.

Ginsberg, Elaine K. *Passing and the Fictions of Identity.* Durham, NC: Duke University Press, 1996.

Hale, Grace Elizabeth. *Making Whiteness: The Culture of Segregation in the South, 1890–1940.* New York: Vintage, 1998.

Sollors, Werner. *Neither Black Nor White, Yet Both: Thematic Explorations of Interracial Literature.* Cambridge, MA: Harvard University Press, 1997.

Wald, Gayle. *Crossing the Line: Racial Passing in Twentieth-Century U.S. literature and Culture.* Durham, NC: Duke University Press, 2000.

Williamson, Joel. *New People: Miscegenation and Mulattoes in the United States.* Baton Rouge: Louisiana State University Press, 1995.

Plessy v. Ferguson

Plessy v. Ferguson was a landmark decision of the U.S. Supreme Court in 1896 that upheld the constitutionality of state laws requiring racial segregation in public accommodations (particularly railroad passenger cars) and that established the doctrine of "separate but equal" as the constitutional standard for such laws. The Supreme Court held that neither the Thirteenth nor the Fourteenth Amendment to the Constitution could be used to challenge intrastate segregation laws. The decision resulted in a proliferation of laws mandating racial segregation in public spaces throughout the South, providing constitutional justification for hardening the de facto separation of the races established by custom into state law. This decision stood for nearly 60 years until the Court reversed itself, beginning in 1954 with

Brown v. Board of Education and other cases that followed. The Court specifically outlawed segregation in all public transportation in 1956 in *Gayle v. Browder.*

With the end of the Civil War, Southern states were occupied by federal troops during the period known as Reconstruction (1866–1877). Military occupation, at first, guaranteed that former slaves could fully exercise their voting rights and their civil rights on an equal basis with whites. However, when Reconstruction ended and federal troops were withdrawn, newly won black rights came under attack. Even before the end of Reconstruction, a pattern of racial separation had developed that, while not compelled by statute, pervaded Southern life. By the 1880s, states began to give these patterns the sanction of law.

In 1890 the Louisiana state legislature passed a law that required "equal but separate accommodations for the white and colored races" on all passenger railroads within the state. An exception was provided for nurses attending children of another race. Almost immediately, the black and French-speaking Creole citizens of New Orleans organized to oppose the law. The Citizen's Committee to Test the

Keith Plessy and Phoebe Ferguson, descendants of the principals in the *Plessy v. Ferguson* court case, pose for a photograph in front of a historical marker in New Orleans, 2011. (AP Photo/Bill Haber)

Constitutionality of the Separate Car Law, known as *Comité des Citoyens,* resolved to establish in court that the law violated the Thirteenth and Fourteenth Amendments to the Constitution. The committee, which included prominent whites in New Orleans, agreed that a 30-year-old shoemaker, Homer Plessy, should test the law. Plessy was a French-speaking resident of New Orleans chosen specifically because he was only one-eighth black (an octoroon in the parlance of the time) and, according to his lawyer, "the mixture [was] not discernible." In this way, the committee hoped to expose the arbitrariness of the law.

Clearly, Plessy could have occupied the white car of any train in Louisiana without trouble. But on June 7, 1892, by prearrangement with the railroad company, he sat in a railway car reserved for whites only and refused to leave when asked. The railroad conductor and a private detective hired by the *Comité des Citoyens* then removed him to the police station, where he was booked and released on $500 bond. The railroad company officials seem to have lent some silent support to the committee's court challenge because they were unhappy about the extra expense of providing separate cars for blacks and whites mandated by the law.

At Plessy's first trial, the presiding judge was John H. Ferguson, a native of Massachusetts. He had earlier struck down as unconstitutional another Louisiana law that had mandated segregated accommodations for travel between states. This time, however, the law was restricted to travel only within Louisiana. Ferguson ruled that the state could impose such restrictions within its borders without violating the Constitution. The decision was appealed to the Louisiana State Supreme Court, which upheld the ruling. The decision at the state level cited other court decisions that had relied for support on the "natural, legal, and customary differences between the black and white races."

Plessy's case was argued before the U.S. Supreme Court by the white, activist, New York lawyer Albion W. Tourgée, who had protested against racial segregation earlier in newspaper columns. He prepared a case that presented a variety of arguments to the Court against the Louisiana law. He argued for a broad interpretation of the Thirteenth Amendment to the Constitution, which had abolished slavery. That amendment, his argument suggested, affirmatively established in law the equality of all citizens. Segregation, therefore, violated the Constitution by perpetuating one of the essential features of slavery.

The case also argued that the Louisiana law deprived Plessy of his right to equal protection of law guaranteed by the Fourteenth Amendment. The purpose of the law was not to promote the public good, but rather to ensure the comfort of whites at the expense of blacks. "The exemption of nurses, "Plessy's lawyer argued, "shows that the real evil lies not in the color of the skin but in the relation the colored person sustains to the white. If he is a dependent it may be endured; if he is not, his presence is insufferable." This could not be called equal protection.

Tourgée also pointed out the arbitrariness of racial classifications, since Plessy had only one-eighth African ancestry and could be taken to be white. Indeed, the definition of who was black and who was white differed from state to state. By granting to railroad conductors (whom the law exempted from civil liability) the power to publicly declare racial designations, the state had deprived Plessy of his reputation (as a white man) without due process of law.

In addition, the arguments for Plessy had to take into account that schools were legally segregated, even in Boston and in Washington, D.C., and that inter-racial marriage was forbidden by law in most states (such laws would eventually be found unconstitutional by the Supreme Court in the following century). Those laws might be acceptable, but the matter of seating on railway coaches was different, Plessy's lawyer argued, being much less serious an issue than education or marriage and not affecting future generations. Therefore, the state had no interest in regulating it.

However, the Supreme Court ruled against Plessy on May 18, 1896. The judges voted 7–1 to uphold the Louisiana law. Justice Brewer did not participate in the case. Justice Henry Billings Brown, a native of Massachusetts and a resident of Michigan, wrote the majority opinion. Justice John Marshall Harlan, a Southerner, wrote a ferocious but solitary dissent.

In the years prior to the *Plessy v. Ferguson* case, this same Court had handed down a number of decisions that limited the scope and effect of constitutional restraints on states' rights. These precedents made the Court's 1896 decision almost inevitable. In 1873, the Supreme Court had rejected a broad interpretation of the Thirteenth Amendment in a collection of suits that became known as the *Slaughter-House Cases.* In that decision, the Court held that the sole purpose of the amendment was to abolish slavery, and perhaps other forms of involuntary servitude. It had nothing to do with equal rights. Furthermore, the decision held that the Fourteenth Amendment was not intended to establish the federal government as the "perpetual censor upon all the legislation of the States." That amendment only forbade state infringement on the rights of U.S. citizenship, which the Court took to be narrow in scope.

In 1876 the Supreme Court had decided (*U.S. v. Cruikshank*) that the Fourteenth Amendment could provide not federal protection against actions committed by private parties, but could only protect against the actions of states. Then, in 1883, the Court had held in five cases collected together as the *Civil Rights Cases* that most of the provisions of the federal Civil Rights Act of 1875 were unconstitutional. The Court again ruled that Congress had authority only to prohibit racial discrimination perpetrated by states, not by private citizens. Such precedents made the legal outlook for Plessy's Supreme Court challenge seem bleak indeed. His lawyer deliberately delayed bringing the case to the Court in hopes of finding a more favorable political climate.

Finally, the Supreme Court ruled against Plessy, citing the precedents mentioned earlier. Plessy's appeal to the Thirteenth Amendment was dismissed in favor of a narrow interpretation of the law. The Court found, as well, that the Louisiana law did not violate the Fourteenth Amendment to the Constitution. Justice Brown wrote:

> The object of the [Fourteenth] amendment was undoubtedly to enforce the absolute equality of the two races before the law, but in the nature of things it could not have been intended to abolish distinctions based upon color, or to enforce social, as distinguished from political equality, or a commingling of the two races upon terms unsatisfactory to either. Laws permitting, and even requiring, their separation in places where they are liable to be brought into contact do not necessarily imply the inferiority of either race to the other.

The majority opinion noted that the Louisiana law had mandated "equal" accommodations be provided for blacks and whites. Therefore, the separation of the races by law was not an issue of equality, since it was just as illegal for whites to sit in the black areas of railway cars as it was for blacks to sit in the white areas. The Court held that the "assumption that the enforced separation of the two races stamps the colored race with the badge of inferiority" was a false one. "If this be so, it is not by reason of anything found in the act, but solely because the colored race chooses to put that construction upon it." The ruling explicitly rejected the idea that racial prejudice could be overcome by legislation and denied that equal rights could be achieved for blacks only by enforcing "commingling" of the races. The Court's majority opinion simply assumed that racial separation was "in the nature of things."

Justice Harlan, who wrote the lone dissent to the majority opinion, was a native of Kentucky and a former slaveowner, although he had fought for the Union in the Civil War and freed his slaves before it ended. Harlan argued forcefully that the Louisiana law was unconstitutional and should be struck down by the courts. He objected that:

> The arbitrary separation of citizens, on the basis of race, while they are on a public highway, is a badge of servitude wholly inconsistent with the civil freedom and the equality before the law established by the Constitution. It cannot be justified upon any legal grounds.

Harlan's dissent specifically accepted a broad interpretation of the Thirteenth Amendment that would exclude laws requiring racial segregation. He states explicitly:

> The Thirteenth Amendment does not permit the withholding or the deprivation of any right necessarily inhering in freedom. It not only struck down

the institution of slavery as previously existing in the United States, but it prevents the imposition of any burdens or disabilities that constitute badges of slavery or servitude. It decreed universal civil freedom in this country.

Harlan's dissent was emphatic. He insisted that the Fourteenth Amendment should bar states from any abridgment, on the basis of race, of civil rights or "personal liberty":

> In respect of civil rights, common to all citizens, the Constitution of the United States does not, I think, permit any public authority to know the race of those entitled to be protected in the enjoyment of such rights. . . . I deny that any legislative body or judicial tribunal may have regard to the race of citizens when the civil rights of those citizens are involved. Indeed, such legislation, as that here in question, is inconsistent not only with that equality of rights which pertains to citizenship, National and State, but with the personal liberty enjoyed by every one within the United States.

Harlan rejected the majority's argument that laws of racial segregation did not discriminate against blacks in language that came close to contempt:

> It was said in argument that the statute of Louisiana does not discriminate against either race, but prescribes a rule applicable alike to white and colored citizens. But this argument does not meet the difficulty. Every one knows that the statute in question had its origin in the purpose, not so much to exclude white persons from railroad cars occupied by blacks, as to exclude colored people from coaches occupied by or assigned to white persons. Railroad corporations of Louisiana did not make discrimination among whites in the matter of accommodation for travellers. The thing to accomplish was, under the guise of giving equal accommodation for whites and blacks, to compel the latter to keep to themselves while travelling in railroad passenger coaches. No one would be so wanting in candor as to assert the contrary.

He went on to say: "The thin disguise of 'equal' accommodations for passengers in railroad coaches will not mislead any one, nor atone for the wrong this day done."

Harlan insisted that the majority's decision would, in time, "prove to be quite as pernicious as the decision made by [the Supreme Court] in the *Dred Scott* case." At the conclusion of his dissent, he waxed prophetic:

> I am of the opinion that the statute of Louisiana is inconsistent with the personal liberty of citizens, white and black, in that State, and hostile to both

the spirit and the letter of the Constitution of the United States. If laws of like character should be enacted in the several States of the Union, the effect would be in the highest degree mischievous. Slavery, as an institution tolerated by law would, it is true, have disappeared from our country, but there would remain a power in the States, by sinister legislation, to interfere with the full enjoyment of the blessings of freedom; to regulate civil rights, common to all citizens, upon the basis of race; and to place in a condition of legal inferiority a large body of American citizens.

Of course, laws "of like character" that enforced racial segregation were eventually enacted in all Southern states, and in some Northern states as well. Such laws relegated African Americans to the status of second-class citizens, excluded from public spaces and vulnerable to public humiliation. Segregated public facilities for blacks were always separate, but very rarely equal to those provided for whites. Nonetheless, the Supreme Court's decision in *Plessy v. Ferguson* protected the constitutionality of such laws and provided them with a legal foundation.

Eventually, the Southern states passed laws that enforced a rigidly segregated society. Every restaurant, every school, every train or public conveyance was segregated by law. Separate facilities for blacks and whites were legislated for hotels, elevators, libraries, colleges and universities, swimming pools, drinking fountains, cemeteries, and prisons. An Oklahoma law segregated telephone booths. Louisiana required separate entryways to circuses for blacks and whites. A Florida law demanded that schoolbooks for white schools be stored separately from schoolbooks used in black schools. Such laws rested on the Supreme Court's standard of "separate but equal" established in *Plessy v. Ferguson*.

This standard was finally repudiated by the Supreme Court in 1954, at least with regard to the legal segregation of public schools, in the famous case of *Brown v. Board of Education*. Other cases would follow quickly that found laws of segregation to be unconstitutional in all circumstances. However, the 1896 *Plessy v. Ferguson* decision found its defenders right up until the end. In 1952, William Rehnquist (then a law clerk and later chief justice of the Supreme Court) composed a memo for the Court during early deliberations that led to the *Brown* case. He wrote: "I realize that it is an unpopular and unhumanitarian position, for which I have been excoriated by 'liberal' colleagues but I think *Plessy v. Ferguson* was right and should be reaffirmed." The Supreme Court disagreed unanimously, and *Brown v. Board of Education* marked the beginning of the end of de jure racial segregation in the United States.

Anthony A. Lee

See also: Jim Crow; Racial Customs and Etiquette; Segregation, Residential.

Further Reading

Lofgren, Charles A. *The "Plessy" Case: A Legal-Historical Interpretation.* New York: Oxford University Press, 1987.

Olsen, Otto H. *The Thin Disguise: "Plessy v. Ferguson."* New York: Humanities Press, 1967.

Plessy v. Ferguson, 163 U.S. 537 (1896). http://www.law.cornell.edu/supct/html/historics/USSC_CR_0163_0537_ZS.html (accessed May 28, 2008).

Thomas, Brook, ed. *Plessy v. Ferguson: A Brief History with Documents.* Boston: Bedford Books, 1997.

Poll Taxes

A levy placed on the right to vote, poll taxes were first established in the years following the American Revolution as a substitute for the traditional requirement that only property owners could cast ballots. Initially, the poll tax expanded the number of eligible voters, but was abandoned as states established unrestricted suffrage for most white males. However, when most male citizens were guaranteed the right to vote as a result of the ratification of the Fifteenth Amendment in 1870, the poll tax was resurrected for a more ignoble purpose. Many whites, alarmed at the sight of former slaves voting and holding elective office, were determined to restrict or even eliminate black political influence in the South. Between 1871 and 1902, the states of Alabama, Arkansas, Florida, Georgia, Louisiana, Mississippi, North Carolina, South Carolina, Texas, and Virginia adopted the poll tax specifically to deny African Americans the right to vote. Georgia was the first state to adopt a poll tax, in 1871. Citizens were required to pay between $1 and $2 to their local election commissions several months before a scheduled primary and general election. On Election Day, voters then had to show proof that the tax was paid in order to cast their ballots. If a voter in Alabama, Georgia, Mississippi, and Virginia failed to pay the levy, then his poll tax bill would double for each subsequent election. This cumulative tax erected an additional barrier between economically disadvantaged Southerners and their constitutional rights.

The poll tax was chiefly designed to prevent African Americans from exercising their franchise, but in this regard, it was unsuccessful. It did make it more difficult for citizens to vote and undoubtedly prevented many from casting ballots especially in the states where the levy was cumulative. However, it fell far short of its goal of entirely disenfranchising black Southerners. Many were able to pay the tax; for example, in Shelby County, Tennessee, 24,086 African Americans registered to vote in 1931. In addition, the poll tax often disenfranchised more white citizens than black. Largely because it restricted white voting, North Carolina repealed the poll tax in 1920, and Louisiana and Florida followed suit in 1934 and 1937, respectively. Around the same time, reformers in the South began to focus a great deal of attention on the inequities of the poll tax. In November 1938, the Southern Conference for Human Welfare was founded by a group of African American and white reformers to address the economic and political inequality that existed in the American South. The conference's Civil Rights Committee investigated the poll tax, and in 1941, it formed the National Committee to Abolish the Poll Tax. Petitioning Congress to abolish the tax in federal elections, the committee played a large role in convincing several Southern states to abolish the excise. Georgia, the first state to enact a poll tax, repealed the law in 1945. South Carolina abolished the poll tax in 1951, and Tennessee did the same in 1953.

Despite the success of the National Committee to Abolish the Poll Tax, Alabama, Arkansas, Texas, and Virginia refused to abandon the levy. As the Civil Rights Movement spread across the South, increased pressure was directed at Congress to abolish the restrictive tax. As a result of this pressure, a constitutional amendment that would eliminate the use of poll taxes in federal elections was introduced. After fierce debate, the amendment passed the House and Senate, and in 1964, the required number of states ratified the Twenty-Fourth Amendment to the Constitution. The ability to charge voters to cast ballots in state and local elections came to an end in 1966 when the U.S. Supreme Court ruled that Virginia's poll tax violated a citizen's right to equal protection under the law as guaranteed by the Fourteenth Amendment to the Constitution. Although it did not accomplish its primary goal of stripping all African Americans of their right to vote, poll taxes were an important tool in preventing blacks from achieving full equality in the segregated South.

Wayne Dowdy

See also: Disenfranchisement; Voting Rights Act of 1965.

Further Reading

Key, V. O. *Southern Politics in State and Nation.* New York: Knopf, 1949.

Martin, Waldo E., Jr. and Patricia Sullivan, eds. *Civil Rights in the United States.* New York: Macmillan, 2000.

Roller, David C., and Robert W. Twyman, eds. *The Encyclopedia of Southern History.* Baton Rouge: Louisiana State University Press, 1979.

Prisons

Southern prisons during the Jim Crow era earned the "dubious distinction" of "America's worst prisons." Jim Crow prisons in the South took various, yet equally brutal, forms—a traditional penitentiary, a penal farm, a former slave plantation, brickyards, or temporary road camps. The prisons were erected in forests, swamps, mines, brickyards, or levees, and the convicts were housed in tents, log forts, and rolling cages. Jim Crow punishment existed in two phases, during the leasing era, which ran from 1890 to the 1920s, and then in the state control system, from the 1920s to 1965. Distinctive in the penal history of this era, the use of state prisons to control black population are deeply rooted in the South.

Immediately after the Civil War, Southern states turned to the criminal justice system in order to control the newly freed slave population. They also needed a labor force to repair Civil War damages. Although Southern states had built penitentiaries before the Civil War, most of them were so badly damaged during the war that they were unusable. By the early 1900s, blacks comprised anywhere from 85 through 95 percent of the prison population, although they comprised no more than half of the total population in the South. Black men, women, and children were summarily convicted and delivered by the local sheriffs to a road camp, penal farm, or, less likely, a penitentiary. Moreover, the penitentiary philosophy—to change prisoners and make them productive citizens—did not fit the Southern perception of their prisoners who were still seen as former slaves and not equipped for reformation and change. The terms "slave," "convict," and "Negro" were interchangeable in the white Southerner's perceptions of blacks after the Civil War.

Leasing

On the surface, leasing appeared to address the issues of prisoner security and safety at a minimum cost to the state. Southern states, including Florida, Texas, Louisiana, Arkansas, Mississippi, Alabama, Georgia, and Tennessee, turned to a variety of leasing arrangements with private individuals and companies, wherein the state turned over the whole prison operation to a private entrepreneur. Virginia never leased its convicts, and the Carolinas did so tentatively and for a short time only. Some states expected the contractor to pay some amount to the state. Others literally gave away complete responsibility for the state prisoners without any monetary or state supervisory expectations; one state even paid the lessee to take the prisoners. Often states signed leases with one individually or organization.

Soon, the leasing of convicts became one of the most exploitative aspects of the prison system during Jim Crow. Prisoners were leased to build railroads, levees, and roads; to work in mines, brickyards, and turpentine camps; and to do agricultural work on former plantations. Conditions under the leasing system were particularly brutal and deadly. Since the lessees did not own the prisoners, they often did not care about their welfare. The life expectancy of convicts in the lease system ranged from 7 through 10 years. Prisoners died of overwork or of violence from the guards or each other, and an ever-growing population of black convicts allowed for the quick replacement of prisoners.

Leasing came to an end by the 1920s for a variety of reasons. In some states, it was no longer economical. In others, railroad building subsided, and road building was generally designated to local governments. Some states had a penitentiary that they used. As it was purported that many companies who leased prisoners had made millions, other states resumed control hoping such large profits would ensue to the state. Still, the change was not fueled by humanitarian concern for the prisoners. Instead, Southern states switched from leasing to chain gangs and prisons in order to transfer manufactured goods via convict labor to the public sector.

Penal Farm Model

After the 1920s, the two most common forms of punishment systems were the penal farms and the chain gangs. The penal farm is the most notorious type of prison system in the South. More than an agricultural production center, the penal farm followed the plantation model of imprisonment. It incorporated both a structure and philosophy of slave plantations, reinforcing black inferiority and subservience to white planters and prison guards. Though they emphasized economy and agricultural work, the penal farm used isolation and neglect of rehabilitation to break down the mostly black prisoners and inculcate convicts with a sense of worthlessness. The purest form of the plantation model of imprisonment emerged in Arkansas, Louisiana, Mississippi, and Texas. Louisiana and Mississippi eventually established one geographical location for its penal farms, while Arkansas used two and Texas used multiple sites. Angola, Louisiana, is now 18,000 acres, while Parchman, Mississippi, was once 20,000 acres. The two farms in Arkansas, Tucker for white convicts and Cummins for black women and men, were located on 4,500 acres and 16,600 acres, respectively.

Although the type of agricultural work has varied through the years, depending upon the economy, natural disasters, and technological developments, the majority of prisoners at these farms worked in the fields. To this day, prisoners admitted to Angola must spend their first 90 days in the fields. The geographical isolation of these farms also served multiple functions. Largely kept out of the public eye, isolation of the prison led to the horrific conditions. On occasion, news reports would filter out and reach the national press. Investigating committees would visit and make recommendations, most often to no avail. No fewer than five recommendations, beginning in the 1930s, were made to move the women prisoners out of Angola. They were not moved until 1961, and not removed from Angola's administration until almost a decade later.

The prevailing belief about the limits of rehabilitation helped maintain bad conditions. Neither state nor federal courts interfered with prison business until the late

Prisoners on a chain gang stand outside a log cabin at their work camp in 1898. The use of prison labor made most state prison systems profitable. (Library of Congress)

1960s. Furthermore, agricultural work was believed to be suited to the limited ability of the imprisoned classes, mostly African Americans and Mexican Americans. Such practices had the effect of perpetuating segregation, as black and Mexican American prisoners were then limited to agricultural work once they were released. The emphasis on maximizing product, coupled with the long-held beliefs about black inferiority, precluded the development of a reform movement or rehabilitation of prisoners.

Convict Road Gang

Spurred by the "good road" movement of the 1920s, chain gangs and road gangs emerged all throughout the South. Generally, county criminal justice agencies oversaw the Southern road gangs, also known as chain gangs. For example, the state of Alabama ran the chain gang system. Alabama's road gang was initially all-black, and even when some white prisoners were introduced, they were always a minority in both number and proportion of convicts, and they were maintained in separate camps. Conditions were hard and exploitative; discipline was often brutal, but not as deadly as under the lease system. Guards routinely whipped prisoners with a three-inch strap, until Alabama outlawed the practice in 1962. Initially, men were housed in portable wooden barracks and sometimes rolling cages. By the mid-1930s, road camps were standardized with wooden buildings that included dormitories, with showers, a mess hall kitchen, and hot and cold running water.

Gender and Race in Southern Prison Systems

States immediately classified all inmates upon their entrance into the system. They were separated according to age, gender, and dangerousness of offense. These classification systems in the South were consistent with assumptions about race and echoed nineteenth-century notions about gendered divisions of labor. Usually, young black male prisoners were sent to do the most strenuous work tasks on the plantation prisons and road gangs, while white prisoners were sent to do industrial or clerical jobs. Both black and white women worked in gender-specific jobs such as washing and sewing uniforms. When needed, however, black women worked alongside the men in the fields, whereas white women usually did no fieldwork. Initially, Louisiana classified prisoners into four categories, beginning with first-class men (almost entirely black) who were assigned to the most arduous labor, and ending with fourth-class men, who were assigned to the hospital. Almost all white men and women were classified as fourth class, although some white men worked on the plantations and levee camps as clerks. When the crop demanded it, all classes of prisoners labored in fields, particularly during the sugar harvest.

Gendered divisions of labor were also segregated. Black women served as cooks, laundresses, and seamstresses exclusively. They also hoed sugar cane stumps and sorted tobacco leaves in the tobacco barn. During leasing in Alabama, black women worked alongside black men in lumber camps, mining camps, and rock quarries. White women sewed uniforms and bedding, or worked in the canneries. Mississippi employed both black and white women as trustees armed with rifles.

The system of Jim Crow in the prison system rationalized that African Americans and Mexican Americans had limited abilities and could do only physical labor. Since black and Mexican American convicts numbered in the majority of prisoners, Alabama, for example, not only used the bulk of the black male population to create the convict road labor force; they designated the convicts on the road gangs to do the most strenuous maintenance work. Black convicts did the weed cutting, shoulder work on the paved roads, and the most arduous work of all—breaking and crushing rock in the quarries, while the free white laborers working alongside them operated the heavy equipment and the trucks. Although it was in use only from 1883 until 1917, one penitentiary in Texas held only white men, and the inmates worked entirely in factories. The Louisiana penitentiary in Baton Rouge housed mainly white men who made the prisoners' uniforms and sewed flags.

Organization and Security

With a structure similar to an antebellum plantation, Southern prisons in Jim Crow amassed several thousand black workers supervised by a small group of rural lower-class whites, who, in turn, worked directly under the direction of sheriffs and wardens. Convicts worked from sunup to sundown, or as they said, from "can to can't." Plagued by boll weevils, floods, and other natural disasters, many Southern states had not made the anticipated profits since the state took over from the lease system. In a cost-savings measure, they turned to the "trusty" convict system. Paid guards were fired and convicts would guard other convicts.

The use of trustees also extended to the living quarters in the prison camp. On the Parchment, Mississippi, prison plantation, prisoners were housed in a number of camps. Each camp had one sergeant, and two assistant sergeants. The sergeant was equivalent to the slave plantation's overseer. He was in charge of the work schedules, disciplining the convicts, and setting the work routine. One assistant sergeant oversaw the fields and functioned as the driver. Called the "rider" in Arkansas, he determined the work quota for the men in the fields. The other assistant sergeant was responsible for the barracks. A number of trusty-shooters watched over the regular convicts, known as gunmen, (rank-men in Arkansas) who worked in the fields. In most circumstances, trusty-shooters and gunmen did not communicate with each other.

Guards and wardens heavily supervised male convicts working in the fields. A typical scenario called for two "high-powers" armed with carbines on horseback and at least three pairs of "shotguns" on foot accompanying the line at different intervals. Usually one pair of guards stood watch some distance from the rear in case of trouble. All these guards were prisoners, or what are commonly called convict-guards. The convict-guards had different ranks and concomitant levels of power, dependent upon the type of prison and work that they supervised. Convict-guards also may have had the ticket to their own release. Occasionally, a convict-guard who shot an escaping prisoner could be rewarded with his freedom. When the federal courts intervened in prison business in the early 1970s, the convict guard or trusty system was declared the worst abuse of power maintained in the Southern prisons.

Treatment and Discipline

Punishment in the penitentiaries, penal farms, and road gangs was brutal and occasionally deadly. Death rates were staggeringly high during leasing. For instance, 216 prisoners died in 1896 in Louisiana, nearly 20 percent of the 1,152 prisoners in the state. Yet in Louisiana State Penitentiary's Biennial Report of the Board of Control for the years 1896–1897, Warden W. H. Reynaud claimed no responsibility for the 1896 death rate but only the 6 percent death rate in 1897, maintaining that he was not appointed warden until August 1896. Since the majority of the prisoners were leased out, his argument that there were no deaths under his watch was correct only in the abstract. Prisoners spoke of killings that happened in camps that were almost hidden away. Scandals of prisoners being beaten to death by sadistic whipping bosses emerged in the other Southern states. Although mortality rates generally fell after the states took control of their prisoners, stories continued about cruel treatment, torture, and beatings under state control, sometimes administered by convict guards and sometimes by free guards. Although figures are not available for Alabama convict mortality rates, the convicts were susceptible to horrific mining disasters. One of the most famous, the Banner Coal Mine tragedy, resulted in 122 convict deaths.

Corporal punishment was the most common penalty for infractions; it was also most often applied without concern for the welfare of the convict. Leather straps known as "Black Annie" in Mississippi and "Old Caesar" in Texas were used for the whippings. Mississippi's "Black Annie" was three feet long and six inches wide. In one year alone, there were 1,547 floggings at Angola, with a total of 23,889 blows. Generally, guards administered whippings on the convict's bare flesh. Men and women alike were required to remove their shirts and/or pull down their pants for the lashings. In order to strike fear or to maintain strict order, guards dispensed punishments in public, requiring convicts to count the number of stripes out loud and in unison.

Prisoners' Resistance

Although they lived under conditions of extreme oppression, Southern prisoners did not always cooperate with the authorities. They used both covert and overt techniques to resist. Whether in penitentiaries, on the plantation prisons or road gangs, prisoners stole, committed arson, faked illness, engaged in sabotage, horribly mutilated themselves, participated in riots and work stoppages, and escaped. Escapes were exceptionally high under the leasing system, as opportunities in the camps and on the farms were greater than inside the penitentiary walls. For instance, from 1872 to 1874, 881 convicts entered the Tennessee prison system. During the same time, 95 escaped. Prisoners, primarily white prisoners, wrote memoirs and some wrote letters to the press revealing the horrible conditions under which they lived and worked. Other prisoners used collective action to start riots.

Although there were few incidents labeled as "riots" in the South, a series of incidents that forced authorities to reform conditions took place. In the "heel-slashing incident" of the early 1950s, 37 white prisoners at Angola, Louisiana, cut their Achilles tendons over two separate occasions to protest work conditions and fears that they would be beaten to death if they went out to the field. In 1935, a group of white Texas prisoners maimed themselves, two by chopping off a lower leg entirely. Self-mutilations became more common over the next decade or more in Texas. The Texas prisoners stated the same reasons that the Louisiana prisoners did—they were afraid of being beaten to death in the fields because they could not make it under the grueling work conditions.

Prisoners also resisted using covert techniques. On the plantation prisons and on the road gangs, convicts used work songs to accompany gang work. Work songs were used exclusively by African American male prisoners. Although black women sang prison songs, there is no record of them using the songs in the fields as the men did. Prison songs functioned to pass the time, pace the work, and provide safety while doing dangerous tasks and gave the men some control over their daily lives. Convicts could protest by singing things that could not be said in ordinary conversation. They expressed tension, frustration, and anger.

Work songs had a structure, the call-response pattern. The "caller," or work group leader, shouted a phrase and the gang responded. In this manner, the leader slowed down the pace when he noticed that some of the men were having trouble keeping up with the work. All the men had to keep up at the same rate, or they would be beaten. The songs regulated the pace of the teams and the strokes of the axes so that they would not cut each other's limbs. A good work song leader did not necessarily have to have a good voice, but he had to be loud. He also had to know the work and the ability of the men on his gang in order to guide them from sunup to sundown without being injured or beaten.

Gender and Housing

Even as separate women's facilities (reformatories) were being built for women up north, between 1870 and 1930, there were no women's reformatories in the Southern states. In Southern penitentiaries, women could be found anywhere from cells at the end of a male cell block, to a cell block of their own, to a building of their own, which sometimes was located close to the male buildings and sometimes further away. Women remained under the administration of the men's institution well into the 1960s.

During the leasing era and under state control, women were sent to the plantations, mining camps, railroads and road gangs. Sometimes they worked alongside the men. Other times, a small group of female convicts cooked and washed for the leased men. When sharing penal farms with men, the women were particularly vulnerable to physical brutality and sexual assault from prison guards and male convicts. On the plantation prisons, women were housed at a separate camp, situated some distance from the men's camps. However, the security was quite lax, and there was considerable unsupervised interaction between the men and women. Prisoners' memoirs report that men and women met each other in all kinds of secluded places on the prison grounds. At Angola, they met in the sugar cane fields when the cane was tall enough.

Although a married couple was often assigned to supervise the women's camps, the husband often had single unsupervised control over the women. Men supervised women in their work places—the fields, the sewing rooms, and in the canneries. Angola's punishment reports reveal that men administered floggings to the female convicts on their bare backs and breasts. Finally when women worked in the fields alongside men, they were required to answer the call of nature right there in the fields in front of the men.

Marianne Fisher-Giorlando

See also: Disenfranchisement; Jim Crow.

Further Reading

Ayers, Edward L. *Vengeance & Justice. Crime and Punishment in the 19th-Century American South.* New York: Oxford University Press, 1984.

Carleton, Mark T. *Politics and Punishment. The History of the Louisiana State Penal System.* Baton Rouge: Louisiana State University Press, 1971.

Mancini, Matthew. *One Dies, Get Another. Convict Leasing in the American South.* Columbia: University of South Carolina Press, 1996.

Oshinsky, David M. *"Worse than Slavery": Parchman Farm and the Ordeal of Jim Crow Justice.* New York: The Free Press, 1996.

Rafter, Nicole Hahn. *Partial Justice: Women, Prisons and Social Control.* New Brunswick, NJ: Transaction Press. 1990.

R

Racial Customs and Etiquette

Racial customs and etiquette predated the period generally designated as the Jim Crow era. The forced physical separation of blacks and whites associated with the period began and ended in the North before the Civil War and pervaded the West and Midwest throughout the period of westward expansion in the United States. Jim Crow was legalized in the South by the U.S. Supreme Court in *Plessy v. Ferguson* (1896), which declared "separate but equal" to be constitutional and permitted the segregation of blacks and whites on railroads in Louisiana. The ruling provided a legal basis for the development of intricate rules of behavior that applied to all areas of life. Their collective design was to reinforce white supremacy and relegate blacks to second-class citizenship. Such customs varied according to gender, geography, hue, and social climate, and they were more rigidly followed in public situations than in private ones. But they were applied to all known African Americans regardless of their educational or social standing. Given the debilitating, even humiliating, nature of these rules, African Americans sought legal and creative ways to counter their negative social, political, and economic impact. They also made a sustained effort to curb, if not altogether neutralize, the psychological impact of such customs, especially on black children.

As Jim Crow laws were initiated with systems of transportation, many of the first rules of etiquette emerged in this area and quickly expanded to include other public spaces where blacks and whites encountered each other from day to day. Regardless of social position, identifiably black passengers were forced to ride in Jim Crow cars, which were often unclean and lacked the comforts of those carrying white passengers. When separate accommodations were not possible, as was sometimes the case with city buses, blacks were to sit at the back of the bus. They were also expected to relinquish their seats if whites exceeded the capacity of the section provided for them. In places of business, whites were served first even if black customers were the first to arrive. Black customers were not allowed to try on certain clothing items, particularly shoes, nor could they return such items once purchased because white store owners feared that whites would not buy products that had been worn by blacks.

In public hospitals, blacks and whites were cared for in separate wards. Black nurses were permitted to care for white patients, but never the reverse, although white doctors were permitted to treat black patients in the colored sections of segregated hospitals. Racial custom nonetheless dictated that white doctors refrain from showing compassion when treating black patients. Blacks in need of blood transfusions were never to be given blood from whites. The reverse was also true. Black writers of the era, and those who wrote fictional works set during the Jim Crow period, often believed this deleterious act captured the quintessence of racism. Lillian Bertha Horace's *Angie Brown* (1949) opens with the death of the protagonist's child, which occurred because the hospital refused to give blood that had been drawn from whites to a black child. Similarly, Toni Morrison's *Song of Solomon* (1978) opens with a black woman in labor in front of "No Mercy Hospital," the name members of the black community gave the hospital because of its treatment of blacks.

An elaborate set of customs governed intimate relations between blacks and whites during the Jim Crow era. Thomas Dixon's novel *The Clansman* (1905) and the subsequent movie based on it, *The Birth of a Nation* (1915), underscored and reinforced white men's profound fear of interracial mixing, namely between black men and white women, as many white men continued to maintain intimate relationships with black women after the emancipation. Rules on interracial relationships were never applied as strictly to white men as they were to black men during the Jim Crow era.

Black males, regardless of the age, were not to even look at white women, nor were they to touch them. Even an accidental brush was considered to be a serious offense. If a black man saw a white woman approaching on a sidewalk, he was to step off the sidewalk until the woman passed. Black men and boys were beaten, castrated, tarred, feathered, and lynched for purportedly getting out their place with white women. Black men had to stay on constant alert for their safety, especially if a white woman in the vicinity had purportedly been raped. White men, on the other hand, engaged in intimate relations with black women without prosecution or public controversy.

White women who maintained intimate relationships with black men were in danger of social ostracism or disinheritance. When pregnancy resulted, the babies were generally aborted or given up for adoption. Many white women whose affairs with black men were discovered cried rape to protect themselves from disgrace or public censure. Gwendolyn Brooks's "Ballad of Pearl May Lee" (1945) offers one of the most riveting presentations of the peril black men faced when they dared have an affair with white women.

Publicly, white men went to great lengths to protect white female purity, but privately, many continued to have intimate relationships with black women, and they did so without prosecution or public controversy. Such relationships were often explored by black and white fiction writers of the period, with the story usually ending in tragedy. Real-life examples also abounded, with one of the most famous cases involving Senator Strom Thurmond, a staunch segregationist, who fathered a daughter, Essie Mae Washington, by a black maid. Given the historic vulnerability of black women to sexual aggression, many black parents from emancipation onward set out to educate their daughters to preclude their having to "work in a white woman's kitchen," where they were often targets of sexual aggression.

In the rural Jim Crow South, racial etiquette was highly articulated and localized. Because most rural black Southerners were farmers, sharecroppers, or tenants, the landlord-tenant relationship shaped most interactions. As a result, segregation, economic exploitation, and oppression were more pronounced in rural areas than in cities.

As the racial composition of towns ranged from predominantly white to predominantly black, variations on the theme existed. In predominantly black towns or predominantly black sections of predominantly white towns, racial etiquette was important when occasional white visitors came for various purposes or when blacks ventured outside a given predominantly black enclave. Writer and anthropologist Zora Neale Hurston often gave primacy to such places in her creative writings. Some predominantly white towns were off limits to blacks. Custom, if not the law, precluded blacks' entering them. Sometimes warning signs were posted on the outskirts of towns to discourage black visitors, such as "Niggers, read and run." Even though there were no laws insisting that blacks not enter, custom dictated as much. Blacks learned from experience and by word of mouth which places were off limits.

Boundaries were less rigid in other rural spaces. Country stores, rural roads, and cotton gins were usually not segregated. Certain recreational activities were also not segregated. Young black and white men sometimes drank and gambled together at cockfights, saloons, and card games. At mutual aid events, white landowners and black hired hands frequently worked together as white farm wives and black domestics prepared meals for the laborers. But in such cases, racial etiquette was decidedly pronounced. African Americans had limited access to most small-town retail shops, but some business, such as barbershops that served whites, were out of bounds. Different from cities, most rural towns had few buses, hotels, or restaurants, all of which provided distinct stages for blacks and whites to play their prescribed roles.

Whites in rural and urban areas generally withheld everyday courtesies from blacks. They did not invite blacks to their homes as guests. Black workers and domestics had to go to the back door of whites' houses, although this rule was not universally applied. Visits and courtesy were avoided because they implied equality, a concept contrary to the racial hierarchy that Jim Crow was designed to reinforce. Whites insisted that blacks use titles that showed deference or respect. Black men and women were to address white men and women as "Sir" and "Ma'am," respectively. In less formal situations, black men might also refer to white men of standing as "boss" or "cap'n" without fear of reprisal. Whites, on the other hand, were never to address black men respectfully. Black men regardless of social standing were addressed by their first names or called "boy," "nigger," or "niggra," a polite substitute for the aforementioned derogatory term. Black men were often called by any name a white interlocutor might conjure on a moment's notice, with the name "Jack" being one of the most common substitutes.

White women sometimes permitted their black servants and acquaintances to address them by their first names, but only if they prefaced the name with the title "Miss." Black women, on the other hand, were never addressed respectfully as "Miss" or "Mrs." The term "wench," which dated back to slavery, still appeared in some legal documents during the Jim Crow period. Although educated whites sometimes referred to black women collectively as "colored ladies," black women were generally referred to as "auntie," "girl," "gal," or by their first names, which black women generally resented. Texas native Lillian Bertha Horace, an educator and writer, noted in her diary that she felt "hurt, indignant, disgusted" when the greeting in a "long formal letter on definite business" opened "Dear Lilly."

White men were careful not to publicly perform any courteous act that hinted that they treated black women like "ladies," a category reserved for white women. They refrained from such polite habits as addressing black women respectfully as "Miss" or "Mrs.," carrying or lifting heavy packages for black women, helping them into street cars, holding doors open for black women and allowing them to enter ahead first, tipping or removing their hats in the presence of black women, or retrieving on their behalf an item that might have fallen to the floor or ground. The lack of courtesy often approached outright discourtesy.

Educational institutions were largely segregated in the Jim Crow South, but black and white educators and administrators still had occasion to interact with each other, particularly during summer certification periods and campus visitations by white supervisors. White officials visiting black schools were often strict, intimidating, and critical as opposed to helpful. Even beyond the South, black students and scholars were not spared the inconveniences of race. In educational institutions in which blacks were admitted, they were often not acknowledged by their professors. Some white professors summarily failed black students, while others never granted black students a grade above "C." The few black scholars who found semipermanent posts at universities outside the South often could not dine in university faculty clubs, nor could they find hotel accommodations when they traveled to professional meetings. Black students, particularly those involved in extracurricular activities such as debate and athletics, faced the same dilemma. Professor Thomas Freeman and members of the Texas Southern University's highly acclaimed debate team had to establish living accommodations with families and religious organizations whenever they had to travel to competitions in the United States. Students, including Barbara Jordan, eventually the first congress woman in the United States, were coached to maintain their dignity despite the bias they faced.

Racist customs and etiquette also impacted blacks in the U.S. military, whose unique position as defenders of the nation and its democratic ideals made their sustained encounter with white supremacy particularly unsettling. Black men in uniform instilled pride in African Americans who appreciated the significance of their sacrifice but incited deep resentment in whites committed to white supremacy. One of the most famous photographs of the Jim Crow era captures in still frame the lynched body of an African American soldier in uniform hanging from a noose in the midst of a crowd of jeering, angry whites.

The deep-seated resentment of white civilians was also evident on military bases, where black men were never treated as equals to white soldiers. They were in segregated units, attended separate training schools, and lived in segregated facilities. They were generally limited to service and supply units and were not allowed to command whites. They also had to bear with the indignities stemming from legalized subjugation. They were often called "nigger" and other derogatory names by their superiors, often mistreated, and generally subject to much harsher reprimand than their white counterparts. The Houston Riot of 1917 is perhaps the most historic event underscoring the tension that permeated such environments. The riot erupted on August 23, 1917, when black soldiers of the 24th Infantry, then stationed in Houston, Texas, armed themselves and challenged the beating of two fellow soldiers by local police. The event resulted in the largest court-martial held in the United States.

Black women in the U.S. military were denied equal treatment as well. They entered the U.S. military first as nurses, with Civil War nurse Susie King Taylor being among the first to record her experiences. During the Spanish-American War, most of the 32 black women recruited as nurses were sent to Santiago, Cuba, in July and August 1898, where they rendered service during the worst years of a yellow fever epidemic. Some black nurses were contracted by the surgeon general to serve in the Spanish-American War. Five black graduate nurses joined the army, according to records at the Tuskegee Institute. Black women nurses were also recruited from various hospitals and training centers in Chicago, Illinois; New Orleans, Louisiana; and Washington, D.C.

During World War I, many black nurses hoped to increase their chances of serving in the Army or Naval Nurse Corps by joining the American Red Cross. Eighteen black Red Cross nurses were offered assignments in Illinois and Ohio not long after the Armistice, but the end of the war precluded the planned assignment of black nurses to other camps. Those who served were limited to caring for German prisoners of war and black soldiers. By August 1919, all were released from duty.

During World War II, black women were permitted to join the nurse course, but their number was limited to 56. On June 25, 1941, President Franklin D. Roosevelt's Executive Order 8802 established the Fair Employment Practices Commission, which initiated the eradication of racial discrimination in the U.S. military. In June 1943, Congresswoman Frances Payne of Ohio introduced an amendment to the Nurse Training Bill to eradicate racial bias. Black women's enrollment in the Cadet Nurse Corps quickly mushroomed to 2,000.

In July 1944, the quota for black army nurses was eliminated, and on January 24, 1945, the U.S. Navy opened its doors to black women. Black women were also enlisted in the Women's Army Auxiliary Corps (WAAC), eventually renamed the Women's Army Corps (WAC), which employed 6,520 black women during the war. Black women also joined the Navy WAVES (Women Accepted for Volunteer Emergency Service) and the Coast Guard SPARS (derived from the Coast Guard motto "Semper Paratus," Latin for "Always Ready"). Similar to black men, black women were assigned to segregated living quarters, ate at separate tables, received segregated training, and used separate recreational facilities. They were not allowed to serve white American soldiers until intervention from Eleanor Roosevelt.

Racial etiquette and customs impacted the lives of black children as well. They learned the rules governing black and white relations by observation and through conversations with their parents and others. For example, Helen Green, the first black woman admitted into Methodist Hospital of the Dallas School of Professional Nursing, as a child wondered why the white woman whom her mother helped with canning never came to their house, especially given that Green's family had at least more space in their front yard for her and the white woman's little girl to play. She also wondered why the little girl always insisted on naming the games, creating the rules, and changing them for her benefit. Green essentially did not enjoy visits to the white woman's house because she was under constant pressure to be careful. The lessons she and other black children learned directly and indirectly were never easy to receive and were often painfully applied. The often-repeated statement "if I don't beat you, the white man will kill you" reflected the rationale some black parents living in Jim Crow cultures used to teach their children respect and even fear of authority, especially given that the ultimate face of authority was white.

Black parents nonetheless found creative ways to insist on a modicum of respect for their children by using titles as first names for their son and daughters, including "King," "Prince," "President," "Princess," "Queen," and "Duke." Others attempted to counter the psychological impact of sustained racism on their daughters by giving them black dolls to help them develop self-respect from their earliest days. Black parents, especially those of aspiring, middle and elite classes, attempted to instill racial pride and "race love" in their children by surrounding them with positive images of blacks, including pictures and Sunday School cards depicting black characters.

Many African Americans masked their displeasure with the racial etiquette and customs when in the company of whites. But they expressed their discontent in private, in their personal writings, or via the black press. The tenor of such relationships continued to change over time. Black domestics of the early twentieth century, for example, did not demonstrate the same deference to whites in public that their enslaved foremothers had shown, and subsequent generations of blacks found it increasingly difficult to respect the rules. Many even resorted to mocking them, sometimes with deadly results, as in the case of Emmett Till. With the help of early black activist scholars, professionals, professional organizations, fraternities, sororities, lodges, clubs, and churches, African Americans and their supporters eventually challenged the legal foundation of Jim Crow, the dismantling of which led to a gradual dissolution of the racial customs and etiquette that legalized discrimination had spawned.

Karen Kossie-Chernyshev

See also: Armed Forces; Minstrelsy.

Further Reading

Brooks, Gwendolyn. *A Street in Bronzeville.* New York: Harper and Row, 1945.

Delany, Sarah L., and A. Elizabeth Delany, with Amy Hill Hearth. *Having Our Say: Delany Sisters' First 100 Years.* New York: Dell, 1994.

Franklin, John Hope. *Mirror to America: The Autobiography of John Hope Franklin.* New York: Farrar, Straus and Giroux, 2005.

Green, Helen. *East Texas Daughter.* Fort Worth: Texas Christian University Press, 2003.

Haynes, Robert V. *A Night of Violence: The Houston Riot of 1917.* Baton Rouge: Louisiana State University Press, 1976.

Johnson, Kevin R. "The Legacy of Jim Crow: The Enduring Taboo of Black-White Romance." *Texas Law Review* 84, no. 3 (February 2006): 739–66. http://www.utexas.edu/law/journals/tlr/abstracts/84/84johnson.pdf (accessed September 2007).

Jones, Jacqueline. *Labor of Love, Labor of Sorrow: Black Women, Work and the Family from Slavery to the Present.* New York: Vintage Books, 1995.

Kossie-Chernyshev, Karen, ed. *Angie Brown.* Acton, MA: Copley Custom Publishing, 2008.

Kossie-Chernyshev, Karen, ed. *Diary of Lillian B. Horace.* New York: Pearson Custom Publishing, 2007.

Love, Spencie. *One Blood, The Death and Resurrection of Charles R. Drew.* Chapel Hill: University of North Carolina Press, 1996.

McGuire, Phillip, ed. *Taps for a Jim Crow Army: Letters from Black Soldiers in World War II.* Lexington: University of Kentucky Press, 1993.

Mitchell, Michele. *Righteous Propagation: African Americans and the Politics of Racial Destiny after Reconstruction.* Chapel Hill: University of North Carolina Press, 2004.

Patterson, Tiffany Ruby. *Zora Neale Hurston and a History of Southern Life.* Philadelphia: Temple University Press, 2005.

Sheldon, Kathryn S. "Brief History of Black Women in the Military." Women in Military Service for America Foundation Web site, http://womensmemorial.org/Education/BBH1998.html#2 (accessed September 2007).

Walker, Melissa. "Shifting Boundaries: Race Relations in the Rural Jim Crow South." In *African American Life in the Rural South, 1900–1950,* ed. R. Douglas Hurt, 81–107. Columbia: University of Missouri Press, 2003.

Reconstruction

Reconstruction refers to an attempt by the federal government to create a new society in the former Confederacy once slavery was eliminated as a basic element of society. Reconstruction began during the war, as Union armies came to control large areas of the South, and found their lines filled with "contrabands," as escaped slaves were termed. With the landowners largely absent, Union commanders began settling former slaves on the abandoned estates. By the end of the war in 1865, the federal government required former states of the Confederacy to adopt the Thirteenth Amendment, which abolished slavery, as a condition of readmittance to the Union.

However, the leaders of the states of the former Confederacy, predominantly the owners of large estates who had led the region into secession and war, began to regain political control of the South. States began adopting "Black Codes," which reduced freedmen, and even blacks who had never been slaves, to a status similar to slavery. Black Codes tied blacks to white landowners, and made a mockery of the constitutional elimination of slavery. Democrats in Georgia went so far as to elect Alexander Stephens, former vice president of the Confederacy, to the U.S. Senate. Enraged by a perceived arrogance of Southern Democrats, Republicans in Congress passed the Reconstruction Acts in 1867 and 1868, which suspended civil government in the former Confederacy and placed the states of the former Confederacy under military rule.

Part of the impetus for Reconstruction was the Republican need to ensure black men voted, as they would overwhelmingly vote Republican. Republicans controlled Congress, but almost all white Southerners were Democrats. Without the black vote in the South, the Republicans would lose control of Congress. The Radical Republicans in Congress were attempting to use the military to create a biracial society. The army ensured black men could vote, and they overwhelmingly voted Republican. Reconstruction state governments created the so-called Negro Militia, which would allow blacks and white Republicans to protect themselves from violent white supremacist groups. But the Radical Republicans never undertook land redistribution. The idea of breaking up the large estates of Southerners who had made war against the United States had been discussed at length, but never implemented. Thus, blacks had a share of political power as long as the federal troops remained in the South, but they had little economic power. The South was overwhelmingly agricultural, and most farmland was owned by white Democrats. Blacks remained economically dependent on the former slaveowners. Thus this nascent two-party, biracial, South would last only as long as federal troops ensured black men were able to vote, and Northern patience with Reconstruction had a limited life span. The rise of white terrorist groups such as the White League and the Ku Klux Klan, which attempted to use extralegal means to prevent blacks from voting, led Congress to pass the Force Act of 1870 and the Civil Rights Act of 1871, also known as the Ku Klux Klan Act. With this authority, the federal government aggressively countered white supremacist terrorist organizations.

Reconstruction saw the passage of two more amendments to the Constitution, which would form the basis for the legal arguments of the later Civil Rights Movement. These were the Fourteenth, in 1868, and the Fifteenth, in 1870. Under the Reconstruction governments that controlled the South, these amendments passed the required amount of states. The Fourteenth Amendment overturned the *Dred Scott v. Sandford* ruling of 1857, which declared that persons of African descent were not citizens. The amendment affirmed that blacks were citizens of their state and of the nation. The Fifteenth Amendment prevented the use of race or previous status as a slave as a factor in denying the right to vote.

In 1875, the U.S. Supreme Court ruling of *U.S. v. Cruikshank* curtailed the ability of the federal government to protect blacks in the South. The final end of Reconstruction came in the Compromise of 1877. As part of the Compromise, the federal government withdrew the few remaining troops from the South, in return for the Democratic backing of Rutherford B. Hayes for president. Northerners were tiring of the continued sectional strife, and the end of Reconstruction was popular in the North as well as in the white South. The federal government, powerless after *Cruikshank,* allowed white Democrats to regain control, and deferred to "Southern sensibilities" on race issues. For over half a century, Reconstruction would be interpreted as a tragic time when an overzealous federal government humiliated the South, and put in power a group of ignorant freedmen, corrupt carpetbaggers, and unscrupulous scalawags.

For white Democrats, Reconstruction was interpreted as the world turned upside down. Whites saw the decade of Reconstruction as a time of great suffering across the South, and saw the great tragedy of the South not in the two centuries of African slavery or even in the four years of bloody Civil War, but in the decade in which the federal government ensured black men could vote. Later, the historian William A. Dunning of Columbia University supported this idea of the white South suffering unimaginable horrors under Reconstruction. He gave birth to a field of interpretation, one that found its greatest popular dissemination in the characterization of Reconstruction state governments portrayed in the film *The Birth of a Nation* in 1915. Only beginning in the 1950s would historians begin to reevaluate Reconstruction, seeing it instead as an opportunity lost, a time when better decisions by the federal government could have perhaps prevented the disenfranchisement of blacks and the rise of Jim Crow.

Barry M. Stentiford

See also: Jim Crow; Ku Klux Klan.

Further Reading

Du Bois, W.E.B. *Black Reconstruction in America, 1860–1880.* New York: The Free Press, 1998.

Foner, Eric. *Reconstruction: America's Unfinished Revolution, 1863–1877.* New York: Harper and Row Publishers, 1988.

Olsen, Otto H., ed. *Reconstruction and Redemption in the South.* Baton Rouge: Louisiana State University Press, 1980.

Stampp, Kenneth M. *The Era of Reconstruction, 1865–1877.* New York: Vintage Books, 1967.

Red Summer

In the summer of 1919, a series of race riots swept across the country. Triggered by mounting racial tensions, the riots resulted in the deaths and injuries of hundreds of African Americans, mostly at the hands of white mobs. Riots took place in at least 26 and as many as 56 cities, with smaller lynch mobs responsible for many more black deaths. The most infamous riots occurred in Charleston, South Carolina; Chicago, Illinois; Longview, Texas; Washington, D.C.; Knoxville, Tennessee; Omaha, Nebraska; and Elaine, Arkansas. Although each riot was sparked by an individual incident, the violence was rooted in competition for jobs, housing, and union wages in Northern urban areas. Ongoing labor struggles and fears of radical political organizations also factored into the hostilities in both the North and South. Just as in other forms of interracial aggression, much of the bloodshed was the result of rumors and lack of proper government intervention. Black journalist and civil rights leader James Weldon Johnson dubbed the season of destruction and violence the "Red Summer" of 1919.

The United States experienced massive change during World War I. Large numbers of African Americans moved to Northern cities, seeking greater employment opportunities in the booming wartime economy and hoping to leave behind the segregation and discrimination of the Jim Crow South. Black workers found factory jobs that had been vacated by laborers who had joined the military effort. White workers often resented the intrusion of black laborers and excluded them from unionization efforts. Employers used the interracial rift and the availability of black workers to hire blacks as strikebreakers. Although black workers did not necessarily want to challenge the unions, they knew that taking jobs as strikebreakers was often the only way to break into a white-unionized industry. Even if their wages were lower than those of unionized workers, black workers were often still earning more money than they did in other occupations.

The influx of black migrants also forced greater competition for housing. African Americans frequently moved into urban neighborhoods that had been dominated by European immigrants. Although it was possible for blacks and other ethnic groups to coexist peacefully, the large numbers of black residents triggered fear in their neighbors. As European immigrants became more commonly accepted as "white," they had greater mobility and could move out of the inner city into less-crowded neighborhoods. During World War I, however, there was little new housing available, and existing buildings often had exorbitant rental rates. Contests over living conditions extended to competition for parks, beaches, and other leisure spaces. Housing and living conditions, educational limitations, and job competition all contributed to rising interracial tensions.

In the early twentieth century, African Americans were organizing as a group in new ways. Organizations such as the National Association for the Advancement of Colored People (NAACP) advocated for equal rights and racial integration. The NAACP's official journal, the *Crisis,* shared stories of injustice and lynchings across the country, and the group lobbied extensively for federal antilynching legislation. The vast number of publications such as the *Chicago Defender,* by the black press and intended for black readers, advocated for greater efforts to end racial injustice.

As black workers left the South for greater opportunities in Northern war industries or to serve as soldiers, the dwindling numbers of Southern laborers gained leverage over their employers. Many sharecroppers demanded higher wages and the ability to regulate their own families, purchases, and leisure time. One of the primary fears of white Southerners was "political agitators" who led local blacks to demand new rights. These agitators, especially the NAACP, were blamed for disrupting long-standing racial relations in the South, even though these relationships were typically based on white dominance and the threat of or actual violence against black workers. White elites tried to prevent their workers from listening to such radical ideas and urged black residents to maintain the old racial order. Stirring up long-standing Southern fears of black and white miscegenation, white leaders argued that political agitators were primarily interested in interracial marriage. As a whole, rural white elites feared the rise of black workers, while in urban areas ethnic immigrants and native-born whites feared a loss of status.

As large numbers of soldiers returned from Europe at the beginning of 1919, even greater competition for jobs, housing, and resources ensued. Returning veterans found that black workers had filled many formerly white jobs and had vastly improved their economic circumstances during the war. White veterans wanted to reclaim their jobs and asked the federal government to guarantee employment and pensions. The American Legion veterans' organization gained tremendous influence in politics and society.

Having proven their loyalty to the United States through their service, returning black soldiers expected to be able to vote in the South and end discriminatory practices. Leaders throughout the country feared that returning black soldiers had high social aspirations and would disrupt prior patterns of racial segregation and discrimination. More than anything, white leaders feared that black veterans would use their military knowledge to forcefully challenge the status quo. The NAACP and black publications had indeed created a "New Negro" who was willing to fight back against injustice. With the rising expectations for racial justice came a rise in black militancy and organization. White-owned newspapers typically interpreted self-defense as black defiance of law and advocated for harsher penalties.

Another important factor in the Red Summer of 1919 was the ongoing Red Scare. Many felt that the recent Bolshevik Revolution of 1917 and high numbers of European immigrants left the United States vulnerable to radical forces. Both government and corporate leaders believed that unionization and contentious labor relations between black and white workers and wealthy white capitalists could cause insurrection. More radical labor unions such as the Industrial Workers of the World (IWW) were open to interracial unionization, which critics feared would lead to both race and class warfare. Returning white veterans used racial hostilities and the Red Scare to gain tremendous social power and discredit anyone who advocated for racial justice.

Perhaps the most well-known riot of the Red Summer occurred in Chicago on July 27–August 2, 1919. A black youth, Eugene Williams, had accidentally crossed the invisible line separating a black swimming area from a white one at Lake Michigan's 25th Street beach. White swimmers threw rocks at Williams until he drowned, but white police officers refused to arrest the instigators. Black and white mobs attacked each other, and the fighting went on for five days. Unlike other riots, the violence was not restricted to just one section of town, but roamed widely over black and white residential and business districts. At least 38 people died and more than 500 were injured. At least 1,000 African Americans were homeless due to fire and other property damage.

The labor unrest of 1919 revealed itself in the steel strike of September and October. Capitalist employers wanted to break the unions, not just end the strike. Knowing that the sight of black workers would make the white unionists furious, corporate leaders hired many black strikebreakers, especially in the area surrounding Chicago. On October 4, black strikebreakers in Gary, Indiana, crossed the picket lines and were attacked by strikers. Two days of rioting followed, and federal troops finally restored order. Corporate rhetoric linked striking workers and black strikebreakers to radical organizations, and public opinion turned against the workers. Capitalists even blamed middle-class African Americans for not controlling the lower class. Government officials soon voted to restrict immigration and enforce segregation to minimize further disorder.

Fear of agitators initiated violence in many cities and minimized the power of unionization and black collective action in the South. In an effort to keep local blacks under control, a White Citizens Council in Leggett, Texas, violently forced the local NAACP president, T. S. Davis, to leave town in August 1919. The town instituted a curfew for black residents and forbade them to hold meetings of any kind. Similarly, a mob in Anderson, South Carolina, forced three NAACP leaders out of town and the branch disbanded. White violence and intimidation against NAACP branches throughout the South greatly undermined the organization's power.

One of the largest massacres of African Americans during the Red Summer took place in the rural delta region of Elaine, Arkansas. There, black sharecroppers and tenant farmers attempted to organize a labor union, the Progressive Farmers and Household Union, in hopes of securing a fair share of their cotton crop. The sharecroppers had earned some money during the wartime rise in wages, which threatened the dominance of white plantation owners. When planters evicted tenant farmers from their homes in the fall, the sharecroppers joined the union and held meetings to discuss ways to fight back. In October, a group of white men fired into a black union meeting in Hoop Spur and the members returned fire, killing one man and wounding another.

White residents quickly spread word of an armed "insurrection" by black workers. The local sheriff deputized men for a posse, and the governor asked for and received 500 federal troops to quell the supposed rebellion. Along with the posse and troops, vigilantes covered a 200-mile radius and killed as many as 200 African American men, women, and children. Some of the victims were burned alive. Many black people were charged and convicted of crimes in connection with the presumed uprising, including 12 men convicted of murder. The highest number of post-riot trials followed the Elaine Massacre, although some convictions were later overturned by the U.S. Supreme Court. Violence, however, continued to operate as the primary social order in the region.

The role of the police and state or federal troops illustrates the vast differences in justice and protection throughout the country. In the Chicago Race Riot of 1919, the police were hampered by a lack of sufficient numbers. African American residents were wary of the police due to long-time injustices, and their hostility was confirmed when white policemen did not always stop white violence against black residents. White police officers focused their attention on Chicago's Black Belt, leaving other areas of the city vulnerable to even higher casualty rates. The Chicago riot ended only with the arrival of the state militia to restore order. However, only the white militia was called out. City leaders feared that black veterans in the state militia would actually lead black citizens to further violence rather than quell the riots.

In some cases, such as Charleston, South Carolina, and Norfolk, Virginia, sailors and soldiers initiated the rioting. Animosities between different races and different branches of the military frequently became violent, and innocent bystanders were often caught in the melee. In Elaine, Arkansas, local white officials controlled the police force and the state militia and quickly deputized many local white landowners, with disastrous results for the black residents.

In other locations, such as Omaha, Nebraska, the military was more effective in controlling the violence. General Leonard Wood was particularly noted for his quick imposition of martial law, his clear chain of command, and his better communication with civilian authorities. He censored news released and prevented newspapers from printing questionable or inflammatory rumors. Most importantly, General Wood prevented his federal troops from participating in the violence, as many local or state troopers were more likely to do. In many instances, later investigatory bodies reprimanded the mayor or other leaders for waiting too long to call in military assistance.

Records of arrests and ensuing legal actions demonstrate the ongoing racial discrimination in the country. Police were more likely to arrest black rioters than white ones, and black rioters on trial were more likely to be convicted. In a time of fear, prejudice, and hostility, African Americans suffered greatly at the hands of their neighbors, their employers, and officials sworn to protect them. The call for black resistance was necessary and timely during the Red Summer of 1919.

Shannon Smith Bennett

See also: Great Migration; World War II.

Further Reading

Arnesen, Eric, ed. *The Black Worker: Race, Labor, and Civil Rights since Emancipation.* Urbana: University of Illinois Press, 2007.

Gilje, Paul A. *Rioting in America.* Bloomington: Indiana University Press, 1996.

Grimshaw, Allen D. "Actions of Police and the Military in American Race Riots." *Phylon* 24 (1963): 271–89.

Schneider, Mark Robert. *African Americans in the Jazz Age: A Decade of Struggle and Promise.* Lanham, MD: Rowman and Littlefield, 2006.

Slotkin, Richard. *Lost Battalions: The Great War and the Crisis of American Nationality.* New York: H. Holt & Co., 2005.

Tuttle, William M., Jr. *Race Riot: Chicago in the Red Summer of 1919.* New York: Atheneum, 1970.

Wormser, Richard. "Red Summer 1919." The Rise and Fall of Jim Crow, Public Broadcasting Service Web site. http://www.pbs.org/wnet/jimcrow/stories_events_red.html (accessed July 2007).

Republican Party

The Republican Party founded in 1854, and in just six years became one of the two major American political parties that have dominated U.S. politics until the present day. The party at its inception contained former Whigs, Free Soil supporters, and Northern Democrats unhappy with their party's stand on the issue of slavery. In essence, the Republican Party maintained the traditional Whig platform of a protective tariff, a national bank, and support for internal improvements, but another major tenet of the new party was opposition to slavery, specifically opposition to the expansion of the institution of slavery into the territories. The Republican opposition to slavery stemmed from several sources; many Republicans opposed slavery on moral grounds, while others sought to preserve the territories to the West as a white man's country. The election of Abraham Lincoln and the outbreak of the Civil War would make the Republican Party's opposition to slavery much more explicit, such that the party platform came to support emancipation and then political and civil rights for African Americans. This transformation was gradual, with Lincoln slowly coming to support immediate emancipation long after many Republican leaders in Congress.

Given that emancipation occurred under a Republican president and the Republican Party's support for political and civil rights for African Americans, the Republican Party gained the loyalty of former slaves for generations to come. Republicans staffed the Reconstruction governments that existed in the South on the conclusion of the Civil War. African Americans from both the North and South held prominent positions in many of these state Reconstruction governments, serving as state legislators and, in some cases, as lieutenant governors and secretaries of state. In addition, under Reconstruction, Southern states elected a number of black Republicans to Congress. African Americans made up a key part of the Republican Party within the South, and support for African American rights was a major tenet of the national Republican Party.

In 1877, the last Reconstruction governments in Florida, South Carolina, and Louisiana fell. In essence, the Republican Party chose to end the Reconstruction project despite the shortcomings of Southern society, due to increasing unpopularity in the North and the high cost of keeping federal troops in the states. With the Democratic Party in firm control of Southern state governments, state legislatures began to curtail the voting and civil rights of African Americans over the course of the 1890s and 1900s, enacting Jim Crow laws that curtailed the spirit of the Fourteenth and Fifteenth Amendments to the Constitution that the Republican Party had worked so hard to enact. The Republican Party did little on the federal level to ensure that the rights of African Americans in the South were protected. Despite this, however, the Republican Party continued to receive overwhelming black support, and African Americans, particularly under Republican president Theodore Roosevelt, received appointments within the federal bureaucracy.

Under William Howard Taft, patronage for blacks was sharply curtailed. Taft gave state's elected representatives a de facto veto over those in federal posts such that Democrats from the South began to bar blacks from federal jobs in their section. In addition, Republicans continued to turn a blind eye to systemic extralegal violence and the violations of black civil rights in the South. In part, this was done in an attempt to gain whites to the Republican Party in the South, though it had little success, as the white South remained staunchly Democratic. Blacks continued to remain in the Republican Party and in some measure, in limited appointments, and in expansive rhetoric, the Republican Party continued to support their cause of equality before the law.

Under Democratic president Woodrow Wilson, segregation was instituted in the federal civil service, and upon the election of Republican Warren G. Harding, the practice continued. The Republican Party failed to pass antilynching legislation despite repeated calls from the black community and prominent Republican leaders. Under Republican presidents Harding, Calvin Coolidge, and Herbert Hoover, the Republican Party consistently failed to meet the demands of the black community as expressed by the National Association for the Advancement of Colored People. This series of presidents, beyond appointments, failed to act on black issues, in part to draw more white Southerners to the party; over time, this destroyed the traditional attachment of African Americans to the Republican Party.

Franklin D. Roosevelt's presidency brought the majority of African Americans firmly into the Democratic Party, where they remained into the twenty-first century. While his presidency failed to address voting and civil rights, New Deal programs helped African Americans, providing jobs and economic assistance. In addition, Roosevelt made a concerted effort to win black support personally. Roosevelt convened a panel of black advisors, called the Black Cabinet. His wife Eleanor Roosevelt in particular actively pushed civil rights issues. Despite the efforts of Eleanor Roosevelt and several other prominent Democratic leaders, President Roosevelt failed to embrace a civil rights agenda. Roosevelt and the Democratic Party were caught in a bind in regard to civil rights. The New Deal programs needed to relieve people hurt by the Great Depression depended on the votes of Southern Democrats who supported Jim Crow laws and segregation. Thus, Roosevelt could not move too far ahead on civil rights lest he endanger support within his own party for his economic agenda. Nonetheless, Roosevelt still garnered black votes, thanks in large part to New Deal programs that provided economic aid to all races. The Republican Party faced no such dilemma in gaining black voters, but their opposition to economic aid during the Depression hurt them with all groups of voters, but African Americans in particular, while Roosevelt's personal charm offensive bore fruit for over three terms.

President Harry S. Truman was the first Democratic president to speak about a civil rights agenda, solidifying the African American drift into the Democratic Party. Truman desegregated the armed services. Still, Truman failed to pass a civil rights act. A number of Northern and Western Republicans recognized that African Americans had started to identify with the Democratic Party, and these Republican leaders were far more active than Truman in calling for a civil rights agenda. Dwight D. Eisenhower enjoyed significant black support and helped to pass the Civil Rights Acts of 1957 and 1960. Both acts largely lacked any enforcement provision, but they were the first civil rights acts passed since the era of the Civil War, and the Republican Party overwhelmingly voted them into being while Democrats remained divided. The 1960 act was the product of Republican senator Everett Dirksen of Illinois. Dirksen, as the Republican leader, would also be pivotal in passing the 1964 Civil Rights Act under President Lyndon B. Johnson, given the opposition of many Southern Democrats to civil rights. The protections given to civil rights under Eisenhower were enacted with Republican votes in combination with Northern Democrats.

In 1954, the Supreme Court in *Brown v. Board of Education* found "separate but equal" unconstitutional. Federal courts then started to make rulings that forced school integration. In 1957, Eisenhower, with the support of the Republican Party, used federal troops to enforce such a court decision in Little Rock, Arkansas, despite the efforts of Governor Orval Faubus and others. Over the course of the 1950s and 1960s, there was an increasingly active Civil Rights Movement. The Republican Party found itself in an odd position. In the first stages of the movement, there were few Republican officeholders in the South invested in the current system. Yet at the same time, there were white voters who might be brought into the party with the decline of segregation, given the divisions inherent in the Democratic Party. Despite this division within the party, the John F. Kennedy administration spoke a great deal about civil rights legislation, and under President Johnson, such legislation was passed, most notably the Voting Rights Act of 1965 that barred literacy tests, poll taxes, and other methods Southern states had used to get around the Fifteenth Amendment to the Constitution. In addition, the act had the enforcement provisions necessary to ensure that the federal government could intervene to monitor the process. Johnson is often quoted as saying shortly after signing the act that he had just lost the South for the Democratic Party, which was largely true, as increasingly from that point the South turned Republican, a trend that had already begun to occur in presidential elections, but that would come to define elections to state legislatures and the U.S. Senate and House of Representatives.

The Republican Party first introduced political and civil rights for African Americans under President Abraham Lincoln and the Radical Republicans in Congress. Over the course of the nineteenth century, however, in an attempt to garner more white votes and create a stronger party in the South, Republicans often soft-pedaled the protection of those rights. It was not until the presidency of Franklin D. Roosevelt that blacks began to become a major constituency of the Democratic Party. Even so, the Republican Party during the 1950s and 1960s often had a better overall record on combating Jim Crow laws in the South, whereas Democrats remained deeply divided, often having the loudest supporters for the Jim Crow system and its loudest detractors. Nonetheless, the Republicans benefited from the ultimate break by Johnson with that Southern Democratic Party support for segregation, as the white South became largely Republican while African Americans became staunch Democratic Party voters.

Michael Beauchamp

See also: Democratic Party; Reconstruction.

Further Reading

Burk, Robert Frederick. *The Eisenhower Administration and Black Civil Rights.* Knoxville: University of Tennessee Press, 1984.

Foner, Eric. *Free Soil, Free Labor, Free Men: The Ideology of the Republican Party before the Civil War.* New York: Oxford University Press, 1970.

Gould, Lewis L. *Grand Old Party: A History of the Republicans.* New York: Random House, 2003.

Jensen, Richard J. *Grass Roots Politics: Parties, Issues, and Voters, 1854–1983.* Westport, CT: Greenwood Press, 1983.

Sherman, Richard B. *The Republican Party and Black America: From McKinley to Hoover, 1896–1933.* Charlottesville: University Press of Virginia, 1973.

Weiss, Nancy J. *Farewell to the Party of Lincoln: Black Politics in the Age of FDR.* Princeton, NJ: Princeton University Press, 1983.

Robinson, Jackie

Jackie Robinson was an African American athlete, activist, and businessman, most famous for his Hall of Fame pioneering career in Major League Baseball. Born in 1919 in Cairo, Georgia, Robinson moved with his mother and four older siblings to Pasadena, California, in 1920, where he grew up in a majority white neighborhood. Although involved in minor acts of vandalism and confrontations with the police as a youth, Robinson moderated his behavior under the influence of Karl Downs, a young black minister in the area. Excelling in a variety of sports in high school, Robinson chose to attend Pasadena Junior College (PJC) to be close to home and his beloved mother, Mallie. At PJC, Robinson set national marks in the broad jump and led the football team to an undefeated season in his sophomore year, earning acclaim in nearly every area newspaper for his brilliant open-field running as the team's quarterback. In February 1939, Robinson enrolled at the University of California at Los Angeles (UCLA), where he became the first athlete in the school's history to letter in four sports: baseball, track, football, and basketball. He earned the most acclaim for his performance on the football field, where, as a junior, he teamed with two other black starters, Kenny Washington and Woody Strode, to lead UCLA to a 6–0–4 record, only narrowly missing the school's first-ever invitation to the Rose Bowl.

After leaving UCLA in February 1941 to earn money to support his mother, Robinson briefly played professional football in Hawai'i before being drafted into the military in March 1943. Sent to Fort Riley, Kansas, for basic training, Robinson earned high marks in a variety of tests, thanks to his intelligence and physical aptitude, but was consistently passed over for admission into Officer Candidate School because of his race. Robinson's friendship with famed heavyweight boxer Joe Louis, also stationed at Fort Riley, helped gain him entrance into the school, where he earned the rank of second lieutenant. After being transferred to Camp Hood, Texas, Robinson faced court-martial charges after

Jackie Robinson is shown in the uniform of the Kansas City Monarchs, which was in a Negro league. Robinson later became the first African American player to sign with a major league team, the Brooklyn Dodgers, and began his major league career in 1947. (Library of Congress)

refusing to move to the back of a military bus when ordered to do so by the bus driver. Asserting his rights as an officer and an American citizen, Robinson was arrested. Eventually acquitted, Robinson was granted an honorable discharge because of an ongoing ankle ailment in November 1944. Robinson then played one year of baseball for the Kansas City Monarchs, a Negro League Baseball team.

Robinson's performance for the Monarchs attracted the attention of Branch Rickey, the president of the Brooklyn Dodgers, a Major League Baseball team. Although there were no formal rules against black players in the major leagues, an unwritten "gentleman's agreement" had kept African Americans out of the sport since the late nineteenth century. Robinson's athletic ability and strong character made him the ideal candidate to integrate Major League Baseball, and Rickey signed him to play that role in August 1945. The decision was announced publicly in October of that year. In 1946, Robinson played for the Dodgers' top minor league affiliate, the Montreal Royals. Although encountering bitter racism from fans, opposing players, and even some teammates and coaches, Robinson excelled and helped lead his team to a league championship. He also married his long-time girlfriend, Rachel Isum, at the conclusion of the 1946 season. The following spring, Robinson trained with the Dodgers and earned a starting spot on the team for the 1947 season.

On April 15, 1947, Robinson became the first African American player to participate in Major League Baseball in the modern era when he took the field with the Brooklyn Dodgers at the age of 28. Robinson faced racist taunting from opposing players and fans, and players often attempted to injure him by throwing pitches directly at him and deliberately "spiking" him with their cleats. African American fans turned out in droves to support him, and some white fans, particularly youths, were also enthusiastic admirers. Robinson initially received little support from his teammates, but an early series against the Philadelphia Phillies, managed by virulent racist Ben Chapman, helped unite the Dodgers. As Robinson withstood a torrent of racial abuse from the Phillies players without responding (a strategy of nonconfrontation he and Rickey had agreed upon), his teammates rallied to his support. In another key incident from that season, team shortstop Pee Wee Reese, a Southerner and one of the Dodgers' best players, silenced a hostile Boston crowd by putting his arm around Robinson and chatting with him on the field. In his nine-year career, Robinson won numerous accolades, including the National League Rookie of the Year in 1947, the National League Most Valuable Player in 1949, and a World Series championship in 1955. Following Robinson's debut, other clubs began to sign African American baseball players, and many consider Robinson's successful turn in baseball, "the national pastime," a pivotal event in the broader struggle for African American civil rights. He was awarded the Spingarn Medal in 1956 by the National Association for the Advancement of Colored People (NAACP) for his contributions to civil rights as a baseball player, the first athlete ever to receive the award.

After retiring from baseball in 1956, Robinson became a vice president for "Chock Full o' Nuts," a popular brand of coffee. He also became active in the NAACP, campaigning as a fund-raiser and supporting a variety of civil rights causes across the country. Although beloved by the black community on the whole, Robinson generated controversy in later years by campaigning for Richard Nixon in the 1960 presidential election, a decision he later regretted. He remained a supporter of the Republican Party until 1964, when the nomination of Barry Goldwater over friend Nelson Rockefeller led him to leave the party. He also resigned from the board of the NAACP in 1967 because he thought that long-time executive director Roy Wilkins had become too autocratic and was not open to new ideas and young leaders. In his last years, as he struggled with diabetes, Robinson bitterly complained in his autobiography *I Never Had It Made* about the lack of black managers in baseball and the ongoing racial inequalities that persisted across the country. One of his last major public appearances was for Major League Baseball's celebration of the 25th anniversary of his first game. He appealed to baseball owners to hire black managers and executives, but did not live to see it happen. He died in October 1972 from complications of diabetes, and was buried in Cypress Hill Cemetery in Brooklyn, New York. Posthumously, he was awarded the nation's highest civilian award, the Medal of Freedom, in 1984. Major

League Baseball also retired his number, 42, in 1997, to honor the 50th anniversary of his debut with the Dodgers.

Gregory Kaliss

See also: Negro League Baseball.

Further Reading

"Baseball and Jackie Robinson." The Library of Congress American Memory Web site http://memory.loc.gov/ammem/collections/robinson/ (accessed May 29, 2008).

Robinson, Jack, with Alfred Duckett. *I Never Had It Made.* New York: G.P. Putnam's Sons. 1972.

Rampersad, Arnold. *Jackie Robinson: A Biography.* New York: Alfred A. Knopf. 1997.

Tygiel, Jules. *Baseball's Great Experiment: Jackie Robinson and His Legacy.* New York: Oxford University Press. 1983.

Roosevelt, Franklin D.

Franklin Delano Roosevelt, who served as U.S. president from 1933 until his death in 1945, did more for racial justice in the United States than had any chief executive had since Abraham Lincoln. The Civil Rights Movement of the 1950s and 1960s had its beginning in the efforts of black and white Americans working under the auspices of the Roosevelt administration to ameliorate the most injurious effects of Jim Crow. Indeed, Roosevelt and his New Deal policies were responsible for the great majority of black Americans to shift their allegiance to the Democratic Party from their traditional base, the Republican Party of Lincoln.

Elected to lift the nation out of the Great Depression, Roosevelt's initial primary focus was resurrecting the American economy, and to do so, he needed the cooperation of the Southern Democrats in Congress. So he did not directly challenge Jim Crow, leaving the states to determine their own laws concerning race. Instead, he relied on liberals in his administration to push the South and the country toward equality and integration. In a sense, Roosevelt traded acquiescence to the South, in terms of segregation, for support for his liberalizing economic policies. In spite of his refusal to actively work toward ending Jim Crow, Roosevelt's administration was the nation's first to promote equality both in the workplace and on Main Street.

Roosevelt's focus on economic restructuring necessarily ate away at the underpinnings of Jim Crow. The New Deal's extensive programs in support of Americans' general welfare, in the areas of health, education, and housing, as well as workplace and agricultural reforms, meant the institution of greater federal planning. Inevitably, Southern states' control of their own racial policies was undermined by federal regulations that had the effect of standardizing even social policies across the nation. Federal efforts to strengthen American society in general worked to enervate local efforts to maintain white supremacy. New Deal programs themselves and the way they touched more blacks, from the use of birth certificates to the introduction of agricultural extension agencies, brought the federal government closer to the average African American and made the idea of political participation more likely.

Roosevelt's belief in the activism of the progressives he had attracted to his administration allowed him to avoid speaking directly to the inequalities of race and class in America. For example, FDR depended on the guidance of social scientists he brought to Washington—many of them from the University of North Carolina at Chapel Hill—to plumb the fallacies beneath the South's racial myths, and to turn new knowledge into practical service. Socialist leader Norman Thomas remembered a meeting with the president, in which Roosevelt refused to back Thomas's call for strong union legislation. "I know the South," Roosevelt told him, "and there is arising a new generation of leaders in the South and we've got to be patient."

Roosevelt hired for the upper echelons of New Deal agencies more than a hundred African Americans. He appointed the first black federal judge and the first black general officer in the U.S. Army. The New Deal disturbed the social, as well as economic, relations that Southern society had developed over decades. Important among the possibilities created by the New Deal was the destruction of Jim Crow laws.

Typical of Roosevelt's approach to racism and Jim Crow was his executive order integrating defense production, signed on June 25, 1941, as Europe was embroiled in World War II and the United States prepared for the possibility of entry into the conflict. Black leaders saw an opportunity to secure work in defense plants and to integrate the armed forces. A. Philip Randolph, president of the Brotherhood of Sleeping Car Porters, the nation's first black labor union, formulated the idea for a march on Washington to demonstrate African Americans' desire for their share of defense work, and the nation's black newspapers overwhelmingly supported the concept.

Roosevelt's response was characteristic. He invited Randolph and Walter White, head of the National Association for the Advancement of Colored People, to the White House and promised fairer treatment in the workplace. Randolph wanted what Roosevelt did not want to give him—a piece of legislation that conservatives could hold against him. With war imminent, the president did not intend to alter the makeup of the military, but he was willing to legislate against job discrimination once he was assured that it would not diminish war production. Randolph called off the march a week before black Americans were set to converge on Washington.

The order promulgated the rationale that the nation needed all the help it could get, "in the firm belief that the democratic way of life within the Nation can be defended successfully only with the help and support of all groups within its borders."

Typically, Roosevelt couched this effort on behalf of black Americans in language that claimed no special prerogatives for minorities, but spoke instead to national security and the general welfare of all Americans. Innocuous as it seemed, the executive order set a precedent against discrimination in hiring that would be cited time and again in the coming years of the Civil Rights Movement.

If Roosevelt thought he could not push to abolish Jim Crow laws, he was happy to be tugged along by the tide created by black leaders, including Randolph, White, and Mary McLeod Bethune, president of the National Association of Colored Women, as well as white civil rights leaders, including—most prominently— Eleanor Roosevelt, his wife.

Eleanor Roosevelt knew her husband's true feelings about civil rights. She wrote about a conversation with FDR and Walter White. "You go ahead," the president told White. "You do everything you can do. Whatever you can get done is okay with me, but I just can't do it." Afterward, she asked, "Well, what about me? Do you mind if I say what I think?" Roosevelt answered, "No, certainly not. You can say anything you want. I can always say, 'Well, that is my wife; I can't do anything about her.'"

The initial steps taken by Roosevelt toward racial equality created an enormous influence on the subsequent generation of Democratic politicians. Among the most ardent, young New Dealers came the sentiment that Roosevelt "was just like a daddy to me always." A died-in-the-wool Texan, Lyndon B. Johnson, would knowingly sacrifice the white Southern vote to the Republicans for generations by sponsoring the most important civil rights legislation since Reconstruction, legislation that finally killed legal Jim Crow. "I don't know that I'd have ever come to Congress if it hadn't been for him," Johnson claimed. "But I do know I got my first great desire for public office because of him—and so did thousands of young men all over the country."

Louis Mazzari

See also: Great Depression; New Deal; World War II.

Further Reading

Egerton, John. *Speak Now against the Day: The Generation before the Civil Rights Movement in the South.* New York: Alfred A. Knopf, 1994.

Freidel, Frank. *FDR and the South.* Baton Rouge: Louisiana State University Press, 1965.

Sitkoff, Harvard. *A New Deal for Blacks: The Emergence of Civil Rights as a National Issue.* New York: Oxford University Press, 1978.

Sullivan, Patricia. *Days of Hope: Race and Democracy in the New Deal Era.* Chapel Hill: University of North Carolina Press, 1996.

Woodward, C. Vann. *The Strange Career of Jim Crow.* New York: Oxford University Press, 1955.

Rustin, Bayard

Bayard Taylor Rustin was an organizer and activist for racial equality around the world. As one of the earliest American proponents of nonviolent direct action, he brought groundbreaking protest strategies out of the pacifist movement to leaders in the Civil Rights Movement. Rustin worked behind the scenes for many organizations, and leaders including A. Phillip Randolph and Martin Luther King Jr. considered Rustin's gifts as a strategist and theorist integral to their campaigns. As an openly gay African American man, Rustin personally faced a good deal of discrimination, even within the progressive organizations with which he worked. Of Rustin's many achievements, he is perhaps best known for serving as the chief organizer for the 1963 March on Washington for Jobs and Freedom. Throughout his life, Rustin sought to illuminate connections between racial discrimination and economic inequality and to reveal the power of nonviolence as a tool for social change.

Born on March 17, 1912, Rustin was raised by his grandparents Julia and Janifer Rustin in West Chester, Pennsylvania. Julia Rustin raised her grandson as

Bayard Rustin, one of the most skillful organizers among the leaders of the Civil Rights Movement. (Library of Congress)

a Quaker and taught him about nonviolence and about respecting all people as part of a human family. Julia Rustin also helped charter West Chester's National Association for the Advancement of Colored People (NAACP) chapter. The Rustin household served as a guest house for African American leaders denied service at local hotels, including W.E.B. Du Bois and James Weldon Johnson. West Chester remained segregated during Rustin's youth, but the town's small size necessitated the integration of West Chester High School. Rustin excelled athletically, academically, and socially in high school, but began to feel the sting of racism more clearly as he got older. Rustin cultivated friendships with students of many different backgrounds, but found that they could not interact freely outside of school or on school trips.

Rustin spent time at Wilberforce University in Ohio and Cheney State Teachers College in Pennsylvania from 1932 to 1936. He joined the Society of Friends (Quaker) in 1937 and soon moved to New York City. Living in Harlem in 1937, Rustin embraced a locally thriving gay community that allowed him a good deal of personal growth, even within a larger African American culture that urged extreme discretion in matters of sexual identity.

Rustin joined the Young Communist League (YCL) at City College of New York in 1938, drawn by the Communist Party of America's commitment to peace and civil rights. Rustin left the YCL in June 1941, and began working with influential African American labor leader A. Philip Randolph. Randolph made Rustin a youth director for a planned "March on Washington for Negro Americans." When President Franklin D. Roosevelt integrated the defense industry to avoid the demonstration, Randolph cancelled the march. Rustin bitterly disagreed with Randolph's decision, but their work in 1941 began a long partnership between the two leaders.

In 1941 Rustin also began working with A. J. Muste at the pacifist Fellowship of Reconciliation (FOR). As a youth secretary with the FOR, Rustin traveled throughout the South teaching about nonviolent direct action, or using techniques of peaceful protest in an organized way to agitate for social change. Rustin's work slowed in 1943, however, when the federal government sent him to prison for resisting the draft as a conscientious objector. In the Ashland, Kentucky, prison where he was held, Rustin led protests against Jim Crow eating areas within the facility. Upon his release in March 1947, Rustin returned to the FOR and worked with Muste, James Farmer, and George Houser in the affiliated Congress of Racial Equality (CORE).

Farmer, Houser, and Rustin planned the Journey of Reconciliation through the upper South to test the U.S. Supreme Court decision in *Morgan v. Virginia* (1946), which prohibited segregation on interstate transportation. The CORE plan called for interracial duos of men to travel from Washington, D.C., on public buses and nonviolently resist orders to abide by Jim Crow seating arrangements on a moral and legal basis. Authorities in Chapel Hill, North Carolina, arrested Rustin and sentenced him to 30 days on a chain gang. While the journey was only marginally successful, it marked a turning point in Rustin's work, and inspired the Freedom Rides attempted by CORE and the Student Nonviolent Coordinating Committee (SNCC) in 1961. Throughout the 1950s, Rustin worked closely under Muste and Randolph and spoke around the world. However, in January 1953, California police arrested and prosecuted Rustin for sodomy (coded as "lewd conduct"), a charge that Rustin denied. Muste then distanced himself from his protégé because of the negative publicity the arrest could bring in the intolerant political climate of the 1950s.

Rustin denied the charges and found his feet quickly as executive secretary for the War Resisters League (WRL). On a short leave of absence in 1956, Rustin traveled South to offer counsel to the new leader of the Montgomery Bus Boycott, Martin Luther King, Jr. Rustin became one of King's closest advisors and strengthened King's commitment to nonviolence in all aspects of his life and work. From New York, Rustin continued to speak with King about effective organizing techniques, and about the need for a permanent organization to build on the success of Montgomery. At meetings in Atlanta and New Orleans, Rustin worked with Stanley Levinson and Ella Baker to draft the original documents that would form the Southern Christian Leadership Conference (SCLC) in 1957; stressing voter education and the use of nonviolent mass protest to force integration. Rustin remained in the SCLC for several years and helped coordinate plans to stage protests at the Democratic National Convention in 1960. Harlem Congressman Adam Clayton Powell Jr. upset at being excluded from planning, jealously threatened to publicize rumors centering on Rustin's sexuality. King flinched at the potential damage the threat held, and accepted Rustin's resignation from the SCLC. Distraught over yet another ousting from the inner circle of movement leadership, Rustin turned to international peace activism in Europe and Africa in the early 1960s.

Rustin's return to the national Civil Rights Movement came again at Randolph's insistence in 1963. Randolph asked Rustin to plan a march in Washington, D.C., to decry the still unrealized promise of freedom for black Americans. Randolph and Rustin sought the involvement of a broad coalition of progressive groups, including the SCLC, the NAACP, the Urban League, CORE, SNCC, and various labor unions. Randolph countered NAACP head Roy Wilkins's objections to Rustin's involvement by agreeing to head a committee to organize the march, and immediately naming Rustin as his deputy. Thus, Rustin controlled of all aspects of the march, delegating responsibility and orchestrating among the sponsor organization. In roughly two months, Rustin planned the "March on Washington for Jobs and Freedom" that took place on August 28, 1963. The march brought hundreds of thousands of people into the capital to peacefully protest continued segregation around the country and to plead for economic equality. Rustin deftly coordinated between leaders of all involved movement groups, metropolitan and police authorities, transportation and sanitation services, thousands of volunteers, celebrities and speakers, and with the U.S. government. The March on Washington proved a success, and has been judged by many to be a high point in the national Civil Rights Movement, anchored by King's "I Have a Dream" speech. National publicity as well as face-to-face meetings between the civil rights leaders, President John F. Kennedy, and members of Congress helped garner support for the legislation that would eventually become the Civil Rights Act of 1964 and the Voting Rights Act of 1965 which invalidated Jim Crow practices around the U.S. After the march, Rustin appeared with Randolph on the cover of *Life* magazine.

Rustin found himself disappointed at the inability of civil rights groups to build upon the success and consensus of the March on Washington. As factionalism grew between and within groups like SNCC and the SCLC, Rustin also found himself becoming more distant from their leadership. Rustin served as an advisor during SNCC's Mississippi "Freedom Summer" in 1964, working to help plan the mass voter registration campaign, and training volunteers in nonviolence at the request of James Lawson. His work with SNCC to fight Jim Crow in Mississippi that summer was among his last operations with SNCC. Once the young radical, Rustin came to view participation in the political process, as opposed to direct action, as the next step in achieving racial equality. His influential essay, "From Protest to Politics: The Future of the Civil Rights Movement" (*Commentary*, February 1965) evinced the widening gap between Rustin and militancy and racial separatism gaining popularity among young activists. In March 1965, Rustin announced the creation of the A. Phillip Randolph Institute (APRI). As head of the organization, Rustin worked to strengthen relationships between civil rights groups and labor unions in order to build coalitions that would affect social and economic equality. Rustin viewed the oppression of racial minorities and systemic poverty as closely intertwined, and saw solving both problems as a necessary and achievable goal.

Rustin continued to work for peace and civil rights throughout the 1960s, leading youth marches for integrated schools in New York and mobilizing for King's Poor People's Campaign in 1968. Rustin remained active internationally through the 1970s, speaking against the Vietnam War and bringing attention to the struggles of refugees in Southeast Asia. In the 1980s, Rustin began to speak out more publicly for gay rights, pointing out the continuities between oppression based on sexuality and race. Bayard Rustin died in August 1987 at the age of 75.

Brian Piper

See also: King, Martin Luther, Jr.

Further Reading

Anderson, Jervis. *Bayard Rustin: Troubles I've Seen.* New York: HarperCollins, 1997.

D'Emilio, John. *Lost Prophet: The Life and Times of Bayard Rustin.* New York: The Free Press, 2003.

Levine, Daniel. *Bayard Rustin and the Civil Rights Movement.* New Brunswick, NJ: Rutgers University Press, 2000.

Rustin, Bayard, Devon W. Carbado, and Donald Weise, eds. *Time on Two Crosses: The Collected Writings of Bayard Rustin.* San Francisco: Cleis Press, 2003.

S

Segregation, Residential

Residential segregation is a spatial isolation based on race rather than income, education, or other factors. While there has not been official, de jure residential segregation in the United States, housing separation by race has been a common, de facto practice justified by cultural, economic, and political policies. Residential segregation becomes cyclical when housing placement influences access to education, job opportunities, or prejudicial cultural practices that reduce the ability to change one's housing circumstances. Poverty, unemployment, and crime are often the results of residential segregation practices.

Racial difference was inscribed in the United States through the institution of slavery, which dictated that one's "place" in society was determined by one's appearance or ethnic background. Prior to the Civil War, some African Americans were not enslaved and lived freely throughout the country, but most experienced some level of discrimination in housing and business practices. Enslaved African Americans in the South typically lived in close proximity to white people, but spatial intimacy was offset by the restrictions of slavery. With emancipation and the end of the Civil War, previously enslaved black people had the opportunity to move or work in other places. While many African Americans moved to cities or other areas to seek work, others could not afford to leave and had to take low-paying jobs as domestic servants or sharecroppers. The desire for mobility and equality was undermined by the reality of poverty and discrimination. In time, Jim Crow laws marked racial difference when the system of slavery no longer fulfilled that role.

In the late nineteenth and early twentieth centuries, immigrants from Europe and other areas often lived in the same neighborhoods as African Americans. During World War I, large numbers of black people left the South and moved into Northern cities as part of the Great Migration. Black workers sought greater job opportunities in the booming wartime industrial economy, while they simultaneously hoped for freedom from Jim Crow laws and discrimination in the South.

Like other immigrant groups, blacks from the South tended to settle in areas near family and friends, often with lower housing costs and less quality housing. Even as they lived near people most like themselves, European immigrants and African American migrants mixed somewhat freely on the streets and in business practices.

As more African Americans competed for jobs and housing with immigrants and native-born Americans, many of whom were becoming commonly recognized as "white," tensions rose in the workplace and in overcrowded neighborhoods. As their wealth and education grew, white immigrants moved out of small urban neighborhoods and into outlying areas with higher-quality housing and better schools. Black tenants, however, were more limited in their housing options. Since few working-class people owned their own homes, landlords could restrict their clientele and many practiced racial discrimination in housing. Assuming that the presence of black tenants would decrease their property values, some landlords even signed restrictive covenants, in which property owners vowed not to sell or rent homes to African Americans, with other landowners to ensure that their buildings would remain white. Middle-class blacks who owned their homes and businesses tended to cluster in particular neighborhoods, such as Chicago's "Black Belt," where they had more freedom to control their own real estate and business practices. This clustering was not necessarily by choice, as local zoning and cultural restrictions limited black opportunities to expand into other neighborhoods. Such segregation resulted in a lack of understanding between groups that often led to riots, economic hardship, and reduced interracial unionization.

Residential segregation reached its height following World War II. More African Americans moved to Northern and Western cities during the Second Great Migration. Returning veterans took advantage of the G.I. Bill by attending universities and buying houses in larger numbers than ever before. Government policies and social practices emphasized consumption as an important form of citizenship, and homeownership was a key element of this practice. People who had previously rented an apartment in the city desired to purchase a home in the suburbs. Using war-industry knowledge of prefabricated materials and supply chain management, new housing developments such as Levittowns made owning a home affordable. However, private contractors assumed that they were building exclusively white communities and enacted policies to preserve their profit margins, including both official and unofficial covenants. Although the U.S. Supreme Court declared in *Shelley v. Kraemer* (1948) that it was unconstitutional for the state to enforce racially based restrictive covenants, voluntary agreements between homeowners continued to impact the composition of suburban neighborhoods. As white renters moved to the suburbs, they were replaced by black residents until many inner-city neighborhoods were almost completely populated by African Americans.

Government practices often supported and perpetuated postwar residential segregation. Local zoning practices in new suburbs typically restricted multifamily housing, thereby limiting residents to those of certain economic classes. Long-standing federal programs to subsidize home repairs and new construction became even more focused on fostering white homeownership. Through tax incentives, selective credit programs, public/private collaborations, and mortgage subsidies, the Federal Housing Administration (FHA) worked with mortgage lenders and banks to address the housing shortage. By insuring private mortgage companies against loss, the government expanded the pool of mortgages available to private homeowners, thus making homeownership feasible for many first-time buyers. Government agencies and other lenders also shifted to long-term, amortized mortgages to accommodate those with smaller incomes, thus freeing other money for further consumption. In the postwar era, the Veterans Administration's (VA) mortgage benefits were primarily reserved for white veterans.

Although the FHA removed explicit language of racial categorization from its policies in the late 1940s, discrimination continued in practice well into the 1960s, especially because integrated neighborhoods continued to be considered risky financial investments.

Historians typically refer to the exodus of white urban residents to the predominantly white suburbs as "white flight." As African Americans continued to move into cities and take vacant tenant positions, white residents became alarmed at the possibility of losing their majority status. Close quarters also fostered the fear of racial mixing, a long-standing dread since the days of slavery and especially post-Reconstruction Jim Crow laws. As African Americans demanded more space, white residents answered by escaping to the suburbs.

Abandoned housing on Chicago's South Side, May 1973. With white flight and the decline of urban industrial jobs in the 1970s, older cities were increasingly inhabited by low-income African Americans and Latinos. (John H. White/National Archives)

Although racial fears explain some of the reasons for white flight, economic factors played perhaps a larger role in the residential shift. White property owners believed that the presence of minority groups would undermine their property values. Many sociological and economic studies demonstrated that such assumptions were unfounded, but white people continued to fear for their investments. By claiming that they were protecting property values rather than discriminating by race, white citizens justified residential segregation in culturally acceptable economic terms.

The arrival of black families in exclusively white neighborhoods was often met with fear and intimidation. Some white occupants resorted to throwing rocks or even burning crosses on lawns, but more often, they exerted political pressure to influence government policies against integration. One of the most common types of intimidation occurred when white residents pressured their neighbors not to sell their houses to black buyers. Although they did not always sign official racial covenants, white sellers often refused to participate in an exchange with black buyers. Some groups even went door-to-door throughout their communities to extract promises from their neighbors not to participate in realtor blockbusting. They typically phrased their concerns in economic rather than racial terms, but the results still amounted to housing discrimination. Such intimidation also caused black home buyers to reconsider moving into predominantly white neighborhoods, thus continuing the cycle of segregation.

Real estate agents played an integral role in maintaining residential segregation. Many realtors refused to assist black families in finding homes in white neighborhoods. When they did help black clients, real estate agents often steered them into predominantly black neighborhoods. The agents claimed that they were protecting the investments of other homeowners by not introducing elements that may reduce property values. Real estate agents often utilized the practice of "blockbusting" to increase profits. If a black family moved into a white neighborhood, agents encouraged white homeowners to sell quickly before their property values declined. The agents then turned around and sold the home to black buyers at exorbitant prices. Both buyers and sellers suffered from this practice, but real estate agents made tremendous profits by feeding off the fears of white residents.

Another practice that supported residential segregation was that of redlining. Mortgage lenders sought stable communities with minor turnover and little threat of mortgage defaults. They assumed that this ideal place was a white neighborhood. Lenders often designated black neighborhoods as high risk and drew a red line around them on a map. The refusal to invest in these areas severely limited the opportunities for African Americans to purchase their own homes. When black buyers were able to obtain loans, they often carried a higher interest rate or shorter payment schedule, making them a greater financial burden than most mortgages for white people. Over time, the lack of investment in black neighborhoods led to a decrease in property values and a general decline in the physical structures of the area. Deteriorating circumstances then made such black neighborhoods prime candidates for urban renewal projects.

At the same time government agencies subsidized white homeownership, they also implemented policies that further segregated public housing. Fearing that too many white residents would move to the suburbs, some urban politicians used new urban renewal legislation to clear existing black neighborhoods. By taking down old apartment buildings and replacing them with new ones, landowners increased their property values and the corresponding rents. New buildings were usually too expensive for the former residents to occupy, so the tenants were forced to leave the vicinity or apply for public housing. Federally funded housing projects contained black tenants in a regulated space with few opportunities for economic or educational advancement. Urban renewal programs frequently undermined vibrant communities and replaced them with institutionalized housing that led to greater rates of poverty and crime. Today, gentrification projects bring new investments to revitalize urban cores, but often drive up housing costs and force lower-income tenants out to continue the cycle of residential segregation.

The government was not always blind to unjust practices, and both government and social organizations sought housing reform. The Fair Housing Act of 1968 was enacted to protect minority groups against discrimination in public and private housing. The act affected all levels of government, from local to federal, and established a system for people to file complaints if they experienced discriminatory practices. Although critics have long-debated the effectiveness of the act, it was one step in civil rights legislation toward the possibility of a more integrated society.

The results of residential segregation are widespread. Predominantly white and predominantly black communities frequently differ in the allocation of resources, their access to consumer goods, the availability of quality housing, and access to upwardly mobile jobs. Income discrepancies result in widely varying tax bases, which in turn impact education, law enforcement, and future investment. Poverty is often concentrated in urban cores and leads to higher rates of crime. Over time, inequalities become more difficult to overcome. As racial difference is mapped onto urban space, the inner city becomes synonymous with crime and poverty, while the suburbs are viewed as a refuge. Residential segregation negates many possibilities for cross-group cooperation and promotes fear and lack of understanding.

Shannon Smith Bennett

See also: Housing Covenants; Jim Crow.

Further Reading

Cohen, Lizabeth. *A Consumers' Republic: The Politics of Mass Consumption in Postwar America.* New York: Vintage Books, 2004.

Freund, David M. P. *Colored Property: State Policy and White Racial Politics in Suburban America.* Chicago: University of Chicago Press, 2007.

Kruse, Kevin M., and Thomas J. Sugrue, eds. *The New Suburban History.* Chicago: University of Chicago Press, 2006.

Massey, Douglas S., and Nancy A. Denton. *American Apartheid: Segregation and the Making of the Underclass.* Cambridge, MA: Harvard University Press, 1998.

Sugrue, Thomas J. *The Origins of the Urban Crisis: Race and Inequality in Postwar Detroit.* 2nd ed. Princeton, NJ: Princeton University Press, 2005.

Sharecropping

Sharecropping, an agricultural labor system, emerged in the Southern United States after the Civil War destroyed the slave labor economy. After emancipation, former slaves suddenly needed to support themselves, and cash-poor planters required cheap labor to raise and harvest crops. Since planters had little capital and freed slaves had no land, equipment, or farm animals, many entered into labor agreements whereby planters furnished land and equipment and former slaves worked the fields. They split the harvest, and the Freedmen's Bureau, established in 1865 to protect the interests of former slaves, initially considered these agreements beneficial. Sharecroppers were provided between 25 and 40 acres to grow their own food and sell what was left over after they provided the planter with his half of the harvest.

Sharecroppers paid for the rental of tools, wagons, animals, and shelter with additional liens on their crop. Provisions like coffee, sugar, flour, cornmeal, and even clothing were available to them through "furnishing merchants" who also accepted liens. After renting and purchasing everything he needed, a sharecropper could find himself down to 25 percent or less of the proceeds of his harvest. Plantations, as in slave days, were closed communities, and sharecroppers were required not only to purchase their supplies and provisions from the landlord's furnishing merchant, but to market their crop through him. All debts were settled at harvest time. A few bad seasons could doom a cropper to a life of revolving debt and credit, and by 1869, the Freedmen's Bureau could no longer advocate for him. President Andrew Johnson not only disbanded the Bureau but also returned most of the confiscated land to Southern planters. This dashed all hope of land redistribution that the Freedmen's Bureau had advocated for the former slaves.

Sharecropping was part of a three-tier system that included tenant farming, share renting, and sharecropping. In a tenant farming arrangement, the landlord provided land, a cabin, and fuel, for which the tenant paid a fixed rental rate per acre. Most tenant farmers were poor whites who had lost their land, but still had tools and farm animals. In share renting, the landlord provided the same things, and the share renter pledged to pay him one-quarter to one-third of his crop. Most share renters were also white. In sharecropping, however, the landlord provided *everything* and the cropper divided the harvest with him—less the cost of supplies and provisions purchased from the furnishing merchant. By law, tenant farmers and share renters owned the crops they produced and therefore could sell

An African American sharecropper plows a field in Alabama, circa 1937. Sharecropping tied landless farmers to white landowners. (Library of Congress)

them wherever they chose. The sharecropper, however, had to sell through the plantation's furnishing merchant.

Since furnishing merchants controlled the commissaries and kept all the accounts, the sharecropping system was fertile ground for abuse. If a cropper challenged the landlord's figures, he and his family could be evicted from the plantation. Sharecropper families often worked 10-hour days and were closely supervised by overseers. Women labored in the fields as well as in the home and child labor was shamelessly exploited. Despite the U.S. Congress passing legislation in 1867 outlawing debt servitude, croppers who owed their landlords money were not permitted to leave the plantation until they worked it off. If they escaped, they were often tracked down and returned by local law enforcement officers. Many of the restrictions imposed on sharecroppers were simply extensions of the slave system.

Organizing sharecroppers into alliances to demand reform was difficult because croppers were spread out over many plantations, and landlords threatened to evict them for even associating with organizers. The Colored Farmers' Alliance, an early attempt, was established in Leflore County, Mississippi, in 1888 by Oliver Cromwell to win the right to trade with stores and cooperatives outside the plantations. Black organizing terrified white planters, who tended to equate it with slave insurrection. In 1889, Cromwell was ordered to leave Leflore County. He refused, and when a group calling themselves the "Three Thousand Armed Men," organized to protect him, the governor sent in the state militia. Cromwell escaped, but 25 Alliance men were killed, and Leflore County's Colored Farmers' Alliance was disbanded. By 1890, however, chapters were operating in Norfolk, Charleston, New Orleans, Mobile, and Houston.

In 1919, a group of black World War I veterans under the leadership of Ike Shaw and C.H. Smith organized the Farmers and Laborers Household Union of America in Phillips County, Arkansas. They drafted a legally binding contract with plantation owners to provide croppers with a written guarantee of their percentage of the harvest as well as a written statement of account at the end of each season. The planters refused to negotiate, but despite their almost constant intimidation, with assistance from allies in law enforcement and the Ku Klux Klan, union membership increased. On September 30, 1919, a sheriff, his deputy, and a black trustee broke up a Farmers and Laborers union meeting at a church in Hoop Spur, Arkansas. In the ensuing struggle, one of the officers was killed and the other wounded. A posse returned the following morning to arrest the union leaders but the armed membership surrounded and protected them. Advised that a race war was imminent, the governor sent in 500 state militia troops who burned the church, killed 29 blacks, and arrested hundreds. The idea of black sharecroppers controlling their own destinies was so terrifying to white planters that they were willing to commit massacres in order to destroy the organizers and intimidate croppers into submission.

In the spring of 1931, black sharecroppers and tenant farmers in Tallapoosa County, Alabama, organized the Croppers and Farm Workers Union under the leadership of Ralph and Tommy Gray and Mack Coad, a black steelworker from Birmingham who organized industrial workers for the Communist Party. During the 1930s the Communist Party succeeded in creating bargaining units of black and white industrial workers in Birmingham and Memphis, and black sharecropper alliances in rural Alabama and Georgia. The Croppers and Farm Workers Union recruited 800 members in just two months, and in July 1931, at a meeting held in a local church, they voted to support cotton pickers in their demand for a one dollar a day wage. (They were earning 50 cents.) Local sheriff Kyle Young and his deputy Jack Thompson, who had been tipped off about the meeting by a cropper who wanted to earn extra points with his landlord, broke up the gathering, killing Ralph Gray, wounding five union members, and arresting dozens more. After Young was wounded, the church was burned to the ground. Once again, the effort to unionize ended in violence and death.

Tommy Gray, his daughter Eula, and black communist Al Murphy reorganized as the Share Croppers Union. By the summer of 1932, they had reclaimed

600 members. The Croppers Union revived the demand for a one-dollar-a-day cotton picker wage, and demanded payment for the cropper's share of the harvest in cash instead of merchant script, credit, or supplies. They also sought freedom to buy what they needed at any store they chose; and the right to sell their crops to whomever they chose. These demands, structured as they were to defeat the planters' monopoly, posed a threat not only to white supremacy but to the planters' cheap labor supply and planters became determined to destroy this union as they had the Croppers and Farm Workers.

In December 1932, Sheriff Cliff Elder went to the Reeltown, Alabama, farm of black Tallapoosa County organizer Clifford James (one of the few black landowners in the county), to impound his two mules and a cow as payment for a six-dollar-debt he owed a white grocer. Without his stock, James could not farm, and he refused to surrender the animals. A dozen armed members of the Croppers Union stood with him. Elder left, but later returned with an armed posse. The subsequent shootout left the sheriff and several deputies wounded, Clifford James dead, and many croppers injured. Thirty-two were arrested, and five were later convicted of assault with a deadly weapon. A search of the James home uncovered a Share Croppers Union membership list, and vigilantes terrorized everyone on it. Many were beaten and jailed and hundreds subsequently left the county. Despite the ongoing violence, however, the union continued to grow. By June 1933 nearly 2,000 members were operating in 73 locales across the Deep South.

During the last decade of the nineteenth century and into the early years of the twentieth century, a sharecropper could net $333 in a good year, a share renter $398, and a tenant farmer as much as $478. The outbreak of World War I, however, disrupted the world cotton market, and prices fell precipitously. They remained depressed throughout most of the 1920s. The end of that decade brought droughts, dust storms, boll weevil infestations, and eventually the Great Depression. Bankrupted Southern planters lost their land at twice the national average as the price of cotton fell from 20 cents a bale (500 pounds) in 1927 to less than 5 cents in 1932. Many croppers found themselves not only unemployed but also homeless. In 1933, in response to Southern planters' pleas for federal assistance, the administration of President Franklin D. Roosevelt established the Agricultural Adjustment Administration (AAA). Planters who agreed to reduce their crop by 30 percent were guaranteed rental payments and the promise of an additional subsidy if their harvests did not cover their costs. It was an attempt to revive the agricultural economy by limiting supplies of cotton, corn, and soybeans and hoping that consumer demand would increase market prices. These federal agreements stipulated that tenant farmers and sharecroppers were to receive a percentage of the payments. Most never did. The New Deal's agricultural policies changed the lives of sharecroppers and tenant farmers forever. After cotton production was drastically reduced, planters no longer needed as many tenants and croppers were turned off the plantations. The cities, plagued by a concurrent industrial depression, could not absorb them and without income or shelter, many starved. Others became radicalized.

As mass evictions from the plantations began, the Share Croppers Union in Tallapoosa County, Alabama (which remained a black Communist organization), grew to almost 8,000. At the same time, a socialist-supported interracial alliance, the Southern Tenant Farmers' Union (STFU), was organized on the Fairview Cotton Plantation near Tyronza, Arkansas, on July 11, 1934. Eleven white and seven black men met at a local schoolhouse and vowed to stop the evictions on the Fairview Plantation and to demand their fair share of AAA money. Founding members included white socialists H. L. Mitchell and Ward Rodgers and black cropper Ike Shaw, who had survived the 1919 Hoop Spur, Arkansas, massacre. Despite its name, the STFU consisted largely of black and white sharecroppers and day laborers. Interracial organizing was rare, since the sharecropping system by its very nature drove poor whites and blacks into competition. Animosity was not unusual, since black sharecropper labor was cheaper, and when times were hard, the landlord accepted fewer tenants. Plantation owners encouraged racial divisiveness because it kept agricultural workers with similar grievances against them divided. New Deal politics, however, had convinced the croppers and tenants that they shared a common misery and that there was strength in numbers. In Arkansas a large percentage of the evicted sharecroppers were white.

Late in 1934, the STFU sent a delegation to Washington, D.C., to meet with Secretary of Agriculture Henry Wallace to demand that planters stop evicting tenants and croppers and pay them their share of the rental and parity subsidies. The Roosevelt administration subsequently created the Resettlement Administration and charged it with assisting destitute landless farmers. When this agency proved bureaucratic and unresponsive, the STFU took matters into its own hands. In August 1935, just before picking season, they threatened to strike. Ultimately they won a 75-cent wage increase without resorting to the strike and grew so rapidly that by 1936, there were over 25,000 members in the South. That year the Farm Security Administration (FSA) replaced the Resettlement Administration. This agency's Tenant Purchase Program bought failed plantations and offered them for sale at low interest rates to croppers and tenants. Most sharecroppers were not in a financial position to buy land, however. Housing projects were also acquired for dispossessed farm workers, but since the program was mandated federally but administered locally, the housing projects were often segregated, and white croppers and tenants ultimately received the largest share of assistance.

Another factor that mitigated against reform was disenfranchisement. Croppers, especially black croppers, did not vote. Some were illiterate, some were too intimidated by their planters to register, and others could not afford to pay the poll tax, a common barrier in the Deep South. Poll taxes compounded every year after age 21 and were required to be paid in full before a citizen could vote. Lack of political clout cut croppers off from the help liberal Southern politicians might have extended to them under the umbrella of New Deal reform.

By 1936, the Alabama Share Croppers Union had chapters in Louisiana and Mississippi and counted 12,000 members. It made several overtures to the STFU, whose membership was spread over Arkansas, Mississippi, Tennessee, and Missouri, to merge, but the socialist STFU leadership was not interested in joining forces with Communists. Traditional Southern racial attitudes had also infiltrated the movement by that time. Although the STFU had been established as a biracial organization, its black membership grew more quickly and ultimately constituted a majority. White croppers and tenants began to drop out and form their own splinter unions. This pleased planters, who feared the threat that interracial organizing posed to their cheap labor supply and to the entire segregated system.

By 1939, the South finally began to recover from the devastation of the Great Depression, and New Deal assistance was no longer either needed or welcome. While Franklin Roosevelt had bailed out planters with his Agricultural Adjustment Administration policies, they had no intention of allowing New Deal liberals and the activist First Lady Eleanor Roosevelt to encourage union organizing or farm worker reform. The region reverted to its traditional distrust of "big government" and its determination to maintain white supremacy.

Despite strikes, protests, the support of many New Deal liberals, and winning some minor reforms, small wage increases, and benefits, the STFU and the SCU were not able to solve the fundamental problems of sharecroppers. Ultimately croppers and tenants were needed less and less, as machinery designed to plant, pick, and harvest cotton became affordable. By 1937, the Share Croppers Union had liquidated and transferred its membership to the Agricultural Workers' Union, an affiliate of the American Federation of Labor. That same year, the Southern Tenant Farmers' Union affiliated with the Congress of Industrial Organization's (CIO) agricultural workers. Two years later, however, it withdrew, and tried to establish itself once again as an independent union. But by that time, membership had fallen drastically, as thousands of sharecroppers left the South. In the end, it was not the reformers or the activists, or even the croppers themselves who ended the system that had locked them into virtual slavery, but economics. It was tractors, mechanical cotton pickers, and the shift in efficiency from tenancy to seasonal wage earners that changed the course of sharecropping.

Mary Stanton

See also: Colored Farmers' Alliance; Reconstruction.

Further Reading

Beecher, John. "The Sharecroppers' Union in Alabama." *Social Forces* 13 (October 1934), 124–32.

Biegert, M. Langley. "Legacy of Resistance: Uncovering the History of Collective Action by Black Agricultural Workers in Central East Arkansas from the 1860s to the 1930s." *Journal of Social History* 32 (Fall 1998), 73–99.

Clark, Thomas D. "The Furnishing and Supply System in Southern Agriculture since 1865." *Journal of Southern History* 12 (February 1946): 28–33.

Kelley, Robin D. G. *Hammer and Hoe: Alabama Communists during the Great Depression.* Chapel Hill: University of North Carolina Press, 1990.

McMillen, Neil R. *Dark Journey: Black Mississippians in the Age of Jim Crow.* Urbana: University of Illinois Press, 1989.

Raper, Arthur F., and Ira De A. Reid. *Sharecroppers All.* Chapel Hill: University of North Carolina Press, 1941.

Rosengarten, Theodore, comp. *All God's Dangers. The Life of Nate Shaw.* New York: Vintage Books, 1984.

Sit-Ins

Sit-ins were a tactic used frequently as a means of nonviolent direct action against racial segregation. In 1960, prompted by a sit-in in Greensboro, North Carolina, a national sit-in movement developed, usually involving students. Between 1960 and 1964, sit-ins were one of the key tactics of the Civil Rights Movement. The sit-ins established many of the philosophical positions and tactics that would underscore the movement. Many activists who would go on to play leading roles in the Civil Rights Movement were first involved in sit-ins.

During the 1940s and 1950s, sit-ins were used sporadically as a tactic by organized labor and early civil rights organizations. Both the Fellowship of Reconciliation (FOR) and the Congress of Racial Equality (CORE) supported the use of sit-ins as a tactic during the 1940s. In Marshall, Texas, a sustained challenge to Jim Crow during the late 1940s and early 1950s saw the use of several sit-ins, which were supported by FOR and CORE. Sit-ins were used in several locations throughout the 1950s to challenge segregation. In July 1958, sit-ins helped desegregate Dockum Drugs in Wichita, Kansas, and one month later, sit-ins were held at the Katz Drug Store in Oklahoma City. Various other sit-ins took place in border states during the last years of the 1950s, often helping to achieve the integration of the establishment targeted. Despite the success of these sit-ins, the tactic failed to grow into the mass movement it would become in the 1960s.

The sit-in movement was sparked by a sit-in in Greensboro, North Carolina. On February 1, 1960, four students at North Carolina Agricultural and Technical

Students protesting racial segregation in the Chicago public schools by staging a sit-in at the office of Benjamin W. Willis, Chicago Superintendent of Schools, July 10, 1963. (AP Photo)

College staged a sit-in at the lunch counter of the F. W. Woolworth's department store in Greensboro. The sit-in was not a spontaneous event: the four protestors—Ezell Blair Jr., Joseph McNeill, David Richmond, and Franklin McClain—had all been members of National Association for the Advancement of Colored People (NAACP) college or youth groups (although the sit-in was not conducted under the auspices of the NAACP), and had spent many hours discussing ways in which they could participate in the integration movement. They had also been exposed to the burgeoning Civil Rights Movement: Greensboro had been visited by both Martin Luther King Jr., and the African American students involved in the Little Rock, Arkansas, desegregation case. The group intended to use the sit-in to illustrate the hypocrisy of allowing African Americans to shop in the store, but preventing them from using the lunch counter. Woolworth's was chosen specifically because it was a national chain and was vulnerable to pressure from outside the South. Having made purchases in the store, the four sat at the lunch counter and asked for service. When they were refused, they remained at the lunch counter until the store closed.

Unlike earlier sit-ins, the Greensboro protest prompted an almost instant movement. While previous sit-ins had been part of local protests and had not necessarily made connections with other local movements, news of the Greensboro sit-in spread quickly through a network of young activists, often connected to black colleges, black churches, and local civil rights groups in the South.

The four protestors themselves contacted Floyd McKissick, an NAACP Youth Council leader, on the evening of the first sit-in. McKissick, along with the Reverend Douglas Moore, who was the Southern Christian Leadership Conference's (SCLC) North Carolina representative, soon arrived in Greensboro, where they helped to organize the sit-ins. Both men had protest experience: Moore in particular had been involved in direct action in Durham, North Carolina, including a sit-in in a segregated ice-cream parlor. The presence of older, more experienced activists like McKissick and Moore helped to maintain the momentum created by the first sit-in and to coordinate the enthusiasm of the growing numbers of student protestors eager to participate.

The next day, the group returned to Woolworth's and again requested service at the lunch counter; once again, they were refused service. However, the group had been joined by 19 other students; by the third day of the protest, over 80 students took part in the sit-in. Over the course of the week, under the guidance of McKissick and Moore, increasing numbers of students from a variety of colleges (including some white colleges) joined the Woolworth's sit-in, and began sit-ins in different stores in downtown Greensboro. By the end of the first week of sit-ins, over 400 students were participating in sit-ins in Greensboro. By this point, white mobs were gathering to harass the protestors, and store managers, who until then had attempted to accommodate the protests, were threatening legal action. When the manager of Woolworth's closed the store at lunchtime, claiming a bomb threat had been received, the protestors decided to halt the sit-ins to allow negotiations to take place. When the store opened on Monday, the lunch counter remained closed.

The Greensboro sit-ins quickly inspired similar protests elsewhere. Moore and McKissick made use of the their connections with activists in other states and were pivotal in helping the sit-in movement to spread other North Carolina cities and into other states. Within days of the first Greensboro sit-in, other protests had taken place in Durham and Raleigh, as well as other communities in North Carolina. Central to the quick spread of sit-ins was the network of civil rights activists that was spread throughout the South. Fred Shuttlesworth of the SCLC witnessed a sit-in in High Point, North Carolina, and was impressed not only by the tactic but also by the way in which the protestors conducted themselves. Such was his enthusiasm for sit-ins that he urged King to get involved. Sit-ins moved quickly from upper South states like North Carolina, and within a week of the first Greensboro sit-in, sit-ins had taken place in Rock Hill, South Carolina, under the auspices of an SCLC minister.

Of all the locations to which sit-ins spread, it was in Nashville, Tennessee, that the movement developed what would come to be its identifying characteristics. Nashville was fertile ground for sit-ins. A cadre of student activists, many of whom, such as Diane Nash and John Lewis, were students at Fisk University, had been searching for a way in which to challenge segregation. Many of these students had been attending nonviolent workshops run by James Lawson, a divinity student at Vanderbilt University, who had been urged to relocate to the South from Ohio by King. Lawson was planning to instigate several protests against segregation in downtown department stores. The Greensboro sit-ins presented themselves as the ideal way in which to do this. Lawson organized a meeting to discuss the use of sit-ins in Nashville, at which over 500 volunteers, as well as the 75 students who had attended the nonviolent workshops, were in attendance. The volunteer's enthusiasm for sit-ins was so overwhelming that, in spite of his reservations, Lawson—who was at least a decade older than most of the students—agreed to begin sit-ins the following day. The meeting closed after Lawson had instructed the volunteers how to behave during the protests. Lawson's greater experience and links to the burgeoning Civil Rights Movement were crucial to establishing the Nashville sit-in movement, articulating its underlying philosophy of nonviolence and organizing it so that pressure could be persistently applied to segregation. However, the enthusiasm and devotion to the cause of the student volunteers drove the movement and provided a constant stream of protestors to participate. The day after the meeting, over 500 neatly dressed protestors entered stores in downtown Nashville to politely ask for service.

For two weeks, daily sit-ins were held in downtown Nashville. As in many cities in which sit-ins were held, the authorities did not react immediately, hoping that the protests would peter out; indeed, the presence of so many students led authorities, as well as the media, to assume that sit-ins would be a short-term movement. As it became clear that the protests were organized, disciplined, and persistent, store owners became increasingly concerned that sales would be lost. The chief of police announced that, at the request of store owners, trespassing and disorderly conduct arrests would be made. This was a development for which many in the Nashville movement had prepared themselves, but it was a particular source of anxiety of the organizers of the movement, who would in effect be advocating that the protestors staged sit-ins in the knowledge that they were likely to be arrested. Sit-in protestors in Raleigh, North Carolina, had already been arrested, and few in Nashville were deterred by this possibility. Indeed, being arrested and jailed would quickly become a mark of honor for protestors; the tactic of "jail, not bail" would soon spread to other forms of direct action.

In response to the Nashville chief of police's announcement, John Lewis committed to paper a code of conduct, by which protestors should abide. These underscored the tenets by which the movement had thus far been conducted and included reminders not to strike back if struck or abused, to be friendly and courteous at all at times, and to remember love and nonviolence. On February 27, as they took up seats at the lunch counters of chosen downtown stores, protestors were attacked by hostile whites; police arrested 77 protestors and 5 whites. Sixteen of the protestors, including Lewis and Diane Nash, declared that they would not accept bail, but would instead serve a jail sentence. Nash told the judge that in refusing bail, they were rejecting the practices that had led to their arrest. On hearing Nash's speech, the majority of the other protestors decided spontaneously also to refuse bail.

The jailing of the protestors sparked outrage in Nashville, but also brought the sit-ins to national attention. As the protestors were sentenced to workhouse detail, support was received from people such as Ralph Bunche, Harry Belafonte, and Eleanor Roosevelt. Further controversy was created when James Lawson was expelled from Vanderbilt's divinity school. If this was designed to distance Vanderbilt from the sit-ins, it backfired: the story made the front page of the *New York Times,* and Lawson was reinstated. In response to growing external criticism, the mayor of Nashville offered a compromise: in return for the ending of protests in the downtown, the jailed protestors would be freed, and a biracial committee to consider the desegregation of downtown would be established. Unbowed by her imprisonment, Diane Nash quickly led a protest at the lunch counter of the Greyhound bus terminal, which was not included in the compromise deal. Unexpectedly, the protestors were served, and segregation at the bus terminal ended suddenly.

The arrest of the Nashville protestors revealed a growing gap between their outlook and that of the wider black community in Nashville, as well as many older activists in the movement. The NAACP's Thurgood Marshall believed the students had made their point through the sit-ins and their arrests. He argued that such protests should now be abandoned and integration pursued through the courts. John Lewis roundly dismissed this approach and identified a fundamental philosophical difference between the protestors and older activists. To Lewis, the sit-ins had created a mass movement that was confronting Jim Crow; the strength of the sit-in movement was the energy and spontaneity of the large numbers of protestors who were willing to risk abuse, violence, and imprisonment to challenge segregation. This difference would find its expression in the formation of the Student Nonviolent Coordinating Committee (SNCC) at a conference at Shaw University, Raleigh, in April 1960, which brought together many of the young activists involved in the sit-in movement. While King hoped that the activists would use their enthusiasm and power for the SCLC, those attending the conference resisted this, and SNCC remained independent of other organizations.

By the point at which SNCC was formed, the sit-in movement had spread to other states. Between February and April, sit-ins were held in over 70 locations, and had reached Georgia, West Virginia, Texas, and Arkansas. As well as capturing the zeal of so many activists who were eager to challenge Jim Crow, sit-ins proved to be a successful method of ending segregation. In Greensboro, the persistence and organization of the sit-in movement offset authorities' hopes that the summer would see a dip in sit-in activity; locals and high school students had been mobilized to carry on the protests when student numbers declined during nonterm time. The pressure brought by continued sit-ins forced the authorities to negotiate. In particular, the economic effects on businesses helped sit-ins to achieve their aims. The combined effects of the sit-ins, the loss of African American business through attendant boycotts and the loss of business from whites who were discouraged from entering stores because of the protests, meant that Woolworth's lost $200,000 in Greensboro in 1960. By the end of July, lunch counters in downtown Greensboro had been integrated.

Other success occurred elsewhere: in Nashville, the city finally conceded in the face of the unstinting pressure of the sit-ins, and downtown lunch counters were integrated in early May. In Durham, downtown businesses began to desegregate as a direct result of sit-ins, while in Virginia, two drugstore chains planned to end the segregation of lunch counters. The federal government also stepped in, and U.S. attorney general William Rogers negotiated with the owners of chain stores in the South to end segregation. Trailways announced that it would desegregate restaurants in bus terminals throughout the South. Although these victories were achieved relatively rapidly, they came as a result of the tenacity and vigor of the protestors, whose refusal to bow to white intimidation and the more moderate approaches of older activists helped to underline the value of sit-ins.

Indeed, the early burst of the sit-in movement helped to frame the Civil Rights Movement that was coalescing under the leadership of King. As well as sit-ins, other forms of direct action, often involving young activists, became keystones of the movement. Many young African Americans were inspired to action by seeing news coverage of sit-ins, and activists like Bob Moses and Cleveland Sellers would later credit the sit-ins as their introduction to the Civil Rights Movement, and for many more, sit-ins were their first active involvement. By the end of 1960, over 70,000 students had participated in sit-ins or direct action inspired by the sit-ins, and more than 3,600 protestors had been arrested. Sit-ins became perhaps the most identifiable tactic of the Civil Rights Movement and were used consistently in the first half of the 1960s.

While the Greensboro sit-ins and the protests they prompted elsewhere helped to erode some of Jim Crow's unassailability, segregation continued to exist in many forms. As the Civil Rights Movement developed, sit-ins were held throughout the South, including those cities in which segregation had already been partly overcome. Organized sit-ins, such as those which sought to integrate the Toddle Inn restaurant chain in Atlanta, Georgia, continued to be a vital source of protest. During the winter of 1962–1963, a boycott of downtown Jackson, Mississippi, was accompanied by sit-ins. The reaction of white mobs, which shouted abuse at protestors, doused them in food, and dragged them from stools, brought to national attention the extent to which whites in that state were resisting integration. Such sit-ins continued to follow the model established by the Greensboro and Nashville movements, and nonviolence remained the underlying philosophy. Other, less prolonged, forms of sit-ins were also employed. During marches and demonstrations, protestors would often spontaneously stage a sit-in, frequently when faced with police brutality, while variants such as pray-ins at segregated churches, or in the face of violence, and wade-ins at segregated beaches were also used.

After the passage of the Civil Rights Act of 1964 and the Voting Rights Act of 1965, sit-ins became less relevant as the goals of the movement shifted. Indeed, in some states, such as Mississippi, sit-ins were a relatively minor tactic, often limited to urban areas. With the passage of legislation outlawing segregation, the frequency of sit-ins declined. Although sit-ins were still used from time to time, as the focus of the movement turned from segregation to voter registration and broader economic goals, new tactics took their place. The emergence of Black Power also undermined the value of sit-ins, as the validity of nonviolence as a tactic and philosophy was increasingly questioned.

Simon T. Cuthbert-Kerr

See also: North Carolina.

Further Reading

Branch, Taylor. *Parting the Waters: America in the King Years, 1954–63.* New York: Simon and Schuster, 1988.

Carson, Clayborne. *In Struggle: SNCC and the Black Awakening of the 1960s.* Cambridge, MA: Harvard University Press, 1981.

Chafe, William H. *Civilities and Civil Rights: Greensboro, North Carolina, and the Black Struggle for Freedom.* New York: Oxford University Press, 1980.

Lewis, John, with Michael D'Orso. *Walking with the Wind: A Memoir of the Movement.* New York: Simon and Schuster, 1998.

Moody, Anne. *Coming of Age in Mississippi.* New York: Bantam Doubleday, 1968.

South Carolina

With South Carolina as the primary architect of the Confederacy that was formed to preserve slavery in America and the first state in 1860 to attempt to leave the Union—severely fracturing the American republic to ignite the Civil War—the state later became an epicenter of Jim Crow violence. The brutality, discrimination, and segregation against blacks following post–Civil War Reconstruction accelerated in the mid-1870s through the zenith of the Civil Rights Movement during the 1960s.

Even at the dawn of the twenty-first century, the National Association for the Advancement of Colored People (NAACP) urged that potential visitors boycott South Carolina because officials refused to remove the Confederate flag flying above the statehouse in Columbia. And although the state's large black population over the years had largely overcome Jim Crow hatred and implemented progressive changes, Greenville County on January 16, 2006, was the last county in America officially to adopt a paid holiday for black civil rights leader Martin Luther King Jr.'s birthday. Ironically, King's associate, Jesse L. Jackson, was born in Greenville in 1941, when the segregation and hate of Jim Crow were still routine.

During and since the Jim Crow days of the early 1900s, King and other black activists, including Ida B. Wells-Barnett, William Pickens of the NAACP, and Fannie Lou Hamer, had protested in South Carolina, where King's mentor Benjamin Mays was born in 1894 and who once called South Carolina the epitome of racist America. In fact, Mays, who became an educator, clergyman, and president of Morehouse College in Atlanta, where King attended as an undergraduate during the mid-1940s, noted that his parents were born into slavery and lived as tenant farmers who experienced the very worst of Jim Crow discrimination.

South Carolina's white power structure had for centuries been very cognizant and wary of black empowerment ever since slavery was introduced there by Spanish explorers in 1526. Countless slave revolts throughout the state's history as the black population exponentially grew would prompt white authorities to form extremely repressive laws to control enslaved Africans with roots to such West African countries as Angola, the Congo, Senegal, Benin, Guinea, and the Gambia. Many such blacks, early on, were imported to the Americas, including South Carolina coastal areas and islands, for their rice-growing skills as practiced in West Africa.

Slave "patrols," which some historians argue developed into the Reconstruction-era Ku Klux Klan, were also instituted to control blacks in South Carolina by 1636 via an act that allowed any white to "apprehend, properly chastise, and send home" slaves found to be outside their master's plantation. Similar acts were passed in 1704 and 1721, and by 1860, such patrols had been combined with "military force" and the local militia. The patrol system thus evolved systems of control designed to institutionalize effective social and economic control of the black population.

There were more blacks than whites in South Carolina, something that white residents watched closely for fear of uprisings. As a result of repeated slave escapes and those rebellions, or attempted insurrections, many "slave codes" or laws were passed in South Carolina as early as 1712 that became a model for many slaveholding colonies, as South Carolina's whites became increasingly concerned about their burgeoning black population. That year, whites learned of a plot for enslaved Africans to destroy Charleston, and to escape with the help of the Yemassee Indians to St. Augustine, Florida. Many blacks, as a result, were hanged and others burned alive. Future rebellions, often led by Angolans, were as well dealt with severely, including a 1739 revolt of 60 to 100 enslaved blacks led by a slave called Jemmy, said to be an Angolan. Although about 40 whites and 20 blacks were killed in the ensuing battle, the revolt was not successful, resulting in many of the black survivors being decapitated, with their heads placed on top of fence posts as a warning to others. The Negro Act of 1740, a harsh measure that resulted from this revolt, became the basis of the slave code in South Carolina.

Such laws became the forerunner of Jim Crow practices starting in the late 1860s and following the Reconstruction period after the Civil War. Before then, though, in 1820 when South Carolina's black slaves skyrocketed to almost 60,000 with whites numbering only about 20,000, ex-slave Denmark Vesey organized a rebellion, with the help of several Angolans, including Jack Purcell or "Gullah Jack," that would have likely wiped out most of the white power structure in and around Charleston. Although Vesey, whose African name was Telemaque, was hanged on July 2, 1822, he is credited with organizing the largest potential slave revolution in American history, utterly terrifying whites. About 35 of Vesey's alleged conspirators were also hanged or executed. Again, very restrictive laws curtailing free and enslaved blacks' travel, congregating, and otherwise communicating were instituted as a precursor for future Jim Crow initiatives.

Blacks in South Carolina, though, continued to push back on white dominance, even during the Civil War. Robert Smalls (1839–1915) became a hero to the Union in 1862 when he commandeered a Confederate steamer near Beaufort, South Carolina, where he had been born a slave. After the war, Smalls returned to South Carolina, purchased his master's home and served in the state's house of representatives, its senate, and then the U.S. House of Representatives for five terms, before becoming the collector of customs for the Port of Beaufort.

The ultimate influx of Union troops during the Civil War in South Carolina, including many of the 180,000 black soldiers who joined the fight to save the Union and wipe out slavery in the South, led to the establishment of black institutions in South Carolina after that great struggle. They included Penn Center School on St. Helena Island off the coast between Charleston and Savannah, Georgia, with the help of black educator Charlotte Forten of Philadelphia, where Martin Luther King Jr. later held strategy sessions during the 1960s Civil Rights Movement.

Furthermore, the African Methodist Episcopal (AME) Church grew to 44,000 members by the end of Reconstruction, with 12 AME ministers serving the South Carolina legislature. With blacks clearly outnumbering whites by

1868 and becoming members of Lincoln's Republican Party, about 68,000 out of 84,000 voted to change South Carolina's constitution. To most whites' consternation, African Americans ascended to such positions as county commissioners, tax assessors, constables, and judges.

Whites were particularly suspicious of black preachers, including Charleston native Daniel Payne (1811–1893), a bishop in the AME Church that had been founded in 1794 by the ex-slave Richard Allen in Philadelphia. Although Payne started a school for African Americans that closed in 1834 because South Carolina would not permit the education of slaves, he founded the first African American–controlled college in America, Wilberforce University of Ohio in 1865. White South Carolinians ultimately realized that such theologians completely countered historical pro-slavery, preaching that blacks were inferior and meant to serve Caucasians. Indeed, black ministers were not immune to the rampant violence during the Jim Crow era, including Payne whose activism endangered him in South Carolina many times.

In 1870, as federal soldiers withdrew from South Carolina, many blacks and their ministers faced great hostility and even death, such as the AME's Wade Perrin, who was assassinated that year. David Wyatt Aiken, who owned a plantation with about 40 slaves before the war, was said to be a primary instigator of such tragedies, declaring in the summer of 1868 that "before the white man should be ruled by niggers, they would kill the last one of them." Aiken County in South Carolina today is named for Aiken's politician cousin, William. David Wyatt Aiken was also implicated in the homicide of B. F. Randolph, a black Methodist preacher and member of the state legislature, who was fatally shot by three men at a train station in Hodges Depot, South Carolina.

In Abbeville County, where the Confederacy was conceived and the first meetings to plot a rebellion against the federal government were held, one federal army officer in 1868 amassed a huge record of incidents where blacks were killed or otherwise assaulted, with homes being burned down, by whites. Black codes were instituted and metamorphosed into the rampant Jim Crow discrimination that would shape the bitter timbre of racial hatred well into the twentieth century in a state where many native whites still viewed South Carolina as separate from the Union.

Born August 1, 1894, in Ninety-Six, South Carolina, the future mentor of Martin Luther King Jr., Benjamin Mays, witnessed the brutality of Jim Crow in Greenwood County during the Phoenix Riot of 1898. That is when several African Americans were lynched over blacks' fight for enfranchisement—an empowerment that racist whites consistently fought to stomp out. One of Mays's earliest memories during that period was watching his father, Hezekiah Mays, kowtowing or sinking to his knees and touching his head to the ground in front of a white mob to avoid certain death.

Such early episodes helped Mays to become a prolific student, graduating vale-dictorian of his 1914 class at South Carolina State College in Orangeburg, where in 1968, four black students would be massacred by city police during a civil rights demonstration. Meanwhile, by the mid-1930s Mays completed his doctorate at the University of Chicago in theology, becoming a highly esteemed educator, preacher, and president of Morehouse where he began to counsel a young student named Martin Luther King Jr. during the 1940s. Mays, via the strong Christian principles of his mother, Louvenia, and inspired to fight the Jim Crow hatred that he had ex-perienced in South Carolina, convinced King that Christian activism through non-violence was an excellent way to fight racism. Some sources indicate that he also helped to introduce King to the concepts of Mahatma Gandhi, who utilized pacifism to oppose the pillars of racism in South Africa and India.

As the 1900s approached, South Carolina's blacks continued to face virulent racism and violence from such groups as the Ku Klux Klan with memberships soar-ing due to anger over losing the Civil War and black advancements. Such whites sought to punish blacks and keep them subjugated, making South Carolina's blacks some of the most prevalent passengers of the early 1900s Great Migration to North-ern cities. African Americans were still hampered from voting and accessing public and private facilities, as well as relegated to primarily menial and sharecropping or tenant-farming jobs in South Carolina and other Southern states.

Indeed, the sharecropping system of the late 1800s and well into the 1900s forced South Carolina's blacks to work the very plantations on which they had been enslaved, as Benjamin Mays' parents had, but usually at very substandard wages that often kept them indebted to unscrupulous white landowners who rented land at unfair prices. Daring to speak out or challenge South Carolina's stupendously racist social norms often meant an agonizing death.

Yet, such brave antilynching warriors as Ida B. Wells-Barnett, born July 16, 1862, in Holly Springs, Mississippi, dared to speak out against such injustices throughout the country and in South Carolina. After participating in a 1913 wom-en's suffrage demonstration in Washington, D.C., she spoke to President William McKinley about the escalating violence against blacks in South Carolina. She wanted it stopped immediately.

William Pickens Sr., born in Anderson County, South Carolina, on January 15, 1881, was destined to become the first field secretary for the NAACP and trav-eled to the deepest reaches of the South, including his home state, to combat Jim Crow during the early 1900s. Credited with recruiting an unparalleled number of members and organizing chapters throughout the United States, Pickens earned de-grees ranging to a doctorate from Talledega College in Alabama, Yale University, Fisk University, Selma University and even a law degree from Wiley University in Marshall, Texas.

National and local news articles of the countless victims of lynching in South Carolina attest to that state's notorious Jim Crow reputation, as revealed in Ralph Ginzburg's "100 Years of Lynchings." For instance, the *Washington Times* reported on February 18, 1900, that a 19-year-old black teen was lynched in Aiken County after a "crowd of 250 tracked the negro fifty miles across Aiken, Edgefield, and Greenwood counties." The young man, "without hesitation," and apparently petrified, had been ordered to climb a tree and jump from a limb after a rope was tied to it and his neck. When the rope broke, he was "hoisted up and then shot to pieces."

White mobs were particularly vicious if a black man was accused of being intimate with a white woman. One black man was killed and another hurt in 1922 near Florence, South Carolina, because the deceased was suspected of having a relationship with a white woman. "The wounded negro was driving a buggy into which the other man had leaped in an attempt to elude the mob. . . . Letters from the white woman were found in the pocket of the dead man after the lynching," according to a January 14, 1922, report in the *Memphis Commercial Appeal.* The white woman realized she too was in trouble for fraternizing with an African American man.

Such abhorrence over interracial relationships certainly reached the highest governmental levels in South Carolina, as indicated by Governor Cole Blease's 1911 statement: "Whenever the Constitution comes between me and the virtue of white women of South Carolina I say 'to hell with the Constitution!'" Indeed, such beliefs reflected the firm attitudes of many white South Carolinians following Reconstruction that their state would never succumb to federal efforts to elevate blacks and absolutely not permit white women and black men to have relationships. Many whites, in fact, viewed the state as separate from the Union, despite losing the Civil War. They realized that the North's military victory, at that point, was simply temporary, and such racist institutions as the Ku Klux Klan and other groups would soon take control. If a black man had been accused of rape, the consequences were often unspeakably horrible, including burning at the stake and dismemberment, especially of the sexual organs that were among body parts often handed out as souvenirs following rallies that were usually attended by thousands of whites.

Although the number of lynching incidents in South Carolina, as well as other states, cannot be pinpointed because countless blacks were killed secretly or without their identities known, it is likely that the figure totals to thousands in South Carolina. Furthermore, the segregation of blacks at public facilities, as well as the hampering of voting rights and economic empowerment, was routine practice in a state that conceptualized and actualized the Confederacy in order to preserve slavery and Jim Crow hatred.

Strom Thurmond, who became the longest serving and oldest U.S. senator before his death in 2003 at age 100, was a former South Carolina governor who became a symbol of racial segregation nationwide, despite his later authenticated sexual relationship with a black worker with whom he fathered a child. During Thurmond's 1948 Democratic bid for president, he said "that there's not enough troops in the Army to force the Southern people to break down segregation and admit the nigger race into our theatres, into our swimming pools, into our homes and into our churches." In 1957, in opposition to the Civil Rights Act, the senator filibustered for a record-setting 24 hours and 18 minutes.

News reports in 2007 also indicate that Thurmond's ancestors owned a slave whose family line developed into the black activist Al Sharpton's family, crystallizing the legacy of South Carolina's pro-slavery and Confederate reality that some observers insist still exists to some degree today.

Although the Confederate flag was removed from the top of the South Carolina statehouse due to pressure from the NAACP and placed on a pole at the street level in July 2000, the divisive symbol of white supremacy and pro-slavery fervor still flies in front of the building.

Donald Scott

See also: Jim Crow; North Carolina.

Further Reading

Documenting the American South. http://docsouth.unc.edu/church/hamilton/hamilton .html (accessed July 22, 2007).

Fry, Gladys-Marie. *Night Riders in Black Folk History.* Chapel Hill: University of North Carolina Press, 1975.

Jim Crow Heroes in South Carolina. http://www.jimcrowhistory.org/scripts/jimcrow/he roes.cgi?state=South%20Carolina (accessed July 29, 2007).

Litwack, Leon F. *Trouble in Mind: Black Southerners in the Age of Jim Crow.* New York: Alfred A. Knopf, 1998.

Negro Plot: An Account of the Late Intended Insurrection among a Portion of the Blacks of the City of Charleston, South Carolina. Boston: Printed and published by J. W. Ingraham, 1822.

Rowland, Lawrence S., et al., *The History of Beaufort County, South Carolina.* Volume 1, 1514–1861. Columbia: University of South Carolina Press, 1996.

Sundown Towns

A sundown town is any organized jurisdiction that for decades kept African Americans or other groups from living in it and was thus "all-white" on purpose. They are so named because some marked their city limits with signs typically reading, "Nigger, Don't Let the Sun Go Down on You In ___."

These towns were not, in fact, all white. "Sundown suburbs" excepted and, to a degree, accepted black live-in servants in white households. Moreover, some communities that took pains to define themselves as sundown towns nevertheless allowed one or even two exceptional black households within their otherwise all-white populations. When Pana, for example, in central Illinois, drove out its African Americans in 1899, killing five in the process, residents did not expel the black barber and his family. With an exclusively white clientele, hence friends in the white community, no one complained about him. Pana did post sundown signs at its corporate limits, signs that remained up at least until 1960, and permitted no other African Americans to move in, so it became a sundown town. Other sundown towns have let in more temporary intruders: flood refugees, soldiers during wartime, college students, and visiting interracial athletic teams and their fans. Most sundown towns and suburbs outside the West—and some in that region—allowed Asian Americans and Mexican Americans as residents. Thus, "all-white" towns may include nonblack minorities and even a tiny number of African Americans.

Sundown towns range from hamlets like Deland, Illinois, population 500, to large cities like Appleton, Wisconsin, with 57,000 residents in 1970. Sundown suburbs could be even larger, such as Glendale, a suburb of Los Angeles, with more than 60,000; Levittown, on Long Island, more than 80,000; and Warren, a Detroit suburb with 180,000. Entire counties went sundown, usually when their county seats did.

These towns and practices date back to the Great Retreat that whites forced African Americans to make between 1890 and 1940. This period is becoming known as the "nadir of race relations," when lynchings peaked, white owners expelled black baseball players from the major (and minor) leagues, and unions drove African Americans from such occupations as railroad fireman and meat cutter. In those years, thousands of towns across the United States expelled their black populations or took steps to forbid African Americans from living in them. Independent sundown towns were soon joined by "sundown suburbs," mostly between 1900 and 1968. Many suburbs kept out not only African Americans but also Jews.

Towns that had no African American residents passed ordinances, or thought they did, forbidding blacks from remaining after dark. In California, for example, the Civilian Conservation Corps in the 1930s tried to locate a company of African American workers in a large park that bordered Burbank and Glendale. Both cities refused, each citing an old ordinance that prohibited African Americans within their city limits after sundown. Some towns believed their ordinances remained in effect long after the 1954 *Brown v. Board of Education* decision and the Civil Rights Act of 1964. The city council of New Market, Iowa, for example, suspended its sundown ordinance for one night in the mid-1980s to allow an interracial band to play at a town festival, but it went back into effect the next day. Other towns never claimed to have passed an ordinance but nevertheless kept out African Americans by city action, such as cutting off water and sewage or having police call hourly all night with reports of threats.

Sundown towns have also maintained themselves all-white by a variety of less formal measures, public and private. As far back as the 1920s, police officers routinely followed, stopped, and harassed black motorists in sundown towns. Suburbs used zoning and eminent domain to keep out black would-be residents and to take their property if they did manage to acquire it. Some towns required all residential areas to be covered by restrictive covenants—clauses in deeds that stated, like this example from Brea, California, "[N]o part of said premises shall ever be sold, conveyed, transferred, leased or rented to any person of African, Chinese or Japanese descent." After a U.S. Supreme Court 1948 decision in *Shelley v. Kraemer* rendered such covenants hard to enforce, some suburbs relied on neighborhood associations among homeowners, allowing them to decide arbitrarily what constituted an acceptable buyer. Always, lurking under the surface, was the threat of violence, such as assaulting African American children as they tried to go to school, or milder white misbehavior, such as refusing to sell groceries or gasoline to black newcomers.

The Civil Rights Movement left sundown towns largely untouched. Indeed, some locales in the border states forced out their black populations in response to *Brown v. Board of Education.* Sheridan, Arkansas, for example, compelled its African Americans to move to neighboring Malvern in 1954, after the school board's initial decision to comply with *Brown* prompted a firestorm of protest. Having no black populations, these towns and counties then had no African Americans to test their public accommodations. For 15 years after the 1964 Civil Rights Act, motels and restaurants in some sundown towns continued to exclude African Americans, thus having an adverse impact on black travelers who had to avoid them or endure humiliating and even dangerous conditions.

At their peak, just before 1970, the United States had perhaps 10,000 sundown towns. Illinois alone probably had at least 500, a clear majority of all incorporated places. In several other Northern states—Oregon and Indiana, for example—more than half of all incorporated communities probably excluded African Americans. Whole subregions—the Ozarks, the Cumberland, a band of counties on both sides of the Iowa-Missouri border, most of the suburbs of Los Angeles—went sundown—not every town, but enough to warrant the generalization. However, except for some suburbs that became all-white mostly after 1930, sundown towns were rare in the traditional South. There, whites were appalled by the practice, not wanting their maids to leave.

The practice of exclusion was usually quite open. Hundreds of towns posted signs. The Academy Award–winning movie of 1947, *Gentleman's Agreement,* was about the method by which Darien, Connecticut, one of the most prestigious suburbs of New York City, kept out Jews, and that publicity hardly ended the practice. In the 1960s, some residents of Edina, Minnesota, the most prestigious suburb of Minneapolis, boasted that their community had, as they put it, "Not one Negro and not one Jew." Residents of Anna, Illinois, still apply the acronym "Ain't No Niggers Allowed" to their town.

Even though proud to be all-white, elite sundown suburbs have usually tried to avoid being known for it. This is the "paradox of exclusivity." Residents of towns such as Darien, Connecticut, for instance, want Darien to be known as an "exclusive" community of the social, moneyed elite rather than as an "excluding" community, especially on racial or religious grounds. So long as elite sundown suburbs like Darien, Kenilworth (near Chicago), Edina, or La Jolla (a community within San Diego) appear to be "accidentally" all white, they avoid this difficulty.

Until 1968, new all-white suburbs were forming much more rapidly than old sundown towns and suburbs were caving in. That year, Title VIII of the Civil Rights Act, along with the *Jones v. Mayer* Supreme Court decision barring discrimination in the rental and sale of property, caused the federal government to change sides and oppose sundown towns. Since then, citywide residential prohibitions against Jews, Asian American, Native Americans, and Hispanics/Latinos have disappeared. Even vis-à-vis African Americans, many towns and suburbs—certainly more than half—relaxed their exclusionary policies in the 1980s, 1990s, and 2000s. Hotels and restaurants, even in towns that continue to exclude black residents, are generally open. However, many towns still make it uncomfortable or unwise for African Americans to live in them.

James W. Loewen

See also: Housing Covenants; Segregation, Residential.

Further Reading

Blocker, Jack S. *A Little More Freedom: African Americans Enter the Urban Midwest, 1860–1930.* Columbus: Ohio State University Press, 2008.

Jaspin, Elliot. *Buried in the Bitter Waters.* New York: Basic Books, 2007.

Loewen, James W. *Sundown Towns.* New York: New Press, 2005.

Newman, Dorothy K., et al. *Protest, Politics, and Prosperity.* New York: Pantheon, 1978, 144.

Pfaelzer, Jean. *Driven Out.* New York: Random House, 2007.

Pickens, William. "Arkansas—A Study in Suppression." In *These "Colored" United States: African American Essays from the 1920s,* ed. Tom Lutz and Susanna Ashton, 34–35. New Brunswick, NJ: Rutgers University Press, 1996.

T

Texas

The institution of slavery in the United States is generally seen as an institution confined to the South, but Texas, which is more Southwestern than Southern, was a slave state from its earliest beginnings. From the early days of Spanish colonialism until the Civil War, slavery was an essential part of the development of Texas. The state legislature passed Black Codes after the Civil War to restrict the rights of blacks and drive them back to the farms and into semi-slavery as victims of peonage. The use of terror to bolster the political, legal, economic, and social systems that regulated black behavior and racial etiquette that was developed during slavery was reestablished in Jim Crow form after Reconstruction. Immediately after the Civil War, during the period from 1865 to 1868, white Texans committed hundreds of acts of violence and murder against blacks. The racial groundwork laid into the social fabric of society by slavery created the narratives for the creation and facilitation of Jim Crow institutions after the Civil War. Although slavery was abolished in 1865, a form of peonage lasted well into the twentieth century and left a legacy that endures in social problems today.

When slavery was abolished, Robert E. Lee, the former commander of Confederate forces, influenced segregated models that were to be established. Lee established a relationship with the Episcopalians and James Steptoe Johnston, a former Confederate soldier, to develop the idea of "Negro education" projects in Texas. One such Jim Crow institution was St. Phillip's College in San Antonio, which sought to keep African Americans in low-paying and servile jobs. Education in Jim Crow institutions consisted of learning how to sew, cook, and wait on white people's needs. This model would be adopted throughout Texas, as whites sought forms of cheap labor, attempted to limit competition with whites for jobs, and sought ways to keep African Americans segregated and in a servile status. The influence of Robert E. Lee helped to give birth to Booker T. Washington's social formula that surrendered to white racism and forged the eventual Jim Crow that governed the South after Reconstruction.

During Reconstruction, former Confederates attempted direct sabotage of the progressive ideas of the period. Texan John Salmon "Rip" Ford, a former commander of the Rio Grande Military District, led a band of ex-Confederates who worked to undermine Reconstruction and the granting of civil rights to African Americans. Ford was also the editor of an Austin newspaper that routinely attacked blacks and Mexican Americans using racist language and stereotypes. In Corpus Christi, during the 1870s, many Mexicans were beaten and hanged for supporting the federal cause and the rights of black people. In San Antonio, racist vigilante forces attempted to destroy Mexican support for blacks and in later years redefined racial models that labeled Mexicans "white" in an attempt to divide and conquer the coalitions between blacks and Mexicans that had been established over many years.

By the 1880s, the constitutional rights guaranteed to African Americans by the Reconstruction amendments had undergone severe setbacks as a result of the removal of Union troops and state elections that removed Radical Republicans from office. Segregation or separate but equal status for African Americans gradually became the norm and codified in the law. Even before the U.S. Supreme Court decision of *Plessy v. Ferguson* (1896), Texas was well on its way in maintaining separation of the "races." Jim Crow laws were numerous in Texas and included about 27 statues and policy changes that were passed in the state.

In many east Texas towns, blacks were systematically removed or forced to leave. Many went to Mexico. The 1877 withdraw of federal troops created the "exodusters," a mass movement to escape the terror of Southern racism. Though this movement peaked in 1879, later attempts eyed Mexico as a refuge for African Americans. The father of poet Langston Hughes was one such advocate of going to Mexico to escape the injustices of Jim Crow in the 1890s. In fact, during this same period, William Ellis, an African American from Victoria, Texas, envisioned a mass exodus to Mexico of African Americans who were being denigrated by Jim Crow laws.

Blacks were forced to pay for their own segregation, when in 1866 a law required that all taxes paid by blacks must be allocated to maintaining segregation in public schools throughout the state. Texas managed to enact only one antisegregation law during Reconstruction in 1871, barring separation of the races on public carriers, but this was invalidated in 1891 by the 22nd Texas Legislature when it passed segregation statutes that became known as the Jim Crow law. In 1876, with Reconstruction defeated, voting laws required electors to pay a poll tax, which was used to prevent African Americans from voting, and a state statute was passed in 1879 that barred interracial marriage. Racial tensions were increased as a result of the separation of the races. After the killing of a black soldier, a riot of black troops occurred at Fort Concho in 1881 near San Angelo, Texas. In the skirmish they destroyed property and wounded a white man.

Other racial riots took place in Texas involving Mexican Americans as well. The Rio Grande City Riot of 1888 occurred after the arrest and killing of a local Mexican American. The killing was justified by a claim that he was attempting to escape, a typical charge used by Southern racists. The incident served as combustible material, and widespread anger against the sheriff increased because he was implicated in the racist lynching of several other Mexicans. In 1899, the Laredo Smallpox Riot was initiated among Mexican American residents who protested being forcefully removed from their homes by Texas Rangers who were responding to reports of a smallpox outbreak. Texas Rangers were often sent in to subdue mobs and often sided with the whites. White racists in border towns often used health issues to remove Mexicans from Texas, and when the Texas Rangers were called in, hundreds rioted. That same year, troops of the Texas Volunteer Guard were dispatched to Orange to suppress a mob organized to drive blacks out of Orange County. The mob was bent on removing all blacks from the area after a black man, accused of rape, was removed from the jail by a mob of between 300 and 500 men. The black man was lynched, and at least 100 shots were fired into his body.

Between 1900 and 1920, the killing of Mexicans and African Americans on the Texas-Mexico border was a frequent event. Some of these killings were the result of a plan by a group of Mexicans to free African Americans from discrimination and help the black community establish six states of their own after Mexico recovered the lands that were taken by Texas slavers to set up the independent Republic of Texas. This plan was called the "Plan of San Diego." When word of this proposal reached the Texas Rangers, they went on a murderous hunt to find the individuals who were planning this insurrection. The revolutionaries managed to destroy a train at Brownsville on October 18, 1915, and carried out numerable raids across the state. When some of these revolutionaries were captured, they were tortured to death or just shot on sight. Many of these revolutionaries were socialists and harbingers of the 1917 Russian Revolution.

During the turbulent years of the prelude to the Mexican Revolt, and the eventual revolution against Porfilio Diaz, 1900–1920, whites in Slocum, Longview, and Waco, Texas, went on rampages and riots in which blacks were burned out and hanged. In Slocum in 1908, approximately 20 African Americans were murdered by a mob of whites. Jesse Washington was burned alive at the stake in 1916 in Waco by a mob of 15,000 to 20,000 whites. In Longview, it was reported that blacks armed themselves and ambushed a train carrying a white racist killer, who they killed. In this period, Jim Crow laws increased as the Mexican Revolution exacerbated the level of terror against African Americans.

After years and years of laws and social rules that produced hate-filled narratives, there were bound to be racial explosions. The Brownsville Raid of August 1906, an alleged attack by soldiers from companies of the black 25th U.S. Infantry, resulted in the largest summary dismissals of troops in the history of the U.S. Army. When these soldiers arrived in Brownsville, they were immediately confronted with racial discrimination at business establishments and reported physical mistreatment. An alleged attack on a white woman, a standard charge in the South and in Texas, infuriated many white residents. When shooting broke out and claimed the life of a white resident and the wounding of a police officer, unsupportable claims were made that the black troops were responsible.

By 1909, the Texas legislature passed further Jim Crow laws that provided separate waiting areas for white and black passengers. Many Jim Crow laws were in part a reaction to the victory of Texas-born boxing champion Jack Johnson over white opponents. White anger grew across the nation, and calls for a "great white hope" echoed across the racial landscape after the defeat of white boxer James J. Jeffries in 1910. In the aftermath of the Johnson victory, racial hatred increased against African Americans and riots broke out across the nation. In 1914, the Texas legislature went so far as to pass laws preventing African American railway porters from sleeping on bedding intended for whites. On a consistent basis, these Jim Crow laws were passed creating a hateful atmosphere in Texas that would soon lead to more violence. In the wake of Jack Johnson's relationships with white women, a state code was approved in 1915 providing imprisonment in the penitentiary from two to five years for interracial marriage.

The Houston Riot of 1917 was started by about 150 black troops of the 24th U.S. Infantry from Camp Logan shortly after the United States entered World War I. Black troops were mindful of the tasks that white supremacy had set for them in fighting Indians and Mexicans while being denied human dignity. The riot, touched off by the arrest of an African American woman in the Fourth Ward of Houston and the beating of a black military policeman by a white Houston police officer, was the culmination of white racial hatred against armed black men. Local white police officers and residents routinely harassed blacks. Many whites were killed in the fighting, and the African American soldiers were court-martialed at Fort Sam Houston in San Antonio. Most of the black men were found guilty. Nineteen African American soldiers were hanged on the Salado Creek, while 63 were given life sentences. Not a single white civilian was brought to trial.

Blacks were being excluded from every aspect of public life, including the use of the public libraries. In 1919, a state statute ordered that blacks use separate libraries. Vagrancy laws were used to force blacks into slave-like conditions by arresting them and forcing them to work off fines on farms. The use of vagrancy laws against blacks and Mexicans to farm out free labor (peonage) was still in use in 1926 and extended well beyond that. Against this backdrop the Longview Race Riot of 1919 occurred, during the "Red Summer." It was also the time of the first "Red Scare," a time in which the federal government began attacking real and imagined "communist" enemies and violating civil liberties.

In Longview, whites needed only to feel threatened by perceived acts of black independence for violence to erupt. In this case, racial tensions were exacerbated because two prominent African American leaders had recommended that black growers bypass established white brokers and sell cotton directly to markets in Galveston, Texas. Governor William P. Hobby ordered Texas Rangers to Longview, and eventually placed some 250 Guardsmen in the town after violence increased. The Democrats increased racial tensions by disenfranchising African Americans in 1922. A voting law preventing blacks from voting in the Democratic Party primary elections in Texas was passed. By 1925, state statutes codified segregation, made miscegenation a felony, and, within about 10 years, went on to create segregated health care facilities. Between 1943 and 1958, segregation was extended to city buses, parks, swimming pools, and other public facilities.

Violence sometimes broke out because of competition over jobs between blacks and whites. In Brenham, rioting broke out over the hiring of a black employee by a railway company. The Beaumont, Texas, Race Riot of 1943 had its roots in the tensions of competition for jobs between blacks and whites and Jim Crow. In 1941, and after the United States entered World War II, Beaumont became a magnet for people seeking work when employment opportunities in the shipyards and war factories were announced. Consequently, large numbers of workers raced to the town, but housing facilities were not plentiful enough to enforce Jim Crow laws. Whites were forced into quarter in proximity to blacks. In the shipyards and factories, blacks began to have access to jobs that were normally reserved for whites. When Jim Crow laws could not be enforced, little excuse was needed for a major eruption of violence. A white mob, outraged at the alleged assault of a white woman by a black, terrorized black residents resulting in two deaths and one hundred homes being destroyed.

Violence in Texas as elsewhere was fueled by the racial structure created by Jim Crow. Even after the Civil Rights Movement pressured for the passage of the Civil Rights Act of 1964, which invalidated Jim Crow laws, the legacy of Jim Crow remained. With the passage of the Voting Rights Act of 1965, Jim Crow laws were eliminated in voting, but the violence continued. In 1967, a riot at Texas Southern University in Houston resulted in the death of one police officer and the wounding of several others. The cause of the riot was the arrest of a student, but the incident was related to general racial tensions created from years of Jim Crowism in Houston. Many social scientists believe police brutality has become one of the racial debris of the Jim Crow legacy. The legacy of Jim Crow extended rioting to

San Antonio when in April 1969, members of Student Nonviolent Coordinating Committee (SNCC) organized a mass demonstration against police brutality that resulted in property damage and the arrest of individuals from a unique group of SNCC Black Panther members.

Mario Marcel Salas

See also: Louisiana.

Further Reading

Barr, Alwyn. *Black Texans: A History of African Americans in Texas, 1528–1995.* Norman: University of Oklahoma Press, 1996.

De Leon, Arnoldo. *They Called Them Greasers: Anglo Attitudes toward Mexicans in Texas, 1821–1900.* Austin: University of Texas Press, 1983.

Gomez, Laura E. *Manifest Destinies: The Making of the Mexican American Race.* New York: New York University Press, 2007.

Till, Emmett

In the summer of 1955, while visiting Money, Mississippi, 14-year-old Chicago native Emmett Till breached Jim Crow etiquette and spoke to a white woman. His punishment was murder. This horrific event revealed that Jim Crow laws and white supremacy were alive and well in the South. With great courage, Emmett's mother, Mamie Till Mobley, turned her personal tragedy into a catalyst for the Civil Rights Movement. Emmett Till's death alerted the nation of the thriving persecution of African Americans under Jim Crow laws.

The son of Mamie and Louis Till, Emmett was born on the South Side of Chicago in 1941. Although Till struggled with a bout of polio at age five, leaving him with a slight stutter, he became a confident child known for his pranks and outgoing personality. In the summer of 1955, Till went to Mississippi to visit relatives and stay with his uncle, Mose Wright. As a Mississippi native, Mobley warned her son of the ways of the South before he boarded the train. While Till had been exposed to segregation in the North, he was unaware of how far white supremacists would go to preserve their Southern way of life.

During his stay in Money, Mississippi, Till and his cousin, Curtis Jones, visited Bryant's Grocery and Meat Market on a Wednesday evening. While Jones started a checkers game with an older man outside the store, Till went inside and bought some gum. As Till left the store, he said "bye, baby" to white cashier Carolyn Bryant, the store owner's wife. The man playing checkers with Jones told the boys they

Emmett Till and his mother, Mamie Till Mobley. The 14-year-old Till was murdered by vigilantes in Mississippi in 1955. (Library of Congress)

should leave before Bryant got her pistol. The scared boys left quickly in Wright's 1941 Ford, and Till begged Jones not to mention the market incident to his uncle. Days passed without incident until Carolyn's husband Roy returned to Money after being away on a trucking job.

Late that Saturday night, Roy Bryant, along with his brother-in-law J. W. Milam, drove to Wright's cabin. Bryant and Milam greeted 64-year-old Wright with a flashlight and a gun. Bryant wanted the boy who talked to his wife. Wright pleaded with the two men asking them not to take the boy. He told them Till was just 14 and from the North; he did not know how to treat white folks. Bryant and Milam pulled Till out of his bed at gunpoint, dragged him into their car, and drove off. The men threatened Wright's life if he mentioned anything of the incident.

The next morning, Curtis Jones called the sheriff to report Till missing. Three days later, a boy fishing in the Tallahatchie River discovered Till's body. His body was so disfigured by the beating that Mose Wright could identify his nephew only by the initialed ring he wore; it was his father's. Before being shot in the head, Till was brutally beaten. His forehead was shattered on one side, an eye was gouged out, and a 75-pound cotton-gin fan was tied around Till's neck with barbed wire. After finding the body, Jones called Till's mother in Chicago.

After the casket arrived in Chicago, the mortician told Mamie Till Mobley that he signed an order for the sheriff of Money that promised Till's casket would not be opened. Mobley opened the casket herself. After seeing her only child's body mutilated beyond recognition, Mobley wanted everyone to see what happened to her 14-year-old son in the Jim Crow South. On September 3, thousands of people came to the open casket ceremony at Rainer Funeral Home. A picture of Till's lynched corpse also appeared in *Jet,* a weekly black magazine, for the whole nation to see.

Less than two weeks after Till's burial, Bryant and Milam were tried for the murder of Emmett Till in Sumner, Mississippi. Although four African Americans, including Mose Wright, were brave enough to testify against Bryant and Milam in the segregated courthouse, the all-male, all-white jury deliberated a little over an hour before returning with not-guilty verdicts for both defendants. That same year, Bryant and Milam sold their confessional story of killing Emmett Till to white journalist William Bradford Huie, for $4,000. Their story appeared in *Look* magazine on January 24, 1956.

Emily Hess

See also: Lynching; Racial Customs and Etiquette.

Further Reading

Hudson-Weems, Clenora. *Emmett Till: The Sacrificial Lamb of the Civil Rights Movement.* Troy, MI: Bedford Publishers, 1994.

Till-Mobley, Mamie, with Christopher Benson. *Death of Innocence: The Story of the Hate Crime That Changed America.* New York: Random House, 2003.

Whitfield, Stephen J. *A Death in the Delta: The Story of Emmett Till.* Baltimore: Johns Hopkins University Press, 1991.

Truman, Harry S.

Harry S. Truman, 33rd president of the United States, was the first chief executive in the twentieth century to take substantive action in support of political and social equality for African Americans. In September 1946, a delegation of African American leaders, including National Association for the Advancement of Colored People (NAACP) executive director Walter White, met with Truman in the White House to discuss the rise of racial violence then occurring across the American South. The president was particularly shocked by the brutal attack upon an African American soldier in South Carolina.

Honorably discharged from the army in February 1946, Sergeant Isaac Woodard was traveling by bus through South Carolina when, during an unscheduled stop, he asked the white driver if he could use the restroom. The driver refused permission and cursed Woodard, who responded in kind. When the bus arrived in Batesburg, the driver informed police chief Lynwood Lanier Shull that Woodard had been unruly during the trip. Boarding the bus, the police chief arrested Woodard for disturbing the peace. When he protested that he had done nothing wrong, Shull savagely beat the discharged sergeant, blinding him in both eyes. The president, deeply troubled by this brutal act, vowed to take action. Under Truman's direction, the Justice Department prosecuted Schull for violating Woodard's civil rights, but an all-white jury found him not guilty. The beating of Sergeant Woodard and the acquittal of his assailant had a profound effect on President Truman. From that point on, he was determined to end legalized discrimination and racial violence from American life.

In December 1946, one month after Schull's acquittal, Truman issued an executive order creating the President's Committee on Civil Rights to investigate civil rights abuses and propose federal statutes that would prevent them in the future. As the committee began its work, Truman continued to call for an end to racial discrimination. On June 29, 1947, the president spoke at the annual meeting of the NAACP, the first chief executive to ever do so. Standing on the steps of the Lincoln Memorial, Truman committed the federal government to ensuring equal rights for African Americans. Four months later, the president was given the tools to make his commitment real when his civil rights committee presented him with its 178-page report on October 29, 1947. Entitled *To Secure These Rights,* the report not only catalogued egregious abuses of civil rights, but also recommended federal action to protect the constitutional liberties of all Americans.

Despite the considerable political risks, Truman sent a special message to Congress on February 2, 1948, proposing a set of laws designed to secure full equality for African Americans. The president's ambitious program included the creation of a civil rights commission and a Justice Department civil rights division to investigate and prosecute violations of civil liberties, establishment of a federal commission to prevent discrimination in the workplace and ensure fair employment practices, antilynching legislation, outlawing segregation in facilities servicing interstate transportation, and further protection for the right to vote.

As might be expected, Truman's message ignited a political firestorm in the American South. Bitterly opposed to his proposals, white Southern Democrats attempted to deny Truman their party's presidential nomination. When that failed, they formed the States Rights or Dixiecrat Party, and nominated Strom Thurmond of South Carolina for president. Although 82 percent of the American people were reportedly opposed to the presidents' civil rights program, Truman defeated

Thurmond and Republican Thomas E. Dewey in the November election. The Dixiecrats were unable to prevent Truman's election, but their allies in Congress did successfully block Truman's civil rights measures from becoming law. In the face of congressional inaction and the hatred of Southern reactionaries, the president remained unbowed. On July 26, 1948, Truman issued two executive orders that weakened the bonds of segregation. Executive Order 9980 required all federal departments to ensure equal employment opportunities for all applicants regardless of race, color, religion, or national origin and established a Fair Employment Board to oversee compliance. The second one, Executive Order 9981, was even more radical.

For decades, one of the most segregated institutions in the country was the U.S. military. Denied opportunities to advance, most black servicemen were prevented from service in combat units and were allowed only to engage in menial activities. In the Marines, for example, blacks could only enlist as kitchen personnel while in the army; only one African American in 70 was a commissioned officer. Appalled by this, Truman ordered military commanders to integrate the armed forces. High-ranking military leaders, most notably army chief of staff General Omar Bradley, bitterly denounced the plan, but again Truman refused to back down. Before the end of his presidency in January 1953, Truman also appointed African American lawyer William Hastie to the U.S. Court of Appeals and integrated federal housing programs.

Truman was the first American chief executive to commit the power of the federal government to the elimination of legalized segregation. Although conservatives in Congress blocked most of his civil rights program, Truman courageously ignored Southern reactionaries such as the Dixiecrats and integrated both the armed forces and federal bureaucracy. At the same time, in calling attention to the discriminatory nature of Jim Crow segregation through the creation of the Presidential Committee on Civil Rights and his address to the NAACP, Truman laid bare the plight of African Americans and emboldened their struggle to achieve social and political equality.

Wayne Dowdy

See also: Democratic Party; Roosevelt, Franklin D.; World War II.

Further Reading

Gardner, Michael R. *Harry Truman and Civil Rights: Moral Courage and Political Risks.* Carbondale: Southern Illinois University Press, 2002.

Haskell, John. "President's Committee on Civil Rights." In *Civil Rights in the United States,* ed. Waldo E. Martin, Jr., and Patricia Sullivan. New York: Macmillan Reference USA, 2000.

Haskell, John. "Truman, Harry S (1884–1972)." In *Civil Rights in the United States,* ed. Waldo E. Martin, Jr., and Patricia Sullivan. New York: Macmillan Reference USA, 2000.

*To Secure These Rights: The Report of the President's Committee on Civil Rights.*http:// www.trumanlibrary.org/civilrights/srights1.htm (accessed May 31, 2007).

Tuskegee Syphilis Experiment

Beginning during the Depression years of Jim Crow segregation in 1932, just before Adolf Hitler came to power in Germany, the Tuskegee syphilis experiment remains one of the most shocking episodes in the troubled history of human experimentation. Sponsored by the U.S. Public Health Service (PHS), the Tuskegee experiment ran for a full 40 years before the disturbing details of the nontherapeutic and unethical medical trial were disclosed to the American public by Jean Heller of the Associated Press in a story published by the *Washington Star* on July 25, 1972.

Jim Crow–era economic deprivations, racial divisions, and white racial prejudices provide an essential framework for understanding what happened to the victims of the Tuskegee study and why the experiment was allowed to continue for so long. The South's post-Reconstruction regime of legally sanctioned and violently enforced racial apartheid trapped many rural African Americans in a vicious cycle of debt peonage, illiteracy, fear, and ill health. Adding insult to injury, white Americans also invented and circulated a number of negative stereotypes of blackness. One of the most common post–Civil War misrepresentations of African American men was that of the "brute" or "black beast." This distorted caricature portrayed black men as primitive, savage, and, in particular, as an uncontrollable sexual threat to white women. White physicians and social scientists echoed and amplified the core ideology of Jim Crow, discovering allegedly high incidences of anatomical irregularities, constitutional weaknesses, and venereal diseases among the black population—with syphilis rates among African American males becoming a chief preoccupation of white public health officials.

The Tuskegee experiment had its immediate origins in a 1929 Julius Rosenwald Foundation–funded PHS study designed to determine the prevalence, and implement methods for control, of syphilis among rural black males in six counties spread across five Southern states. This privately financed health plan initiative was discontinued in the fall of 1930, but not before researchers had identified Macon County, Alabama, as the study's area of greatest need. Tragically, as few of the syphilis sufferers discovered in Macon County had ever received any treatment, they were later targeted (by then–assistant surgeon general Taliaferro Clark) as an "unparalled opportunity" to develop a new research project, examining "the effect of untreated syphilis on the human economy." In total, 400 men, already infected with syphilis, and a further 200 serving as uninfected controls, were selected for the experiment, centered at Tuskegee Institute's John A. Andrew Memorial Hospital. In addition to prominent white physicians and public health officials, several black medical professionals played key parts in the research. Perhaps the most notable African American involvement came from public health nurse Eunice Rivers, who acted as a trusted liaison between the men in the study and the PHS doctors. There has been much debate as to nurse Rivers's knowledge of and complicity in the experiment. By way of understanding her position, historian Susan Reverby explains that the complex world of Tuskegee's race, class, gender, and professional politics created peculiar pressures that sometimes forced individuals like Rivers into contradictory and compromising roles.

The men were recruited via a number of coercive and deceptive incentives—such as the offer of "special free treatment" (including painful diagnostic procedures, such as spinal puncture), free transport to and from hospital, free hot lunches, and free burial insurance (but only after permission for an autopsy had been granted). None of the subjects enrolled in the study were ever provided with appropriate or adequate treatment; indeed, they were discouraged and even actively prevented from seeking treatment outside the program and were also denied the most effective antibiotic therapy against the disease—penicillin—when it eventually became widely available in the 1940s. Nor were the men properly or fully informed that they were human guinea pigs participating in a medical research experiment. Instead they were told that they were being treated for "bad blood," a vernacular term used to describe several illnesses in the rural black community (including syphilis, anemia, and fatigue). This was a group of very vulnerable patients, with few alternatives, who were victims of a long-term cruel combination of racial discrimination and medical callousness.

Racism and exploitation have deep roots in American medicine, especially in the Southern states. For example, in neighboring Montgomery County, Alabama, during the era of antebellum slavery, Dr. James Marion Sims performed a variety of medical experiments on slave men, women, and infants. Between 1844 and 1849, Sims developed a method of repairing injuries suffered during childbirth and later gained international fame as the "father of American gynecology." However, Sims owed the perfection of his surgery to the role of enslaved women, upon whom he conducted repeated operations (without anesthesia). In the same era, Southern medical schools demonstrated what has been termed "postmortem racism," encouraging the use of black cadavers (many obtained without permission and stolen from graveyards) in anatomical training and the use of black body parts in medical museums. This long history of medical abuse and differential treatment created a legacy of mistrust and fear toward white physicians in the African American community, often resulting in an understandable reluctance to participate in clinical trials.

The 1972 media exposé led to the termination of the study. However, by this stage, a number of the men had died and many family members had been infected. The most positive outcome of the tragedy was the crucial role it played in making Americans rethink the ethics of human experimentation. It gave impetus to the National Research Act of 1974, making written informed consent of human subjects a fundamental condition of participation in medical research trials. Furthermore, in July 1973, Macon County civil rights attorney Fred Gray filed a $1.8 billion class-action lawsuit, which resulted in an out-of-court settlement a year later for $10 million

Herman Shaw, a Tuskegee Experiment victim, smiles after receiving an official apology from President Bill Clinton on May 16, 1997, in Washington, D.C. Clinton apologized on behalf of the U.S. government to African American men, whose syphilis, unknown to the sufferers, went untreated by government doctors so that the long-term effects could be studied. (AP Photo/Greg Gibson)

to be divided among the study's living participants and heirs of the deceased.

On May 16, 1997, in the presence of eight survivors of the study, family representatives of the deceased, political activists, and historians, President William J. Clinton issued a formal federal apology for the Tuskegee Syphilis Experiment. As a commitment to long-term efforts to heal the wounds inflicted by the study, the Clinton administration also supported the building of a National Center for Bioethics in Research and Health Care at Tuskegee University, which opened in 1998. The study also left a cultural legacy, becomingthe subject of poems, documentaries, a play, and HBO award-winning movie, *Miss Evers's Boys*.

Stephen C. Kenny

See also: Health Care.

Further Reading

Brandt, Allan M. "Racism and Research: The Case of the Tuskegee Syphilis Study." In *Sickness and Health in America,* ed. Judith Walzer Leavitt and Ronald L. Numbers. Madison: University of Wisconsin Press, 1997.

Hornblum, Allen M. *Acres of Skin: Human Experiments at Holmesberg Prison.* London: Routledge, 1998.

Jones, James H. *Bad Blood: The Tuskegee Syphilis Experiment.* New York: Free Press, 1981, revised 1992.

Reverby, Susan M., ed. *Tuskegee's Truths: Rethinking the Tuskegee Syphilis Study.* Chapel Hill: University of North Carolina Press, 2000.

Virginia

During the Jim Crow era, the Commonwealth of Virginia, an Upper South state, had some of the strictest laws in the nation that kept nonwhites subordinated to whites. Additionally, Virginia led the nation in its antimiscegenation laws and in its zealous pioneering efforts at eugenics. The state was also the scene of some of the key events in the Civil Rights Movement, which led to the disestablishment of Jim Crow.

Virginia had been the birthplace of black slavery in the United States, and as a colony and into the federal period, Virginia slaveowners made much of their wealth exporting surplus slaves for an expanding national market. Laws from the 1830s required emancipated blacks to leave the state within one year of gaining their freedom. The Virginia slave code went beyond that of most slave states, forbidding conversion to Christianity as grounds for granting freedom to slaves. Slaveowners had no legal liability for causing the death of their slaves, either by accident or intentionally. Fearing that literacy in part tended to lead to slave rebellions, the act of teaching a slave to read became a crime.

Following the Civil War and Reconstruction, Virginia followed the Mississippi Plan to deprive blacks of the right to vote, mainly using poll taxes and property qualifications, which also tended to disenfranchise poor whites. Virginia also used understanding tests, in which an election official would ask the potential registrant to explain a given passage in the Constitution. Usually, the responses of blacks were judged to be insufficient to allow the black person to register to vote.

Virginia's real pioneering efforts were in eugenics, the pseudoscience of improving the population by preventing those deemed "less fit" from reproducing. Its Racial Integrity Act of 1924 required that each child born in the state be assigned to a racial category, and its defining racial characteristics described. The act also specifically outlawed marriages between white and nonwhite persons. Virginia's law went further in this respect than similar laws in other states in that Virginia made the state of marriage itself a crime if it was between a white and a nonwhite person. Thus, an interracial couple legally married in New York could be arrested if they came to Virginia. Most states with similar laws simply refused to issue marriage licenses to couples of different "races." Virginia also in 1924 passed the Sterilization Act, allowing the state to sterilize anyone deemed "unfit." The law fell hardest on poor uneducated whites and nonwhites who were institutionalized. Virginia's eugenics policies were upheld by the U.S. Supreme Court in 1924 in the *Buck v. Bell* ruling, which held that the state had a vested interest in preventing those found mentally deficient from reproducing. Virginia's eugenics program would later be the model for similar programs created by the Nazi Party in Germany in the 1930s.

The linkage of Virginia's antimiscegenation law and its sterilization law stemmed from the work of Professors Arthur Estabrook and Ivan McDougle, who published a deeply flawed 1924 study of a mixed population near Lynchburg of what they termed the "WIN" tribe, which stood for "White, Indian, and Negro." According to Estabrook and McDougle, throughout history, whenever white populations lived for long periods with blacks, the result was the "mongrelization" of the whites, and the decline of society. The heavily biased study concluded that mixed-race persons inherited the "worst" traits of each parent stock, and thus allowing mixed-race people to be created was to be prevented using the full power of the state. Virginia had little interest in preventing the interbreeding of various nonwhite peoples, and state laws specifically applied only to preventing white and nonwhite mixing.

Despite this fear of racial mixing, and Virginia's strict racial classification laws, where the "one-drop rule" prevailed, as opposed to the one-eighth rule that was more common in the South, a notable exception was enshrined in Virginia law. Most of the so-called First Families of Virginia claimed descent from the Powhatan Pocahontas from her marriage to John Rolfe. To accommodate these families, many of whom were prominent politically or economically, the law declared that persons who were one-sixteenth or less of Indian descent, and otherwise white, were to be considered 100 percent white under Virginia law.

In the years after World War II, Virginia's Jim Crow laws came under increasing pressure from several sources. The massive expansion of the federal government under the New Deal and especially during the war had led to enormous growth in the northeast part of the state, directly across the Potomac from Washington. Many of the state's new residents were from outside the South and far less inclined to support overt discrimination. Additionally, the State Department put specific pressure on Maryland and Virginia to abolish racial discrimination, at least in the areas around Washington, as they created international difficulties for the United States in trying to bring newly emerging African nations into alliances with the United States and a rejection of the Soviet bloc. However, Virginia politicians, backed by politicians throughout the South, proved unsympathetic to State

Department difficulties, and took no immediate actions to lessen at least the more obvious signs of Jim Crow.

Virginia's strict enforcement of Jim Crow led to two important legal challenges that would lead to great victories in abolishing the entire system. In a case that began when a black Virginia woman traveling to Maryland was arrested in 1944 for refusing to get to the back of a Greyhound bus, the U.S. Supreme Court ruled in *Irene Morgan v. Commonwealth of Virginia* (1946), that racial segregation of bus passengers in interstate travel was unlawful. In 1960, the Court extended the ruling in *Boynton v. Virginia,* which outlawed segregated waiting rooms and other facilities for passengers at bus terminals serving bus lines involved in interstate travel.

Other Jim Crow laws in Virginia would provide fodder for other legal challenges to legalized discrimination. The 1954 *Brown v. Board of Education* case was based in part on the earlier *Davis v. Prince Edwards County School Board, Virginia* case, which was filed by National Association for the Advancement of Colored People (NAACP) attorneys. The *Davis* case began in 1951 out of student protest against the disparities between spending on white and black public school in Virginia.

Following the *Brown* decision, Governor Thomas B. Stanley announced that Virginia would resist integration of its public schools. He then formed the all-white Gray Commission, ostensibly to study the impact of the *Brown* decision, but in reality to attempt to avoid implementing it. Its chairman and namesake, Garland Gray, was a staunch segregationist. Five years after *Brown,* few school districts were integrated. Some Virginia counties closed their public schools rather than integrate. This tactic was ruled unconstitutional in the 1964 U.S. Supreme Court ruling of *Griffin v. School Board of Prince Edward County, Virginia.*

A legal challenge to Virginia's strict anti-interracial marriage law ended with the nullification of all such state laws nationwide. The 1967 U.S. Supreme Court ruling in *Loving v. Virginia* held that all state laws banning interracial marriages were unconstitutional. In the ruling, Chief Justice Warren noted "the fact that Virginia prohibits only interracial marriages involving white persons demonstrates that the racial classifications . . . [were] measures designed to maintain White Supremacy." Thus the very extreme nature of Virginia's law helped abolish all such laws nationwide.

Barry M. Stentiford

See also: Cold War; Marriage, Interracial.

Further Reading

Heinemann, Ronald L. *Old Dominion, New Commonwealth: A History of Virginia, 1607–2007.* Charlottesville: University of Virginia Press, 2007.

Smith, J. Douglas. *Managing White Supremacy: Race, Politics, and Citizenship in Jim Crow Virginia.* Columbia: University of South Carolina Press, 2001.

Wallenstein, Peter. *Cradle of America: Four Centuries of Virginia History.* Lawrence: University Press of Kansas, 2007.

Voting Rights Act of 1965

The Voting Rights Act of 1965 was passed on August 6, 1965, under the administration of President Lyndon B. Johnson. Its overall purpose was to outlaw the many discriminatory voting practices that were in put in place in Southern states following Reconstruction.

The act was passed in an attempt to uphold the intention of another edict ratified 95 years earlier: the Fifteenth Amendment to the U.S. Constitution. The amendment, adopted in 1870, was the first legislative action taken against "discrimination on the basis of race, color, or previous condition of slavery." As the attempted Reconstruction ended in failure, Southern states began to find ways to keep blacks from voting by using means that were not stated in the Fifteenth Amendment. State officials did this through violence, intimidation, and enacting Jim Crow laws that included literacy tests, poll taxes, and grandfather clauses that gave otherwise disqualified voters whose grandfathers voted the right to vote. The effect of putting racially motivated restrictions on the voting process ultimately prevented blacks from gaining any political and economic power.

In 1954, state-sponsored segregation in public schools was ruled unconstitutional in the *Brown v. Board of Education* case. The Civil Rights Act of 1964 and the Voting Rights Act eventually overruled any Jim Crow laws that were still in existence. Despite the fact that the Fifteenth Amendment was used to clarify and solidify voting rights, many Southern blacks and other minorities were still denied voting rights through the 1960s. By the mid-1960s, the rights of African Americans and other minorities in the United States was a matter of great importance within the American political system. Each month went by with more demonstrations, more rallies, and more violence toward them. The tipping point was an incident in Selma, Alabama, when peaceful protestors were meaninglessly attacked by state troopers. President Johnson immediately began pressuring Congress more to generate civil rights legislation. Some of his goals were met when, in 1965, the Voting Rights Bill was passed.

Congress resolved that the antidiscrimination laws of the day were not strong enough to hold up against state officials who were reluctant to enforce the Fifteenth Amendment. This spurred legislative hearings that discovered how ineffective much of the legislation had been. Taking one discriminatory practice at a time made no difference—as soon as one biased practice was prohibited, a new tactic, which was not mentioned in any legislation, was instantly adopted.

John Lewis of the Student Nonviolent Coordinating Committee (currently a U.S. congressman) is clubbed to the ground by an Alabama state trooper during the first Selma voting rights march on March 7, 1965. (AP Photo)

The National Voting Rights Act of 1965 banned the idea that in order to be considered an eligible voter in the United States, one must first pass a literacy test. This also required for the federal registration of voters in regions that had less than 50 percent of eligible voters registered.

The act also gave the Department of Justice power to act on any unlawful voting practices. It now had jurisdiction over the registration process, changes in voting laws, and any "devices" that could be used to limit voting. The Voting Rights Act had an immediate impact on the empowerment of the African American population throughout the country by doing away with many of the restrictions that state laws had enacted. In 1966, the U.S. Supreme Court upheld the constitutionality of the Voting Rights Act, stating that "after enduring nearly a century of systematic resistance to the Fifteenth Amendment, Congress might do well to shift the advantage of time and inertia from the perpetrators of evil to its victims."

Three months after the passing of the Voting Rights Act of 1965, nearly 8,000 African Americans had registered to vote in Dallas County, Alabama. Only months earlier, violence was used against peaceful demonstrators wanting nothing more than to be treated equally. In Mississippi, African American voter registration skyrocketed from 6.7 percent of the population prior to the enactment of the Voting Rights Act to 59.8 percent by 1967. The Voting Rights Act of 1965 also resulted in a huge increase of African American elected officials. According to the Joint Center for Political and Economic Studies, fewer than 1,500 blacks held elective office in 1970, compared to the current estimate of 9,000. Section Five of the act was interpreted very loosely by the Supreme Court until 1970, when Congress eventually decided that the Supreme Court's interpretations were too broad and hearings on the matter were held. The hearing testimonies were filled with examples of discriminatory practices. The testimonies made clear that on the local level, "gerrymandering, annexations, adoption of at-large elections, and other structural changes" were all loopholed through the national legislation. Furthermore, recognition of the same kinds of discrimination against other ethnic minority groups materialized in the hearings. Regardless, Congress ultimately validated the Supreme Court's position by extending the bill for 12 years.

The *White v. Regester* decision (412 U.S. 755 [1973]) shaped law through the 1970s against many unfair gerrymandered redistricting plans. It determined that some multimember districts were unconstitutionally being used to restrict the power of minority votes. Even in the twenty-first century, restrictions on ballet access and minority vote intensity remain as serious obstacles to voting rights. Such policies as last-minute location changes of heavily minority polling places, discouragement of non-English-speaking citizens from voting, the use of extremely confusing registration requirements, racially centered campaigning, and intimidation and violence all are discouragements and hindrances for many African Americans to be a part of the voting process.

The Voting Rights Act of 1965 undoubtedly empowered African Americans and other minority groups with the right to vote. It is also directly responsible for giving members of those communities a say in shaping the social and economic problems that have plagued them for so long, through local, state, and county-elected officials. The Voting Rights Act of 1965 remains as a pivotal piece of American legislation and the fight for equality among races. It is a frontier peace of legislature in maintaining ideals of quality, fairness, and tolerance.

Certain provisions of the Voting Rights Act were set to expire in 2007. Congress responded and the Fannie Lou, Rosa Parks, and Coretta Scott King Voting Rights Act Reauthorization was signed for a 25-year extension by President George W. Bush on July 27, 2006.

Arthur Holst

See also: Civil Rights Act of 1964.

Further Reading

The Avalon Project. "Voting Rights Act of 1965. August 6, 1965." http://www.yale.edu/lawweb/avalon/statutes/voting_rights_1965.htm (accessed May 8, 2007).

U.S. Department of Justice. "The Voting Rights Act of 1965." http://www.usdoj.gov/crt/voting/intro/intro_b.htm (accessed June 15, 2007).

W

Wallace, George

George Corley Wallace was an Alabama governor who fought desegregation efforts during the 1960s. Wallace was born in Clio, Alabama, on August 25, 1919. As a child, Wallace expressed a great desire to involve himself in politics, seeing it as a way to help him, and others, out of poverty. After receiving an undergraduate degree from the University of Alabama, he enrolled in law school. Shortly after graduation, he was called to serve his country in the Army Air Corps during World War II. Almost immediately upon his return from the Pacific theater, he began a long career of public service. He served as a circuit judge, and later, he served in the Alabama House of Representatives. Wallace initially took a progressive stand on issues of civil rights and integration in particular. This changed dramatically after he lost a gubernatorial election in 1958 to a candidate who took a stronger stand against integration. Wallace blamed his loss on his moderate stand on civil rights issues.

Wallace first gained national attention when he physically stood in the door-way of the building where students at the University of Alabama registered for classes. His intention was to fulfill a campaign promise to physically prevent African American students from registering for classes at an all-white school. While the stand was largely symbolic and completely ineffective in preventing his goal of preserving segregation, this scene was displayed to a national audience by way of network television. This event propelled his political career that would span two decades as an elected official.

During this time in office, he campaigned against the expansion of integration. He regularly spoke against integration and used his position as governor to slow the progress of integration and impede the spread of civil rights for African Americans. He served as Alabama governor for four terms, 1963 to 1967, 1971 to 1975, 1975 to 1979, and 1983 to 1987. He was a presidential candidate for the Democratic Party in 1964, 1972, and 1976. He also ran as an independent in 1968. During Wallace's first term as governor, an Alabama governor could not succeed himself. After a failed attempt to eliminate this restriction, he convinced his wife, Lurleen, to run for governor. She succeeded and was governor from 1967 until her death in May 1968. Having his wife in office enabled him to continue to influence Alabama's state government and provided a base of support for his campaign for president through his American Independent Party. Although he won the electoral votes of several Southern states, he came up short in his presidential bid.

After his reelection to the Alabama governorship in 1970, he began his third attempt to run for the presidency. This time, he ran for president as a Democrat. After a respectable showing in early primaries, he was shot by a gunman while campaigning at a shopping mall in Maryland. One of the bullets lodged near his spinal cord and left him paralyzed from the waist down. This injury effectively ended his presidential campaign and any future hopes of becoming president. After an easy reelection as Alabama's governor in 1974, he attempted his fourth and final run for the presidency. After weak showings in early primaries, he withdrew from the race. He mounted his final gubernatorial campaign in 1982. Once again, he was successful. He decided not to run for reelection in 1986, citing complications from injuries stemming from the gunshot wounds, which took a toll on his health.

After his retirement from public service, Wallace spent a great amount of time apologizing for his actions and words that caused so much harm to so many people. He visited with many of the leaders of the civil rights era and other elected African Americans for the purpose of asking their forgiveness. Many of his former adversaries publicly forgave Wallace for his actions and stated he had a changed heart. Wallace died of heart failure on September 13, 1998.

James Newman

See also: Segregation, Residential.

Further Reading

Carter, Dan T. *The Politics of Rage.* New York: Simon and Schuster, 1995.

Lesher, Stephan. *George Wallace: American Populist.* Reading, MA: Addison-Wesley Publishing Company, 1994.

McMillen, Neil R. *The Citizens' Council: Organized Resistance to the Second Reconstruction, 1954–64.* Urbana: University of Illinois Press. 1971.

Rohler, Lloyd. *George Wallace: Conservative Populist.* Westport, CT: Greenwood Press, 2004.

Washington, Booker T.

African American leader Booker Taliaferro Washington was born into slavery in a slave cabin on a Virginia tobacco plantation to a white father who he did not know and a slave mother who could not read or write. His mother taught him lessons in thrift and virtue. These lessons, in addition to the slave code of ethics, in which it was acceptable to steal from those who enslaved you, would prove useful to Washington throughout his life. After the Emancipation Proclamation was signed, he and his family moved to West Virginia. As a young man, he learned of Hampton Institute and, on October 1, 1872, began his journey to Hampton, Virginia. He completed this journey, by foot and by railroad. Part of Washington's entrance requirements to Hampton Institute included sweeping the auditorium. He cleaned the auditorium more than once, which is a testament to Washington's diligence, hard work, and personal development.

While Washington had his challengers, he also served as an inspiration to many around the world. His approach has been criticized and dismissed for more overt displays of racial protest and petition for social change. Washington was called "the great accommodator" by W.E.B. Du Bois and has even been called an "Uncle Tom" for being too compromising with whites and for going so far as telling jokes in black dialect to white audiences. Washington's accommodating stance and compromise with whites can be understood within the context of the Jim Crow South, his Tuskegee project, and his demands for blacks' individual and economic development.

Washington wanted blacks to be self-sufficient but to understand the collective struggle. He pushed for advancement despite oppression and was very devoted and committed to his efforts, despite the overt and more covert obstacles that he faced. Washington believed

Educator Booker T. Washington, head of the Tuskegee Institute, advocated accommodation with white racism. (Library of Congress)

that both blacks and whites were responsible for making blacks productive and valuable to America's industrial growth. This great compromise was achieved through soliciting the support of whites while urging blacks not to agitate whites or challenge the status quo in demand of civil rights. Washington also called for blacks to forego social parity with whites in favor of greater economic development, and he felt it was possible to be segregated from whites but for there to still be economic ties to whites. He accomplished this by gaining middle- and upper-class whites' economic support for Tuskegee Institute.

Washington wanted to change black America from all angles and did not believe that blacks would forever be second-class citizens. He believed that there were contexts in which blacks would be advanced and have educational and economic opportunities. Washington, therefore, asked blacks to reflect on the accomplishments since the Emancipation Proclamation and how much more can be accomplished if blacks work together and form an economic base for self-sufficiency. This self-sufficiency would also make blacks and whites economically interdependent, rather than blacks being solely dependent on whites, and allow blacks to be prepared for their full citizenship rights and integration in American society.

With integration and assimilation in American society, Washington pushed for blacks to advance but not to isolate themselves socially by servicing blacks only or only supporting businesses because they were black-owned. Washington's challenge to blacks was to maintain an individual will through which the collective will can be mobilized and realized. Individual will included skill attainment, higher education when attainable, sobriety, and devoutness.

Washington was greatly inspired by abolitionist Frederick Douglass because Douglass was also born into slavery and learned and understood the virtues of being self-made and focusing on individual development. Douglass argued that blacks failed to attain a skill base, and this failure was the foundation for the "Negro problem." Douglass, therefore, was an advocate of blacks learning a trade so that they can gain parity with whites and have greater opportunities. In agreement with this sentiment, Washington thought that earning a dollar through a trade was worth more than the opportunity to spend a dollar in white establishments. Industrial education was deemed a necessity by Washington, whereas higher education was an option, not a priority. Washington knew that the majority of blacks would not have access to higher education, although Washington's own children did.

Washington and Douglass both believed that the South was the best place for blacks, that blacks should not move to the North, and that blacks should accumulate wealth in order to be more self-sufficient and have greater opportunities. Both Washington and Douglass also compared the potential for the development and advancement of blacks with the realized development and advancement of Jews. The Jews were admired for their pride, their unity, and their success upon assimilation, despite obstacles. Instead of complaining, blacks should have individual motivation and advancement so that they can advance as a people and actually contribute to society. The importance of learning a trade and the belief that blacks were to blame for the "Negro problem" was deemed simplistic in its logic by the critics of both Douglass and Washington because economic development was not *the* solution to the "Negro problem."

Washington and Douglass differed in that Washington placed greater emphasis on the individual accountability, self-sufficiency, and self-reliance components of Douglass's message whereas Douglass's overall message was more militant. In his militancy, Douglass maintained an assimilation stance without mocking blacks and making jokes about black dialect in front of white audiences. Douglass was often critical of whites' acts of oppression and partially attributed the conditions of blacks to this oppression. Unlike Washington, Douglass did not make jokes about blacks in front of whites or appear to go too far in his attempts at assimilating. Washington criticized this militancy because it had generally lost its effectiveness. Political and social agitation did not have a substantial grounding in economic development. However, Douglass did not live in the South and, despite the obstacles that Northern blacks faced, could afford to take a more militant approach.

Washington and Du Bois are often presented as adversaries with contrasting and conflicting views; however, they shared the ultimate objective, but differed mostly in strategy. Washington was similar to Du Bois in that he was committed to social change and social action and used various institutions to bring about such change, including Tuskegee Institute and the National Negro Business League. He did not openly discuss all of his affiliations and strategies for change but rather covertly fought for change. Washington knew that change was a process.

Among Du Bois's criticisms of Washington was that his advice was sought by presidents, politicians, philanthropists, and scholars, and that he was made into the Negro representative. Washington's appointment as the Negro representative was seen as a contradiction to the funding and support whites provided to Washington's Tuskegee Institute. This creates the image that Washington's interests and efforts are not purely in the interests of Negroes but are, instead, greatly influenced by whites. Whites supported Tuskegee and upheld him as the only valued black leader as long as he advocated segregation. Washington solicited this support of middle- and upper-class whites to back Tuskegee financially and to keep lower-class whites from interfering with Washington's efforts.

To understand Washington's stance, he must be placed within the context of the Jim Crow South, just as to understand Du Bois's and Douglass's approaches, they must be placed in the more Northern contexts in which they lived. Northern blacks faced inequality but in a different type of an environment, and were more educated, economically independent, and critical. Washington's approach of entrepreneurship and thriftiness appealed to Northern blacks. However, Northern blacks did not support Washington's belief that there can and should be protest without the appearance of protest and that fights for civil and political rights should be abandoned in favor of individual and economic development. He felt as though Du Bois and others were showing whites "their hands" rather than focusing on silent protest that would result in the development and true advancement of the Negro. Tuskegee Institute was one example of slow change and long-term investment for a larger goal. In the Jim Crow South, revolt and overt protest would have resulted in Washington being lynched and the struggle being lost.

Washington's efforts had been overshadowed and largely overlooked, while Du Bois's and his counterparts' efforts of desegregation and social justice were advanced. Washington's platform appealed to blacks' needs and urged blacks to forego their more immediate wants. As a result of the increased unpopularity of Washington's approach in favor of the approach of Du Bois and his counterparts, there continued to be a shortage of black entrepreneurs, and blacks' consumerism and dependency on whites increased with desegregation and an increase in voting and civil rights. Therefore, the efforts of Du Bois and his counterparts were successful in the short term, but blacks failed to become more self-sufficient as Washington envisioned. Washington's message is not completely lost because he continues to serve as a motivation and challenge to black entrepreneurs and blacks who are concerned with individual and collective moral and economic development.

Rutledge M. Dennis

See also: Albany Civil Rights Movement; Atlanta Compromise, The.

Further Reading

Adegbalola, Gaye Todd. "Interviews: Garvey, Du Bois, and Booker T." *Black Books Bulletin* 3 (Spring 1975).

Brock, Randall E. "Cast Down Your Buckets Where You Are." *Crisis* 99 (1992): 2.

Burns, Haywood. *Afro American Studies: An Interdisciplinary Journal* 1, no. 1 (May 1970).

Champion, Danny. "Booker T. Washington versus W.E.B. Du Bois: A Study in Rhetorical Contrasts." In *Oratory in the New South,* ed. Waldo W. Braden. Baton Rouge: Louisiana State University Press, 1979.

Cunnigen, Donald, Rutledge M. Dennis, and Myrtle Gonza Glascoe, eds. *Research in Race and Ethnic Relations.* Vol. 13, *The Racial Politics of Booker T. Washington,* 105–31. Oxford: JAI Press, 2006.

Flynn, John P. "Booker T. Washington: Uncle Tom or Wooden House." *Journal of Negro History* 54 (July 1969).

Hancock, Gordon B. "Booker T. Washington: His Defense and Vindication." *Negro Digest* 13, no. 7 (May 1964).

Harlan, Louis R. "Booker T. Washington in Biographical Perspective." *American Historical Review* 75 (1970): 1581–99.

Washington, Booker T. *Up from Slavery.* Garden City, NY: Doubleday, 1900.

Wells-Barnett, Ida B.

Ida Bell Wells-Barnett fought a battle against slavery's legacy of racism and segregation. She was born enslaved on July 16, 1862, in Holly Springs, Mississippi. Under the institution of slavery, her father, James Wells, had learned carpentry, thereby acquiring a higher social status than other enslaved persons. Ida Wells gained an education in schools operated by the Freedmen's Bureau, an organization set up after the Civil War. For a short while, she attended Shaw University, called Rust College until 1890, until her frequent clashes with the president, W. W. Hooper, led to her expulsion. In 1878, a yellow fever epidemic killed over 200 whites and about half as many blacks in Holly Springs, including Wells's parents and her baby sister. Because she was visiting her grandmother, she escaped the deadly virus. She learned of her parents' deaths and her siblings' whereabouts by letter and traveled back to her home after doctors reported safe conditions. Determined to keep the family together, Wells secured a job as a public school teacher at the age of 16. In 1881, she and her brother George and sister Annie joined their aunt in Memphis, where Wells soon began teaching in the city schools.

In September 1883, Wells directly attacked Jim Crow segregation by refusing to leave the first-class railroad car to sit in the smoky car reserved for blacks. Whites in the South

Ida B. Wells was a civil rights activist, journalist, and crusader against lynching. (Library of Congress)

were unaccustomed to the well-dressed and articulate African Americans more visible as access to education and transportation networks improved. Although middle-class blacks were an affront to social customs and Southern norms, many adopted respectability to counter racism. Wells, like other blacks who challenged segregation on streetcars and railroads, reasoned that she paid the price to sit in the nicer car and should be treated as such. Her defiance led the railroad conductor to use physical force to remove her from the car. She fought back, biting the conductor and clinging to her seat, but was no match for the other passengers who helped carry her to the second car. Wells filed suit after this incident and another and won cash settlements for both. The Tennessee Supreme Court eventually overturned the rulings but was not able to quiet Wells or end her activism. The incidents and others actually proved to be a major catalyst in her decision to pursue a career in journalism.

Wells's first articles dealt with her proceedings with the railroad company. She soon adopted the pseudonym, Iola, for her essays, and by the end of 1885, her work commonly appeared in newspaper columns. Wells often used her words to defend black women's virtue from the popular attacks in white and even black writings. Female writers faced resistance from some black men who felt threatened by sharing the literary field with females. The stereotypes surrounding black womanhood, especially the images of the Jezebel and Mammy, proliferated throughout the Jim Crow era. Many white-authored histories portrayed black women as Jezebels, the exact opposite of the ideal woman of the Victorian age. Mammy represented the antithesis of the libidinous Jezebel. Whites portrayed Mammy, who usually served in domestic capacities or as a caregiver to white children, as a woman without sexual desires. Wells wrote to attack the many institutions that became conduits for perpetuating these controlling images of black women. Many times, black men criticized Wells for ignoring society's definition of the proper roles for women.

Along with her teaching, in 1889, Wells became a co-owner of, and a writer for, the *Free Speech and Headlight,* a newspaper founded in Memphis by Taylor Nightingale and J. L. Fleming. Wells used the *Free Speech* as a mouthpiece for the unequal justice meted out to blacks and whites. Her classroom teaching ended in 1891, when the Memphis school board fired her for her criticism of the school system printed in the *Free Speech.* Since her salary as editor paid little, Wells worked to increase the circulation of the newspaper to make ends meet. These experiences mark the beginning of a lifelong crusade to inform the whole society about discrimination in general and lynching in particular.

After Wells reported the brutal murders of her associates and prominent members of the Memphis black community, Thomas Moss, Calvin McDowell, and Lee Stewart, antilynching became her main cause. The investigation of the brutal murders did not lead to any arrests since local law officials often cooperated with lynch mobs, the pinnacle of white terrorism in the United States. Understood later as motivated by the economic competition the African American businessmen represented, Wells used her reports on the lynching to encourage blacks to leave Memphis. She also chastised the white press that sensationalized the murders and demonized the upstanding black men. On May 21, 1892, the *Free Speech* published a piece by Wells that proclaimed the falsity of the often-echoed charges of rape that drove mobs to action. She hinted at some white women's willful participation in sexual liaisons with black men, angering whites in Memphis who destroyed her printing press and threatened her life. Wells fled Memphis for Chicago where she joined the staff of the *Age,* a black newspaper edited by T. Thomas Fortune.

In Chicago, Wells worked to correct the conception that mob members were mostly poor or ignorant whites. She also revealed that charges of criminality leveled at the victims of lynch mobs often resulted from racism rather than attempted or actual offenses. At first, Wells, like many whites, believed the charges of rape leveled at lynching's victims until she learned of its falsity firsthand. White men claimed the protection of white womanhood as a major validation for lynching. Like the Jezebel myth, the stereotype of the black male rapist emerged as evidence of the need for the separation of blacks and whites that defined Jim Crow. Wells worked to correct these assumptions on black personalities to end the deadly consequences these negative caricatures often elicited.

Wells was an example of the "new" African American woman in the context of Women's Rights and the Black Clubwomen's Movement of the late nineteenth century. A network of black women supported her crusade from the start. Like larger society, these clubs also reflected racial separation. In the fall of 1892, African American women in New York, Philadelphia, and Boston organized a well-attended reception where Wells delivered an emotional address about the Moss, McDowell, and Stewart lynchings and her exile from Holly Springs. The event drew support from the black press and an audience of over 200 people who provided the finances needed for Wells to publish *Southern Horrors,* her first pamphlet on lynching.

Ida B. Wells's antilynching campaign pamphlets *Southern Horrors* (1892), *A Red Record* (1892), and *Mob Rule in New Orleans* (1900) reflected a massive increase in violence toward black people after emancipation. In *Southern Horrors,* Wells argued that whites lynched blacks in response to the franchise, since access to the vote represented another privilege many whites in the South reserved for themselves. As such, Wells's essays protested the disenfranchisement of African Americans even though her gender barred her own participation in electoral politics. She then implicated the press that played an integral role in perpetuating the myth of the uncontrolled lust of black men. She also chided those men and women who refused to speak out against lynching. Wells declared that white men shamelessly murdered black men to protect white economic interest rather than white women.

In *A Red Record,* Wells recorded reported lynchings and their supposed causes. The plethora of descriptions of lynchings, all from white-authored sources, proved the compliancy of state police departments and elected officials. Wells played on whites' religious sensibilities by referring to the mobs as Christians. She also laid bare the issues she held with Women's Christian Temperance Union president Frances Willard, who defended the mobs in the name of white women. She finished her second pamphlet by calling for readers to be proactive in spreading the word on lynching. It ended by encouraging readers to support the 1894 Blair Bill that called for investigations into mob violence. Wells's final pamphlet chronicled the life and death of Robert Charles, whose actions in self-defense set off a mob of whites in New Orleans who then indiscriminately targeted the whole black community. The white press presented Charles as a murderer, but in actuality, his crime was working alongside Henry McNeil Turner in garnering support for emigration to Liberia. This detailed case of unbridled white violence disproved the black beast theory as justification for lynching, and reiterated that perpetrators remained unpunished. Like Wells's other writings, it used religious references and the gendered rhetoric of manhood to plead her case.

Following in the footsteps of the abolitionist Frederick Douglass, Wells carried her message to Europe to gain support for her campaign against lynching in 1893. Many foreign leaders considered America a symbol of freedom and democracy. Wells sought to provide a more nuanced vision of the nation that included the nature of Jim Crow legislation and the extent whites took to keep the races socially separate. She worked to inform other countries about the second-class status afforded African Americans in hopes that these countries would pressure leaders in the United States to protect the black civil rights. She returned to England a year later to conduct a second tour and further articulate her disgust of the U.S. government for seeming to ignore the continued humiliation and discrimination practiced on the basis of race.

In many ways, Wells was the antithesis of the theoretical model of true womanhood, though she did adhere to some prescribed gender roles. In 1895, she married Ferdinand Barnett, a lawyer and owner of the *Chicago Conservator.* After the marriage, she became editor of the *Conservator* and continued to use print media to wage a battle against Jim Crow. As a wife and mother of four children, Wells-Barnett's national influence declined, but not her zeal for antilynching and reform. Before her renown as the major voice of the antilynching campaign, Wells joined with other black leaders to dismantle segregation and discrimination. She held memberships in the National Afro-American League and the Southern Afro-American Press Association, and she became the National Colored Press Association's first female officer. She was also a member of the National Association of Colored Women and the National Association for the Advancement of Colored

People and supported suffrage for women. Her writings called for organization and concrete strategies to fight segregation and discrimination. Although Congress never passed the Blair Bill or any other form of antilynching legislation, Wells-Barnett's efforts did lead to a decrease in instances of lynching in the United States.

Christina L. Davis

See also: Lynching.

Further Reading

Duster, Alfreda M., ed. *Crusade for Justice: The Autobiography of Ida B. Wells.* Chicago: University of Chicago Press, 1970.

McMurry, Linda O. *To Keep the Waters Troubled: The Life of Ida B. Wells.* New York: Oxford University Press, 1998.

Royster, Jacqueline Jones. *Southern Horrors and Other Writings: The Anti-Lynching Campaign of Ida B. Wells, 1892–1900.* Boston: Bedford Books, 1997.

Schechter, Patricia. *Ida B. Wells-Barnett and American Reform, 1880–1930.* Chapel Hill: University of North Carolina Press, 2001.

White Citizens Council

White Citizens Councils were established to thwart the spread of civil rights in the South by means of economic retribution against citizens who supported civil rights workers or their cause. Membership consisted primarily of wealthy white business owners and elected officials. Most White Citizens Councils were first established following the U.S. Supreme Court decision of May 17, 1954, in the case of *Brown v. Board of Education,* when the Court reversed the 1896 ruling in *Plessy v. Ferguson,* declaring that racial segregation in schools was unconstitutional. The first White Citizens Council was formed in Greenwood, Mississippi, shortly before the *Brown v. Board of Education* ruling.

The councils were created to counteract the activities of the National Association of for the Advancement of Colored People (NAACP) and prevent the advancement of integration. Their formation met with varying degrees of success. Councils in Mississippi tended to possess more members than those in other states. The Deep South states of Alabama, Georgia, Louisiana, and South Carolina typically had more councils with more members than in other Southern states such as Tennessee, Arkansas, and North Carolina.

Often referred to as "the white-collar Klan," this organization sought to use its economic and political clout to deter and punish an individual's involvement in the NAACP and advancing civil rights. Typically, their activities would involve firing a person, denying a loan, or boycotting the person's business if that person was believed to be involved in supporting integration. Some groups sought to gain public support through advertising. Groups would often purchase advertising space in local newspapers to present their thoughts on integration and recruit members.

Some elected officials and other white community leaders openly favored laws that would maintain the status quo in the state's segregation practices. These individuals were often members of White Councils, or worked closely with them. A good example of this is the relationship Alabama governor George Wallace enjoyed with White Citizens Councils in his state. These groups would often support his candidacy through votes and monetary contributions. Mississippi's governor during the 1960s, Ross Barnett, also possessed close political ties with these organizations. Despite the strong ties with particular governors in the Deep South, White Citizens Councils were largely ineffective in other parts of the country.

The demise of White Citizens Councils came quickly in many parts of the South, but slowly in the Deep South. The last organized councils existed in Mississippi into the 1970s. Many of their official records were destroyed or sealed by state and local judges. In the later part of the twentieth century, most of the sealed records became available for viewing by the public. It provided a glimpse into the activities and meticulous records some White Citizens Councils kept on the activities of civil rights workers of the time.

James Newman

See also: Jim Crow; Ku Klux Klan.

Further Reading

McMillen, Neil R. *The Citizens' Council: Organized Resistance to the Second Reconstruction, 1954–1964.* Urbana: University of Illinois Press, 1971.

World War I

World War I involved the United States directly for only about a year and a half. The war occurred during one of the worst periods of oppression of black people in the United States since the end of slavery. Yet, the war also began to unleash forces that would, in the long run, begin the dismantling of Jim Crow. About 400,000 black men, and some black women, served in the American military during the war, which subjected them to the military's version of Jim Crow, while at the same time exposing many of them to a world beyond Jim Crow in Europe. Additionally, the economic mobilization of the war years brought new economic possibilities, and began the Great Migration of blacks from the rural South to the urban South, and eventually to the urban North. However, in the two years following the end of the war, blacks were victims of the worst racial violence since Reconstruction.

Jim Crow was justified in part by the idea that black men were naturally cowards, or that they would not fight for the United States. Most history of black participation in previous wars had been largely purged from historical memory. Men who would not fight were not fit to vote. Thus, many in the military and government, especially Southern whites, were hesitant over the idea of using blacks in combat. While most racists had little problem with using blacks in the military in support or transportation units, the idea of arming blacks and training them to kill Germans threatened to undermine the whole Jim Crow system. Black leaders put pressure on the federal government to allow black men to serve in the infantry, hoping that a strong showing of black men defending the United States would give

Officers of the 367th Infantry Regiment, 92nd Division in France during World War I. Most African Americans who fought in World War I served in the segregated 92nd Division or the 93rd Division, where all of the enlisted men were black. Most of the officers were white, but some black officers also served. (National Archives)

a moral argument for allowing black men to vote. Under pressure from blacks and their white liberal allies, the government adopted a policy whereby Selective Service was instructed to induct blacks as well as whites, and for the army to create new infantry regiments and even divisions of black men.

When the United States declared war on the Central Powers in April 1917, the regular army contained two infantry and two cavalry regiments of African Americans, for a total of almost 10,000 black men. This number included an influx of 4,000 men who joined during a recruiting drive in 1916. Of these four black regiments, three remained in the United States throughout the war, while one served in the Philippines. The National Guard contained another 10,000 black men, almost all of whom were from Northern states. However, most black men who served in the military during World War I, like their white counterparts, entered the military through Selective Service. Thirty-four percent of black registrants were later drafted, compared to 24 percent for whites. A total of 13 percent of draftees were black, although blacks constituted only around 10 percent of the total population. However, in the spring and early summer of 1917, whites were actively sought for voluntary enlistment into the military, whereas most blacks were denied enlistment, so that the eventual wartime army roughly reflected the ratio of blacks to whites in the nation. W.E.B. Du Bois, among other black intellectuals, urged blacks to support the war effort fully, believing that black opposition would be used to justify further oppression, whereas faithful support of the nation during wartime would bring recognition of the rights of blacks as Americans. In September 1917, Emmett J. Scott, former secretary to Booker T. Washington, was appointed special assistant to the U.S. secretary of war. Scott's mission was to assure that Selective Service did not discriminate.

With the war coming at the height of the Progressive era, the army attempted to use "scientific" intelligence testing to place drafted men into the most suitable position. Two professors, Walter D. Scott and Robert Yerkes, developed a series of questions that they believed measured innate intelligence, but actually tested familiarity with upper middle-class white culture. With 90 percent of blacks from the rural South illiterate, their knowledge of, for example, characters in the works of Charles Dickens was limited. According to the tests, almost half of all white and 89 percent of black draftees rated as "morons." While white supremacists tried to use the tests as "proof" that blacks were inferior to whites, the tests also showed that, on average, black Northerners outscored rural white Southerners. Such reports angered white Southerners, and the army disregarded the tests.

Most blacks who served in the military during the war served in the army. The Marine Corps admitted no blacks, while the navy took in about 1 percent. Of 400,000 blacks who served in the war, some 42,000 served in combat, a ratio slightly lower than for whites. Before the war, the black regular army regiments were stationed in the West or at overseas posts, as with most white regiments. However, the needs of the rapid mobilization for the war made necessary the construction of large mobilization and training camps, the majority of which were in the South, where land was cheaper and the warmer climate would allow more training over the winter of 1917–1918. Many blacks in the army assumed that their status as soldiers of the United States would protect them from Jim Crow, and for many Northern blacks, their time at training camps in the South would be their first experience with Jim Crow.

However, the army was sensitive to the opposition it faced from Southern political leaders over the very idea of arming and training black men, and bringing large numbers of them together. Southern political leaders often protested to the federal government when they found a black unit was to be stationed nearby. Among Southern whites, the use of black men by the federal government during the Civil War and Reconstruction was seen as an act of barbarity. The army feared the backlash from any incident that might occur. As a result, the army imposed strict Jim Crow–style regulations over its black soldiers, and in general sought to ship black units to Europe quickly, often before they had been properly trained or equipped. However, much the army attempted to mollify Southern whites by keeping the black soldiers under tight control, incidents were bound to occur.

The worst incident came on August 23, 1917, at Camp Logan, near Houston, Texas, involving soldiers from the 24th Infantry regiment, one of the four black regular army regiments. Many members of the 24th were relatively new soldiers, and the regiment had only recently been transferred to the South, where it was providing protection for a new training facility while it was under construction. However, the 24th, as with many regular regiments, had recently lost many of its long-term noncommissioned officers who had been assigned to the newly forming regiments in the national army. Additionally, many of the soldiers in the 24th had little firsthand experience with Jim Crow, and assumed their status as soldiers of the United States would shield them. Instead, the soldiers found themselves constantly harassed by civilians and police. When one of their own was arrested by local police, about 100 soldiers from two battalions used their army weapons in an attempt to free him. In the resulting melee, 16 white people died, including five policemen, and about a dozen others wounded. In the aftermath, the army tried by courts-martial 155 men in all. Nineteen of the men were hanged by the army, with no advanced public notice. The incident shocked blacks, who saw it as a lynching. Throughout the South, white communities interpreted the violence in Houston as an example of what happens when Northern blacks come to the South, and whites in the South became even more vigilant in ensuring Northern blacks respect the color line. The secretary of war, Newton D. Baker, a liberal, told President Woodrow Wilson that Jim Crow was the cause of the problems with the black units.

Racial violence between white civilians and black soldiers, such as in Houston, was used to justify keeping black soldiers in labor battalions and not issuing them weapons. As labor units, the African Americans performed superbly. One regiment, working as stevedores at a French port, was expected to unload 6,000 tons a month, based on French estimates. In September 1918 alone, they unloaded 800,000 tons. But many blacks, both soldiers and civilians, resented their serving only as laborers and clamored for black combat units. The army relented and reluctantly agreed to create more infantry units. Since segregation was the rule of the day in the army, black units were not comingled with white units. Instead, the army took the various black National Guard regiments and battalions and mixed them with newly formed regiments of black draftees, to create two new divisions, the 92nd and the 93rd.

Blacks also wanted to see black officers, not just black enlisted men. The army had, at the start of the war, very few black officers. Indeed almost all of the officers in the four black regular army regiments were white, although almost all of the officers in the black National Guard units were black. The highest-ranking black officer at the start of the war was Lieutenant Colonel Charles A. Young, a West Point graduate who served with the 10th Cavalry in Arizona. The army received complaints from Southern congressmen when white Southern junior officers were assigned to the 10th, which would mean serving under Colonel Young. Despite a flawless record, including combat in Cuba and Mexico, Young was forcibly retired, extensively on medical grounds, but in reality to placate Southern congressmen. Colonel Young appealed his retirement, but was not returned to active service until just before the war ended. Southern congressmen insisted that in no situation would white men be commanded by a black man. They dropped their opposition to the army creating a black Officers Candidate School only when the army assured them that black officers would never command white troops. At Fort Des Moines in Iowa, some 639 black men received commissions—106 as captains and the rest as lieutenants—out of 1,250 candidates. Almost all of these black officers were then assigned to the new black infantry regiments in the national army. However, even as officers, these men soon found that the army treated them as inferiors and subjected them to the same Jim Crow as enlisted black soldiers.

Prejudice against black soldiers within the army created the self-fulfilling prophecy of failure of black soldiers in battle. The most notorious example was the 92nd Division. The division suffered from poor training, lack of equipment, no artillery, and uneven officer quality. While some of the officers, especially the lower-ranking officers, were black, most officers, including all the higher-ranking officers, were white. Many of the white officers assigned to black units were either the castoffs from other divisions or self-identified racists in the belief that they "knew how to handle blacks." Thrown into battle on unfamiliar terrain two days after arrival in the Argonne, two battalions from the 368th Regiment failed in combat, while others performed well. The failure of some elements of the 92nd was projected to the entire division, and then to all black soldiers. The failure of the 92nd was cited as "proof" that blacks were naturally unfit for combat. As a result, most black combat soldiers had their weapons taken away and were employed in manual labor, especially as stevedores. This stigma would last through World War II.

In sharp contrast to the experience of the 92nd Division was that of the 93rd. The 93rd Division was "loaned" to the French Army, in part to ward off pressure from the French to take control of the entire American Expeditionary Force. While the French army was segregated by colonial or metropolitan origins of each regiment, it was not technically segregated on the color line. More importantly, the French had no stereotype of Africans or blacks being cowards or unfit to serve as soldiers. The French separated the four regiments of the 93rd and attached them to French divisions. Black American officers were shocked to find that French officers treated them as equals, as brother officers, something that never occurred in the U.S. Army. With French equipment, proper training, and capable leadership, the African American regiments performed well, earning 550 French decorations, including 180 of the Croix de Guerre, while suffering 35 percent casualties. They held their front for 191 days without losing territory, while capturing many Germans. The French government was so pleased with the performance of the black American soldiers that it heaped honors and praise on the fighting ability of the black Americans, which in turn led to the U.S. government requesting that the French cease its high praise, lest the black Americans come home demanding that they be treated as equals.

The worst period of violence against blacks came in the two years after the war, when postwar economic readjustment put many strains on American society. While labor violence erupted in Washington State and Oregon, and in Boston, the police strike took the occupation of the city by the State Guard to restore order, the worst violence in the nation was racial. Mississippi had the worst violence since the end of Reconstruction. Some whites bemoaned that they would have to lynch thousands of black men in order to restore the status quo as it had been before the war. Whites feared black men who had fought Germans—a white people—in Europe, and who had been "spoiled by French whores," would forget their place in America. While black Americans would celebrate units such as the 369th Regiment, the "Harlem Hellfighters," which saw heroic service with the French army, white America soon forgot all about black service and loyalty during the war, and instead subjected blacks to increased racism and savage violence, lest blacks think the war might change race relations in the nation. The experience would be a bitter lesson for black Americans.

Barry M. Stentiford

See also: Armed Forces; Great Migration.

Further Reading

Barbeau, Arthur, and Florette Henri. *Black American Troops in World War I*. Philadelphia: Temple University Press, 1974.

Buckley, Gail L. *American Patriots: The Story of Blacks in the Military from the Revolution to Dessert Storm*. New York: Random House, 2002.

Donaldson, Gary A. *The History of African-Americans in the Military*. Malabar, FL: Krieger Publishing Company, 1991.

Edgerton, Robert B. *Hidden Heroism: Black Soldiers in America's Wars*. Boulder, CO: Westview Press, 2001.

World War II

World War II was a pivotal event in history as it marked the emergence of modern America. The country came out of the war as a world economic and military power. Thousands of war veterans moved to the middle class thanks to housing and education loans through the federal G.I. Bill (officially known as the Serviceman's Readjustment Act). The role of government changed as did the place of African Americans and women in society. During the war, factories increased production to provide war goods to the armed services. The creation of this defense industry allowed African Americans and women to attain better-paying factory jobs that were never open to them before. After working in factories during the war, American women began to permanently move out of the home and into the workforce, changing gender and family dynamics. Many African American workers left the rural South to take advantage of job opportunities in the cities of the North and West. New types of jobs were open to black women, as many moved out of domestic positions and into the service sector. Most African Americans were eager to contribute to the war effort. Many black men, in an attempt to show their patriotism, joined the armed forces. Segregation in the military and the treatment of blacks as second-class citizens at home angered many blacks and prompted them to advocate for equality in America as the country was fighting for freedom and against Fascism in Europe.

Migration

During the war, the nation's factories increased production to make goods for the war, providing much-needed jobs in the wake of the Great Depression. Since many white men had gone to war, women and African Americans took their places in factories. The availability of better-paying factory jobs attracted rural blacks to industrial centers all over the country. African Americans living in rural areas of the South migrated to Southern cities, which were industrializing for war production. Hundreds of thousands of Southern blacks who wanted to escape violence and Jim Crow chose to leave the South completely, migrating to cities in the North and West. This migration, often referred to as the Second Great Migration, caused various effects in the places from which migrants left and those to which they traveled. Many blacks found better-paying positions during the war in factories producing goods for the military. This notwithstanding they also faced discrimination in their new homes. Moreover, overcrowding of black communities and subsequent expansion of black residence into other communities, competition over war industry employment, unequal access to skilled employment, and race antagonisms were all effects of the World War II migration.

Blacks moved en masse to cities in the West such as Oakland and Los Angeles, where huge shipyards and new aerospace industries were located. African Americans also moved to cities with heavy industry—for example, steel and automobile factories, which could be easily converted to produce war goods. The black populations of Detroit and Chicago skyrocketed during the war. Black migrants also continued to settle in New York City even though the city's factories converted to wartime production much later than other cities because of the lack of heavy industry.

The influx of blacks in Northern and Western cities caused changes to the population of these cities, which often led to racial tension and competition over jobs and resources. As more and more blacks moved into Western cities in areas where they had never lived, African American faced increased discrimination from white residents. In these new areas of black settlement like Los Angeles and Richmond, California, black residence was restricted to declining neighborhoods.

In Detroit and Chicago, cities with a large black population, more and more blacks moved there, settling in the existing black neighborhoods and straining the community resources available. Because the number of blacks skyrocketed in these cities and the areas where they could reside did not, the migration resulted in overcrowding of black neighborhoods, higher mortality rates, and increased crime. The standard of living in many of these urban black communities declined.

Black Labor

Though the industries of the North and West attracted Southern blacks, there were factors pushing them to leave the South. Technological innovations displaced agricultural black laborers in the South, prompting many to look for employment in urban factories. The mechanical cotton picker made the sharecropper system obsolete. Mechanization of farming through the adoption of tractors, harvesters, and sprayers made the need for black farm workers decline. Therefore, World War II provided industrial opportunities for blacks looking to leave a Southern economy that had less and less of a place for them. As the migration continued, the black community in Southern rural areas was gradually erased.

Many black migrants were not initially able to take advantage of the labor shortages in the early years of the war, especially in construction, heavy industry, and the aircraft industry. Employers hired white workers, ending white unemployment, while blacks remained without jobs, without training, and deprived of income because of reductions in Depression-era federal relief programs. Many companies, especially aviation factories that produced planes for the military, refused to employ black workers, a policy supported by the trade unions representing white workers. The United States Employment Service (USES), a federal agency, continued to fill "white only" requests from factory employers. The USES's general policy was to operate according to the pattern of the local community; therefore, if industries in a community did not hire black workers, their office would not, either. The policy of the USES reinforced discriminatory hiring practices of employers. For these reasons, during the early war years, African Americans often had trouble finding any position other than custodian in war industries.

In the South, where much defense industry was located, the National Youth Administration could not enroll blacks in training programs. There were no technical schools for blacks in the South, and because of Jim Crow laws, blacks could not enroll in white schools to learn these skills. In their efforts to exert greater control in government worker recruitment, Southern governors increasingly relied on closed shop agreements with trade unions of the American Federation of Labor (AFL). This collusion

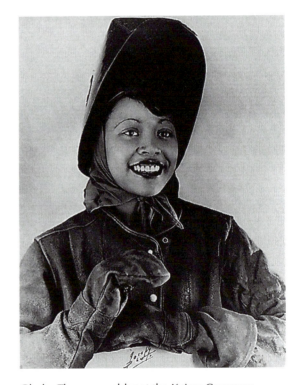

Gladys Theus, a welder at the Kaiser Company Permanente Metals Corporation yards near Oakland, California. During World War II, women occupied many positions in industry previously held by men. (National Archives)

between local governments and the AFL would restrict who received the expanding employment benefits, a fact that had large implications for African Americans since they were often excluded from AFL membership. Southern employers preferred to use white women instead of blacks to fill labor vacancies in order to preserve the racial configuration and power relations of Southern society. In this way, federal mobilization agencies became the battleground over labor control in the South.

In 1943, circumstances in the labor market changed that prompted factories nationwide to open their doors to black workers. Increased demands for war production and a manpower shortage forced factories to hire black workers. With labor shortages becoming more acute each day and the government considering plans for manpower allocation, employers began to relax the bars to hiring, and unions found it more difficult to maintain restrictive policies. African Americans began to find skilled and semiskilled positions in the nation's factories, earning more money than they had before. Black women in particular moved out of domestic jobs and into jobs in factories and service industries.

Social Effects of the Migration

In the South, employment of blacks in factories unsettled race relations. Whites in the rural South who were anxious about miscegenation openly resented wage increases for African Americans. These advances made Negroes too independent in their eyes, which was a dangerous development because it would foster African Americans' quest for social equality. Many blacks received war jobs, and some even managed to obtain skilled positions in plants. In general, however, the most menial and work-intensive jobs were given to black workers. White workers largely rose in status and income, but black workers entering the labor market took over the worst positions. Moreover, the traditional labor system of the South was being disrupted. To ensure adequate and efficient war production, the War Manpower Commission recruited Southern black workers to move to the Midwest and West Coast. This further undermined the low-wage labor system of Southern industries and large-scale agriculture.

The migration affected social and racial patterns in Northern and Western cities also. In Western cities, where few blacks had lived before the war, the migration had enormous employment and social effects. The massive wartime influx of black migrants to Los Angeles and San Francisco changed the racial and regional composition of the population. The arrival of unskilled migrants who would work for less pay prompted a restructuring of production methods from craftsmanship to mass production. In response, unions tightened their control on membership, excluding black workers. The Brotherhood of Boilermakers, the AFL craft union for shipyard workers, was the most vocal opponent of the new labor process.

In reaction to black migration, white residents often placed more stringent social controls on African Americans. Between 1940 and 1945, over 340,000 black people migrated to California to take advantage of employment opportunities in the new war industries. After the passage of Executive Order 8802 banning race discrimination in defense industries, black workers accelerated their movement into the state. As black newcomers flooded the cities, whites abandoned them, confining African Americans to isolated neighborhoods. Increased racial segregation, changing economic and social relations, forging of bonds between black old-timers and newcomers, and expansion of the black industrial workforce were all results of the migration. Municipalities from Los Angeles to San Francisco responded to the influx of black migrants by establishing more stringent social, political, and economic restrictions on all black residents, newcomers, and longtime residents alike. Local newspapers and police departments began to characterize crime in racial terms, giving a distorted picture of black criminal activity and stigmatizing the entire community.

The new migration also had political effects. The influx of new black working-class voters and the corporatist nature of municipal politics during the war enabled a coalition of labor, blacks, and other progressive groups to mount an attack on conservative rule. Under the leadership of a united labor movement, this coalition grew to become major contenders in postwar urban politics, especially in Oakland.

Variations of the patterns and processes in California were at work in Detroit, Chicago, and New York City as well. Centers of production provided blacks with greater economic and social opportunities, and facilitated the rise of the black middle. However, due in part to migration, the cities' blacks faced pervasive discrimination and competition from whites, which caused blacks to have to endure inferior employment opportunities; substandard housing; inadequate health facilities; inferior education; and problems with drugs, crime, and insecurity. The migration of blacks to urban areas during World War II indelibly affected the social, political, and economic landscape of American cities.

Blacks in the Military

African Americans had been treated as second-class citizens for more than a century in the United States. Many blacks believed that white Americans would more likely see blacks in this country as full citizens if they proved their love for and dedication to the country. As in World War I, black men volunteered as soldiers fighting to defend the nation and its democratic principles in an effort to demonstrate their bravery and their status as American citizens. Most black soldiers, however, were never accepted as equals. When blacks enlisted in the military, many were placed in segregated combat units, training schools, and camp facilities. Moreover many black soldiers, though trained, never saw actual combat. Instead they made up the service and supply units, often acting as porters and messmen, the same positions to which many black men had been relegated as civilians.

African American organizations like the National Association for the Advancement of Colored People (NAACP), the National Urban League (NUL), and the Brotherhood of Sleeping Car Porters (BSCP) pressured the government to end segregation in the armed forces. Walter White, executive secretary of the NAACP, and A. Philip Randolph, president of the BSCP, met with President Franklin D. Roosevelt and other military officials to express their views. These leaders advocated for integration of the military and asked the federal government to denounce discriminatory practices, goals that were not fully reached until President Harry S. Truman's executive order in 1948.

Black soldiers were also targets of racial violence in American cities. Mobs of whites attacked black soldiers, many of whom were in uniform. During the war, incidents of racial violence increased as they had in previous American wars. Racial violence took place involving white and black soldiers in several American cities, including Alexandria, Louisiana (1942); Florence, South Carolina (1942); Phoenix, Arizona (1942); Flagstaff, Arizona (1943); and Vallejo, California (1943). Violence broke out between black soldiers and white soldiers, police, and civilians in these incidents.

The Riots of 1943

The challenges to equality that African Americans faced during the war exploded in 1943. More than 240 racial incidents occurred in 47 different towns and cities during that year. Full-scale race riots broke out in Detroit, Harlem, and Los Angeles, and numerous lynchings occurred in a number of different states. Tensions between whites and blacks in many cities were exacerbated by migration, overcrowding in defense centers, competition for jobs, and conflict over housing. These tensions erupted in violence and in some cases escalated to race riots.

The Detroit Race Riot of 1943 was the most infamous and destructive race riot that year. A dispute between black youths and whites over access to the Belle Isle amusement park started the riot. The violence moved to the black section of the city, and African Americans began to stone white-owned stores and cars driven by whites. Many blacks rioted out of frustration about limited economic opportunities, police brutality, substandard housing, segregation, and inadequate recreational facilities. White rioters were acting out racial prejudice, and many were angry about having to compete with blacks for jobs, housing, and recreational facilities. The two days of racial violence ended with 9 whites and 25 blacks dead. Nearly 700 people were injured. The riot resulted in nearly $2 million worth of property stolen or damaged before state and federal troops regained order.

Similar dynamics set off a riot in Harlem less than two months later. The frustration blacks felt at employers' continued refusals to employ them in higher-paying war industries contributed to an explosion of discontent in the summer of 1943. On the night of August 2, a riot began in response to a white police officer shooting an off-duty black soldier. The police charged the soldier with interfering in the arrest of a black woman in the lobby of a Harlem hotel. False rumors circulated accusing the officer of having killed the soldier who was trying to defend his mother. In response to the rumors, black rioters broke store windows, looted, damaged property, and attacked policemen. By the morning of August 3, five persons had been killed, 400 injured, and hundreds of stores had been looted. Property damage was estimated at $5 million. Many African American leaders believed this burst of violent action was an outgrowth of the lack of economic opportunities for New York City's African Americans.

The underlying causes of the racial violence in Detroit and New York City illustrate how African Americans felt in other centers of defense production during the war. Police violence and competition over limited resources and jobs contributed to a rash of racial conflicts between whites and blacks during the war. Though violence was one manifestation of black frustration, black leaders and black organizations sought other methods to alleviate some of the problems blacks in cities faced.

1940s' Jim Crow and the Beginning of Civil Rights Activism

Increasingly, scholars have identified World War II as a catalyst for black activism and a more militant African American consciousness. African Americans linked the issues of victory over Fascism abroad with victory over racism at home and began a campaign for racial equality. The Double V campaign was the term used for the myriad of activities undertaken by black leaders and organizations to achieve full citizenship for African Americans. "Double V," a term initially used in a newspaper article appearing in the *Pittsburgh Courier,* stood for "Victory at Home and Abroad."

Black workers used the mobilization process and federal programs to gain economic and social mobility. Labor activism was especially important to African Americans because legislation was passed in 1941 prohibiting discriminatory hiring practices in war industries. During the war African American demands for civil rights were focused on the workplace. Black workers and activists, following in the footsteps of A. Philip Randolph, emerged as leaders in local and national struggles for black rights. African Americans used the need for factory workers and fair employment to force the federal government into acting for the equality of black

workers. Southern black activists in trade unions and civic organizations, local offices of the NUL and NAACP, and other locally based grassroots groups comprised
a national effort to get African Americans jobs in war projects.

Black organizations took action to resist discrimination in 1941. In April, Lester
Granger, executive secretary of the NUL, Walter White, leader of the NAACP,
Channing Tobias of the YMCA, Mary McLeod Bethune of the National Youth
Administration and A. Philip Randolph of the Brotherhood of Sleeping Car Porters
asked President Roosevelt to forbid discrimination in the armed forces and defense
industries. Secretary of War Henry Stimson and Secretary of the Navy Frank Knox
refused to desegregate the armed forces, and Roosevelt did not insist. Afraid of angering employers and Southern Democrats, the president merely issued a statement
condemning discrimination. The black delegation felt that this was not enough and
proposed a march on Washington, D.C., at a meeting in Chicago. Randolph agreed
to lead the March on Washington Movement and publicly announced plans for
such a march to demand an executive order to end racial discrimination in defense
industries.

This outpouring of black discontent and the threat of a mass protest forced
the federal government to relent. On June 25, 1941, the pressure from the March
on Washington Movement pushed President Roosevelt to issue an executive
order banning discriminatory hiring practices in industries with government war
contracts. Not only did Executive Order 8802 prohibit discrimination in hiring
practices but also prohibited government training programs from discriminating
against black workers. Finally, the executive order established the Fair Employment Practices Commission in the Office of Production Management. The committee was to receive and investigate complaints of discrimination in violation
of the executive order, and take appropriate steps to redress grievances which it
found to be valid.

The March on Washington Movement was the beginning of a newer, more militant, outright demand for civil rights: a demand spurred by economic hardships.
Black organizations pressured government agencies to enforce fair employment
legislation. In 1945, a breakthrough in fair employment legislation came in New
York with the passage of the Ives-Quinn Law, which outlawed discriminatory hiring practices in the state. Black newspapers continuously ran stories on discrimination against black soldiers and workers, informing black readers of the prejudice
and rallying support for the activities of black organizations to alleviate these problems. There is also evidence that black servicemen after fighting in the war refused
to accept prewar racial practices. Black veterans, many of whom had lived in the
South, were more likely to reenlist, and twice as likely to relocate to a different
region after the war.

Legacy

Many historians believe that World War II was a catalyst for processes that ended in the ghettoization of urban black communities. Moreover, many use the end of the war as the marker of the beginning of urban decline. They argue that racism prevented blacks from moving into the middle class, and restrictive covenants, redlining, and denial of federal housing loans kept blacks out of the growing suburbs. Consequently, many African Americans were trapped in decaying cities. Moreover, racist implementation of the federal G.I. Bill also gave unfair economic advantage to white war veterans who could use government loans for housing to buy homes in the suburbs and tuition loans to go to college. Using the G.I. Bill, white veterans and their families entered the middle class, while black veterans were not afforded those opportunities. Some link the more militant protests it engendered to the beginning of the Civil Rights Movement.

No matter the arguments about the long-term effects of the war, World War II was very significant for African Americans. The availability of factory jobs to African Americans, which prompted migration, changed the face of American cities. Black men and women were able to find better-paying jobs in factories, and black women moved out of domestic occupations and into clerical and service positions after the war. For the first time, the majority of blacks no longer resided in rural Southern areas. In fact, after the 1940s, the African American population was no longer concentrated in the South, but spread more evenly throughout the country. World War II created not only modern America but modern black America as it was known for the rest of the twentieth century.

Carla J. DuBose

See also: Detroit Race Riot of 1943; Double V Campaign; March on Washington Movement; Roosevelt, Franklin D.

Further Reading

Blum, John M. *V Was for Victory: Politics and American Culture during World War II.* San Diego, CA: Harcourt Brace Jovanovich, 1976.

Capeci, Dominic J., Jr., and Martha Wilkerson. *Layered Violence: The Detroit Rioters of 1943.* Jackson: University of Mississippi, 1991.

Chamberlain, Charles D. *Victory at Home: Manpower and Race in the American South during World War II.* Athens: University of Georgia Press, 2003.

Dalfiume, Richard M. "The 'Forgotten Years' of the Negro Revolution." *Journal of American History* 55, no. 1 (June 1968): 90–106.

Johnson, Marilynn S. *The Second Gold Rush: Oakland and the East Bay during World War II.* Berkeley: University of California Press, 1993.

Lemann, Nicholas. *The Promised Land: The Great Black Migration and How It Changed America.* New York: Albert A. Knopf, 1991.

Lynch, Hollis R. *The Black Urban Condition: A Documentary History, 1866–1971.* New York: Crowell, 1973.

McGuire, Phillip. "Desegregation of the Armed Forces: Black Leadership Protest and World War II." *Journal of Negro History* 68, no. 2. (Spring 1983): 147–58.

Polenberg, Richard. *War and Society: The United States, 1941–1945.* Philadelphia: J. B. Lippincott Company, 1972.

Wynn, Neil. *The Afro-American and the Second World War.* New York: Holmes and Meier, 1976.

Wynn, Neil. "The 'Good War': The Second World War and Postwar American Society." *Journal of Contemporary History* 31, no. 3 (July 1996): 463–82.

Primary Documents

EXCERPTS FROM *PLESSY V. FERGUSON* (1896)

Plessy v. Ferguson *was one of the most important decisions about the meaning of the Thirteenth Amendment and Fourteenth Amendment to be handed down during the 19th century. In the* Civil Rights Cases *(1883), the U.S. Supreme Court ruled that Congress did not have the power to remedy individual acts of racial discrimination that were not the result of state action. By contrast, in* Plessy v. Ferguson, *the Court upheld one of Louisiana's Jim Crow laws requiring that white and black passengers be seated in separate train cars. This law was challenged by Homer Plessy, who was seven-eighths white and one-eighth black, after he was denied seating on a car reserved for whites. (See also Louisiana;* Plessy v. Ferguson*)*

That petitioner was a citizen of the United States and a resident of the state of Louisiana, of mixed descent, in the proportion of seven-eighths Caucasian and one-eighth African blood; that the mixture of colored blood was not discernible in him, and that he was entitled to every recognition, right, privilege, and immunity secured to the citizens of the United States of the white race by its constitution and laws; that on June 7, 1892, he engaged and paid for a first-class passage on the East Louisiana Railway, from New Orleans to Covington, in the same state, and thereupon entered a passenger train, and took possession of a vacant seat in a coach where passengers of the white race were accommodated; that such railroad company was incorporated by the laws of Louisiana as a common carrier, and was not authorized to distinguish between citizens according to their race, but, notwithstanding this, petitioner was required by the conductor, under penalty of ejection from said train and imprisonment, to vacate said coach, and occupy another seat, in a coach assigned by said company for persons not of the white race, and for no other reason than that petitioner was of the colored race; that, upon petitioner's refusal to comply with such order, he was, with the aid of a police officer, forcibly ejected from said coach, and hurried off to, and imprisoned in, the parish jail of

New Orleans, and there held to answer a charge made by such officer to the effect that he was guilty of having criminally violated an act of the general assembly of the state, approved July 10, 1890, in such case made and provided. . . .

We consider the underlying fallacy of the plaintiff's argument to consist in the assumption that the enforced separation of the two races stamps the colored race with a badge of inferiority. If this be so, it is not by reason of anything found in the act, but solely because the colored race chooses to put that construction upon it. The argument necessarily assumes that if, as has been more than once the case, and is not unlikely to be so again, the colored race should become the dominant power in the state legislature, and should enact a law in precisely similar terms, it would thereby relegate the white race to an inferior position. We imagine that the white race, at least, would not acquiesce in this assumption. The argument also assumes that social prejudices may be overcome by legislation, and that equal rights cannot be secured to the negro except by an enforced commingling of the two races. We cannot accept this proposition. If the two races are to meet upon terms of social equality, it must be the result of natural affinities, a mutual appreciation of each other's merits, and a voluntary consent of individuals. [. . .]

Mr. Justice HARLAN dissenting [excerpt]

In respect of civil rights, common to all citizens, the constitution of the United States does not, I think, permit any public authority to know the race of those entitled to be protected in the enjoyment of such rights. Every true man has pride of race, and under appropriate circumstances, when the rights of others, his equals before the law, are not to be affected, it is his privilege to express such pride and to take such action based upon it as to him seems proper. But I deny that any legislative body or judicial tribunal may have regard to the race of citizens when the civil rights of those citizens are involved. Indeed, such legislation as that here in question is inconsistent not only with that equality of rights which pertains to citizenship, national and state, but with the personal liberty enjoyed by every one within the United States. [. . .]

Source: Plessy vs. Ferguson, Judgement, Decided May 18, 1896; Records of the Supreme Court of the United States; Record Group 267; Plessy v. Ferguson, 163, #15248, National Archives.

EXECUTIVE ORDER 9981 (1948)

Signed by President Harry Truman on July 26, 1948, Executive Order 9981 created the President's Committee on Equality of Treatment and Opportunity in the Armed Forces. It led to the desegregation of the U.S. military. Truman had promised presidential action on the issue of civil rights in a speech before Congress on

February 2, 1948. This executive order, in conjunction with Executive Order 9980 (which established the Fair Employment Board in the Civil Service Commission), fulfilled that promise. (See also Armed Forces; Executive Order 9981)

Establishing the President's Committee on Equality of Treatment and Opportunity in the Armed Forces.

WHEREAS it is essential that there be maintained in the armed services of the United States the highest standards of democracy, with equality of treatment and opportunity for all those who serve in our country's defense:

NOW THEREFORE, by virtue of the authority vested in me as President of the United States, by the Constitution and the statutes of the United States, and as Commander in Chief of the armed services, it is hereby ordered as follows:

1. It is hereby declared to be the policy of the President that there shall be equality of treatment and opportunity for all persons in the armed services without regard to race, color, religion or national origin. This policy shall be put into effect as rapidly as possible, having due regard to the time required to effectuate any necessary changes without impairing efficiency or morale.

2. There shall be created in the National Military Establishment an advisory committee to be known as the President's Committee on Equality of Treatment and Opportunity in the Armed Services, which shall be composed of seven members to be designated by the President.

3. The Committee is authorized on behalf of the President to examine into the rules, procedures and practices of the Armed Services in order to determine in what respect such rules, procedures and practices may be altered or improved with a view to carrying out the policy of this order. The Committee shall confer and advise the Secretary of Defense, the Secretary of the Army, the Secretary of the Navy, and the Secretary of the Air Force, and shall make such recommendations to the President and to said Secretaries as in the judgment of the Committee will effectuate the policy hereof.

4. All executive departments and agencies of the Federal Government are authorized and directed to cooperate with the Committee in its work, and to furnish the Committee such information or the services of such persons as the Committee may require in the performance of its duties.

5. When requested by the Committee to do so, persons in the armed services or in any of the executive departments and agencies of the Federal Government shall testify before the Committee and shall make available for use of the Committee such documents and other information as the Committee may require.

6. The Committee shall continue to exist until such time as the President shall terminate its existence by Executive order.

Harry Truman
The White Hous0065
July 26, 1948

Source: Truman, Harry. Executive Order no. 9981. *Federal Register,* 13 FR4313 (July 28, 1948).

EXCERPTS FROM *BROWN V. BOARD OF EDUCATION* (1954)

In Brown v. Board of Education *(1954), the U.S. Supreme Court ruled that segregated educational institutions were unconstitutional. The Topeka Board of Education, in Topeka, Kansas, had allowed for segregated elementary schools, which led to the lawsuit on the part of the National Association for the Advancement of Colored People (NAACP). In the* Brown *decision, the Supreme Court overturned the "separate but equal" doctrine that had been sanctioned by* Plessy v. Ferguson *(1896). In the unanimous decision, Chief Justice Earl Warren wrote that separating children by race contributed to feelings of inferiority. The Court also had found that segregated education violated the equal protection clause of the Fourteenth Amendment. (See also* Brown v. Board of Education*;* Brown v. Board of Education, *Legal Groundwork for)*

Segregation of white and Negro children in the public schools of a State solely on the basis of race, pursuant to state laws permitting or requiring such segregation, denies to Negro children the equal protection of the laws guaranteed by the Fourteenth Amendment—even though the physical facilities and other "tangible" factors of white and Negro schools may be equal.

(a) The history of the Fourteenth Amendment is inconclusive as to its intended effect on public education.

(b) The question presented in these cases must be determined, not on the basis of conditions existing when the Fourteenth Amendment was adopted, but in the light of the full development of public education and its present place in American life throughout the Nation.

(c) Where a State has undertaken to provide an opportunity for an education in its public schools, such an opportunity is a right which must be made available to all on equal terms.

(d) Segregation of children in public schools solely on the basis of race deprives children of the minority group of equal educational opportunities, even though the physical facilities and other "tangible" factors may be equal.

    (e) The "separate but equal" doctrine adopted in Plessy v. Ferguson has no place in the field of public education.

    (f) The cases are restored to the docket for further argument on specified questions relating to the forms of the decrees.

MR. CHIEF JUSTICE WARREN delivered the opinion of the Court [excerpt]

The plaintiffs contend that segregated public schools are not "equal" and cannot be made "equal," and that hence they are deprived of the equal protection of the laws. Because of the obvious importance of the question presented, the Court took jurisdiction. Argument was heard in the 1952 Term, and reargument was heard this Term on certain questions propounded by the Court.

Reargument was largely devoted to the circumstances surrounding the adoption of the Fourteenth Amendment in 1868. It covered exhaustively consideration of the Amendment in Congress, ratification by the states, then existing practices in racial segregation, and the views of proponents and opponents of the Amendment. This discussion and our own investigation convince us that, although these sources cast some light, it is not enough to resolve the problem with which we are faced. At best, they are inconclusive. The most avid proponents of the post-War Amendments undoubtedly intended them to remove all legal distinctions among "all persons born or naturalized in the United States." Their opponents, just as certainly, were antagonistic to both the letter and the spirit of the Amendments and wished them to have the most limited effect. What others in Congress and the state legislatures had in mind cannot be determined with any degree of certainty.

An additional reason for the inconclusive nature of the Amendment's history, with respect to segregated schools, is the status of public education at that time. In the South, the movement toward free common schools, supported by general taxation, had not yet taken hold. Education of white children was largely in the hands of private groups. Education of Negroes was almost nonexistent, and practically all of the race were illiterate. In fact, any education of Negroes was forbidden by law in some states. Today, in contrast, many Negroes have achieved outstanding success in the arts and sciences as well as in the business and professional world. It is true that public school education at the time of the Amendment had advanced further in the North, but the effect of the Amendment on Northern States was generally ignored in the congressional debates. Even in the North, the conditions of public education did not approximate those existing today. The curriculum was usually rudimentary; ungraded schools were common in rural areas; the school term was but three months a year in many states; and compulsory school attendance was virtually unknown. As a consequence, it is not surprising that there should be so little in the history of the Fourteenth Amendment relating to its intended effect on public education.

Today, education is perhaps the most important function of state and local governments. Compulsory school attendance laws and the great expenditures for education both demonstrate our recognition of the importance of education to our democratic society. It is required in the performance of our most basic public responsibilities, even service in the armed forces. It is the very foundation of good citizenship. Today it is a principal instrument in awakening the child to cultural values, in preparing him for later professional training, and in helping him to adjust normally to his environment. In these days, it is doubtful that any child may reasonably be expected to succeed in life if he is denied the opportunity of an education. Such an opportunity, where the state has undertaken to provide it, is a right which must be made available to all on equal terms.

We come then to the question presented: Does segregation of children in public schools solely on the basis of race, even though the physical facilities and other "tangible" factors may be equal, deprive the children of the minority group of equal educational opportunities? We believe that it does.

In Sweatt v. Painter, supra, in finding that a segregated law school for Negroes could not provide them equal educational opportunities, this Court relied in large part on "those qualities which are incapable of objective measurement but which make for greatness in a law school." In McLaurin v. Oklahoma State Regents, supra, the Court, in requiring that a Negro admitted to a white graduate school be treated like all other students, again resorted to intangible considerations: ". . . his ability to study, to engage in discussions and exchange views with other students, and, in general, to learn his profession." Such considerations apply with added force to children in grade and high schools. To separate them from others of similar age and qualifications solely because of their race generates a feeling of inferiority as to their status in the community that may affect their hearts and minds in a way unlikely ever to be undone.

Source: Brown v. Board of Education, 347 U.S. 483 (1954).

THE SOUTHERN MANIFESTO, *AKA* DECLARATION OF CONSTITUTIONAL PRINCIPLES (1956)

The Supreme Court's Brown v. Board of Education *(1954) decision, which ruled that the segregationist system of "separate but equal" in education was unconstitutional, is widely hailed as a victory for U.S. civil rights. Not so, however, by Southern pro-segregation legislators (mostly Democrats) of the time who were fervently opposed to racial integration and the overthrow of the white supremacist system of the 1950s' South. To protest the federal government's support of integration, during February and March 1956, the segregationist legislators wrote "The Southern*

Manifesto," which spelled out their opposition to what they perceived as a threat to their region's way of life and the Supreme Court's abuse of judicial power.

The first and most radical draft of the manifesto was written by South Carolina's Senator Strom Thurmond—1948 presidential candidate for the States Rights Democratic Party (Dixiecrats) and one of the Senate's most fervent segregationists— though the caucus demanded that the document be rewritten by more temperate senators. The final draft was written by Georgia's Richard Russell, with additions by Florida's Spessard Holland and Texas's Price Daniel. The document was signed by 19 senators and 81 members of the House of Representatives, including the entire congressional delegations of Alabama, Arkansas, Georgia, Louisiana, Mississippi, and South Carolina. The following is the full text of "The Southern Manifesto." (See also Brown v. Board of Education; *Jim Crow)*

The unwarranted decision of the Supreme Court in the public school cases is now bearing the fruit always produced when men substitute naked power for established law.

The Founding Fathers gave us a Constitution of checks and balances because they realized the inescapable lesson of history that no man or group of men can be safely entrusted with unlimited power. They framed the Constitution with its provisions for change by amendment in order to secure the fundamentals of government against the dangers of temporary popular passion or the personal predilections of public officeholders.

We regard the decision of the Supreme Court in the school cases as a clear abuse of judicial power. It climaxes a trend in the Federal Judiciary undertaking to legislate, in derogation of the authority of Congress, and to encroach upon the reserved rights of the States and the people.

The original Constitution does not mention education. Neither does the 14th amendment nor any other amendment. The debates preceding the submission of the 14th amendment clearly show that there was no intent that it should affect the system of education maintained by the States.

The very Congress, which proposed the amendment subsequently, provided for segregated schools in the District of Columbia.

When the amendment was adopted in 1868, there were 37 States of the Union. Every one of the 26 States that had any substantial racial differences among its people either approved the operation of segregated schools already in existence or subsequently established such schools by action of the same law-making body, which considered the 14th amendment.

As admitted by the Supreme Court in the public school case (*Brown v. Board of Education*), the doctrine of separate but equal schools "apparently originated in *Roberts v. City of Boston* (1849), upholding school segregation against attack as being violative of a State constitutional guarantee of equality." This constitutional doctrine began the North, not in the South, and it was followed not only in Massachusetts, but also in Connecticut, New York, Illinois, Indiana, Michigan, Minnesota, New Jersey, Ohio, Pennsylvania, and other northern States until they, exercising their rights as States through the constitutional process of local self-government, changed their school systems.

In the case of *Plessy v. Ferguson* in 1986 the Supreme Court expressly declared that under the 14th amendment no person was denied any of his rights if the States provided separate but equal public facilities. This decision has been followed in many other cases. It is notable that the Supreme Court, speaking through Chief Justice Taft, a former President of the United States, unanimously declared in 1927 in *Lum v. Rice* that the "separate but equal" principle is "within the discretion of the State in regulating its public schools and does not conflict with the 14th amendment."

This interpretation, restated time and again, became a part of the life of people of many of the States and confirmed their habits, custom, traditions, and way of life. It is founded on elemental humanity and Government of the right to direct the lives and education of their own children should not deprive common sense, for parents.

Though there has been no constitutional amendment or act of Congress changing this established legal principle almost a century old, the Supreme Court of the United States, with no legal basis for such action, undertook to exercise their naked judicial power and substituted their personal political and social ideas for the established law of the land.

This unwarranted exercise of power by the Court, contrary to the Constitution, is creating chaos and confusion in the States principally affected. It is destroying the amicable relations between the white and Negro races that have been created through 90 years of patient effort by the good people of both races. It has planted hatred and suspicion where there has been heretofore friendship and understanding.

Without regard to the consent of the governed, outside agitators are threatening immediate and revolutionary changes in our public-school systems. If done, this is certain to destroy the system of publish education in some of the States.

With the gravest concern for the explosive and dangerous condition created by this decision and inflamed by outside meddlers:

We reaffirm our reliance on the Constitution as the fundament law of the land.
We decry the Supreme Court's encroachments on rights reserved to the States and to the people, contrary to established law, and to the Constitution.
We commend the motives of those States, which have declared the intention to resist forced integration by a lawful means.
We appeal to the States and people who are not directly affected by those decisions to consider the constitutional principles involved against the

time when they too, on issues vital to them, may be the victims of judicial encroachment.

Even though we constitute a minority in the present Congress, we have full faith that a majority of the American people believe in the dual system of government which has enabled us to achieve our greatness and will in time demand that the served rights of the States and of the people be made secure against judicial usurpation.

We pledge ourselves to use all lawful means to bring about a reversal of this decision, which is contrary to the Constitution, and to prevent the use of force in its implementation.

In this trying period, as we all seek to right this wrong, we appeal to our people not to be provoked by the agitators and troublemakers invading our States and to scrupulously refrain from disorder and lawless acts.

Source: Congressional Record, 84th Cong., 2nd sess. (March 12, 1956).

EXCERPTS FROM CIVIL RIGHTS ACT OF 1964

The Civil Rights Act of 1964, a landmark in American legal history, provided much of the legal basis for the modern civil rights movement. Enacted on July 2, 1964, the law is lengthy and covers many areas of discrimination, most notably voting rights and segregation. Although it was originally passed to protect the rights of African Americans, sections of the law have since been used by a variety of groups in their fight against discrimination. (See also Civil Rights Act of 1964; Voting Rights Act of 1965)

Public Accommodation

SEC. 201. (a) All persons shall be entitled to the full and equal enjoyment of the goods, services, facilities, and privileges, advantages, and accommodations of any place of public accommodation, as defined in this section, without discrimination or segregation on the ground of race, color, religion, or national origin.

(b) Each of the following establishments which serves the public is a place of public accommodation within the meaning of this title if its operations affect commerce, or if discrimination or segregation by it is supported by State action:

(1) any inn, hotel, motel, or other establishment which provides lodging to transient guests, other than an establishment located within a building which contains not more than five rooms for rent or hire and which is actually occupied by the proprietor of such establishment as his residence;

(2) any restaurant, cafeteria, lunchroom, lunch counter, soda fountain, or other facility principally engaged in selling food for consumption on the premises, including, but not limited to, any such facility located on the premises of any retail establishment; or any gasoline station;

(3) any motion picture house, theater, concert hall, sports arena, stadium or other place of exhibition or entertainment; and

(4) any establishment (A)(i) which is physically located within the premises of any establishment otherwise covered by this subsection, or (ii) within the premises of which is physically located any such covered establishment, and (B) which holds itself out as serving patrons of such covered establishment.

(c) The operations of an establishment affect commerce within the meaning of this title if (1) it is one of the establishments described in paragraph (1) of subsection (b); (2) in the case of an establishment described in paragraph (2) of subsection (b), it serves or offers to serve interstate travelers or a substantial portion of the food which it serves, or gasoline or other products which it sells, has moved in commerce; (3) in the case of an establishment described in paragraph (3) of subsection (b), it customarily presents films, performances, athletic teams, exhibitions, or other sources of entertainment which move in commerce; and (4) in the case of an establishment described in paragraph (4) of subsection (b), it is physically located within the premises of, or there is physically located within its premises, an establishment the operations of which affect commerce within the meaning of this subsection. For purposes of this section, "commerce" means travel, trade, traffic, commerce, transportation, or communication among the several States, or between the District of Columbia and any State, or between any foreign country or any territory or possession and any State or the District of Columbia, or between points in the same State but through any other State or the District of Columbia or a foreign country.

Source: Civil Rights Act of 1957. Public Law 85–315. U.S. Statutes at Large 71 (1957): 634.

Selected Bibliography

Books

Anderson, James. *The Education of Blacks in the South, 1860–1931.* Chapel Hill: University of North Carolina Press, 1988.

Ayers, Edward. *The Promise of the New South: Life after Reconstruction.* New York: Oxford University Press, 1992.

Barbeau, Arthur, and Florette Henri. *Black American Troops in World War I.* Philadelphia: Temple University Press, 1974.

Bay, Mia. *The White Image in the Black Mind: African American Ideas about White People, 1830–1925.* New York: Oxford University Press, 2000.

Bogle, Donald. *Toms, Coons, Mulattoes, Mammies, and Bucks: An Interpretative History of Blacks in American Films.* New York: Viking Press, 1973.

Branch, Taylor. *Parting the Waters: America in the King Years, 1954–1963.* New York: Simon and Schuster, 1988.

Branch, Taylor. *Pillar of Fire: America in the King Years, 1963–1965.* New York: Simon and Schuster, 1998.

Brown, Nikki. *Private Politics and Public Voices: African American Women's Activism from World War I to the New Deal.* Bloomington: Indiana University Press, 2007.

Carson, Clayborne, et al. *The Eyes on the Prize Civil Rights Reader: Documents, Speeches, and First Hand Accounts from the Black Freedom Struggle.* New York: Penguin Books, 1991.

Carson, Clayborne. *In Struggle: SNCC and the Black Awakening of the 1960s.* Cambridge, MA: Harvard University Press, 1981.

Clark-Lewis, Elizabeth. *Living In, Living Out: African American Domestics in Washington, D.C., 1910–1940.* Washington, DC: Smithsonian Institution Press, 1994.

Collier-Thomas, Bettye, and V.P. Franklin, eds. *Sisters in the Struggle: African American Women in the Civil Rights—Black Power Movement.* New York: New York University Press, 2001.

Cooper, Anna Julia. *A Voice from the South.* New York: Oxford University Press, 1988.

Crawford, Vickie, Jacqueline Rouse, and Barbara Woods, eds. *Women in the Civil Rights Movement: Trailblazers and Torchbearers.* Brooklyn, NY: Carlson Publishing, 1990.

Dray, Philip. *At the Hands of Persons Unknown: The Lynching of Black America.* New York: Modern Library, 2003.

Du Bois, W.E.B. *The Souls of Black Folk.* New York: Library of America, 1903.

Egerton, John. *Speak Now against the Day: The Generation before the Civil Rights Movement in the South.* New York: Alfred A. Knopf, 1994.

Floyd, Samuel A. *The Power of Black Music: Interpreting Its History from Africa to the United States.* New York: Oxford University Press, 1995.

Franklin, John Hope, and August Meier. *Black Leaders of the Twentieth Century.* Urbana: University of Illinois Press, 1982.

Frederickson, George. *The Black Image in the White Mind: The Debate on Afro-American Character and Destiny, 1817–1914.* New York: Harper and Row, 1971.

Gibson, Jo Ann Robinson. *The Montgomery Bus Boycott and the Women Who Started It.* Knoxville: University of Tennessee Press, 1987.

Giddings, Paula. *Ida, A Sword among Lions: Ida B. Wells and the Campaign against Lynching.* New York: Amistad, 2008

Giddings, Paula. *When and Where I Enter: The Impact of Black Women on Race and Sex in America.* New York: William Morrow, 1984.

Gilmore, Glenda Elizabeth. *Gender and Jim Crow: Women and the Politics of White Supremacy in North Carolina, 1896–1920.* Chapel Hill: University of North Carolina Press, 1996.

Hahn, Steven. *A Nation under Our Feet: Black Political Struggles in the Rural South from Slavery to the Great Migration.* Cambridge, MA: Harvard University Press, 2003.

Hall, Jacquelyn Dowd Hall. *Revolt against Chivalry: Jessie Daniel Ames and the Women's Campaign against Lynching.* New York: Columbia University Press, 1993.

Hampton, Henry, and Steve Fayer, eds. *The Voices of Freedom: An Oral History of the Civil Rights Movement from the 1950s through the 1980s.* New York: Bantam Books, 1990.

Harlan, Louis T. *Booker T. Washington: The Making of a Black Leader, 1856–1901.* New York: Oxford University Press, 1972.

Harlan, Louis T. *Booker T. Washington: The Wizard of Tuskegee, 1901–1915.* New York: Oxford University Press, 1983.

Harris-Perry, Melissa. *Sister Citizen: Shame, Stereotypes, and Black Women in America.* New Haven, CT: Yale University Press, 2011.

Hine, Darlene Clark, Elsa Barkley Brown, and Rosalyn Terborg-Penn, eds. *Black Women in America: An Historical Encyclopedia.* Brooklyn, NY: Carlson Publishing, 1993.

Hunter, Tera. *To 'Joy My Freedom: Southern Black Women's Lives and Labors after the Civil War.* Cambridge, MA: Harvard University Press, 1997.

Jones, Jacqueline. *Labor of Love, Labor of Sorrow: Black Women, Work, and the Family from Slavery to the Present.* New York: Basic Books, 1995.

Kellogg, Charles. *NAACP: A History of the National Association for the Advancement of Colored People.* Baltimore: Johns Hopkins University Press, 1967.

Kelly, Robin D. G. *Hammer and Hoe: Alabama Communists during the Great Depression.* Chapel Hill: University of North Carolina Press, 1990.

Lewis, David Levering. *W.E.B. Du Bois: Biography of a Race, 1868–1919.* New York: Henry Holt and Co., 1993.

Lewis, David Levering. *W.E.B. Du Bois: The Fight for Equality and the American Century, 1919–1963.* New York: Henry Holt and Co., 2001.

Lewis, David Levering. *When Harlem Was in Vogue.* New York: Alfred A. Knopf, 1981.

Litwack, Leon. *Been in the Storm So Long: The Aftermath of Slavery.* New York: Vintage, 1980.

Litwack, Leon. *Trouble in Mind: Black Southerners in the Age of Jim Crow.* New York: Knopf, 1998.

Lomax, Alan. *Mr. Jelly Roll: The Fortunes of Jelly Roll Morton, New Orleans Creole and "Inventor of Jazz."* New York: Grove Press, 1950.

Marable, Manning. *Malcolm X: A Life of Reinvention.* New York: Penguin Books, 2001.

Marable, Manning. *Race, Reform, and Rebellion: The Second Reconstruction in Black America, 1945–1982.* Jackson: University Press of Mississippi, 1984.

Marks, Carole. *Farewell—We're Good and Gone: The Great Black Migration.* Bloomington: Indiana University Press, 1989.

McMillen, Neil. *Dark Journey: Black Mississippians in the Age of Jim Crow.* Urbana: University of Illinois Press, 1989.

Moody, Ann. *Coming of Age in Mississippi.* New York: Dell Press, 1968.

Patterson, James. *Brown v. Board of Education: A Civil Rights Milestone and Its Troubled Legacy.* New York: Oxford University Press, 2000.

Payne, Charles. *I've Got the Light of Freedom: The Organizing Tradition and the Mississippi Freedom Struggle.* Berkeley: University of California Press, 1995.

Rabinowitz, Howard. *Race Relations in the Urban South: 1865–1890.* New York: Oxford University Press, 1978.

Ransby, Barbara. *Ella Baker and the Black Freedom Movement: A Radical Vision.* Chapel Hill: University of North Carolina Press, 2003.

Stovall, Tyler. *Paris Noir: African Americans in the City of Light.* New York: Houghton Mifflin, 1998.

Sullivan, Patricia. *Days of Hope: Race and Democracy in the New Deal Era.* Chapel Hill: University of North Carolina Press, 1978.

Washington, Booker T. *Up from Slavery: An Autobiography.* New York: Doubleday, 1902.

Watkins, Mel. *On the Real Side: A History of African American Comedy.* New York: Lawrence Hill Books, 1999.

Woodward, C. Vann. *The Strange Career of Jim Crow.* New York: Oxford University Press, 1957.

X, Malcolm. *The Autobiography of Malcolm X.* With the assistance of Alex Haley. New York: Ballantine Books, 1973.

Web Sites

American Radio Works. State of Siege: Mississippi Whites and the Civil Rights Movement. http://americanradioworks.publicradio.org/features/mississippi/ (accessed January 21, 2014).

Cruz, Bárbara C., and Michael J. Berson. "The American Melting Pot? Miscegenation Laws in the United States." *OAH Magazine of History* 15, no. 4 (Summer 2001), 80–84. The Fight for Desegregation. http://library.thinkquest.org/J0112391/the_fight_for_desegregation.htm (accessed January 21, 2014).

Library of Congress. "From Jim Crow to Linda Brown: A Retrospective of the African-American Experience from 1897 to 1953." http://memory.loc.gov/learn/lessons/97/crow/crowhome.html (accessed January 21, 2014).

"*Plessy v. Ferguson* (1896)." Landmark Cases, Supreme Court, http://www.streetlaw.org/en/landmark/cases/plessy_v_ferguson (accessed January 21, 2014).

Public Broadcasting Service. "The Rise and Fall of Jim Crow." http://www.pbs.org/wnet/jimcrow/ (accessed January 21, 2014).

Index

Note: Page numbers in **boldface** reflect main entries in the book.

Abernathy, Ralph David, xxxiv, **1–5**, 21–23, 178

Abolitionists, 43, 47, 64, 188, 208, 213, 221, 235, 298, 422, 428

Acheson, Dean, 107

Advertising, **5–12**, 179, 284, 430

Affirmative Action, **12–14,** 278

Africa, xxiv, xxv, 20, 64, 65, 67, 68, 71, 89, 100, 111, 112, 169, 171, 172, 186, 207, 231, 265, 283, 284, 299, 300, 367, 389, 392, 447

African Blood Brotherhood, 161

African diplomats, 111

Ahmadiyyah movement, 262–63

Alabama, xxx, xxxiv, 1, 2 3, **14–17**, 17–21, 23, 33, 41, 55, 59, 72, 100, 101, 102, 109, 112, 117, 120, 121, 130, 131, 137, 138, 140, 165, 166, 174, 188, 202, 224, 225, 235, 240, 241, 245, 256, 278, 292, 293, 294, 297, 317, 331, 332, 333, 336, 338, 378, 379, 380, 381, 392, 409, 410, 416, 417, 419, 420, 429, 430, 453

Alabama Council on Human Relations, **17–21**

Albany Civil Rights Movement, **21–24**, 177

American Medical Association, 197, 199

American Negro Labor Conference, 161

Anti-immigration laws, 146

Anti-Semitism, 229

Arkansas, xxxiv, **24–29**, 39–41, 72, 78, 100, 110, 118, 129, 137, 180, 187, 195, 228, 236, 247–49, 296, 331–34, 337, 350, 353–54, 358, 378, 380, 381, 383, 386, 396, 429, 453

Armed Forces, **29–32**, 78, 95, 140, 150, 153, 188, 268, 269, 276, 363, 408, 436, 441, 443, 448–49

Atlanta Compromise, The, **33–35**, 174

Back to Africa Movement, 169, 172, 186, 299

Baker, Ella, 161, 245, 367, 459

Baker, Josephine, 108

Baker, Ray Stannard, 298

Baldwin, James, **37–38**, 108, 161

Baptist Church, 1, 2, 3, 16, 20, 21, 43, 102, 144, 163, 174, 198, 223, 224, 231, 244, 293

Baseball, xxx, xxxiii, xxxiv, 295, 298, 303–7, 359, 360, 361, 362, 395

Basketball, 359

Bates, Daisy, 28, **39–41**

Baton Rouge Bus Boycott, xxvi, **41–42**

Berea College v. Kentucky, **42–44,** 83

Bethune, Mary McLeod, **44–46,** 51, 161, 166, 364, 443

Birmingham, Alabama, 3, 14, 15, 16, 19, 20, 21, 23, 102, 111, 112, 130, 163, 223, 225, 231, 245, 306, 378

Birth of a Nation, The, xxxii, **46–49,** 92, 93, 176, 229, 282, 298, 299, 342, 350

Black Cabinet, The, xxxiii, 45, **49–51,** 357

Black Codes, xxii, **51–59,** 204, 251, 286, 348, 391, 399

Blackface, 10, 48, 208, 210, 213, 280–82, 284

Black Like Me, **59–63,** 96, 323

Black Muslims, 187, 262, 264–65

Black nationalism, **63–67**, 95, 124, 164, 171, 262, 266

Black Panther Party, 4, 32, 66, 404

Black Power, xv, 4, 37, 66, 117, 124, 211, 225–26, 324, 388

Blues, **67–71**, 186, 209

Brown v. Board of Education, 19, 28, **72–79**, 79–82, 108, 109, 120, 123, 151, 163, 188, 200, 202, 213, 222, 231, 242, 247, 273, 275, 277, 289, 314, 325, 330, 357, 395, 396, 415, 416, 429, 450–53

Brown v. Board of Education, legal groundwork for, xxi, xxvi, xxxiv, 28, 40, **79–82**, 108, 109, 120, 123, 151, 163, 188, 200, 213, 222, 231, 242, 247, 273, 277, 289, 314, 325, 330, 357, 395, 396, 415, 416, 429, 450–53

Buchanan v. Warley, **82–84,** 222

California, 66, 158, 187, 188, 205, 217, 219, 250, 258, 271, 296, 359, 367, 395–96, 437–38, 440–41

Chicago Race Riot of 1919, **85–88,** 237–38, 354

Children, xxiii, xxvi, 1, 6, 14, 17, 55, 58, 72, 73–74, 76–78, 86, 102, 109, 110, 120, 144, 149, 192, 198, 202, 206, 215, 217, 254, 258–59, 266, 271, 277, 282, 288, 303, 308, 313, 315, 318, 320, 325, 333, 341, 346–47, 354, 396, 422, 426, 428, 450–52, 454

Chinese, xxx, 52, 235, 238, 254, 396

Churches, 3, 18–19, 42–43, **88–92**, 98, 124, 177, 183–84, 186–87, 195, 197–99, 221, 223, 288, 347, 383, 388, 394

Cinema, **92–97**

Civil disobedience, xxv–xxvi, 1, 3, 163

Civil Rights Act of 1875, **98–99,** 104, 327

Civil Rights Act of 1964, xxvi, xxxv, 12, **99–104**, 113, 131, 199, 200, 213, 215, 232, 242, 277, 368, 388, 395, 403, 416, 455–56

Civilian Conservation Corps, **104–6,** 395

Civil War, xxi–xxii, 17, 24–25, 26, 30, 43, 47, 51, 52, 53, 89, 92, 94, 95, 98, 119, 120, 127, 136, 137, 145, 153, 165, 175, 182, 183, 196, 221,

227, 229, 233, 251, 254, 269, 282, 296, 297, 299, 300, 312, 319, 325, 328, 333, 341, 345, 350, 355, 356, 357, 371, 376, 388, 390, 392, 393, 399, 409, 413, 425, 433

Cold War, **106–15**, 130, 231, 300

Colored Farmers' Alliance, **115–19**, 377, 378

Confederate Flag, **119–21**, 389, 394

Congress for Racial Equality (CORE), xxvi, xxxiii, 9, **121–25**, 162, 245, 269, 290, 314, 366, 382

Creoles, 251, 252, 325

Customs, xxi, xxiv, 59, 149, 271, 286, 291, 301, 341–48, 390, 426

Darwinism, 146, 283, 297

Davis, Benjamin O., 140

Davis, Frank, 117

Davis, Olethia, xix, 79, 124

Davis, R.T., 10

Davis v. Prince Edwards County School Board, 72, 74, 415

Debt peonage, 26, 115, 118, 409

Democratic Party, xxii, xxxi, xxxiii, 95, 120, **127–32**, 136, 167, 188, 230, 252, 290, 356, 357, 358, 362, 403, 420, 453

Desegregation, xxxiv, 17, 18, 20, 37, 78, 103, 109, 112, 123, 153–54, 162, 178, 199, 202, 223, 245, 269, 276–78, 383, 386, 419, 424, 448

Detroit Race Riot of 1943, **132–35**, 441

Discrimination, xxi, xxiii, xxvi, xxxiv, 7, 12, 28, 34, 44, 63, 73, 88, 90, 91, 95, 98, 99, 100, 103, 105, 106, 107, 116, 122, 134, 135, 139, 140, 153,

154, 157, 158, 159, 166, 169, 180, 191, 193, 194, 196, 205, 206, 215, 222, 226, 233, 236, 237, 239, 240, 241, 252, 267–68, 269, 275, 276, 303, 310, 311, 313, 314, 319, 322, 327, 329, 346, 347, 351, 352, 354, 363, 364, 365, 371–75, 388, 389, 391, 397, 401, 402, 407, 410, 414–15, 416, 418, 426, 428, 429, 437, 440, 443, 447, 455

Disenfranchisement, xvi, xxx, xxxi, xxxv, 25, **135–39**, 159, 163, 227, 350, 380, 427

Dixiecrats, 120, 130, 154, 188, 265, 266, 407–8, 453

Double V campaign, 31, 100, **139–42**, 153, 442

Du Bois, W.E.B., xxi, xxxi, 35, 65, 107, 108, 139, 161, 172, 173, 174, 184, 224, 238, 299, 300, 302, 320, 366, 421, 423, 424, 432

East St. Louis Riot, **143–45**

Emancipation, xvi, xxix, 7, 26, 52, 53, 56, 57, 176, 269, 282, 285, 298, 342, 343, 355–56, 371, 376, 421, 422, 427

Equal Protection Clause (Fourteenth Amendment), xxix, 73, 75, 76, 77, 78, 80, 82, 83, 99, 103, 136, 213, 277, 326, 327, 328, 332, 349, 450–51

Eugenics, **145–48**, 297, 300, 413, 414

Evers, Medgar, xxxv, 97, 102, 139, **148–52**, 163

Executive Order 8802, xxxiii, 135, 140, 154, 157, 158, 269, 346, 440, 443

Executive Order 9346, 158
Executive Order 9981, xxxiv, 31,
    152–55, 276, 408, 448, 449
Executive Order 10925, 12

Fair Employment Practices Commis-
    sion (FEPC), 134, 135, **157–59,**
    269, 270
Fair Housing Act (1968), 205, 375
Fair Labor Standards Act (1938), 308,
    309, 310
Farmer, James, xxxiii, 121, 122, 162,
    366
Faubus, Orval, 28, 40, 78, 110, 248,
    358
Federal Bureau of Investigation (FBI),
    66, 97, 142, **159–65,** 176, 179,
    266
Federal Housing Administration
    (FHA), 204, 373
Fellowship of Reconciliation, 121,
    162, 243, 268, 366, 382
Ferguson, John H., 253, 324–30
Fifteenth Amendment, 25, 127, 128,
    136, 166, 252, 295, 296, 313, 331,
    349, 356, 358, 416, 417
Florida, 44, 45, 72, 90, 137, **165–68,**
    182, 195, 234, 330, 331, 332, 333,
    356, 390, 453
Football, 150, 359
Fourteenth Amendment, xxix, 25, 58,
    73, 75, 76, 77, 78, 80, 82, 83, 99,
    103, 136, 138, 213, 253, 277, 324,
    326, 327, 328, 329, 332, 349, 447,
    450, 451
Free blacks, xxix, 29, 52, 53, 54, 55,
    57, 136, 152, 182, 251
Freedom Rides, xxxv, 3, 20, 101, 111,
    122, 123, 124, 163, 243, 245, 290,
    293, 367

Freedom Summer, 113, 124, 290–91,
    368
Freemasons, 263

Gandhi, Mahatma, 2, 65, 107, 122,
    224, 225, 243, 392
Garvey, Marcus, xxxii, 64, 161,
    169–72, 186, 187, 261, 262, 263,
    264, 299
Georgia, xxxi, 4, 21, 23, 31, 33, 44,
    72, 95, 101, 107, 117, 118, 120,
    121, 130, 137, 139, 163, 165, 166,
    172–79, 182, 187, 192, 195, 197,
    209, 223, 229, 256, 258, 259, 299,
    318, 331, 332, 333, 348, 359, 378,
    386, 387, 390, 429, 453
G.I. Bill, 311, 372, 436, 444
Gone with the Wind (film), 93, 94, 95,
    177, 298
Grandfather clause, xxvii, 137, 416
Great Depression, 8, 50, 65, 93, 94,
    97, 104, 105, **179–81,** 187, 240,
    241, 262, 267, 274, 299, 307, 357,
    362, 379, 381, 436
Great Migration, xxv, xxxi, 71, 85–86,
    90, 118, 143, **181–89,** 230, 282,
    299, 300, 371, 372, 392, 431, 437
Great Retreat, 166, 298, 300, 395
Greensboro, North Carolina, 244, 314,
    382–84, 385, 386, 387, 388

Haiti, 52, 107
Hampton Institute, xxix, 33, 197, 421
Harlem, xxi, xxv, xxxii, 37, 38, 113,
    171, 186, 265, 266, 267, 322, 366,
    367, 435, 441–42
Health Care, xxiii, 26, 66, 143, 181,
    191–200, 302, 403, 411
Historically Black Colleges and
    Universities, xxi, 90, **200–203**

Homosexuality (and gay), 37, 365, 366, 368
Hoover, J. Edgar, 142, 160
Housing Covenants, **203–6**, 276
Howard University, 12, 79, 80, 193, 197, 202, 274, 295
Hughes, Langston, 59, 186, 211, 274, 400
Hughes, Robert, 18–21
Humor and comedic traditions, **206–12**

"I Have a Dream" speech (King), xxvi, xxxv, 163, 225, 266, 368
Immigration, 145, 146, 296, 297, 299, 353
Indians (Native Americans), xxx, 73, 105, 165, 182, 226, 251, 270, 296, 313, 390, 397, 402
Industrial Workers of the World (IWW), 162, 237, 352
Integration, xxi, 4, 16, 17, 19, 23, 28, 31, 32, 35, 40, 75, 78, 98, 108, 110, 121, 130, 145, 149, 151, 154, 155, 163, 168, 178, 199, 202, 227, 231, 243, 245, 247, 248, 249, 250, 264, 276, 277, 278, 279, 286, 307, 314, 315, 351, 357, 362, 366, 367, 374, 382, 383, 386, 388, 415, 419, 422, 429, 430, 441, 452, 454
Intelligence, 283, 297, 359, 432
Interracial marriage, 48, 53, 82, 214, 270–73, 286, 327, 352, 400, 402, 415

Jamaica, 169–72, 186
Japanese Americans, xxxiii, 107
Jazz, xxx, xxxiv, 186
Jet (magazine), 91, 323, 406

Jews, 60, 128, 167, 175, 204, 227, 229, 230, 231, 299, 395, 397, 422
Jim Crow, 1, 2, 3, 14, 15, 79, 82, 85, 88, 89, 90, 91, 92, 102, 103, 104, 106, 107, 108, 109, 110, 112, 114, 118, 120, 122, 123, 127, 129, 135, 139, 140, 141, 145, 146, 147, 148, 149, 150, 151, 152, 153, 154, 159, 161, 162, 163, 164, 165, 166, 167, 168, 172, 173, 174, 175, 176, 177, 178, 181, 182, 184, 185, 187, 188, 191, 192, 193, 194, 195, 196, 197, 198, 199, 200, 201, 203, 204, 205, 208, 209, 211, **213–16**, 222, 229, 230, 231, 232, 233, 235, 236, 238, 239, 240, 241, 242, 245, 246, 251, 252, 253, 254, 255, 256, 262, 263, 268, 270, 281, 285, 286, 287, 288, 289, 290, 291, 292, 294, 295, 301, 303, 307, 308, 310, 311, 312, 313, 314, 315, 316, 317, 318, 319, 320, 321, 322, 323, 332, 333, 336, 337, 341, 342, 343, 344, 345, 346, 347, 350, 351, 356, 357, 358, 362, 363, 364, 366, 367, 368, 371, 373, 382, 386, 387, 388, 389, 390, 391, 392, 393, 399, 400, 401, 402, 403, 404, 406, 408, 409, 413, 414, 415, 416, 421, 423, 424, 425, 426, 427, 428, 430, 431, 433, 434, 437, 438, 442–43, 447, 453
Johnson, Jack, 161, 210, **216–19**, 402
Johnson, Lyndon Baines, xxvi, 12–13, 100, 102, 113, 124, 129, 130, 164, 188, 200, 215, 278, 357, 364, 416
"Jump Jim Crow," 213
Justice Department, 102, 108, 151, 159, 163, 279, 407

Kansas, 72, 73, 74, 75, 140, 185, 196, 219, 234, 257, 277, 296, 298, 304, 305, 306, 359, 360, 382

Kennedy, John F., xxxv, 1, 12, 13, 17, 100, 101, 102, 110–13, 124, 130, 131, 151, 266, 278, 279, 289, 290, 358, 368

Kennedy, Robert F., 4, 101, 121, 130, 164, 232, 245

Kentucky, 10, 42–44, 47, 72, 82–83, 123, 193, 204, 213, **221–22**, 249, 296, 298, 306, 328, 366

King, Martin Luther, Jr, xxvi, xxxiv, xxxv, 1, 2, 16, 18, 21–22, 23, 65, 91, 100, 101, 112, 114, 123, 130, 161, 163, 177, 187, 188, 217, **223–27**, 243, 244, 266, 293, 318, 365, 367, 383, 389, 390, 391, 392

Ku Klux Klan, 14, 16, 19, 32, 46, 47, 48, 49, 65, 92, 102, 119, 120, 134, 140, 161, 163, 166, 172, 175, 183, 222, **227–32**, 258, 261, 263, 265, 291, 298, 299, 349, 378, 389, 392, 393

Labor Unions, 27, 65, 180, **233–43**, 268, 310, 352, 353, 363, 367, 368

Lawson, James Morris, Jr., **243–46**, 368 385, 386

Little Rock Nine, 28, 40, 41, 109, **247–50**

Lincoln, Abraham, 48, 118, 136, 153, 188, 269, 355, 358, 362, 391

Lincoln Memorial, xxvi, xxxiii, 40, 407

Literacy, xxvii, xxx–xxxi, 23, 103, 104, 128, 137, 172, 173, 188, 238, 297, 358, 409, 413, 416, 417

Los Angleles, 132, 158, 186, 204, 246, 250, 359, 395, 396, 437, 439, 440, 441

Louisiana, 24, 41, 42, 56, 57, 59, 61, 72, 117, 124, 129, 130, 137, 165, 166, 186, 187, 193, 199, 202, 204, 235, 237, **251–54**, 256, 259, 308, 325, 326, 327, 328, 329, 330, 331, 332, 333, 334, 336, 337, 338, 339, 341, 346, 356, 381, 429, 441, 447, 453

Loving v. Virginia, 147, 273, 415

Lynching, xxiv, xxv, xxx, 15, 18, 26, 33, 34, 46, 64, 65, 70, 96, 144, 160, 167, 173, 174, 175, 176, 182, 188, 213, 230, 231, **254–60**, 272, 283, 287, 298, 303, 321, 351, 393, 395, 401, 424, 425, 426, 427, 428, 429, 433, 441

Malcolm X, xxxv, 66, 113, 139, 161, 187, 226, **261–67**

March on Washington, xxvi, xxxiii, xxxv, 4, 40, 102, 112, 124, 140, 154, 157, 163, 266, **267–70,** 363, 365, 366, 368, 443

Marriage, interracial, 48, 53, 82, 214, **270–73**, 286, 327, 352, 400, 402, 415

Marshall, Thurgood, 72, 80, 151, 161, 188, **273–79**, 386

Marxism, 167, 236, 237, 240

Maryland, 80, 112, 123, 182, 257, 273, 274, 275, 276, 296, 414, 415, 420

Meredith, James, xxxv, 101, 111, 120, 151, 246, **279–80**, 289

Mexicans, 153, 185, 204, 254, 308, 310, 335, 336, 395, 400, 401, 402

Mexico, 62, 219, 401, 402, 434

Middle class, xv, xxi, xxiii, xxx, 1, 4, 7, 9, 18–19, 26, 32, 60, 96, 167, 174, 184, 195, 201, 223, 224, 231, 232, 273, 284, 302, 311, 353, 372, 432, 436, 444

Minstrelsy, 7, 208, 209, 210, 213, **280–85**

Miscegenation, 146, 147, 214, 271, 321, 352, 403, 413, 414, 439

Mississippi, xxx, xxxi, xxxiv, xxxv, 14, 24, 28, 53, 54, 55, 56, 57, 59, 62, 67, 68, 70, 71, 72, 96, 97, 101, 102, 107, 111, 113, 117, 120, 121, 124, 128, 129, 130, 131, 136, 137, 139, 148, 149, 150, 151, 160, 163, 164, 180, 192, 194, 195, 198, 202, 245, 252, 256, 278, 279, 280, **285–92**, 293, 295, 296, 297, 298, 299, 311, 322, 331, 333, 334, 336, 337, 338, 368, 377, 381, 387, 388, 392, 404, 405, 406, 413, 417, 425, 429, 430, 435, 453

Missouri, 24, 72, 80, 196, 205, 257, 276, 296, 298, 305, 381, 396

Mixed race, 147, 174, 319, 320, 322, 414

Montgomery Bus Boycott, xxvi, 2, 3, 15, 18, 66, 91, 109, 123, 177, 244, 278, **292–94**, 317, 367

Muhammad, Elijah, xxxiii, 161, 187, 261, 262, 264, 265, 266

Mulattos, 48, 153, 271, 318, 319, 320, 322, 323

Music, xxx, 67–71, 89, 91, 174, 177, 186, 210, 282, 283

Nadir of the Negro, xxiv, xxx, 35, 236, **295–301**, 395

National Association for the Advancement of Colored People, xxv–xxvi, xxxi, 9, 15, 21, 28, 35, 39, 48, 65, 72, 79, 83, 87, 93, 101, 107, 124, 134, 140, 148, 149, 153, 161, 171, 176, 184, 199, 211, 243, 248, 253, 255, 267, 273, 279, 289, 292, 317, 321, 351, 356–57, 361, 363, 366, 383, 389, 406, 415, 428–29, 441, 450

National Association of Colored Women, xxx, 45, **301–3**, 364, 428

National Guard, 4, 28, 40, 66, 101, 110, 120, 131, 144, 247, 248, 249, 289, 293, 432, 434

National Urban League, 51, 184, 441, 443

Nation of Islam, xxxiii, 38, 95, 261, 262

Native Americans (Indians), xxx, 73, 105, 165, 182, 226, 251, 270, 296, 313, 390, 397, 402

Negro League Baseball, **303–7**

New Deal, xxxiii, 15, 18, 45, 50, 105, 129, 131, 160, 180, 187, 267, **307–12**, 357, 362–64, 379, 380–81, 414

New Negro, xxv, 87, 211, 302, 352

New Orleans, xxx, xxxi, 61–62, 115, 124, 138, 152, 193, 194, 198–99, 209, 236, 239, 251, 306, 319, 325–26, 346, 367, 378, 427–28, 447, 448

New York City, 8, 37, 87, 111, 113, 132, 167, 182, 186, 187, 188, 261, 264, 266–67, 299, 366, 397, 437, 440, 442

North Carolina, xxxi, xxxv, 44, 54, 72, 101, 116, 117, 118, 123, 128, 137, 182, 193, 196, 198, 219, 244, 245,

297, **312–16**, 320, 331, 332, 363, 367, 382, 384, 385, 429

Oklahoma, xxxii, xxxiv, 24, 72, 80–81, 87, 185, 187, 230, 257, 276, 296, 298–99, 330, 382, 452
One drop rule, 270, 320, 414
Owens, James Cleveland "Jesse," xxxiii

Parks, Rosa, xxxiv, 2, 16, 65, 123, 224, 292, 293, **317–18**, 418
Passing, **318–24**
Paternalism, 283
Plantations, 11, 24, 26, 28, 47, 52, 56, 64, 93, 95, 173, 180, 182, 198, 199, 206, 207–8, 221, 256, 281, 282, 284, 313, 318, 333–34, 336, 337, 338, 339, 340, 353, 376, 377, 378, 380, 389, 391, 392, 421
Plessy v. Ferguson, xxiii, xxx, 77, 79, 82, 83, 88, 166, 213, 251, 275, 296, 301, **324–31**, 341, 400, 429, 447–48, 450, 454
Poetry, xxi, 211
Police, xxxi, xxxii, 4, 16, 19, 23, 28, 40, 42, 66, 86, 87, 95, 97, 102, 113, 133, 134, 144, 145, 159, 160, 163, 175, 178, 231, 244, 245, 249, 314, 326, 345, 353, 354, 359, 367, 368, 385, 386, 388, 392, 396, 402, 403, 404, 407, 428, 433, 435, 440, 441, 442, 447
Poll Taxes, xxvii, xxx, xxxi, 14, 15, 25, 46, 56, 128, 137, 166, 167, 173, 188, 313, **331–32**, 358, 381, 400, 413, 416
Poverty, xxiv, xxxiii, 13, 34, 40, 48, 62, 90, 130, 148, 150, 170, 173,

176, 179, 191, 226, 243, 246, 291, 302, 307, 368, 371, 375, 419
Prisons, 27, 101, 154, 171, 219, 229, 235, 243, 254, 262, 264, 272, 314, 330, **332–40**, 366
Property rights, 82–83

Race riots, xxxi, xxxii, 17, 85–88, 132–35, 175, 176, 237–38, 321, 350, 354, 403
Racial customs and etiquette, **341–48**
Randolph, A. Philip, xxxii, xxxiii, 140, 154, 157, 161, 162, 172, 267–70, 363, 364, 365, 366, 367, 368, 441–43
Reconstruction, xvi, xxi, xxii, xxvi, xxix, 14, 23, 25, 27, 30, 31, 43, 46, 47, 48, 49, 51, 53, 58, 59, 64, 90, 92, 94, 98, 99, 117, 120, 127, 131, 136, 165, 167, 172, 173, 175, 183, 188, 199, 201, 204, 217, 222, 228–29, 233, 251, 252, 285, 286, 289, 291, 295, 298, 300, 301, 313, 319, 325, **348–50**, 356, 364, 373, 388, 389, 390, 393, 399, 400, 409, 413, 416, 431, 433, 435
Redlining, 204–5, 374, 444
Red Summer, 87, 88, 299, **350–55**, 403
Republican Party, 25, 118, 128, 129, 137, 166, 235, 252, 313, **355–59**, 362, 391
Residential segregation, 83, 203–5, 222, 315, 371–76
Robinson, Jackie, xxxiii, xxxiv, 100, 307, **359–62**
Roosevelt, Franklin D., xxxiii, 45, 49, 90, 104, 105, 129, 135, 140,

154, 157, 160, 179, 187, 267, 307, 346, 357, 358, **362–64**, 366, 379, 381, 441

Rosewood, Florida, 167

Rustin, Bayard, 121, 123, 161, 268, 269, 270, **365–69**

Sambo, 94, 207, 218, 282

Segregation, residential, 83, 203–5, 222, 315, **371–76**

Segregation, school, 72, 74, 276–77, 450, 453

Self-determination, 88, 123

Separate but equal, xxiii–xxiv, xxv, 74, 77–83, 88, 166, 200, 202, 213, 251, 253, 275–76, 301, 321, 324, 330, 341, 357, 400, 450–54

Sharecropping, 26–28, 50, 56, 115–16, 118, 143, 173, 175–76, 180, 183, 256, 286–87, 343, 352–53, 371, **376–82**, 392, 437

Sit-Ins, 65, 101, 122–23, 162, 243–44, 314, **382–88**

South Carolina, xxx, 7, 44, 53, 54, 57, 117, 120, 130, 137, 165, 182–83, 188, 191, 193, 195–96, 277, 285, 312, 323, 331–32, 350, 353–54, 356, 384, **388–94**, 406–7, 429

Southern Christian Leadership Conference (SCLC), xxvi, xxxiv, 2–3, 16, 91, 102, 112, 151, 163, 178, 225, 244, 367, 384

Southern Manifesto, 452–55

Southern Tenant Farmers; Union, 27, 180, 380, 381

Soviet Union, 107–8, 110, 111, 231

State Department, 108, 112, 414

Stereotypes, xxiv, 5, 8, 31, 97, 207, 208, 210, 281, 283, 298, 400, 409, 426, 427

Stowe, Harriet Beecher, 94, 208

The Strange Career of Jim Crow (Woodward), xvii, 295

Strikes, 4, 25, 42, 91, 118, 135, 143, 169, 186, 235–36, 239–40, 243, 246, 310, 338, 351, 353, 380–81, 385, 435

Student Nonviolent Coordinating Committee, xxxv, 4, 21, 65, 124, 151, 177, 225, 243, 290, 367, 386, 404, 417

Sundown Town, 298, 300, **394–97**

Syphilis, 409–12

Teachers, xvi, xix, xxi, xxiii, 15, 18–19, 23, 74, 81, 172, 184, 202, 243, 264, 273, 276, 287, 288, 297, 313–15, 317, 366, 425

Teacher training, 288

Television, xxiv, 8, 10, 97, 102, 198, 206, 209, 211, 261, 284, 419

Tennessee, xxiii, xxix, 24, 73, 91, 123, 137, 193, 201, 226, 228, 239, 243, 244, 245, 280, 331–33, 338, 350, 381, 384, 429

Texas, 11, 24, 56, 70, 73, 81, 115, 129–30, 137, 185, 187–88, 217, 296, 305, 331–34, 337–39, 344–45, 350, 353, 359, 382, 386, 392, **399–404**, 453

Thirteenth Amendment, xxii, xxix, 25, 27, 103, 136, 222, 251, 326–28, 348, 447

Till, Emmett, xxxiv, 91, 109, 151, 289, 347, **404–6**

Truman, Harry S., xxxiv, 31, 95, 107–9, 120, 129–30, 139, 154, 159, 167, 176, 188, 276, 357, **406–9**, 441, 448–50

Turner, Nat, 64, 96

Tuskegee Airmen, xxxiii

Tuskegee Syphilis Experiment, **409–12**

Universal Negro Improvement Association (UNIA), xxxii, 170, 261

University of Alabama, 17–19

University of Georgia, 178

University of Kentucky, 222

University of Mississippi, xxxv, 101–2, 111, 120, 151, 202, 279–80, 289

U.S. Supreme Court, 100–101, 109, 120, 123, 147, 162, 205, 213, 222, 231, 247, 273, 276, 278, 314, 324, 326, 332, 366, 372, 396, 400, 414, 415, 417, 429

U.S. v. Cruikshank, xxii, xxix, 327, 349

Vagrancy, 27, 52–53, 55, 58, 402

Veterans, xxv, 1, 21, 47, 64, 87, 96, 117, 120, 150, 203, 288, 307, 311–12, 352, 354, 372–73, 378, 436, 443–44

Vietnam War, 4, 32, 114, 131, 225, 368

Virginia, xxx, 33, 43, 72, 74, 103, 117, 123, 147, 182, 197, 204, 209, 241, 258–59, 271–73, 276–77, 296, 306, 312, 314, 331–33, 354, 366, 387, **413–16**

Voting Rights Act of 1965, 17, 113, 124, 131, 139, 242, 358, 368, 388, 403, **416–18**

Walker, Madam C.J., 186

Wallace, George C., 15–17, 101, **419–20**

Warren, Earl, 76, 277, 415, 450–51

Washington, Booker T., xxix, xxx, xxxi, 26, 33, 70, 170, 174, 184, 196, 197, 202, 298, 302, 399, **421–25**, 432

Washington, D.C., xxvi, xxx, xxxv, 4, 25, 40, 87, 102, 109, 111, 112, 124, 140, 154, 157, 163, 164, 182, 193, 198, 202, 205, 225, 245, 255, 258, 266, 267–70, 272, 274, 302, 304, 327, 346, 350, 366, 380, 392, 411

Wells-Barnett, Ida B., 302–3, 389, 392, **425–29**

West Virginia, 73, 103, 296, 386, 421

White, Walter, 75, 176, 267, 321–23, 363, 364, 406, 441, 443

White Citizens Council, 15, 19, 120, 151, 289, 353, **429–30**

White flight, 373–74

White League, 227, 304, 349

White supremacy, xxi, xxiv–xxv, xxx–xxxi, 3, 25, 48, 63–64, 92, 95, 119–21, 136–38, 213, 231–32, 261, 263–64, 284, 286, 289, 296, 297, 300, 301, 341, 345, 363, 379, 381, 394, 402, 404, 415

Women, xvi, xxiv, xxx–xxxiii, 2, 10, 26, 32, 35, 38, 40, 43, 45, 46, 62, 65–66, 86, 87, 90, 92, 104, 105, 117, 133, 140–41, 144, 158, 166, 175, 183, 192, 196, 216–19, 236, 237, 241, 254, 257, 258, 259–60, 264, 266, 271–72, 282, 292, 294, 301–3, 317, 322, 333–34, 336, 338–40, 342–46, 354, 364, 377, 392–93, 402, 409–10, 426–30, 436, 438, 439, 444

World War I, xxv, xxxi, xxxii, 17, 30, 64, 85, 87, 135, 139, 140, 143, 144, 171, 179, 180, 184, 185, 219, 276, 299, 346, 351, 371, 378, 379, 402, **430–36**

World War II, xxv, xxvi, xxxiii, 2, 15, 30, 31, 46, 60, 64, 100, 107, 134, 135, 139, 140, 153, 157, 162, 181, 187, 188, 193, 203, 209, 215, 219, 265, 267, 284, 288, 300, 311, 314, 346, 363, 372, 403, 414, 419, **436–45**

Zip Coon, 282

About the Editors

NIKKI L. M. BROWN is an associate professor and undergraduate studies co-ordinator in the History Department at the University of New Orleans. Her first book, *Private Politics and Public Voices: African American Women's Activism from World War I to the New Deal,* won the 2007 Letitia Woods Brown Memorial Book Prize for the best book in African American women's history.

BARRY M. STENTIFORD is a professor of military history at the U.S. Army's School of Advanced Military Studies, Command and General Staff College. He earned his PhD from the University of Alabama in history. Among his publications are such works as *The Richardson Light Guard of Wakefield, Massachusetts: A Town Militia in War and Peace, 1851–1975* (2013), *The Tuskegee Airmen* (2011), and *The American Home Guard: The State Militia in the Twentieth Century* (2002).